CABO

JOE CUMMINGS & NIKKI GOTH ITOI

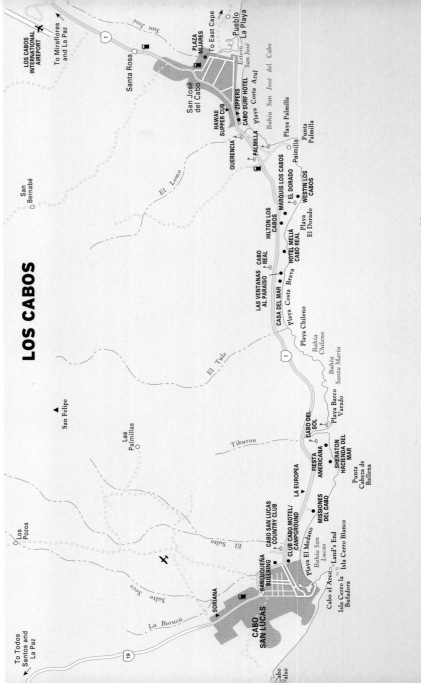

LOS CABOS

To Todos Santos and La Paz

Los Pozos

San Felipe

San Bernabé

Santa Rosa

LOS CABOS INTERNATIONAL AIREPORT

To Miraflores and La Paz

San José

To East Cape

Pueblo La Playa

PLAZA MIJARES

San José del Cabo

Estero San José

ZIPPERS
HAWAII SUPPER CLUB
CABO SURF HOTEL
Playa Costa Azul

PALMILLA
Bahía San José del Cabo
Playa Palmilla

QUERENCIA
Punta Palmilla

Palmilla

El Lomo

MARQUIS LOS CABOS
WESTIN LOS CABOS
EL DORADO
Playa El Dorado

HILTON LOS CABOS
HOTEL MELIA CABO REAL

CABO REAL

LAS VENTANAS AL PARAISO

CASA DEL MAR
Playa Costa Brava

Playa Chileno

Bahía Chileno

El Tule

El Tule

Bahía Santa María

Playa Barco Varado

CABO DEL SOL

FIESTA AMERICANA

SHERATON HACIENDA DEL MAR

Punta Cabeza de Ballena

LA EUROPEA

Tiburon

Las Palmillas

MISSIONES DEL CABO

CABO SAN LUCAS MOTEL/ CAMPGROUND

CLUB CABO MOTEL/ CAMPGROUND

CABO SAN LUCAS COUNTRY CLUB

Playa El Medano

Bahía San Lucas

El Salto

El Salto

SORIANA

SANLUQUEÑA BULRING

CABO SAN LUCAS

Land's End

Cabo el Arco

Isla Cerro la Bufadora
Isla Cerro Blanco
Isla Cerro Blanco

La Boruca

Salto Seco

Cabo Cabo Falso

PACIFIC OCEAN

© AVALON TRAVEL PUBLISHING, INC.

0   2 mi

0   2 km

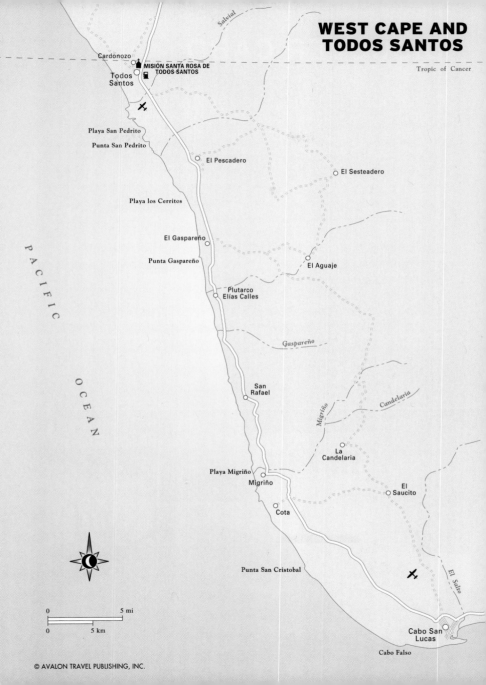

WEST CAPE AND TODOS SANTOS

Tropic of Cancer

Cardonozo

MISIÓN SANTA ROSA DE
TODOS SANTOS

Todos
Santos

Salvial

Playa San Pedrito

Punta San Pedrito

El Pescadero

El Sesteadero

Playa los Cerritos

El Gaspareño

Punta Gaspareño

El Aguaje

Plutarco
Elías Calles

Gaspareño

San
Rafael

Candelaria

Migriño

La
Candelaria

El
Saucito

Playa Migriño

Migriño

Cota

Punta San Cristobal

El Salto

PACIFIC

OCEAN

Cabo San
Lucas

Cabo Falso

0   5 mi

0   5 km

© AVALON TRAVEL PUBLISHING, INC.

DISCOVER CABO

Once upon a time, the typical Cabo visitor chose this destination for one reason: to catch big fish. These days, any number of pastimes might inspire a trip to the southern tip of the Baja peninsula. At the Los Cabos International Airport, retirees mingle with tipsy spring breakers. Newlyweds wait in line with artists and anglers. And scuba divers roll bags full of gear through the crowd.

What brings them all to the western edge of the Mexican republic? Striking tropical-desert scenery, uncommon wildlife, pristine beaches, friendly residents, five-star resorts, and nearly perfect weather all year round. And that's just the beginning of the list.

Scuba divers enjoy tropical conditions in a variety of underwater environments. Surfers find waves on both sides of the peninsula, depending on the season. Kayakers can paddle from island to island or beach to beach in the lower Sea of Cortez. Eco-minded travelers can participate in sea turtle conservation programs.

Las Ventanas al Paraíso

Outdoor recreation may be the primary draw, but Baja offers plenty of opportunities for cultural experiences as well. A distinctive *bajacaliforniano* cuisine is emerging in the larger towns, where chefs are opening new restaurants that focus on creative preparation of seafood with fresh, locally grown ingredients. In addition, San José del Cabo and Todos Santos host vibrant contemporary art scenes, while La Paz offers opportunities to learn about Baja's colonial history. Local museums, live music, and annual festivals complete the picture.

With its crystalline shores embracing verdant mountains, Cabo, or more broadly, the Cape Region of Baja California Sur, resembles a diamond-and-emerald pendant floating on azure seas. It extends from Cabo San Lucas to La Paz – the state capital of Baja California Sur – and from the Pacific Ocean to the Sea of Cortez, and it contains one of the most popular and fastest-growing destinations in all of Mexico, the Los Cabos Corridor. World-famous resorts, including

room with a view

Las Ventanas al Paraíso, Esperanza, and the One&Only Palmilla, have staked their claim to secluded beaches along this stretch of coastline, bringing with them international chefs, luxurious spas, and championship golf courses.

Beyond the five-star resorts, many out-of-the-way places in the interior and along the coast receive but a trickle of visitors, many of them annual returnees for whom Cape explorations have become a pleasurable obsession. The historic mining and farming towns of San Pedro, El Triunfo, and San Bartolo take you back in time. A network of hiking trails traverses the Sierra de la Laguna, leading to a number of freshwater springs and waterfalls. And many miles of undeveloped beach lie along the West Cape, a short drive from Cabo San Lucas, and along the East Cape north of Punta Pescadero and south of Bahía Los Frailes. Depending on the time of year and weather conditions, you might spend a week camping and surfing, or an afternoon sunbathing, boogie-boarding, or volunteering to escort baby sea turtles from their nest to the water's edge.

Two protected marine parks help safeguard the abundance

boards galore

of marinelife. Just beyond the Cabo San Lucas harbor, Bahía San Lucas is easily accessible by kayak or water taxi. Farther afield, Bahía Pulmo supports a living coral reef that begins in waist-deep water just beyond the village center. You can be swimming among moray eels, puffer fish, guitarfish, and gentle nurse sharks within minutes of your arrival in Cabo Pulmo.

Short, direct flights from the West Coast of the United States draw a majority of visitors from California, Oregon, Washington, and western Canada. For example, flights from Los Angeles to La Paz or Los Cabos take only about two hours.

Long-time Baja travelers will tell you that the Cape Region has changed – that it's not the offbeat destination it once was. In many ways, they are right. Costco and Home Depot have arrived. The coastal real estate market is in a frenzy. And there are more upscale options than ever before. But though they may pine for the days of deserted beaches and long gas lines, these seasoned travelers are still returning year after year. Whether you are planning your first trip or your 20th, you are sure to find your own tropical paradise.

tropical display

Contents

The Lay of the Land 16
Planning Your Trip... 18
Explore Cabo 21
Los Cabos Weekends 21
Seaside Romance 23
Around the Cape in Seven Days 24
Scuba Diving and Snorkeling..................................... 26
Riding the Waves.. 28

Los Cabos 29
San José del Cabo.. 35
The Corridor.. 59
Cabo San Lucas... 71

East Cape and the Sierra de la Laguna 106
East Cape 108
Sierra de la Laguna and Vicinity................................. 130

La Paz and Vicinity 141

Sights 147

Beaches 149

Islands... 154

Sports and Recreation 157

Entertainment and Events.. 166

Shopping.. 168

Accommodations.. 169

Food.. 175

Information and Services.. 180

Getting There and Around 182

Southeast of La Paz 184

West Cape and Todos Santos 190

West Cape... 194

Todos Santos 203

Background.. 225

The Land.. 225

Climate 229

Flora 231

Fauna... 235

History 241

The People 252

Essentials 254

Getting There... 254

Getting Around 260

Visas and Officialdom... 271

Sports and Recreation 277

Accommodations. 288

Food and Drink. 291

Health and Safety 302

Money 307

Information and Services. 309

Communications 311

Measurements and Standards 314

Resources 315

Glossary 315

Spanish Phrasebook 317

Suggested Reading. 323

Internet Resources 326

Index. 328

Accommodations Index 328

Restaurant Index. 330

General Index. 333

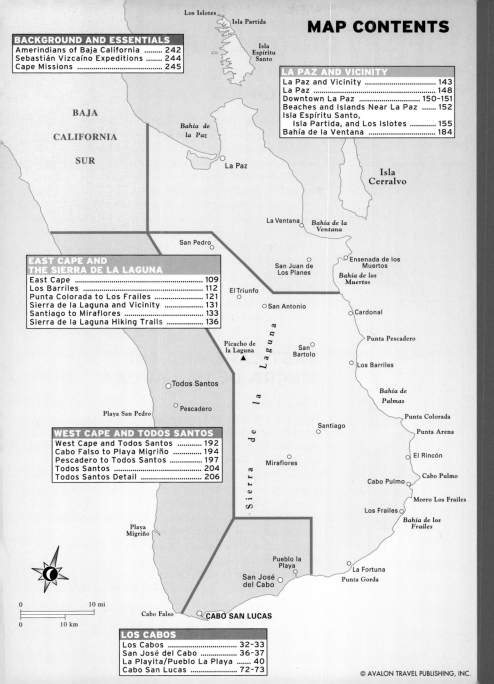

MAP CONTENTS

BACKGROUND AND ESSENTIALS
Amerindians of Baja California 242
Sebastián Vizcaíno Expeditions 244
Cape Missions 245

LA PAZ AND VICINITY
La Paz and Vicinity 143
La Paz 148
Downtown La Paz 150-151
Beaches and Islands Near La Paz 152
Isla Espíritu Santo,
   Isla Partida, and Los Islotes 155
Bahía de la Ventana 184

EAST CAPE AND THE SIERRA DE LA LAGUNA
East Cape 109
Los Barriles 112
Punta Colorada to Los Frailes 121
Sierra de la Laguna and Vicinity 131
Santiago to Miraflores 133
Sierra de la Laguna Hiking Trails 136

WEST CAPE AND TODOS SANTOS
West Cape and Todos Santos 192
Cabo Falso to Playa Migriño 194
Pescadero to Todos Santos 197
Todos Santos 204
Todos Santos Detail 206

LOS CABOS
Los Cabos 32-33
San José del Cabo 36-37
La Playita/Pueblo La Playa 40
Cabo San Lucas 72-73

BAJA

CALIFORNIA

SUR

Los Islotes

Isla Partida

Isla
Espíritu
Santo

Bahía de
la Paz

La Paz

Isla
Cerralvo

La Ventana   Bahía de la
Ventana

San Pedro

San Juan de
Los Planes

Ensenada de los
Muertos

Bahía de los
Muertos

El Triunfo

San Antonio

Cardonal

Punta Pescadero

Picacho de
la Laguna ▲

San
Bartolo

Los Barriles

Bahía de
Palmas

Todos Santos

Pescadero

Playa San Pedro

Santiago

Punta Colorada

Punta Arena

Miraflores

El Rincón

Cabo Pulmo

Cabo Pulmo

Morro Los Frailes

Los Frailes

Bahía de los
Frailes

Playa
Migriño

Sierra   de   la   Laguna

Pueblo la
Playa

San José
del Cabo

La Fortuna

Punta Gorda

0   10 mi

0   10 km

Cabo Falso   CABO SAN LUCAS

© AVALON TRAVEL PUBLISHING, INC.

The Lay of the Land

LOS CABOS

It's with good reason that the majority of first-time visitors to Baja plant themselves along the southernmost tip of the peninsula: The contrast of rock cliffs, white-sand beaches, and turquoise water produces **scenery** unlike any other in the world; plentiful **five-star resorts** pamper guests with luxury amenities; and the weather defines perfection.

Once a pair of quiet fishing villages, today's Cabo is a town, resort, and region all wrapped up into one. Los Cabos, as the tourist corridor is now known, refers to the twin cape towns of **San José del Cabo** and **Cabo San Lucas.** San Lucas entertains the young and young at heart with **beach clubs,** bars, and discos, while quieter San José offers a growing number of gourmet restaurants serving *alta cocina mexicana.* Many come to fish and dive, but **world-class golf** and luxurious spa treatments can also be part of the experience.

EAST CAPE AND THE SIERRA DE LA LAGUNA

Travelers with a passion for water sports and a willingness to forgo the conveniences of a fully developed tourist infrastructure will find paradise along the eastern shores of the lower Baja peninsula. Here, the Sea of Cortez serves up secluded beaches, steady winds, abundant game fish, a **living coral reef,** and days of 100-foot visibility underwater. For **fishing, diving, kayaking,** and **windsurfing,** conditions don't get much better than this. Development at the northern and southern edges of the region is changing access to some beaches and inviting a less adventurous set to enjoy the views; overall, however, the East Cape remains a place of solar power, dirt roads, *panga* boats, and *palapa* restaurants.

Inland, the **Sierra de la Laguna** attracts hikers, mountain bikers, and horseback riders with cascading **waterfalls,** 7,000-foot peaks, and a chance to experience the rancho way of life.

LA PAZ AND VICINITY

Unlike Cabo San Lucas and other Mexican resort towns, La Paz has little need to preen for tourists. Shockingly beautiful sunsets viewed from its five-kilometer-long (3-mi-long) *malecón,* or waterfront promenade, pristine **white-sand beaches** nearby, and a string of **uninhabited islands** just offshore all speak for themselves. This authentic city of 200,000 residents offers a mix of colonial influences and modern conveniences. Stay downtown, within walking distance to shops, restaurants, and the waterfront. Or stay at a beachfront resort a few kilometers away from the city center. With its own international airport and proximity to the peninsula's interior, La Paz is the perfect place to study Spanish, enjoy the emerging Baja California cuisine, or launch an **outdoor expedition**—whether by kayak, dive boat, yacht, or bicycle.

WEST CAPE AND TODOS SANTOS

North of Cabo San Lucas, strong winds and heavy swell from the Pacific Ocean have sculpted a **rugged shoreline** that extends to the modern-day artist community of Todos Santos and beyond. Experienced surfers camp out here for weeks on end hoping to catch the perfect wave, and a few pioneers have built vacation homes near the water's edge, but for the most part, the West Cape remains the least developed stretch of coastline on either side of the peninsula south of La Paz.

A well-maintained paved road makes **Todos Santos** and neighboring **El Pescadero** easily accessible from La Paz or Los Cabos. Set back from the ocean in a lush oasis environment, Todos Santos has become a crossroads where artists, yoga students, surfers, and retirees all mingle in pursuit of their activities. There is no shortage of **art galleries** to browse, beaches to comb, or interesting people to meet.

Planning Your Trip

A sense of adventure is a must for any Cabo vacation. Things will not always go as planned, and the traveler who embraces unexpected challenges as part of the fun will enjoy the trip infinitely more.

Full-service resorts and online resources make it easy to plan every aspect of a Cabo visit in advance. Those who prefer to make decisions on the fly can do so, with a couple of exceptions: Places book up in La Paz and Los Cabos during the Christmas/New Year's and Semana Santa (the week leading up to Easter) holidays, and La Paz fills up during the November Baja 1000 off-road race. Travelers who build some flexibility into their trip can allocate time as they go, view rooms and restaurants before committing to them, discover new places, and bargain for significant discounts. Of course, if you decide to wing it, you'll spend a good chunk of your vacation looking for places to stay, so this approach works best for longer trips.

WHEN TO GO

The flat end of the peninsula from San José del Cabo to Cabo San Lucas is warm year-round. Pacific influences generally moderate the heat July–September, while the tropic waters of the Gulf Current make this stretch the warmest coastal zone on the peninsula during winter months. Cabo San Lucas receives about 45 percent of its measurable annual rainfall—a total of 15–18 centimeters (6–7 in) a year—in September, so if there's a month to avoid for weather reasons, that's the one.

For some travelers, August and September may also be intolerably hot. Todos Santos on the Pacific coastline is cooler than Cabo San Lucas in the summer, and Cabo San Lucas is usually cooler than San José del Cabo or La Paz.

The two months when you're least likely to have Los Cabos beaches to yourself are December and January, when large numbers of Americans and Canadians come here seeking respite from rainstorms and blizzards. Crowds dwindle in summer and early fall due to the heat, although anglers and divers keep at least some hotels fully booked during these months as well.

Activity Seasons

If you'd like to time your visit around a specific outdoor activity, consider the following as a guideline:

Sportfishing: The greatest variety and number of game fish swim the widest range of Cape waters April–October, when water temperatures are relatively warm. In winter, many species migrate south, but fortunately for winter anglers, exceptions abound.

Scuba Diving: Water visibility is best July–October, when it exceeds 30 meters (100 ft); this is also when the air temperature is warmest, often reaching well over 32°C (90°F).

Surfing: Cape Region surfers are blessed; they can enjoy both winter and summer wave action within a radius of roughly 100 kilometers.

Kiteboarding and Windsurfing: November–March, the Sea of Cortez is a windsurfer's paradise, particularly along the East Cape. La Paz attracts windsurfers even in summer, when a strong breeze called *el coromuel* comes in just about every afternoon.

Whale-Watching: California gray whales and calves are a common sight offshore December–April, as they pass through Cape waters on their way to birthing lagoons on the Pacific Coast of the Central Baja region. The closest lagoon for viewing the whales up close, Bahía Magdalena, lies 200 kilometers (120 mi) northwest of La Paz.

EXTENDED STAYS

Wanderlust comes on strong in this part of the world. Many a traveler arrives in the Cape Region with some free time, a little money, a passion for the outdoors, and little else in the way of a plan. Whether you are a student off for the summer, a marine biologist on sabbatical, or a business professional in between jobs, you can easily spend a month or half a year immersing yourself in all that the region has to offer. An extended Baja stay rejuvenates the soul, and you'll likely make new friends for life. Be warned, however: The longer you stay, the harder it gets to leave. Here are some ways to while away your time:

- Enroll in a Spanish language school in La Paz.
- Volunteer to teach English.
- Participate in a local environmental conservation program.
- Sign up for cooking classes in La Paz.
- Join a yoga retreat in Todos Santos.
- Rent a secluded *casita* and use it as a writing, painting, music, or sculpture studio.
- Learn to fish using only a hand line.
- Master every surf break on the East and West Capes.
- Become a professional timeshare presentation attendee and stockpile the freebies.

WHAT TO TAKE

Seasoned Baja travelers pride themselves on the detailed nature of their packing lists. (Spreadsheets with multiple tabs for each kind of gear are not unheard of.) Below are some items to consider. See the *Essentials* chapter for lists of camping, diving, fishing, and surfing supplies.

Documents: The first thing to pack is your passport, required for U.S. citizens as of January 2007. Then print out confirmations and contact information for your flight, rental car, hotel, and any prebooked activities. Pack driving maps if you plan to venture beyond the Los Cabos region.

Gadgets: A camera is a must-have for any trip to Cabo. A GPS, laptop, cell phone, and portable music player may also come in handy while on the road in Baja, but the more electronics you pack, the heavier your bags will be and the more you'll have to keep track of your belongings. Even if you don't plan to camp, a headlamp is useful in places like Cabo Pulmo, where there are no streetlights for getting around at night.

Toiletries and First Aid: You can buy just about anything you need in San José or La Paz, but bring any favorite specialty items from home, just in case. Tums and Pepto come in handy when you OD on the hot sauce. Bug repellent and anti-itch lotion help prevent and soothe insect bites. Hand sanitizer is always a good idea.

Shoes, Clothes, and Accessories: Bring sturdy footwear for walks and hikes, and Tevas or other water-friendly footwear for the beach. Sunhat, sunglasses, and sunscreen are essential. Bring a cute wrap for the beach, but leave the strappy heels behind unless you want to risk going home with a

surfing the Corridor

broken ankle. Layers come in handy. Pack your reading material of choice; English-language books and magazines are hard to find and more expensive here.

Sports Equipment: Consider the size of your rental car when packing up the sports closet. Golf clubs, fishing rods, scuba gear, and surfboards take up lots of room. Bring straps for securing gear on the roof and repair kits for fixing dings and leaks. Renting equipment is an option in the more developed towns, including Cabo San Lucas, San José del Cabo, and La Paz. Even out-of-the-way places such as Cabo Pulmo, Los Barriles, and Todos Santos have kayaks, surfboards, and scuba gear available for rent.

Explore Cabo

LOS CABOS WEEKENDS

Winter blues got you down? A long weekend in the Baja sun may be just the answer. Travelers based in the western United States can reach Los Cabos by air in a matter of hours. Choose a home base in high-energy Cabo San Lucas or sophisticated San José del Cabo (30 minutes apart by car), or in the exclusive atmosphere of the Corridor that connects the two. Once settled, you'll have white-sand beaches, water sports, restaurants, shops, and galleries all within easy reach of your hotel.

SAN JOSÉ DEL CABO
Day 1
Arrive at Los Cabos International Airport (SJD); transfer to a hotel in downtown San José or a resort along the Corridor. Consider El Encanto Suites for modest accommodations or Casa Natalia for something more upscale. A condo at Playa Costa Azul on the outskirts of San José is another good option. If it's Thursday, browse open galleries on the weekly evening **Art Walk** in downtown San José. Savor the tastes of *alta cocina mexicana* at one of San José's stylish restaurants, such as La Panga Antigua, Tequila Restaurant, or Don Emiliano.

Day 2
Grab a pastry for breakfast at the French Riviera. Relax with a good novel by the pool. Later, walk or kayak along the **Estero San José;** snorkel the rock reefs at **Playa Chileno** or **Playa Santa María,** looking for green moray eels, spotted eagle rays, and an array of tropical fish; or catch some waves at **Playa Costa Azul.** Book a sunset horseback riding tour along **Playa California.** In the evening, order a refreshing *michelada* followed by a seafood dinner at an oceanview restaurant along the Corridor, such as Puerta Vieja or Sunset Da Mona Lisa. Finish the evening at LaSanta Wine Bar or Morgan's Restaurant and Cellar, both near the plaza in San José.

Day 3
Head out for a day of **fishing** from La Playita or **surfing** at Playa Costa Azul. Alternatively, you could travel to Cabo San Lucas to go **diving.** Or browse the many interior design shops in San José, dreaming of ways to decorate your own vacation home. Better yet, sign up for a massage at one of the luxurious spas at the Westin Los Cabos, Marquis Los Cabos, or Esperanza resorts.

Ask Restaurant-Bar Pepe's to prepare your fresh catch for dinner, head to Carnitas El Michoacano to order *carnitas* by the kilo, or try the stone bowls filled with flank steak and avocado at Guacamaya. Afterward, head to Havana Supper Club or Zippers at Playa Costa Azul for some live music.

Excursion: To see a more remote side of Baja, drive to **La Playita** (15 minutes) and along the southern stretch of the East Cape. Retrace your steps, allowing time to get back to your hotel before dark.

Day 4
Last chance to work on a tan by the pool. Stroll **Boulevard Mijares** one last time to pick up gifts and souvenirs at Sol Dorado or Antigua Los Cabos. Pack your bags and leave time for lunch at Mariscos Mazatlán II on your way to the airport. Finish reading your book on the plane.

Playa El Médano

CABO SAN LUCAS

Day 1

Arrive at Los Cabos International Airport (SJD); transfer to accommodations in downtown Cabo San Lucas or a resort along the Corridor. Consider Cabo Villas for a central location, or Club Cascadas or the Hotel Finisterra for a somewhat quieter setting. Head to **Playa El Médano** to dip your feet in the bay. Order a cocktail at Billygan's Island or The Office, and watch the sun sink behind the arch at **Land's End.**

After dark, explore downtown Cabo San Lucas by foot, taking in the shops and clubs along Boulevard Marina and Plaza Bonita. Savor the flavors of Japan at Nick-San Restaurant, then head to Sancho Panza Wine Bistro and Jazz Club Restaurant to taste Baja California wines, or Cabo Wabo for live music. Finish the evening with a Cuban cigar at Hemingway's.

Day 2

Pack a beach bag and hire a water taxi to take you to **Playa del Amor,** or rent a kayak and paddle there yourself before the wind kicks up.

Sunbathe and snorkel around Pelican Rock before catching a boat ride back to town. Head to Las Gardenias for an authentic Mexican lunch. Spend the afternoon browsing the shops in Plaza Bonita and the Puerto Paraíso mall, and head to the rooftop bar at the Cabo Villas for drinks and a **sunset view.** In the evening, enjoy Continental fare at Peacocks Restaurant and Bar or seafood at Mi Casa de Mariscos, followed by **live jazz** at Edith's.

Day 3

Grab a latte at Theory Café in Plaza Bonita before you head out for a **day at sea.** Bring lunch, and spend most of the day on a guided fishing, kayaking, diving, or snorkeling tour. Don't forget the sunblock; and divers, remember to allow 24 hours before your return flight. When you return, take a nap or lounge by the pool before another night out on the town. For dinner, order **shrimp by the bucket** at El Shrimp Bucket or Italian dishes at Capo San Giovanni.

Start the night's festivities at the Giggling Marlin or The Nowhere Bar on the waterfront, then move to one of Cabo's notorious **late-night discos,** such as El Squid Roe, until the wee hours of the morning.

Excursion: The bohemian town of **Todos Santos,** with art galleries and a pleasant small-town atmosphere, is just an hour away by car.

Day 4

Browse the traditional **Mexican handicrafts** at the Mercado Mexicano or the **silver jewelry** at Taxco or Joyería Albert. Admire ceramic sculptures at the Sergio Bustamante gallery and professional photographs of Baja California in the Tomas Spangler gallery. Take one last chance to fill your shoes with sand at Playa El Médano. Then off to the airport you go.

SEASIDE ROMANCE

Weddings, honeymoons, and anniversaries often inspire a quiet retreat. Sunset beach walks, couples' spa treatments, shopping for fine art or jewelry, dinner by candlelight, and movies on the beach are just a few of the ways to celebrate the occasion. With swim-up bars, private soaking tubs, and full-service spas, several resorts along the Los Cabos Corridor excel in creating that intimate setting. Farther afield, bohemian Todos Santos adds a layer of art and culture to the romance.

Most Romantic Resorts

- Spacious luxury suites at **Dreams Los Cabos** in the Corridor's Cabo Real development are a favorite for celebrating special occasions.

- Select linens for your bed from a menu when you check in at **Las Ventanas al Paraíso,** then enjoy a private movie showing on the beach at night.

- The remote Pacific Coast setting and no-kids policy of **Pueblo Bonito Pacifica** appeals to those in search of a quieter Los Cabos experience.

Best Candlelight Dinners

- In the heart of downtown La Paz, **Las Tres Virgenes** serves creative *bajacaliforniano* cuisine.

- **La Panga Antigua,** in San José del Cabo, offers contemporary Mexican cuisine in an outdoor courtyard setting.

- At the Marquis Los Cabos along the Corridor, **Canto del Mar** seats just 21 guests for an elegant French dinner.

Most Intimate Boutique Hotels

- Watch stunning sunsets from the pool or bar at **Posada de las Flores,** on the *malecón* in La Paz.

- Enjoy the natural surroundings of a freshwater lagoon at secluded **Posada La Poza,** in Todos Santos.

- Relax in contemporary European style at

Casa Natalia, in the heart of downtown San José del Cabo.

Best Beaches to Walk at Sunset

- Watch surfers catch their last waves of the day at **Playa Costa Azul,** just outside of San José del Cabo.

- See the sun melt into the Pacific from **Playa Solmar,** which runs along the southwestern edge of the Cape.

- Observe the wildlife in action along the **Estero San José** or **Playa Las Pocitas,** near Todos Santos.

Best Spas

- Enjoy treatment rooms with a view at the **Marquis Los Cabos.**

- Heavenly body wraps and oceanside massage sets the mood at the **Westin Los Cabos** near San José del Cabo.

- Soak in the indoor steam caves and waterfalls at **Esperanza,** close to Cabo San Lucas.

Shopoholics, Rejoice

- Browse **contemporary fine art** on display in the galleries of Todos Santos and San José del Cabo.

- Find a **Mexican fire opal** in one of San José's jewelry shops.

- Watch artisans making ceramics at **Ibarra's Pottery** in La Paz.

AROUND THE CAPE IN SEVEN DAYS

Travelers with a week or more can experience the many dimensions of the lower Baja peninsula by making a circular route around the Cape Region via paved highways Mexico 1 and Mexico 19. Extending a total distance of approximately 564 kilometers (350 mi), this route takes visitors along the lower slopes of the Sierra de la Laguna, through the sierra's former mining towns, across the plains of La Paz, and along the coastlines of the East and West Capes as well as the Corridor between San José del Cabo and Cabo San Lucas.

It's possible to complete the loop by bus, but expect to do a fair amount of walking to get from the stops along the highway to the scenic coastal areas. A rental car affords more flexibility and convenience, and you can park easily in all of the towns along the route.

This loop can be comfortably driven in two or three days, but since there are many towns worth exploring and activities to enjoy at each stop, most travelers prefer to allow a week or longer. For more of an adventure, consider widening the loop by taking the sandy Camino Rural Costero, or Rural Coastal Road.

Day 1

Arrive at Los Cabos International Airport (SJD); transfer to a hotel in downtown **San José del Cabo** and spend the evening around town. Browse the art galleries and Mexican fire opal stores downtown before sitting down to a leisurely dinner at a restaurant serving *alta cocina mexicana*.

Day 2

Drive to **Cabo Pulmo** via Mexico 1 (1–1.5 hrs), exiting at La Ribera and heading east to pick up the coastal road. The last few miles will be on dirt road. Head straight for the beach and spend the rest of the day **snorkeling** the live coral reef that comes all the way into shore. Order fish tacos and an icy *michelada* for dinner at the *palapa* restaurant on the beach, or stop by Nancy's Restaurant and Bar for a more upscale experience. Book your activity of choice for the next morning: Fishing, kayaking, and diving top the list.

Sidetrip: At Santiago, head west to reach the **Cañon de la Zorra** and a 30-foot waterfall, just a 10-minute walk from the parking lot.

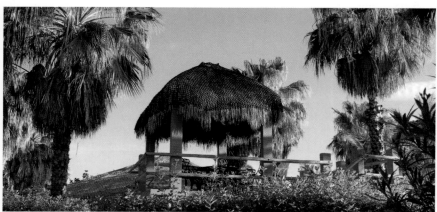

palapa-roofed *casita*, Cabo Pulmo

Alternate Route: To avoid the off-road driving and relatively primitive accommodations, skip Cabo Pulmo and stay on Mexico 1 until **Los Barriles,** popular with anglers, windsurfers, and kiteboarders.

Day 3

Spend the morning out at sea, and in the afternoon continue north along Mexico 1 to **La Paz** (1.5–2 hrs). Check in to a downtown hotel and walk the *malecón* at sunset. Seek out seafood at Mariscos Moyeyo's or *arranchera* at Rancho Viejo, then head to Casa de Villa or Las Varitas for drinks and live music.

Day 4

Take a *panga* shuttle to **Isla Espíritu Santo** for a day of kayaking and snorkeling, or book a day of diving. Alternatively, paddle or drive to a few of the beaches along the Pichilingue Peninsula. Enjoy the views from one of the waterfront seafood restaurants at **Playa Tecolote.** Spend the next morning exploring the **Museo Regional de Antropología e Historia** in downtown La Paz, and shopping for pottery and other crafts.

Depart La Paz in the afternoon, heading south on Mexico 1 to Mexico 19, which leads to **Todos Santos** (1 hr). Check in to a hotel in town, such as the Todos Santos Inn, or a vacation rental near the beach, such as Los Colibrís. For dinner, choose casual Mexican fare at Miguel's or Barajas Tacos, or something more upscale at Tres Gallines.

Sidetrip: Travelers with extra time can add a day for a **whale-watching** tour in **Bahía Magdalena,** approximately 3.5 hours by car from La Paz.

Day 5

Walk the **historic district** in Todos Santos, with brick buildings and colorful facades that date back to the town's status as Baja's sugarcane capital in the late 19th century. Admire the artwork in a few of the town's dozen **galleries.** Drive north along the coast to **Playa La Pastora** or south along Mexico 19 to **Playa Los Cerritos,** at Km 64, to stroll the beach in the afternoon. Continue south along Mexico 19 to reach **Cabo San Lucas** before dark (1 hr). Check in to a hotel in downtown Cabo San Lucas or a resort along the Corridor, such as the Sheraton Hacienda del Mar. Make a reservation at Nick-San Restaurant for outstanding sushi, and later taste Baja California's best wines at Sancho Panza Wine Bistro and Jazz Club Restaurant.

Day 6

Hire a water taxi, paddle a kayak, or rent a Wave-Runner to visit **Playa del Amor,** or plan a day of fishing or diving out of Cabo San Lucas. Wander the shops and enjoy afternoon cocktails at The Nowhere Bar or the Giggling Marlin along the marina. Take a nap so you can rally for the nightlife at Cabo Wabo or El Squid Roe after dark.

Day 7

Schedule a massage for your last morning in paradise. Take a dip in the pool, hit the shops, and return to the airport with sand in your shoes.

SCUBA DIVING AND SNORKELING

Certified divers with limited time to travel have some difficult choices to make when planning a trip to the inviting waters of the Sea of Cortez. The good news is that wherever you go, you'll encounter one of the world's richest marine ecosystems, with sea lions, numerous whale and dolphin varieties, manta rays, amberjacks, and schooling hammerhead sharks all living amid the more than 100 islands and islets that dot the sea. Larger species native to temperate northern waters mix with colorful, smaller species of tropical origin that have found their way north from Central and South American waters, providing underwater scenery that is especially vivid and varied. Water temperatures are comfortable most of the year; visibility rarely falls below 20 feet and can exceed 100 feet on the best of days.

WHERE TO GO
Cabo San Lucas

One option is to stay close to the lively scene in Cabo San Lucas. Short boat rides are an advantage to diving here; crowds and noise from harbor traffic are the main deterrents.

A **deep submarine canyon** just 45 meters offshore offers exciting underwater topography for experienced divers. The canyon is known for its intriguing "sandfalls," streams of falling sand channeled between rocks along the canyon walls. But even when the rivers aren't running, the dive offers varied marinelife, large and small.

Another popular dive from San Lucas begins in the surge under a sea lion colony on the Sea of Cortez side of **Land's End** and concludes

with an underwater swim around to the Pacific side. Guitar fish, schooling amber jacks, green sea turtles, and countless other species are likely to make an appearance on this dive.

Snorkeling near **Playa del Amor** is surprisingly good, despite the crowds. More snorkeling opportunities await at **Playas Chileno and Santa María** on the Corridor.

Cabo Pulmo

Alternatively, you can sacrifice nightlife and amenities to explore the **living coral reef** and national marine park offshore from Cabo Pulmo in the East Cape region. The coral attracts a wide variety of fish of all sizes and colors; other smaller reefs, as well as shipwrecks, lie in the general vi-dive center, Cabo Pulmo Beach Resort

cinity. Drift dives are common here, and boat rides are short. Several sites, including a sea lion colony, are ideal for novices. Guides tend to have smaller groups and visit more advanced sites during the week. On Saturday mornings, tour vans from Cabo San Lucas bring mostly novice divers to Cabo Pulmo to see the reef. Snorkelers can access the reef in waist-deep water directly in front of the **Cabo Pulmo Beach Resort**.

La Paz

The islands and seamounts offshore from La Paz harbor some of the most exciting underwater topography and the largest marine creatures in the sea. Boat rides are long—an hour or more—and currents tend to be strong at these sites. The reward is the chance to experience the deep blue and to spot schooling hammerhead sharks, giant mantas, and the majestic whale shark. In addition, the snorkeling in the bays around **Espíritu Santo** and neighboring islands is as good as it gets.

Popular dive sites near La Paz include Playa Balandra (mostly snorkeling), Roca Suwanee, Isla Espíritu Santo, Isla Partida, the *Salvatierra* shipwreck, El Bajito Reef, Los Islotes, and El Bajo Seamount. **El Bajo** is famous for its summer population of giant manta rays. Schooling hammerhead sharks are also common during the summer months—they're very rarely aggressive toward divers when swimming in schools, so El Bajo makes an excellent observation area.

Pacific Coast

Heavy swells and surging along the Pacific coast mean that Pacific diving should be tackled only by experienced scuba divers or with an experienced underwater guide.

Dive Operators

Dive operators in all of these locations provide expert guiding and instruction services. For those who are seriously dedicated to the sport, liveaboard trips are another option. Plan on a five-day trip to allow for multiple dive days and at least one rest day. A full week allows time for an excursion to one of the other dive areas.

WHEN TO GO

From La Paz south, onshore water temperatures usually hover between 21°C (70°F) and 29°C (85°F) year-round, making the southern Cortez the most popular diving destination on this side of Baja. Water visibility is best July–October, when it exceeds 30 meters (100 ft); this is also when the air temperature is warmest, often reaching well over 32°C (90°F).

RIDING THE WAVES

Novice and experienced surfers find waves aplenty in the West Cape, the Corridor, and the lower East Cape regions. In winter, a west-northwest groundswell combines with the year-round north-west windswell to stoke point breaks along the Pacific shore from Punta Márquez all the way to Migriño. During summer's southern swell, point breaks fire all along the Corridor between Cabo San Lucas and San José del Cabo. Large swells can send surfable waves up the Sea of Cortez as far north as Los Barriles.

Los Cabos

Most of the action in the Los Cabos region takes place near **Playa Costa Azul,** just outside of San José del Cabo. When summer's south swells roll in, experienced surfers wait for a turn at Zippers and The Rock, while beginners can usually handle the waves at **Playa Acapulquito,** the next cove to the west. Book a condo within walking distance to the breaks, and sign up for lessons through the Costa Azul Surf Shop across the highway from Playa Costa Azul, or the Cabo Surf Shop inside the Cabo Surf Hotel at Playa Acapulquito.

East Cape

Nine miles northeast of San José, **Shipwreck** picks up the south swell, and farther north, **Nine Palms** is popular with longboarders. During the late summer/early fall *chubasco* season, op-portunistic surfers often find surprisingly good waves at **Punta Arena,** near La Ribera and the Camino Rural Costero. Load up on supplies in San José, and plan to camp on the beaches.

West Cape and Todos Santos

Guests of the Pescadero Surf Camp head to **Playa Los Cerritos.** Beginners appreciate the sandy bottom and can learn to stand up on the whitewater on the inside. Closer to Todos Santos, the cobblestone point at **Punta San Pedro** breaks on both north and south swells. Several inns and vacation rentals in El Pescadero are located within walking distance to the break. Surfers looking for big waves head to **Playa La Pastora** north of Todos Santos. You can rent boards and buy gear at two shops in Todos Santos or at the beach at Los Cerritos.

LOS CABOS

Something magical happens at the point where the cool green Pacific Ocean crashes into the blue sapphire Sea of Cortez at Land's End. The fish that inhabit these waters drew the original visitors 30 years ago. Then the anglers began to bring their golf clubs, dive gear, and college-age kids. Today, stunning geography, perfect weather, endless opportunities for outdoor recreation, and federal funding from the Mexican government have transformed the area from a cluster of fishing villages into a full-scale tourist corridor.

From Cabo San Lucas to San José del Cabo, and everywhere in between, highway exit ramps are replacing dirt-road turnoffs, new resorts and condo buildings are under construction, golf courses are opening, and restaurant menu prices are reaching for the stars. Some say Los Cabos is well on its way (if not already there) to becoming Mexico's most expensive destination.

Adventure travelers, fear not: Los Cabos offers much more than nine-bedroom villas and 110-foot yachts. Beneath the upscale veneer, quaint B&Bs, modest hotels, free snorkeling beaches, authentic taquerías, and affordable *panga* boat tours invite exploration.

Cabo San Lucas and San José del Cabo enjoy equal access to a string of beautiful beaches along the Corridor between the two towns, but because the San Lucas harbor provides shelter for a sizable sportfishing and recreational fleet, the preponderance of yearly Los Cabos visitors station themselves here rather than in San José or along the Corridor.

Although it's located closer to Los Cabos

© NIKKI GOTH ITOI

HIGHLIGHTS

Plaza Mijares: A shady plaza at the intersection of San José's two main streets features the twin-towered **Iglesia San José,** built in 1940 on the site of the original 1730 Misión San José del Cabo (page 39).

Estero San José: The freshwater Río San José meets the Pacific Ocean at a 50-hectare (125-acre) estuary that hosts more than 200 species of birds (page 40).

Playas Chileno and Santa María: Two of the Corridor's most popular and accessible beaches offer safe swimming and good snorkeling (page 60).

Land's End: A large cluster of granitic batholiths, carved by wind and sea into fantastic shapes, tumbles into the sea at the Cape's southernmost point (page 75).

Playa del Amor: The Sea of Cortez meets the Pacific Ocean at this two-sided beach just outside the Cabo San Lucas harbor. Calm waters on Bahía San Lucas invite underwater exploration, while pounding surf on the Pacific side warns sunbathers to keep their distance (page 76).

LOOK FOR **(** TO FIND RECOMMENDED SIGHTS, ACTIVITIES, DINING, AND LODGING.

International Airport, San José del Cabo is a quieter, more traditional resort town than neighboring Cabo San Lucas. A somewhat older tourist crowd frequents San José (pop. 25,000), leaving Cabo San Lucas to partying college students, bachelor parties, and young couples. That said, San José is experiencing some growth pains of its own—in the form of heavier traffic and noise pollution from pervasive construction. And there is concern that the town is becoming unaffordable for local residents.

The Transpeninsular Highway's 29-kilometer (18-mi), four-lane stretch between San José del Cabo and Cabo San Lucas—known as the Corridor—provides access to numerous beaches, coves, points, and tidal pools along the Pacific Ocean and Sea of Cortez.

PLANNING YOUR TIME

In a couple of days, you can easily explore the main sections of downtown San José and sample a few restaurants, plus have time for the beach. Add extra days for any special activities, such as scuba diving, fishing, or mountain biking. The drive from San José del Cabo to Cabo San Lucas along the Corridor takes about 30–45 minutes. Surfers and beachcombers will happily spend a full week at a resort along the Corridor. But aside from the beaches (which are spectacular) and associated activities, there is little else to see—meaning, you don't need a lot of time to cover the area if you're just passing through.

For some travelers, a half day in Cabo San Lucas will be more than enough time; others will be content to spend a week. It all depends on whether you prefer nightlife or a more remote setting for your vacation.

CHOOSING AN ACCOMMODATION

Whether you are a first-time or veteran Los Cabos visitor, finding a place to stay involves an overwhelming variety of choices. There are all-inclusive resorts, boutique hotels, basic motels, bed-and-breakfast inns, condominiums, timeshares, and villas of all sizes. (And some resorts mix and match, to give even more choice.) You can be at the beach, on a golf course, or in town. You can book directly with a resort or private owner, or use a booking service or property management company. And you can spend US$50 to US$950 a night, depending on your budget and the level of comfort you seek.

If you'd like a quieter location where you can look at the beach but swim in a pool, the Corridor or hotel zone of San José would be good choices. If you want to surf, consider Playa Costa Azul, just outside of San José. For swimming and nightlife within walking distance of your hotel, head to Cabo San Lucas.

High-end resorts feature a full list of amenities, usually including air conditioning, direct-dial phones, satellite TV, multiple swimming pools, swim-up bars, tennis courts, hot tubs, fitness centers, kids' club, and beach *palapas,* plus onsite restaurants and bars. Some resorts also have their own dive centers, spa services, horseback riding, and ATV rental services. High-speed wireless Internet, voice-over-IP phones (free long distance), and flatscreen TVs are some of the newest amenities that hotels and condo owners are adding to differentiate themselves.

Vacation rental condos or villas, or condo-style hotels, afford the most flexibility, as you can cook some of your own meals and venture out for others. Many of the newest condo complexes are concentrated near Playa Costa Azul, between San José and the Corridor. Most are on or near the beach and many have tennis courts, swimming pools, and laundry facilities; however, the persistent sound of traffic on Mexico 1 is a drawback to this location. You can rent units directly from private own-ers by searching for list .craigslist.com and www.vr ple), or by contacting a propert service. (Many of these services a on the private-owner sites.)

Planning Ahead

If you are thinking about a year-end holiday vacation, book as far in advance as possible. Repeat visitors reserve many of the most popular rooms and rentals as much as a year in advance for the weeks around Christmas and New Year's. February and March are popular too, and despite the number of choices for accommodations, there are a handful of resorts—including the One&Only Palmilla, Dreams, and Riu Palace—that seem to be full almost all the time. Flexible travelers need not plan so far ahead, and they are often rewarded with better deals.

Booking Services and Property Management Companies

If you haven't yet decided on a specific location within Los Cabos, or you have a very specific set of criteria for choosing a place to stay, contact a booking service agent, who can give you an overview of several different properties that meet your criteria and your budget. The following companies specialize in Los Cabos area bookings: **Delfin Hotels & Resorts,** also called **Cabo Hotels** (U.S. tel. 800/524-5104) lists a wide variety of villas, condos (Terrasol, Las Mañanitas, Mira Vista, Mykonos) all-inclusive resorts, and bed-and-breakfast inns. It also publishes several Cabo accommodations websites, including www.cabohotels.com, www.cabocondos.com, and www.allinclusivecabo.com. **Baja Properties** (Doblado and Morelos, San José tel. 624/142-0988, Cabo San Lucas tel. 624/143-2560, U.S. tel. 877/462-2226, www.bajaproperties.com) has 20 years of experience in Los Cabos real estate marketing, eight office locations, and a team of 25 agents.

Watsonville, California–based **Earth, Sea, and Sky Vacations** (ESSV, U.S. tel. 800/745-2226, www.cabovillas.com) specializes in

LOS CABOS

luxury vacation packages to the Los Cabos area. It represents 90 villa rentals, ranging from two- to nine-bedroom units, with a starting pricepoint of US$1,500 per night, as well as 30 resorts. For an extra fee, ESSV staff will stock your villa prior to your arrival with the foods and supplies you request. Guests can also opt for in-villa services, such as pilates or yoga classes, spa treatments, and chef services (for one special meal or three meals daily). Since ESSV also handles activity bookings for whale-watching, fishing, and snorkeling, many travelers work with the company to coordinate group trips, such as large family vacations or small weddings.

Companies that focus exclusively on Cabo San Lucas or San José del Cabo (as opposed to the entire region), are listed in the accommodations section for those towns.

GETTING THERE

The majority of Los Cabos visitors arrive by air, but you'll meet many who have traveled by car, boat, bicycle, or even on foot. Public transpor-

tation by bus is also a possibility. Once you've arrived, you can do without a car if you plan to stay at an all-inclusive resort or at a hotel in town. Rent a car if you want to take a day trip to the East Cape or Todos Santos.

By Air

Los Cabos International Airport (SJD), located about eight miles north of San José del Cabo via a speedy four-lane section of Mexico 1 (Km 44, tel. 624/142-5111), serves both San José and Cabo San Lucas. The airport does not have Jetways, so have your shades at the ready as you exit the plane and climb down the stairs to the tarmac.

The process of going through customs can take more than an hour, depending on how many people are working and if other flights have arrived at the same time. After you go through passport control, you'll proceed to the baggage claim area. Claim your bags and have your paperwork ready to show the customs official. You'll be asked to run your bags through a scanner and to press a button

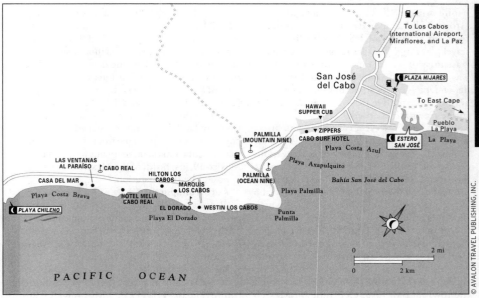

To Los Cabos
International Aireport,
Miraflores, and La Paz

San José
del Cabo

PLAZA MIJARES

To East Cape

HAWAII
SUPPER CUB

Pueblo
La Playa

PALMILLA
(MOUNTAIN NINE)

ZIPPERS
CABO SURF HOTEL

ESTERO
SAN JOSÉ

La Playa

Playa Costa Azul

LAS VENTANAS
AL PARAÍSO

CABO REAL

Playa Axapulquito

CASA DEL MAR

HILTON LOS
CABOS

MARQUIS
LOS CABOS

PALMILLA
(OCEAN NINE)

Bahía San José del Cabo

Playa Costa Brava

HOTEL MELIÁ
CABO REAL

Playa Palmilla

PLAYA CHILENO

EL DORADO

WESTIN LOS CABOS

Playa El Dorado

Punta
Palmilla

PACIFIC OCEAN

0   2 mi
0   2 km

© AVALON TRAVEL PUBLISHING, INC.

that determines whether your bags will be randomly searched.

The airport has three terminals served by several major airlines, including:

- Terminal 1: American, Aeromexico, US Airways, Continental, Mexicana

- Terminal 2: General aviation and cargo

- Terminal 3: Alaska, Delta, Frontier, United

Terminal 1 holds a few food kiosks (Domino's Express, Subway Sandwiches, Dunkin' Donuts), two snack bars, souvenir shops, a money-exchange service, and an upstairs restaurant, but has no seats in the waiting area for arriving flights—a minor inconvenience for those meeting incoming passengers.

There are no seats in the waiting area for arriving flights at the new terminal either, except at the small bar. The second level (inside security) has a bar in the center and a cafeteria at one end.

A *colectivo* (shared) van into the San José area runs US$12 per person and US$15 to the Cabo San Lucas area. A private taxi from the airport to any destination in San José del Cabo costs US$35; US$70 to Cabo San Lucas.

BY PRIVATE AIRCRAFT

Private pilots will find a 1,550-meter (5,100-ft) paved airstrip just north of Cabo San Lucas. Contact Baja Bush Pilots (www.bajabushpilots.com) for up-to-date information about making the trip to Los Cabos.

By Car

Most of the big auto rental agencies have desks at Los Cabos International Airport, as well as offices in or near town. (See the sidebar *Where to Rent a Car in Baja* in the *Essentials* chapter.) Rates will be similar across most companies, and since car rentals don't require a deposit up front, it doesn't hurt to make a reservation in advance. You can always cancel if you change your mind. When you reserve or prepay for a car online, the price typically will not include Mexican liability insurance. Be sure to factor this cost (around US$25 per day for the minimum required coverage of US$50,000) into your travel planning. Vehicles range from standard transmission subcompact sedans to SUVs, wagons, jeeps, pickup trucks, and vans. Independent agencies sometimes include insurance in the rates (see *Insuring Your Rental Car* in the *Essentials* chapter).

If you don't reserve a car before you arrive in Los Cabos, you can look at price lists at the airport. By comparing rates across the various desks, you can sometimes negotiate the price downward. It's usually cheaper to rent a car at Los Cabos International Airport than in Cabo San Lucas or San José, but it's always worth shopping around.

If you're driving yourself, there are two ways to reach the towns along the Los Cabos Corridor from the airport: Follow signs for Mexico 1 south through town, passing through several stoplights before you reach the town of San José. Continue on Mexico 1 another 10–20 minutes for destinations along the Corridor, or about 30 minutes to Cabo San Lucas. Alternatively, if you don't mind paying a toll of US$2, you can exit the airport onto the *quota,* a fast four-lane road with no exits until you enter San José at the junction of Paseo Los Cabos and the Mega grocery store plaza. If you pick up a rental car offsite, you'll have to return to the terminal to get to the toll road.

By Bus

Buses to/from La Paz: Autotransportes Águila (tel. 624/143-7880) operates 17 buses a day to La Paz (US$14 from Cabo San Lucas and US$17 from San José), a dozen via Todos Santos. This is the quickest route at 3.5 hours total; the rest go via San José del Cabo, Los Barriles, and the East Cape, totaling 4–4.5 hours. The first bus leaves Cabo San Lucas at 5:45 A.M.; the last leaves at 8:30 P.M. Buses that depart at 7:40 A.M., 9:40 A.M., and 12:30 P.M. continue to Pichilingue for the ferry; if you miss these, take any La Paz bus and transfer to one of the hourly buses to Pichilingue from the La Paz bus station. Cabo's main intercity bus terminal is on Mexico 19, just north of the Mexico 1 junction, opposite the Pemex station.

Autotransportes La Paz also has buses to La Paz, usually slightly cheaper than the competition. The bus stop is on the opposite side of the road, just south of the same junction. Buses depart at 6, 7, 8:30, and 9:30 A.M., then roughly every 90 minutes thereafter.

Buses Farther North: Each day at 4 P.M. a first-class bus also leaves for the 24-hour trip to Tijuana (US$125), with stops in Ciudad Constitución (US$25), Loreto (US$33), Mulegé (US$35), Guerrero Negro (US$57), and Ensenada (US$90).

By Sea

The nearest ferry service to the mainland operates between La Paz and Mazatlán (see *Getting There and Around* in the *La Paz and Vicinity* chapter).

Marina Cabo San Lucas is the main docking facility for transient recreational boats; bow-stern anchorages are also permitted in the outer bay (see *Boating* in the *Cabo San Lucas* section).

San José del Cabo

The Jesuit padres who founded a mission community here in the 18th century situated San José on a mesa a couple of kilometers north of the beach. Century-old brick and adobe buildings, many of them proudly restored, line the main streets radiating from the plaza and church. These are interspersed with Indian laurel trees and other greenery, making San José one of the most pleasant pedestrian towns in the Cape Region.

The architecture thins out and becomes more modern as you descend toward the beach, culminating in a golf course, condos, resort homes, and the *zona hotelera*. Because of the town's mesa geography, the beachfront hotels don't obscure the view from town. Areas to the north and east of town are dotted with irrigated orchards producing mangoes, avocados, bananas, and citrus.

As the *cabecera* (roughly equivalent to "county seat") of the Municipio de San José del Cabo, the town enjoys well-maintained streets and city services. Employment in the public as well as private sector has lured a variety of talented *bajacalifornianos* to establish residence here. A number of foreigners also have retirement or vacation homes in the area, although the overall gringo presence, whether resident or visiting, is much smaller than in Cabo San Lucas.

HISTORY

The Pericú who frequented the San José area before the Spanish *entrada* called the area "Añuiti," a name whose meaning has been lost. Spanish galleons first visited Estero San José—the mouth of the Río San José—to obtain freshwater near the end of their lengthy voyages from the Philippines to Acapulco in the late 17th and early 18th centuries. During this period the estuary was known among seamen as Aguada Segura (Sure Waters) and, less commonly, San Bernabe, a name left behind by Sebastián Vizcaíno

© PAUL ITOI

Playa California

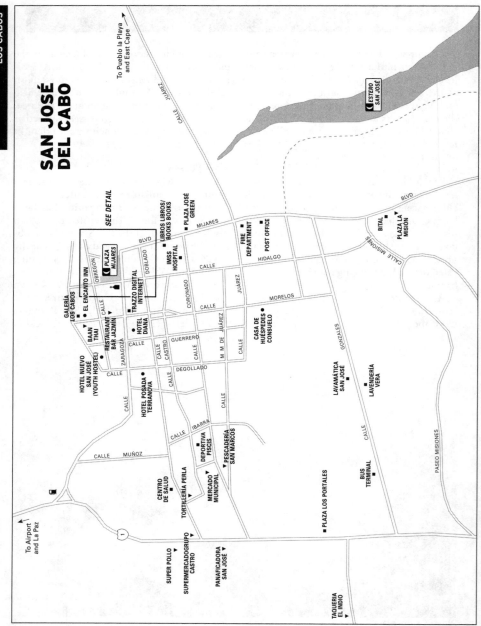

SAN JOSÉ DEL CABOS

To Pueblo la Playa and East Cape

ESTERO SAN JOSÉ

SEE DETAIL

GALERÍA LOS CABOS

EL ENCANTO INN

PLAZA MIJARES

TRAZZO DIGITAL INTERNET

LIBROS LIBROS/ BOOKS BOOKS

PLAZA JOSÉ GREEN

BLVD

OBREGÓN

CALLE JUÁREZ

DOBLADO

MIJARES

FIRE DEPARTMENT

POST OFFICE

BITAL

PLAZA LA MISIÓN

BLVD

BAAN THAI

RESTAURANT BAR JAZMÍN

HOTEL DIANA

IMSS HOSPITAL

CALLE

HIDALGO

CALLE MISIONES

HOTEL NUEVO SAN JOSÉ (YOUTH HOSTEL)

ZARAGOZA

CORONADO

CALLE

JUÁREZ

MORELOS

HOTEL POSADA TERRANOVA

CALLE CASTRO

GUERRERO

DEGOLLADO

M M DE JUÁREZ

CALLE

CASA DE HUÉSPEDES CONSUELO

GONZALES

CALLE

IBARRA

DEPORTIVA PISCIS

PESCADERÍA SAN MARCOS

LAVAMÁTICA SAN JOSÉ

LAVENDERÍA VERA

CALLE MUÑOZ

CENTRO DE SALUD

TORTILLERÍA PERLA

MERCADO MUNICIPAL

BUS TERMINAL

PASEO MISIONES

PLAZA LOS PORTALES

To Airport and La Paz

SUPER POLLO

SUPERMERCADOGRUPO CASTRO

PANAFICADORA SAN JOSÉ

TAQUERÍA EL INDIO

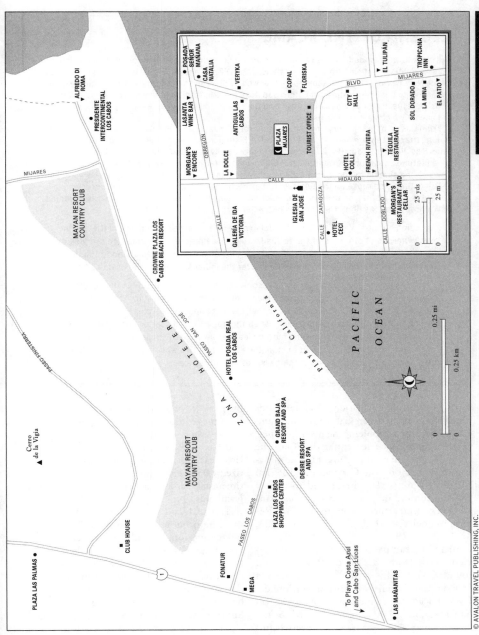

LEGEND OF THE FLAME

A little-known episode featuring a shipwrecked Irishman footnotes San José's colorful history. Fleeing political strife in 18th-century Ireland, John O'Brien and several of his countrymen sailed to the New World – along the same route followed by Sir Francis Drake and earlier English explorers – only to become stranded at Estero San José in 1795. After marrying a local Pericú woman, O'Brien refused rescue when his father and the rest of the Irish crew were later picked up by a ship on its way back to the British Isles.

From this point in the story onward, facts merge with fable as O'Brien gained legendary status among the *bajacalifornianos* as "La Flama" (The Flame) for his red hair and fiery disposition. Also known as Juan Colorado (Red John), or more prosaically as Juan Obregón, the Irishman set out on a lifetime adventure throughout the Californias as far north as San Francisco, working as a cowboy and singing the nostalgia-tinted praises of San José del Cabo everywhere he went. For O'Brien, San José replaced the Emerald Isle as his homeland, and one imagines him crying in a shot of tequila instead of ale as he expresses his longing for "San José del Arroyo," as imagined in Walter Nordhoff's book *The Journey of the Flame:*

> On seeing our dear Valley of San José del Arroyo for the last time, with the cattle grazing everywhere, on both sides of the fertile land, on the hillsides, I remembered the violent stampedes of the wild bulls and the delicious sips of warm milk I stole, and I thought: If heaven is like this valley, I can only repeat after the Indians, "Father, lead us there!"

> How many times, in subsequent years, someone galloping by my side in the desert has asked me, "Where are you from, countryman?" And when I answered him "From San José!" something crept into his voice that no other place is capable of evoking when he asked: "Would that be San José del Arroyo?" Then the horses could scatter, the cattle begin a stampede, the water be a thousand burning leagues away, or death lie close by in ambush for us, and nevertheless we had to stop. Because when two who love this Arroyo Valley meet and know each other, everything else loses importance.

during his coastal navigations. As pirate raids along the coast between Cabo San Lucas and La Paz became a problem, the need for a permanent Spanish settlement at the tip of the Cape became increasingly urgent. The growing unrest among the Guaicura and Pericú south of Loreto also threatened to engulf mission communities to the north; the Spanish had to send armed troops to the Cape Region to quell Amerindian uprisings in 1723, 1725, and 1729.

In 1730 Jesuit padre Nicolás Tamaral traveled south from Misión La Purísima and founded Misión Estero de las Palmas de San José del Cabo Añuiti (or Misión San José del Cabo, for short) on a mesa overlooking the Río San José, about five kilometers north of the current town site. Because of the overwhelm-

ing presence of mosquitoes at this site, Tamaral soon moved the mission to the mouth of the estuary, on a rise flanked by Cerro de la Vigía and Cerro de la Cruz. During the mission's first year, Jesuit records show the padre baptized 1,036 *salvajes* (savages), while at the same time establishing fruit orchards and irrigated farmlands.

Tamaral and the Pericú got along fine until he pronounced an injunction against polygamy, long a tradition in Pericú society. After Tamaral punished a Pericú shaman for violating the antipolygamy decree, the Amerindians rebelled and burned both the San José and Santiago missions in October 1734. Tamaral was killed in the attack. Shortly thereafter, the Spanish established a garrison to protect the community from

© NIKKI GOTH ITOI

Plaza Mijares, San José's central plaza

insurgent natives and the estuary from English pirates.

By 1767, virtually all the Amerindians in the area had died either of European-borne diseases or in skirmishes with the Spanish. Surviving Pericú were moved to missions farther north, but San José del Cabo remained an important Spanish military outpost until the mid-19th century, when the presidio was turned over to Mexican nationals.

During the Mexican-American War (1846–1848), marines from the U.S. frigate *Portsmouth* briefly occupied the city. A bloody siege ensued, but the Mexicans prevailed under the leadership of Mexican naval officer José Antonio Mijares. Plaza Mijares, San José's town square, is named for him, as is Boulevard Mijares, the main avenue connecting the town center and the hotel zone. As mining in the Cape Region gave out during the late 19th and early 20th centuries, the population of San José and the rest of the region decreased. A few sugarcane farmers, cattle ranchers, and fishermen began trickling into the San José

area in the 1930s, and in 1940 the church was rebuilt.

San José remained largely an agricultural backwater known for its avocados, mangoes, citrus, and other fruits until the Cape began attracting sportfishers and later the sun-and-sand set in the 1960s and 1970s. Since the late 1970s, Fonatur (the Mexican tourist bureau) has sponsored several tourist and residential development projects along San José's shoreline. Fortunately, the development has done little to change San José's Spanish-colonial character, and local residents take pride in restoring the town's 18th-century architecture and preserving its quiet, laid-back ambience.

SIGHTS
Plaza Mijares

Most town festivals are centered at Plaza Mijares. The shady plaza, at the intersection of Boulevard Mijares and Calle Zaragoza (San José's two main streets), is a well-tended expanse of brick with benches and a gazebo. At the plaza's west end is the twin-towered **Iglesia San José,** built in 1940 on the site of the original 1730 Misión San José del Cabo. A mosaic over the main entrance depicts a scene from the infamous 1734 Pericú uprising, with Amerindians shown dragging Padre Tamaral toward a fire, presumably to be burned alive.

Estero San José

The freshwater Río San José meets the Pacific Ocean at this 50-hectare (125-acre) estuary just east of the Presidente InterContinental Los Cabos hotel. A sandbar at the mouth of the river forms a scenic lagoon surrounded by tall palms and marsh grasses—habitat for more than 200 species of birds, including brown pelicans, ring-necked ducks, common egrets, and herons. Bird connoisseurs should keep their eyes peeled for Belding's yellowthroat, also commonly seen here. You can rent canoes at Tío Sports, next to the Presidente, for paddling around the lagoon.

A public footpath, **Paseo del Estero,** follows the estuary and river through scenic fan palms, river cane, and tule—a perfect place for bird-watching. The path begins at the Presidente and comes out on Boulevard Mijares near a modern water-treatment plant. There is plenty of street parking near the hotel.

Zona Hotelera

Fonatur has developed 4,000 shoreline acres adjacent to San José into a hotel and recreation zone. Thus far, the zone contains several resort hotels, a golf course, shopping center, and several condo and housing developments. Between the Presidente InterContinental and Crowne Plaza resorts, the new Cabo Azul Resort & Spa, under construction by Pacific Monarch Resorts, will house 292 vacation villas. Mayan Resorts is also developing a new resort next door. Some of the nicest homes in the Fonatur zone are located along the north side of the golf course.

The wide, sandy beach here, known as either Playa Hotelera or Playa California, is perfect for sunbathing, but the undertow is strong.

La Playita and Pueblo La Playa

Just east of San José via Calle Juárez, adjacent to the village of Pueblo La Playa, is La Playita (Little Beach). An ocean beach away from the hotel zone, La Playita offers *pangas* for hire. Walk along the beach northeast of the Presidente InterContinental Los Cabos about a kilometer, or you can walk or drive a similar distance east along Calle Juárez from downtown. Continue along a dirt road through the middle of the village, past a radio tower, to reach the most secluded spots.

Along the dirt road from here to Pueblo La Playa and beyond to the East Cape are large banyan *(zalate)* and mango trees as well as wild sugarcane. Much of the Río San José valley was once planted in sugarcane.

Home development continues in the area. Fonatur has begun to develop a new tourist zone called Puerto Los Cabos (www.puertoloscabos) at La Playita. At last check, a four-lane boulevard with a landscaped median led the way through several traffic circles to the beach. Cranes were moving rocks one by one to

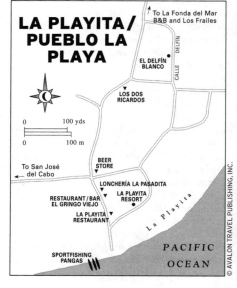

LA PLAYITA / PUEBLO LA PLAYA

To La Fonda del Mar B&B and Los Frailes

EL DELFÍN BLANCO

CALLE DELFÍN

LOS DOS RICARDOS

0   100 yds
0   100 m

To San José del Cabo

BEER STORE

LONCHERÍA LA PASADITA

LA PLAYITA RESORT

RESTAURANT/BAR EL GRINGO VIEJO

LA PLAYITA RESTAURANT

La Playita

SPORTFISHING PANGAS

PACIFIC OCEAN

© AVALON TRAVEL PUBLISHING, INC.

© NIKKI GOTH ITOI

dining under a *palapa* roof at Mariscos El Puerto, at La Playita

form a protected harbor around the sportfishing *pangas* that line the beach. When complete, the 2,000-acre development will include more five-star hotels and designer golf courses and a new marina that will allow large seagoing vessels to dock, ushering thousands of passengers into town.

Playa Costa Azul

Connecting San José to the Corridor, Plaza Costa Azul is gently washed by low breakers and often safe for swimming, except during the *chubasco* season (see *Surfing*). Several condo complexes line the beach. For travelers coming from San José, there is a new and unmarked exit ramp just after Havanas Restaurant and before the wide arroyo. Turn left off the ramp and park in the sandy lot that divides Mira Vista condos and Zippers Restaurant.

FISHING

Whether you're a seasoned veteran or you've never fished a day in your life, there are plenty of options near San José. For newbies, your captain and crew will find the right spot for the day, rig up the bait, and handle boating the fish. All you have to do is reel and smile for the picture. Later, top off the day by taking your fresh catch to a local restaurant to have it prepared to your liking.

Fishing boats for hire fall under two general categories: *pangas* and cruisers. Cruisers are the larger boats you'll see in the marina slips. They're often equipped with tuna-towers, enclosed cabins, bathroom, and other amenities. *Pangas* are the ubiquitous open launches, powered by outboard motor and sometimes featuring a sunshade and center console. If you see a *panga* with a newer four-stroke outboard, center console, sunshade, and mounted radio, jump in—you've got a winner. The fish don't care what kind of boat you're in, but the cruisers can handle the larger game fish and a nonfishing passenger in comfort.

Don't forget to pack a hat, sunglasses, sunscreen, water, food, waterproof camera, sandals/Tevas, and windbreaker. Take motion sickness medicine the night before and morning of the trip if you are prone to seasickness (or if you aren't sure).

All hotels in the *zona hotelera* can arrange guided fishing trips. Since San José has no harbor or marina (until the new one is completed in La Playita), all trips are in *pangas.* Well-known **Francisco's Fleet** (formerly Victor's Sportfishing, U.S. tel. 800/521-2281, www.jigstop.com) is based at Palmilla beach. A six-hour *panga* trip for 2–3 people costs US$190; bring your own food and drinks. An eight-hour trip aboard a 28- to 32-foot cabin cruiser can accommodate up to six anglers for US$395. **Gordo Banks Pangas** (tel./fax 624/142-1147, U.S. tel. 800/408-1199, www.gordobanks.com) launches out of La Playita and rents 22-foot *pangas* for US$200 (six hours, 1–3 anglers) or 23-foot super *pangas* for US$240 (six hours, 1–3 anglers), and cruisers for US$350–530.

There are a few extra costs to factor into the planning: Tips for the captain and fish-cleaning crew are the norm. Live bait is often not included in the cost of the *panga,* so expect to pay US$20 per boat. Fishing licenses cost US$11/day, US$23/week. You do not need a fishing license to fish from the shore. For details on fishing seasons and on-shore and inshore catches, see *Fishing* in the *Essentials* chapter.

Deportiva Piscis (tel. 624/142-0332, daily 8 A.M.–7 P.M.), on the south side of Calle Castro near the Mercado Municipal, sells fishing tackle as well as bait.

SNORKELING AND DIVING

San José visitors must head to the East Cape, the Corridor, or Cabo San Lucas for suitable snorkeling and diving sites. Expert divers who are comfortable in strong currents and choppy seas and interested in exploring the offshore Gorda Banks seamounts may be able to hire a *panga* from La Playita; however, be aware that even groups of experienced dive instructors have run into complications when attempting to turn a fisherman into a dive-boat captain for the day. The safer approach is to book a trip through one of the PADI-certified dive shops in Cabo San Lucas.

SURFING

Summer is the peak season for catching waves here, but good-sized swells occasionally roll through as late as mid-November. On the outskirts of San José, **Playa Costa Azul** (Blue Coast Beach) boasts two good summer breaks: a short fast inside known as Zippers, and a middle right point break called The Rock. Spectators watch the action below from a lookout at Km 28. At the next little bay south, almost invisible from the highway, **Playa Acapulquito** (Little Acapulco Beach, also known as Old Man's) gets an outside break that sometimes connects with the Costa Azul waves in larger summer swells. This spot is a popular choice for surf lessons. There are many lesser-known breaks along the Corridor that break on different sized swells (see *Surfing* under *The Corridor*).

Other options within an hour's drive of San José await along the East and West Cape shores. If you have a sturdy rental car or your own vehicle, you can drive northeast of San José along the coastal dirt road to several spots that break on south swells. Nine miles from San José, Shipwreck is a right point that tends to catch more of the south swell than the Corridor spots. There are several take-off zones from which to choose, and camping on the beach can be a relaxing way to escape the Corridor crowd. If you are going for the day, bring water, food, and shade.

Just up the road is Nine Palms. Waves here are a little softer than at Shipwreck and more popular with longboarders. When the waves get well overhead, the spot can transform into a high-performance, steeper wave that justifies its popularity. Don't bother counting the palms, as they've multiplied since the spot was named. The wreck at Shipwreck was also carried off by a storm long ago.

Equipment

Several shops near San José rent boards and other equipment. The **Cabo Surf Shop** (Km

28, tel. 624/178-6188, U.S. tel. 858/964-5117, www.cabosurfshop.com), located at the Cabo Surf Hotel, offers private or group instruction on Playa Acapulquito through the Mike Doyle Surf School (8 A.M.–8 P.M. daily, US$65/hr), as well as board rentals. Drop-ins are welcome. The **Costa Azul Surf Shop** (Km 28, Plaza Costa Azul, tel. 624/142-2771, www.costa-azul.com, Mon.–Sat. 8 A.M.–7 P.M., Sun. 9 A.M.–5 P.M.) rents short boards, hybrids, and longboards to experienced surfers, as well as beginner boards with rubber fins, and offers lessons. Stop in for beach umbrellas, beach chairs, and snorkeling gear, too.

KAYAKING

Next to the Presidente InterContinental Resort, **Tío Sports** (tel. 624/142-4599, daily 8 A.M.–5:30 P.M.) rents sit-on-top kayaks for paddling the estuary.

MOUNTAIN BIKING

NaturAdventure (tel. 624/105-2050, www.naturadventure.com) leads half-day and full-day trail rides of varying levels around the Los Cabos area on Gary Fisher, Trek, and Specialized bikes. Destinations include Punta Gorda (US$65 pp), Cabo Pulmo (US$95 pp), and the Sierra de la Laguna (US$90 pp, US$75 half-day). Previous clients (only) can rent bikes for a self-guided tour (US$35–55 per day). MTB shoes and Shimano pedals are also available.

GOLF

The former Campo de San José got a makeover and new owner in 2006. The new **Mayan Resorts Country Club** (www.mayanresorts-golf.com) has an attractive, nine-hole, par-35 course surrounded by landscaped residential properties and has a sea view. Rates are US$130 for 18 holes, with considerable discounts for resort guests (US$89). Discounted twilight rates (US$69) begin at 2 P.M. An additional resort course designed by Jack Nicklaus and Greg Norman is scheduled to open in 2008. For other courses a short drive from town, see *Golf* under *The Corridor*.

YOGA

Yoga instructors Caryl Leffel and Victor Ramirez (tel. 624/105-2230) offer classes Monday–Saturday at 8:30 A.M. and 10 A.M. in a small chapel on El Encanto Suites property in downtown San José. They also teach evening classes Tuesday–Thursday at the Mayan Palace Gym at 7 P.M. and 8 P.M. They welcome all levels, with a maximum of 15 students per class (US$7 at the El Encanto).

SPA SERVICES

In addition to spa services at the resort hotels, **Equilibrium** (Plaza Catedral 8, tel. 624/128-7434, 10 A.M.–2 P.M. and 4 P.M.–9 P.M.) on Zaragoza at Plaza Mijares offers massages for US$38. Another option is a massage on the beach in front of the Coral Reef resort for US$40/hour or US$20/half hour.

ORGANIZED TOURS

Nomadas de Baja (Calle Zaragoza near the Pemex, tel./fax 624/146-9642, www.nomadas-debaja.com) organizes a full range of guided expeditions throughout southern Baja. You can choose from a desert hot springs walking tour (US$65), kayak adventures around Cabo Pulmo (nine hours, US$105), diving (two-tank dive, US$140), and mountain-bike tours (2.5–5 hours, US$85). Rates include a bilingual guide, all related gear, lunch and/or snacks, and beverages.

You can also tour the back roads of Baja in a fleet of Hummers with **Baja Outback** (tel. 624/142-9200, www.bajaoutback.com, US$165–220 pp). Single- and multi-day tours go to Todos Santos, Santiago, Rancho La Verdad, and Rancho Antares (between Cabo Pulmo and Los Frailes).

Located in front of the Presidente InterContinental hotel, **Baja's Activities** (tel. 624/142-2922, www.bajasactivities.com, 9 A.M.–6 P.M.) organizes horseback rides along the estuary and beach (US$35/1 hr, US$55/2 hrs), snorkeling tours to Santa María Bay (US$35 pp), and ATV tours of the East Cape (US$60/single, US$89/double). Credit cards are accepted. **Rancho Tours** (tel. 624/143-5464, www.ranchotours.com) leads walking tours of La Paz and Todo Santos for US$65 per person.

Ecotourism specialist **Baja Wild Outfitters** (tel. 624/172-6300, www.bajawild.com) leads a variety of adventure trips, including kayaking, snorkeling, surfing, hiking, ATV, Jeep safaris, whale-watching, and turtle release programs. Half-day trips range US$60–98, and all-day trips are US$105–410, depending on the activity. Group and multisport packages are available.

ENTERTAINMENT AND EVENTS
Bars and Nightclubs

While San José doesn't offer as much of a nighttime party scene as Cabo San Lucas, neither does the town close down at sunset—although in low season it may seem that way.

Behind Plaza Mijares and close to El Encanto Suites, █ **LaSanta Wine Bar** (Obregón 1732 at Hidalgo, tel. 624/122-1898, www.lasanta.com.mx, Mon.–Thurs. 6 P.M.–1 A.M., Fri.–Sat. 6 P.M.–2 A.M.) opened in 2005 as a trendy bar and lounge featuring 27 wines by the glass (and 135 bottled labels) from California, Spain, and France, as well as some Baja labels, for US$6–24/glass. The atmosphere is historic Mexico meets Manhattan chic, complete with beamed ceilings, stone walls, red drapes, mood lighting, and contemporary suede sofas. To complement the wine, you can order oysters on the half shell, Spanish gazpacho with scallops, a charcuterie plate, risotto, foie gras, and salads for US$11–30. LaSanta plays live music every Wednesday and Thursday and has DJs on Saturdays.

The popular **Tropicana Bar and Grill** (Mijares 30, tel. 624/142-1580, Sun.–Thurs. 8 A.M.–midnight, Fri.–Sat. till 2 A.M.) features lounge-lizard folk music in the front room and canned music in the back. Both bars host a two-drinks-for-the-price-of-one happy hour in the late afternoon. Live Latin bands play on weekends from 10 P.M. on.

Morgan's Restaurant and Cellar (Hidalgo and Doblado, tel. 624/142-3825, morgans@prodigy.net.mx, daily 6–11 P.M.) often hosts live music, usually jazz, in the popular and comfy bar.

Shooters Bar & Grill (Doblado and Mijares, tel. 624/142-9900), above Tulipán Restaurant, is an open-air, rooftop bar with seating in plastic chairs and jazz music.

The nautical theme is a bit cheesy, and tunes are country oldies, but otherwise the **Cielito Lindo Sky Bar** (Paseo San José, tel. 624/142-9292, Tues.–Sun. 5 P.M.–midnight), in the lighthouse tower of the Crowne Plaza, is a great place to catch the sunset.

Behind the Mega shopping center, the **Rusty Putter Bar and Grille** (Hotelera Plaza Los Cabos, tel. 624/142-4546) is a sports bar/restaurant with some outdoor tables—the *palapa*-covered area is a great spot to catch an ocean breeze. Prices are reasonable considering the size of the portions (entrées start at US$6). The restaurant serves breakfast, lunch, and dinner daily from 8 A.M. till late, and the bar features live music on weekends. Satellite TV and an 18-hole miniature golf course provide additional entertainment.

Havana Supper Club (Km 29, tel. 624/142-2603, daily from breakfast till late night) perched on a rise overlooking Mexico 1 and Playa Costa Azul, hosts live jazz nightly. Nearby **Zippers** (Km 28.5, tel. 624/172-6162, daily 11 A.M.–10 P.M.), near Costa Azul, is a bar and grill with live "baby boomer music" Friday and Saturday nights.

Events

On most Saturday evenings during the December–March high tourist season, San José hosts a fiesta in Plaza Mijares. Although the fiestas are mostly held for the benefit of tourists, lots of locals attend as well. Typical events include folk dances, mariachi performances, cockfight demonstrations, and piñata-breaking. Numerous vendors sell arts and crafts and food; profits from food and beverage sales go to local charities and service clubs.

Many art galleries stay open late for weekly Art Walks on Thursday evenings.

San José's biggest annual festival is held March 19, the feast day of its patron saint. In

© NIKKI GOTH ITOI

Calle Zaragoza, opposite the plaza

SAN JOS

LOS CA

46

see individ
turnarou
your r
late

LOS CABOS

LOS CABOS

addition to music, dancing, and food, celebratory activities include horse races and parades.

SHOPPING

From souvenirs to collectible furnishings, you can find a little of everything along the streets of San José. And unlike in Cabo San Lucas, here you can browse at a leisurely pace without worrying about aggressive shop owners encouraging you to make a purchase.

Arts, Crafts, and Souvenirs

Near the intersection of Boulevard Mijares and the road to Pueblo La Playa, about halfway between the *zona hotelera* and the plaza, is a large open-air market selling inexpensive Mexican handicrafts; it's generally open 11 A.M.–9 P.M.

Higher-quality, higher-priced arts and crafts are offered in shops along the east end of Calle Zaragoza and the north end of Boulevard Mijares. **Antigua Los Cabos** (Mijares 5, tel. 624/146-9933, antiguabcs@yahoo. com) has some antiques, as well as handmade rugs, folk art, ceramics, and tequilas. Across

the street, **Veryka** (tel. 624/142-0575) and **Copal** (tel. 624/142-3070) both carry Mexican crafts. **Sol Dorado** (Mijares 33, across from the Tropicana, tel. 624/142-1950) is a multilevel store filled with ceramics, glassware, ironworks, mirrors, and furnishings. For large or fragile items, the store ships via DHL (fully insured). It will also deliver purchases to your hotel for US$10–85, depending on the location. The smaller **Mejicanisimo** (Zaragoza 8, tel. 624/142-3090, daily 9 A.M.–10 P.M.), next to the plaza, has much of the same.

Shop 12 Leather Factory, on the corner of Mijares and Coronado, has been in business since 1927 with a large selection of leather goods, including purses, shoes, belts, and even shotgun cases.

Jewelry

Several stores sell high-quality Mexican fire opals and other gemstones. Ask to see the opals in natural light—the more "fire," the higher the price. If you don't see what you want, ask to

al stones. Most stores offer 24-hour
nd for custom settings, but don't plan
ickup time to the minute, or you may be
to catch your flight home.
Martha Rodriguez at **El Rincón del Ópalo**
jewelry factory (Mijares 6, tel. 624/142-2566,
beltran_018@hotmail.com, Mon.–Sat. 9 A.M.–
9 P.M., Sun. till 2 P.M.) can help you choose a
stone and setting in a pleasant gallery off the
main plaza. **Jewelry Factory** (Mijares 5, tel.
624/142-6394) on the plaza next to Antigua
Los Cabos, has some of the highest quality
jewels in town, and service to match. **La Mina**
(Mijares 33, tel. 624/142-3747, lamina788@
hotmail.com) displays costume jewelry on the
porous walls of a small cave and has a second
location in Cabo San Lucas.

Fine Art Galleries

San José has a legitimate art district that is
home to a number of first-rate galleries. Run by
a graduate of the Parsons School of Design in
New York City and a full-time Los Cabos resident, the three-story **Galería de Ida Victoria**
(Guerrero 1128, tel. 624/142-5772, www
.idavictoriaarts.com) has been recognized as
one of the finest art galleries south of Los Angeles. State-of-the-art lighting and hanging
systems were custom designed to showcase
paintings, photography, sculpture, and other
works of art. A fire in 2007 severely damaged
the gallery, but the owner was planning to re-
build as quickly as possible.

The **Old Town Gallery** (Obregón 20, tel.
624/142-3662, www.oldtowngallery.net,
Mon.–Sat. 10:30 A.M.–7:30 P.M., Thurs. till
9 P.M.) displays works by contemporary Mexican, American, and Canadian artists. **Galería
Arenas** (Obregón 10, vicjorge71@hotmail.
com, Mon.–Sat. 10 A.M.–2 P.M. and 4 P.M.–
8 P.M.) has original Mexican pottery.

The eclectic **Pez Gordo Gallery** (Obregón
19, tel. 624/142-5788, www.pezgordogallery.
com, Mon.–Sat. 10 A.M.–8 P.M.) represents
more than 40 contemporary artists based in
Baja and throughout Mexico. Works range
from oil and acrylic to wax, collage, and photography.

Several galleries in this part of town stay
open late on Thursday evenings (5–9 P.M.) for a
weekly Art Walk that includes wine and food.

Home Decor

San José has amassed quite a collection of shops
dealing in interior design products of all kinds.
Galería Los Cabos (Hidalgo north of Obregón,
tel. 624/142-0044) sells a unique assortment of
antique and rattan furniture, stoneware, crafts,
decorator items, and locally made barrel-back
chairs. **Casa Paulina** (tel. 624/142-5555), on
Obregón across from El Encanto Suites, sells
high-quality, original home accessories and
furniture in a two-level store—a perfect detour for anyone looking to furnish a vacation
home. **Casa Maya** (Km 31.5, tel. 624/142-
6611) displays handcrafted furnishings, fabrics,
upholstery, bedding, and home accessories in a
15,000-square-foot showroom.

Sporting Goods

The **Big Tony** (tel. 624/142-0744) beachware
store has locations in town on Zaragoza and
next to Zippers Restaurant at Playa Costa
Azul. Across the highway in a small shopping
plaza, the **Costa Azul Surf Shop** (Km 28,
tel. 624/142-2771, www.costa-azul.com.mx,
Mon.–Sat. 8 A.M.–7 P.M., Sun. 9 A.M.–5 P.M.)
has board rentals and surf and snorkel maps.
You can also have your board repaired after a
rough day in the water.

The **Cabo Surf Shop** (Km 28, tel. 624/178-
6188, www.cabosurfshop.com, daily 8 A.M.–
8 P.M.), located at the Cabo Surf Hotel, offers
board rentals.

Deportiva Piscis (tel. 624/142-0332, daily
8 A.M.–7 P.M.), on the south side of Calle Castro near the Mercado Municipal, sells fishing
tackle and bait *(carnada)* when it's available.

Bookstores

A branch of **Libros Libros/Books Books** (tel.
624/142-4433, daily 9 A.M.–7 P.M.), on the west
side of Boulevard Mijares just north of Plaza
José Green, carries one rack of English-language paperbacks, plus *USA Today* and a limited selection of maps and books about Baja.

ACCOMMODATIONS

Besides the major hotels and condotels in the *zona hotelera* along the beach, San José offers some smaller, reasonably priced inns in the town itself. A downtown location puts you close to shops and restaurants, with a short drive or long walk to the beach. Condos and hotels along Playa Azul are about a 5- to 10-minute drive from town, depending on traffic. Rates are given for double occupancy in the high season (holidays may be higher) and do not include 12 percent tax and 10 percent service, unless otherwise noted. Discounts may be available for stays of a week or longer.

Hotels in Town

Under US$50: The basic but clean **Hotel Ceci** (Calle Zaragoza 22 opposite the church, tel. 624/142-0051, US$34) contains 14 basic rooms with fans. Bathrooms are tiny and rather primitive, and at night, busy Calle Zaragoza might make this a noisy choice, but most of the noise subsides by 11 P.M. **Hotel Diana** (Zaragoza 30, tel. 624/142-0490, US$30), a bit west of the Hotel Ceci, has spartan rooms with air conditioning, TV, and hot water.

You'll find two **Posada Señor Mañana** lodging options in San José; more confusing, they sit side by side on Calle Obregón behind the plaza at the northeast edge of town, overlooking some *huertas*. A few years back, half of the original operation was bought out, including the name. The founder changed the original name for a couple of years but has reverted to the former appellation, thus the confusion. The original Posada Señor Mañana (Obregón 1A, tel./fax 624/142-0462, www.srmanana. net, US$40–67) is a rambling affair; rooms are clean and a variety of group sizes can be accommodated. Just to the east sits the other Posada Señor Mañana (tel./fax 624/142-1372, US$40–70). A small pool and open *palapa* sitting areas with hammocks are a bonus, as is the common kitchen area with individual locked pantry cabinets. Take a look at a few rooms here, as there is a variety.

Friendly and economical 【 **Hotel Colli** (Hidalgo btw Zaragoza/Doblado, tel. 624/142-0725, US$49) offers 12 simple but clean and comfortable rooms in a family-run operation. This is the best deal in town under US$50. Some rooms have fans, others are air-conditioned, and all have a private bath.

US$50-150: The hospitable **Hotel Posada Terranova** (on Degollado just south of Zaragoza, tel. 624/142-0534, www.hterranova. com.mx, US$60) is a converted home that has been expanded to encompass 29 clean, air-conditioned rooms, each with satellite TV and two beds. Direct-dial phones are a plus (but make sure not to use the multiple-digit prefix option that allows use of a credit card, as this reaches one of the infamous price-gouging American phone companies). The inn also features a good Mexican restaurant (daily 7 A.M.–10 P.M., mains US$9–14) with an intimate dining room and an outdoor eating section, plus a bar.

The quiet, Mexican colonial–style **El Encanto Inn** (Morelos 133, tel. 624/142-0388, U.S. tel. 512/465-9751, www.elencantosuites.com, US$79–133) has expanded to two buildings, with the more upscale 【 **El Encanto Suites** diagonally across from the original inn. Designed in grand hacienda style, the new, V-shaped building wraps 14 large, elegant suites around a small swimming pool and fountain. Fluffy towels, king-size beds, and remote-control air-conditioning are a few of the special touches. More economical standard and garden suites are located in the original inn. Rooms here are popular with travelers who plan a one-night stopover before heading to or from the East Cape. Yoga instructors Caryl Leffel and Victor Ramirez (tel. 624/105-2230) offer classes Monday–Saturday at 8:30 A.M. and 10 A.M. in a small chapel on the property. Wireless Internet works intermittently (15 minutes free, US$4 for 30 minutes, or US$10 for one hour), and there is an iMac for guest use in the lobby. A café near the pool serves breakfast and drinks, and you can park for free in a gated, but not guarded, lot across the street.

Behind the Tropicana Bar and Grill, **Tropicana Inn** (Mijares 30, tel. 624/142-1580,

THE PITCH

Few visitors board their flight to Los Cabos intending to buy a timeshare. Yet the timeshare market is booming as the destination evolves. Timeshares now command higher prices and higher occupancy rates than hotels. Nearly six million people now participate in fractional ownership vacation models (also called vacation clubs), and they spend US$1 billion a year on their condos and villas. How do so many travelers come to change their minds between arrival and departure?

LOS CABOS IS A BEAUTIFUL PLACE
It's a lot easier to pack up and head home when you know you can return again and again.

THE PITCH IS ALL AROUND
Timeshare salespeople disguise themselves as activities coordinators, concierges, restaurant hosts, and even grocery store staff. Europcar's Mexican office told at least one customer in early 2007 that they had to sign up for a timeshare presentation in order to get a rental car at the rate they had reserved. When the customer balked, the agent refused to give the customer a rental car. In another example, the Mayan Palace reportedly pays Mega thousands of dollars a month to have its reps roam the supermarket aisles. Their

goal is to draw unsuspecting visitors into a friendly conversation – *Is this your first time in Los Cabos? Where are you staying? Would you like to go whale-watching today? Can I help you find the sugar?* – and then invite them to a 90-minute presentation over breakfast in exchange for any number of giveaways. With prices ranging US$15,000-25,000, "owning" a timeshare in a world-class destination can be an attractive proposition. Why not hear what they have to say?

THE FREEBIES ARE ENTICING
Salespeople may offer US$200 in cash, free whale-watching or snorkeling tours, sunset horseback rides, restaurant coupons, and more. The deal gets better the longer you resist. Not a bad way to finance part of your trip if you don't mind giving up part of a day.

Everyone thinks they can work the system, and many who participate in a presentation do resist the temptation to buy. Some even sign up for a second pitch on their next visit. But here's the catch:

TIMESHARES ARE NOT REAL ESTATE
They are vacations. When you buy a timeshare, you prepay for vacations at a dis-

---

www.tropicanacabo.com, US$80–130) features 37 attractively decorated rooms around a tile-and-cobblestone fountain courtyard. Each room comes with air conditioning, satellite TV, coffeemaker, minibar, and direct-dial telephone; other amenities include a swimming pool and free transportation to La Playita and Playa Palmilla. A free continental breakfast is served in a gardenlike pool area.

Over US$250: The posh **Casa Natalia** (Mijares 4, tel. 624/142-5100 or 888/277-3814, www.casanatalia.com, US$295) is a contemporary European-style boutique hotel located right off the plaza with 14 deluxe rooms, two spa suites, and two connecting rooms, all individually decorated with authentic artwork

from San Miguel de Allende, Oaxaca, and Puebla. Besides the usual amenities found at accommodations in this price range, all rooms have small, private bougainvillea-covered terraces hung with hammocks. Other features include a heated pool, outdoor *palapa* bar, and in-room spa services. The attached Mi Cocina restaurant (daily 6:30–10 P.M., mains US$20 and up), run by owner Natalie Tenoux's husband, Loïc Tenoux, gets high marks for gourmet fare.

Beach Hotels
Occupancy rates for the hotels along Playa Hotelera have been climbing in recent years to match those of their busier Cabo San Lucas

counted rate. If you like the idea of returning to a familiar place in Los Cabos for one or two weeks each year, this model can make a lot of sense.

IT'S HARD TO SAY NO

Sales reps choreograph every aspect of the pitch, from the upbeat music to the champagne and cheers of congratulations echoing around the room. They face intense pressure to sell, so if the first approach doesn't win you over, there will be one or two more pitches as you attempt to leave the room. (Biannual weeks? Off-season weeks? Trial membership? Free Jet Ski tour? Take our survey before you go?) As prices come down, the deal gets sweeter, and suddenly you either begin to feel guilty for accepting all the freebies or you think you're crazy for not taking advantage now that you've negotiated the terms so low. Bottom line: That 90-minute breakfast presentation could result in a US$10,000 charge on your credit card.

YOU MAY NOT GET WHAT YOU PAID FOR

Timeshare developments typically begin selling when construction has just begun — sometimes they don't get finished, or when they do, they don't always shape up as promised. Stories abound of frustrated timeshare purchasers who don't get the weeks they originally bought, or whose reservations seem to get lost every time they book. Services may not be available as promised, and the quality of the accommodations may change as the years go by.

Also, because timeshare owners aren't year-round residents, they usually lack both a sense of community and a sense of responsibility toward the local environment. For the developer, timeshares mean huge profits, as the same space is sold repeatedly in one-week segments. Because land in Baja is relatively inexpensive, considering the charming scenery and climate, it seems to attract get-rich-quick developers who show a decided lack of respect for the fragile Baja environment.

PROCEED WITH CAUTION

Timeshares are not all bad, and attending a presentation may be a worthwhile experience for a variety of reasons. Just be sure you know what's coming before you give away any of your precious vacation time. And don't buy without considering all the options.

---

peers, though you may still be able to negotiate a deal during off-peak seasons. Whether you choose a hotel or condo, beware that demolitions, renovations, and new construction are in progress all over this area, even during the peak travel season. There's a good chance you'll end up next to, above, or below a noisy construction zone. The hammering, sawing, and drilling typically begins at 8:30 A.M. and lasts till 5:30 P.M. Do your homework before you book.

Over US$250: Although its brand name may conjure images of a business convention, the **Crowne Plaza Los Cabos Beach Resort** (tel. 624/142-9292, U.S. tel. 866/365-6932, www.cploscabos.com, US$250–400) is one of few resorts in Los Cabos where you can enjoy a stay free of condo sales pitches, as the property does not have timeshares onsite. Large guestroom terraces and a saltwater infinity pool are two more distinguishing features. Children four and up can play in the kids club while mom and dad relax by the pool. High-speed Internet access costs US$15 per day. All-inclusive meal plans are available.

Situated between the Desire and Posada Real resorts along the Zona Hotelera, **The Grand Baja Resort & Spa** (U.S. tel. 800/745-2226, www.grand-baja.com, US$265–390) has one-, two-, and three-bedroom suites and was transitioning to new owners in 2007. All-inclusive plans are no longer offered. A coffee shop/deli with Internet access is open all day Sunday, when most other cafés are closed, but the rates are the highest we found anywhere on the peninsula: US$8 per hour (prorated).

At the far northeastern end of the *zona hotelera,* next to the Estero San José, the 400-room **Presidente InterContinental Los Cabos Resort** (tel. 624/142-0211, U.S./Canada tel. 888/567-8725, www.ichotelsgroup.com, US$290–425) serves some of the best meals around for all-inclusive package guests. This resort in recent years completed a US$11 million expansion and renovation. The resort also maintains a playground and offers special children's activities. Tío Sports next to the hotel rents ATVs and sit-on-top kayaks.

All-Inclusive (Only) Resorts: The well-maintained **Hotel Posada Real Los Cabos** (tel. 624/142-0155, U.S. tel. 800/528-1234, www.posadareal.com.mx, US$130–195 pp) is a Best Western property with 156 rooms and suites that feature air conditioning, telephone, and satellite TV. Hotel facilities include a heated pool, swim-up pool bar, tennis courts, two seaside hot tubs, and restaurant. Most rooms offer ocean views. Rates cover meals, drinks, tips, and tax.

Next to the Crowne Plaza, the **Royal Solaris Los Cabos Hotel** (Lte. 10, Zona Hotelera, tel. 624/145-6800, U.S. tel. 866/289-8466, www.clubsolaris.com, US$125 pp) is targeting families with young children with a new water park. Most of its 389 rooms have ocean views. Entertainment options include a Tehuacan dinner theater show. A free snorkeling tour comes with a stay of six nights or more.

Clothing is optional at **Desire Resort & Spa Los Cabos** (formerly the Fiesta Inn, Blvd. Malecón Zona Hotelera, tel. 624/142-9300, U.S. tel. 888/201-7551, Canada tel. 800/655-9311, www.desireresorts.com, US$150–355 pp). Reactions ranged from shock to awe when this couples-only establishment opened in 2006, catering to upscale, "liberated" adults. A red and dark brown color scheme with hand-painted murals of scenes from the *Book of Kama Sutra* set the mood. A clothing-optional pool and jacuzzi, L'Alternative Disco, and Sensuous Playroom take it over the top. The resort's 150 rooms and suites have king-size beds and flatscreen TVs, among a complete list of standard amenities. From the beach, curious onlookers can recognize the resort by shoulder-height bamboo screens on the terraces that allow for private sunbathing.

Bed-and-Breakfasts

Next to the public golf course, **Casa del Jardín** (Paseo Finisterra 107, tel. 624/142-1964, www.casajardin.com, US$85–95) offers four rooms in a renovated former residence. Each room is named and decorated according to a different nature theme. All rooms have ceiling fans, air conditioning, and private balconies. The property is lushly planted with citrus trees, flowers, palms, and a large herb and vegetable garden. Guests have free run of the house (including an upstairs sitting room and downstairs living room, both equipped with TVs) as well as access to a telephone, fax, and computer. A full breakfast is served on a covered terrace overlooking the garden and swimming pool or in the formal dining room. Smoking is not permitted in the house.

Condominiums and Condotels

Condominium complexes are sprouting up on the outskirts of San José as fast as all-inclusive resorts. Las Olas (closest to the lookout point at Zippers surf break), El Zalate (next to the Coral Baja timeshare resort), and Sampiguita (closer to the hotel zone) are just a few of the newcomers. Owners rent vacant units to visitors for anywhere from US$120 a night for a studio or one-bedroom to around US$450 or more for a deluxe two- or three-bedroom unit. Rates can vary quite a bit even within the same complex, depending on location and views and how the unit is furnished. Be sure to inquire how close the unit is to the highway and whether there is construction underway inside the building. At Mykonos and other complexes nearby, the persistent sound of heavy traffic on Mexico 1 can drown out the sound of waves crashing onto the beach. Discounted weekly and monthly rates are sometimes available.

ALL-INCLUSIVE RESORTS

If making decisions about food adds stress to your vacation experience, look for a rate plan that includes meals, activities, and entertainment. The following resorts offer all-inclusive packages:

SAN JOSÉ DEL CABO

- Crowne Plaza Los Cabos Beach Resort (p. 49) – Business conventions

- Presidente InterContinental Los Cabos Resort (p. 50) – Good variety and quality of food

- Hotel Posada Real Los Cabos (p. 50) – Good deal for the money

- Royal Solaris Los Cabos Hotel (p. 50)– Families with young kids

- Desire Resort & Spa Los Cabos (p. 50) – Clothing optional

THE CORRIDOR

- Dreams Los Cabos (p. 66) – Weddings, honeymoons, anniversaries

- Meliá Cabo Real (p. 67) – Safe swimming beach

CABO SAN LUCAS

- Riu Palace (p. 93) – Largest of the all-inclusive set, with 642 guestrooms

- Tesoro Los Cabos Hotel (p. 95) – College students on spring break

Delfin Hotels & Resorts maintains a current list of all-inclusive resorts in the Los Cabos area at www.allinclusivescabo.com.

The payment process for a condo is different from reserving a hotel room: Property managers typically require a deposit of 50 percent of the rental fee by check or direct deposit to a U.S. bank account, and the remaining amount by cash upon arrival. Cleaning fees are often added to the rental fee. Sometimes full payment is required before arrival—all the more reason to get the information you need before committing to a particular unit.

Southwest of San José del Cabo proper, near Playa Costa Azul, **Mira Vista Beachfront Condos** (tel. 624/144-5049, US$110–160) rents one-bedroom condos by the week.

White-and-blue Mediterranean-style **Mykonos Bay Resort** (Km 29, tel. 624/142-3789, one bedroom US$130–290) rents one- and two-bedroom condos in three buildings, each with air conditioning, satellite TV, kitchen, and washer/dryer. Amenities include a basic gym and lighted tennis court. Buildings B and C have larger units and are closest to the beach and quieter than Building A, which has smaller units and picks up more noise from the highway.

Within walking distance of the Mega shopping plaza as well as the beach, the sprawling **Las Mañanitas** complex has some of the nicest condos around for US$225–475 per night. Next door, **Sampaguita Luxury Townhouse/ Condominiums** is newer and smaller, with only 14 units in a quiet, gated complex that has a pool, hot tub, and tennis court. Two-bedrooms run about US$200–300/night.

Booking Services and Property Management Companies

Baja Properties (Doblado and Morelos, tel. 624/142-0988, U.S. tel. 877/462-2226, www. bajaproperties.com) manages one-, two-, and three-bedroom rentals in Las Mañanitas for US$225–475 per night, as well as a few less expensive locations. **Nash Group Properties** (Paseo Finisterra #107, www .bajaholidays.com), run by the owners of the Casa del Jardín B&B (see *Bed-and-Breakfasts*), manages several rental properties in Mykonos, Las Olas, and a few other complexes. **SeaSide Vacations** (tel. 624/142-3789, Canada tel. 604/484-8488, www.sea-side.com) has a variety of units in several buildings in the area, as does **Sunshine Services** (tel. 624/142-2212, U.S. tel. 888/545-4310, www .sunshineservices.com), with an office location next to the bus terminal.

La Playita

Under US$50: Northeast of San José, in the village of La Playita and within walking distance of the beach in Pueblo La Playa itself, cozy **El Delfín Blanco** (Delfínes, tel. 624/142-1212, tel./fax 624/142-1199, www.eldelfinblanco.net, US$39–50) offers simple cabañas facing the beach. Accommodations here are more traditionally Mexican style than resort-oriented. Some have private baths, others are shared.

US$50-100: Three miles past La Playita toward the East Cape, **La Fonda del Mar Bed and Breakfast** (U.S. tel. 951/303-9384, www.buzzardsbar.com, US$75–95) has three solar-powered *palapa* structures with comfortable beds and tile floors, all with private half-bath and shared shower, plus a suite with private bath. Breakfast for two at the adjacent Buzzards Bar & Grill is included.

A short walk from the sportfishing *pangas* on the beach, **La Playita Inn** (Pueblo La Playa, tel./fax 624/142-4166, www.laplayitahotel.com, US$69–109) offers well-tended rooms with air conditioning, ceiling fan, TV, and large shower. Standard rooms have two queen beds. A third-floor penthouse has one queen bed; another has two queens; and a third a kitchen and sitting area. Cash or travelers checks only.

Camping and RV Parks

Camping options are becoming increasingly limited in the wake of pervasive resort development. One of the last holdouts, Brisa del Mar RV Park, enjoyed its last winter season in 2006–2007. You can still camp for free on the beach at La Playita between San José and Pueblo La Playa, but that too may change as the Puerto Los Cabos project takes shape. For safe and secluded camping, best to head north along the East or West Cape Regions.

FOOD

Most of San José's growing number of fashionable restaurants are along Boulevard Mijares and Calle Zaragoza near the plaza. These eateries are for the most part geared to Mexican

diners as well as foreigners—so far the town harbors no equivalents to Cabo San Lucas's Giggling Marlin or Squid Roe.

As a general rule, the closer a restaurant is to the plaza, the more expensive the menu. To save money and experience local flavor, seek out the spots where San José residents eat—most are in the western part of town toward Mexico 1.

Alta Cocina Mexicana

Restaurants specializing in Mexican foods prepared in the *alta cocina* ("high cuisine," or gourmet) style have proliferated in San José. **Tequila Restaurant** (Doblado 1011, tel. 624/142-1155, www.tequilarestaurant.com, daily for dinner, mains US$20 and up), in a restored classic adobe just west of Boulevard Mijares on the south side of Doblado, was the first of the high-class eateries to open. It looks small from the entryway but opens onto a sizable open-air, tree-shaded courtyard in back. In addition to a prime list of tequilas and a walk-in humidor, the restaurant blends Asian, Mexican, and Mediterranean flavors into a menu that highlights seafood cooked on the grill or baked in a wood-fired oven. Produce comes from its own organic farm, which also supplies some of the area's top resorts.

A member of the Slow Food movement emphasizing locally grown and prepared foods, **Don Emiliano** (Mijares 27, tel. 624/142-0266, daily 6–11 P.M., mains US$20–36) is run by a well-known chef from Mexico City, Margarita C. de Salinas. Try the six-course tasting menu (US$49) paired with Mexican wines (US$88) or order a la carte. At the upscale **Mi Cocina** (Mijares 4, tel. 624/146-7100, daily 6–11 P.M., mains US$20 and up), the husband of the owner of Casa Natalia serves nouvelle Mexican-Euro cuisine in a beautiful, contemporary outdoor setting.

Next to the plaza, **La Panga Antigua** (Zaragoza 20, tel. 624/142-4041, www.lapanga.com, daily for lunch and dinner, prix fixe US$18) is set in a colonial ambience, with a courtyard, lounge bar, and wine cellar. A menu of contemporary Mexican cuisine with a focus on

© NIKKI GOTH ITOI

pizza on the plaza at La Dolce

seafood is prepared by a chef who is a graduate of the Culinary Institute of America. Credit cards are accepted.

Chilies in all their forms take center stage at **El Chilar** (1497 Juárez at Morelos, tel. 624/142-2544, Mon.–Sat. 3–10 P.M., mains US$10–30). A Oaxacan chef prepares an ever-changing menu of Mexican specialties at this small restaurant located near the Telmex tower. Cash only.

If you don't mind the strip-mall setting, **Habañeros Mexican Bistro** (Mijares in Plaza La Misión, tel. 624/142-2626, Mon.–Sat. 11 A.M.–10 P.M., lunch mains US$5–14, dinner mains US$9–18) doubles as an organic market. Dinner specials include roast pork tenderloin or surf and turf for US$20; Corona and Pacifico beers are only US$1.50.

Mexican

Restaurant Bar Jazmín (Zaragoza and Obregón, tel. 624/142-1760, daily 7 A.M.–10 P.M., mains US$13–40), just off Zaragoza on Morelos opposite the *nevería,* is a casual eatery

serving fresh juices and *licuados,* Mexican breakfasts, French toast and pancakes, *chilaquiles,* burgers, tortilla soup, *tortas,* tacos, tostadas, fajitas, and seafood—plus occasional live music. *Huachinango* (whole red snapper) and *carne asada a la tampiqueña* are served on sizzling hot platters. Credit cards, including American Express, are accepted.

Damiana (Mijares 8, tel. 624/142-0499, www.damiana.com.mx, daily 10:30 A.M.–10:30 P.M., dinner mains US$10–17), on the plaza, named for the Cape Region's legendary herbal aphrodisiac, is housed in a restored 18th-century townhouse and is one of the original romantic courtyard restaurants in Los Cabos. Rooms include a tastefully decorated bar, an indoor dining area, and a patio dining area—candlelit in the evening—surrounded by lush foliage. House specialties include cheese soup, shrimp, lobster, abalone, and steak. A free taste of *damiana* liqueur is served to guests upon request.

La Terraza Sidewalk Café (Mijares 30, tel. 624/142-1580, daily 8 A.M.–10:30 P.M., mains

US$10–15), at the Tropicana Bar and Grill, is a large, touristy restaurant/bar with outdoor patio, big-screen TV, and live music and dancing at night. The menu is basic Tourist Mex/Fake Caribbean, but the drinks are strong.

The family-run **Posada Terranova** (on Calle Degollado just south of Zaragoza, tel. 624/142-0534, daily 7 A.M.–10 P.M., mains US$5–18) features a small dining room and bar as well as outdoor seating. In addition to standard Mexican dishes, the menu offers a good variety of high-quality Mexican and American breakfasts.

(**Mariscos Mazatlán II** (Km 35, Mexico 1, tel. 624/143-8565, daily for lunch and dinner, mains US$10–14), near Soriana on the way to the airport, is a favorite among expats for fresh fish at reasonable prices in a nontouristy atmosphere. Look for a green *palapa*-roof building with outdoor seating on the west side of Mexico 1. There is also a sister location in Cabo San Lucas.

American and International

El Tulipán (The Tulip Tree, on Calle Doblado just off Mijares, tel. 624/146-9900, mains US$10–20), is a casual place open for lunch and dinner. The menu features hamburgers, rib-eye steak, veggie burgers, salads, stir-fries, and pastas—all served in large portions.

Baan Thai (Morelos and Comonfort, tel. 624/142-3344, daily noon–10:30 P.M., mains US$11–25) serves pad thai, wok-tossed salmon, and an assortment of curries, as well as a few other Pacific Rim dishes. Dining areas are nicely appointed with Asian furniture, and the food is light and tasty, a nice break from heavy Mexican fare.

Morgan's Restaurant and Cellar (Hidalgo and Doblado, tel. 624/143-3825, morgans@prodigy.net.mx, daily 6 P.M.–midnight, dinner till 10 P.M. only, closed Sept., mains US$20 and up) brings Mediterranean culinary influences to San José del Cabo. All breads and pastries are baked on the premises, and the wine list is stellar. The separate bar makes a favorite gathering place for residents and tourists alike. **Morgan's Encore** (Morelos and Obregón, tel.

624/142-4727, daily 6 P.M.–midnight, dinner till 10 P.M. only, closed Sept., mains US$20 and up), near the El Encanto Inn, is quieter, with a different menu and fewer tourists.

In a new plaza behind the Casa Paulina interior design store, **Voila! Bistro** (Plaza Paulina on Morelos and Comonfort, tel. 624/130-7569, www.voila-events.com, daily for lunch and dinner) serves a few wines by the glass, as well as soup, salads (US$9), and entrées like rib eye steak for US$28.

On Plaza Mijares, **La Dolce Ristorante Italiano & Pizzeria** (Hidalgo and Zaragoza, tel. 624/142-6621, daily 2 P.M.–11 P.M., mains US$7–14) serves pastas and pizzas, plus Italian starters and desserts. The upscale **Alfredo di Roma** (formerly Da Antonio, Mijares at the Presidente InterContinental Resort, tel. 624/142-1001, Tues.–Sat. 1–10:30 P.M., mains US$13–30), on the Estero San José, resembles an Italian trattoría. Outdoor tables have a pleasant view of the scenic estuary.

Pair the meat cut of your choice with one of four house sauces, add a side or two, and you have a fantastic meal at **La Bodega Steak and Wine House** (Zaragoza btw Guerrero/Morelos, tel. 624/142-6619, www.labodegasanjose.com, Mon.–Sat. 6–11 P.M., mains US$17–29). Credit cards are accepted.

Antojitos and Fast Food

At the west end of Calle Doblado are several inexpensive taco stands and *fruterías*. The Mercado Municipal features a section of side-by-side, clean *loncherías* (Mon.–Sat. 6 A.M.–6 P.M., Sun. 6 A.M.–4 P.M.).

Restaurant El Descanso (daily 24 hours, mains US$5–10), an outdoor *palapa*-roofed place on Calle Castro diagonally opposite the Mercado Municipal, serves inexpensive *menudo, pozole, birria, barbacoa,* tamales, and other Mexican soul food 24 hours a day. Look for large vats on a wood fire. **Cafetería El Portón** (tel. 624/142-4115, Mon.–Sat. 8 A.M.–5:30 P.M., mains US$5–10), on the north side of Doblado east of Calle Muñoz, offers good basic Mexican fare in clean surroundings. **Restaurant Las Hornillas** (daily noon–

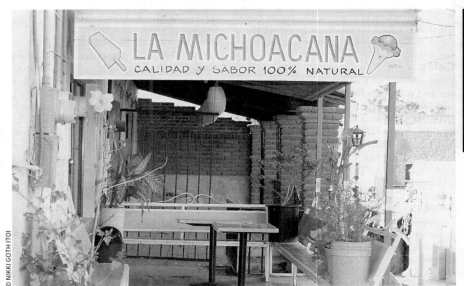

© NIKKI GOTH ITOI

I scream, you scream; we all scream for *helado.*

9 P.M., mains US$5–10), toward the west end of Calle Doblado, specializes in inexpensive mesquite-grilled chicken, steaks, and burgers for a mostly local clientele. **Super Tacos de Baja California Hermanos Gonzales,** on the north side of Calle Doblado west of the Centro de Salud, is a branch of the famous taco stand of the same name in La Paz. Look for inexpensive fish, shrimp, and clam tacos (US$1–2), with a large selection of condiments.

Taquería Erika (daily for lunch and dinner), near Mexico 1 on the south side of the street, serves *tacos de carne asada* and *tripa,* as well as quesadillas. Two tacos al pastor cost about US$2.50.

Adventurous eaters should head to **Taquería El Ahorcado,** known among gringos as **The Hangman** (Pescadores and Marinos, tel. 624/172-2093, Tues.–Sun. 6 P.M.–midnight, mains US$5–10), in the Chamizal neighborhood across Mexico 1, for beef tongue tacos and other unusual fare. This funky, rustic outdoor place has a full selection of quesadillas (including *huitlacoche,* mushroom, squash-flower, and

cactus fillings), tacos, *frijoles charros, champurrado,* and *café de olla.* Bring your own beer and enjoy live music while you dine. In the same neighborhood, 【 **Guacamaya** (open for dinner daily, mains US$8–12), off Calle Doblado, on the north side of Mexico 1, has become a local favorite for meat and fish tacos, including mouthwatering *tacos al pastor,* carved from a rotisserie spit and served with the signature toss of a pineapple slice. Huge stone bowls filled with flank steak and avocado are a super deal for US$7.

La Picazón (tel. 624/147-3857, Mon.–Sat. lunch and dinner, mains US$5–8), just east of the bus terminal on Calle González, serves good, basic *antojitos* at low prices in a pleasant outdoor *palapa* atmosphere. You can get *taquitos, tacones* (wraps), quesadillas, and even good burgers; more substantial fare includes chicken, lots of seafood, and steaks.

Good fish and shrimp tacos are available at **Cafetería El Recreo** (Hidalgo btw Zaragoza and Obregón, Wed.–Mon. 7 A.M.–9 P.M., mains US$5–10), a small stand with a few tables just north of the church on the Plaza Mijares. It's open for breakfast at 7 A.M., then 2–9 P.M. Wednesday–Monday for tacos.

Cafés

Enjoy coffee and pastries in air-conditioned comfort at **French Riviera** (corner of Hidalgo and Doblado, tel. 624/142-3350, www.fren-chrivieraloscabos.com, daily 8 A.M.–11 P.M., breakfast mains US$5–10, lunch mains US$6–13). The menu offers a long list of hot and cold coffee drinks, chai, smoothies, Italian sodas, pies, cookies, and pastries along with cigars and liquors.

Sweets

For Mexican-style ice cream or fresh-fruit popsicles, try **Paletería y Nevería La Michoacana** on Calle Morelos near Zaragoza across from Restaurant Jazmín, or on Zaragoza across from the plaza. The *paletas de mango* (mango popsicles) are quite refreshing.

Dulcería Arco Iris, on the north side of Calle Doblado, west of Green, and **La Bonita del Señor San José,** on the south side of Doblado east of Morelos, both feature all types of Mexican candies.

Groceries

These days, the best place to stock up on food and other supplies is the **Mega** supermarket (tel. 624/142-4524), at the intersection of Paseo Los Cabos and Mexico 1. Choose from a full array of Mexican and American brands, decent produce, and a wide selection of cheeses and meats. There is a well-stocked pharmacy, and those traveling with youngsters will find all manner of supplies, from pacifiers to bouncy seats. The friendly "staff" wearing orange shirts and offering to help you find your groceries are actually timeshare reps. In the adjoining plaza are a Telcel store, surf shop, public restrooms, and numerous fast food options.

For a more authentic shopping experience, the **Mercado Municipal,** between Calles Castro and Coronado in the west part of town, provides fresh fruits and vegetables, fish, meats, a *licuado* stand, and a cluster of *loncherías;* it's open from dawn to dusk daily.

On the east side of Mexico 1, just north of Calle Doblado, **Supermercado Grupo Castro** (tel. 624/143-0566) is larger than the other stores in town. A half kilometer north of town on the east side of Mexico 1, **Soriana** (tel. 624/142-6132) is a Walmart-style store with everything from beach towels to deli-meats. If you are heading directly to the East Cape, this is a good place to stock up on supplies for the week.

Tortillería Perla (diagonally opposite the Centro de Salud health center on Calle Doblado, tel. 624/142-0034, Mon.–Sat. 6 A.M.–1 P.M., Sun. 6 A.M.–3 P.M.) sells corn tortillas by the kilo. On the west side of Mexico 1, almost opposite the west end of Calle Doblado, **Tortillería de Harina** supplies flour tortillas during roughly the same hours.

The most convenient place in town to buy fresh seafood is **Pescadería San Marcos,** a small fish market near the Mercado Municipal on Calle Coronado.

On Calle Gonzalez, near the Corona supermarket and down the street from the bus terminal, **Panadería 1 de Mayo** has freshly baked breads and pastries with the usual tray-and-tong service.

La Playita and Pueblo La Playa

Just east of San José via Calle Juárez, **Los Dos Ricardos** (tel. 624/142-3068, Fri.–Wed. 9:30 A.M.–10:30 P.M., mains US$5–10) is a typical but out-of-the-way open-air seafood *palapa* on the road through Pueblo La Playa.

Palapa-roofed **La Playita** (daily for dinner, mains US$10–15), in Pueblo La Playa near the beach, has long held a good reputation for serving fresh seafood in a laid-back, beachy atmosphere. It changes management from time to time so it unfortunately lacks consistency, but it's worth a try in case it's going through a good phase. There's occasional live music.

La Playita Ali's International Place (mains US$5–10), the second thatched-roof building on the right as you enter La Playita proper, does fish tacos a little differently.

Instead of dunking the fillets in batter and deep-frying them, the cooks stir-fry unbattered fish in an onion and pepper sauce and serve it with large flour tortillas. Ali's will also be happy to cook (or smoke) any fish you may have caught.

Before you get to Tacos Ali and La Playita, look for **Mariscos El Puerto** (daily for lunch and dinner, mains US$4–7), which has about 10 tables with colorful checked tablecloths under a *palapa* roof and a menu of seafood cocktails, fish tacos that come with a tray of especially fresh condiments, and burgers.

Playa Costa Azul
Surfers, wannabes, and tourists head to **Zippers** (Km 28.5, tel. 624/172-6162, daily 11 A.M.–10 P.M., mains US$8–20), a round, *palapa*-topped beach restaurant at the southwest end of Playa Costa Azul. The menu offers tasty mesquite-grilled hamburgers, fish burgers, teriyaki chicken sandwiches, chili, chiles rellenos, and quesadillas. Indoor seating areas feature air conditioning, while the large outdoor patio offers a great ocean view. Enjoy live music on weekends during the tourist season.

INFORMATION AND SERVICES
Tourist Assistance
The Baja Sur **state tourism office** (tel. 624/146-9628, www.loscabos.gob.mx) is located at Boulevard Mauricio Castro, Plaza San José, Locales 3&4.

Money-Changing
There are now ATMs aplenty in San José, and several banks in town can still change dollars to pesos, for a fee. They are generally open Monday–Friday 8:30–11:30 A.M. **Santander Serfín,** two blocks west of Bancomer on Calle Zaragoza, usually has shorter lines. **HSBC,** in a small, relatively new shopping center on Boulevard Mijares just south of Calle Misiones, also offers exchange services. Another money exchange service is located in the Mega shopping plaza at the intersection of Mexico 1 and Paseo Los Cabos.

Major hotels will gladly take your dollars at a lower exchange rate. Use your credit card and ATM machines as much as possible to get the most pesos for your dollar.

Post and Telephone
San José's **post and telegraph office**, on Boulevard Mijares, is open Monday–Friday 8 A.M.–5 P.M. Next to the post office, the Telecomm office sends and receives Western Union telegrams.

Mail Boxes Etc. maintains an outlet at Plaza Las Palmas (Km 31, tel. 624/142-4355, fax 624/142-4360). MBE carries mailing supplies, postage stamps, and magazines and rents mailboxes.

The **public telephone office** on Calle Doblado, opposite the hospital, offers direct-dial long-distance phone service. Ladatel booths, the most convenient public phones for making international calls, can be found at Calles Doblado and Muñoz and on Calle Hidalgo between Obregón and Comonfort. The pharmacy counter of the Mega supermarket sells Ladatel phone cards, as does Havana's Restaurant near Plaza Costa Azul.

Internet Access
One of the best-operated Internet centers in town, **Trazzo Digital Internet** (Zaragoza 24 btw Hidalgo/Morelos, tel. 624/142-0303, www.trazzodigital.com, Mon.–Fri. 8 A.M.–9 P.M., Sat. 9 A.M.–7 P.M.) was also the fastest when we last checked. Trazzo has 15 comfortable workstations with wireless mice for US$1 up to 10 minutes, US$2.50 for 30 minutes, and US$0.30 for each additional 5 minutes. It also offers copies, printing, and scanning. Credit cards, including American Express, are accepted. **Ciber Espacio** (Mon.–Fri. 8 A.M.–9 P.M., Sat. 9 A.M.–9 P.M., US$2/hour) has 10 computer stations in an air-conditioned space near the school. There is also wireless access at the airport.

Medical Services
For medical assistance, visit the **Walk-in MediClinic** (Km 28, tel. 624/130-7011) in the El Zalate Plaza on Mexico 1. The facility has an

SAN JOSÉ DEL CABO PHONE NUMBERS

San José del Cabo area code: 624
General Hospital: 142-2770
Highway Patrol: 146-0573
Police, Fire Department, Red Cross (emergency): 066
Police (nonemergency): 142-2835
Tourism Office: 142-2960, ext. 150

emergency room, lab, pharmacy, and ambulance. Another option is **Médica Los Cabos** (Zaragoza 128, tel. 624/142-2770), near the Pemex station. Both will respond to emergencies 24/7.

Laundry

Lavandería Vera (tel. 624/124-1013) and **Lavamática San José** (tel. 624/142-4150), both on Calle González east of the bus terminal, offer washing, drying, and folding services Monday–Saturday 8 A.M.–8 P.M. **Eco Lavandería,** on Calle Obregón near Morgan's Encore, is a full-service laundry open Monday–Saturday 8 A.M.–9 P.M. and Sunday 8 A.M.–3 P.M. A small load costs about US$5.

RV Service and Supplies

Wahoo RV Center, near the CFE electric utility office in Colonia Chula Vista, off Mexico 1 (turn west between the Super Pollo and the turnoff for the Pemex station, tel./fax 624/142-3792, Mon.–Fri. 8 A.M.–1 P.M.), sells RV parts and accessories and does maintenance and repairs—including air conditioning and refrigeration—for trailers and motor homes, and it offers the use of a dump station.

   Los Cabos Mini and RV Storage (Km 37 Mexico 1, tel. 624/142-0976, cell 624/147-3117, bombardelli@prodigy.net.mx) offers locked, garage-style storage units within a fenced and lighted complex with 24-hour security. One of the few services of its kind anywhere in southern Baja, the storage facility is located about five kilometers from Los Cabos International Airport.

Canadian Consulate

The office of the Canadian consulate is on the second floor of Plaza José Green (Blvd. Mijares, tel. 624/142-4333, www.loscabos@canada.org.mx, Mon.–Fri. 9 A.M.–1 P.M.).

GETTING AROUND

Detailed information on how to get to Los Cabos is given at the beginning of this chapter. Once you've arrived, you can get around by foot, bike, bus, rental car, taxi, or shuttle.

By Bus

From San José's main bus station on Calle González (tel. 624/142-1100), Águila/ABC runs 15 buses a day to La Paz (US$17), with four buses a day from 7 A.M. and 3 P.M. continuing to Pichilingue for the ferry and six buses to Cabo San Lucas (US$3). The last bus to Cabo San Lucas leaves around 7 P.M. There is also hourly bus service between Cabo San Lucas and San José via the Flecha Verde and Estrella de Oro bus lines. The blue-and-orange Subur Cabo buses run between the two towns for US$2. It's easy to pick them up anywhere along Mexico 1. Officially, they're supposed to run till around 10 P.M.

By Car

You can do without a car if you plan to stay at an all-inclusive resort or a downtown hotel. Rent a car if you want the convenience of being able to drive yourself into town from a more remote location, or if you plan to take a day trip to the East Cape or Todos Santos. Most of the big auto rental agencies have desks at Los Cabos International Airport, as well as offices in or near town. Note: When renting in Mexico, you must buy Mexican liability insurance (typically about US$25/day). For details, see *Getting Around* in the *Essentials* chapter. The sidebar *Where to Rent a Car,* also in the *Essentials* chapter, has specific agency locations and contact information.

By Taxi and Shuttle

Visitors staying in town or at the beach are able to see most of what San José has to offer on foot. If you tire of walking, cabs are available; typical taxi fares are US$5 from the *zona hotelera* to the plaza downtown or from downtown to Pueblo La Playa, US$35 from town to Los Cabos airport or to Cabo San Lucas. Taxis congregate in front of the bus station, the beach hotels, and along Boulevard Mijares toward the plaza. Look for a taxi stand signed Sitio San José on Boulevard Mijares, just south of Plaza José Green. Call 624/142-0401 or 624/142-0105 for pickups.

The Corridor

This 29-kilometer (18-mi) section of Mexico 1, connecting San José del Cabo and Cabo San Lucas, represents one of Mexico's finest nontoll routes and passes by secluded beaches, rocky points, and tidal pools. It's known officially as the Corredor Náutico (Nautical Corridor), or more commonly in English simply as "the Corridor."

This section of Mexico 1, four lanes all the way, represents one of Mexico's finest nontoll routes. However, most of the roads branching south of the highway are unpaved. Almost all can be negotiated by ordinary passenger vehicles, though the overall number of public access roads continues to decline because of private development. Although it's illegal for any hotel or other private development to block all access to any beach along the Corridor, guarded gateways may dissuade all but the very bold. In some cases it's necessary to park along the highway or in a nearby hotel parking lot and walk down to the beach.

There aren't really separate towns along the Corridor; instead, the area is divided into several *fraccionamientos,* or districts for development, each containing several resorts, golf courses, spas, and the like. At Km 19.5, the Cabo Real development presides over scenic Bahía El Bledito and comprises the Marquis Los Cabos, Meliá Cabo Real Convention Center Beach and Golf Resort, Hotel Casa del Mar, and Casa del Mar Condos, as well as the renowned Cabo Real Golf Course and the Jack Nicklaus–designed El Dorado Golf Course (see *Golf*). Stretching between Km 10 and Km 20, Cabo del Sol consists of the Sheraton and Fiesta America resorts and the Cabo del Sol golf course.

BEACHES

One after another, beautiful beaches and coves hug the coastline between San José and Cabo San Lucas. Some are hidden from highway view by bluffs, and others are marked by resort development, of which increasingly restricted access is an unfortunate side effect. To find the beaches that are still open, follow the blue-and-white signs along Mexico 1, sometimes labeled *Acceso a Playa* but more often than not simply bearing a simple outline of a snorkel mask or swimmer. Strong undertows and rocks make many of these beaches unsafe for swimming. Playas Chileno and Santa María are two exceptions. The sidebar *Beaches Along the Corridor* lists all beaches accessible from the highway.

Playa Palmilla

Playa Palmilla at Km 26 is a decent swimming beach—local kids dive here for golf balls that have dropped into Neptune's realm from the Palmilla Golf Club Ocean Course links. **Restaurant-Bar Pepe's** (Km 27, tel. 624/144-5040) will cook your catch for a few dollars, or you can rely on the restaurant's own dependable source of seafood (see *Food*).

Playa El Mirador/Playa Bledito

Farther southwest, a breakwater has tamed the waters along Playa El Mirador, a lengthy stretch of beach north of the Hotel Meliá Cabo Real and part of Bahía El Bledito. Look for an access road just north of Km 20. As the Cabo

Real development expands, public access may change.

◖ Playas Chileno and Santa María

A little more than halfway to Cabo San Lucas, the wide crescents of sand rimming Bahía Chileno and Bahía Santa María constitute two of the Corridor's most popular and accessible swimming beaches. At Playa Chileno, visitors walk through a gate in the chain-link fence protecting the beach from vehicles and follow a path through a grove of fan palms to reach the beach itself. The palms provide natural shade, a component lacking at most other Corridor beaches. Beneath the houses perched on headlands at either end of the bay are rocky areas with good snorkeling. Once run-down, primitive restrooms were refurbished in 2006.

Though picturesque and suitable for swimming, Playa Santa María offers a smaller beach without shade; it's best enjoyed by snorkelers and divers rather than swimmers, and there are now snorkeling equipment and beach umbrellas for rent. Both of these beaches can get crowded with shoulder-to-shoulder snorkelers when the tour boats come in mid-morning to mid-afternoon. Best to get an early start if you'd like to have the bay to yourself.

Playa Las Viudas

Playa Las Viudas (Widows Beach), more commonly known as Twin Dolphin Beach, is reached via a rough sand turnoff at Km 11–12 next to the private entrance to the former Hotel Twin Dolphin. Vehicles with high road clearance will fare better than ordinary sedans. The tan-colored beach—actually several scalloped beaches separated by small rocky points—tends to be on the pebbly side, though the swimming is usually excellent.

Northeast of Cabo San Lucas at Km 4, little-known and uncrowded **Playa Cemeterio** offers calm swimming and white sands.

La Concha Beach Club

Just northeast of the Meliá Cabo Real at Km

BEACHES ALONG THE CORRIDOR

BEACH	NEAREST KM MARKER	DISTANCE WEST OF KM MARKER (IN METERS)
Costa Azul	29	500
Acapulquito	27	800
Playa Palmilla	26	400
Punta Bella	24	400
Buenos Aires	22	400
El Mirador	20	–
San Carlos	19	–
El Zalate	17	500
Costa Brava	17	100
Cantamar	16	700
Del Tule	15	400
Punta Chileno	14	–
Santa María	12	200
Las Viudas (Twin Dolphin)	12	500
Barco Varado (Shipwreck)	9-10	–
Cabo Bello	5-6	200
Cemeterio	4	–

19.5 is the upscale La Concha Beach Club and Restaurant (tel. 624/144-0102, daily 10 A.M.–10 P.M.). This beautiful secluded spot consists of three small, curving, sand-fringed bays. The club offers a splash pool, showers, beach umbrellas, and beach chairs and rents towels and snorkeling equipment. The restaurant serves international cuisine and is open for lunch and dinner daily 11 A.M.–10 P.M. Instead of an entrance fee, there's a reasonable food-and-drink minimum purchase requirement (easily achieved in the club's well-run open-air dining areas). No pets, ice chests, or food from the outside.

SURFING

Although Los Cabos is less famous than Baja's northern and central Pacific coast for surf, the summer southwest swell brings consistent wave action to the tip of the peninsula, when most of the west coast points are flat. The surf reaches peak height during the *chubasco* season, late summer to early fall. The most dependable surfing area between San José and Cabo

San Lucas is **Playa Costa Azul,** at Km 29–28, where a grinding shore-breaker called Zippers is sometimes backed by Hawaii-style outside breaks in heavy swell.

Punta Palmilla, below the One&Only Palmilla at Km 28–27, whips out a sometimes large right point break, while the bay to the point's immediate north, **Playa Acapulquito,** between Costa Azul and Palmilla, offers a good reef break in heavy swell.

Reef breaks sometimes occur at **Playa Buenos Aires,** Km 22 (beware strong rips), and at **Playa Cabo Real,** Km 20; then there's a gap until **Playa Cantamar** at Km 16 and **Punta Chileno** at Km 14, both offering workable point breaks. To reach Cantamar—which is often confused with **Playa El Tule** (also known as Puente del Tule)—you need eagle eyes. Coming from Cabo San Lucas in your own vehicle (the turnoff is accessible only from this side of the highway), cross Arroyo El Tule and then immediately turn right off the highway as the road begins to rise toward the Solidaridad monument. Here look for a small dirt road through a gate in a barbed-wire fence (usually open), after which a sand road leads around to the northeast end of Puente El Tule, a good spot to park and camp.

In summer, a good-sized, nicely shaped right point break sometimes forms off **Playa Barco Varado,** at Km 9—access comes just northeast of the turnoff for the Cabo del Sol golf course/ hotel complex.

Playa Cabo Bello, between Km 6 and Km 5, is known for a consistent left point break nicknamed Monuments for the H-shaped concrete monument that used to stand next to the highway near here. Northwest swell refracted off Cabo San Lucas fuels this band easternmost break for winter surfing. During heavier swell, it may be joined by an outer reef break. The spot seems to amplify the available swell and is one of the few left point breaks along the Corridor. Be prepared to wait your turn at the takeoff spot and keep an eye out for rocks and urchins.

Most of these beaches now feature some sort of condo or resort development in prog-ress, but there's always a way to drive through or around them; it's illegal to restrict public beach access.

DIVING

Several beaches along the Corridor feature rock reefs suitable for snorkeling and scuba diving, particularly **Playa Santa María** (Km 12), **Playa Chileno** (Km 14), and **Playa Barco Varado** (Shipwreck Beach, Km 9–10). Santa María offers rock reefs at either end of a protected cove at depths of 13 meters (40 ft) or less. The north point displays sea fans and gorgonians, along with the usual assortment of tropical fish. The south end has sea caves, coral outcroppings, and large rocky areas inhabited by reef fish and lobster.

The remains of the Japanese tuna boat *Inari Maru No. 10*, stranded on rocky shoals in 1966, is the main diving destination at Shipwreck Beach. A local story says that when Cabo *pescadores* noticed the Japanese vessel fishing illegally, they extinguished the nearest lighthouse beacon and rigged a light of their own that lured the boat onto the shoals after nightfall. The hull and other wreckage lie 2–26 meters (6.5–85 ft) underwater, near scenic rock reefs. Tidal pools along Shipwreck Beach support starfish and sea urchins.

GOLF

Golf is king in the Corridor, which is home to three Jack Nicklaus–designed golf courses (the 27-hole Palmilla, 18-hole El Dorado at Cabo Real, and the 18-hole Cabo del Sol), the 18-hole Robert Trent Jones II–designed Cabo Real course, the Tom Fazio–designed 18-hole Querencia, and the 18-hole Tom Weiskopf addition to Cabo del Sol. The Cabo San Lucas Country Club, formerly known as the Raven Golf Club, was designed by Roy Dye. Keeping all of those fairways groomed and green in a desert environment doesn't come cheap: Greens fees average US$250. Discounted twilight rates begin at 2 P.M. Rates may vary according to the travel season and day of the week.

These courses boast landscapes and playing terrain comparable to those found in many Arizona and California desert courses, the main difference being the visual addition of the sparkling Sea of Cortez.

Palmilla

Opened in 1992, the Jack Nicklaus–designed 27-hole golf course at the One&Only Palmilla (Km 26, tel. 624/144-5250) is divided into arroyo, mountain, and ocean courses, splendid by all accounts. Nearly every hole has a view of the Sea of Cortez in the distance. This course hosted the 1997 PGA Senior Slam, 1997 Taylor Made Pro-Am, and 1998 World Pro-Am tournaments. Nicklaus himself, though admitting his bias as the designer (this was his first course in Latin America), claims the 17th and 18th holes are the best finishing holes in the world. The course's signature hole is the 440-yard, par-4 Mountain Five, which necessitates a long drive across two desert arroyos. Gray water irrigates the fairways and greens, easing the strain on the Los Cabos water supply. The public pays US$209–269 per 18 holes. Fees include golf cart, practice balls, bottled water, and use of the driving range. Callaway clubs rent for US$50 plus tax. The golf course serves as the centerpiece of a 384-hectare (950-acre) development surrounding the original hotel with fairway homes, a network of paved roads, a clubhouse, and a tennis complex.

Cabo Real

The Cabo Real complex at Km 19.5 boasts two world-class golf courses. The 18-hole, par-72 **Cabo Real Golf Course** (tel. 624/144-0040, U.S. tel. 800/393-0400, reservations@caboreal.com) stretches over more than 7,000 yards of verdant landscape with three ocean holes. There are five sets of tees from which to choose. The course is open to the general public for US$260–280 for 18 holes (9 holes US$180), including tax, golf cart, practice facilities, club service, and bottled water. Hotel guests staying at the Westin Los Cabos, Meliá Cabo Real, and Casa del Mar receive a 10 percent discount. King Cobra brand golf club rentals are US$50.

The Jack Nicklaus–designed **El Dorado Golf Club** (Km 10, tel. 624/144-5450) is the second championship course in the Cabo Real development. The 18-hole, par-72 course features six oceanfront holes; the rest are carved out of two picturesque canyons surrounded by trees, cacti, and rock formations. Six holes come into play beside four lakes. This 7,050-yard course has been called the finest course in Mexico and one of the best in the world. Greens fees run US$260–280 and include tax, golf cart with laser range finder, practice facilities, club service, and bottled water. The clubhouse and restaurant afford views of the Sea of Cortez and the 9th and 18th holes.

Cabo del Sol

Jack Nicklaus designed his second set of Mexican fairways on 730 hectares (1,800 acres) of land between Playa Barco Varado and Cabo Bello. Cabo del Sol (Km 10.5, tel. 624/145-8200, U.S. tel. 877/703-4394) is Los Cabos's highest-rated golf course so far. *Golf Digest* has rated it as one of the top 10 public golf courses anywhere; Nicklaus himself insists that it includes some of the greatest ocean holes in the world. Seven of the course's holes feature dramatic oceanfront play along the shore of Bahía de Ballenas. The front nine is 3,597 yards, par 36, while the back nine extends 3,440 yards, also par 36.

A newer desert course, a 7,100-yard, par-72 piece of eye-candy designed by PGA great Tom Weiskopf (his first golf course in Mexico), spreads across 57 hectares (140 acres) of desert landscape. A third 18-hole course for Cabo del Sol is still in the planning stages.

Fees start at US$350 for 18 holes on the ocean course (taco lunch included), or US$220 on the desert course, which includes tax, a golf cart, practice facilities, club service, and bottled water. Guests of the Fiesta Americana and Sheraton resorts receive a 10 percent discount. Callaway clubs rent for US$55.

Cabo San Lucas Country Club

This Roy Dye–designed, 300-hectare (745-acre), 18-hole course (501 Palo Blanco, tel.

seaside massage at the Westin Los Cabos

624/143-4653/4, U.S. tel. 888/328-8501) lies just one kilometer northeast of Cabo San Lucas, on sloping terrain facing the sea, with views of Land's End and Bahía San Lucas from each fairway and five tees for each hole (back, championship, member, forward, and front). At 610 yards (par 5), the seventh hole is said to be the longest in Mexico. The front nine is 3,651 yards (par 36), the back nine is 3,569 yards (par 36). Greens fees are among the lowest in the area, US$95–169 for 18 holes for nonmembers, including cart. Taylor-Made clubs rent for US$49. To avoid drawing excessively from the Cape's precious aquifer, gray water from the resort spends a month cycling through a series of duckweed ponds until the fast-growing plant renders the water safe for irrigation. Along with fairway homes, the resort features tennis, swimming, and fitness clubs.

SPA SERVICES

Most of the resorts listed in this chapter have their own spa facilities, with a menu of treatments from body wraps and massages to facials and pedicures. Services are typically offered inside or under a tent on the beach. Some of the standouts include heavenly body wraps at **The Spa at the Westin Los Cabos** (Km 22.5, tel. 624/142-9000, U.S. tel. 800/598-1864, www.westinloscabos.com), and indoor steam caves and waterfalls, plus holistic treatments using local fruits and vegetation at **Esperanza Resort** (Km 7, Punta Ballena, tel. 624/145-6400, U.S. tel. 866/311-2226, www.esperanzaresort.com), where 90-minute treatments cost US$198. The **Marquis Los Cabos** (Km 21.5, tel. 624/144-2000, U.S. tel. 877/238-9399, www.marquisloscabos.com) also boasts a gorgeous 10,000-square-foot spa with six additional massage tents on the beach. A 50-minute facial runs US$100–115; deep-tissue, Shiatsu, Thai, or sports massage services are US$115–125 for 50 minutes; mud therapy treatments are US$115 for 50 minutes; and body scrubs are US$79 for 25 minutes. Nonguests can use the spa facilities (steam room, whirlpool tubs, and spa swimming pool) without reserving a treatment for US$25. At the Palmilla exit (Km 27.5), **Hive Day Spa** (tel. 624/144-6123, U.S. tel. 312/602-9556, www.hivespa.com, Mon.–Fri. 10 A.M.–9 P.M.) offers 90-minute treatments for US$125–145. Credit cards are accepted.

SHOPPING

For jewelry, clothing, antiques, and home furnishings, look for an upscale shopping plaza called **Tiendas de Palmilla** (Km 27.5, Palmilla, 624/144-6999, www.lastiendasdepalmilla.com) on the north side of Mexico 1 at the Palmilla Resort exit. Among other boutiques, the eclectic **Pez Gordo Gallery** (tel. 624/144-5292) has opened a second location here. **Artesania Mágica** (tel 624/144-6046, www.artesania-magica.com, daily 10 A.M.–8 P.M.) has a selection of upscale Mexican handicrafts. Cabo San Lucas's outstanding sushi restaurant, **Nick-San** (tel. 624/144-6262, www.nicksan.com, Tues.–Sun. 12:30–10:30 P.M.) has opened a second location here.

ACCOMMODATIONS

The priciest and best-situated hotels in Los Cabos grace the coast along the Corridor. Designed to appeal to the well-heeled hedonist seeking a degree of privacy and seclusion not found in Mexican beach resorts such as Puerto Vallarta, Cancún, Mazatlán, or Acapulco (and avoiding the hot, rainy summers elsewhere in coastal Mexico), these resorts take full advantage of their desert remoteness. *Conde Nast Traveler* magazine named five of the Los Cabos resorts to its Gold List 2007, an annual ranking of the best places to stay worldwide: Las Ventanas, Esperanza, the Hilton, One&Only Palmilla, and Fiesta Americana Grand.

Prices for these resorts begin around US$300–400 for the Sheraton and Hilton, climb to US$500 for the Westin and Marquis, and top out at US$700–1,000 per night or more for the Palmilla, Esperanza, and Las Ventanas. The lowest rates at each resort typically require full payment at the time of booking, and cancellation fees apply.

Travel club memberships such as AAA can yield a discount of US$100 or more per night. The standard rates do not include 12 percent tax and 15 percent service, unless otherwise noted. Even if you have no plans to stay in the area, the hotel restaurants or bars are well worth a visit for a meal or drink and the ocean view.

Cabo Surf Hotel

Hidden away below Mexico 1, just two kilometers southwest of San José, Cabo Surf Hotel (Carr. Transp. Km 28, tel. 624/142-2676, www.cabosurfhotel.com, US$250–355) offers a small cluster of 10 remodeled comfortable apartments and villas overlooking Playa Acapulquito. All units come with a minibar, coffeemaker, satellite TV, and seaview terraces. Kitchenettes and kitchens are available. The grounds include a large barbecue area, restaurant/bar, hot tub, swimming pool, and plunge pool. Its **7 Seas** (www.7seasrestaurant.com, daily 7 A.M.–10 P.M., lunch mains US$7–13, dinner mains US$18–28) serves Mexican, Mediterranean, and seafood entrées under an open-air *palapa*.

Sheraton Hacienda del Mar

You won't have to get up at the crack of dawn to reserve a chaise lounge at the Sheraton (Km 10.5, Cabo del Sol, tel. 624/145-8000 or 800/903-2500, U.S. tel. 888/625-5144, www.sheratonhaciendadelmar.com, from US$400)—an abundance of patio furniture was part of the resort design. Even better, a poolside concierge helps guests plan the day's activities without having to leave the pool.

Part of the Cabo del Sol development, the Sheraton is a plush Mediterranean-style resort with 270 rooms and 31 suites; the latter were renovated in late 2006. Some rooms also contain hot tubs. Other amenities include a three-tier pool, two outdoor whirlpool tubs facing the ocean, a gym, spa, and tropical gardens.

The hotel boasts five bars and five restaurants, including the renowned **Pitahayas** (tel. 624/145-8010, daily for breakfast, lunch, and

TYING THE KNOT

Destination weddings are becoming big business in Los Cabos. Inviting your friends and family to a seaside marriage ceremony and wedding reception will create memories to last a lifetime. But the choices can be overwhelming, and there seems to be no upper limit on what you can spend. Consider these tips before you start planning the big day:

HIRE A WEDDING COORDINATOR

Different legal system, languages, and event business norms can make for a difficult planning process. Do yourself a favor and get help early. Dozens of wedding specialists operate from the area and can advise on reception sites, flowers, music, and food. Some are affiliated with a particular resort; others work independently. Booking service Earth, Sea, & Sky Vacations (www.cabovillas.com/weddings.asp) works with a professional coordinator to plan weddings in the area. Baja Weddings (www.bajawedding.com) is another reputable service.

CHOOSE YOUR PRIORITIES

When planning from afar, you won't be able to oversee every last detail of the event in person. Decide in advance what matters most and focus your attention there. Leave the other details in the hands of an experienced wedding coordinator.

FIND THE RIGHT SETTING FOR YOU AND YOUR GUESTS

An all-inclusive resort may simplify the logistics for some couples; others will prefer to select food, music, cake, photography, and flowers à la carte.

SET A BUDGET AND STICK TO IT

You may fall in love with the gourmet lunch at the One&Only Palmilla, but it may not be the place to host your 100-person event.

READ THE FINE PRINT BEFORE YOU BOOK

Are you committing to rent all the rooms in the inn? Make sure you know the terms of the deal before you pay a deposit.

DIG FOR DEALS

Join an online forum, such as CaboWeddings on Yahoo Groups (http://groups.yahoo.com/group/CaboWeddings), to learn from the experience of others. Brides report finding bands and vendors for as low as half the cost of vendors their coordinator recommended. The Los Cabos Guide keeps an online list of local wedding service providers (www.loscabosguide.com/services/weddings.htm).

---

dinner, mains US$15–40), which offers a creative menu of Pacific Rim cuisine. Dine inside or out at the more casual **Tomates** (tel. 624/145-8000, daily for breakfast, lunch, and dinner, mains US$10–15), serving a fusion of Mexican and international dishes. Look for the beautifully landscaped Cabo del Sol exit ramp near Km 10.

Dreams Los Cabos Suites Golf Resort & Spa

A favorite among wedding parties, honeymooners, and anniversary celebrants, Dreams Los Cabos (Km 18.5, Cabo Real, tel. 624/145-7600, U.S. tel. 866/237-3267 www.dreamsresorts.com, from US$600)

has 308 large and private luxury suites and all the amenities of a full-service resort. Its honeymoon packages include a champagne breakfast in bed. Book ahead if you have your heart set on a stay at Dreams; this popular resort has one of the highest occupancy rates in Los Cabos.

Hilton Los Cabos Beach & Golf Resort

Next door, the Hilton (Km 19.5, Cabo Real, tel. 624/145-6500, from US$400) features Mediterranean architecture, a beautiful infinity pool, and a complete list of luxury-style amenities, plus a favorable location near Playa Bledito. Rooms were recently renovated by designer Paul

Duesing and have large baths with soaking tubs, separate showers, and L'Occitane products.

Meliá Cabo Real

The Meliá Cabo Real (Km 19.5, tel. 624/142-2222, www.solmelia.com, from US$388) offers 305 well-appointed rooms plus several suites, almost all with ocean views—laid out like a squared-off horseshoe around a huge glass-and-onyx, pyramid-topped, open-air lobby. Guests can swim at the beach (tamed by the addition of a rock jetty) or in the hotel's freeform pool. On the beach, Tío Sports rents sports equipment and organizes scuba tours and instruction. Three restaurants prepare meals, although recent visitors have expressed disappointment in food quality and service. All-inclusive rates available.

Casa del Mar Golf Resort and Spa

The Casa del Mar (Km 19.5, tel. 624/145-7700, U.S. tel. 800/227-9621, www.casadelmarmexico.com, US$415–450) is a smaller place containing 24 oceanview rooms plus 32 deluxe one-bedroom suites with spacious bathrooms and complete kitchenettes. The premises also hold a full-service European-style spa, six pools, four tennis courts, the adjacent Cabo Real Golf Club, three bars, and a restaurant called **El Tapanco** (daily 5–10:30 P.M., mains US$10–20), serving Nuevo Mexican cuisine.

Fiesta Americana Grand Los Cabos

Adjacent to the Cabo del Sol golf course is the family-oriented Fiesta Americana Grand Los Cabos (Km 10.3, Cabo del Sol, tel. 624/145-6200, U.S. tel. 800/343-7821, www.fiestaamericana.com, US$476–662), with 250 oceanview guestrooms and suites and a secluded beach in front. Rooms are spread across six floors and feature private balconies. The resort's restaurant, **Rosato,** serves northern Italian cuisine.

Westin Resort & Spa Los Cabos

If you've been doing some research on resorts in Los Cabos, you've likely seen pictures of a dramatic architectural interpretation of the arch at Land's End. This is the Westin Los Cabos (Km. 22.5, tel. 624/142-9000, U.S. tel. 800/598-1864, www.westinloscabos.com, US$379–705), designed by renowned Mexican architect Javier Sordo Magdaleno, who endowed the bold curvilinear design with a bright palette of colors abstracted from the surrounding geological, floral, and marine environment. A Zenlike rock-and-cactus garden on a hillside overlooks a dramatic seaside pool fed by a sophisticated water-recycling system. A nine-hole putting green with its own shaded outdoor bar provides added entertainment. On the opposite hillside to the immediate north of the hotel stand numerous pastel timeshare and residential units managed by the hotel.

The chain's signature Heavenly Beds are reason enough to stay here. Separate tubs and showers in large marble bathrooms add even more of a distinctive touch. Flatscreen TVs, initially in premier World Club rooms, are in the plans for all guestrooms.

Several restaurants on-site provide a variety of dining experiences; they include eclectic **Arrecifes** and **La Cascada,** which serves *tapas* from around the world.

A state-of-the-art European spa offers body wraps, mud baths, and massage treatments inside or on the beach. Guests have golf privileges at the Cabo Real golf course, about 2.5 kilometers southwest.

Marquis Los Cabos

From the inlaid turquoise stones that accent resort corridors to perfectly filtered light in the spa rooms, meticulous attention to detail and contemporary Mexican decor set the tone for a stay at the Marquis Los Cabos (Km 21.5, tel. 624/144-2000, U.S. tel. 877/238-9399, www.marquisloscabos.com, US$445–700). Opened in 2003, the Mexican-owned resort was designed to reveal ocean views from every angle. Guests can move from their room to a restaurant, the spa, or the gym without losing sight of the sea. The Marquis' 237 rooms have soaking tubs and showers, Bulgary bath fixtures, mahogany woodwork, flatscreen TVs, and

COURTESY MARQUIS LOS CABOS

Marquis Los Cabos

exquisite linens. Each morning, hotel staff delivers breakfast to guests through a private pass-through alcove. In addition, rooms and common areas showcase contemporary Mexican paintings and sculpture. And if you fall in love with the eclectic furnishings, as many guests apparently have, you'll soon be able to buy your own from a furniture store on the premises. Twenty-eight *casitas* have their own swimming pools. A 10,000-square-foot spa and an award-winning, 21-seat French restaurant, **Canto del Mar** (dinner only, prix fixe US$60 pp), set the hotel apart. Close proximity to the highway and small balconies are the only obvious disadvantages at this resort. A service charge of US$35 per day applies.

Las Ventanas al Paraíso

Romance defines the experience at Las Ventanas (tel. 624/144-0300, U.S. tel. 888/767-3966, www.lasventanas.com, junior suites US$650–1,350), just northeast of Km 20, which celebrated its 10th anniversary in 2007. Accordingly, one of your first choices upon

arrival here will be selecting bed linens from the sheet menu. Under the auspices of Rosewood Hotels and Resorts, Las Ventanas was designed using an innovative combination of Mexican-Mediterranean architecture and interior design. Unlike the bright primary colors favored by many Mexican beach resorts, here pastels and earth tones are emphasized. Underground tunnels hide many of the day-to-day guest service activities to keep aboveground architecture to a minimum, adding to the overall sense of intimacy.

Guest suites average 90 square meters (960 sq ft)—among the largest standard room sizes in Mexico. Highlights include custom-made furniture, inlaid stone-and-tile floors, an adobe fireplace, private furnished patio with individual splash pool/hot tub, computerized telescope aimed at the sea (for viewing the whales offshore), freshly cut blooms, and a huge bathroom. Each room also comes with a small bottle of high-end tequila. Three spa suites have space for in-room treatments, as well as rooftop terraces with outdoor hot tubs.

Guests have free use of a full-service spa and fitness center. The beach in front of the resort, Playa Costa Brava, is a little too *brava* for most swimmers, but overlooking the beach is a large freeform horizon pool with "high tech" pebbles that change color according to the color of the sky and sea. The resort's restaurant, simply called **The Restaurant** (daily for breakfast, lunch, and dinner), has been managed by a new chef since 2005. Other dining options include a less formal restaurant and a tequila-and ceviche-tasting bar. Friday evening Tequila Nights, open to guests and nonguests, are run as tasting classes. Private movie nights on the beach, complete with wine and gourmet Mexican *botanas,* are another signature Las Ventanas diversion. Multiday spa and meal packages are available. For guests who want to venture away from the resort, Mini Cooper S convertibles, BMW motorcycles, and off-road Hummers are available for rent.

Esperanza Resort

By many accounts, Esperanza (Km 7, Punta

Esperanza Resort

Ballena, tel. 624/145-6400, U.S. tel. 866/311-2226, www.esperanzaresort.com, US$675–1,325) leads the pack for outstanding guest service. Located close to Cabo San Lucas, its 50 *casitas* and six suites feature original Mexican artwork and hand-crafted furnishings. A signature spa has indoor steam caves and waterfalls, with treatments that incorporate local fruits and vegetation. And the oceanfront Mediterranean restaurant, the **Signature Restaurant at Esperanza,** completes the picture; it's open for breakfast, lunch, and dinner. Esperanza also has its own art gallery with works by contemporary Mexican painters and sculptors for sale. A four-night minimum stay is required for all weekend bookings January–April except February and March, when a seven-night stay is required.

One&Only Palmilla

Today, the oldest resort in Los Cabos is also one of the destination's most expensive—and most popular—places to stay. The former Hotel Palmilla Resort received an $80 million makeover and opened as the One&Only Palmilla (Km 27, tel. 624/146-7000, U.S. tel. 866/829-2977, www.oneandonlyresorts.com, US$550–775) in early 2004. Covering 384 hectares (950 acres) of Punta Palmilla near Km 27, the resort was the Cape's first major resort; it was built in 1956 by "Rod" Rodríguez, son of former Mexican president Abelardo Luis Rodríguez. Coconut palms, clouds of hibiscus, and sweeping seaviews dominate the grounds. Facilities at the resort's latest incarnation include two infinity-edge pools and a children's pool; fitness center, yoga garden, and spa with 13 private treatment villas; and a rustic chapel used for weddings. All 172 rooms and suites feature flatscreen satellite TV with DVD and CD player with Bose system surround-sound, state-of-the-art voice and data lines, and separate sitting area. Rates include personal butler service, twice-daily maid service, daily fruit delivery, and an aromatherapy menu. The One&Only Palmilla maintains a sportfishing fleet and offers *panga* fishing trips, scuba diving, and snorkeling. Palmilla also boasts a world-class golf course (see *Golf*).

Guests enjoy 24-hour room service from the resort's two restaurants: **Restaurant C,** created by Charlie Trotter of Chicago restaurant fame, and the *palapa*-style **Agua Restaurant,** which offers a Mediterranean menu.

FOOD

Most restaurants along the Corridor are tucked inside full-service resorts (see *Accommodations*). Expect to pay at least US$100 for two (without drinks) at most of the restaurants in this section. Here are a few stand-alone eateries and some of the resort standouts.

Seafood and International

Restaurant-Bar Pepe's (Km 27, tel. 624/144-5040), on Playa Palmilla, will cook your catch for a few dollars, or you can rely on the restaurant's own dependable source of seafood.

Pecan-encrusted sea bass, mesquite grilled prawns, and live lobster anchor the menu at **Pitahayas** (Km 10, Cabo del Sol, tel. 624/145-8010, daily 5:30–10:30 P.M., mains US$15–40), at the Sheraton Hacienda del Mar, a large open-air restaurant with an impressive underground wine cellar, serves an innovative menu of Pacific Rim cuisine focusing on fresh seafood and a mesquite grill. Formal resort attire is required.

At the Cabo Surf Hotel, **7 Seas** (Km 28, tel. 624/142-2676, www.7seasrestaurant.com, daily 7 A.M.–10 P.M., lunch mains US$7–13, dinner mains US$18–28) serves breakfast, lunch, and dinner under an open-air *palapa*. The dinner menu features Mexican, Mediterranean, and seafood entrées with a decent wine list. Seafood-stuffed poblano peppers are one of the more unusual dishes.

At the Westin Los Cabos, **Arrecifes** (Km. 22.5, tel. 624/142-9000) commands a view of the wave-battered beach below and offers an eclectic menu emphasizing seafood and standout desserts; **La Cascada** underwent a US$900,000 renovation in 2006 featuring illuminated onyx cube tables, a new fire pit lounge, and a menu of creative *tapas del mundo,* or small plates from around the world paired with wines that match the flavors of the food.

And at the One&Only Palmilla, diners can choose between the *palapa*-style **Agua Restaurant,** featuring Mediterranean cuisine and a view of the sea, and Charlie Trotter's first overseas restaurant, called **Restaurant C** (Km 7.5, tel. 624/146-7000, www.charlietrotters.com, mains US$20 and up). Representative entrées at C include rockfish with ratatouille, quinoa, and a black olive–caper vinaigrette and steamed and spit-roasted duck with spiced carrots, parsnips, and a tangerine-merlot reduction. Both restaurants are open for breakfast, lunch, and dinner.

Italian and Continental

In the Misiones del Cabo complex, **Sunset da Mona Lisa** (formerly Da Giorgio, Km 5.5, tel. 624/145-8160, www.sunsetmonalisa.com, daily 8:30 A.M.–11 P.M., mains US$18–35) draws a crowd for sunset views and Italian fare. A multilevel patio overlooks the bay and Cabo San Lucas. Credit cards are accepted.

Dinner at the award-winning French restaurant **Canto del Mar** (tel. 624/144-2000, dinner only, prix fixe US$60 pp), inside the Marquis Los Cabos resort, is an Old World

affair, complete with acoustic guitar music and a collection of masks from Florence on the walls. There are just 21 seats in the house for the nightly six-course tasting menu. An adjoining cigar room has a hardwood floor and ornate upholstered armchairs.

American and Eclectic

The Mediterranean-inspired **French Riviera** in San José and Cabo San Lucas has a third location between Cabo Bello and Misiones del Cabo (Km 6.3, tel. 624/104-3124, www.frenchrivieraloscabos.com, daily noon–11 P.M., mains US$33).

Mexican

Close to Cabo San Lucas, **◖ Puerta Vieja** (Km 6.3, tel. 624/104-3252, www.puertavieja.com, mains US$13–23) offers a fantastic view and hearty fare like Sonora beef and fresh shellfish, prepared with Asian accents and offered at incredibly reasonable prices—a rare find along the Corridor. One more kilometer east, the same owners run the popular **Villa Serena Restaurant** (Km 7.5, tel. 624/145-8244, daily 7 A.M.–10 P.M., mains US$12–25) next to the Villa Serena RV Park. Tasty seafood platters or beef and chicken dishes are a great deal.

Groceries and Supplies

La Europea (Km 6.7, tel. 624/145-8755, Mon.–Fri. 9 A.M.–8 P.M., Sat. 9 A.M.–9 P.M.) stocks a wide variety of international gourmet foods, from prosciutto to wasabi, as well as an impressive selection of fine wines and liquor. Look for the main store at the first stoplight as you enter Cabo from the east. Smaller, satellite stores are located at the marina level of the Puerto Paraíso plaza in Cabo San Lucas and on the south side of Mexico 1, east of the Mega plaza in San José. Credit cards are accepted. **Costco** (Km 4.5, tel. 624/146-7180, daily 9 A.M.–9 P.M.) and **Home Depot** (Km 6.5, tel. 624/105-8600) have also opened stores close to Cabo San Lucas.

INFORMATION AND SERVICES

Pemex stations are located at Km 5 just outside of Cabo San Lucas and near the Westin between Km 24 and Km 25. Most of the resorts offer Internet access and phone services for guests. For medical needs, see *Information and Services* in the *San José del Cabo* and *Cabo San Lucas* sections.

GETTING AROUND

Resorts along the Corridor are a 30- to 60-minute drive from the airport. Many, including the Westin, offer shuttles to San José del Cabo and Cabo San Lucas for guests who want to see a little more than their hotel grounds. Car rental agencies have offices at many of the larger resorts. (See the sidebar *Where to Rent a Car in Baja* in the *Essentials* chapter.) For advice on how to get to Los Cabos from the United States, see *Getting There* at the beginning of this chapter.

Cabo San Lucas

Cabo San Lucas has a tourist-to-resident ratio higher than elsewhere in the Cape Region, especially during the peak November–March tourist season. Several cruise lines also feature Cabo San Lucas on their itineraries. Yet in spite of all the visitors—most of whom confine themselves to the waterfront—Cabo manages to retain something of a funky, small-town feel. Away from Boulevard Marina, many of the unpaved, sand streets are lined with the *tortillerías,* hardware shops, and markets typically found in any small coastal Mexican town.

Named for the slender cape extending eastward from Baja California's southernmost tip, Cabo San Lucas is the only city in Mexico with a marine preserve within its city limits. Created in 1973, the protected 36-square-kilometer (14-sq-mi) patch of sea and shore designates special boat lanes, boating speed limits, and restricted fishing and recreation craft areas, all under the watchful eye of Grupo Ecológico de Cabo San Lucas. Nowhere else among Mexico's top-drawing seaside resorts will you find such pristine beaches within so short a distance (5–10 minutes by boat taxi) of the town center.

Outside this area, however, hotel and condo development marches ahead full steam. Pedregal—a fashionable hillside district to the west—the marina, and Playa El Médano to the east are all chockablock with condos and villas. Next to undergo development will probably be the large section of unused harborfront property near the inner harbor entrance, where an old cannery and ferry pier sit abandoned.

While yachting and sportfishing bring an older, early-to-bed crowd to Cabo, the town's nightlife attracts an energetic youth market, creating a more vibrant ambience than at relatively staid San José del Cabo, 29 kilometers (18 mi) northeast. As the last stop on the 1,700-kilometer (1,000-mi) Transpeninsular Baja road trip, Cabo also acts as a receptacle for old Baja hands looking for a few days or weeks of R&R before beginning the long return drive across relatively unpopulated desert landscapes.

Thus, as residents and repeat visitors will point out, you never know who you'll run into in Cabo; yachties on their way to and from exotic South Pacific ports, cops on a fishing vacation, Baja road warriors, honeymoon couples, Mexico City denizens cleaning out their lead-filled lungs, rockers resting up after a continental tour, or Montana cowboys escaping the snow—they've all set themselves temporarily adrift in the Pacific.

HISTORY
The Pericú and the English

In pre-Cortesian times, the only humans enjoying Cabo San Lucas were the Pericú, one of the nomadic Guaycura Amerindian groups that inhabited the Cape Region for hundreds if not thousands of years. Standard anthropology says that, like other Amerindians in North and South America, the Pericú were descendants of Asian groups who traversed the prehistoric land bridge between the Eurasian and

CABO
SAN LUCAS

To Candelaria and
Todos Santos

To San José del Cabo,
Los Cabos Airport

To Club Cabo

To Todos Santos
and bus terminal

© AVALON TRAVEL PUBLISHING, INC.

16 DE SEPTIEMBRE
GÓMEZ FARIAS
MENDOZA
LEONA VICARIO
MORELOS
ZARAGOZA
OCAMPO
ABASOLO
MATAMOROS
HIDALGO
CABO SAN LUCAS

CARRANZA
REVOLUCIÓN
OBREGON
CALLE
CALLE
LIBERTAD
16 DE SEPTIEMBRE
20 DE NOVIEMBRE
NIÑOS HÉROES

CÁRDENAS
PESCADORES
CAMINO
MARINA

CALLE
MIJARES
ORTEGA
JUVENTUD
ALIKAN
CALLE
12 DE OCTUBRE
CALLE
CONSTITUCIÓN
MADERO
ZAPATA

SUPER
POLLO
FRUTERÍA
LIZARRAGA
HOTEL
SANTA FE
COTP
LOLITA'S
RESTAURANT
TORTILLERÍA PERLA
LA PERLA
LOS
MILAGROS
HOTEL
HOTEL MAR
DE CORTEZ
CAPO SAN
GIOVANNI
SWISS
PASTRY
MI CASA
HOTEL DOS MARES
MERCADO MEXICANO
PANCHO'S
SIESTA
SUITES
CABO
WABO/KAZ
GIGGLING
MARLIN
PLAZA
DEL SOL
PLAZA
NÁUTICA
CARLOS'N
CHARLIE'S
LAS
QUESADILASSS
PLAZA
ARAMBURO
EL SQUID
ROE
HOTEL CASA BLANCA
TAQUERÍA LOS
PAISAS
CARNITAS EL
MICHOACANO
CABO INN
HOTEL LOS
ARCOS
OLAS
HOTEL
IMMIGRATION
OFFICE
BANCOMER
BANAMEX
MCDONALD'S
DOLLAR
RENT-A-CAR
POST
OFFICE
MARISCOS
MOCAMBO
FUMARI CAFÉ
HOOKAH BAR
DOLLAR/ ALAMO
BUS
STOP
HARD ROCK CAFÉ
PLAZA
BONITA
PUERTO
PARAÍSO MALL
MARINA CABO
SAN LUCAS OFFICE
BOAT RAMP
MARINA FIESTA
RESORT
PLAZA
FIESTA
LENNY'S DELI
PEACOCKS
BAHIA CONDO HOTEL
MARINA SOL
CONDOS
CABO VILLAS
CASA RAFAEL'S
EDITH'S
JAZZ CAFE
LAS PALMAS
HOTEL MELIÁ
SAN LUCAS
PUEBLO BONITO
BLANCO RESORT
PUEBLO
BONITO
ROSÉ RESORT
VILLA DEL PALMAR
CABO BEACH
RESORT & SPA
CLUB CASCADAS
LAS GARDENIAS
SCHOOL
TELMEX
THE
BUNGALOWS

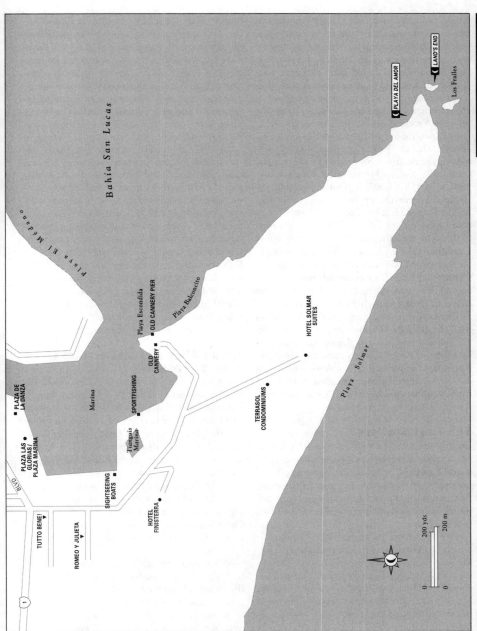

American continents. One fringe theory, however, suggests that the Pericú may have descended from Tahitian mariners blown off course on their way to Hawaii. English accounts from the 17th and early 18th centuries lend at least partial credence to this theory by pointing out how much the physical and social characteristics of the Pericú differed from that of other Amerindians of the same era.

Spaniard Juan Rodríguez Cabrillo made first contact with the Pericú here in 1542 while exploring the coastline. Sir Francis Drake stopped off in 1578, followed by privateer Thomas Cavendish in 1587. English pirating exploits inspired the Spanish to gain a stronger foothold on the Cape. Spanish explorer Sebastián Vizcaíno spent a week here in 1596, then returned in 1602 to map the region with cartographer Gerónimo Martín Palacios. Vizcaíno strongly recommended the establishment of a colony at Cabo San Lucas; Loreto, farther north on the Sea of Cortez, was selected instead, leaving Cabo to the English for another hundred years.

Until the mid-18th century, English pirates used the harbor as a hiding place for attacks on Manila galleons. Woodes Rogers anchored here in 1709, when he and his crew captured the Spanish galleon *Encarnación*. Another English corsair, George Shelcocke, landed in 1721 and carried out a regional survey that included extensive drawings of the Pericú.

The First Settlers

During the remainder of the Spanish colonial era, Cabo's natural harbor was periodically used by passing galleons, but since it offered no source of freshwater and scant protection from late-summer *chubascos* rolling in from the southeast, it was largely ignored in favor of San José del Cabo.

The Mexican independence movement largely bypassed San Lucas, although the Chilean ship *Independence* visited Cabo in 1822 in support of the Mexican struggle. The visit accomplished little as a military exercise because Mexico had gained independence from Spain the previous year, but it may have sparked renewed interest in San Lucas as a convenient

harbor in this part of the world. By the end of the 19th century, an enterprising group of *bajacalifornianos* began processing and shipping bark from the local *palo blanco* tree, a key ingredient in leather tanning. The principal route for the bark trade ran between Cabo San Lucas and San Francisco. Shipping traffic gradually increased, and port authorities built the lighthouse now known as Faro Viejo at nearby Cabo Falso in 1890.

In 1917, an American company floated a tuna cannery from San Diego to San Lucas to take advantage of the abundance of tuna in the area. As San Lucas gathered a small population, a roadbed to San José del Cabo, the nearest federal government seat, was laid in the 1920s. By the 1930s, a cannery and a small fishing village inhabited by around 400 hardy souls occupied the north end of the Cabo San Lucas harbor. Fish-canning remained the backbone of the local economy until the cannery was heavily damaged by a hurricane in 1941. During World War II, the area was all but abandoned as Japanese submarines cruised the Pacific coast; Cabo seemed destined for obscurity.

Marlin Alley and La Carretera Transpeninsular

Fortunately for *sanluqueños* (residents of San Lucas), post–World War II leisure travel brought fly-in anglers, who spread the word that Cabo was a game fish paradise. The Cape sportfishing craze of the 1950s and 1960s—when the waters off the peninsula's southern tip earned the nickname Marlin Alley—expanded the population to around 1,500 by the time the Transpeninsular Highway was completed in 1973. After the establishment of the highway link between the United States and Cabo San Lucas, the town was transformed from a fly-in/sail-in resort into an auto-and-RV destination.

When Baja California Sur received statehood in 1974, a ferry route from Puerto Vallarta on the mainland was established, thus opening the area to increased Mexican migration. The construction of Los Cabos International Airport near San José del Cabo in the 1980s brought

LOS CABOS

© JOE CUMMINGS

El Arco

Cabo within reach of vacationers who didn't have the time for a six-day drive from border to Cape and back. The establishment of a water pipeline between San José and San Lucas further loosened the limits on development.

Today the local economy rests on the provision of tourism services and a booming construction industry, which supplies the growing need for leisure, residential, and business structures throughout the lower Cape Region.

◖ LAND'S END

You know you've reached the end of the road in Baja when the towering rock formations and signature arch at Land's End come into view. Forming the coccyx of a rocky spine that reaches northward all the way to Alaska's Aleutian Islands, the formations are collectively known as **Finisterra,** or Land's End. Take a water taxi beyond the harbor to get a closer look at the cliffs and watch sea lions play in the surge.

El Arco, a rock outcropping at the tip of

Land's End, has become Cabo San Lucas's most immediately recognizable symbol. During low tide you can walk along Playa del Amor to the 62-meter (200-ft) rock formation, which features an eroded passage through the middle. El Arco is also known as the Arch of Poseidon since it marks the entrance to a precipitous submarine canyon—the perfect throne room for the King of the Seas—just offshore. Running northwest from El Arco and Playa del Amor are several more unnamed rock formations, including two large granite clusters as tall or taller than El Arco.

Just offshore stand **Los Frailes** (The Friars), two rock islets shaped like clusters of hooded monks and frequented by sea lions. A smaller, bird-limed rock pinnacle off the northeast side of the Cape, **Roca Pelícanos** (Pelican Rock), serves as a crowded pelican roost. The base of the pinnacle, about six meters (20 ft) down, is richly endowed with marinelife, including coral, sea fans, gorgonians, sea urchins, and numerous tropical fish. Recent reports from divers say visibility at the rock is declining,

Land's End

© PAUL ITOI

however, because of discharge from cruise ships moored in the outer harbor.

Cerro La Vigía, rising 150 meters (500 ft) above the harbor, once served as a lookout point for English pirates awaiting Manila galleons to plunder. Today it's still an excellent vantage point for viewing Land's End, the town, the marina, Playa Solmar (the beach next to the Hotel Solmar), and Cabo Falso. A steep trail begins just behind the old cannery on the harbor and leads to La Vigía's summit, which is marked by a crucifix.

BEACHES

Beachgoers can choose among five beaches close to the downtown area and a string of beaches and coves along the San José del Cabo to Cabo San Lucas Corridor.

Playa El Médano

The most popular and easily accessible local beach, Playa El Médano (Dune Beach) extends several kilometers along Bahía San Lucas northeast from the inner harbor's entrance channel. Baja's most heavily used beach is packed with swimmers and sunbathers during peak vacation periods—and is one of the few local beaches where swimming is safe year-round. Beach vendors rent *pangas,* personal watercraft, inflatable rafts, windsurfing and snorkeling equipment, kayaks, volleyball equipment, *palapas,* and beach furniture. Several *palapa* bars and restaurants scattered along the beach offer cold beverages, as well as burgers, seafood, and Mexican fare.

Minor annoyances at Playa El Médano include the many vendors who plod up and down the beach hawking jewelry, rugs, hammocks, hand-painted plates, and the like (they won't persist if you show no interest) and the sprawling condo developments in the background that mar the view of the Sierra de la Laguna foothills.

◖ Playa del Amor

Cabo's next most popular beach can be reached only by boat or by a difficult climb over two rock headlands along the ocean. Playa del Amor (Love Beach), also known as Playa del Amante (Lover's

Beach), lies near the tip of Cabo San Lucas—the cape itself, not the town—just northwest of the famous arch-shaped rock formation featured in virtually every Los Cabos advertisement. The wide, sandy, pristine beach extends across the cape behind the arch to the other side, forming two beachfronts—one on Bahía San Lucas and one on the Pacific. The latter is sometimes whimsically called "Divorce Beach."

Only the beachfront facing the bay is generally safe for swimming. The beach is supposed to be free of vendors and commercial enterprises; however, vendors do occasionally sell cold drinks out of a cooler. Unless you have a portable beach umbrella, go early in the day to command one of the shady rock overhangs. The southeast end of the bay features a series of coral-encrusted rocks suitable for snorkeling; a deep submarine canyon lying only 50 meters (164 ft) offshore is a popular scuba diving site.

You can reach Playa del Amor by water taxi from the marina, or take a glass-bottomed boat tour (US$10 round-trip for either option) and arrange a drop-off at the beach. Ask to see the boat before you pay, as some are in much better shape than others. Should the engine fail and cut your trip short, the person you paid will likely be nowhere in sight. Any tour boat in the vicinity should give you a ride back to the marina upon presentation of your ticket stub; the last tour boat leaves the marina around 3 P.M. In calm seas, you can also rent a kayak (US$10 pp/hr) on Playa El Médano and paddle across the inner harbor entrance to the beach. It's best to go in the morning, when the water is calm; the paddle takes about 40 minutes one-way.

Those skilled at bouldering can reach the south side of the beach by climbing from the east end of Playa Solmar (in front of the Hotel Solmar) over two rocky points that separate the two beaches. The climb is best attempted during low tide, when the cove between the rock formations reveals a sandy beach useful as a midway rest stop. The second set of rocks, to the east, is more difficult than those to the west; turn back after the first set if you've reached the limit of your climbing skills.

© PAUL ITOI

Playa El Médano

Playa Solmar

This very wide, very long beach running along the southwestern edge of the Cape is accessible via the road to Hotel Solmar. The strong undertow and heavy surf make it suitable for sunbathing and wading only. Solmar's biggest advantage is its lack of people, even during peak tourist seasons.

Cannery Beaches

Next to the abandoned Planta Empacadora (the old tuna cannery on the south side of the inner harbor entrance) are two small public beaches virtually ignored by most Cabo visitors. The first, **Playa Escondida** (Hidden Beach), lies next to the cannery pier and is easily reached by walking along the west bank of the marina and alongside the main cannery building. The sand extends only around 50 meters (164 ft), less in high tide, but it's popular with local Mexican families because Dad can fish from the pier while the kids play in the calm water.

Playa Balconcito (Little Balcony Beach), a bit larger than Playa Escondida, lies beyond the pier on the other side of the cannery toward the sea. You must walk along a stone ledge—part of the cannery foundation—to get there.

Corridor Beaches

Northeast of Cabo San Lucas—on the way to San José del Cabo—a number of uncrowded, relatively pristine beaches are suitable for swimming, fishing, camping, snorkeling, and scuba diving (see *Beaches* in *The Corridor* section).

FISHING

Other than swimming and lying on the beach, sportfishing is Cabo's number-one outdoor activity. Tens of thousands of billfish are hooked off the Cape each year. The biggest trophy of all, the *marlín azul* (blue marlin), can reach five meters (16 ft) in length and weigh close to a ton. In the Cape area, it's not unusual to hook 200- to 400-kilogram (440- to 880-lb) blues. A smaller species, the *marlín rayado* (striped marlin), grows to more than 270 kilograms (600 lbs), while the *marlín negro* (black marlin) is almost as big as the blue.

yellowfin tuna

© JOE CUMMINGS

To catch a glimpse of these huge game fish, stop by the sportfishing dock on the marina's west side around 3–4 P.M., when sportfishing boats return with their catches. Note the flags flown over the boats: A triangular blue flag means a billfish has been bagged, while a red flag with a T means one has been tagged and released. All Cabo sportfishing outfits request that anglers release billfish to fight another day; some even require it. Instead of skinning and mounting these beautiful fish, they recommend bringing a video camera along to record the catch from start to finish. Even where customers demand to keep a billfish, the Sportfishing Association of Los Cabos stipulates that only one billfish per boat may be killed (you can catch and release as many as you like).

Good marlin-fishing spots include **Banco San Jaime,** 29 kilometers (18 mi) southwest of Cabo Falso, and **Banco Golden Gate,** 31 kilometers (19 mi) west of Cabo Falso. Dorado and wahoo are also common in those areas. Sportfishing cruisers—powerboats equipped with electronic fish-finders, sophisticated tackle,

FISH TRANSLATOR

Mexican guides who lead sportfishing trips often use the local terms for game fish; when they don't, the English terms they use aren't always correct. This works the other way, too – many gringos use incorrect Spanish names for Baja fish, which can cause confusion when asking about local fishing conditions. Here is a key to some of the more common translations:

albacore tuna – *albacora*
barracuda – *picuda*
black sea bass – *mero prieto*
bluefin tuna – *atún de aleta azul*
blue marlin – *marlín azul*
dolphinfish (mahimahi) – *dorado*
grouper (generic) – *garropa*
halibut – *lenguado*
hammerhead shark – *cornuda*
jack crevalle – *toro*
ladyfish – *sabalo*
mackerel – *sierra, makerela*
manta ray – *manta*
marbled scorpionfish – *cabezón*
octopus – *pulpo*
Pacific amberjack – *pez fuerte*
perch (generic) – *mojarra*
pompano – *palometa*
puffer (generic) – *bolete*
red snapper – *huachinango*

roosterfish – *papagallo, pez gallo*
sailfish – *pez vela*
seabass (cabrilla) – *cabrilla*
shark (generic) – *tiburón*
small shark – *cazón*
squid – *calamar*
stingray (generic) – *raya*
striped marlin – *marlín rayado*
swordfish – *pez espada*
triggerfish – *cochi*
wahoo – *sierra wahoo, peto*
whale shark – *pez sapo*
white seabass – *corvina blanca*
yellowfin tuna – *atún de aleta; amarilla*
yellowtail – *jurel*

Pez is the generic word for fish. Once fish has been caught and is ready for cooking (or has been cooked), it's called *pescado*.

fighting chairs and harnesses, and wells for keeping live bait—are the angler's best chance for landing large game fish.

Almost unbelievably, marlin are also somewhat common just beyond the steep drop-offs between Los Frailes and Cabo Falso, an area easily reached by *panga* or skiff. Without the technology of a fishing cruiser, *panga* marlinfishing becomes the most macho hook-and-line challenge of all—the resulting fish stories reach *Old Man and the Sea* proportions. For anglers with more humble ambitions, black sea bass, cabrilla, sierra, and grouper are found in inshore waters; surfcasters can take corvina, ladyfish, sierra, and *pargo*.

Guided Sportfishing

Several outfitters arrange sportfishing trips aboard cruisers and *pangas*. Rates average US$350 a day on a four-angler, 28-foot cruiser and US$550 a day for a six-person, 36-foot fishing cruiser. Charter boats generally hold 4–6 anglers; rates usually include tax, license, gear, and ice. **Pisces Fleet** (Blvd. Marina at Madero, tel. 624/143-1288, www. piscessportfishing.com) is one of the more reliable independent outfitters. Bareboat rates are US$355 and US$450 for 28- and 31-foot boats (US$500/630 all-inclusive), US$850–1,650 for 35- to 42-foot boats. The fleet tops out with a 111-foot yacht that accommodates 12 anglers for US$9,500. Half-day rates are available.

Dream Maker Sportfishing (Locale 20, Hotel Tesoro complex, tel. 624/143-7266, www.dreammakercharter.com) leads five-hour and eight-hour trips with a fleet of nine boats that includes everything from a 22-foot *panga* (US$175/5 hrs) to a 42-foot

WORLD FISHING RECORDS SET IN BAJA

The nonprofit International Game Fish Association (IGFA) tracks world records set for each species of game fish according to weight, weight/test ratio (fish weight to line test), place where the catch was made, and other significant record details. World-record catches achieved by Baja anglers for specific line classes include those for the following fish: Pacific blue marlin, striped marlin, Pacific sailfish, swordfish, roosterfish, dolphinfish *(dorado)*, gulf grouper, California yellowtail, Pacific bonito, bigeye trevally, spotted cabrilla, spearfish, giant sea bass, white sea bass, California halibut, Pacific jack crevalle, black skipjack, yellowfin tuna, Pacific bigeye tuna, and chub mackerel.

Baja anglers hold all-tackle records – high-est weight of any fish species regardless of line test – for gulf grouper, olive grouper, roosterfish, Pacific amberjack, white sea bass, spotted cabrilla, rainbow runner, black skipjack, yellowfin tuna, Pacific jack crevalle, chub mackerel, and California yellowtail.

For information on IGFA membership and record entries, contact IGFA (300 Gulf Stream Way, Dania Beach, FL 33004, igfahq@aol.com, www.igfa.org). Membership includes a copy of the IGFA's annual *World Record Game Fishes Book*, which contains a list of all current fishing records, as well as the bimonthly *International Angler* newsletter. IGFA members are also eligible for discounts on fishing charters offered by several sportfishing outfitters in Cabo San Lucas.

---

sportfisher (US$1,250 all-inclusive or US$1,050 boat only).

Located at the Bahia Hotel, **Gaviota Sportfishing** (U.S. tel. 800/932-5599, www.grupobahia.com) has experienced captains and 11 boats ranging from 26- to 36-foot cruisers. All-inclusive packages for four (US$755 including tax or US$595 boat charter only) come with tackle, bait, lunch, and a case of beer, soda, or bottled water. The same package for two aboard a 26-foot cruiser is US$440 (US$360 boat charter only). Boats leave at 7 A.M. and return at 3 P.M.

Guided cruiser trips are also easy to arrange through any major Cabo hotel. Solmar, Finisterra, and Meliá Cabo Real all have their own fleets, while other hotels typically use local brokers.

Whomever you go with, be sure to get a breakdown of exactly what to expect on any guided trip. One reader wrote to us and complained that he paid for eight hours of marlin fishing but got two hours of marlin fishing, three hours of bottom fishing, one hour waiting to buy bait, and two hours of idle boating. If you know that you're expected to provide your own bait, shop ahead. And expect that the farther out

you go, the more time you'll spend in transit to and from your intended fishing destination.

Panga Trips

The least expensive fishing trips of all are those arranged directly with local *pangeros,* the men who own and operate single fishing *pangas.* Such *pangas* are sometimes available in Cabo San Lucas, but most *panga*-fishing trips operate out of La Playita near San José del Cabo. The typical *panga* trip costs US$175 for five hours in a three-person, 22-foot boat. *Panga* rates usually don't include rental gear or fishing licenses. When inquiring about rates—*panga* or cruiser—ask whether the quote includes filleting of edible game fish. The better outfits include fish preparation and packing among their services at no extra charge.

Surf Casting

Cheaper yet is to forgo boating altogether and drop a line from the beach. The best surf casting in the immediate area is at **Playa Solmar,** but watch the surf closely, as large waves sometimes seem to arrive out of nowhere. You can also fish from the old pier extending from the abandoned tuna cannery at the entrance to the harbor, where the water is relatively calm. On **Playa El Médano,** you can fish only at the far northeastern end of the beach.

Bait, Tackle, and Fish Processing

Minerva's Baja Tackle (on Blvd. Marina at Madero, tel. 624/143-1282, Mon.–Sat. 9 A.M.–7 P.M.), next door to Pisces Fleet, is well stocked with lures and other tackle designed specifically for Cabo sportfishing. Minerva's is also the area's official International Game Fish Association (IGFA) representative.

Buy fresh bait at the San Lucas harbor docks for a few dollars. Locals here will also clean and fillet your catch on the spot for tips. You can arrange to have fish cleaned, processed, vacuum-packed, and frozen through **Gricelda's Smoke House** (Loc 19 & 20 in the Tesoro Hotel complex, tel. 624/143-7266, www .dreammakercharter.com) on the marina.

DIVING AND SNORKELING

Cabo is a unique diving destination because it's in the middle of a transition zone between tropical and temperate waters. Strikingly large fish such as amberjack, hammerheads, and manta rays—which are partial to temperate waters—mix with the smaller, more colorful species typical of tropical waters. It's also unique in that some of the best snorkeling and scuba sites are only a 5- to 25-minute boat ride from the marina (compared to boat rides of 1–2 hours to the islands off La Paz).

Snorkelers explore the base of the cliffs on each side of **Playa del Amor,** about three meters (10 ft) deep, for coral and tropical fish. Nearby Pelican Rock, some six meters (20 ft) deep, is a bit more challenging. Strong swimmers, on calm days, can swim south around the arch to the sea lion colony at Los Frailes and frolic with the creatures. Several spots along the Corridor between San Lucas and San José feature good snorkeling, including **Playa Chileno** and **Playa Santa María** (see *Diving and Snorkeling* in *The Corridor* section).

Guided scuba dives tour many of the same sites as snorkelers, making it convenient to ac-commodate mixed groups (but also making it more crowded, both above and below the surface). Also, given the proximity of these dive sites to the harbor, the loud and constant rumble of boat traffic overhead makes for an annoying distraction.

The most popular dive sites in the Cabo Marine Preserve include Pelican Rock, Neptune's Finger, and the point at Land's End. Pelican Rock and Neptune's Finger begin at shallow depth (20–25 ft), and then descend over boulders or along a wall into a vast submarine canyon, as diver skill, air consumption, and visibility allow.

Part of a national marine preserve, the canyon begins just 50 meters (164 ft) off Playa del Amor and is famous for its "sandfalls"—streams of sand tumbling over the canyon rim at a depth of around 30 meters and forming sand rivers between rock outcroppings. At a depth of around 40 meters (130 ft), the outcroppings give way to sheer granite walls, where the sand rivers drop vertically for more than two kilometers (to a depth of around 2,750 m/9,000 ft). The phenomenon was first documented by a Scripps Institute of Oceanography expedition in 1960 and later made famous in one of Jacques Cousteau's television documentaries. The size of the sandfalls and sand rivers depends to a large extent on climatic conditions; during long spells of calm weather they may even come to a halt. But there is plenty to see, whether or not the rivers are running. The edges of the canyon walls are layered with colorful coral, sea fans, and other marinelife. These in turn attract schools of tropical fish, including many open-ocean species not ordinarily seen this close to shore. Graceful eagle rays, good-sized grouper, and tiny zebra eels are just a few of the sightings divers may experience on these dives.

The Land's End dive begins in the surge under a sea lion colony on the Sea of Cortez side of the point and ends with an underwater swim around to the Pacific side, covering varied underwater topography along the way. Guitar fish, schooling amber jacks, green sea turtles, and countless other species are likely to make an appearance on this dive.

HOW MUCH DOES IT COST?

GUIDED DIVE AND SNORKEL TOURS

Discounts apply for multiday dives.

Snorkel tour (equipment included)	US$25-45
One-tank boat dive	US$45-65
Two-tank boat dive	US$70-85
Night dive	US$50-65
Cabo Pulmo day trip	US$120-155
Gorda Banks day trip	US$120-185
Nondiver passenger	US$10-15

SCUBA INSTRUCTION

Open Water referral (4 dives, for students who have completed classroom and pool work prior to arrival)	US$210-250
Open water certification (classroom and dives)	US$375-430
Discover Scuba/resort course (introduction to scuba)	US$90-100
Refresher dive	US$100
Advanced certification	US$280-330
Rescue diver course	US$300

EQUIPMENT RENTAL

Snorkel gear (usually included with tour)	US$4-12
Scuba package with dives (discounts for multiday dives)	US$20-25/day
Weight belt and weights	US$8
Regulator	US$12
Tanks	US$12
BCD	US$12
Wet suit	US$8
Airfills	US$45

Cabo San Lucas dive shops can also arrange trips to **Cabo Pulmo** for reef dives in a protected marine park (see *East Cape* in the *East and Central Cape* chapter) and the Gorda Banks, where advanced divers with experience in strong currents can explore seamounts at a depth of around 41 meters (135 ft) that are famous for sightings of hammerhead sharks, whale sharks (the world's largest fish), huge tuna, amberjack, grouper, and manta rays.

Dive Guides and Outfitters

Many Cabo hotels can arrange guided dive trips and equipment rentals. Some have their own shops onsite, while others book through one of the many independent shops in town. Dive operators typically organize two outings per day, weather permitting. Morning boats leave the harbor around 9 A.M., and the afternoon shift departs around 1 P.M. Mornings tend to be less crowded above and below the surface. In the afternoon, the wind kicks up and boat traffic increases, making water entries and exits a little trickier.

Manta (tel. 624/144-3871, www.caboscuba. com) is a professionally-run PADI shop conveniently located at Playa El Médano. Its custom-designed 35-foot boat holds 15 divers comfortably; additional 28-foot and 26-foot boats accommodate up to 10 divers each. All three boats are equipped with radios, first aid kits, and oxygen. For local dives in the Cabo Marine Preserve, advanced and novice divers often share the same boat, but have separate dive guides, since easy and advanced dives start at the same points. (Experienced divers go deeper and stay under longer than beginner groups.) Knowledgable boat captains and a friendly international guide staff make for a safe and enjoyable dive experience. An earlier morning start (8:30 A.M.) helps avoid the crowds. Rental gear is in good shape, with Sherwood regs, Aqualung and Genesis BCDs, and Akona, Body Glove, and Scuba Pro wetsuits. In addition to standard 80 cft tanks, smaller (63 cft) and larger (100 cft) sizes are available.

Underwater Diversions (tel. 624/143-4004, U.S. tel. 949/226-8987, www.divecabo. com) is another reputable shop in the Plaza Marina. **Blue Adventures** (tel. 624/144-4680, www.aventurasazul.com), also in the Plaza Marina, takes divers to sites in the Cabo Marine Preserve and along the Corridor. Longer trips to Gorda Banks and Cabo Pulmo are also possible. Nondivers can ride along for US$10 with a reservation. **Amigos del Mar** (tel. 624/143-0505, U.S./Canada tel. 800/344-3349, fax 624/143-0887) is next to Solmar Fleet on the west side of the harbor; and **Tío Watersports** (tel. 624/143-2986, daily 8 A.M.–5:30 P.M.) has facilities at the Meliá San Lucas, Meliá Cabo Real, and Marina Fiesta hotels.

See the sidebar *How Much Does It Cost?* for costs of guided tours, instruction, and equipment rental. During the slower summer season, some dive shops offer certification courses at heavily discounted rates; since underwater visibility is at its best during these months, this is a real bargain.

Liveaboards

Amigos del Mar (tel. 624/143-0505, U.S./Canada tel. 800/344-3349, fax 624/143-0887), next to Solmar Fleet on the west side of the harbor, arranges luxury liveaboard dive trips to the Socorro Islands, Guadalupe Island, Gorda Banks, Los Fraires, El Bajo, Cabo Pulmo, and other more remote sites aboard the 112-foot *Solmar V* (www.solmarv.com). The wood-and-brass-fitted boat features two onboard air compressors and a dive platform for easy exits. Prices run around US$2,100 for eight-day Sea of Cortez trips, including all land transfers, food and beverages, accommodations in air-conditioned staterooms, and up to three guided dives per day. Longer nine-day trips to the remote Socorro Islands run around US$3,000. The boat holds a maximum of 22 divers and 10 staff members.

Blue Adventure (tel. 624/144-4680, www. aventurasazul.com) also runs custom multiday trips to La Paz, Cabo Pulmo, and Gorda Banks for US$385 per person per day.

Snorkel Tours

Pez Gato (Camino Del Cerro 215, El Pedregal, tel. 624/143-3797, www.pezgatocabo. com, Mon.–Sat., US$45), offers four-hour sail and snorkeling tours to Bahía Santa María along the Corridor, aboard one of three catamarans. The tour includes two hours of swimming and snorkeling at Santa María, plus ceviche, tuna salad, guacamole, salsa and chips, open bar, bottled water, sodas, and cold beer on the way back. The boat departs at 10 A.M. and returns around 2 P.M. Monday–Thursday and Saturday; departure and return times are an hour later on Friday. Kids under 12 are free.

SunRider Adventure (tel. 624/143-2252, www.sunridertours.com) has a 60-foot vessel with a restaurant onboard. A snorkeling lunch tour to Playa Santa María for US$45 per person includes a Mexican buffet and open bar. Cash only.

Equipment

Most dive shops rent snorkel and dive equipment in packages or à la carte, so if you forget your fins or your mask strap breaks, you'll be able to borrow a replacement for the day. Repairs are a different story, however. If you're bringing your own gear, have it serviced before you leave home; check your computer batteries, and bring spare parts. Despite the number of dive shops, replacement parts are difficult, if not impossible, to come by in Baja.

Recompression

Clinica de Especialidades (Lopez Mateos btw Morelos/Vicario, tel. 624/143-3914 or 143-2919) maintains a hyperbaric recompression chamber that is available to recreational divers for emergencies.

SURFING

The nearest surfable waves occur well outside the city limits at **Playa Cabo Bello,** between Km 5 and Km 6 (see *Surfing* in *The Corridor* section). Well-known Monuments, a left point break at Misiones del Cabo, is another option close to town. Most good surf occurs here only during summer and early fall. Cabo Bello, recipient of a winter northwestern swell, is the one exception. The Pacific coast near Todos Santos is the place to head for waves in winter. If you need equipment or ding repair in Cabo San Lucas, try the **Cabo San Lucas Surf Shop** at the Plaza Marina.

PADDLING, SAILING, AND WINDSURFING

The onshore surf at Playa El Médano is mild enough for launching wind- and paddle-powered craft easily, and you can rent from a number of vendors along the beach. Kayaks cost US$10 per person/hour or US$50 for a half-day.

The water is calmest in the morning, and it takes about 40 minutes to get to Playa del Amor, so it's best to get an early start. Tell the vendors where you plan to take the craft; they'll know the conditions and advise accordingly. Watch out for powerboats, yachts, and cruise ships; larger craft have the de facto right of way. Novices should stick close to Playa El Médano, no matter what the conditions.

BOATING

With thousands of yacht arrivals per year, Cabo San Lucas is a major Baja California boating center. Even though harbor size and marine-repair facilities don't match those of La Paz, the greater variety of other services, nightlife, shopping, and dining venues more than compensates.

The outer harbor anchorages are mostly occupied by sportfishing cruisers; recreational boaters can moor off Playa El Médano to the northeast. Ringing the inner harbor, first dredged in the early 1970s, is **Marina Cabo San Lucas** (Lote A-18 De la Darsena, tel. 624/143-1251, U.S. tel. 310/541-3830, www. cabomarina.com.mx). Facilities include hot showers, restrooms, a pool, snack bar, laundry, dry storage and personal storage facilities, a chandlery, fuel (both diesel and gas), water, and 380 slips (20–416 ft) complete with electricity, telephone hookups, and satellite TV. Also available are a 75-ton lift and full-ser-

Cabo San Lucas marina

vice boatyard. Permanent and monthly renters at Marina Cabo San Lucas have priority over short-term visiting boaters; daily rentals are available on a first-come, first-served basis. Visiting boaters should contact the marina 15 days before arrival to check on the availability of slips. The Marina Cabo San Lucas office is open Monday–Saturday 9 A.M.–5 P.M., Sunday 10 A.M.–3 P.M. The marina's condos are occasionally available as rentals, and the adjacent Marina Fiesta Resort usually has vacant rooms. A convenience store and wireless Internet are also open Monday–Saturday 6 A.M.–7 P.M. and Sunday 6 A.M.–6 P.M.

Also in the inner harbor are two boat ramps, one near the old ferry pier and one at the northeast end of the harbor near the Tesoro Hotel. A fuel dock is between the old ferry pier and the abandoned cannery, just inside the entrance to the inner harbor. Cabo San Lucas is an official Mexican port of entry; the **COTP** office is on Calle Matamoros at 16 de Septiembre.

Cape Marine (Plaza Marina, Local J2-3, tel. 624/143-4970, Mon.–Sat. 8 A.M.–6 P.M.) carries hardware, apparel, yachting supplies and tools, and fishing equipment. Credit cards are accepted.

CRUISES

An abundance of glass-bottomed tour boats depart frequently from the marina and from Playa El Médano 9 A.M.–4 P.M. each day. The standard 45-minute tour costs US$8–12 per person and covers Pelican Rock, the famous Land's End arch, and the sea lion colony. For no extra charge, the crew will let passengers off at Playa del Amor near the arch; you can flag down any passing boat from the same fleet and catch a ride back to the marina later in the day. Be sure to see the boat you will board before you pay, as engines can be old and unreliable, and you may not get your money back if the trip is aborted due to engine failure. **Dos Mares** (tel. 624/143-4339) is one of the oldest fleet operators; **Esperanza's Fleet** (tel. 624/144-4666, www.esperanzas-fleet.com, US$12 or US$22 with snorkeling gear rental) is another option. Simpler launches without glass bottoms will do the same trip, including beach drop-off and pickup, for slightly less.

Sunset cruises with all the beer and margaritas you can drink are also popular and usually last around two hours and 15 minutes. You can make reservations at the marina or at most hotels; tickets cost US$25–50 per person depending on whether dinner is included.

Pez Gato (Camino Del Cerro 215, El Pedregal, tel. 624/143-3797, www.pezgatocabo. com, Mon.–Sat.) offers an all-the-margaritas-you-can-drink sunset cruise that leaves from the main dock at 6 P.M. and returns at 8 P.M. for US$35 per person. (Book through any hotel or online.) **Jungle Cruise Tours** (tel. 624/143-7530, www.cabobooze-cruise.com) does an adults-only catamaran cruise that leaves from the marina at 6 P.M. in spring and summer and 5 P.M. in fall and winter for US$35 per person. A couple of similar boats operate sunset cruises from the west side of the harbor near the Tesoro Hotel. During high season these companies may offer sunset cruises on two separate boats simultaneously—a "romantic" cruise oriented toward couples, and a "booze cruise" for young singles.

A larger cruise ship, **Caborey** (tel. 624/143-8269, www.caborey.com) runs a dinner cruise for US$74 per person and a margarita cruise with appetizers for US$49.

Whale-Watching

Whales pass within a few hundred meters of Cabo San Lucas throughout the year, but the most activity occurs during gray whale migration season, January–March. The **Dos Mares** tour-boat fleet operates whale-watching trips from the marina during the migration season for US$35 per person. With binoculars you can also see passing whales from the Hotel Finisterra's Whale Watcher's Bar.

Swimming with Dolphins

At **Cabo Dolphins** (tel. 624/173-9500, www. cabodolphins.com, Mon.–Fri. 10 A.M., noon, 3 P.M., and 5 P.M., Sat.–Sun. 10 A.M. and noon), you can spend a half hour swimming alongside playful bottlenose dolphins for US$165 per person. Children under 10 must be accompanied by a paying adult.

ATVS AND WAVERUNNERS

The sandy beaches and dunes in the Cabo San Lucas area are open to all-terrain vehicles (ATVs), as long as they're kept away from swimming areas (Playa El Médano) or turtle-nesting areas (Cabo Falso). Any of the hotels in town can arrange tours for around US$60 per person single/US$80 double. The basic route visits sand dunes, the ruins of El Faro Viejo, and a 1912 shipwreck; the six-hour tour adds La Candelaria, an inland village known for its pottery (see the *West Cape and Todos Santos* chapter). All-day trip rates include a box lunch and refreshments. Vendors along Boulevard Marina also book these trips. **Baja's Activities** (tel. 624/143-2050, www.bajasactivities.com), with locations at many local hotels and beaches, allows two riders per ATV at a discounted rate.

On a calm day, a WaveRunner can be a fast and fun way to explore the bay and Playa del Amor, and you don't have to be a speed demon to enjoy the ride. A number of vendors along Playa El Médano offer rentals for around US$70/hour.

MOUNTAIN BIKING

NaturAdventure (tel. 624/105-2050, www. naturadventure.com) leads half-day and full-day trail rides of varying levels around the Los Cabos area on Gary Fisher, Trek, and Specialized bikes. Destinations include Punta Gorda (US$65 pp), Cabo Pulmo (US$95 pp), and the Sierra de la Laguna (US$90 pp, US$75 half-day). Previous clients (only) can rent bikes for a self-guided tour (US$35–55 per day). MTB shoes and Shimano pedals available.

HORSEBACK RIDING

Red Rose (La Rosa) Riding Stables (Km 4, across from Cabo San Lucas Country Club, tel. 624/143-4826) appears to be the area's most serious saddle outfit. Choose Western or English tack. A one-hour ride along Playa El Médano costs about US$30; a two-hour mountain ride is US$45. Custom horseback trips and riding lessons are also available.

Rancho Collins (Camino Viejo a San José, tel. 624/143-3652, daily 8 A.M.–6 P.M.), across from Club Cascadas, offers 60-, 90-, and 120-minute horseback riding tours of nearby beaches and desert for US$30 per person/hour. Plan your ride in the morning or at sunset for maximum scenic effect. Its 45 horses are healthy and in good shape. Look for a pretty palomino near the road.

La Sanluqueña Bullring (tel. 624/143-8144), at the junction of Mexico 1 and Mexico 19, offers well-fed, well-trained horses for private trail rides or for rides along Playa El Médano. Horses are available for beginners as well as experts. A 75-minute ride runs about US$30.

SKYDIVING AND PARASAILING

Look for **Skydive El Sol** (tel. 624/129-7173, www.skydiveelsol.com, open daily year-round), a relative newcomer to Cabo San Lucas, near Club Cascadas on Playa El Médano, where the going rate is US$200 for a tandem jump that includes one minute of freefall time. Plan on a two-hour outing, from start to finish. For an additional US$90, you can return home with a DVD of the entire experience. Skydive El Sol needs at least two jumpers to book a trip.

The **Caborey** luxury cruise ship (tel. 624/143-8260, www.caborey.com) offers parasailing trips at a rate of US$35 for an eight- to ten-minute ride.

GOLF

About one kilometer north of the Cabo city limits, the 300-hectare (746-acre) **Cabo San Lucas Country Club** (tel. 624/143-4654, U.S. tel. 888/328-8501) offers a Roy Dye–designed course with views of Land's End and Bahía San Lucas from each fairway.

YOGA

Cabo Mind Body Fitness offers pilates and Bikram-method yoga sessions in the privacy of your own villa, but prices are correspondingly steep: Pilates sessions run US$158–190 per person/hour, down to US$50 per person/hour for groups of seven or more. Yoga classes cost US$139 per person/hour, down to US$38 for groups of 11 or more. Discounts apply for pairs and triples too, so it pays to buddy up. Visit www.cabovillas.com for details.

SPA SERVICES

Most of the larger Cabo resorts have their own spas onsite. For example, **Armonia Spa** (tel. 624/142-9797, www.pueblobonito .com) opened in 2005 at the Pueblo Bonito Pacifica resort and offers 50-minute massage treatments for US$100. Choices include hot stone, Shiatsu, four hands, deep tissue, Swedish, and pregnancy massage. **Nahui Beauty & Day Spa** (tel. 624/143-7066, www.nahuibeautyspa.com, Mon.–Sat. 10 A.M.–8 P.M.) at the Marina Sol Resort, one block off Playa Médano, offers a full menu of massage therapy, including deep tissue, reflexology, and aromatherapy (US$49–59 for 50 minutes), plus facials, manicures, and pedicures.

ENTERTAINMENT AND EVENTS

With an emphasis on booze and music, Cabo nightlife begins early and ends late. The action starts in the bars downtown near the marina and after midnight moves to the discos, which stay open till 3 or 4 A.M.

Bars

Tourists bent on getting well-primed for the evening pack **Giggling Marlin** (Matamoros at Blvd. Marina, tel. 624/100-6956, www.gigglingmarlin.com). Among the row of bars and restaurants along the marina in Plaza Bonita, **The Nowhere Bar** (tel. 624/143-4493, www.nowherebar.com, daily 11 A.M.–1 A.M., margaritas US$5) is a popular stop, especially during March madness NCAA basketball championships, with a happy hour 5–9 P.M.); you'll get two drinks (served in glasses, not plastic) for the price of one, whether you need them or not.

For a taste of Manhattan, **Red** (Zaragoza, around the corner from Squid Roe, tel. 624/143-5645, Mon.–Sat. 6 P.M.–3 A.M.) is an open-air wine and martini lounge.

The quirky **Latitude 22+ Roadhouse** (Km 4.5, tel. 624/143-1516, www.lat22nobaddays.com, Wed.–Mon. 8 A.M.–11 P.M.) attracts Corridor residents and Baja old-timers with ocean views, reasonably priced cocktails, and giant flatscreen TVs and offers a Croatian-influenced menu. Formerly a downtown hangout, "Lat 22" is now located next to Costco and behind the power plant. Credit cards are accepted.

At **Hemingway's** (Guerrero btw Cardenas/Madero, tel. 624/143-9845, www.jnjhabanos.com), you can order a US$150 sip of tequila (the bottle costs more than US$1,000). Or the knowledgeable bartenders can help you taste a variety of high-end tequilas in the range of US$7–10 per taste. There are more than 345 tequilas from which to choose. The immense walk-in humidor has a full selection of Cuban cigars from Cohiba, Montecristo, and Partagas. A cigar roller, or *torcedor,* rolls well-made cigars for US$11–15.

If wine is your beverage of choice, **Sancho Panza** (tel. 624/143-3212) off Blvd. Marina in the Tesoro Hotel complex, offers the best wine list in southern Baja. This is the perfect place for a quiet drink, and the tapas menu is tops.

Fumari Café Hookah Bar (Lázaro Cárdenas across from the Paraíso mall, Mon.–Thurs. 4–11 P.M., Fri.–Sat. 4 P.M.–2 A.M., drinks US$2–4) is a cozy second-story café with several tables inside and a large roof deck outside. Curl up on a sofa and play a game of chess while you smoke a flavored hookah (US$13) or sip a chai tea.

Friday is tango night at super chic **Barometro** (tel. 624/143-1466, 10 P.M.–2 A.M.) on the Plaza Marina.

The **Whale Watcher Bar** (tel. 624/143-3333) at the Hotel Finisterra has a more sedate but popular 3:30–5:30 P.M. happy hour. The bar hosts an excellent mariachi group Thursday–Sunday and offers great Pacific views any day of the week.

Edith's (tel. 624/143-0801, www.edithscabo.com, daily 6 P.M.–1 A.M.), near Playa El Médano on the west side of the Camino de los Pescadores, presents live and recorded jazz (mostly 1940s and 1950s vintage).

Hard Rock Café (Blvd. Marina, Plaza Bonito, tel. 624/143-3779, daily 11 A.M.–2 A.M.), marked by a pink vintage Cadillac protruding from the front of the building at Plaza Bonita, is a lively place featuring sports-oriented TV rather than music videos, the entertainment staple of HRCs elsewhere. The Hard Rock hosts occasional live rock bands from La Paz and the mainland.

Dance Clubs

Cabo's discos begin filling up around 11 P.M., but the crowd doesn't really break a sweat till around midnight or later. A perennial favorite is the two-story dance floor at **El Squid Roe** (Lázaro Cárdenas at Zaragoza, tel. 624/143-0655), where bleacher-balconies offer a bird's-eye view of the swirling masses below. Balloons and confetti falling from the sky, table dancing, centipedes, and two-for-one drinks are all part of the experience. The Squid may stay open as late as 3 A.M., depending on the crowd.

Californians are partial to **Cabo Wabo** (Guerrero btw Madero/Lázaro Cárdenas, tel. 624/143-1188, www.cabowabo.com, 7 P.M.–2 A.M.), a dance club/restaurant owned by California rock 'n' roller Sammy Hagar. The music

---

WABORITA

The signature Cabo Wabo drink looks like a tropical fish, blue on the bottom and green on top. Here's how to make one when you get home:

1 oz tequila
½ oz Damiana liquor
½ oz orange liquor
½ oz lime juice
Shake and serve straight up with a dash of blue curaçao.

here alternates between a recorded mix (with video) and live bands. Cabo Wabo was built in 1989 and named for a Van Halen song describing the "wobble" exhibited by tourists walking around town after a night of club-hopping. Sammy and his band play at the club at least twice a year (on the club's April anniversary and again for the Red Rocker's birthday in October) and occasionally more often—Christmas and New Year's are good bets.

Among the newer clubs targeting a younger crowd is **Zoo Bar & Dance** (Blvd. Marina across from Plaza Bonita, tel. 624/143-5500, 9 P.M.–4 A.M.). Ladies drink free Thursdays 9 P.M.–midnight.

Cinema

On the second floor of Puerto Paraíso mall, **Cinema Paraíso** (tel. 624/143-1515) shows first-run Mexican, American, and international films.

Charreada

Despite the name, **La Sanluqueña Bullring** (tel. 624/143-8144), a small wooden stadium at the northeast corner of Mexico 19 and Mexico 1, actually hosts horseback-riding shows rather than bullfights. One of the performances, here billed as "Ladies on Horseback Ballet"—is *escaramuza,* a female equestrian event from the traditional *charreada.* The facility also rents horses for private rides.

Race and Sports Book

Casino Real Casino Sports Bar (tel. 624/143-1934, daily 9 A.M.–11 P.M.), in Plaza Náutica near the marina, features a full-service bar and restaurant, and a bank of closed-circuit television screens tuned to various sporting events.

Also in Plaza Náutica next to Baskin-Robbins is **Caliente Race and Sports Book** (tel. 624/143-1934), where customers can place bets based on Las Vegas odds. Satellite-linked TV monitors show thoroughbred and greyhound races, as well as American football, basketball, baseball, and other games.

Events

Bike races, fishing to[...] tivals, and national [...] of the gatherings th[...] San Lucas each year. [...] (www.loscabosguide[...] to-date listing of ev[...] of the fishing tournaments is **Bisbee's and Blue Marlin Jackpot Tournament** (tel. 624/143-1622, www.bisbees.com), held for three days each October. The purse for the contest has approached US$5 million in recent years, making it the world's richest billfish tournament. Proceeds go to local charities.

Another notable yearly event falls around the Festival of San Lucas on October 18; look for a week of music, dancing, and feasting in the Mexican tradition.

SHOPPING

The streets of Cabo are filled with souvenir shops, street vendors, clothing boutiques, and galleries—probably more shops of this type per capita than anywhere else in Baja. A number of new, upscale shops now line the Plaza Fiesta, near the Marina Fiesta hotel.

Arts, Crafts, and Souvenirs

For inexpensive handicrafts—rugs, blankets, baskets, leatherwork—from all over Mexico, try the outdoor **Mercado Mexicano** on Hidalgo at Obregón; for the best prices, you'll have to bargain. Get good deals on Talavera ceramics at the **Mexican Pottery Factory Outlet** (Madero btw Guerrero/Hidalgo, tel. 624/105-0046).

Taxco (Guerrero and Blvd. Marina, tel. 624/143-0551) has the best selection of silver jewelry in town. **Joyería Albert,** on Matamoros between Niños Héroes and Lázaro Cárdenas, is a branch of the reputable Puerto Vallarta jeweler.

The newer shopping centers are all along the marina side of Boulevard Marina. **Plaza Bonita** has **Dos Lunas** (tel. 624/143-1969, www.doslunas.com), which offers hand-painted clothing, with a second location in

...íso; and **Cartes** (tel. 624/143-...n.–Sat. 9 A.M.–9 P.M., Sun. 9 A.M.–...with rustic colonial furniture, Talavera ...ry, arts and crafts, and classy home-...cor accessories. The presence of a **Sergio Bustamante** gallery (Loc. 25 and 27, tel. 624/144-4894, daily 9 A.M.–9 P.M.) here (and second location in Puerto Paraíso) shows that Cabo San Lucas has attained a market rank similar to that of Cancún and Puerto Vallarta. People tend either to love or to hate Bustamante's whimsical but costly ceramic sculptures, with their angelic faces and otherworldly, Peter Max–like themes.

Across from Mi Mariscos restaurant at the corner of Paseo a la Marina and Camino Viejo a San José, **Chile & Anis** (tel. 624/143-7454, Mon.–Sat. 9 A.M.–8 P.M.) is a Baja arts and crafts store with silver jewelry, wood crafts, mirrors, and ceramics for sale. Upscale crafts line the shelves of **Mi Mexico Magico** (Loc. 52, tel. 624/143-5153, daily 8 A.M.–9 P.M.) in the Marina Fiesta plaza.

local pottery

© JOE CUMMINGS

Puerto Paraíso

The first enclosed shopping mall in Los Cabos, the glitzy Puerto Paraíso (tel. 624/144-3000), adjoining the marina, is Cabo's most upscale shopping and entertainment plaza. So far what you'll find for the most part are three levels of art galleries and international fashion franchises such as Quicksilver, Nautica, Mossimo, Guess, and Harley-Davidson, and even a Curves exercise center. American restaurants and food outlets include Ruth's Chris Steak House, Häagen-Dazs, Houlihan's, and Johnny Rockets. There is also a bowling alley on the third level. When finished, the mall will contain more pricey shops, a convention center, two hotels, condo units, and a spa. Clean public restrooms and free parking are added conveniences.

Fine Art Galleries

In the lobby of the Tesoro Los Cabos Hotel, a photography gallery displays prints by **Tomas Spangler,** whose work depicts images and scenes unique to the Baja peninsula. A rep-

resentative is available Monday–Saturday 10 A.M.–2 P.M. (www.fotomas.com).

Golden Cactus Gallery (Guerrero and Madero, tel./fax 624/143-6399, www.golden-cactusgallery.com) features the works of artist Chris MacClure in a second-story studio. MacClure's work captures local Baja imagery, and he has created commissioned paintings of yachts, airplanes, and the like for celebrity clients including John Travolta.

Home Decor

San José and the Corridor have a higher concentration of home furnishing stores, but there are a few in Cabo San Lucas as well. **Decor America Interiors** (Mendoza and Obregón, tel./fax 624/143-0575, www.decoramericainteriors.com, Mon.–Fri. 9:30 A.M.–6 P.M., Sat. 9:30 A.M.–1 P.M.) is a full-service interior design shop offering a wide selection of furniture, custom upholstery, and accessories.

Northeast of town, **Artesano Mexicano** (Km 2.5, tel. 624/143-7161, daily 9 A.M.–1 P.M. and 3 P.M.–8 P.M.) is a large shop selling rustic furniture, hand-painted Mexican tiles, colorful ceramic sinks, terra-cotta wall sconces, glassware, pewter, and many other ceramic and iron decorating accessories, all at low (for Cabo) prices.

Cigars

Many stores sell Cuban cigars in Los Cabos, but fakes are rampant. Buy from a reputable merchant if you want the real thing. And remember, Cubans never go on sale. **La Casa del Habano** (formerly J&J Habanos, Blvd. Marina near Madero, tel. 624/143-6160 or 877/305-6242, www.jnjhabanos.com) has a walk-in humidor and a few tables inside. Prices are steep, but you can be confident that you're getting what you pay for. The owners have also opened a new cigar bar called **Hemingway's,** across from the entrance to Cabo Wabo (see *Bars*).

Wine

La Europea (tel. 624/145-8755, Mon.–Fri. 9 A.M.–8 P.M., Sat. 9 A.M.–9 P.M.) has opened a small street-level store in the Puerto Paraíso complex. This satellite of the larger, main store on the Corridor features a good selection of discounted wines, including some California labels, plus just about every other type of booze and upscale deli items such as balsamic vinegar, crackers, olives, cheeses, rose petal marmalade, and fresh baguettes. Credit cards are accepted.

Sporting Goods

Cabo Sports Center (Plaza Náutica, tel. 624/143-4272, daily 9 A.M.–7 P.M.) sells beach supplies, sports sandals, and varied equipment for golf, swimming, surfing, snorkeling, boogie-boarding, and mountain biking. **Minerva's Baja Tackle** (on Blvd. Marina at Madero, tel. 624/143-1282, Mon.–Sat. 9 A.M.–7 P.M.), next door to Pisces Fleet, is well stocked with lures and other tackle designed specifically for Cabo sportfishing.

Books and Magazines

Libros Libros/Books Books (Plaza de La Danza, tel. 624/143-3172, daily 9 A.M.–9 P.M.) stocks a few English-language paperbacks, magazines, maps, books on Baja, children's books, and U.S. newspapers. A second, larger branch in Plaza Náutica, next to Dairy Queen, had no English titles at last check.

ACCOMMODATIONS

Cabo San Lucas offers a greater number and variety of hotels than neighboring San José. Most are in the US$50–150 range, although the high-end resorts cost well over US$250 in winter and early spring.

Unless otherwise noted, rate ranges quoted below are for double rooms, peak season, usually November–May. Some hotels may offer a 15–20 percent discount March–October and a discount for stays longer than a week. Add 12 percent tax to all rates; some hotels may charge an additional 10–15 percent service charge.

Downtown Hotels

Although Cabo's beaches are the average visitor's preferred address, you can save considerably by staying downtown and walking or driving to the beach.

Under US$50: A bit off the beaten track (and close to the bus terminal), **Hotel Casa Blanca** (on Calle Revolución a half block east of Morelos, tel. 624/143-5360, US$45–50), offers 20 newly renovated rooms with king-size beds and air conditioning. In the same vicinity, **Olas Hotel** (Revolución at Gómez Farías, tel. 624/143-1780, fax 624/143-1380, US$45) feels more like a hostel, with 28 rooms (some with one king-size bed, others with two single beds). Amenities include cable TV, fan, fridge, microwave, and patio. Budget travelers might also check out relative newcomer **Hotel Oasis,** across from the CCC (Centro Comercial California) on the west side of Mexico 19 just north of the junction with Mexico 1, where the going rate is US$35–45. The friendly **Hotel Dos Mares** (Zapata, tel. 624/143-0330, hoteldosmares@cabotel.com.mx, US$40–90) rents 37 quite adequate, air-conditioned rooms with TV and phone. A small pool is on the premises.

US$50-100: Cabo Inn Hotel (20 de Noviembre btw Vicario/Mendoza, tel./fax 624/143-0819, US$58) is a cash-only place with nice courtyard areas downstairs and small, clean rooms with air conditioning, ceiling fans, and tiny bathrooms. A shared TV is usually on in the downstairs lobby, though it's turned off at a reasonable hour. The roof patio has a seating area furnished with a sofa, chairs, and a cabinet full of books, as well as a "social pool." One *palapa* unit features a whirlpool and another can sleep up to six people.

One of the best values downtown is the friendly and efficient **Siesta Suites Hotel** (Zapata btw Guerrero/Hidalgo, tel./fax 624/143-2773, U.S. tel. 866/271-0952, www.cabosiestasuites.com, US$59), near the better downtown restaurants and one block from the marina. All 15 suites and five hotel-style rooms are clean and quiet. Suites come with a kitchen and separate bedroom. All rooms have air conditioning, cable TV, and telephone (local calls are free). The hotel also features a sundeck, barbecue area, and secured parking. Because of price and location, Siesta Suites is a popular (and somewhat noisy) spot; reservations are recommended, even in summer—ask for the highest floor available to minimize the noise. Credit cards are accepted.

The **El Dorado** (Morelos btw Obregón/Carranza, tel. 624/143-2810, US$55) offers basic rooms. The **Hotel Los Arcos** (Vicario and Revolución, tel. 624/143-0702, US$55) opened in December 2005 with 32 clean rooms in a two-story building with cable TV and air conditioning.

Three blocks back from the marina, old gringo standby **Hotel Mar de Cortez** (Blvd. Lázaro Cárdenas at Guerrero, tel. 624/143-0032, U.S./Canada tel. 800/347-8821, www.mardecortez.com, US$50–67) stays full virtually all season. Its clean, air-conditioned rooms surround a small pool and patio area planted with date palms; some of the rooms have small patios attached. Facilities include a restaurant and outdoor bar area.

A large arched metal door leads to the attractive walled courtyard of the **Los Milagros Hotel** (Matamoros 116, tel. 624/143-4566, U.S. tel. 718/928-6647, info@losmilagros.com.mx, US$75–115). The 12 spacious rooms—some with kitchenettes—are well appointed. An inviting splash pool/hot tub and free Wi-Fi are added conveniences.

Now owned by The Villa Group, **Hotel Santa Fe** (southwest corner of Zaragoza and Obregón, tel. 624/143-4401, U.S. tel. 877/845-5247, gerenciasantafe@prodigy.net.mx, US$74–95) is a tidy, Mexican-style compound containing 46 studios set around a pool. Each studio has a sliding glass door, recently renovated bath, kitchenette, new furnishings, air conditioning, satellite TV, and phone. Amenities include wireless Internet, offstreet parking, 24-hour security, a small counter restaurant with outdoor seating (daily 7 A.M.–7 P.M.), laundry, and a mini super (daily 7 A.M.–7 P.M.). A free beach shuttle was in the works for 2007.

One block off the marina on the second floor of Plaza de la Danza, **Viva Cabo Hotel** (Blvd. Marina, Plaza La Danza, tel./fax 624/143-5810, US$89–100) has eight studios with kitchens, air conditioning, satellite TV, and sitting areas. Amenities include a restaurant and bar, with a pool and fitness center next door.

Playa El Médano Hotels

The preponderance of Cabo's beach hotels are along this long strip of sand southeast of the town center.

US$50-100: East along Playa El Médano, behind San Vicente and Vagabundos RV Parks, **Club Cabo Hotel and Campground Resort** (tel./fax 624/143-3348, www.clubcaboinn.com, US$65–95) rents several suites and bungalows with air conditioning, verandas, and king-size beds. Other amenities include laundry facilities, wireless Internet access, table tennis, swimming pool, hot tub, large refrigerator for storing your catch, and shuttle to town. English, Spanish, and Dutch are spoken. Club Cabo is also an RV park (see *Camping and RV Parks*). It's a 15–20 minute walk from the park to the marina/downtown and a short walk to the beach, which is separated from the park by a dirt road and one of the last stands of natural thorn forest in the Cabo area—a good birding site.

Not on the beach, but close to it, is the 10-room **Casa Rafael's** (Pescador at El Médano, tel. 624/143-0739, www.casarafaels .com, US$75–100), tastefully decorated in Mexican-colonial style. Rooms with access for people with disabilities are available; some rooms have hot tubs and some have ocean views. The premises are planted in banana and papaya and feature exotic caged birds, a pool, hot tub, small gym, piano bar, cigar lounge, and a restaurant with a good wine collection (mains US$16–35). Credit cards are accepted.

US$150-250: Families particularly like **Villa del Palmar Cabo Beach Resort & Spa** (Km 0.5, tel. 624/145-7000, U.S. tel. 877/845-5247, www.villadelpalmarloscabos.com, junior suites US$200–400), which stands along a secluded area of El Médano and offers 458 suites, including junior suites and one- to three-bedroom oceanview deluxe suites, all with kitchens, marble bathrooms, and furnished balconies. Other amenities include two pools (one with poolside bar), two lighted tennis courts, a fitness center, a water-sports facility, and rooftop and beachside restaurants. Some units are available only by the week. The onsite Spa at Villa del Palmar offers individual and package treatments in a 10,000 square-foot European-style spa. Prices include tax; three-night minimum.

Over US$250: Next door to the Villa del Palmar, **Villa La Estancia** (Km 0.5 Camino Viejo a San José, tel. 624/143-8121, U.S. tel. 619/683-7883, www.villalaestancia.com) has 158 units ranging in size from one bedroom (US$550–650) to three bedrooms, as well as standard guestrooms (US$301–370) and junior suites. Still under construction at press time, **Villas del Arco** (tel. 624/145-7000, U.S. tel. 888/880-8512, www.villadelarcocabo.com) was to have three buildings when complete, with junior suites for around US$300, as well

as one- and two-bedroom units. Prices at both of these resorts include tax, and there is a three-night minimum.

The **ME Cabo** resort (Playa El Médano, tel. 624/145-7800, U.S. tel. 800/336-3542, www. solmelia.com, US$335–796) is a Spanish-owned Sol Meliá property with 108 recently remodeled rooms and suites built in a horseshoe shape around a large pool and patio area. Distinctive touches include an adults-only floor, free preloaded iPods, and home theaters. Most rooms have ocean views.

A couple hundred meters northeast along the beach is the striking **Pueblo Bonito Los Cabos** (tel. 624/142-9797, U.S. tel. 800/990-8250, www.pueblobonito.com, US$378–550), a white, five-story Mediterranean-style building topped by blue-tiled domes and arrayed in a horseshoe around gardens and a freeform pool with a waterfall. Purified water throughout the resort makes teeth-brushing less of an ordeal. The 148 junior and luxury suites come with kitchenettes and ocean views.

Farther northeast is another Pueblo Bonito resort, the **Pueblo Bonito Rosé** (tel. 624/142-9898, U.S. tel. 800/990-8250, www.pueblobonito.com, suites US$340–995). The 260 suites are situated on 2.2 hectares (5.5 acres). Not-especially-new rooms feature comfortable beds, private balconies, ocean views, hand-painted terra-cotta floors, kitchens, and original artwork. One of the hotel's finest features is its lavish lobby, which is decorated with velvet draperies, a 17th-century Flemish tapestry, and fountains surrounded by 16th-century Italian baroque cherubs.

Three miles east of Cabo San Lucas, beachfront **Riu Palace** (Km 5.5, Camino Viejo a San José, tel. 624/146-7160, U.S. tel. 888/666-8816, www.riu.com, US$248–310) comprises a town unto itself, with 642 guestrooms—that are booked almost all of the time, according to travel agents—and all-inclusive (only) meal plans. Part of a large international hotel chain, the lively Riu has so many dining and entertainment options that many guests never leave the resort during their visit. Rates include taxes. Riding the success of its first Los Cabos property, the company is reportedly building another resort next door.

Pacific Beach Hotels

Two of Cabo's most distinguished hotels are secluded from the rest of town by the rocky ridge leading to Land's End.

US$150-250: Impressively constructed high on the ridge itself, overlooking the beach and Pacific Ocean, is the 1971-vintage, 287-room **Hotel Finisterra** (tel. 624/143-3333, U.S. tel. 800/347-2252, www.finisterra.com, US$175–225). A newer tower wing, known as the Palapa Beach Club, offers spacious suites with ocean views and extends from the beach below all the way to the original hotel and lobby area, to which it is connected by a bridge. A gorgeous business center makes for a comfortable office away from home. It is equipped with leather chairs, five flatscreen TVs, and several Dell computer stations. Wireless Internet costs US$10/day. A 1,040-square-meter (11,200-sq-ft) swimming pool with whirlpools and swim-up bar sits on the beach at the foot of the Palapa Beach Club. Beds are on the firm side, and some of the rooms and suites in the original Finisterra section feature city, marina, or garden views rather than bay views. Amenities include lighted tennis courts, sauna, pool, massage service, and wedding chapel.

The sleek, V-shaped **Hotel Solmar Suites** (tel. 624/143-3535, U.S. tel. 310/459-9861 or 800/344-3349, www.solmar.com, US$170–330) features 180 rooms and suites built right on the beach directly into the rocks that form Land's End, plus additional timeshare/condo units overlooking the beach. Some of the suites have a private hot tub on the terrace. An older section of units directly on the beach has lower ceilings and less natural light; newer units are set back from the sand but have high ceilings, better lighting and newer furnishings. Down at the original beach wing are tennis courts, an aquatic center, an indoor-outdoor restaurant that cooks your fish anyway you like it (mains US$6–15), and two heated pools with swim-up *palapa* bars and hot tubs. The Solmar

is renowned for its fishing fleet; all-inclusive fishing packages are popular during the late-summer fishing season. The hotel's liveaboard dive boat, the *Solmar V* (www.solmarv.com) is one of the finest in Baja.

Over US$250: Open since 2002, the **Pueblo Bonito at Sunset Beach** (Cabo Pacifica, tel. 624/142-9999, U.S. tel. 800/990-8250, www.pueblobonito.com, US$394–550) has 327 suites on a 50-acre hillside overlooking the Pacific, behind the Pedregal development. Amenities include a hilltop "sky pool," a main pool that overlooks the beach, tennis courts, and a free shuttle into town (drop off at the Pueblo Bonito Blanco on Playa Medano). Fitness facilities cost extra (US$15/day) and massages run a steep US$130 at the Spa at Sunset Beach (daily 8 A.M.–7 P.M.). Two-for-one happy hour lasts exactly one hour, so best to load up on beverages during that time. Eat tacos and chicken sandwiches and the like poolside, or enjoy sushi in the bistro.

In the vicinity, the newest Pueblo Bonito property, **Pueblo Bonito Pacifica** (Cabo Pacifica, tel. 624/142-9696, U.S. tel. 800/990-8250, www.pueblobonito.com, US$400–494), opened in 2005. Couples in search of a romantic getaway like the no-kids factor at this boutique-style resort. Its 154 rooms, including 14 suites, are appointed in minimalist fashion, with a sand and ivory color scheme. Those who want a little more nightlife find the location a bit too remote. Strolling along the beach is discouraged due to heavy surf; you can, however, rent a bed on the beach for US$20 an hour. There is a free shuttle to town, or cabs for US$10 one-way. Meals at **Siempre,** the resort's main restaurant, are pricey, and food quality gets mixed reviews. The onsite **Armonia Spa** offers a variety of massage treatments, including hot stone, Shiatsu, four hands, deep tissue, Swedish, and pregnancy massage (US$100 for 50 minutes).

Marina Hotels

US$50-100: Overlooking the east side of the marina, the **Marina Cabo Plaza** (tel. 624/143-1833, US$100/day or US$700/week) has 63 rooms with a pool and location adjacent to a shopping center with restaurants, stores, and a private mail center. Playa El Médano is a 10-minute walk away. Kitchenettes are available.

US$150-250: Largest of the marina hotels, and the most basic all-inclusive resort in Los Cabos, the **Tesoro Los Cabos Hotel** (tel. 624/173-9300 or 800/716-8770, U.S. tel. 800/543-7556, www.tesororesorts.com, US$165–176 EP or US$183–194 AI)—formerly the Costa Real, and before that, the Hotel Plaza Las Glorias—is nicknamed "Cabo Jail" because it takes so long to walk from one end to the other. All rooms come with air-conditioning, telephones, refrigerators, and in-room safety box. Facilities include a beach club at Playa El Médano. All-inclusive (AI) and European (EP) rate plans are available.

Next to Plaza Fiesta, near the Marina Cabo San Lucas office, stands the **Marina Fiesta Resort & Hotel** (tel. 624/145-6020, U.S. tel. 877/243-4880, www.marinafiestaresort.com, US$202–299). The hotel's well-designed, comfortable suites come with kitchenettes. Among the facilities are a sundeck and solarium (both with hot tubs), a massage and therapy room, 24-hour supermarket, drugstore, children's playground, and a freeform heated pool with a swim-up *palapa* bar.

Bed-and-Breakfasts

US$50-100: A few blocks from the town center, **Casa Pablito Bed and Breakfast Hotel** (Hidalgo and Ortega, tel. 624/143-1971, U.S. tel. 866/444-1139, www.casapablitoloscabos. com, US$90) is a new property opened by the owner of Club Cascadas. Originally built to house employees of the condo resort, the building has been converted into a traditional Mexican hacienda-style inn with 14 suites set around a pool and *palapa*-shaded breakfast area. Rooms have either one queen or two twin beds, plus kitchenettes, air conditioning, and cable TV.

US$100-150: Off Calle Constitución in the residential western part of town, **The Bungalows Breakfast Inn** (Dorado and Lienzo Charro, tel. 624/143-5035, U.S. tel. 888/424-2226,

www.cabobungalows.com, US$135–185) offers eight well-decorated one-bedroom suites, each with ceiling fan, air conditioning, fridge, stove, and TV; one larger, deluxe one-bedroom suite; one honeymoon suite with a private veranda and view of town; and six two-bedroom bungalows, each sleeping 4–6 guests. Smoking isn't permitted anywhere on the premises, inside or out. The small but well-landscaped grounds also contain a heated swimming pool, hot tub, and outdoor barbecue, plus a small gift shop selling many of the Mexican decor accessories seen in the guestrooms. A Mexican cook and pastry chef prepare the full breakfast.

US$150-250: One mile east of Cabo San Lucas and a half mile above Mexico 1, **Casa Contenta** (tel. 624/143-6038, www.cabocasacontenta.com, US$160–195/day or US$1,050–1,300/week) has five air-conditioned rooms with private baths in a three-story home with a swimming pool and wireless Internet throughout. Take a yoga class, book a spa treatment, or simply enjoy the view of Land's End on the rooftop terrace. There's a three-night minimum.

Condominiums and Condotels

Some of the best deals for families or small groups are rental condos, which usually sleep up to four for US$120–250 per night. Some condos take reservations directly, while others have booking services (some do both). And many different property management companies may have listings in the same complex. Rates do not include tax and service unless otherwise noted.

US$100-150: Well-managed, four-story **Bahía Condo Hotel** (tel. 624/143-1888, U.S. tel. 800/932-5599, www.grupobahia.com, US$129–149), just off Camino de los Pescadores above Playa El Médano, rents simple, clean, air-conditioned units, some with ocean views, all with minimally equipped kitchenettes, satellite TV, and direct-dial phones. Giant sculpted concrete shells frame the beds as headboards, and bamboo doors enclose the bathroom and closet. Faucets and tiling have aged a bit. The property includes laundry facilities, a decent restaurant, pool with hot tub and swim-up *palapa* bar, and free parking. Its studios feel more like basic hotel rooms than condos, but for the price, you can't beat the location and friendly service. Rates here include tax. Construction in front of the hotel detracts somewhat from the view, and like many affordable downtown locations, the place is overrun with college students on spring break during the month of March.

Close to downtown but also within easy walking distance of El Médano, **Marina Sol Condominiums** (tel. 624/143-3231, U.S. tel. 877/255-1721, www.marinasolresort.com) features simple one- and two-bedroom condos built around a garden courtyard with a pool. A room accessible to the disabled is available. The complex also has a hot tub, swim-up bar, and small gym. An independently operated grocery store, spa, and laundry service are located in the lobby.

US$150-250: Club Cascadas (Camino Viejo a San José, tel. 624/143-1882, U.S. tel. 800/365-9190 ext. 400, www.clubcascadasdebaja.com, one bedroom US$199–335), at the east end of El Médano, is a nicely designed timeshare complex with 110 interconnected villas, two pools, and tennis courts.

Near Casa Rafael's off Camino de los Pescadores, a short walk from Playa El Médano, stand the two round, whitewashed towers of **Cabo Villas** (tel. 624/143-9166, fax 624/143-2558, cabovillasresort@prodigy.net.mx). One-bedroom, one-bath units and two-bedroom, two-bath units are available.

The **Hotel Solmar Suites** (tel. 624/143-3535, U.S. tel. 310/459-9861 or 800/344-3349, www.solmar.com) rents a number of timeshare/condo units on the hill overlooking Playa Solmar. Next door, **Terrasol Condominiums** (tel. 624/143-1803, U.S. tel. 800/524-5104, www.terrasolcabo.com, one bedroom US$130–250) consists of studio, one-bedroom, and two-bedroom units, all with kitchens, ocean views, and wireless Internet access. On the premises are two pools, a tennis court, swim-up *palapa* bar, and snack bar. You can walk to the beach from both the Solmar and Terrasol.

Timeshares and Villas

As the new Pedregal develement takes shape on the west side of town, a number of large, luxury beach homes have come on the rental market in Cabo San Lucas. Ranging in size from two to five or more bedrooms, these townhouses or private homes accommodate small groups with a creative list of in-villa services. For an extra fee, the property manager will stock your villa prior to your arrival with the foods and supplies you request. (You can also head to Costco and buy what you want when you get there.) Guests may schedule pilates or yoga classes, spa treatments, and chef services (one special meal or three meals daily). Prices start at about US$1,500 per night for a three-bedroom villa.

Booking Services and Property Management Companies

Delfin Hotels & Resorts (U.S. tel. 800/524-5104), described at the beginning of this chapter in the *Choosing an Accommodation* section, has Cabo San Lucas condos in the Terrasol complex. It also books for Casa Contenta B&B and most of the all-inclusive resorts. **Cabo Villa Rentals** (U.S. tel. 877/473-1946, www.cabovillarentals.com, 8:30 A.M.–5 P.M.) manages condos in the Terrasol and Villa La Estancia complexes and three- to five-bedroom villas in the Pedregal development. **Earth, Sea, and Sky Vacations** (U.S. tel. 800/745-2226, www.cabovillas.com), also described earlier, represents 90 luxury villa rentals, ranging from two- to nine-bedroom units with a starting pricepoint of US$1,500 per night, as well as 30 resorts. **Pedregal Escapes** (Camino de La Plaza 145, Fraccionamiento Pedregal, tel. 624/144-3222, www.pedregalescapes.com) is the vacation rental division of the company that developed the Pedregal gated community on the west side of Cabo San Lucas. It manages two- to five-bedroom villas, plus even a few larger homes. Prices start at about US$450 per night, and some properties require a security deposit.

Camping and RV Parks

Three kilometers northeast of Cabo San Lucas off Mexico 1, the **Vagabundos del Mar RV**

Park (Km 3, tel. 624/143-0290, www.vagabun-dosrv.com) has 52 slots with full hookups for US$20/day or US$120/week; discounts are available for members of the Vagabundos del Mar travel club (see *Travel Clubs* in the *Essentials* chapter). November–June, this park is usually booked up for weeks or months at a time, so be sure to make contact well in advance if you want to park here. Caravans are not accepted. Facilities include a restaurant, bar, flush toilets, *palapas,* showers, a pool, and laundry.

Behind the Vagabundos RV Park and Playa El Médano is the rustic **Club Cabo Hotel and Campground Resort** (tel./fax 624/143-3348, www.clubcaboinn.com, US$20). To get there, turn east off Mexico 1 onto the road to Club Cascada, then turn onto the first dirt road on your left and follow the signs. This small campground offers 10 tent sites and 10 slots for smaller RVs—some shaded, some not, all for US$20 per site. Facilities include well-kept toilets, hot showers, a hot tub, hammock lounge area, table tennis, trampoline, pool, wireless Internet and secure parking. Club Cabo also rents eight suites with kitchens (see *Playa El Médano Hotels).*

Nowadays Club Cabo is more likely to have a vacancy than Vagabundos; it is also closer to the beach than the others. The proprietor, an accomplished pilot, can arrange ultralight flights and instruction in the area. Visiting pilots may receive discounts on accommodations. Inquire about kayaking, sailing, horseback riding, and mountain biking. The adjacent natural thorn forest is a habitat for many resident and migratory bird species.

Villa Serena RV Park (Km 7.5, U.S. tel. 800/932-5599, www.grupobahia.com, US$21/day, US$112/week, US$391/month) has 54 spaces with full hookups but no shade, as well as a laundry room and bathroom with hot showers. In the adjacent *palapa* restaurant, a La Paz native serves delicious food (coconut shrimp, whole *huachinango*/red snappper) at reasonable prices (tel. 624/145-8244, daily 7 A.M.–10 P.M., mains US$12–25).

You can camp on the beaches farther northeast along Mexico 1 (see *The Corridor*) or northwest along Mexico 19.

FOOD

Downtown Cabo San Lucas is riddled with restaurants and bars, most of open-air design. Menus usually attempt to cover the main bases demanded by any Mexican resort area—seafood, Italian, Mexican, and steak. Because Cabo is Baja's number-one resort town, prices are higher than what you'd find in La Paz, Ensenada, Tijuana, or other tourist areas: Dinners run north of US$100 for two. Quality is also generally high since Cabo attracts chefs from all over Mexico and beyond. One complaint: Cabo restaurants sometimes hold back on the chilies in Mexican dishes and table salsas; hence *picante*-lovers may be forced to request extra chilies or fresh *salsa cruda* to bring things up to the proper level of heat.

Mexican
Mi Casa (Calle Cabo San Lucas opposite the plaza, tel. 624/143-1933, dinner daily 5:30–10:30 P.M., lunch Mon.–Sat. noon–3 P.M., mains US$13–30) is often cited as the most authentic Mexican restaurant in Cabo. The tastefully designed, half-*palapa,* half-open-air dining room is encircled by pastel murals intended to look like a small Central Mexican village. The menu lists dishes from all over Mexico, including fajitas, *mole verde, mole poblano, pipián, carne asada a la tampiqueña, pollo borracho,* and *cochinita pibil.* The food is good but doesn't always match the menu descriptions.

Just to the northeast of Plaza Náutica, in Plaza del Sol, **O Mole Mío** (tel. 624/143-7577, daily 11:30 A.M.–11:30 P.M., mains US$10–20) features original Mexican recipes such as El Solo Mío (grilled red snapper seasoned with Cajun spices and served with mango salsa) or Camarones Frida y Omar (shrimp baked in a tequila sauce and topped with julienned potatoes). The interior, decorated with unusual custom-designed wicker-and-iron furniture, is as interesting as the menu. The bar section is a fun place for drinks and *botanas.*

For authentic Mexican dishes that won't cost a lot, try **La Perla** (Blvd. Lázaro Cárdenas at Guerrero, Mon.–Sat. 9 A.M.–4:30 P.M., restaurants along the Cabo San Lucas marina

© PAUL ITOI

mains US$4–5), a simple Mexican eatery supported by a mainly local clientele. The menu features inexpensive *desayuno, tortas, molletes, tingas,* tacos, burritos, quesadillas, and *licuados.* **Lolita's Restaurant** (Niños Héroes near Matamoros, Mon.–Sat. 7 A.M.–7:30 P.M., mains US$7–13) serves authentic *antojitos mexicanos (huachinango,* crab, fish filet), plus *champurrado* (hot chocolate made with cornstarch).

Among the best nontourist Mexican eateries in town is **◖ Las Gardenias** (mains US$6–12), a family-owned spot on the road to Playa El Médano. It's divided into two sections, the right side serving tacos of various kinds and the left side a changing menu that includes dishes such as chiles rellenos, *cochinita pibil, nopales,* and *chicharrón.*

Back in gringolandia, **Pancho's** (Hidalgo off Blvd. Marina, tel. 624/143-0973, daily 7 A.M.–11 P.M., dinner mains US$18–40) serves huge Mexican platters with somewhat inflated prices, plus tasty Mexican breakfasts and more than 190 varieties of tequila. All the waiters speak English, and there is pleasant outdoor seating.

Carlos'n Charlie's (Blvd. Marina, tel. 624/143-1280, daily 11 A.M.–midnight, mains US$10–20) functions primarily as a place for tourists to drink themselves silly. But this Grupo Anderson restaurant serves good Mexican food. **El Squid Roe** (Blvd. Lázaro Cárdenas at Zaragoza, tel. 624/143-0655, daily noon–3 A.M., mains US$10–20) is one of the many Grupo Anderson restaurant/bars in Mexico that combine zany, tourist-on-the-loose fun with tried-and-true menus based on regional cuisine. Drinks are served in plastic cups.

Casa Rafael's (Pescador and Médano, tel. 624/143-0739, Mon.–Sat. 6–10 P.M., mains US$20 and up) is a small hotel with an elegant dining room specializing in nouvelle Mexican cuisine—served à la carte or as a seven-course, fixed-price meal. The changing menu also features international dishes and seafood. The wine list is impressive, and there is live music nightly. Reservations are suggested.

Cilantro's Bar & Grill (tel. 624/143-2900, daily 11 A.M.–11 P.M., mains US$10–20) at the Pueblo Bonito Resort on Playa El Médano, is one of Cabo's better hotel-oriented Mexican restaurants, featuring mesquite-grilled seafood and homemade tortillas. For a casual lunch or dinner at the beach, **Cascadas Beach & Grill** (Playa El Médano, tel. 624/143-0307, daily 7 A.M.–11 P.M., mains US$8–13) has reasonably priced Mexican plates.

Amber glassware and a free pomegranate tequila aperitif are nice touches at **Los Garcia** (mains US$8–15), one of the newer restaurants located at the street level of the Puerto Paraíso mall, serving upscale tacos, barbecued ribs, lobster salad, and other Mexican fare.

Tequila shrimp, made with the restaurant's own label, and lobster burritos are standout entrées at Sammy Hagar's **Cabo Wabo Restaurant** (Guerrero btw. Madero/Lázaro Cárdenas, tel. 624/143-1188, www.cabowabo.com, daily 11 A.M.–11 P.M., mains US$17–28). Try the Waborita cocktail to start the meal off right. Downstairs, the Cabo Wabo Cantina serves a more casual menu.

Seafood

Mocambo de Los Cabos (Vicario and 20 de Noviembre, tel. 624/143-6070, daily noon–10 P.M.; mains US$10–20) is a casual, local-style place with a huge seafood menu. Equally fresh but more creative and more expensive, **Fish House** (Plaza La Danza, upstairs from Nick-San and KFC, tel. 624/144-4501, daily noon–10 P.M., mains US$14–24) specializes in fresh clams and oysters, salmon pasta, and live Maine lobster. Despite the name, steak also holds a place of honor here, and the wine selection is good.

Try the *pescado zarandeado* (red snapper served whole in a tomato-based broth) or grilled fish *meniore* style (in a sauce of garlic, butter, white wine, and capers) at **Mariscos Mazatlán** (Mendoza and 16 de Septiembre, tel. 624/143-8565, mains US$10–14). The menu also includes 12 different preparations of shrimp. This restaurant has a second, less touristy location in San José del Cabo, on the West

side of Mexico 1 on the way to the airport. Near the Ace Hardware store at the corner of Camino Real and Paseo de la Marina, **Mi Casa de Mariscos** (tel. 624/143-6898, micasa@cabonet.net.mx, daily 1 P.M.–10:30 P.M., mains US$13–29) has a raw bar with shrimp, scallops, oysters; "barely touched" dishes like ceviche and seared fresh catch; and fully cooked entrées like *huachinango frito a la talla* (fried whole red snapper).

El Shrimp Bucket (in the Plaza Fiesta shopping center on the marina, tel. 624/143-2598, daily 6 A.M.–11 P.M., mains US$10–20), near Marina Fiesta Resort, is a transplant from Mazatlán and the best of the several restaurants in town with the word "shrimp" in the name. The pink crustaceans are served in every conceivable fashion, including the ever-popular fried shrimp served in a terra-cotta bucket. Breakfasts are also good. At **The Shrimp Factory** (Blvd. Marina at Guerrero, tel. 624/143-5066, daily noon–11 P.M., mains US$10–20), order shrimp or lobster by the kilo (US$20–30 per half kilo), served with bread, salad, and crackers, and go to town.

Las Palmas (tel. 624/143-0447, daily 10 A.M.–11 P.M., mains US$10–15), on Playa El Médano, was the first *palapa* restaurant on Médano, and most residents agree it's still the best, in spite of the ugly concrete addition. The grilled seafood is always a good choice.

Another perennial favorite at the marina, **Solomon's Landing** (tel. 624/143-305, daily 7 A.M.–11 P.M., mains US$10–30), behind the Tesoro Hotel, specializes in lobster and shrimp dishes. Credit cards are accepted.

Italian and Continental

Capo San Giovanni (Guerrero at Madero, tel. 624/143-0593, Tues.–Sun. 5–11 P.M., mains US$13–32), just across the road and south of Cabo Wabo, has a spacious courtyard out back and an inventive southern Italian menu of seafood combos and pasta dishes.

Romeo & Julieta (Camino al Pedregal, tel. 624/143-0225, daily 4–11 P.M., mains US$10–20), near the Hotel Finisterra, offers a popular Italian menu featuring fresh pasta and wood-fired pizzas. In the plaza below the Puerto Paraíso mall, **Amarone** (Store #107, tel. 624/105-1035) prepares starters like antipasti or proscuito and melon for US$12 and lobster or veal filet for US$38. Also downtown, **La Dolce Italian Restaurant & Pizzeria** (Hidalgo and Zapata, tel. 624/143-4122, daily 6–11 P.M., mains US$10–20) serves a full menu of pastas and pizzas, plus Italian starters and desserts.

A German chef presides over a highly regarded kitchen at 【 **Peacocks Restaurant and Bar** (Camino de los Pescadores, tel. 624/143-1858, daily 6–10 P.M., mains US$15 and up), next to the driveway of Hotel Meliá San Lucas. The changing menu at this large, *palapa*-roofed, open-air restaurant is diverse and creative, and the wine list is extensive.

American and Eclectic

Popular with Corridor residents and Baja old-timers, **Latitude 22+ Roadhouse** (Km 4.5, tel. 624/143-1516, www.lat22nobaddays.com, Wed.–Mon. 8 A.M.–11 P.M., mains US$10–20) prepares a Croatian-influenced menu of slow-roasted prime rib, steak, burgers, ribs, shrimp, fish, chicken fried steak, and pastas. Ocean views, reasonably priced cocktails, and giant flatscreen TVs add to the dining experience. Formerly a downtown hangout, "Lat 22" is now located next Costco and behind the power plant. Credit cards are accepted.

In the Tesoro Hotel complex overlooking the marina, **Café Canela** (tel. 624/143-3435, daily 6 A.M.–5 P.M., mains US$6–10) has sandwiches, soups, salads, fresh-squeezed juices, and Mexican dishes with a twist, such as blue cheese quesadillas with smoked tuna. Canela also offers box lunches.

Olé Olé (Plaza Bonita Loc. 3A, tel. 624/143-0633, daily 7 A.M.–11 P.M., mains US$13–32) faces the marina at Plaza Bonita. The large outdoor tapas bar features Spanish cuisine and dinner combos such as *gazpacho andaluz,* *tortilla española,* and *jamón serrano* (Spanish-style cured ham). Try the *gambas a la ajo,* a plate of shrimp in garlic sauce, also available

in an octopus version. Paella is served from 1 P.M. only on Sunday (and sometimes on Friday, US$22).

Cozy 【 **Sancho Panza Wine Bistro and Jazz Club Restaurant** (Locales D19-22, Plaza Tesoro Hotel, tel. 624/143-3212, www.sanchopanza.com, daily 4 P.M.–11 P.M., mains US$10–20) is one of the best establishments of its kind in the entire Cape region. To find it, walk under the pedestrian bridge that connects the wings of the Tesoro Hotel Plaza and look for it on your right. Aided by an artistic and colorful Miró-esque decor, the proprietors have created a first-class wine bar that stocks such hard-to-find, top-of-the-line Baja labels as Monte Xanic and Chateau de Camou along with more than 150 other wines. The short menu offers delicious "new world tapas" that mix New American, Mediterranean, and Latin American influences with outstanding results.

Ruth's Chris Steak House (Puerto Paraíso, tel. 624/144-3232, daily 1 P.M.–11:30 P.M., mains US$20 and up), a branch of the U.S. chain of the same name, serves its trademark fresh broiled beef on an open-air patio with a marina view.

Giggling Marlin (Matamoros near Blvd. Marina, tel. 624/143-0606, www.gigglingmarlin.com, daily 8 A.M.–2 A.M., mains US$10–20) is better for appetizers and booze than entrées. Most tourists come here to snap photos of themselves hanging upside down—like landed marlins—from the restaurant's block-and-tackle rig. Others come for the big-screen satellite TV.

Serious carnivores should head to **Brasil Steakhouse** (Zapata at Hidalgo, tel. 624/143-8343, www.brasilcabo.com, daily 5 P.M.–11 P.M., US$28 pp) for an all-you-can-eat feast of top sirloin, New York strip, *arranchera,* sausage, ribs, and more. The chef slices meats from a serving skewer at the table, while the wait-staff delivers fresh salads and vegetables. The chicken wings that come as an appetizer rival the best you can find in the United States. Try the *carperinia* cocktail to start—essentially a mojito without the mint. **French Riviera** (Plaza del Rey btw Misiones/Cabo Bello, tel. 624/142-3350, www.frenchrivieraloscabos.

com, daily noon–11 P.M., mains US$33), an extension of the popular San José bakery, prepares Mediterranean specialties.

The English-speaking staff at the **Stop Light Bar and Grill** (Lazaro Cárdenas and Morelos, tel. 624/143-4740, mains US$6–19) serves a decent breakfast of eggs, pancakes, or *chilaquiles.* Portions are large, and cocktails are served in glasses, not plastic. Dinner fare includes ceviche, snails, sandwiches, salads, and enchiladas, as well as lobster, steak, and pasta.

Enjoy a sunset meal at the aptly named **Sunset Grill** (tel. 624/143-9199) atop the Cabo Villas complex at Playa El Médano. The restaurant serves breakfast (mains US$5–10), lunch (mains US$5–9), and dinner (mains US$13–22) daily. Empanada appetizers come with a side of guacamole; fish ceviche goes well with a martini. Cash only.

At **Edith's** (tel. 624/143-0801, www .edithscabo.com, daily 6 P.M.–1 A.M., mains US$10–20), near Playa El Médano on the west side of the Camino de los Pescadores, enjoy views of Bahía Cabo San Lucas and Land's End as long as the sun's up, and a hearty dinner of prime rib, rack of lamb, or any number of regional specialties through the evening hours.

Asian
C Nick-San Restaurant (Lte. 10, Blvd. Marina, tel. 624/143-4484, www.nicksan.com, Tues.–Sun. 11:30 A.M.–10:30 P.M., mains US$20 and up) is centrally located along the main strip and serves excellent Japanese barbecue, seafood, and sushi. This is probably the most reliably high-quality restaurant in San Lucas, regardless of cuisine. Don't miss the sashimi salad.

Tacos and Fast Food
The local fast-food scene is concentrated along Calle Morelos, where you'll find a string of stands offering tacos, carne asada, and *mariscos* at the lowest prices in town. The taquerías seem to change owners and names every other year or so but rarely close down completely. A cluster of inexpensive restaurants serve seafood cocktails, chicken, and *tortas* at the south end of Calle Ocampo where it meets Boulevard Lázaro Cárdenas. At the corner of Revolución and Morelos, **Tacos Condi** draws a crowd for *asada cabeza* and other tacos. North of Hemingway's on Guerrero, **Cheto Tacos** serves dependable fish tacos and licuados.

Las Quesadillasss (Blvd. Marina at Lázaro Cardénas, tel. 624/143-1373, daily 7 A.M.– 2 A.M., mains US$6–13), opposite Arámburo Plaza, is a good bet for late-night dining. Enjoy tacos, quesadillas, grilled lobster, steak, French dessert crepes, coffee drinks, and beer in a little two-story outdoor spot under a *palapa* roof.

A string of inexpensive Mexican restaurants lies along Calle Leona Vicario, north of Revolución. One is **Taquería los Paisas** serving tacos and stuffed potatoes (with two other locations—another along Leona Vicario and one opposite Hotel Casa Blanca). A bit farther north past Carranza is **Carnitas El Michoacano** (tel. 624/105-0713), where you can order carnitas by the kilo.

In the plaza below Cabo Wabo, **Taco Loco** serves bean, chicken, pork, and shrimp tacos for US$1 each. **La Luna** (tel. 624/105-0132, Tues.–Sat. noon–10 P.M., Sun. noon–6 P.M.), behind the Pueblo Bonito Rosé resort, serves wraps, burgers, and tacos.

Delicatessens
"Almost-kosher" **Lenny's Deli** (tel. 624/143-8380, daily 7 A.M.–4 P.M.), just east of Camino Pescadores and south off Lázaro Cárdenas, sells fresh-baked breads, imported cheeses, and cold cuts. You can also order sandwiches at **La Europea** (mains US$5–12) just outside the Puerto Paraíso mall. There are a few tables out front, overlooking the marina. Air-conditioned booths are a comfortable place to grab a sandwich (and check your email with free Wi-Fi) at **Señor Greenberg's Mexicatessen** (Plaza Náutica, tel. 624/143-5630, daily 24 hours, mains US$5–12), which has several locations, including a new deli next to Johnny Rockets in the Puerto Paraíso mall.

Cafés

◖ **Theory Café** (tel. 624/143-5518, daily from 10 A.M., mains US$3–7) in the center of Plaza Bonita serves lattes, mochas, and frappucinos, and plays music like the Red Hot Chili Peppers. Use your laptop or theirs for wireless Internet. **Cabo Coffee Company** (tel. 624/105-1130) has expanded to a new Internet café with high-speed wireless connections on the corner of Hidalgo and Madero, across from its original roasting facility. A satellite location is also available outside the Giggling Marlin. **San Francisco Coffee Company** (Blvd. Marina 38, tel. 624/144-4387, www .sanfranciscocoffeecompany.com) brews hot and cold espresso drinks (US$2.50–5.50) and blends smoothies (US$4.50–5.50). It also has wireless Internet (US$2 for up to 15 minutes), DVD rentals, and English-language books.

Among the many dockside restaurants by the marina, **Baja Cantina** (Dock L–M, tel. 624/143-1591, mains US$7–15) serves tasty jalapeño poppers, artichoke and spinach dip, and other starters for US$5–8, as well as fish, burgers, and Mexican plates for dinner. Wireless Internet is a plus. Look for a second location at Playa El Médano (tel. 624/143-9773).

Palapa Restaurants

Several *palapa* bars and restaurants scattered along Playa El Médano—including **Billygan's Island** (tel. 624/143-0402), **The Office** (tel. 624/143-3464), and **Las Palmas** (tel. 624/143-0447)—offer cold beverages, as well as burgers, seafood, and Mexican plates (lunch mains US$8–15; dinner menus are more expensive).

Groceries

Cabo's several supermarkets stock Mexican and U.S. foodstuffs—from fresh Mexican cheeses to Sara Lee frozen cheesecake—plus cooking and cleaning supplies and even auto parts. Varying from small to huge, they include **Almacenes Grupo Castro** (southwest corner of Morelos and Revolución, tel. 624/143-0566), **Supermercado Sánliz** (three locations: Blvd. Marina at Madero,

Ocampo at Matamoros, and Vicario at López Mateos), and **Supermercado Arámburo** (at Arámburo Plaza, Lázaro Cárdenas at Zaragoza, tel. 624/143-1450). Supermercado Arámburo stocks a large selection of both domestic and imported foods, as does the **CCC** (Centro Comercial California, tel. 624/146-7200) on the east side of Mexico 19 just north of the junction with Mexico 1. A few hundred yards farther toward Todos Santos is **Soriana** (Carr. Todos Santos and Calle Guajitos, tel. 624/105-1290, www.soriana .com), a Walmart-esque superstore. On the other side of town, the same outfit runs warehouse-style **City Club** (Blvd. Lázaro Cárdenas at Paseo del Pescador, tel. 624/143-9492, www.soriana.com), with groceries, produce, and baked goods.

Pescadería El Dorado (tel. 624/143-2820), on the south side of 5 de Febrero between Abasolo and Ocampo, stocks a large selection of fresh finfish and shellfish. The most convenient place to buy fresh tortillas is **Tortillería Perla** (on Morelos btw Hidalgo/Matamoros, tel. 624/143-1381).

Panaficadora la Moderna, on Calle Leona Vicario across from Mariscos Mocambo, is a small bakery with a decent selection of Mexican baked goods.

La Baguette (tel. 624/142-1125, Mon.–Sat. 8:30 A.M.–7:30 P.M.), on Boulevard Lázaro Cárdenas next to the entrance for Pedregal, carries European and American-style baked goods including pastries, bagels, and breads. **Swiss Pastry** (Hidalgo at Lázaro Cárdenas across from the plaza, tel. 624/143-3494, Mon.–Sat. 7 A.M.–4 P.M.) serves chicken potpie, sandwiches, fresh bagels, and other pastries, as well as coffee. It has a few tables in front as well as inside.

Frutería Lizarraga (Matamoros at Av. de la Juventud, tel. 624/143-1215) stocks a good selection of fruits and vegetables; several local hotel and restaurant chefs shop here.

Tutto Bene! (Blvd. Marina opposite the Tesoro Hotel, daily 9:30 A.M.–9 P.M.), near the traffic circle, stocks an impressive selection of organic foods and imported wines.

The best shopping area for beer and liquor is the string of *subagencias* and *licores* along Calle Matamoros.

INFORMATION AND SERVICES
Tourist Assistance
The nearest Baja Sur state tourism office is located in San José del Cabo (Blvd. Mauricio Castro, Plaza San José, Locales 3&4, San José del Cabo, tel. 624/146-9628, www.loscabos.gob.mx). **Fonatur** (tel. 624/142-0146, www.fonatur.gob.mx) maintains an office on the marina. Its representatives are always interested in speaking with potential investors, but they don't distribute general tourist information.

Money-Changing
American dollars are readily accepted throughout Cabo, but you'll save money if you pay in pesos. Foreign-currency exchange service is available Monday–Saturday 8:30 A.M.–noon at **Bancomer** (Hidalgo at Guerrero), **Banamex** (Hidalgo at Lázaro Cárdenas), and **Santander Serfín** (in Arámburo Plaza). All three banks have ATMs. Hotel cashiers also gladly change dollars for pesos, albeit at a lower rate than at the banks.

There's a full-service **American Express office** in town near the marina in Plaza Bonita (tel. 624/143-5766, fax 624/143-5988, Mon.–Fri. 9 A.M.–6 P.M., Sat. 9 A.M.–1 P.M.). It offers emergency check cashing, cardmember services, foreign exchange, and tours.

Except in emergencies, stay away from Cabo's money changers, which charge high commissions or sell currency at low exchange rates.

Post and Telephone
Cabo's **post office**, on Boulevard Lázaro Cárdenas near 16 de Septiembre, is open Monday–Friday 8 A.M.–4 P.M., Saturday 9 A.M.–noon. Public telephone booths are at various locations throughout town, including the main plaza and Arámburo Plaza.

Mail Boxes Etc. (Blvd. Marina 39-F, Plaza Fiesta, tel. 624/143-3033, fax 624/143-3031) carries mailing supplies, postage stamps, and magazines and rents mailboxes.

CABO SAN LUCAS PHONE NUMBERS

Cabo San Lucas area code: 624
Cabo San Lucas Hospital: 144-3434
COTP (Captain of the Port): 143-0048
Hyperbaric chamber: 143-3666
Immigration: 143-0135
Police, Fire Department, Red Cross (emergency): 066
Police (nonemergency): 143-3977, 143-5123
Red Cross (nonemergency): 143-3300
U.S. Consulate: 143-3566

Internet Access
Cabo San Lucas has experienced a proliferation of Internet cafés, although they seem to come, change hands, and go as fast as taco stands. Coffee shops and real estate offices are good places to check. Prices have come down quite a bit in recent years, settling at about US$2–6 per hour. A few places are beginning to offer Internet phone services as well. The following list is by no means exhaustive.

BajaTech (tel. 624/143-4240), on Boulevard Lázaro Cárdenas across from the Pemex, sells computer time for email and Web surfing in a comfortable café/bar atmosphere. Free parking. A more expensive option is **Internet Café Cabomail** in Arámburo Plaza (tel. 624/143-7797, Mon.–Fri. 9 A.M.–9 P.M., Sat. 9 A.M.–6 P.M., Sun. noon–6 P.M.), which offers Internet calls to the United States for US$2 per 10 minutes. At **Cabo Clipper Internet & Computers Business Center** (Level 3 Puerto Paraíso Plaza, tel. 624/105-0482, caboclipper@gmail.com, daily 10 A.M.–10 P.M.), you'll pay US$2 for up to 15 minutes or US$6 for one hour. There was no wireless access last we checked, and you'll pay the same prices if you bring your own laptop. Credit cards are accepted.

A minimarket in the lobby of the Marina del Sol condo complex has three ancient PCs connected to the Internet. Better yet, the on-site **Oasis Bar and Grill** (tel. 624/143-6285, www.marinasolresort.com, Thurs.–Tues. 9 A.M.–10:30 P.M.) now has wireless Internet. The lobby of the Siesta Suites Hotel also has three fast PCs (with USB ports) for US$3/hour.

There are several places in town where you can enjoy a latte or cappucino while you check your email: **Theory Café** (tel. 624/143-5518), in the center of Plaza Bonita, opens at 10 A.M. daily. **Cabo Coffee Company** (tel. 624/105-1130, www.cabocoffee.com) has expanded to a new Internet café with high-speed wireless connections on the corner of Hidalgo and Madero, across from its original roasting facility. A satellite location is also available outside the Giggling Marlin. **San Francisco Coffee Company** (38 Blvd. Marina, tel. 624/144-4387, www.sanfranciscocoffeecompany.com) has wireless Internet for US$2 up to 15 minutes. **Baja Cantina** (Dock L–M, tel. 624/143-1591) offers wireless Internet along with a full lunch and dinner menu.

Laundry

Cabo has a number of self-serve and full-service laundry facilities scattered about town. One of the most reputable is **Lavandería Evelyn** (tel. 624/143-0920, daily 7 A.M.–7 P.M.), opposite El Faro Viejo Trailer Park on Calle Matamoros, with banks of washing machines for self-service laundry; ask the attendants to start the machines for you. Or you can pay (by weight) to have the washing, drying, and ironing done by the staff—one-day service is the norm.

Magazines and Newspapers

The annual magazine *Los Cabos Guide* (www.loscabosguide.com) contains a number of features, ads, annotated lists, and announcements concerning hotels, restaurants, clubs, and recreational events, as well as local social and business news. Its online listings are fairly complete, though some pages are more up to date than others. Pop into any real estate office for a free copy. Another handy resource is the **Gringo Pages of Los Cabos** (cell tel. 624/141-6471, http://worlddirectories@sbcglobal.net), an annual yellow pages listing covering the entire Los Cabos Region, with some listings for Todos Santos and the East Cape as well.

The local Spanish-language newspaper is *El Heraldo de los Cabos*. *Gringo Gazette,* a tourist newspaper written and edited locally but printed in the United States, carries whimsical local news stories and events listings. Another tourist rag, *Destino,* contains less news and more ads. The bi-lingual *Los Cabos News* reports on happenings from Cabo San Lucas to San José.

USA Today and *The News* (from Mexico City) are usually available at **Supermercado Sánliz** (Blvd. Marina at Madero), as well as at other larger grocery stores catering to gringos. **Libros Libros/Books Books** in Plaza de la Danza carries *The News, USA Today,* and the *Los Angeles Times.*

Medical Services

Dial 066 for emergency situations. English-speaking doctors advertise in Los Cabos media and a couple of clinics specialize in gringo care. **AmeriMed,** in the Pioneros Building along Lázaro Cárdenas (Loc. 1, tel. 624/143-9670), is a 24-hour clinic with bilingual staff who specialize in urgent and emergency services, along with OB/GYN care, family practice, and more. Most insurance programs are accepted.

Immigration

Cabo's *migración* office is on Boulevard Lázaro Cárdenas between Gómez Farías and 16 de Septiembre.

U.S. Consular Agent

A U.S. consular agent in Cabo, under the auspices of the U.S. consul general in Tijuana, maintains a small office at Plaza Naútica (C-4, Blvd. Marina, tel. 624/143-3566, usconsulcabo@hotmail.com, Mon.–Fri. 10 A.M.–1 P.M.). The consular agent can assist U.S. citizens with lost or stolen passports and other emergency situations.

© JOE CUMMINGS

panga at Playa del Amor

GETTING AROUND

In Cabo itself, you can easily get around on foot, bicycle, or scooter, though car taxis are available for around US$5–10 a trip. **Checker Cabo** is a fleet of mountain bikes welded to two-wheeled carts to produce Asian-style pedicabs.

You can hire **harbor skiffs** from the marina in front of the Tesoro Hotel to Playa El Médano and Playa del Amor (US$10 round-trip only). In the reverse direction, skiffs are plentiful at El Médano, but for Playa del Amor, arrangements for a pickup are necessary.

Vendors along Boulevard Marina rent mopeds, ATVs, and—less often—motorcycles. These are hard to come by without going on a three-hour, US$60 tour of some sort, usually to the Old Lighthouse. If you can find them by the hour, typical prices are US$20 per hour, US$60 for a half day, US$80 for a full day.

EAST CAPE AND THE SIERRA DE LA LAGUNA

The promise of calm seas, steady winds, and abundant game fish lures many adventure-seekers away from the resorts of Los Cabos to the remote beaches and rocky points of the Cabo del Este, or East Cape. Indeed, the opportunities for deep-sea fishing, windsurfing, kayaking, and scuba diving here are among the best in the world. And when you've had your fill of white-sand beach and salty air, the Sierra de la Laguna beckons, with 7,000-foot peaks, freshwater springs, and waterfalls.

In September 2006, Hurricane John made landfall at Bahía de Los Frailes, causing severe wind and flood damage. Although roofs and roads took a beating, the towns in its path had mostly recovered by year-end.

PLANNING YOUR TIME

Towns along the East Cape are small and don't take much time to explore; you could easily take in a little of each in a four- to five-day trip. However, if you've come to the East Cape for a specific activity, such as fishing, diving, or windsurfing, you'll likely want to stay in one place for a while. If fishing is your top priority, then it makes sense to stay in Los Barriles or Buena Vista and add a day of diving. But if diving is the draw, best to head north or south to be closer to the dive sites. And if you plan to drive along the coastal road, as opposed to Highway 1, note that the unpaved 77-kilometer (48-mi) stretch between El Rincón and San José del Cabo can take up

HIGHLIGHTS

◖ **Bahía de Palmas:** Anglers, kiteboarders, and windsurfers all find paradise in the Sea of Cortez near Los Barriles and Buena Vista (page 108).

◖ **Cabo Pulmo:** Reef-building corals, crystal waters, and white-sand beaches attract divers, snorkelers, and kayakers to Bahía Pulmo and Playa La Sirenita (page 122).

◖ **Gorda Banks:** Six miles from shore, this pair of seamounts draws anglers from across the world for unrivaled marlin and wahoo fishing (page 129).

◖ **San Bartolo:** A pleasant central Cape Region settlement overlooking a lush arroyo makes a perfect stopover on the drive from La Paz to Los Barriles (page 132).

◖ **Cañon de la Zorra:** At the edge of the Sierra de la Laguna, near Santiago, a 30-foot waterfall plunges over smooth granite rock into a swimmable lagoon below (page 137).

LOOK FOR ◖ TO FIND RECOMMENDED SIGHTS, ACTIVITIES, DINING, AND LODGING.

EAST CAPE

to four hours, depending on your vehicle and its ability to handle washboard roads.

Santiago, at the foothills of the Sierra de la Laguna, is an easy day trip from San José del Cabo, or a good place to stretch your legs during the drive between San José and La Paz. Allow 3–5 nights if you want to explore the backcountry of the Sierra de la Laguna.

East Cape

Consisting of a succession of scenic arid-tropical coves and beaches along the Sea of Cortez, the East Cape extends from the northern end of Bahía de Palmas south to San José del Cabo, at the tip of the Cape. Below La Ribera, several tiny seaside communities remain off the grid—though mainstream power and phone service loom in the not-too-distant future. Coastal development is ongoing from Buena Vista to Cabo San Lucas, with land prices skyrocketing in recent years. Most of these developments resemble Southern California–style subdivisions, complete with signed gate, paved entrance, and concrete curbs. But few, if any, of the developments are fully built yet. So aside from the gates and model homes, many parts of the coast still look pretty secluded; the challenge is finding access to the sea.

There are a few remaining spots where the fishing and camping are free. The coastline north of El Cardonal as far as Bahía de los Muertos (also called Bahía de los Sueños, or Bay of Dreams, by optimistic developers) remains relatively untouched. But although beaches are officially public, access is increasingly limited.

◖ BAHÍA DE PALMAS

The gently curving shore of Bahía de Palmas, stretching 32 kilometers (20 mi) from Punta Pescadero south to Punta Arenas, began its commercial life in the 1960s as a fishing resort accessible only by yacht or private plane. Now that the Transpeninsular Highway swerves to within a couple miles of the bay, it has become a full-fledged fishing and windsurfing mecca.

In many places along the bay, anglers can reach the 100-fathom line less than a mile from shore, especially toward Punta Pescadero (Fisherman's Point) at the north end. (See *Fishing* in the *Essentials* chapter for details on common catches.) The world-famous "Tuna Canyon," about 6.5 kilometers (4 mi) directly south of Punta Pescadero, reaches depths of 50 fathoms and has a year-round population of sizable yellowfin tuna; rocks along Tuna Canyon's sub-

merged walls tend to cut the lines of all but the most skilled sportfishers. Guided fishing trips, arranged at any of the hotels along the bay, cost US$200–260 a day for a *panga,* US$200–325 a day aboard a fishing cruiser. Launch trailered or cartopped boats off sandy beaches or at the boat ramp just north of the Hotel Buena Vista Beach Resort (see *Buena Vista*).

Windsurfers and kiteboarders flock to Los Barriles November–April when sideshore winds—collectively called *El Norte* and aided by thermals from the Sierra de la Laguna—blow 18–30 knots for weeks at a time. The rest of the year, you'll have to settle for around 12–14 knots—not too shabby. During the high-wind season, inshore water temperatures average 22–24°C (72–75°F), with air temperatures in the 25–29°C (78–85°F) range. The same basic conditions can be found all the way north to El Cardonal. Several hotels on the bay rent equipment and provide basic instruction.

With such favorable recreational conditions, it's little wonder that legions of *norteamericano* anglers, boaters, and windsurfers are buying up property along the bay to build vacation and retirement homes. The Barriles–Buena Vista area is starting to look like a San Diego suburb. Several roads branch east off Mexico 1 between Km 110 and 105 to hotels and trailer parks—most owned by foreigners—scattered along the central section of Bahía de Palmas. Because zoning regulations are virtually nonexistent, construction varies from flimsy *palapa* extensions to impressive beach homes. Those seeking more solitude and less development can head north of Los Barriles to Punta Pescadero at the northern end of Bahía de Palmas, or farther north to El Cardonal.

PUNTA PESCADERO AND EL CARDONAL

There are now two ways to reach the northern end of Bahía de Palmas and the southern end of Bahía de los Muertos: A sandy, washboard

EAST CAPE

El Cardonal
Los Algodones
Punta Pescadero
Punta Pescadero

Sea of

To **SAN BARTOLO**,
El Triunfo, and La Paz

San Bartolo

BAHÍA DE PALMAS

Los Barriles

Buena Vista

Cortez

La Ribera

Punta Colorada

Surgidero

CAMINO COSTERO

Punta Arena

CAÑON DE LA ZORRA

El Rincón

La Abundancia

Santaiago

La Trinidad

Cabo Pulmo   Tropic of Cancer

TROPIC OF CANCER MONUMENT

CABO PULMO

Cabo Frailes

Miraflores

Los Frailes   *Bahía los Frailes*

Sierra la Trinidad

0   5 mi
0   5 km

San José

Punta Boca del Tule

Rancho la Vinorama

Santa Anita

GORDA BANKS

San Bernabé

La Fortuna

To Cabo San Lucas

San José del Cabo

PACIFIC OCEAN

© AVALON TRAVEL PUBLISHING, INC.

road heads north from Los Barriles—look for a turnoff from Mexico 1 signed Punta Pescadero. The road crosses a couple of arroyos that could be problematic in heavy rains. Alternatively, a relatively new, paved road continues along an inland route from Los Barriles directly to El Cardonal.

Punta Pescadero

At the extreme north end of Bahía de Palmas (13.6 km/8.5 mi north of Los Barriles), **(Hotel Punta Pescadero** (tel. 612/141-0101, U.S. tel. 800/426-2252, www.puntapescadero.com, US$150) is a small fishing resort on 125 palm-studded acres overlooking a sandy beach. The resort is popular with private pilots, since it has a paved landing strip (1,065 m/3,500 ft, Unicom 122.8, US$25 landing fee), and you'll likely hear regular fly-in guests trading stories at the bar. (As at other Baja airfields, plane theft is a very real concern here; throttle locks and prop chains are essential. Contact Baja Bush Pilots, www.bajabushpilots.com, for more information. Baja Bush Pilot

and AAA discounts available.) A small housing development is growing up next to the airstrip, so the Punta Pescadero's once-secluded nature is changing, but compared to the congestion of Los Barriles, it remains off the beaten track.

Each of 21 spacious rooms comes with a seaview, private veranda, air conditioning, satellite TV, and refrigerator; some have cathedral ceilings and fireplaces (quite nice on winter evenings), and all were renovated in 2005. King-size beds are made in crisp white linens with fluffy pillows and down comforters. During the windy season, ask for a room that faces southwest for a terrace that's sheltered from the El Norte gusts. A gracious staff speaks excellent English, and public areas include a restaurant with large picture windows, outdoor patio dining, dive shop with compressor, small pool, lighted tennis court, and rental equipment for scuba and free diving, boating, and fishing. Petroglyphs are visible in nearby rock caves that once served as Amerindian burial sites. The unpaved side road out to the actual point is not recommended for RVs or trailers.

© PAUL ITOI

view from Punta Pescadero

El Cardonal

A new, paved highway makes it much easier and faster to reach El Cardonal, located past Punta Pescadero and technically at the south end of Bahía de los Muertos (23 km/14 mi from Los Barriles). Inshore coral heads here provide worthwhile underwater scenery, while nearby prehistoric cave paintings reportedly depict marlin, turtles, and human figures.

The Canadian-owned **El Cardonal's Hide-A-Way** (tel./fax 612/141-0040, www.elcardonal.net) offers six sparsely furnished suites for US$72/482 per night/week as well as spaces for RV and tent camping. Each of the large beachfront studios comes with two full-size beds, a sofa, kitchen, and ceiling fan. Small campers and tent camping on large campsites costs US$10 per day; sites with electricity and water only are US$12; full hookups cost US$13. A dump station is available, as are fishing boats (*pangas* and a 32-foot cruiser), hot-water showers, a 24-hour restaurant, launderette, public telephone, horseshoe pit, badminton court, picnic tables, ice, and rental shop with equipment for fishing, windsurfing, diving, kayaking, and snorkeling.

Beyond El Cardonal, the road continues northward along the coast, then west across the Sierra El Carrizalito to San Juan de los Planes (see *Southeast of La Paz*).

LOS BARRILES

The defining image of day-to-day life in Los Barriles these days is that of early retirees happily speeding along dirt roads on ATVs, which they ride to the supermarket, the hardware store, the beach, and everywhere in between. No longer the sole domain of sports fishermen and windsurfers, the town has broadened its appeal with more guest accommodations, restaurants, and services—and a vibe that is friendly and relaxed.

A strip mall on the main access road from Mexico 1 is the defacto town center, with another row of commercial businesses along Calle 20 de Noviembre, heading north to Punta Pescadero. A row of gringo McMansions front the beach behind a stone retaining wall, and several

rolling dock at Los Barriles

EAST CAPE

LOS BARRILES

To Punta Pescadero

KARINA'S HAMBURGUESA

EL BARRILITO

20 DE NOVIEMBRE

Sea of Cortez

To Mexico 1

OTRA VEZ

EL ANCLA

EAST CAPE RV RESORT

OASIS COFFEE BAR

TAQUERÍA EL VIEJO

SUPERMERCADO FAYLA

THE OFFICE

CAMPESTRE TRINY

BAJA PAPA'S EAST CAPE SMOKEHOUSE

MARTIN VERDUGO'S RESORT

HOTEL PLAYA DEL SOL

LOS BARRILES HOTEL

To La Paz

1

TIO'S TIENDA

TIENDA POPULAR

20 DE NOVIEMBRE

CALEB'S CAFÉ

PALMES DE CORTEZ

SUPERMERCADO CHAPITO'S

ATM

Plaza del Pueblo

CALLE LOS BARRILES

EL TORO Y LA LUNA

SCALE NOT AVAILABLE

To Cabo San Lucas

© AVALON TRAVEL PUBLISHING, INC.

developments are in varying stages of completion in the hills above and to the north of town. However, those in search of the "real" Baja should not despair; Los Barriles retains an authentic *tortillería,* plus roosters that roam the streets, a cement factory where blocks are still made by hand, numerous taco stands, and countless other family-owned businesses. Local Mexicans know each other by their *sobrenombres* (nicknames), and the untamed backcountry is just minutes away.

Windsurfing

During the high-wind season, November–March, hotels in Los Barriles can arrange package deals that include windsurfing seminars, use of state-of-the-art equipment, air transportation, and accommodations. Keep in mind that although lessons are typically geared to your level, wind and surf conditions at Los Barriles are best enjoyed by experienced boardsailors rather than novices.

Fishing

Martin Verdugo's Resort and the Hotel Palmas de Cortez offer fishing packages; the concierge at the Hotel Palmas de Cortez can arrange fishing trips for guests and nonguests. In addition, **Congo's Awesome Sportfishing** (tel. 624/141-0231, U.S. tel. 208/726-1955, www.awesome-fishing.com), headquartered at the East Cape RV Resort and run by Jeronimo "Congo" Casio, operates two cruisers, a 30-foot island hopper (US$450 for 1–4 anglers) and a 32-foot Blackfin sportfisher (US$600 for 1–4 anglers). A popular day trip when the conditions aren't too windy is to travel north by boat to Bahía de los Muertos, fish on the way, and stop for lunch at the Giggling Marlin.

East Cape Tackle (Plaza del Pueblo, www.eastcapetackle.com, Mon.–Fri. 9 A.M.–5 P.M., Sat. 9 A.M.–2 P.M.) sells bait and tackle and also rents surf rods, pole spears, and snorkeling gear; plus, you can pay with plastic.

Guided Tours

ATVs are a popular mode of transportation in Los Barriles. Inquire about rentals and tours at **Amigos ATV Tours** on the main access

© PAUL ITOI

Vela Windsurf Resort

road (Calle Los Barriles near Plaza del Pueblo, tel. 624/141-0430, www.amigosactivities .com). Tours cost US$60–70 for a single rider, and US$75–90 for a double. Rental rates are US$20/100 per hour/day. Amigos also rents Wave-Runners and leads horseback rides and snorkeling tours. Other possibilities include hikes, bird-watching, mountain biking, and snorkeling. You can book any of these activities through the concierge at the Hotel Palmas de Cortez, whether or not you are staying at the resort.

Quadman, across from the Amerimed clinic, on the north side of Calle Los Barriles near the T intersection at 20 de Noviembre, also rents ATVs (US$50/4 hrs) and Rhinos (US$150/day and US$1,000 deposit). Rhinos seat four people and you must be 35 or older to drive. ATVs have racks for fishing poles, though riders must stay at least 60 feet from the high tide line to protect turtle nests.

Spa Services

Above the gym in the Hotel Palmas de Cortez, at the end of Calle Los Barriles, **Spa de Cortez** (tel. 624/141-0050 ext. 616, massagewithchristene@hotmail.com) offers Swedish, therapeutic, and sports massage, plus aromatherapy, body scrubs, facials, and waxing services. A one-hour massage is US$80, and a 90-minute treatment is US$115.

Shopping

Tío's Tienda (20 de Noviembre, approximately one block north of Calle Los Barriles, daily 7:30 A.M.–10 P.M.), next door to Tío Pablo's, carries everything from fishing tackle and souvenirs to apparel, gift wrap, and office supplies. It also stocks one of the most impressive collections of books about Baja California found on either side of the border. Many of the titles are self-published memoirs written by gringo transplants; others are field guides, travel books, and novels that take place in Mexico. **Baja Beach Company** (Plaza del Pueblo, Mon.–Fri. 9 A.M.–5 P.M., Sat. till 3 P.M., Sun. till 1 P.M.), in the strip mall near Buzzard Bay, has ceramics, textiles, gifts, and a few books and maps. Back on the highway, across from the main entrance to town, **El Toro y La Luna** (Mexico 1 Entrada a Los Barriles, tel. 624/141-0696, www.eltoroylaluna.net, daily 8 A.M.–5 P.M.) carries ceramic sinks, tiles, and other home furnishings.

Accommodations

Choices of accommodations in Los Barriles include two all-inclusive hotels, several hotels and RV parks, and private vacation homes available for rent either by the owner or through a property manager.

US$50-100: Martin Verdugo's Beach Resort (20 de Noviembre, approximately one block north of Calle Los Barriles, tel. 612/141-0054, www.verdugosbeachresort.com, US$60–70) has updated air-conditioning units in each of its 29 well-kept rooms, located in a two-story hotel next to the beach. Facilities include a small pool, boat launch, and restaurant. Kitchenettes are a plus here (though not in every room), but when the wind is blowing hard, the pool at the Los Barriles Hotel offers more shelter.

Off the beach but within walking distance to

restaurants and shops, the exceptionally clean **Los Barriles Hotel** (20 de Noviembre, approximately one block north of Calle Los Barriles, tel. 624/141-0024, www.losbarrileshotel.com, US$53) looks unremarkable from the outside, but feels something like a well-kept Swiss chalet inside. It has 20 spacious rooms set around a swimming pool, each with high ceilings, two firm but comfortable queen-size beds, large tiled showers, and remote-controlled air conditioning. Minimal but quality furnishings include rustic wooden dressers, tables, and headboards. A cedar hot tub is the latest addition to the pool area. Popular with families, this hotel is a great value for the price.

All-Inclusive: The Van Wormer family runs two all-inclusive resorts in Los Barriles: **Hotel Playa del Sol** (tel. 624/141-0050, U.S. tel. 877/777-8862, www.vanwormerresorts.com, US$120–130), on the beach off 20 de Noviembre north of Calle Los Barriles, has 26 air-conditioned rooms, an oceanfront pool, tennis and volleyball courts, an outdoor terrace restaurant, bar with satellite TV, rental gear (for fishing, kayaking, mountain biking, and windsurfing), charter boats for sportfishing (US$220–300 per day, not including fishing permits), and a full-service Vela windsurfing center. The hotel is closed in September.

On the beach at the end of Calle Los Barriles, about 300 meters south of Hotel Playa del Sol and just a half mile off the highway, the all-inclusive **Hotel Palmas de Cortez** (tel. 624/141-0050, U.S. tel. 877/777-8862, www.vanwormerresorts.com, US$190–220) offers 50 poolside, oceanfront, and garden-view rooms, plus several cabanas and condos that sleep up to six guests. Facilities include a restaurant and bar, ping pong tables, driving range, infinity pool, tennis and racquetball courts, an 868-meter (2,850-ft) landing strip (Unicom 122.8), windsurfing gear, charter boats (US$250–660, not including fishing permits), and equipment for fishing. The Van Wormer family also runs the Hotel Punta Colorada farther south along the East Cape.

Vela Windsurf Resort (U.S./Canada tel. 831/461-0820 or 800/223-5443, www.velawindsurf.com) is based at the Hotel Playa del

TO BUY OR NOT TO BUY: TIPS FOR PURCHASING REAL ESTATE IN BAJA

It started as a trickle, and by 2003 had progressed into a full-scale land rush. As Mexican law and real estate services make it easier for foreigners to own property, many Baja-bound Americans and Canadians are answering the call.

1. THE TERMS

Foreigners can only purchase coastal property (within 31 miles of the coast) in Mexico through a limited real estate trust (*fideicomisos*). Trusts are renewable every 50 years, with no limit on the number of renewals. In most cases, you will need a Mexican real estate attorney to complete a transaction.

2. FINANCING

You can finance the purchase through several lenders: Mortgages are now available for financing up to 70 percent of appraised property values with terms of 15-20 years. Lending rates run around 3 percent higher than in the United States, and closing costs for a mortgage deal are high.

Some sellers ask that the full purchase price be paid up front. Because a large number of gringos buy land in Mexico with cash, some Mexicans assume this is customary for all Americans and Canadians. Paying up front is not the typical procedure for Mexicans themselves, who usually make down payments and send in monthly time payments; mortgage terms similar to those found in Canada and the United States are available in Mexico, though they are difficult for nonresidents to obtain. Even if you have the cash, don't hand over more than half the full amount until you have the *fideicomiso* papers in hand.

3. TITLE INSURANCE

You can purchase title insurance, previously unavailable, from several providers.

4. PRICES

Prospective buyers can find small plots in subdivisions near the beach from US$20,000. Completed small vacation homes range US$200,000-500,000, and full-scale mansions are in the millions.

5. REAL ESTATE AGENTS

Choose a reputable agent: A lot of people get burned in Mexican real estate deals. It's best to deal through an established, reputable agent. Mexican tourist offices in Baja often carry information on residential property. Talk to current owner-residents about which real estate companies have the best and worst reputations.

6. CONDOS AND SUBDIVISIONS

In condominium and subdivision situations, a master *fideicomiso* is created. Only as the units are sold does the trust pass to the buyer, and then only if proper procedures are followed – which they often aren't. If you buy a condo or subdivision unit, you should receive a document naming you as beneficiary, thus transferring property from the master trust holder to the buyer. If you don't, you'll have to get the master trust holder's signature before you can sell or otherwise transfer the property to someone else.

7. DO YOUR HOMEWORK

Mexico doesn't require salespeople or brokers to obtain any sort of real estate license. Investigate agents and properties thoroughly before signing on the dotted line.

Sol. Seven-night packages start at US$945–1,280 and include all windsurfing equipment, instruction at every level except novice, accommodations, meals, tax, and service. Guests also have free use of kayaks and mountain bikes; the staff provides good maps and descriptions of nearby kayaking and biking routes. Snorkeling, tennis, and volleyball are also available through the center at no cost to package guests. Scuba diving, kiteboarding lessons, and horseback riding can be arranged at additional cost.

Vela opens just before Thanksgiving and closes the first week in March. Outside the center's peak period (Dec. 20–Jan. 20), nonpackage guests at Hotel Playa del Sol may be able to rent windsurfing boards, kayaks, and bikes.

Camping and RV Parks

A trendsetter among parks in Mexico, the **East Cape RV Resort** (tel. 624/141-0231, U.S. tel. 208/726-1955, www.eastcaperv.com) designed its property with big rigs in mind. Located a short walk from the beach, at the intersection of 20 de Noviembre and Ocean Drive (unmarked at last check), the resort has 51 spaces with full hookups for US$25/150/525 per night/week/month. Another dozen spaces with limited hookups are located in an adjacent palm garden that sometimes floods during the rainy season (US$18/105 per night/week). Bathrooms are modern and clean, and the wall around a new pool and hot tub got its first coat of paint in late 2006. High-speed wireless Internet costs US$4/15/40 per day/week/month. Washing machines and dryers require U.S. quarters. Owner Theresa Comber is the closest thing Los Barriles has to a chamber of commerce. Ask her for advice on day trips and activities in the area.

North of Hotel Playa del Sol, **Martin Verdugo's Beach Resort** (20 de Noviembre, approximately one block north of Calle Los Barriles, tel. 612/141-0054, www.verdugosbeachresort.com) caters to families and retirees with lower rates and a beachfront location. This well-run and well-maintained park has dump stations, flush toilets, showers, boat ramps, laundry facilities, and full hookups for US$15 for two people, plus US$3.50 for each additional person. Weekly/monthly rates are US$100/345 (credit cards are accepted). Tent sites cost US$12 per night. Kids play Marco Polo in the beachfront swimming pool, and locals gather for breakfast in the third-story restaurant. Fishing rates are US$380 for a 28-foot cruiser and US$240 for a 23-foot super-*panga*. Inquire about fishing packages that include accommodations and meals, and be sure to make reservations well in advance during the peak windsurfing season, January–March.

Another big-rig-friendly park, **Playa Norte RV Haven** (harnecker@gmail.com, US$18–22), on the beach off Calle 20 de Noviembre, past the wide arroyo, has upgraded its infrastructure in recent years to include hot showers, electricity, a dump station, and Wi-Fi. Caravans are welcome.

Free primitive camping is available in the area north of these parks, usually referred to by gringos as Playa Norte.

Vacation Rentals

Many American owners rent their Baja vacation homes by the night, week, or month. **East Cape Property Management and Vacation Rentals** (Plaza del Pueblo, tel./fax 612/141-0381, www.abajavacation.com, Mon.–Sat. 10 A.M.–2 P.M.) handles rental properties in Los Barriles, Buena Vista, Punta Pescadero, Rancho Leonero, and Los Frailes. **Sunset Rentals** (20 de Noviembre, just past the Hotel Los Barriles, tel. 624/141-0416) offers short- and long-term rentals in studios as well as one- and two-bedroom condos. All have kitchens, garages, balconies, wireless Internet, and air conditioning. **Vacation Rentals by Owner** (www.vrbo.com) also has a few dozen East Cape listings. Rates range US$75–195 a night for one-bedroom homes.

Food

The number and variety of restaurants in Los Barriles is multiplying by the day. Today's menus feature grilled fish and meats, traditional Mexican *platos*, pasta, sushi, pizza, sandwiches, soups, espresso, and, of course, mouthwatering tacos.

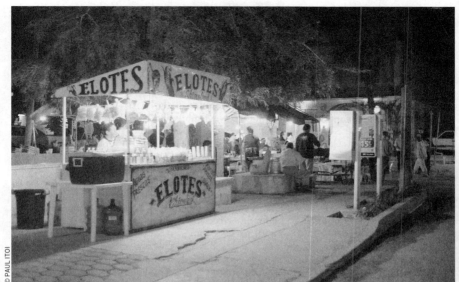

© PAUL ITOI

fiesta in Los Barriles

Restaurants: In a strip mall just off Mexico 1 on the access road to Los Barriles, **Buzzard Bay Sports Cantina** (Plaza del Pueblo 21, daily for lunch and dinner, mains US$7–15) offers a menu of burgers, sandwiches, appetizers, and Mexican food, and has both outdoor and indoor seating. Next door, **Baja Pizza Kitchen** (Plaza del Pueblo 19, tel. 624/150-8372, Mon.–Fri. 4 P.M.–8 P.M.) makes pizzas during limited hours. A small pizza costs US$7 and a large is US$15.

Tío Pablo's (20 de Noviembre, tel. 612/142-1214, daily 11 A.M.–10 P.M., mains US$7–20), on the main north–south road through Los Barriles, is a large, smartly designed *palapa*-style structure with ceiling fans, a well-stocked bar, sports TV, and a menu of salads, sandwiches, and burgers. In the same complex, Tío's takeout window offers pizzas to go.

Martin Verdugo's Restaurant (20 de Noviembre, approximately one block north of Calle Los Barriles, tel. 612/141-0054, daily 6 A.M.–noon, mains US$4–7) is a third-story restaurant that serves Americanized breakfast fare. *Chilaquiles* arrive smothered in melted cheese but without the signature *queso fresco* on top. Omelets come with seasoned hash browns and a choice of toast or tortillas. Seaviews and air conditioning are the main draw. Service is friendly, though slow even by Mexican standards.

Run by the same owners as the once-famous Restaurant Balandra in Cabo San Lucas, which closed more than 30 years ago, **◖ Campestre Triny** (20 de Noviembre across from the East Cape Smokehouse, daily noon–10 P.M., mains US$9–20) offers freshly prepared traditional Mexican fare, including specialties of *huachinango frito* (whole fried red snapper), paella, and imperial shrimp. High-quality ingredients and a somewhat upscale presentation are reflected in menu prices. This is also one of the few places in town that serves Negro Modelo beer. Dine family-style under a canopy of trees behind the main house or at your own table on the porch. Check out the collection of arrowheads hanging on the wall while you're there.

About a quarter mile farther on 20 de Noviembre, **Otra Vez** (20 de Noviembre, tel. 612/141-0249, Mon.–Sat. 5–10 P.M., mains US$8–20) occupies a long, low, whitewashed building with a colorful arch out front. Popular with local gringos, the menu includes freshly prepared parrot fish, burgers, steaks, fresh salads, and pasta dishes.

Another favorite among locals for dinner, **❰ El Barrilito** (20 de Noviembre, daily for lunch and dinner, mains US$6–15) serves large portions of fresh seafood under a large *palapa* at the bend in the road heading out toward Pescadero. Ceviche is a standout. In a smaller *palapa* next door, the same owners have opened **Kenichi Sushi & Bar,** with all-you-can-eat specials for US$20. More sushi can be found at **Yako's Sushi-Bar** (tel. 624/141-0050) in the Hotel Palmas de Cortez, on the beach at the end of Calle Los Barriles.

Antojitos and Fast Food: During American football season, you're likely to find a number of tourists watching the game at **Taquería El Viejo** (20 de Noviembre near El Oasis Coffee and Baja Land Deals, daily for breakfast and lunch). The restaurant has about a dozen shaded outdoor tables where you can enjoy a breakfast of eggs, omelets, or *chilaquiles* for US$5–6, tacos for US$1–2, and burgers for US$5. Lunch specials vary daily (US$7–8). **Taquería Los Barriles,** at the junction with the beach road, is packed all afternoon and evening for the great seafood and carne asada tacos; the breakfasts are cheap. The enormous super burros at **La Palma Taquería** are a great value, too. Look for the sign on a surfboard just off 20 de Noviembre near Tio Pablo's.

Across the street from El Barrilito, on the inside of the bend that turns to Pescadero, **Karina's Hamburguesas** serves carne asada, *papas rellenos,* and other quick meals from a restaurant cart.

Cafés: Oasis Coffee Bar (20 de Noviembre, past The Office) serves a US$2-cup of coffee, as well as hot and cold espresso drinks and smoothies for US$2–4. It shares the space with Baja Land Deals, so you can browse pictures of real estate for sale while you wait for your drink. High-speed wireless Internet service is free, and there are a few shaded tables outside.

Groceries: Closer to Los Barriles on the main Los Barriles access road, between Plaza del Pueblo and 20 de Noviembre, **Supermercado Chapito's** is the largest grocery store in town, with a pharmacy. A new market, **Tienda Popular** (daily 7 A.M.–10 P.M.), west of 20 de Noviembre, about one block north of the intersection with Calle Los Barriles, recently opened just up the hill from Tio Pablo's. **Supermercado Fayla,** on 20 de Noviembre just past the Hotel Los Barriles, is more gringo-oriented, stocking basic food supplies as well as souvenirs, videos, and U.S. newspapers on Fridays. During the peak winter season, a bakery truck from La Paz visits town on Fridays and a fresh produce vendor comes on Saturday mornings.

Buy frozen or smoked fish or have yours prepared and vacuum-packed at the **Baja Papa's East Cape Smokehouse** (20 de Noviembre at Calle Don Pepe, tel. 624/141-0294, www.bajapapas.com, daily 9 A.M.–6 P.M.). Allow 48 hours turnaround time.

Information and Services

East Cape RV Resort owner Theresa Comber is the closest thing Los Barriles has to a chamber of commerce. Stop by to ask for advice on restaurants, day trips, and activities in the area.

La Plaza del Pueblo shopping center, near the highway on the main access road, has clean public restrooms and public telephones. The post office recently closed. Near the end of the main access road to Los Barriles, an **Amerimed Clinic** is open Monday–Saturday 8 A.M.–2 P.M. and 4 P.M.–6 P.M. for medical needs. Call 624/141-0797 for emergencies.

If you don't already have a car, **National Car Rental** maintains an outpost at the Oasis Coffee Bar, but in most cases an ATV would be a better vehicle for getting around town. The closest PEMEX is just south of town on Mexico 1. **El Lavadero/The Washroom** (20 de Noviembre near the Los Barriles Hotel, Mon.–Sat., hours vary), is the only place to have your clothes washed, unless you're staying at one of the full-service RV parks.

For high speed Internet, head to **The Office** (20 de Noviembre across from Sunset Rentals, tel. 624/141 0142, fax 624/141 0259, theoffice@prodigy.net, Mon.–Sat. 8 A.M.–8 P.M., Sun. 10 A.M.–6 P.M.). Work on one of 10 Samsung desktop machines, or bring your laptop, for US$0.10/minute. Fax, phone, and copy services are also available. Better yet, enjoy free wireless Internet while you sip a latte at Oasis Coffee Bar, just a few doors away. East Cape RV Park, Sunset Rentals, and many private home owners have wireless Internet, too.

Several businesses in town accept credit cards, but you'll still need cash (dollars or pesos) for tacos and the like. **Baja Money Exchange** (Mon.–Sat. 9 A.M.–5 P.M.), near the Oasis Coffee Bar, can trade your dollars or travelers checks for pesos. At last check, the ATM that had been located near The Office had been removed. The only ATM in town is next to the Amerimed clinic on Calle Los Barriles.

BUENA VISTA

Smaller and quieter than its neighbor to the north, Buena Vista attracts a similar crowd of families, fishermen, and retirees—many of them reportedly former law enforcement professionals from Southern California. It won't be long before the two towns are connected by the homes and businesses that are spreading out between them. Southbound travelers may have difficulty finding the unsigned entrance to town: Look for the turn on a curve between Km 104 and 105.

Scuba Diving

Buena Vista has a reputable dive center located on the beach, next to the Vista del Mar trailer park. **Vista Sea Sport** (tel. 624/141-0031, www.vistaseasport.com) is run by two PADI-certified dive instructors from Southern California who own three super-*pangas* and one cruiser. However, boat rides to the major sites—Cabo Pulmo, Los Frailes, Punta Pescadero, and Isla Cerralvo—are long and rates are higher (US$110–120 for a two-tank dive) than at shops based in La Paz or Cabo Pulmo. Scuba gear rental is US$20 with a tour. Airfills

cost US$8; snorkeling gear US$10. Look for a giant earthmover that serves as the boat launch. To find the shop from Mexico 1, take the turn across from the Calafia Hotel, then turn left at the T in the dirt road and follow the signs.

Ecotours

Ángel Ortiz and Paul Ortiz Meza offer guided ecotours and adventure tours through **Ángel Eco Tours** (tel. 624/141-0838). Options include snorkeling and kayaking in the Cabo Pulmo Marine Sanctuary, whale-watching in Magdalena Bay on the Pacific coast, tours of ceremonial rock-art sites near Santiago, and visits to an inland oasis, canyon, and rancho, also near Santiago. Tours last 7–8 hours and include refreshments.

Accommodations

US$100-150: Old-timer **Rancho Buena Vista** (Km 106, U.S. tel. 805/928-1719 or 800/258-8200, www.ranchobuenavista.com, US$105 pp) features a nice restaurant and bar facing the sea, as well as a pool, whirlpool, tennis and volleyball courts, a weight room, fitness programs, fishing tackle (including fly-fishing equipment), cruisers, windsurfing gear, a boat ramp, boat storage, unpaved airstrip, and 57 air-conditioned cottages. All meals are included. It's easy to miss the entrance to Rancho Buena Vista if you're coming south on Mexico 1. The left turn comes just after a small mountain pass that obscures it; watch for a blue highway sign on the right that says Hotel.

US$150-250: Popular with families and retirees, the **Hotel Buena Vista Beach Resort** (Km 105, tel. 624/141-0033 or 800/623-0710, U.S. tel. 619/429-8079 or 800/752-3555, www.hotelbuenavista.com, US$150–180) offers 60 air-conditioned Mediterranean-style bungalows with private baths, sitting areas, and private terraces. Buildings are arranged close together against a hillside, and the resort feels somewhat dated, but the location just across from the beach is ideal. Facilities include a garden, two pools, a swim-up bar, cocktail lounge, beachfront dining, water aerobics center, tennis courts, two whirlpool tub–powered hot springs mineral spas, spa services, kayaks, horseback riding, and equipment for diving, snorkeling, fishing, and hunting. The resort organizes various outings, such as tours of cave paintings and waterfalls, as well as bird-watching, hiking, and snorkeling tours. All meals, snacks, nonalcoholic beverages, beer, and domestic well drinks are included. Lower European plan rates are available. Fishing and diving packages are also offered.

The sportfishing fleet at the resort features a 23-foot *panga* (US$240), a 28-foot cruiser (US$350), a luxury 29-foot twin-engine cruiser (US$410), and a 31-foot twin-engine cruiser (US$450). Tax, tips, tackle, bait and fishing licenses are extra.

Round-trip or one-way transportation from the airport can be arranged by the U.S. reservations office.

Food

Restaurant Calafia (mains US$7–17), on Mexico 1 near the Buena Vista police station, offers good shrimp tacos, chiles rellenos, and tables with views of Bahía de Palmas. It's usually open for lunch and early dinner only. Popular **Flag's Sports Bar,** on Mexico 1 opposite the Pemex, isn't really a sports bar, but it has lots of libation options. A **Tienda Popular** minimarket is located north of the main entrance to town.

LA RIBERA

To reach the Coastal Road from the north, take the paved road signed La Ribera east at Km 93 off Mexico 1 (at Las Cuevas), and watch for potholes. This 20-kilometer (12-mi) road passes through La Ribera (La Rivera), a small town of around 2,000 with a Pemex station, church, *tortillería,* cemetery, banana and mango trees, trailer shelters, and simple homes lined up along a network of sandy roads overlooking a sand beach. Worn *palapa* shelters at the south end of the beach can be used for camping when not occupied by fishermen. Several *mercaditos* in the village offer local produce and other supplies for long-term visitors.

A sandy road just south of La Ribera Trailer Park leads 0.6 kilometer (0.4 mi) to a casuarina-shaded beach where you can camp for free. A point at the north end of the small bay (also accessible from La Ribera) creates a surf break during heavy southwest swells.

Food

A new restaurant has opened at the Y in La Ribera, where the road turns south to Cabo Pulmo (9 A.M.–10 P.M., breakfast mains US$6–8, dinner mains US$9–25). It serves steak, lobster, fish, shrimp, Caesar salad, and chiles rellenos. **Mercado Rey,** on El Camino Rural Costero, just past the Y and across from the Pemex, carries tools, propane tank parts, chains, and beer, plus basic groceries and a good selection of American liquors.

Shopping

A branch of the Los Barriles home decor store, **El Toro y La Luna** (tel. 624/141-0698, www. eltoroylaluna.net, daily 8 A.M.–5 P.M.), on Avenida Santa Maria at the turn for the road to Cabo Pulmo, has ceramic sinks, tiles, and other home furnishings at the Y.

Information and Services

A medical clinic and pharmacy are collocated next to the athletic fields on the way into town, on the south side of Avenida Santa Maria past the turnoff to Cabo Pulmo. An Internet café on Calle 29 de Enero is open daily 8 A.M.–3 P.M. and 5–8 P.M. (tel. 624/130-0302).

AROUND PUNTA COLORADA

Punta Colorada lies at the south end of the bay, 16 kilometers (10 mi) east of Mexico 1 via the La Ribera road.

Accommodations

US$100-150: Perched on a seaside cliff near La Ribera, the █ **Hotel Punta Colorada** (tel. 612/121-0044, U.S. tel. 818/222-5066 or 800/368-4334, www.vanwormerresorts.com, US$110–160) is a longtime favorite of roosterfish fanatics; the roosterfishing off nearby Punta Arena is usually the best in Baja, as evidenced

PUNTA COLORADA TO LOS FRAILES

Laguna Salina

PACIFIC OCEAN

La Ribera

Salinas Punta Colorada

La Trinidad

Punta Colorada
Punta Colorada

Matanza

Punta Arena

Tropic of Cancer

Miramar

Parque Marina Nacional Cabo Pulmo

Los Mangles

Cabo Pulmo

CABO PULMO

La Boquita

San Miguel

Los Frailes

Cabo Frailes

0   2 mi

0   2 km

© AVALON TRAVEL PUBLISHING, INC.

EAST CAPE

cruisers. The hotel is closed September and the first week of October.

US$150-250 (All-Inclusive): South of Buena Vista lies the secluded **Rancho Leonero Resort** (tel./fax 612/141-0216, U.S. tel. 760/634-4336 or 800/646-2252, www. rancholeonero.com, US$150–250). Perched on a low promontory overlooking the sea, this comfortable, quiet, and rustic resort features 30 spacious, rock-walled, *palapa*-roofed rooms, suites, and bungalows. All have seaviews, but none contains a phone or TV. As at Punta Pescadero, a small development now adjoins the resort, with new homes built on land sold by the owner of Rancho Leonero.

The expansive grounds hold a restaurant and bar, pool, hot tub, fully equipped dive center, sportfishing fleet, and 20 miles of running/ hiking trails. A rock reef in front of the hotel is suitable for snorkeling. Three meals a day are included in the room price. Fishing charters start at US$250 for a super-*panga*, US$385 and up for cruisers. Snorkeling equipment costs US$10 per day. Horseback riding, kayaking, scuba, and hiking trips can also be arranged. US$25 discount August–September and November–March, excluding December 20–January 1.

Surfing

One of Baja's least-known surfing spots—simply because no one expects surf this far up the Sea of Cortez—can be found at **Punta Arena,** just below Punta Colorada. A left point break can crop up here anytime during the March–November southwest swell, but the peak surf usually comes in late summer or early fall—*chubasco* season.

EL CAMINO RURAL COSTERO

La Ribera is the northern end of the notorious El Camino Rural Costero (The Rural Coastal Road), which runs all the way to Pueblo La Playa. About halfway along the route stands a brass plaque commemorating the road's May 1984 grading. For first-time drivers who have braved washouts and sandpits to read it, the sign never fails to elicit a few chuckles.

In general, driving conditions along the

by the photo of a record-setting 93-pound catch on the wall in the bar. The hotel offers 40 large rooms, all but eight of which have ocean views. About half of its rooms were renovated in 2006. Three meals daily are included in the price, and the restaurant serves a buffet dinner open to the public on Wednesdays and Saturdays. Call by noon for reservations. The hotel also has an indoor/outdoor bar and its own airstrip (1,000 m/3,300 ft, Unicom 122.8). All tap water at the resort comes from a mountain well. Guided fishing trips are available starting at US$220 a day for a super-*panga* and US$330–385 for

EAST CAPE

DRIVING WASHBOARD ROADS

Whether you rent a car or drive your own, exploring Baja's back roads takes a toll on vehicle and driver alike. Follow the tips below to enjoy a safe and smooth ride:

Less is more: Lower the air pressure in your tires for driving on softer sand.

Stay to the side: You can often find a smoother track on the far left or right side of the road.

Pick up the pace: Faster speeds often smooth out the bumps, but be sure to slow down when approaching turns to avoid skids and unexpected obstacles.

Know your clearance: Watch for large rocks and deep potholes that can wreak havoc on low-hanging oil pans.

Travel with tools: At a minimum, a spare tire and jack are essential. Old carpet remnants work well for getting traction on soft sand.

Ask around: For less traveled routes, inquire when the road was last graded and what kind of vehicle you need to pass through safely.

Coastal Road are suitable for passenger cars of average road clearance; even smaller RVs sometimes manage to make it all the way. Sand can be a problem in places, and shoulders are invariably soft. Weather plays an important role in day-to-day conditions; after late-summer or early-fall storms, parts of the Coastal Road can be impassable. Make inquiries before embarking on the trip and be prepared to turn back if necessary.

Eventually the Coastal Road is supposed to be paved all the way to San José del Cabo. In early 2006, local government officials staged a press event to commemorate the beginning of work on a five-mile-long paved road to Los Frailes; however, the earthmover that was to be the star of the show reportedly got a flat tire and the event was canceled. The machine stayed by the side of the road for weeks after, but no dirt was ever moved. Plans to pave the road have been repeatedly delayed in recent years, to the relief of local residents, who fear the arrival of mainstream power and phone service will change their towns forever.

In spite of the rough access, certain areas along the route—including Cabo Pulmo and Los Frailes—are filling up with small-scale housing and resort developments. Open space for beach camping is still available, but access is becoming increasingly limited as new developments lay cinder blocks and finish their first few homes. Several ranchos along the central and southern sections still raise cattle, goats,

pigs, and sheep—mostly without fencing. If you substitute fiberglass *pangas* for dugout canoes, the ranchos today appear much as they must have in 1941, when John Steinbeck described Cabo Pulmo:

On the shore behind the white beach was one of those lonely little rancherías we came to know later. Usually a palm or two are planted nearby, and by these trees sticking up out of the brush one can locate the houses. There is usually a small corral, a burro or two, a few pigs, and some scrawny chickens. The cattle range wide for food. A dugout canoe lies on the beach, for a good part of the food comes from the sea. Rarely do you see a light from the sea, for the people go to sleep at dusk and awaken with the first light.

◖ CABO PULMO

Heading south from La Ribera, the Coastal Road is paved for a short way, then turns to dirt. The unpaved part of the 26.5-kilometer (16.5-mi) stretch between La Ribera and Cabo Pulmo is usually in fair condition.

Bahía Pulmo

Noted for its reef-building corals, this shallow bay is bounded by Cabo Pulmo to the north and Corral de los Frailes to the south. Coarse white-sand beaches ring the bay, most of them readily accessible from the parallel Coastal Road. Baja California pearling once reached its southernmost point here.

Playa La Sirenita

A pristine, fine-sand beach known as Playa La Sirenita (Mermaid Beach, named for a rock formation whose silhouette resembles the head and bust of a female figure) lies against the north escarpment of Corral de los Frailes at the bay's southeastern tip. Best reached by small boat or kayak from the village of Cabo Pulmo, the beach's crystal waters are protected from southerly winds in the summer and early fall; rock reefs close by offer snorkeling opportunities. There's just enough room above the tideline for undisturbed overnight camping.

Farther south around the wide headland of **Corral de los Frailes** (named for a rock formation with a resemblance to hooded friars), a colony of sea lions lives among geometric boulder piles.

Take the first sand road north of Corral de los Frailes that isn't barbwired to reach **Playa Corral de los Frailes,** a secluded beach sheltered from most onshore winds.

Pulmo Reef System

The bay's reef system, the northernmost of only three coastal reefs in North America and the only coral reef in the Sea of Cortez, is rich with tropical marine life and hence a favorite snorkeling and scuba diving destination. Its accessibility from shore adds to the attraction. You can watch a wide variety of tropical fish, eels, and rays—as well as the occasional nurse shark—in waist-deep water.

The reef consists of eight hard coral fingers scattered throughout the bay, from Cabo Pulmo at the north end to Corral de los Frailes at the southern end. Four finger reefs extend from the center of the bayshore: two solid lengths called **Las Navajas;** an unnamed broken length used by (harmless) nurse sharks as a breeding zone; and a solid, kilometer-long finger known as **El Cantil.** Water depths along these four reefs range 4.5–10.5 meters (15–35 ft).

Farther offshore (up to 3.2 km/2 mi), running

a panga bound for the reef at Cabo Pulmo

ENDANGERED SEA

In 2005, the United Nations Educational, Scientific and Cultural Organization (UNESCO) added the Gulf of California to its World Heritage List of close to 200 areas of outstanding natural and cultural value around the globe. Citing its striking beauty and critical role as a natural laboratory for the study of thousands of marine species, UNESCO identified a site of 244 islands, islets, and coastal areas within the Gulf of California, or Sea of Cortez. Also important was the fact that all major oceanographic processes occurring in the planet's oceans take place in this body of water.

Environmental conservation groups heralded the designation as a critical step forward in curbing severe damage wrought by commercial fishing and bottom trawling, which destroy eelgrass beds and shellfish that sustain many other species in the sea. But World Heritage status is only the beginning of a long and costly battle. Two international organizations, Conservation International (www.conservation.org) and the World Wildlife Fund (www.worldwildlife.org) are funding projects in the area in an effort to protect the fragile ecosystem for generations to come. Meanwhile, the Mexican government is stepping up its commitment to fund marine parks and conservation activities throughout the region.

more or less parallel to the bayshore, are the reef fingers of **La Esperanza** (at depths of around 18 m/60 ft), **El Bajo de los Meros** (15 m/50 ft), and **Outer Pulmo** (30 m/100 ft).

Soft coral heads can be found at **El Islote**—a rock island near La Esperanza—and at **Las Casitas,** rock caves just off Corral de los Frailes at a depth of 13 meters (45 ft).

The reef system here is very delicate; reef corals can't tolerate temperatures lower than 21°C (70°F) and must have clear water since debris settling on their disks and tentacles will kill them. The reefs are important breeding grounds for several marine species, so if the corals die it will negatively affect all manner of fish in the area.

The Mexican government established the Cabo Pulmo National Marine Park in 1995, and no fishing or anchoring at the reef (or anywhere in Bahía Pulmo) is permitted. Shore development remains among the reef's biggest ecological challenges, because the corals rely on unpolluted and unimpeded runoff. If resorts or housing developments further expand along Bahía Pulmo, the reef will probably perish.

Diving

Optimum visibility in the waters around Pulmo Reef occurs March–October. Aside from the natural reefs cited above, directly off Cabo Pulmo (the cape itself) lies the wreck of *El Vencedor,* a tuna boat that sank in 1981 and now forms an excellent artificial reef. Pilot whales are commonly seen in the vicinity in April, large jack crevalles August–September.

Three dive centers run guided tours from Cabo Pulmo. All are located within 100 yards of each other. In the village center, the **Cabo Pulmo Beach Resort** (El Camino Rural Costero, tel. 612/141-0244, U.S. tel./fax 208/726-1306 or 888/997-8566, www.cabopulmo.com) operates a PADI-certified dive center with two boats, well-maintained gear, and experienced, professional dive guides. A two-tank boat dive costs US$75 and an equipment rental package is US$20 with a boat dive. You do not need to be a guest of the resort to snorkel or dive with the shop. On weekends, the dive center often hosts groups of day-trippers from resorts in the Cabo San Lucas area. These dives tend to be more crowded with novice divers. Plan to dive midweek if you want to do more advanced dives. Snorkeling tours are US$35 with gear, and single kayaks rent for US$35 a day. Experienced divers can rent tanks and a kayak for self-guided beach diving.

Pepe's Dive Center (tel. 877/733-2252, www.cabopulmo.com.mx), across from El Ca-

© PAUL ITOI

dive center at Cabo Pulmo Beach Resort

ballero restaurant, also offers a complete diving service, as does **Cabo Pulmo Divers** (www.cabopulmodivers.com)—located in the Castro family complex, next to the Miscellanea Market. Rates at both are comparable to those at the Cabo Pulmo Beach Resort, although readers have reported higher rates (up to US$72 pp) for tours of only one or two people. It pays to shop around.

The dive operators are also happy to arrange boat trips for nondivers interested in touring the bay, Playa La Sirenita, and the Corral de los Frailes seal colony.

Fishing

Neither sport nor commercial fishing is permitted in Bahía Pulmo, but inshore north of Cabo Pulmo, anglers can find giant sea bass, snapper, *pargo,* ladyfish, and roosterfish. Offshore are grouper, sierra, skipjack, dorado, marlin, and tuna. The tuna are found closer in at Bahía de los Frailes farther south, but anywhere along this coastal stretch the heavyweights can come within three kilometers (2 mi) of the shoreline.

Tuna season begins most years in late March or early April, and peak months for most varieties are May–June and October–November. Kiki and Paco Castro offer half-day (US$160) and full-day (US$260) tours in their super-*pangas,* including gear and bait. Inquire at the dive center behind the El Palapa beachfront restaurant.

Accommodations and Camping

As new owners build and acquire properties in Cabo Pulmo, the number of rental options has increased. Expect most high-season rates to climb even higher during the peak season around Christmas and New Year's.

US$50-100: In the midst of Cabo Pulmo village, **Cabo Pulmo Beach Resort** (El Camino Rural Costero, tel. 612/141-0244, U.S. tel./fax 208/726-1306 or 888/997-8566, www.cabopulmo.com, US$60–125) offers 25 *palapa*-roofed, solar-powered units by the day, week, or month. The bay is just a short walk from each. The choice of accommodations here includes a beach house that accommodates 4–6 people, *casitas,* and basic and deluxe bungalows;

all come with kitchenettes or full kitchens, plus bed and bath linens. Some feature patios, roof decks, and barbecue grills. Marly Rickers and Clint Fultz, a friendly young American couple with longtime ties to Cabo Pulmo, also manage a handful of rentals in the same group of *casitas* for US$65–125 per night. Contact **Cabo Pulmo Casas** (tel. 877/754-5251, www.cabo-pulmocasas.com).

Across the dirt road from the Cabo Pulmo Beach Resort, Kent Ryan rents **Baja Bungalows** (www.bajabungalows.com, US$45–125), with a main house that has spectacular views from the upstairs master suite, plus a two-bedroom unit on the lower level and an additional bungalow and *palapa* suite with shared bath and full outdoor kitchen. The beach is a three-minute walk away. **Nancy's Restaurant and Bar,** adjacent to the Cabo Pulmo Beach Resort, also has a few basic rooms for US$40–50.

Over US$250: Just north of Cabo Pulmo Beach Resort stands **Villa and Casa del Mar** (U.S. tel. 208/726-4455 or 888/225-2786, www.bajaparadise.com, US$170–375), a large, deluxe beachfront house with a full kitchen, spacious living areas, shaded terraces, and a rooftop sundeck. All rooms come with fan and air conditioning, which must be run sparingly since the house is solar-powered. The main part of the house rents for US$375 a night or US$2,500 per week for two guests in peak season. The smaller attached studio apartment costs US$170/night or US$1,150/week. A newer, self-contained cottage called El Nido goes for US$215/night or US$1,400/week and includes a fully equipped kitchen.

Camping: At the other extreme, you can camp for free on the beach at the south end of Bahía Pulmo, or for US$2 per night at the north end.

Food

Adjacent to the Cabo Pulmo Beach Resort, **Nancy's Restaurant and Bar** (Thurs.–Tues., mains US$16–20) began as a trailer and two tables 12 years ago, and has evolved into a charming venue with a rustic collection of tables beneath a *palapa* shelter. Fresh guacamole

sushi for supper

© PAUL ITOI

with homemade chips is a delightful way to begin the meal. Lobster enchiladas, crab cakes, and fresh catch (yours or Nancy's) are accompanied by crisp side salads. Popular with divers during the dive season, the simple restaurant has an especially cozy ambience at night when illuminated by hurricane lamps. Nancy also offers occasional cooking classes. The **Coral Reef Bar and Grill** (Wed.–Mon., mains US$10–20) is a cozy restaurant with a TV and bar located above the blue building that serves as the resort dive center. Enjoy a cocktail at sunset and then choose from a limited menu of the day.

At last check, ◖ **Restaurant El Caballero** (Mon.–Sat. 7 A.M.–10 P.M., Sun. 7 A.M.– 12 P.M., mains US$6–14), on the opposite side of the road near Nancy's, had the best menu in town, thanks to a professional chef who came from San José del Cabo initially to work at the Coral Reef and then moved next door. Caballero also has a bar and small assortment of groceries, drinks, and snacks for sale. **El Palapa** (formerly called Restaurant Lupita, Tues.–Sun., lunch plates US$4–10, dinner mains US$8–18) offers casual beachfront dining from a menu of fish tacos, carne asada, and other traditional fare. Cabo Pulmo's restaurants are notoriously understaffed even during peak season. It can take up to 45 minutes or longer to be served, even at lunch.

For groceries, several vendors make the rounds through town during the week. A bakery truck comes from La Paz on Wednesdays; Polo brings fresh fruit, vegetables, and meats in his pickup truck on Wednesdays and Sundays; Ysidro delivers fish, scallops, and shrimp on Tuesdays. Strawberries and ice cream come intermittently as well. You can buy fresh tortillas (10 for less than US$2), homemade tamales (US$1), and empanadas (US$1) for takeout at **Elvira's Kitchen,** near the Cabo Pulmo Divers shop. The **Miscellanea Market** (daily 9 A.M.–7 P.M., limited summer hours), with colorful snails painted on the side of the building, is located next to the Cabo Pulmo Divers shop and stocks basic supplies, including dairy, juice, produce, bread, toiletries, candy, and canned goods. For a long stay, it's best to load up on groceries at Soriana or one of the other supermarkets in San José del Cabo or at Supermercado Chapitos in Los Barriles. Mexican food brands generally cost less than their U.S. counterparts. It's a good idea to buy ice, as the propane refrigerators in most Cabo Pulmo rentals cool very slowly, and a car full of groceries will take a long time to chill.

Information and Services

Internet access via satellite is possible in Cabo Pulmo, but service is by no means reliable, and it will cost you. Inquire at Pepe's Dive Center. At last check, rates were US$5 for 10 minutes, and US$1 per additional minute. In an emergency, the owners of the Cabo Pulmo Beach Resort or Cabo Pulmo Casas can usually get a message out. For casual correspondence, plan to connect in San José or Los Barriles.

There are no banks or ATMs in Cabo Pulmo or Los Frailes, and few places except the largest resorts accept credit cards. U.S. or Mexican currency is accepted, and you can load up on cash at an ATM machine in San José or Los Barriles. Be sure to get plenty of small bills, as many businesses cannot change larger bills.

Basic medical services are available in La Ribera and Los Barriles, and the closest hospital is in San José.

Getting There

Most visitors drive themselves to Cabo Pulmo via El Camino Rural Costero. From San José del Cabo, follow Highway 1 north 50.6 kilometers (31.5 mi) to an overpass at Las Cuevas, and bear right (east) onto the single lane road to La Ribera. From La Paz, pass Buena Vista heading south, and take the exit for La Ribera. As you approach La Ribera (9.6 km/6 mi), turn right before the soccer field. Follow the coastal road 26 kilometers (16 mi) south to Cabo Pulmo. The drive should take about 40 minutes from the time you leave Highway 1.

If you are flying into San José and plan to drive the same day to Cabo Pulmo, aim to arrive no later than noon. By the time you get through passport control, retrieve your luggage, rent a car, and buy your groceries, several hours will have passed, and it is not advisable to drive the highway or coastal road after dark. If you arrive in the afternoon, consider staying overnight in San José before departing for Cabo Pulmo the next day.

The closest gas to Cabo Pulmo is at La Ribera to the north. Be sure to fill up before heading south along the coastal road.

Aguila bus service from San José will get you as far as Las Cuevas for about US$11 one-way, but from there, you'll have to hitch a ride or arrange in advance for someone to pick you up. Another option for traveling sans auto is to contact one of the companies that transport divers from the Los Cabos area to Cabo Pulmo for the day. For example, **Impala Transportation** (tel. 624/141-0726 or cell 122-0141) has a van that holds 14 passengers. With notice, Cabo Pulmo Resort can arrange round-trip transportation from Los Cabos airport for a fee; a stop at a grocery store near the airport on the way up can be included.

BAHÍA DE LOS FRAILES

About eight kilometers (5 mi) south of Cabo Pulmo village is a sandy spur road east to gently curving, white-sand Bahía de los Frailes. With Bahía Pulmo just to the north serving as a protected nursery, onshore and inshore fishing is unusually good here. Surfcasters can land roosterfish, while boating anglers can hook yellowfin tuna, leopard grouper, skipjack, dorado, and marlin, all within a couple miles of shore.

The north end of the bay is protected from November–April northern winds by Cabo Los Frailes, but windsurfers will find a steady crossshore breeze at the bay's south end. The bay plummets here as deep as 210 meters (688 ft).

Accommodations and Camping

Villa Los Frailes (El Camino Rural Costero, U.S. tel. 206/984-3483, www.bajavilla.com, US$550) is an oceanfront home that sleeps 10 people in four bedrooms and five baths with a hot tub and pool deck. Cabo Villa Rentals manages a few vacation properties along the East Cape, including Casita Luna Azul at Estancia (U.S. tel. 877/473-1946 or 310/943-7614, www.cabovillarentals.com). This one-bedroom *casita* is set on a point overlooking the sea and costs US$225 per night.

Beach camping is permitted along the north end of the bay—a nominal fee of US$2–3 per site may be collected to pay for trash collection.

Information and Services

Los Frailes has little commercial infrastructure of its own, but a new "mini-super" market named **Quitos** has opened across the street from the Villa Los Frailes on El Camino Rural Costero. The airstrip was closed in 2007 but scheduled to reopen in the near future.

SOUTH TO SAN JOSÉ DEL CABO

South of Los Frailes the Coastal Road deteriorates rapidly, but those with sturdy vehicles and steady nerves will be rewarded by secluded arroyo campsites and vignettes of disappearing ranch life.

a burro looking for lunch

© NIKKI GOTH ITOI

La Vinorama

About 12.5 kilometers (7.5 mi) south of Los Frailes is **Rancho Tule,** followed after 5.5 kilometers (3.5 mi) by **Rancho Boca de la Vinorama.** The coastal desert scenery along this stretch can be particularly impressive, with lots of green cacti and *torotes* (elephant trees). A late-summer beach break sometimes hits at Boca del Tule, sending a few clued-in surfers scurrying across the landscape in this direction. Near La Vinorama, the **Crossroads Country Club Beachfront Playa** isn't really a country club in the traditional sense, but it has a bar and restaurant with Internet service, public phone, and even a book exchange. For breakfast, choose eggs any style for US$3 or a cheese omelet for US$4. For lunch or dinner, there are fish tacos (US$6), quesadillas, and ham and cheese sandwiches. Jesse Ventura, of Montana governorship fame, lives in a new beachfront mansion just up the road. **Villa del Faro** (www.villadelfaro.net, US$125–450) consists of four deluxe *casitas* and a primitive stone cottage on the beach.

Palo Escopeta

Just south of Vinorama, a graded dirt road heads west across the lower Sierra La Trinidad to the ranching settlement of **Palo Escopeta.** From there it continues on to meet Mexico 1 near San José Viejo, a distance of 34 kilometers (22 mi). Although roughly the same distance as the remainder of the Coastal Road to San José, the Palo Escopeta road often rides more smoothly and quickly. Hence, unless you're heading for a specific spot along the coast between Pueblo La Playa and La Vinorama, it's normally faster to cut across the hills here to Mexico 1 rather than follow the coast.

From La Vinorama along the coast, it's another five kilometers (3 mi) and 1.5 kilometers (one mile) southwest, respectively, to **Rancho San Luis** and **Rancho Santa Elena.** This section of road is often the most rugged along El Camino Rural Costero, with lots of soft spots and washouts. Beyond another 5.5-kilometer (3.5-mi) section is the small dairy farm of

La Fortuna. Nearby, Oregonians Lloyd and Marti Miesen host a small bed and breakfast, **Boca de Los Palmas** (U.S. tel. 503/922-0465 or 866/781-8159, www.martimiesen.com, US$225). Accommodations are in a one-bedroom guesthouse with a king-size bed, private bath, and luxury linens; an additional guestroom is available in their home on the same property for US$85 (only with rental of the guesthouse).

After La Fortuna, the road improves a bit for 24 kilometers (15 mi) before terminating at **Pueblo La Playa,** a fishing village on the eastern outskirts of San José del Cabo.

Jutting from the coast about 10.3 kilometers (6.4 mi) before Pueblo La Playa is **Punta Gorda,** known for good onshore/inshore fishing and, in a south or southwest swell, surfing. Surfers know the breaks here as "Santa Cruz," the name of a small *ranchería* nearby (actually Santa Cruz de los Zacatitos). Beach campsites are free and plentiful in this area.

After 15 years in business, Sharon and Robert Ruyg, the owners of the once-loved Casa Terra Cotta B&B in San José, have moved on to a more upscale and remote location: **Hacienda Soleada del Mar** (Manzana A-Lote 7, tel. 624/113-6386, www. haciendasoleada.com) is available as a B&B, with seven rooms for US$100–230 a night, or as a 9,200-square-foot vacation rental that sleeps 14 for US$1,000/night. There is a small pool on the property, and kayaks, snorkeling gear, and beach umbrellas and chairs are provided.

𝗖 Gorda Banks

Around 10 kilometers (6 mi) offshore lie the world-famous Gorda Banks, a pair of seamounts that are a hot spot for marlin and wahoo fishing. *Pangeros* are sometimes available for guided fishing trips out to the banks, but it's easiest to hire someone at La Playita, the beach behind Pueblo La Playa farther on. If you have your own boat, beach launching is generally easier at La Playita. Guided scuba trips to the Gorda Banks can be arranged through dive outfitters in Cabo San Lucas.

Sierra de la Laguna and Vicinity

Along Mexico 1 between La Paz and San José del Cabo, a number of mining-turned-farming towns sport cobblestone streets and 19th-century stone-and-stucco architecture. Nestled among well-watered arroyos in the Sierra de la Laguna, these neglected settlements now support themselves growing citrus, avocados, mangoes, corn, and sugarcane, and, to a lesser extent, serving the needs of passing travelers. Many of the families living in the central Cape Region are descended from Spanish settlers of the 18th and early 19th centuries. Others are newcomers—including a few Americans and Canadians—drawn by the area's solitude and simplicity.

SAN PEDRO TO SAN BARTOLO
San Pedro
This town of only a few hundred inhabitants appears—and quickly disappears—just before the junction of Mexico 1 and Mexico 19. *Carnitas* connoisseurs swear by **El Paraíso** and **El Pin** (featuring *carnitas, chicharones,* and hot dogs), two unassuming roadside cafés on the west side of Mexico 1. The junction itself is reached at Km 185; if Cabo San Lucas is your destination, you must decide whether to take Mexico 19 via Todos Santos or the Transpeninsular Highway (Mexico 1) via El Triunfo, San Antonio, San Bartolo, Santiago, and Miraflores.

Unless you're in a hurry to reach Cabo San Lucas, Mexico 1 is the most scenic choice for drivers of autos and light trucks. South of San Pedro, Mexico 1 winds through the Sierra de la Laguna and features a succession of dizzying curves and steep grades. Hence for trailers, RVs, and other wide or lengthy vehicles, Mexico 19 is the better choice since it runs along relatively flat terrain (see the *West Cape and Todos Santos* chapter).

El Triunfo and San Antonio
During the Jesuit missionary period, this section along the lower northern slopes of the sierra was earmarked for cattle ranching. But mining concessions moved in after the discovery of silver in 1748, and San Antonio quickly grew into a town of 10,000 people, many of them Yaqui laborers. Then known as Real de Minas de Santa Ana, it was the first nonmission town founded in Baja. The Spanish crown took over the mines in 1769 and struggled to turn a profit from a relatively low quality of ore. When Loreto was heavily damaged by a hurricane in 1829, San Antonio briefly served as capital of the Californias before the capital was transferred to La Paz in 1830.

In 1862, better gold and silver deposits were uncovered at El Triunfo (Triumph), seven kilometers (4.5 mi) north of San Antonio. By 1878 the large Progreso mining concern had established seven gold and silver mines around the village, attracting a number of Mexican, French, English, Italian, German, and American immigrants. The company paid for the region's first post office and installed the first electrical and phone lines to La Paz.

Both San Antonio and El Triunfo bustled with frontier commerce through the end of the 19th century, when the ore began running out. Then a hurricane flooded the mines in 1918 and sounded the death knell; by 1925, both towns were virtually abandoned. Today El Triunfo has only around 400 residents, most of them involved in small-scale mining (extracting ore from leftover tailings) or the weaving of palm baskets. A few *artesanías* can be found on the main road through town. San Antonio, in a lushly planted valley that descends eastward all the way to the Sea of Cortez, has developed into a farming community with around 800 residents, a Pemex station, a post office, and a few markets.

A number of historic adobe buildings in both towns have been restored, including El Triunfo's Casa Municipal and San Antonio's unusual 1825 church exhibiting train and paddle-wheeler motifs. A fun time to visit San Antonio is June 13, the feast day of St. Anthony, when everyone from both San Antonio and El Triunfo turns out for music and dancing.

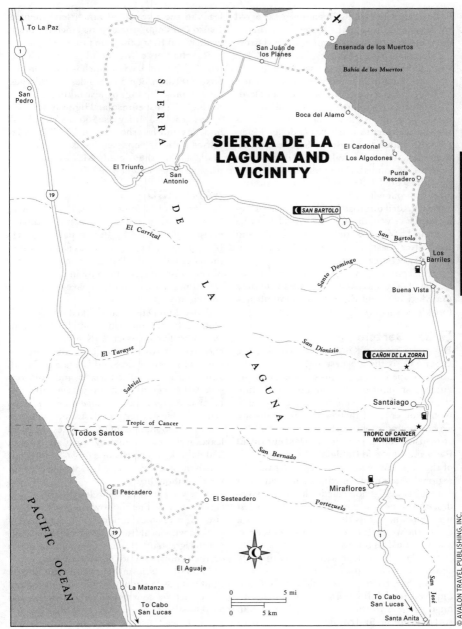

Baja travelers have also mentioned lots of old mines and mining paths throughout the region, often good for exploratory hikes. Hiring a guide is always a good idea; locals in El Triunfo and San Antonio know who's good.

Near San Antonio, between Km 158 and 159, a road heads north off Mexico 1 and leads 22 kilometers (14 mi) to BCS 286, the highway to San Juan de los Planes and La Paz. This is the shortest way to reach Bahía de los Muertos (also called Bahía de los Sueños) and La Ventana from the Central Cape. The unsigned road is easy to miss. (Look for an intersection near the school zone.) Although the road surface starts out with asphalt, it quickly becomes a wide, graded dirt road traversable by most vehicles. Once you hit BCS 286, turn left for La Paz and La Ventana, right for Los Planes and the Cortez coast. There is a Pemex station at this intersection as well.

In El Triunfo, two markets have a modest selection of groceries: **Abarrotes La Escondida** (on Mexico 1) and the **Tienda Comunitaria** (off Mexico 1 in the center of town).

(San Bartolo

Beginning just past Km 128, San Bartolo (pop. about 550) is the greenest and lushest of the central Cape settings, thanks to a large spring gushing straight out of a mountainside into the arroyo. To complete the tropical picture, many homes sport thatched roofs. Mangoes, avocados, and other fresh fruits are available at roadside stands or in town. **Restaurant El Paso** and **Dulcería Daniela's,** on the east side of the highway, serve meals. (**El Oasis** sells regional *dulces* made of fruit such as guava or mango, as well as homemade cheese, empanadas, *bistec ranchero,* quesadillas, and the coldest beer in town. Across the street, grab a seat on one of the wrought iron benches that overlook a valley of palms below.

San Bartolo's patron saint day is June 19, conveniently close to San Antonio's.

From San Bartolo, a 26-kilometer (16-mi) unpaved road follows an arroyo lined with huge *güeribos* to the tiny settlement of **San Antonio de la Sierra.** This arroyo in turn leads to the arroyo and ranch settlement of **Santo Domingo,** where rustic ranch furniture, leather, and fruit candy are produced.

Rancho Verde (Mexico 1 btw Km 143/142, tel. 612/126-9103, www.rancho-verde.com) offers 3,400 acres of mountain desert wilderness for camping, biking, or just taking time out during a Transpeninsular Highway journey. Spaces cost US$11/day (US$66/week) with full hookups and hot showers, or US$7 if you're self-contained. Food service isn't ordinarily available, but the friendly Mexican staff can prepare simple *antojitos* on request.

SANTIAGO

The largest of the central Cape Region towns, Santiago was founded as Misión de Santiago el Apóstol in 1723 by Italian padre Ignacio María Nápoli. The mission was abandoned in the latter half of the 18th century after a series of Pericú rebellions, and only in relatively recent times has agriculture revived the arroyo community.

A two-kilometer road flanked by vegetable plots, leafy fruit orchards, and blue fan palms leads west from Mexico 1 (Km 85) across the wide, flat Arroyo de Santiago, dividing the town into Loma Norte and Loma Sur (North and South Slopes). Santiago and environs serves the region as an important source of palm leaves for making *palapa* roofs. *Palmeros* claim the fan-shaped fronds are best cut during a full moon, as rising sap makes the palm leaves last longer. Properly dried and stored, 250 palm leaves equals one *carga,* or load, for which the *palmeros* receive US$30–50, depending on leaf quality.

A newly paved road circles the town, and various *tiendas* line the town plaza; the town also offers a Pemex station, hotel, supermarket stocked with local fruit and vegetables, post office, telegraph office, church, and the only zoo on the peninsula south of Mexicali.

A small, rustic museum adjacent to the church at the corner of Calzada Misioneros and Calle Victoria contains colonial artifacts and local fossils. It's open Monday–Friday 8 A.M.– 1 P.M.; free admission.

SANTIAGO TO MIRAFLORES

To Cañon San Dionisio and La Laguna

To El Triunfo and La Paz

⟨ **CAÑON DE LA ZORRA** ★

Cerro el Tepetate ▲

Palo Verde ○

Santiago ○

GRADED ROAD

SANTA RITA (HOT SPRINGS) ■

San Jorge

El Encinal ○

San Jorge ○

San   Jorge

Mesa   Cerralvo

1

Agua Caliente

EL CHORRO (HOT SPRINGS) ■

Agua Caliente ○

Las Cabras ○

Las Escobas

Las Vinoramas ○

Mesa las Vinoramas

Cerro la Ventanita ▲

To Cañon San Bernardo

Boca de la Sierra

GRADED ROAD

Miraflores ○

El Ranchito ○

0   2 mi

0   2 km

San Martín ○

Mesa el Capulin

La Tinaja

1

Mesa los Difuntos

Caduaño ○

GRADED ROAD

Boca de la Sierra

To Cañon San Pablo

To San José del Cabo

EAST CAPE

© AVALON TRAVEL PUBLISHING, INC.

Santiago celebrates its patron saint day, the feast day of St. James, on July 25.

Accommodations and Food

Decorated with local fossils, the highly regarded ◖ **Palomar Restaurant-Bar** (tel. 612/130-2126, Mon.–Sat. 11:30 A.M.–8 P.M., mains US$11–15), south of the plaza on the east side of Calzada Misioneros, serves seafood, enchiladas, steak, and burgers. Fresh guacamole is made from avocados grown in the courtyard. Homemade soups and *pescado mojo de ajo* (fish cooked in garlic butter) are house specialties. It also offers six plain but tidy rooms with air conditioning around a quiet courtyard for US$40. Manager Luis Castillo can also radio guides from Rancho Dionisio for hikers.

Sonido y Silencio Garden Nursery (tel. 624/113-5362, Mon.–Fri. 9 A.M.–11 A.M.) sells baskets of organically grown produce, including tomatoes, chilies, lettuce, kale, broccoli, herbs, and whatever else is in season, for US$12 (small) and US$20 (large).

Vicinity of Santiago

The dirt road to the zoo continues southwest nine kilometers (5.5 mi) to the village of **Agua Caliente** (also known as Los Manantiales), where a hot spring in a nearby canyon (about 7 km/4 mi west of the village) has been channeled into a concrete tub for recreation. Camping is permitted in the canyon. Ask directions to two other hot springs in the area: **El Chorro** (west of Agua Caliente) and **Santa Rita** (north). The network of roads behind Santiago passes through dense thorn forest in some spots, and it's easy to get lost unless you keep a compass on hand or a good fix on the sun. If you can bring along a copy of the Mexican topographic map for this area (Santiago 12B34), all the better; each of these locales is clearly marked. Do not attempt these roads at night. If you continue south along the sandy road past Agua Caliente, you'll reach the town of Miraflores after 8.7 kilometers (5.4 mi).

At the north end of Santiago, another dirt road leads northwest to **Rancho San Dionísio**

(23.5 km/14.5 mi), where the Cañon San Dionísio approach to Picacho La Laguna begins (see *Sierra de la Laguna*).

At **Las Cuevas,** eight kilometers (5 mi) northeast of Santiago on Mexico 1 (around Km 93), is the turnoff to La Ribera and the East Cape. Services include a Pemex, minisuper, and bus stop.

Three kilometers (2 mi) south of Santiago, a large painted concrete sphere marks the **Tropic of Cancer** (latitude 23.5° N), south of which you are "in the tropics." As if to sanctify the crossing, an impressive Guadalupe shrine has been built next to the rather unattractive marker.

MIRAFLORES

A 2.5-kilometer (1.5-mi) paved road to Miraflores branches west off Mexico 1 at Km 71 next to a Pemex station. This ranching and farming community is known for leatherwork; **Curtiduría Miraflores** (Miraflores Tannery), just off the access road between the highway and town (look for a small sign reading Leather Shop on the north side of the road), sells handmade leather saddles, bridles, whips, horsehair lariats, and other ranching gear, as well as a few souvenir items such as leather hats, belts, and bags, and the occasional bleached cow skull.

Owned and operated by the Beltrán family, the tannery is particularly known for its rustic ranch saddles. One saddle may use up to eight cowhides, each tanned in the traditional *sudcaliforniano* manner with local *palo blanco* bark and powdered *quebrache,* a reddish-brown, tannin-rich extract from a type of dogbane tree grown on the mainland. Saddle frames are fashioned out of local woods—*ciruelo, copal*—or *cardón* skeletons. Custom orders are accepted. The *curtiduría* also sells engraved knives made from salvaged car springs—a source of particularly strong metal for knife blades—and sheathed in handtooled leather.

The town's **Casa de Cultura** has been completely renovated, and it now contains a collection of modest displays chronicling local history.

Miraflores honors the Virgin of Guadalupe as its patron saint, so Fiesta Guadalupana (December 12), celebrated throughout Mexico, is especially fervent here.

Well past the tannery, after you've crossed an arroyo and are just getting into the center of Miraflores, a large hedge of bougainvillea nearly obscures the open-air, *palapa*-roofed **Restaurant Las Bugambilias,** to the left on a small side street off the main road. All manner of inexpensive, *bajacaliforniano*-style *antojitos* are available here from morning till evening. **Restaurant Miraflores,** next to Mini Super El Nidito near the market and plaza, makes good tacos with shrimp, fish, or beef. Several *mercaditos* in town provide local produce and *machaca*.

Vicinity of Miraflores

A dirt road northwest of Miraflores leads to **Boca de la Sierra** (Mouth of the Sierra), a settlement at the mouth of Cañon San Bernardo—the second of the three canyons providing access deep into the Sierra de la Laguna. *Ejido* farms in the Boca de la Sierra area cultivate vegetables and herbs—especially sweet basil—for Cape Region supermarkets and restaurants as well as for export to the United States.

Another dirt road southwest of town leads to the mouth of Cañon San Pablo, a third Laguna hiking route. Inquire at the tannery about guided trips into the sierra to view Amerindian rock-art sites.

SIERRA DE LA LAGUNA

The mountainous heart of the Cape Region extends southward from the Llano de la Paz (the plains just south of La Paz) to Cabo San Lucas, a distance of around 135 kilometers (81 mi). Originally called Sierra de la Victoria by the Spanish, the interior mountains were renamed Sierra de la Laguna in the early Mexican era. These peaks are unique among sierras in the southern half of Baja California in that they're granitic rather than volcanic. And unlike the sierras to the north, the entire Laguna range is tilted eastward instead of westward; i.e., its steepest slopes are on the west side of the escarpment rather than the east.

Picacho de la Laguna (elevation 2,161 m/7,090 ft), roughly in the sierra's center, is usually cited as the highest peak in the range, although according to some sources **Cerro las Casitas**—approximately 6.5 kilometers (4 mi) southeast of Picacho de la Laguna and measuring 2,083 meters (6,835 ft) by most accounts—may be higher. Between these two peaks is a large, flat meadow called **La Laguna** (elevation 1,707 m/5,600 ft). This depression held a mountain lake until around 1870, when Cañon San Dionísio became sufficiently eroded to drain away accumulated water.

The sierra flora has been little researched; the most recent detailed studies were undertaken in the 1890s by botanist T. S. Brandegee for the California Academy of Sciences. The foothills and mesas below 500 meters are covered with dry *matorral*—low-growing cacti, succulents, thornscrub, and abundant herbs. Common species include barrel cactus, cholla, *palo verde,* ironwood, damiana, and oregano. Canyon walls may be draped with *zalate* (wild fig). At elevations of 500–750 meters (1,640–2,460 ft), tropical-subtropical deciduous forest and columnar cacti are the dominant flora (e.g., *mauto, palo blanco,* prickly pear, *cardón, palo adán*). At 750–1,200 meters (2,460–3,940 ft), live-oak woodlands (*encino*, madrone) dominate, and above 1,200 meters a mix of live oak and piñon pine prevails. At its highest elevations, La Laguna qualifies as a cloud forest during the moist summer months, when the peaks are consistently shrouded in mist or rain.

Islands in the Sky

The range's highlands receive more annual precipitation—up to 89 centimeters (35 in) per year in some microclimates—than any other place in Baja California. As a result, the meadow of La Laguna and other flats and high canyons in the sierra contain a number of "relic environments" preserving flora and fauna long ago lost on the arid plains below.

These "islands in the sky" support a sensational mix of desert, tropical, and subalpine

EAST CAPE

plant species that are found together nowhere else in North America. Among the unlikely combinations seen growing side by side: mosses and cacti, madrone and monkey flower, palm and willow. Of the 447 plant species known to grow in the sierra, at least 70 are reportedly indigenous. Undisturbed by human progress, deer, coyote, mountain lion, Pacific tree frog, and dozens of hummingbird species also thrive in the highland areas of the sierra.

For many years, naturalists and outdoor enthusiasts clamored for the upper sierra to be declared a national park or preserve, and in June 1994 the Mexican government finally granted the Sierra de la Laguna official recognition as a "biosphere reserve." Such status prohibits development within the reserve's 32,519-hectare core zone; local ranchers are permitted to graze livestock in a buffer zone surrounding the protected core.

Hiking and Backpacking

The Sierra de la Laguna is a popular hiking area for Cape residents, as it offers the op-

portunity to leave behind the fig trees and palms of the arid-tropical environment for a walk among cottonwoods and subalpine meadows. Three lengthy east–west canyons—Cañon San Dionísio, Cañon San Bernardo, and Cañon San Pablo—provide the principal access into the sierra. All three routes enable hikers to cross the sierra's spine from east to west or vice versa. Primitive campsites are available along each of the three routes.

The northernmost and most popular route, via Cañon San Dionísio, leads directly to La Laguna, the range's largest and highest meadow. La Laguna lies at an altitude of just under 1,800 meters (6,000 ft), between Picacho de la Laguna and Cerro las Casitas, the sierra's tallest peaks. The scenery on this hike is impressive. A straight traverse of this route, starting from either side, is possible in three days, although this would allow little time for taking it easy. Add at least another day to allow some time to enjoy La Laguna once you've reached it.

© PAUL ITOI

Sierra de la Laguna entrance

🌙 Cañon de la Zorra

Freshwater is a sight to behold in the Baja desert landscape. For those travelers who would like to venture into the Sierra but do not have time for a multiday hike, there is a 30-foot waterfall just six miles beyond Santiago that has a swimmable lagoon and is reachable by foot. At the far end of the divided avenue that leads into Santiago (as you approach the plaza), turn right and set your trip odometer to zero. At 0.48 kilometer (0.3 mi), go straight through the dirt road intersection and head up the hill, past a sign for San Dionísio. At 1.29 kilometers (0.8 mi) and the crest of the hill, turn left. At 1.77 kilometers (1.1 mi), turn right across a small arroyo and follow this road to 4.02 kilometers (2.5 mi), where the road forks and there is a sign pointing to the right fork marked Cañon de la Zorra. Follow this fork to the end of the road at 9.66 kilometers (6.0 mi) and park at the trailhead. Small wooden outhouses are popping up in remote areas of the Cape, and you'll find one of them here. Go through the gate and follow the trail for 10 minutes down to the river bottom and the falls.

Cañon San Dionísio: Western (Todos Santos) Approach

Most hikers ascend to La Laguna from the west side, which is a steeper but more straightforward hike (and about 2 km shorter) than from Rancho San Dionísio. Unlike the network of cattle trails on the east side—which are best negotiated with local guides—the western ascent can be easily accomplished without a guide. From the west side a round-trip can be completed in two days.

Near Todos Santos, the sandy road to La Burrera leaves Mexico 19 about 100 meters south of the Punta Lobos turnoff. Past an old water tower, take the first left and continue straight through several intersections till the road ends at a gate and parking area. From the gate, follow the dirt road till you reach La Burrera (about 25 minutes away), where a sign in English advises hikers to follow marked trails (ironic since we've never seen any marked trails in the sierra). Also known as San Juan del Aserradero, this village on the sierra's western slopes lies around 17.5 kilometers (11 mi) northeast of Todos Santos. Continue along this road another 20 minutes or so till you see a clearing on the right that has been used for camping; look for a sign reading No Tire Basura (Don't Throw Trash). Just past this sign, the road ascends to a small rise, at the top of which the main trail begins. After 30 meters or so of easy grade, the trail begins its long, steady climb straight up the mountain. Following this wide, established (rutted in places), 11-kilometer (7-mi) trail, you should reach La Laguna in 5–8 hours, depending on your pace. Along the way the vegetation changes quickly from desert and thorn forest into lush piñon-oak woodlands; about 20 minutes before you reach La Laguna the forest canopy opens to magnificent views of the sierra and Pacific Ocean.

Follow the arroyo that drains La Laguna at its southeast corner, near where the trail comes in from Rancho San Dionísio, to reach a

EAST CAPE

20-meter (66-ft) cascade with deep pools suitable for swimming.

The return descent along the same trail takes about four hours to reach La Burrera.

If you need a ride to La Burrera from Todos Santos, your best bet is to inquire at Siempre Vive (at the corner of Calles Juárez and Márquez de León) in the late morning, when ranchers from the western sierra sometimes turn up for supplies and gossip. Fees for such a ride are negotiable—some ranchers will give you a lift for gas money and a six-pack of Tecate, others ask up to US$30. You might also inquire at the Todos Santos taxi stand next to the town park.

Cañon San Dionísio: Eastern (Santiago) Approach

From the east side of the sierra, count on 3–4 days to La Laguna and back with time to explore the area. The eastern mouth of the main canyon is reached via a dirt road to Rancho San Dionísio from Santiago (19 km/12 mi). From there it's a 13-kilometer (8-mi) hike west through the canyon mouth, then into a side arroyo and finally along the southern rim of the canyon to La Laguna. Piñon pine and cape live oak began appearing about two-thirds of the way up. This trail is relatively difficult to follow and is intersected by potentially confusing animal paths; a guide, available at Rancho San Dionísio or in Santiago, is highly recommended. If you decide to go it alone, be sure to carry a topo map and compass, and watch out for cattle trails branching off the main trail in every direction. Scout ahead at questionable junctions, even if it means going slower. Once you're up on the ridgeline you should be able to spot La Laguna in the distance and then confidently follow any trail heading in that direction.

Those wishing to explore a bit can follow the canyon four kilometers (2.5 mi) straight west of the ranch into a steep area of boulders; where the arroyo forks there's a 20-meter (66-ft) waterfall and deep pools suitable for swimming. Don't attempt to follow the canyon all the way to the meadow unless you're into some very serious bouldering and scrambling.

Near the northwest edge of the meadow itself are a couple of herder's shacks. Just past these the trail cuts into the forest and divides; the southern branch descends to La Burrera, while the north branch ascends Picacho de la Laguna, a 90-minute hike away. (A lesser third trail leads to an arroyo with freshwater.) Easy to climb, the peak is bare of trees and provides splendid views of the surrounding terrain. Closer to the meadow, a hill surmounted by radio towers also makes a good vantage point.

Those wishing to traverse the sierra can descend westward from La Laguna another 11 kilometers (7 mi) to La Burrera; see *Cañon San Dionísio: Western (Todos Santos) Approach.* About 20 minutes into the descent from the meadow, you'll come upon terrific views all the way to the Pacific Ocean. Roads from La Burrera meet Mexico 19 south and north of Todos Santos; the area east of these junctions is honeycombed with other dirt roads, but if you continue in a westerly direction you'll eventually come to the highway.

Cañon San Bernardo

The next route to the south, via Cañon San Bernardo, is a relatively easy (from east to west) hike that crests at around 900 meters (3,000 ft). The canyon trailhead is accessible via an eight-kilometer (5-mi) dirt road from Miraflores to Boca de la Sierra, where the trail skirts a dam and follows the canyon to the crest, 16 kilometers (10 mi) northwest. Several pools along the way provide freshwater year-round. From the 900-meter crest, the trail continues over the sierra to the village of Santo Domingo on the western side, for a total traverse of 22.5 kilometers (14 mi). The Cañon San Bernardo crossing makes a good four- to five-day hike, although it's possible to make a quick overnight to the crest and back from the eastern approach.

Cañon San Pablo

Cañon San Pablo provides the southernmost route into the sierra, reaching an elevation of around 1,000 meters (3,300 ft). The canyon mouth is best approached by taking a 6.5-kilometer (4-mi) dirt road west from Caduaño, a village four kilometers (2.5 mi) south of Miraflores, to Rancho El Salto. From Rancho El Salto, it's approximately 10.5 kilometers (6.5 mi) to the crest; the trail continues over the ridge and along a steeper 4.8-kilometer (3-mi) westward descent to the village of El Güerigo on the other side, where a network of dirt roads leads west to Mexico 19. A leisurely El Salto–El Güerigo hike takes 4–5 days.

Seasons

The best backpacking season here is late fall, after the rainy season has passed and sierra streams and *tinajas* are full. Temperatures above 1,500 meters (5,000 ft) typically measure 12–22°C (54–72°F) during the day, 5–12°C (41–54°F) at night. In January and February, temperatures can dip below freezing at night, while daytime temps run around 10–20°C (50–68°F).

The warmest temperatures are usually encountered in May and June, when the mercury reaches around 25°C (77°F) during the day, 10–15°C (50–60°F) at night. Although the scenery isn't as spectacularly green this time of year, it's a fine time to beat the heat down on the coastal plains.

July–October rains may wash out trails and flood the canyons. Rainfall peaks in August, averaging 7.5 centimeters (3 in) but sometimes reaching a drenching 20 centimeters (7.8 in) for the month.

Supplies

A compass and good topographic map are musts for any trip into the Sierra de la Laguna. To cover all three routes, you should possess copies of Mexico's relevant 1:50,000-scale topos: El Rosario F12B23; Las Cuevas F12B24; Todos Santos F12B33; and Santiago F12B34 (see *Hiking and Backpacking* in the *Essentials* chapter). Bring warm clothing and sleeping bags for the summit; morning frost isn't uncommon even in fall and spring. Long pants and sturdy hiking shoes are rec-

ommended as a defense against the abundant cactus and nettles.

On the Cañon San Dionísio trail, bring all the water you'll need to reach La Laguna, as there are no dependable sources on the way up, even in wet weather. An arroyo at La Laguna itself carries water year-round. On the Cañon San Bernardo trail, pools of water can be found along the way year-round. Water may be available from ranchos along the Cañon San Pablo trail, but bring your own to be safe. Be sure to use a water-purification system of some kind on all water sources in the mountains; although the water is generally uncontaminated, the presence of livestock precludes absolute safety.

Guides

For eastern ascents into the sierra, those unsure of their backpacking and orientation skills should consider hiring a local guide, since trails across the eastern escarpment are often obscured and junctions not always obvious. A guide can also prepare simple camp meals and point out items of natural interest— Amerindian rock art, flora and fauna—that first-timers might otherwise miss. Ask around for guides in Santiago or Miraflores. For the Cañon San Dionísio route, you can sometimes arrange a guide at Rancho San Dionísio, just before the eastern trailhead.

The going rate for guides in Santiago is US$30–35 per day per person, plus an extra US$15 per day per pack animal. Rancho San Dionísio charges US$30 for a guide without mules, no matter how many people are hiking.

Many hikers make the western approach to Cañon San Dionísio from Todos Santos without a guide; the main difficulty is finding your way (or arranging a ride) to the trailhead. If you decide to hire a guide, there are a couple of options in Todos Santos. Fernando Arteche (sierradelalaguna@hotmail.com) is fluent in English and knowledgeable about the Sierra de la Laguna. His guided trips usually take three days, and you can go on foot or by mule. Another local guide, Juan Sebastián López (onejohnone@hotmail.com), offers three-day trips on horseback, with packhorses to carry the gear. He also leads two-day trips to the hot springs.

Information and Services

Services are few and far between in this part of the Cape Region. San Antonio (Km 157) and Miraflores (Km 71) have Pemex stations. Buses stop at Santiago, for access to the Sierra de la Laguna, and at La Ribera/Las Cuevas, Km 93, for access to Cabo Pulmo (no connecting service).

Driving Across the Sierra

Visitors with sturdy, high-clearance vehicles may be able to traverse the Sierra de la Laguna in dry weather via a road that leaves Mexico 1 about 16 kilometers (10 mi) south of Miraflores (about 8 km/5 mi north of Santa Anita) near Km 55. Among gringo road hogs this route is often called the "Naranjas road"; the correct name is Ramal Los Naranjos (*naranjo* means "orange tree," a probable reference to the many small citrus farms in the area). Because parts of it may suffer from washouts, this is not a road to tackle during the rainy season (July–Sept.), and you should make inquiries at

any time of year to determine whether the road is clear all the way.

From the Mexico 1 turnoff the road leads west-northwest 42 kilometers (26 mi) to the village of **El Aguaje,** past the *ranchitos* of San Miguelito, Cieneguita, San Pedro de la Soledad, and El Remudadero. The ungraded road passes a couple of 1,500- to 1,800-meter (5,000- to 6,000-ft) peaks before cresting at around 1,035 meters (3,400 ft) and descending into a challenging set of sharp curves and grades approaching 30 percent. At 27 kilometers (17 mi) from Mexico 1 you get your first view of the Pacific Ocean, by which point the road begins hugging the edge of a rock mountain. Shortly thereafter the road may be washed out or blocked by rock slides and you may not be able to continue. The track eventually widens to a graded, gravel road near El Aguaje, then continues another 12.8 kilometers (8 mi) before terminating at Mexico 19 near Playa Los Cerritos south of Todos Santos. Two INEGI topo maps, San José del Cabo F12B44 and La Candelaria F12B43, would make helpful—though not required—companions on this cross-sierra road trip.

LA PAZ AND VICINITY

Ensconced along the largest bay on Baja's Sea of Cortez coast, La Paz is a city of more than 200,000 noted for its attractive *malecón* (waterfront walkway) backed by swaying palms and pastel-colored buildings, its splendid sunsets, easygoing pace, sunny climate, and its proximity to uncrowded beaches and pristine islands. Many Baja travelers—Mexicans and gringos alike—cite La Paz (Peace) as their favorite city on the Baja California peninsula; a few even go so far as to pronounce it their favorite in all of Mexico. La Paz is ideal for the traveler who wants more than a beach and booze vacation; here, you'll get some history, eco-adventure, and a taste of the real Mexico mixed in.

Cabo San Lucas, 221 kilometers (137 mi) farther south, still receives more attention than

La Paz in the American press, which suits La Paz fans fine since it means fewer tourists—around 4,500 gringos in all spend the winter season here; and some stay year-round. But the Baja Sur state government is investing heavily in tourism in the area around La Paz, and new direct flights from California to the city's international airport may herald a new wave of visitors in coming years.

Indeed, as the real estate market becomes saturated in Los Cabos, developers are looking northward. Three large-scale resort developments are already underway: Like Cabo San Lucas, La Paz now has its own hilltop Pedregal neighborhood in the making, at the northeastern edge of town on the way to Pichilingue. Cobblestone roads and utilities are the first step in the creation of a

HIGHLIGHTS

◖ *Malecón:* You haven't experienced La Paz until you've strolled the waterfront promenade at sunset. Visitors and residents alike pause to watch the dramatic display of color. Stop for a cocktail or an ice cream, and enjoy the evening breeze (page 147).

◖ Museo Regional de Antropología e Historia: Think you know your Baja history? Save time for a tour of the fossils, minerals, and maps of rock-painting sites in this well-run museum. Exhibits depict Amerindian and colonial life throughout central and southern Baja (page 147).

◖ Playa El Tecolote: A drive to the end of the road along Bahía de La Paz leads to this wide, sandy beach. Wade into clear, shallow waters and enjoy views of Isla Espíritu Santo across the channel. A steady breeze keeps the bugs away if you decide to spend the night (page 151).

◖ Isla Espíritu Santo: The best-known of the islands offshore from La Paz entertains paddlers, divers, and boaters with white-sand beaches and rock reefs. You can camp in several places on the island and enjoy endless opportunities for outdoor adventure (page 154).

◖ Bahía de la Ventana: A short drive south of La Paz, this L-shaped bay offers steady winds for kiteboarders and windsurfers, plus easy access to Isla Cerralvo for scuba diving adventures. Enjoy the remote feel while it lasts (page 184).

LOOK FOR ◖ TO FIND RECOMMENDED SIGHTS, ACTIVITIES, DINING, AND LODGING.

128-acre (52 hectare) private, gated community of 370 lots, a 200-room hotel, condos, and a shopping plaza. Nearby, a second beach development, the 500-acre CostaBaja Resort & Marina (www.costabajaresort.com) already has an operational 280-slip marina and Fiesta Inn resort. When complete, the development will include 50 villas, plus shops and restaurants. The real estate fever has spread to the south as well, with five hotels, a residential neighborhood, and airport planned for the Bay of Dreams.

The most controversial development is taking shape on the Mogote Peninsula, a spit of land that juts out in the bay. Environmentalists are concerned that the future site of the Paraíso del Mar (www.paradiseofthesea.com) project, consisting of two golf courses, a 535-slip marina, 2,000 hotel rooms, and 2,000 private homes, will permanently destroy hundreds of acres of mangrove essential to the health of the marine ecosystem.

Despite the feverish pace of real estate activity, La Paz remains steeped most

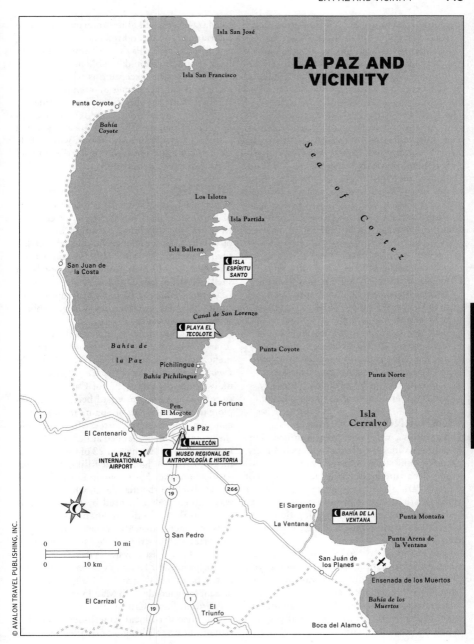

LA PAZ AND VICINITY

Isla San José

Isla San Francisco

Punta Coyote

Bahía
Coyote

LA PAZ AND
VICINITY

S e a

o f

Los Islotes

Isla Partida

C o r t e z

Isla Ballena

ISLA
ESPÍRITU
SANTO

San Juan de
la Costa

Canal de San Lorenzo

PLAYA EL
TECOLOTE

Bahía de
la Paz

Punta Coyote

Pichilingue

Bahía Pichilingue

Punta Norte

Pen.
El Mogote

La Fortuna

Isla
Cerralvo

1

El Centenario

La Paz

MALECÓN

LA PAZ
INTERNATIONAL
AIRPORT

MUSEO REGIONAL DE
ANTROPOLOGÍA E HISTORIA

1

19

266

El Sargento

BAHÍA DE LA
VENTANA

Punta Montaña

La Ventana

San Pedro

Punta Arena de
la Ventana

San Juán de
los Planes

0   10 mi

0   10 km

El Carrizal

19

1

El
Triunfo

Ensenada de los Muertos

Bahía de los
Muertos

Boca del Alamo

© AVALON TRAVEL PUBLISHING, INC.

profoundly in mainland Mexico's traditions; it was the first major European settlement on the peninsula and has long been a haven for Mexicans dissatisfied with life on the mainland. Many *Paceños* (La Paz residents) are descendants of mainlanders who sailed to La Paz to avoid the political turmoil of the 19th and early 20th centuries. And it's not uncommon to meet more recent Mexican émigrés who have resettled in La Paz after becoming fed up with modern-day political machinations in Mexico City, Guadalajara, or Monterrey. *Paceños* are proud of the many ways in which their city lives up to its name.

Along the bay, La Paz remains much as John Steinbeck described it in 1941:

> La Paz grew in fascination as we approached. The square, iron-shuttered colonial houses stood up right in back of the beach with rows of beautiful trees in front of them. It is a lovely place. There is a broad promenade along the water lined with benches, named for dead residents of the city, where one may rest oneself.... [A] cloud of delight hangs over the distant city from the time when it was the great pearl center of the world.... Guaymas is busier, they say, and Mazatlán gayer, but La Paz is antigua.

PLANNING YOUR TIME

La Paz offers a wide variety of accommodations and dining venues, well-stocked supermarkets, marine supply stores, and a ferry terminal with a daily departure for Mazatlán across the Sea of Cortez. Parking can be a bit tight, and minor traffic snarls are common in *el centro,* the city center, but can be avoided by using Boulevard Forjadores, a wide avenue skirting the southern section of the city.

Allow several days to explore the city and surrounding beaches; a week or more if you plan to fish, snorkel, dive, or kayak around the islands just offshore. If you're coming to learn Spanish, local schools recommend a minimum stay of two weeks, up to a month if you can swing it. Travelers planning to take the ferry

to Mazatlán should allow an extra day or two to arrange permits and reservations.

February is La Paz's peak tourist month. Even then, you should be able to find a hotel room easily. One exception is when the Baja 1000 off-road race comes to town in mid-November. With the race finish just outside the city limits, every room, condo, and vacation rental books up months in advance. If you roll into La Paz without reservations, you'll likely have to continue south to Los Barriles to find a place to crash for the night.

HISTORY

When the Spanish first landed on the shores of Bahía de la Paz in the early 16th century, the area was inhabited by migrating bands of Guaicura and Pericú, who allegedly called their homeland "Airapi." Hunters and gatherers, these Amerindian groups lived mostly on shellfish, small game, and wild plants. As artifacts on display at La Paz's Museum of Anthropology demonstrate, they were also skilled weavers and potters.

Into this peaceful scene entered the first European, a Basque mutineer named Fortún Jiménez, who commandeered the Spanish ship *Concepción* on the Sea of Cortez in 1533. Originally under the command of Captain Diego Becerra, the *Concepción* had been sent to explore the sea on behalf of Spain's most famous conquistador, Hernán Cortés. After executing the captain, Jiménez landed at Bahía de La Paz in early 1534, where he and 22 of his crew were killed by Amerindians while filling their water casks at a spring. The survivors sailed the *Concepción* back to the mainland, where the ship was immediately captured by Cortés's New Spain rival, Nuño de Guzmán. At least one crew member managed to escape and returned to Cortés with descriptions of a huge, beautiful bay filled with pearl-oyster beds.

Cortés himself landed at the northeast end of the bay, probably at Pichilingue near the present ferry terminal, in May 1535 and named it Puerto de Santa Cruz. Cortés was able to effect a truce with local Amerindians, but his attempt at establishing a permanent Spanish

ENGLISH PIRATES ON THE SEA OF CORTEZ

Sir Francis Drake, Thomas Cavendish, William Dampier, Woodes Rogers, Thomas Dover, and other English privateers left behind a colorful Baja legacy. In spite of Spain's repeated attempts to colonize the peninsula, throughout the Spanish colonial period the pirates probably gained more wealth in the Californias than the Spanish themselves. For 250 years they plagued the Manila galleons off the coast of the Californias, finding the bays and lagoons of Baja's Cape Region perfect hiding places from which to launch attacks on treasure-laden ships.

In La Paz, using their knowledge of the strong breeze that blows into the harbor every summer afternoon, the pirates attacked Spanish galleons while the vessels were effectively trapped in the bay. Four centuries after the first Manila-Acapulco voyages, this afternoon wind is still known as *el coromuel*, named for the Puritan Cromwells – father and son – who ruled successively as Lord Protectors of England.

THE DISAPPEARANCE OF THE *DESIRE*

The most notorious of the Pacific privateers was Sir Thomas Cavendish, whose greatest feat of plunder occurred at Cabo San Lucas in 1587. There had been two English vessels, *Desire* and *Content*, commandeered the Spanish galleon *Santa Ana* after a protracted sea battle.

Cavendish set fire to the *Santa Ana* after looting its cargo holds and setting its crew and passengers ashore. The Spanish crew later retrieved the burned hulk and restored it for a return to Acapulco.

The plundered treasure, meanwhile, was divided between the *Desire* and the *Content*. The ships set sail for England immediately, but during the first night of their triumphant voyage the *Desire* disappeared. Cavendish reported in England that the captain and crew of the *Desire* must have scuttled the ship on a nearby island and disappeared with the loot. Neither the wreckage of the vessel nor the treasure was ever discovered; some historians speculate that at least part of the missing wealth remains buried near the Cape.

A VISIT BY ROBINSON CRUSOE

In 1709, famed corsair Woodes Rogers landed in La Paz after rescuing a seaman who'd been marooned five years on a deserted island off Chile's coast. The rescued man was Alexander Selkirk, whose island sojourn became the inspiration for Daniel Defoe's *Robinson Crusoe*, published in 1719. Selkirk was aboard Rogers's *Dover* when the crew captured the Spanish galleon *Encarnación* off Cabo San Lucas in 1709; he served as sailing master on the ship's return voyage to England the following year.

colony lasted only through 1538, when the colonists were forced to abandon the peninsula because of supply problems.

The next Spaniard to visit the bay was famed explorer Sebastián Vizcaíno, who landed here in 1596 during his long voyage around the peninsula's perimeter and north to California. Because he and his crew were treated so well by the Pericú, Vizcaíno named the bay Bahía de La Paz (Bay of Peace).

Pirates and Colonization

Baja California remained free of Spaniards another 100 years before the successful establishment of a mission colony at Loreto to the north. By this time, English and Dutch pirates were plundering New Spain's Manila galleons as they returned from the Orient weighted down with gold, silks, and spices. One of the freebooters' favorite staging areas was Bahía de La Paz, which contained numerous *ensenadas* (coves) and inlets perfect for concealing their swift corsairs. When Spanish crews put in for water, the pirates raided the galleons, often using their knowledge of strong afternoon winds to attack the ships when they were effectively pinned down.

Increased pirate activity in the late 17th and early 18th centuries created the need for a Spanish presence in the Cape Region. In 1719,

Padre Juan de Ugarte, then president of the missions, contracted a master shipbuilder to construct a ship for the specific purpose of exploring the Sea of Cortez coast and improving supply lines with the mainland. The barque *El Triunfo de la Cruz,* assembled of native Baja hardwood at the Mulegé estuary, made its first sailing to Bahía de La Paz in 1720 with Ugarte and Padre Jaime Bravo as passengers.

Ugarte and Bravo founded the mission community of Nuestra Señora del Pilar de la Paz at the current city site. The padres didn't find the Pericú to be as friendly this time around; the mission lasted only until 1749, when it was abandoned after a series of Amerindian rebellions. By this time, another mission and a presidio had been founded farther south at San José del Cabo—a better location for monitoring pirate activity.

La Paz Reborn

Left with European diseases and without the support of the mission system, the local Pericú population dwindled quickly. By 1811, Mexican ranchers and *pescadores* who had settled along the Bahía de La Paz started their own town, which they named La Paz after the bay. After Loreto was severely damaged during a hurricane in 1829, the capital of Baja California Sur was moved to burgeoning La Paz, where it has remained ever since.

During the Mexican-American War (1846–1848), U.S. troops occupied the city; the soldiers left when the Californias were split by the 1848 Treaty of Hidalgo. But American general William Walker, dissatisfied with the treaty and hoping to add another slaveholder state to counter the growing U.S. abolitionist movement, formed his own army of "New York Volunteers" and retook La Paz in November 1853. Proclaiming himself "president of the Republic of Sonora," Walker lasted only six months; he and his mercenaries fled upon hearing that the United States wouldn't back their claims, and that the Mexican army was on its way to La Paz from the mainland. Walker was tried in the United States for violation of neutrality laws, fined, and two years later was executed by the Nicaraguan army for attempting a similar takeover of Nicaragua.

La Paz remained a sleepy tropic seaport, known only for pearl harvesting, until it was declared a duty-free port after World War II. After an epizootic disease killed off the entire pearl-oyster population, the city's economic focus turned to farming and trade with the mainland. During Mexico's postwar economic boom, mainland Mexicans crossed the Sea of Cortez in droves to buy imported merchandise; enchanted by La Paz itself, many stayed on.

In the 1950s, La Paz became well-known as a fishing resort and was visited by a succession of North American literati and Hollywood celebrities, thus initiating the city's reputation as an international vacation spot. But until the Transpeninsular Highway was completed in 1973, the city remained for the most part a tourist destination for mainland Mexicans.

Statehood was bestowed on the Territory of Baja California Sur in 1974, and La Paz was made state capital. Linked by air, ferry, and highway to mainland Mexico and the United States, the city has grown considerably in the decades since; yet it manages to maintain its tropic port ambience.

Sights

【 *Malecón*

The pleasant five-kilometer *malecón*, a seawall promenade along the northwest side of Paseo Alvaro Obregón extending from Calle 5 de Febrero (Mexico 1 south) to the northeastern city limits, is looking better than ever these days. Decorative paving, newly painted crosswalks, and wrought-iron benches invite visitors and residents alike to take a walk along the bay. Water quality has improved too, making it possible to swim once again (though most people continue northeast to the beaches along the Pichilingue Peninsula).

The best time of day for people-watching is around sunset, when the city begins cooling off, the sun dyes the waterfront orange, and *Paceños* take to the *malecón* for an evening stroll or jog. Snacks and cold beverages are available at several *palapa* bars along the way. Restaurants, shops, real estate offices, car rental agencies—and a brand new Applebees chain—line the opposite side of Obregón.

© PAUL ITOI

cucumbers for sale

An archway marks the entry to the Muelle Turístico (Tourist Pier), with cobblestone paving, potted plants, and well-lighted wrought-iron seating areas. With locals strolling and hanging out on the pier on warm evenings, it has taken on the feel of a traditional Mexican plaza.

【 Museo Regional de Antropología e Historia

Baja California history buffs shouldn't miss this well-designed museum (5 de Mayo and Altamirano, tel. 612/125-6424, daily 9 A.M.–6 P.M., admission free). Three floors of exhibits cover Cape Region anthropology from prehistoric to colonial and modern times. On display are fossils, minerals, Amerindian artifacts, dioramas of Amerindian and colonial life, and maps of rock-painting sites throughout central and southern Baja. Labels are in Spanish only.

Plaza Constitución (Jardín Velazco)

La Paz's tidy downtown *zócalo* is enclosed by Avenida Independencia and Calles 5 de Mayo, Revolución de 1910, and Madero. At the southwest side of the plaza is the post-missionary-style **Catedral de Nuestra Señora de La Paz,** which replaced La Paz's original mission church in 1861. Although the twin-towered brick edifice looms over the plaza, it lacks the charm of earlier Jesuit missions. Inside, only an image of Nuestra Señora del Pilar and a few theological books survive from the earlier 1720 mission. A couple of blocks southwest of the plaza, on Calle Zaragoza between Arrival and Lerdo de Tejada, a plaque commemorates the original mission site.

At the northwest side of Plaza Constitución, opposite the cathedral, is the **Biblioteca de História de las Californias** (Library of Californias' History). Housed in the 1880s-era former Casa de Gobierno (Government House), the library is filled with Spanish- and English-language volumes on Alta and Baja California history. The

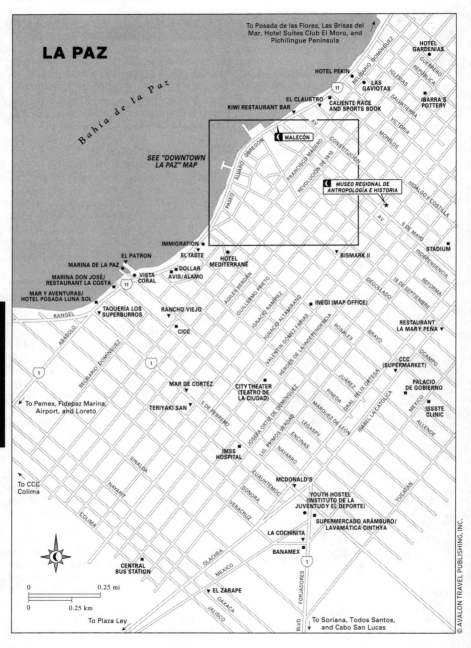

LA PAZ

Bahía de la Paz

To Posada de las Flores, Las Brisas del Mar, Hotel Suites Club El Moro, and Pichilingue Peninsula

HOTEL GARDENIAS

HOTEL PEKIN

LAS GAVIOTAS

EL CLAUSTRO

KIWI RESTAURANT BAR

CALIENTE RACE AND SPORTS BOOK

IBARRA'S POTTERY

MALECÓN

SEE "DOWNTOWN LA PAZ" MAP

MUSEO REGIONAL DE ANTROPOLOGÍA E HISTORIA

IMMIGRATION

EL PATRON

EL TASTE

MARINA DE LA PAZ

HOTEL MEDITERRANÉ

STADIUM

BISMARK II

MARINA DON JOSÉ/ RESTAURANT LA COSTA

VISTA CORAL

DOLLAR AVIS/ALAMO

MAR Y AVENTURAS/ HOTEL POSADA LUNA SOL

RANGEL

TAQUERÍA LOS SUPERBURROS

RANCHO VIEJO

INEGI (MAP OFFICE)

RESTAURANT LA MARY PEÑA

CICC

CCC (SUPERMARKET)

To Pemex, Fidepaz Marina, Airport, and Loreto

MAR DE CORTÉZ

CITY THEATER (TEATRO DE LA CIUDAD)

PALACIO DE GOBIERNO

ISSSTE CLINIC

TERIYAKI SAN

To CCC Colima

IMSS HOSPITAL

MCDONALD'S

YOUTH HOSTEL (INSTITUTO DE LA JUVENTUD Y EL DEPORTE)

SUPERMERCADO ARÁMBURO/ LAVAMÁTICA CINTHYA

LA COCHINITA

BANAMEX

CENTRAL BUS STATION

0   0.25 mi

0   0.25 km

EL ZARAPE

To Plaza Ley

To Soriana, Todos Santos, and Cabo San Lucas

© AVALON TRAVEL PUBLISHING, INC.

general public is welcome to use the library for research. Officially, the library hours are Monday–Friday 9 A.M.–6 P.M., Saturday 9 A.M.–3 P.M., though these are not always strictly adhered to. For library information, call 612/122-0162.

La Unidad Cultural Profesor Jesús Castro Agúndez

This cultural center (Navarro btw Altamirano/Independencia, tel. 612/125-0207, Mon.–Fri. 8 A.M.–3 P.M.) includes an art gallery, community art school, city archives, and the **Teatro de la Ciudad** (City Theater), a 1,500-seat performing-arts facility that hosts musical, the-atrical, and dance performances throughout the year.

Universities

As Baja California Sur's educational center, La Paz supports a large number of schools at the primary, secondary, and tertiary levels. The prominent **Universidad Autonomía de Baja California Sur** (University of Baja California South), on Boulevard Forjadores, has reputable programs in agriculture, engineering, and business. The **Instituto Tecnológico de La Paz** (Technological Institute of La Paz), also on Boulevard Forjadores, is primarily known for its commercial-fishing department.

Beaches

BAHÍA DE LA PAZ

Bahía de La Paz is scalloped with 10 signed, public beaches. Most inviting are the seven beaches strung out northeast of La Paz along Península de Pichilingue—they get better the farther you get from the city.

Playa Palmira and Playa el Coromuel

Playa Palmira, around four kilometers (2.5 mi) east of downtown La Paz via the La Paz–Pichilingue Road, has been taken over by the Araiza Inn Palmira and Club de Yates Palmira, leaving little remaining beachfront. A kilometer farther, the small but pleasant Playa el Coromuel is popular with local residents and offers restaurant/bar service, a waterslide, *palapas,* and toilets.

Playa Caimancito

In front of La Concha Beach Resort near Km 5, Playa Caimancito (named for an offshore rock formation that resembles a small gator) features a rock reef within swimming distance of the grayish beach. Although it's close to the city and resort developments, you can see a surprising number of tropical fish here; incoming tide is the best time for swimming and snorkeling.

Playa del Tesoro and Playa Punta Colorada

Playa del Tesoro, 14 kilometers (8.5 mi) from the city, is another casual, semiurban beach with *palapas* and a sometimes-open, often-closed restaurant. The beach was purportedly named for a cache of silver coins unearthed by crews building a road to the Pichilingue ferry terminal near the beach. Just southwest of El Tesoro, a dirt road leads to hidden Playa Punta Colorada, a small, quiet cove surrounded by red-hued hills that protect it from the sights and sounds of the La Paz–Pichilingue Road.

Playa Pichilingue

At Km 17, just beyond the SEMATUR ferry terminal, is Playa Pichilingue, the only public beach in the La Paz vicinity with restrooms available 24 hours for campers. The beach also has a modest *palapa* restaurant (tel. 612/122-4565, mains US$5–10). A taxi from the *malecón* to the ferry terminal will run US$20.

Playa Balandra

After Pichilingue, the once-sandy track has been replaced by pavement as far as Playa El Tecolote. An unsigned left turnoff for Playa

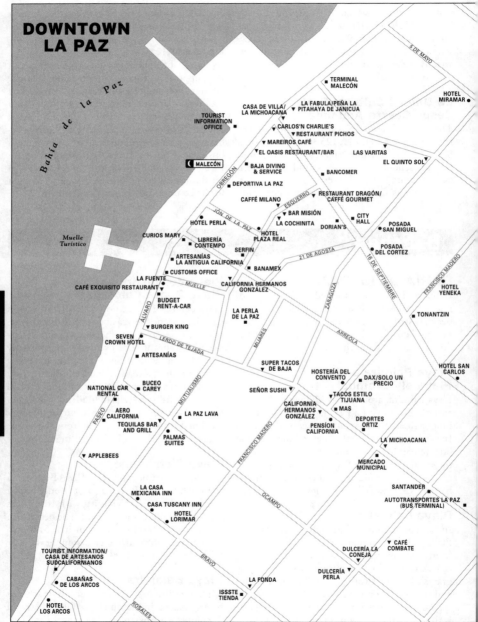

DOWNTOWN LA PAZ

Bahía de la Paz

Muelle Turístico

5 DE MAYO

TERMINAL MALECÓN

HOTEL MIRAMAR

CASA DE VILLA/ LA MICHOACANA

LA FABULA/PEÑA LA PITAHAYA DE JANICUA

TOURIST INFORMATION OFFICE

CARLOS'N CHARLIE'S

RESTAURANT PICHOS

MAREIROS CAFÉ

LAS VARITAS

EL QUINTO SOL

MALECÓN

EL OASIS RESTAURANT/BAR

BAJA DIVING & SERVICE

BANCOMER

OBREGÓN

DEPORTIVA LA PAZ

ESQUERRO

RESTAURANT DRAGÓN/ CAFFÉ GOURMET

CAFFÉ MILANO

BAR MISIÓN

CITY HALL

JON. DE LA PAZ

LA COCHINITA

DORIAN'S

POSADA SAN MIGUEL

HOTEL PERLA

CURIOS MARY

HOTEL PLAZA REAL

POSADA DEL CORTEZ

LIBRERÍA CONTEMPO

SERFIN

ARTESANÍAS LA ANTIGUA CALIFORNIA

21 DE AGOSTA

16 DE SEPTIEMBRE

FRANCISCO MADERO

CUSTOMS OFFICE

BANAMEX

LA FUENTE

CAFÉ EXQUISITO RESTAURANT

MUELLE

CALIFORNIA HERMANOS GONZÁLEZ

HOTEL YENEKA

ALVARO

BUDGET RENT-A-CAR

LA PERLA DE LA PAZ

ZARAGOZA

TONANTZIN

BURGER KING

SEVEN CROWN HOTEL

LERDO DE TEJADA

MIJARES

ARBEOLA

ARTESANÍAS

SUPER TACOS DE BAJA

HOSTERÍA DEL CONVENTO

DAX/SOLO UN PRECIO

HOTEL SAN CARLOS

NATIONAL CAR RENTAL

BUCEO CAREY

SEÑOR SUSHI

TACOS ESTILO TIJUANA

MUTUALISMO

MAS

AERO CALIFORNIA

CALIFORNIA HERMANOS GONZÁLEZ

PASEO

TEQUILAS BAR AND GRILL

LA PAZ LAVA

DEPORTES ORTIZ

PALMAS SUITES

PENSIÓN CALIFORNIA

LA MICHOACANA

APPLEBEES

FRANCISCO MADERO

MERCADO MUNICIPAL

LA CASA MEXICANA INN

SANTANDER

CASA TUSCANY INN

AUTOTRANSPORTES LA PAZ (BUS TERMINAL)

HOTEL LORIMAR

OCAMPO

TOURIST INFORMATION/ CASA DE ARTESANOS SUDCALIFORNIANOS

BRAVO

DULCERÍA LA CONEJA

CAFÉ COMBATE

CABAÑAS DE LOS ARCOS

DULCERÍA PERLA

HOTEL LOS ARCOS

ROSALES

LA FONDA

ISSSTE TIENDA

Balandra appears five kilometers (3 mi) beyond Pichilingue, and then it's another 800 meters (0.5 mi) to the parking area and beach, which has several *palapas* and brick barbecue pits. Depending on the tide, the large, shallow bay of Puerto Balandra actually forms several beaches, some of them long sandbars. Ringed by cliffs and steep hills, the bay is a beautiful and usually secluded spot, perfect for wading in the clear, warm waters. Clams are abundant, and a coral reef at the south end of the bay offers decent snorkeling. Climb the rock cliffs—carefully—for sweeping bay views. Camping is permitted at Balandra, but oftentimes a lack of breeze brings out the *jejenes* (no-see-ums), especially in the late summer and early fall. The beaches sometimes draw crowds on weekends.

Playa El Tecolote

About three kilometers (1.5 mi) beyond the Playa Balandra turnoff is Playa El Tecolote, a wide, long beach backed by vegetated dunes. Because El Tecolote is open to the stiff breezes of Canal de San Lorenzo, the camping here is usually insect-free. Two *palapa* restaurants, **El Tecolote** (tel. 612/127-9494, mains US$8–15) and **Palapa Azul** (tel. 612/122-1801, mains US$8–15), sell seafood and cold beverages and rent *pangas,* beach chairs and umbrellas, fishing gear, and plastic canoes. Both restaurants have pay showers. Free municipal *palapas,* barbecue grills, and trash barrels dot the beach north and south of the restaurants.

Isla Espíritu Santo, 6.5 kilometers (4 mi) away, is clearly visible in the distance; for around US$40–50 you can hire a *panga* to cross the channel (see *Islands*).

FARTHER AFIELD

From El Tecolote, the road returns to sand as it winds across the peninsula for about 13 kilometers (8 mi) before ending at remote **Playa Coyote.** Along the way, shorter roads branch off to rocky coves suitable for camping. Don't tackle this road expecting to find the perfect white-sand beach; the farther northeast from El Tecolote you go, the stonier and browner the beaches become.

LA PAZ AND VICINITY

South of Playa Coyote, you can navigate a network of sand roads to Puerto Mejia and **Las Cruces.** Named for three crosses topping a bluff near the cove where Cortés supposedly landed, Las Cruces served as a supply port for Isla Cerralvo pearl beds during the pearl era. It was abandoned in the 1930s after the pearl-bearing oysters died out. In 1949, Abelardo L. Rodríguez III, grandson of a former Mexican president, designed and built at Las Cruces a fly-in getaway resort for Hollywood celebrities, including Desi Arnaz and Bing Crosby. The 20,000-acre resort was incorporated as Club de Caza y Pesca Las Cruces (Las Cruces Hunting and Fishing Club) in 1961 and today remains a private association counting around 225 members. Although the resort's popularity peaked in the 1950s and 1960s, some of the fabulous beach villas are still occupied on occasion. The road's final approach is so difficult (intentionally so, according to rumors) that few people arrive by road; instead, guests use the resort's private airstrip or arrive by yacht. Membership is conferred by invitation and sponsorship only.

PENÍNSULA EL MOGOTE

This 11-kilometer (7-mi) thumb of land juts across the top of Ensenada de la Paz directly opposite the city. The southern shore of the peninsula is rimmed by mangroves, while the north side facing the open bay offers clean water and a long beach sullied only by everyday flotsam. It's not uncommon to see dolphins swimming by. Local myth says that if you eat the wild plums of the *ciruelo (Cryptocarpa edulis)* growing on El Mogote's sand dunes, you'll never want to leave La Paz.

Access to El Mogote is changing rapidly as a new US$240 million real estate project takes shape. The Paraíso del Mar plans call for two golf courses, a club house, hundreds of homes, a shopping mall, church, hotels, marina, and park. Necessary infrastructure will include desal plants, water and sewage treatment plants, and a ferry terminal. (Although there is a dirt road leading out to the peninsula from El Comitá, north of La Paz, primary access for

© AVALON TRAVEL PUBLISHING, INC.

visitors will be by ferryboat, since the distance is only one-half mile from the *malecón*.) The project has come under criticism from environmentalists, including Greenpeace, for endangering hundreds of acres of mangroves, which provide a habitat and nutrients for thousands of marine species in the Sea of Cortez.

Unless you're interested in touring the de-

THE PEARLS OF LA PAZ

Pearls develop from sand grains or other small particles that manage to get between an oyster's mantle and its shell. The oyster secretes a substance that cushions it from the irritation of the particle – if the grain moves freely during the secretion buildup, the pearl is more or less spherical; if it stays in one place or is embedded in the shell, it becomes a "baroque" pearl. Even when an oyster doesn't contain a pearl, the interior of the shell is valued for its rainbow luster, known as mother-of-pearl. Only particular mollusk varieties within the family Pteridae, found only in certain coastal areas off East Asia, Panama, and Baja California, can form pearls.

Pearl gathering in the New World goes back at least 7,000 years. When the Spanish found Amerindians along the Sea of Cortez coast wearing pearls and pearl shells as hair ornaments in the early 16th century, they quickly added pearls to the list of exploitable resources in Mexico. Finding the source of the luminescent, milky-white spheres – oyster beds – became a priority of marine expeditions off Mexico's west coast.

After a Spanish mutineer reported the presence of pearls in Bahía de la Paz in 1533, harvesting them became one of Cortés's primary interests in exploring Baja's lower Sea of Cortez coast. Between 1535, when Cortés finally managed to establish a temporary settlement at Bahía de la Paz, and 1697, when Jesuit padres began missionizing the Baja peninsula,

untold thousands of pearls were harvested. The Jesuits, however, strongly objected to any secular exploitation of the peninsula, preferring to keep Baja within the domain of the church. Hence during the mission period (1697–1768), pearling was restricted to sporadic illegal harvests; still, many pearls found their way to Europe, where they encrusted the robes of bishops and Spanish royalty.

In the mid-19th century, after the secularization of Baja missions, the Baja pearl industry was revived by *armadores* (entrepreneurs), who hired Yaqui divers from Sonora to scour the shallow bays, coves, and island shores between Mulegé and La Paz. The invention of diving suits in 1874 revolutionized pearling by allowing divers access to deeper waters. By 1889 the world pearling industry was dominated by Compañía Perlífera de Baja California, based in La Paz.

Intensive harvesting rapidly depleted the oyster beds, and between 1936 and 1941 most of the remaining pearl oysters were wiped out by an unknown disease. Many La Paz residents today believe the disease was somehow introduced by the Japanese to eliminate Mexican competition in the pearl industry, but it's more likely the disease simply took advantage of an already weakened population.

The mystique of La Paz pearls continued long after the industry's demise. John Steinbeck based his novella *The Pearl* on a famous pearl story he heard while visiting La Paz in 1941.

velopment, the easiest way to reach the peninsula is by kayak from the Marina de La Paz area (see *Kayaking* under *Sports and Recreation* later in this chapter for more information).

Most kayakers land on the mangrove side facing Ensenada de la Paz and then walk across the peninsula's narrow isthmus to reach the bay/ocean side.

Islands

The large and small islands clustered just north of Península de Pichilingue offer an amazing variety of recreational possibilities both in and out of the water. The 22.5-kilometer-long (14-mi-long) Isla Espíritu Santo and its smaller immediate neighbor to the north, Isla Partida, are excellent destinations for all manner of watercraft from sea kayaks to yachts. Sandy beaches and large coves along the western shores of both islands provide numerous opportunities for small-craft landings and camping. In full sun, the sand-bottom reflections of these bays create such a bright, translucent color that white seagulls flying over them are transformed into glowing blue-green UFOs.

◖ Isla Espíritu Santo

Formerly owned by a local *ejido,* this island was "sold" to the Mexican government in 2003, through the cooperative efforts of several nonprofits, which raised US$3.3 million to compensate *ejido* members for the land. For the traveler in search of outdoor adventure, this means the island has a good chance of remaining undeveloped, even as large real estate projects take shape on the peninsula.

Around Isla Espíritu Santo, rock reefs provide good **snorkeling** at Punta Prieta, at the north end of Bahía San Gabriel toward the island's southwestern tip; at the west end of Isla Ballena, an islet off the northwest coast of Espíritu Santo; at three islets in Caleta El Candelero, toward the island's northern end; and off Punta Bonanza on Espíritu Santo's southeast side.

Even if you don't snorkel, picturesque, sand-bottom **Bahía San Gabriel** is worth a visit to see the ruined walls of a pearlery dating to the early 20th century. The low walls form an inner lagoon that fills and empties with the tides, creating little waterfalls along the edges of the bay.

Just north of Ensenada La Ballena (directly opposite Isla Ballena), near a spot where the Guaicura found year-round water, several small rock shelters known as **Las Cuevitas** bear petroglyphs. More caves formerly used by the Guaicura can be found in the dry arroyo behind Ensenada La Ballena.

Espíritu Santo's most interesting **hike** starts from the beach at Caleta El Candelero and follows a deep, rocky arroyo inland into the 200-meter-high (650-ft-high) volcanic bluffs. The trail passes wild fig and plum trees clinging to the arroyo's rock sides; if you're lucky you might even spot a rare, endemic black jackrabbit.

Isla Partida

On the northern tip of Isla Partida you can hike to the top of a bluff called **El Embudo** for sweeping sea and island views. At the north and south ends of Isla Partida a couple of fish camps may have drinking water and food, but don't count on it. Plenty of yachts frequent the area. A narrow sandbar almost bridges Partida and Espíritu Santo, leaving a tight channel for small boat movement between the two islands.

Los Islotes

Just north of Isla Partida lie Los Islotes, a cluster of guano-covered volcanic rock islands popular among divers, anglers, birds, and sea lions. The sea lions and their pups often join divers and snorkelers for a swim. However, be cautious around lone adult male elephant seals. While these animals may appear friendly, their great size, strength, and large teeth have the potential to inflict serious injury; local dive operators advise that you not approach lone males or attempt to swim with them (see *Diving* under *Sports and Recreation*).

Camping

Caleta El Candelero and El Cardonalcito, on the west sides of Isla Espíritu Santo and Isla Partida, respectively, are generally considered the best camping beaches because each has a freshwater well suitable for bathing. To be certain of hauling some water out, you should

ISLA ESPÍRITU SANTO,
ISLA PARTIDA, AND LOS ISLOTES

Los Islotes

Sea of Cortez

El Embudo

Arroyos

Isla Partida

Punta Tintorera

Ensenada Grande

Punta Tijeretas

Las Cuevitas

El Cardonal

FRESHWATER WELL

Sand Spit

El Cardonalcito

Caleta Partida

Arroyo

Bahía el Mesteño

Isla Espíritu Santo

FRESHWATER WELL

Arroyos

ISLA ESPÍRITU SANTO

Bahía la Salinita

Punta Lobos

Caleta el Candelero

Isla Ballena

Playa Ballena

Arroyos

HOT SPRINGS

Isla Gallo

Playa Gallina

LIGHTHOUSE

Punta Bonanza

Isla Gallina

Arroyo

Puerto Ballena

Arroyo

Bahía Bonanza

Playa Coralito

Bahía de la Paz

Punta Prieta

Bahía San Gabriel

Punta Morito

Punta Colorada

Playa Dispensa

Punta Lupona

Punta Dispensa

0   1 mi

0   1 km

To La Paz

© AVALON TRAVEL PUBLISHING, INC.

LEAVE NO TRACE

Visitors intent on setting foot on the delicate islands of the Sea of Cortez should heed the recommendations proffered by Conservation International, as follows:

- Check your equipment and provisions thoroughly before landing to avoid the introduction of rats, mice, insects, or seeds from other islands or from the mainland. Check your shoes and cuffs.

- Don't bring cats, dogs, or any other animals to the islands.

- Don't take plants, flowers, shells, rocks, or animals from the islands.

- The animals and plants that live on the islands are not used to human presence. Keep this in mind during your visit.

- Keep a minimum distance of 45 meters (150 ft) from all sea bird and sea lion colonies, and keep at least 300 meters (1,000 ft) away from pelicans during their nesting period (Apr.–May).

- Don't cut cacti or shrubs. Don't gather wood; plants take a long time to grow on these arid islands. Dry trunks are the home of many small animals. If you need to cook, take your own stove, and avoid making fires.

- Don't make new walking paths. Don't remove stones or dig holes; you will cause erosion.

- Don't camp on the islands unless you are familiar with low-impact techniques. Conservation International Mexico can provide you with that information.

- Help keep the islands clean. Don't throw or leave garbage on the islands or in the sea. Help even more by bringing back any garbage you find.

- To camp or even land for any activity on the islands of the Sea of Cortez you need a permit from the Secretaría de Medio Ambiente y Recursos Naturales (SEMARNAT). To obtain a permit, contact Instituto Nacional de Ecología, Dirección de Aprovechamiento Ecológico, Periferico 5000, Col. Insurgentes Cuicuilco, C.P. 04530, Delegación Coyoacán México D.F. 01049, México, www.ine.gob.mx.

For more information, contact Conservation International, Calle Banamichi Lote 18 Manzana 1, Lomas de Cortés, Guaymas, Son. 85450, México, tel./fax 622/221-1594, 622/221-2030, m.carvajal@conservation.org, www.conservacion.org.mx, or its main U.S. office at 1919 M St., NW Suite 600, Washington, DC 20036, tel. 202/912-1000 or 800/406-2306, www.conservation.org.

---

bring your own bucket and five meters (15 ft) of rope. For drinking, bring enough purified water for the duration of your stay. If you must drink from the well, treat the water with purification tablets/iodine or boil it for at least 10 minutes.

Because these islands are part of an ecological preserve, you must obtain permission from the La Paz SEMARNAT office (2nd floor, Ocampo 1045 btw Rubio/Verdad, tel. 612/128-4171, Mon.–Fri. 8 A.M.–3 P.M.) before setting up camp. Camping is not allowed on Ensenada Grande or Playa Ballena. No pets or harvesting wood for campfires.

Getting to the Islands

Punta Lupona, on the southern tip of Espíritu Santo, lies within kayaking range—just 6.5 kilometers (4 mi)—from Península de Pichilingue. Once at Espíritu Santo, it's easy to explore Isla Partida by kayak; the shallow channel between the two islands is only a few hundred meters across. Playa El Tecolote or the smaller beaches just to its east are good put-in points for kayak trips to the island. Because of winds and tidal currents, this isn't a trip for the novice paddler. Even experienced sea kayakers on a first voyage to the island should follow someone who knows the tricky interplay of currents, shoals, tides, and winds. Outfitters in La Paz lead kayak trips to the islands with experienced guides (see *Kayaking* under *Sports and Recreation*).

Several companies in La Paz arrange two-hour powerboat jaunts to Isla Espíritu Santo and Isla Partida for around US$140 per boat including lunch. At Palapa Azul (tel. 612/122-1801), on Playa El Tecolote, you can arrange a four-hour trip around the west side of Espíritu Santo to a large island bay (Ensenada Grande) on Isla Partida and to the sea lion colony at Los Islotes; the cost for this trip, US$100 for up to

six people, includes lunch. A one-way shuttle out to the island costs US$60.

Whether booking with an agency in town or at the beach, remember to inquire about the quality and contents of the lunch. If the lunch situation sounds iffy or awful (a prominent La Paz company at one time was serving a single lousy sandwich of white bread glued to two slices of processed American cheese), demand more food or carry your own lunch. Life preservers are another variable worth inquiring about; some boats don't carry them.

Sports and Recreation

FISHING

Outer bay and offshore fishing in the La Paz area are very good; a boat is mandatory since onshore and surf-fishing opportunities are limited. The bay and canals west of the islands hold roosterfish, *pargo,* cabrilla, needlefish, bonito, amberjack, jack crevalle, yellowtail, sierra, and pompano. Beyond Isla Espíritu Santo are the larger game fish, including dorado, grouper, marlin, tuna, and sailfish. Yellowtail usually run in the area January–March, while most other game fish reach peak numbers April–November. Canal de Cerralvo, around the east side of Península de Pichilingue, provides excellent fishing for roosterfish and *pargo colorado* January–July.

Any of the major La Paz hotels will arrange fishing trips. One of the oldest operations is **Jack Velez Sport Fishing Charters** (tel. 612/128-7518, jackvelez@hotmail.com). Another established outfit is **Fisherman's Fleet** (tel. 612/122-2744 ext. 628), also with a desk at Los Arcos. Both offer fully equipped boats with guides, tackle, ice, and fish-cleaning and -filleting service at daily rates ranging from US$200 (for a 22-foot *panga*) to US$375 (for a 30-foot cabin cruiser).

You can also arrange guides and boats at the pier just east of the Pichilingue ferry terminal. From here, *panga* fishing trips in the bay generally cost US$100 a day for two people, while trips beyond Isla Espíritu Santo or to Canal de Cerralvo cost around US$200. Long-range fishing cruises run US$275–380 a day and usually accommodate up to four anglers.

Anglers with a sturdy set of wheels and their own tackle can drive the desolate road north from El Centenario (west of La Paz on the way to Ciudad Constitución) to **Punta El Mechudo** and **San Evaristo** at the northernmost end of Bahía de la Paz, where the onshore and inshore fishing—for grouper, snapper, *pargo,* cabrilla, sierra, dorado, and yellowfin—is almost as good as in the Canal de Cerralvo. Most visiting anglers camp on either side of Punta El Mechudo. The road is paved for the first 40 kilometers (25 mi) as far as the phosphate-mining town of San Juan de la Costa, then it becomes graded gravel interspersed with ungraded sand for the final 53 kilometers (33 mi) to San Evaristo. This road is best traversed by high-clearance vehicles only.

Buy fishing tackle at **Deportiva La Paz** (Mutualismo, tel. 612/122-7333), one block in from the Applebees on the *malecón.*

DIVING AND SNORKELING

The islands offshore from La Paz present divers of all skill levels with some of the

HOW MUCH DOES IT COST?

GUIDED DIVE/SNORKEL TOURS

Discounts apply for multiday dives (overnight in La Paz hotel, typically the Los Arcos). Hotel/dive packages are available.

Snorkel tour (equipment included)	US$50-65
Two- or three-tank boat dive	US$85-135
Night dive	US$60
Package of two days/three nights, with accommodations and meals	US$300-400
Package of six days/seven nights, with accommodations and meals	US$700-800
Nondiver passenger	US$10-15

LIVEABOARD DIVE TRIPS

Types of liveaboard trips: Socorro Island, Whale Shark Expedition, Island Tour

Six days/seven nights	US$1,565
Eight days/nine nights	US$1,495-2,500
Night dive on liveaboard trip	US$30

DIVE INSTRUCTION

Open water certification (classroom and dives)	US$420
Discover Scuba/resort course (Introduction to scuba)	US$110-140
Advanced certification	US$390
Nitrox certification	US$220

GUIDED KAYAK TOURS

Day trips	US$35-95
Two-day trip	US$250-300
Four-day trip	US$400-500
Six-day trip	US$1,100
Ten-day trip	US$2,000

DIVE AND KAYAK EQUIPMENT RENTAL

Snorkel gear (usually included with tour)	US$6-15
Scuba package with dives (discounts for multiday dives)	US$20-30/day
Rebreather	US$65
Airfills	US$5
Nitrox refills	US$8-12
Panga shuttle to Espíritu Santo (round-trip from Playa Tecolote)	US$200-400
Double kayak	US$60/day
Single kayak	US$40/day
Truck shuttle to Playa Tecolote	US$25
Island camping fee	US$4

most interesting underwater topography in the Sea of Cortez, as well as opportunities to spot some of the largest pelagics in the sea. Sea lions frolic at Los Islotes, while hammerhead sharks school around the El Bajo seamount and giant mantas cruise against the current. From the surface, you may see flying mantas, schools of dolphins, and giant bait balls. But unlike the reef and wall diving in Cabo Pulmo and Cabo San Lucas, where dive sites are a 5- to 15-minute boat ride from shore, long, choppy boat rides are the norm here (45–60 minutes)—hence the higher rates. Remember to take your seasickness medicine the night before. (Many divers swear by Bonine, found over the counter in the United States and Mexico.) A day of diving typically begins around 7–8 A.M. and finishes in the late afternoon. Lunch is usually included at no extra cost. *Note:* Most operators require a minimum of at least two divers to send a boat out to the islands. Some require four divers to visit the more remote sites. See the sidebar *How Much Does It Cost?* for standard prices.

Dive Sites

Most boats frequent about a dozen different sites around the islands offshore from La Paz. A sea lion colony at Los Islotes (25–50 ft) provides loads of underwater entertainment. Also suitable for beginners, the *Salvatierra* wreck (60 ft) presents an opportunity to explore the remains of a cargo ferry that sank in 1976. If conditions permit, advanced divers might request a trip to the El Bajo seamount (60–100+ ft) in hopes of encountering a school of hammerhead sharks, as well as giant mantas, whale sharks, and towers of schooling amber jacks and tuna. (See the sidebar *Diving and Snorkeling Around La Paz.*)

Day Trips

In business since 1992, **Buceo Carey** (Legaspy and Topete, tel. 612/128-4048, U.S. tel. 877/239-4057, www.carey.com.mx) is one of the more respected dive centers in town. A staff of local captains and international dive guides leads one-day and multiday dive trips to Espíritu Santo sites for US$85 a day, and to El Bajo and Isla Cerralvo for US$95. The cost includes guide, transportation, lunch, unlimited sodas and beer, weight belt, and two tanks. Rental equipment includes regulators, BCDs, wetsuits, masks, snorkels, fins, tanks, weight belts, booties, and portable air compressors. Carey prides itself in the fact that it offers its clients a choice of 15 different lunch menus. The company maintains a second office at Marina de La Paz. Inquire about accommodations packages: Two days/three nights at the Los Arcos runs US$317; six days/seven nights is US$773.

The granddaddy of all dive outfits in La Paz is Fernando Águilar's **Baja Diving and Service** (B.C.S. 11/Carr. a Pichilingue, past the ferry terminal, tel. 612/122-7010, www.clubcantamar.com). Based at the Club Cantamar Resort and Sports Centre on the Peninsula Pichilingue, the company operates a fleet of eight vessels, including some of the largest dive boats on the Sea of Cortez, holding more than 20 divers. Its custom-built 53-foot *Liberación* is the newest dive boat in La Paz, with air conditioning and hot water, two heads, and a pleasant sundeck for warming up after each dive. The boat accommodates 30 divers for day trips and 10 divers as a liveaboard (see *Liveaboard Trips*). The company was putting the finishing touches on a new 70-foot catamaran in 2007. They also run *pangas* for divers who consider the larger boats to be too much like cattle cars. Besides the sheer scale of the operation, shorter boat rides are a significant advantage of diving with the Cantamar staff. Boats typically depart at 8:30 A.M. and return by 5 P.M. For divers who aren't staying at the resort, a shuttle service is provided at no additional cost.

Dive rates are US$95 per person per day for two or three tanks, depending on conditions. Day trips include transportation, boat ride, lunch, and drinks. The resort has an ultralight plane used for spotting whale sharks (extra charge of US$20 pp). Shorter boat rides also make the more

DIVING AND SNORKELING AROUND LA PAZ

Some of Baja's best dive sites lie in the vicinity of La Paz, but most are accessible only by boat. Along the western shores of **Isla Espíritu Santo** and **Isla Partida** lie several good diving reefs. Bahía San Gabriel, a large cove along Espíritu Santo's southwest shore, features a shallow boulder reef (San Rafaelito) at its northern end suitable for both scuba diving and snorkeling. Similar rock reefs – along with submarine caves – can be found farther north off Espíritu Santo's western shore near Caleta El Candelero, extending from the west side of **Isla Ballena**. The latter islet also features a black coral forest and is protected from strong prevailing winds. All of these sites lie 1-2 hours from La Paz by boat.

LOS ISLOTES

One of the most colorful dive sites in the vicinity is Los Islotes, the tiny islet group off the north end of Isla Partida. Boulder reefs and underwater pinnacles off the north and northeast shores draw large marine species, including schools of hammerhead sharks, manta rays, and other pelagic (open-ocean) fish. A nearby cove is home to around 300 sea lions, who seem to enjoy swimming alongside divers and performing tricks for the camera. Late in the breeding season (Jan.-May) is the best time to visit the colony, since this is when the adolescent pups are most playful. The south side of Los Islotes is well protected from prevailing winds virtually year-round.

EL BAJITO

To the southwest of Los Islotes lies El Bajito, a large rock reef that extends to within six meters (20 ft) of the sea's surface; the base of the reef meets a sandy bottom at about 24-28 meters (80-90 ft). The diverse marinelife frequenting the reef includes grouper, cabrilla, and an unusually large number of morays living among the many cracks and crevices in the reef; attached to the rocks are gorgonians, sea fans, and other invertebrates. Wind protection here is scant.

EL BAJO

A group of three sea pinnacles called El Bajo (also known as Marisla Seamount), about 13 kilometers (8.2 mi) northeast of Los Islotes, is renowned for the presence of large pelagics such as marlin, sharks (hammerhead, blacktip, tiger, and silvertip), dorado, corvina, and

distant dive sites like Las Animas and the San Diegito Reef more accessible for day-trippers (extra charge of US$25 per diver for trips to these sites).

Dive packages for 3–14 nights with half- or full-board cost US$370–1,522 and US$402–1,692; nitrox and rebreather dive packages are also available at additional cost. Included are round-trip airport transfers and lunch on dive days.

Rental gear is available (snorkel set US$6/day, dive gear US$21/day). Certified divers can also get nitrox refills for US$8–12 and rent rebreathers for US$65. New divers can get certified in the resort's own pool (US$420, includes two days open-water dives) or try an introductory Discover Scuba course (US$140). Advanced certification costs US$390. Nitrox certification is US$220. In case of a dive emergency, the Cantamar has the only recompression chamber in La Paz. For more information or to make a reservation, drop in to the Cantamar's downtown sales office (Obregón 1665-2, Plaza Cerralvo, near the Hotel Perla, tel. 612/122-1826, daily 9 A.M.–8 P.M.).

Another multiboat operation is based at the La Concha Beach Resort. **The Cortez Club Dive Center** (Km 5 Carr. a Pichilingue, tel. 612/121-6120, www.cortezclub.com) has 12 dive boats, its own classroom for dive instruction, and a private jetty and ramp. Rates are a little higher than other shops for day trips, but lower for scuba courses.

Day excursions aboard Baja Expeditions' 45-foot *Don Cano* or 48-foot *Pez Sapo* cost manta rays. Mantas frequent El Bajo July–mid-October and here seem unusually friendly. Whale sharks, the largest fish in the world, are occasionally seen near El Bajo during the same months, as are pilot whales. Depths range 18–43 meters (60–140 ft). Boats typically take 2–3 hours to reach El Baja from La Paz.

Because of strong tidal currents and lack of wind protection, El Bajito and El Bajo are best left to experienced open-ocean divers.

SALVATIERRA

The wreck of the *Salvatierra*, a 91-meter (300-ft) La Paz-Topolobampo ferry that went down in the Canal de San Lorenzo in 1976, presents one of the more challenging dives. The hull lies about 2.5 kilometers (1.5 mi) southeast of the southern tip of Isla Espíritu Santo at a depth of approximately 10 fathoms (18 m/60 ft). Encrusted with sponges, sea fans, mollusks, and gorgonians, the wreck attracts numerous varieties of tropical fish, including groupers, barracuda, angelfish, goatfish, parrotfish, moray eels, and rays.

ISLA CERRALVO

Southeast of Península de Pichilingue, the somewhat more remote Isla Cerralvo offers several additional diving opportunities. **La Reinita,** a rock reef off the island's northern shore, attracts large pelagic fish. Even more remote – generally reached by liveaboard boat trips – are **Isla Santa Cruz** and **Islas Las Animas** to the north. The former is known for rock reefs at depths of around 17 meters (35 ft) with a profusion of sea horses, while the latter reportedly offers the greatest variety of diving experiences – caves, hammerheads, whale sharks, sea lions – of any site in the Sea of Cortez. Only Baja Expeditions leads Santa Cruz and Animas dives.

WHEN TO GO

Optimum diving months are May–August, when visibility reaches 30 meters (100 ft) or more and water temperatures run around 27°C (80°F). In September, tropical storms can be an obstacle. October conditions are often spectacular, but during the late fall and winter high winds and changing currents reduce visibility to 10–15 meters (35–50 ft). A light wetsuit is necessary any time except June–August.

LA PAZ AND VICINITY

US$125 per day (Mar.–Dec.), which covers three dives, breakfast, lunch, snacks, and happy hour (tel. 612/125-3828, U.S. 800/843-6967, www.bajaex.com).

Liveaboard Trips

If viewing underwater marinelife is the focus of your trip to La Paz, consider a multiday trip aboard one of these custom-designed dive boats. Packages typically include the first and last nights in a La Paz hotel, usually the Los Arcos. Rates below are for double occupancy. An additional fee often applies for single occupancy.

Baja Diving and Service (see *Day Trips*) runs several liveaboard trips through the summer and fall months. A nine-night trip to Socorro Island (eight days of diving) costs US$2,500. A seven-night (six days of diving) whale shark expedition is US$1,565. **Buceo Carey** (see *Day Trips*) runs multiday trips on two boats: *Marco Polo* holds 6–8 divers, six days/five nights for US$1,399; first and last night at the Los Arcos. **Baja Expeditions** (tel. 612/125-3828, U.S. 800/843-6967, www.bajaex.com) offers liveaboard trips on the air-conditioned, 80-foot *Don José*. Trips are booked out of the U.S. office, but it's occasionally possible to sign up in La Paz when space is available. The company runs eight-day expeditions aboard the *Don José* May 28–November 30, from US$1,445 per person for standard rooms to US$1,645 per person for superior rooms (double occupancy). Three eight-day excursions specifically dedicated to viewing the magnificent whale shark are offered in May and June from US$1,495 per person for standard rooms to US$1,695 per person for superior rooms (double occupancy). The boat holds 16 divers. The *Don José* has a loyal following since the staff allows divers to go on their own schedule by running constant shuttles to many different sites.

Operated by a Mexican-Japanese couple, **Baja Quest** (Rangel 10 btw Sonora/Sinaloa, tel. 612/123-5320, www.bajaquest.com.mx) offers two-night/three-day dive-trip packages May–December, for US$850 including hotel and airport transfers, and longer trips for US$1,040–1,190. Luxury accommodations aboard *The Sandman* cost US$993–1,395. Baja Quest also organizes dive/cruise/camping combinations (Apr.–Nov. only). Whale-watching and camping tours include campsite with large kitchen, tents, cots, sleeping bags, sun showers, toilets, round-trip transportation, kayaking equipment and instruction, and *pangas,* but not airfare, hotel, airport to hotel transfers, meals on arrival and departure dates, airport taxes, or crew tips.

Another dive operator in town is **Toto's Dive Shop and Service** (Guerrero btw Revolución de 1910/Serdán, tel. 612/122-7154, fax 612/123-4521). **Deportiva La Paz** (Mutualisimo, tel./fax 612/122-7333) sells diving equipment and airfills but doesn't organize dive trips.

Snorkel Tours

Most dive and kayak outfitters also run snorkel tours. Less expensive trips visit the beaches along Peninsula Pichilingue; the more expensive ones go to the islands for the day. For example, **Buceo Carey** (see *Day Trips*) offers snorkeling trips for US$65 to Playa Encantada and the sea lion colony. **Baja Diving and Service** (see *Day Trips*) at the Cantamar does local snorkel trips for US$50. And **Azul Tours** (Obregón 774, tel. 612/122-4427, azultours@gmail.com) brings snorkelers to Espíritu Santo for US$55 per person.

El Tecolote Rest/Bar/Playa (tel. 612/127-9494, www.eltecolote.net) transports snorkelers to Espíritu Santo in *pangas* for US$40. The price includes gear and lunch. Boats depart between 10–11 A.M. for a four-hour tour. Stop by the booking office, just off the plaza next to the Hotel Miramar, for more information. Other water activities include: WaveRunners, kayaks, banana boat, and water skiing.

WHALE-WATCHING

There are several ways to see gray and blue whales in action: Dive and kayak outfitters offer special whale-watching tours. Some tours go to the Sea of Cortez, while others go to the San Ignacio Lagoon on the Pacific side of the Baja Peninsula. Some trips involve snorkeling and paddling; others are just boat cruises. You can go for one day or eight, depending on your budget and how much time you want to spend with the mammals.

Baja Outdoor Activities (tel. 612/125-5636, U.S. tel. 888/217-6659, www.kayakin-baja.com) offers a package with two three-hour boat trips plus an overnight stay and all meals for US$250 per person.

Johnny Friday and Maldo Ficher lead ecotours in the area through **Baja Adventure Company** (tel. 612/124-6629, U.S. tel. 877/650-2252, www.bajaecotours.com), a division of Mar de Cortez sports. Its marine biologists, zoologists, and other professionally trained guides lead whale-watching trips.

KAYAKING

Several local outfits operate excellent guided kayak trips in the region. Packages usually include the first and last nights in hotel accommodation, with camping on the nights in between. Meals, transportation to the islands, and airport transfers are also typically covered by the price. Some trips return to a base camp every night, while others move to a new place each day. Some supply camping gear, others ask that you bring your own.

Baja Expeditions (tel. 612/125-3828, U.S. tel. 800/843-6967, www.bajaex.com) has been running seven-day trips to Espíritu Santo (US$1,045) since 1985. Other destinations include the Loreto to La Paz coast (10 days) and Magdalena Bay (8 days). An adventurous

10-day, open-water kayak trip hops among the islands of Espíritu Santo, Los Islotes, San José, Santa Cruz, and Santa Catalina (Oct.–Apr. only).

Owned by a La Paz native, **Mar y Aventuras** (Topete 564 btw 5 de Febrero/Navarro, tel. 612/123-0559, U.S. tel. 800/355-7140, www.kayakbaja.com), near La Marina Don José and Marina de La Paz, leads one-day and multiday trips and rents kayaks and gear to experienced paddlers. Its boats are a mix of doubles and singles made of fiberglass and some plastic. All have rudders. Day trips range US$35–95 per person, depending on the destination and size of the group. Two- to four-day tours cost US$250–495. Magdalena Bay whale-watching trips cost US$300–795 for two to five days. Longer trips to Espíritu Santo are available as well.

Experienced kayakers can also rent kayaks from Mar y Aventuras for paddling to El Mogote or to the islands on their own. The company rents single kayaks for US$40 a day, including PFD (personal flotation device), paddle, bilge pump, and spray deck. Double kayaks go for US$60/day. You can also rent snorkeling gear, wetsuits, dry bags, tents, small stoves, and sleeping bags. Boat shuttles out to Isla Espíritu Santo (US$200–400 round-trip for 1–2 people) as well as truck shuttles to Playa El Tecolote for beach launches to Espíritu Santo (US$25 one-way for 1–2 people), can be arranged. There is a camping fee of US$4/day for the island camping, which can be paid at the Mar y Aventura office.

Several other outfitters lead paddling trips to Isla Espíritu Santo. **Baja Quest** (Rangel 10 btw Sonora/Sinaloa, tel. 612/123-5320, www.bajaquest.com.mx) organizes three- to six-day kayaking/hiking/camping trips (Mar.–May and Oct.–Dec., US$540–1,080 pp). **Baja Outdoor Activities (BOA)** (tel. 612/125-5636, www.kayakinbaja.com) offers two different styles of kayak trips: "Cooperatively catered" trip participants carry their own gear each day and help guides prepare meals, making for a more self-sufficient experience, but with heavier boats to paddle. Others prefer a fully catered trip, in which guides prepare all meals and camping supplies are transported by motorboat. Four-day island tours range US$420–490. Daily dolphin sightings are common on the 10-day Loreto to La Paz trip (US$1,090). Participants should expect to paddle about four hours per day on this trip.

The half-day tour for US$35 is a nice way for beginners to get a feel for the sport without committing to a full-day adventure. BOA also offers a one-day tour of Balandra Bay for US$60. BOA rents sit-on-top kayaks and sea kayaks by the day or week (US$35–60/day and US$110–220/week).

BOATING

With a huge, protected bay, several public and private marinas, and several boatyards and marine supply stores, La Paz is Baja California's largest and best-equipped boating center.

At the west end of the *malecón,* the **Marina de La Paz** (Topete 3040 at Legaspy, tel. 612/122-1646, www.marinadelapaz.com) has completed numerous upgrades in recent years: New docks and a new layout came in 2004, followed by a fixed breakwater system in 2005, and an additional 120 feet of fixed breakwater plus a new 160-foot dock for accommodating large vessels in 2006. Facilities at this floating marina now include a launch ramp, fuel dock (diesel), market with groceries and marine supplies, café, water and electricity outlets, cable TV, laundry, showers, restrooms, wireless Internet, a chandlery, and boat and vehicle maintenance and storage. **Club Cruceros de La Paz** (www.clubcruceros.org, Mon.–Sat. 9 A.M.–6 P.M.) is a local nonprofit association that maintains a clubhouse at the marina and offers incoming mail service, as well as a book exchange library.

Rates for one of the marina's 150 slips range from US$19/day and US$350/month for a 30-foot craft to US$88/day and US$1,650/month for a 100-foot craft. Discounts also apply for stays of 4–21 days, if paid in advance. Showers cost US$1.30 daily. Cable TV is US$1 per day or US$15 per month. Parking for slip clients is US$1 daily or US$22 per month. Prices include tax.

Marina de La Paz is the most popular marina in the bay and is often full November–May; check for vacancies before sailing in. A US$200 deposit will hold your space on the waiting list. Reserve online, or by mailing a personal check.

Northeast of town, on the Canal de La Paz at Km 2.5, the well-planned **Marina Palmira** (tel. 612/123-7000 or 877/217-1513, www.marinapalmira.com) offers 186 full-service slips accommodating yachts up to 130 feet long and 12 feet deep. The marina recently reinforced its breakwater and launching ramp. There is free wireless Internet, and a free shuttle to downtown is available at various times each day. Other services include dry-storage facilities, a market, laundry, water, showers, bathrooms, a pool, hot tub, tennis court, two restaurants, a bar, 24-hour security, parking for one car per registered guest, a public phone, marine supplies, a fuel dock (diesel as well as gas), and boat launch. Crewed and bareboat yacht charters are available. Daily slip rates range US$15.75–60 depending on the size of the boat; monthly rates are US$10–21 per foot for slips of 30–100 feet. Electrical service costs extra. Condos and hotel rooms adjacent to the marina available for rent by the day, week, or month.

Based at the Club Cantamar Resort and Sports Centre, **Marina Pichilingue** (tel. 612/122-7010, www.clubcantamar.com) has 35 slips for boats up to 75 feet long (US$8.10/ft/month). Water, electricity, and dry storage are available.

La Marina Don José (Encinas 15, tel./fax 612/122-0848), at the end of Calle Encinas, one street south of Marina de La Paz, offers mooring facilities but is often full. Rates run US$8.80 per foot per month. The marina office is open Monday–Friday 8 A.M.–noon and 2–6 P.M., Saturday 8 A.M.–1 P.M.

A newcomer on the Peninsula Pichilingue, **Marina CostaBaja** (tel. 612/121-6225, www.costabajaresort.com) can accommodate megayachts up to 200 feet in 250 slips. Rates start at US$11.50/foot up to 39 feet for one month, up to US$22/foot for a 150- to 200-foot boat.

Daily rates are subject to availability (US$1.10/ft/day up to 99 feet and US$1.65/ft/day for 100–200 ft boats). Liveaboards require special permission from the marina. Amenities include Internet, TV, and phone; at-slip pumpout service, dry storage, restrooms and showers, parking, pool, and shuttle to La Paz. Some travelers who have used this marina report problems with black soot from the nearby oil refinery damaging canvas on their boats. A reservation form is available online.

The new Marina Fidepaz (Mexico 1/Constituyentes, near Km 4.5, tel. 612/124-2206), part of the Mexican government's Sea of Cortez Project, is being constructed near the airport, with 40 boat slips.

You can launch trailered and cartopped boats at Marina de La Paz, Marina Palmira, La Marina Don José, Aquamarina RV Park, and Pichilingue. Smaller boats and kayaks can put in at any of the public beaches.

Parts and Repairs: Marina de La Paz is the best local source of information about boating needs; **Ferretería Marina SeaMar** (SeaMar Marine Chandlery, Topete and Legaspy, tel. 612/122-9696, Mon.–Fri. 8:30 A.M.–1:30 P.M. and 3–6 P.M., Sat. 8:30 A.M.–1:30 P.M.), opposite the marina entrance, stocks many everyday nautical items. **López Marine Supply** (Vista Coral Plaza, tel. 612/125-4160, Mon.–Sat. 8 A.M.–5 P.M.) accepts Visa and MasterCard. Club Cruceros keeps a list of local marine service providers at www.clubcruceros.org/services.

Buying a *Panga*: La Paz is the *panga* capital of Mexico. Until 1968, when American Mac Shroyer designed and built the first molded fiberglass *pangas,* many Sea of Cortez fishermen still used dugout canoes of Amerindian design; glass *pangas* made in La Paz are now sold all over Mexico. **Embarcaciones Arca** (tel. 612/122-0874, fax 612/122-0823) makes and sells *pangas* at a factory on Calle Guillermo Prieto between Juárez and Allende. The standard *panga* is sold in 16- to 26-foot lengths, but the factory can accommodate special orders as long as 36 feet. The standard *panga* outboard motor is a *cinco-cinco caballos,* 55 horsepower.

Boat Charters

Baja Coast SeaFaris (Dock B, Marina de La Paz, tel. 612/125-9765, www.bajaseafaris.com) can organize customized charters aboard its *Irish Mist* 50-foot sailing yacht and *Tesoro del Mar*, a Beneteau 50 sailboat. Multiday trips (3–5 days or longer) include visits to Espíritu Santo, Isla Partida, and Los Islotes, with stops along the way for swimming with sea lions, scuba diving, kayaking, tubing (for kids), sailing, beachcombing, whale-watching, birdwatching, snorkeling, or fishing. Rates start at US$695–865 per person per day, based on a group of two, with substantial discounts for larger groups (US$145–165 additional pp per day). Rates include all onboard meals, snacks, and cocktails, lodging at Los Arcos Hotel on the last evening, and airport transfers. Scuba diving and rental gear are also available. Reservations should be made at least four months in advance for trips during the spring, fall, or major holidays. A 10 percent discount is offered for families and special occasions like honeymoons and anniversaries.

ATVS

ATV tours have become a popular way to explore the Baja Peninsula, and La Paz now has its first tour operator: **La Paz ATV's Adventures** (cell 612/131-0784, www.lapaza-tvs.com, US$75/90 s/d) runs three-hour tours on Honda Rancher 350 ATVs. The ride includes safety equipment, instruction, and bottled water, and the route goes from the village of El Comitán, a half hour north of La Paz, through El Mogote sand dunes, to the end of the peninsula and back. Shuttle service is provided from La Paz to the departure site.

MOUNTAIN BIKING

Colocated in the Baja Outdoor Activities (BOA) office next to the El Moro hotel, Mexican-owned **Katún** (tel. 612/348-7758, www.katuntours.com) runs guided tours of the Sierra de La Laguna (US$1,980/two weeks, US$1,299/one week, US$50–75/day). Combination kayak/bike trips cover travel from the Sea of Cortez to the Sierra de la Laguna in

10 or 14 days (US$1,350/US$1,980). And the weeklong Jesuits trail tour traces historic routes through the Sierra la Giganta, from the Sea of Cortez to the Pacific (US$1,199).

Katún also rents 2006 Giant Yukon bikes with front suspension for US$10 an hour, US$15 for four hours, or US$20 per day. **Azul Tours** (Obregón 774, tel. 612/122-4427, azul-tours@gmail.com) rents mountain bikes for US$15/day.

HIKING AND HORSEBACK RIDING

Antonio Moller (tel. 612/123-1370, t_moller@hotmail.com) leads one-day and overnight trips into the Sierra de La Laguna from La Paz. Day trips (US$120 for one person, US$70 pp for two people, US$60 pp for a group of 3–6) include transportation from La Paz to the biosphere, lunch at a local ranch, and a one-hour horseback ride. Student discounts available.

SPA SERVICES

The Hotel Los Arcos offers spa services at reasonable rates: A 45-minute massage is US$45, and a 50-minute sports massage is US$55. Hacienda del Cortez was adding a full-service spa in 2007.

ORGANIZED TOURS

Travel companies and outfitters offer a variety of guided tours and organized activities, from island kayak trips and whale-watching to language immersion and cooking classes. Here are a few additional options:

Readers have reported pleasant outings with **Eduardo's Tours** (044-612/105-2609, eduar-doviajes@hotmail.com). Eduardo Gomez provides ground transportation and leads guided trips to Los Cabos (US$99 pp), Todos Santos (US$77 pp), and El Triunfo (US$77 pp). A La Paz city tour costs US$27.50 per person. Whale-watching (US$120) and snorkeling (US$77 pp) tours are also possible. **Azul Tours** (Obregón 774, tel. 612/122-4427, azultours@gmail.com) offers a La Paz city tour for US$30 per person, as well as island trips (see *Diving and Snorkeling* and *Kayaking*).

LA PAZ AND VICINITY

Mar y Aventura (Topete 564 btw 5 de Febrero/Navarro, tel. 612/123-0559, U.S. tel. 800/355-7140, www.kayakbaja.com) offers a Spanish language immersion and cooking class package, in partnership with Se Habla La Paz. Packages include seven nights/eight days accommodations in the Posada Luna Sol, 25 hours of Spanish classes, and three nights of cooking classes (US$495 pp, double occupancy).

Once a year in April, May, or November, travel photographer Jim Cline leads a **Wonders of Baja** photo tour (U.S. tel. 877/350-1314, www.jimcline.com) of La Paz, Loreto, Mulege, Todos Santos, and Cabo San Lucas, including three boat trips to islands on the Sea of Cortez. Participants get to try their hand at capturing the seascapes, cacti, historic missions, and wildlife through the lens of their camera. Tours include accommodations and seafood dinners.

Entertainment and Events

BARS AND MUSIC

Bar Pelícanos (Paseo Obregón 498, tel. 612/122-2744, www.losarcos.com, daily 10 A.M.–1 A.M.), in Hotel Los Arcos, overlooking the *malecón,* is a large, sedate watering hole popular among tourists and old hands. It's worth at least one visit to peruse the old photos along the back wall; subjects include a motley array of unnamed vaqueros and revolutionaries, as well as Pancho Villa, General Blackjack Pershing, President Dwight Eisenhower, Emiliano Zapata, and Clark Gable (posed with a marlin).

On Calle Esquerro near the Hotel Perla, the slightly seedy **Bar Misión** features live *norteña* bands nightly.

Tequilas Bar and Grill, in a rustic house next to El Palmar Suites on Calle Mutualismo near Bravo, is an intimate bar with pool tables and a small private room popular with local politicians.

The rather interesting-looking **El Claustro** (Obregón btw Hidalgo/Costilla, tel. 612/122-1609, Tues.–Sun.) is a rock 'n' roll bar ensconced in a two-story pseudo-Italianate structure, complete with heavy faux-painted "marble" pilasters around the doors and stained-glass windows, plus lots of ironwork. It's decorated inside and out with an angel motif.

Caliente Race and Sports Book (Paseo Obregón at Morelos, tel. 800/027-3354, www.caliente.com.mx, Mon.–Fri. 10 A.M.–midnight, Sat.–Sun. 9 A.M.–midnight) has the usual array of satellite-linked TV monitors for viewing international sports events—and betting on them if the mood strikes you.

Living up to its laid-back reputation, La Paz isn't big on discos. A slightly older crowd frequents **Las Varitas** (Independencia 111, tel. 612/125-2025, www.lasvaritas.com), downtown near El Quinto Sol natural foods store and Plaza Constitución. The club offers dancing to recorded and live music. It also has a second location in Cabo San Lucas.

Carlos'n Charlie's, on Paseo Obregón, has an attached dance club, **La Paz Lapa** (Obregón and 16 de Septiembre, tel. 612/122-9290), that experiences occasional waves of popularity, especially on Thursday evenings when women are admitted without having to pay the usual cover charge. Above Pizza Fabula and La Pitahaya, **Casa de Villa** (Obregón and 16 de Septiembre, tel. 612/122-5799) is a rooftop bar and nightclub that's popular with locals.

Nightclub La Cabaña (Paseo Obregón 1570, tel. 612/122-0777, daily 9 P.M.–3 A.M.) at the Hotel Perla, usually offers live *norteña* music and attracts a local crowd. There's live music on Thursday and Sunday, and no cover charge on Wednesday.

In a courtyard behind La Fabula Pizza on Obregón, **Peña La Pitahaya de Janicua** (Obregón 15, tel. 612/126-2234) is an almost hidden spot with a bohemian ambience and live Latin folk music nightly.

BULLFIGHTS AND CHARREADAS

The municipal stadium at Constitución and Verdad occasionally hosts *corridas de toros* in the late winter, usually February–March.

Paceños are more active in *charrería* than in bullfighting, and you can attend *charreadas* (Mexican-style rodeos) at **Lienzo Charro Guadalupano,** just south of the city on the west side of Mexico 1 south (heading toward San Pedro). For information on the latest schedules for *charreadas* and *corridas de toros,* contact the state tourism office (tel. 612/124-0199), between Km 6 and 5 on Mexico 1 (Avenida Abasolo), opposite the Fidepaz marina. A *gran charreada* is usually held to celebrate Cinco de Mayo (May 5).

CINEMAS

In the city center, **Cinema Versalles Plus** (Revolución de 1910, tel. 612/122-9555) shows first-run movies on four screens. The largest and most popular cinema in town is the 14-screen **Cine Gemelos** in the new Soriana shopping complex out on Boulevard Forjadores at the corner of Avenida Luis Donaldo Colosio.

EVENTS

Carnaval

La Paz's biggest annual celebration is Carnaval, held for six days before Ash Wednesday in mid-February. Carnaval is also held in the Mexican cities of Mazatlán, Ensenada, and Veracruz, but Carnaval connoisseurs claim La Paz's is the best—perhaps because the city's *malecón* makes a perfect parade route.

As at all Mexican Carnavals, the festival begins with the Quema de Mal Humor, or "Burning of Bad Humor," in which an effigy representing an unpopular public figure is burned. Other events include the crowning of La Reina del Carnaval (Carnaval Queen) and El Rey Feo (Ugly King), colorful costumed parades, music, dancing, feasting,

© JOE CUMMINGS

costumed Carnaval celebrant in La Paz

LA PAZ AND VICINITY

cockfights, and fireworks. The festival culminates in El Día del Marido Oprimido, or "Day of the Oppressed Husband" (23.5 hours of symbolic freedom for married men to do whatever they wish), followed by a masquerade ball on the Tuesday evening before Ash Wednesday.

Fiesta de La Paz

Also prominent on the city's yearly events calendar is the Fiesta de La Paz (officially known as "Fiesta de la Fundación de la Ciudad de La Paz"), held May 3, the anniversary of the city's founding. The state tourist office (tel. 612/124-0100, turismo@correro.gbcs.gob.mx), between Km 6 and 5 on Mexico 1 (Avenida Abasolo), opposite the Grand Plaza Resort, can provide up-to-date details on festival scheduling and venues.

Baja 1000

The Baja 1000 off-road race comes to town in mid-November. Produced by SCORE International (U.S. tel. 818/225-8402, www.score-international.com), the event is the sixth and last in a series of desert races that take place in the southwestern United States and Mexico each year. The Baja 1000 attracts more than 400 pro contestants who drive trucks, motorcycles, ATVs, and every imaginable variation of off-road vehicle. They start in Ensenada and cruise at breakneck speeds through the desert to the outskirts of La Paz. Only about half of the race entrants complete the challenging 1,000-mile course.

In its 40th year in 2007, the race draws thousands of support crew and spectators to the most remote parts of the peninsula. The course opens for pre-running approximately three weeks before the race start. Travelers on Mexico 1 during this time will often see vehicles kicking up a cloud of dust in the distance, moving at speeds faster than highway drivers go. *Note:* This is one of the only times a year you may encounter traffic on the more remote stretches of Mexico 1.

Shopping

Before the city's duty-free status was recalled in 1989, imported merchandise could be purchased in La Paz free of import duties and sales tax. Nowadays, sales tax is commensurate with the rest of Mexico's. But the city still offers some of Baja's best shopping in terms of value and variety.

DEPARTMENT STORES

La Paz's main department stores are **Dorian's** (16 de Septiembre at Esquerro) and **La Perla de La Paz** (Arrival at Mutualismo), which was temporarily closed in late 2006 due to a fire. A newer Dorian's can be found in the Soriana shopping complex on Boulevard Forjadores, at the southwestern edge of town.

MAS (Madero at Degollado, daily 9 A.M.–9 P.M.) is a three-story discount department store that stocks everything from clothing to luggage to housewares. Next door on Madero between Tejada and Arreola, opposite Hostería del Convento, **DAX** (Mon.–Thurs. 8 A.M.–9 P.M., Fri.–Sat. 8 A.M.–10 P.M.) is an American-style pharmacy with many hard-to-find cosmetic and toiletry items. And next to DAX is the popular **Solo Un Precio** ("Only One Price," Madero btw Tejada/Arreola, daily 8 A.M.–9 P.M.), where everything in the store is only 10 pesos (US$1). You can find some great deals here.

ARTS AND CRAFTS

Along Paseo Obregón in the vicinity of the Hotel Perla and Hotel Los Arcos are a number of souvenir and handicraft shops of varying quality. One of the better ones is **La Antigua California** (Paseo Obregón 220, tel. 612/125-5230), which sells quality folk arts and crafts from the mainland. There are a few similar shops on Obregón between Degollado and Ocampo. **México Lindo** (Paseo Obregón at 16 de Septiembre), next to Carlos'n Charlie's, is also good for *artesanías*. **Curios Mary** (Arreola 25 at Obregón, tel. 612/122-0815) specializes in Majorcan pearls.

Casa de Artesanos Sudcalifornianos, a government-supported shop next door to the Tourist Information/Tourist Police office on Paseo Obregón between Allende and Rosales, focuses on *artesanías* from Baja California Sur.

Away from the city center, the **Centro de Arte Regional** (Calle Chiapas at Encinas) produces and sells pottery, as does **Ibarra's Pottery** (Prieto 625 btw Iglesias/República, tel. 612/122-0404, Mon.–Fri. 9 A.M.–3 P.M., Sat. 9 A.M.–2 P.M.), where you can watch pottery being made. **Artesanía Cuauhtémoc** (Av. Abasolo btw Jalisco/Nayarit) weaves rugs, blankets, wall hangings, tablecloths, and other cotton and wool items. Custom orders are possible, and customers are welcome to watch the weavers at their looms in the back of the shop.

Artesanías Colibri (Paseo Obregón btw Muelle/Arreola, tel. 612/128-5833, Mon.–Sat. 10 A.M.–1 P.M. and 3–8:30 P.M.) carries a good selection of *artesanías,* rustic furniture, and decorating accessories, plus cute clothes for babies and kids.

For bottom-dollar bargains on clothing, housewares, and leather, browse the **Mercado Municipal Francisco E. Madero** (Revolución de 1910 at Degollado). Inexpensive electronics, watches, and jewelry are available at a string of shops along Calles Domínguez and Madero between Avenida Independencia and Calle 16 de Septiembre, and along a pedestrian alley off Calle 16 de Septiembre near Dorian's department store.

Santander (tel. 612/125-5962), a large store at the corner of Serdán and Degollado, stocks a wide variety of useful *artesanías,* including saddles, guitars, and huaraches.

SPORTING GOODS
Deportes Ortiz (Degollado 260, almost opposite Pensión California, tel. 612/122-1209) carries a modest selection of camping, diving, and other sports equipment.

BOOKSTORES
Librería Contempo (Calle Arrival at Paseo Obregón) carries Mexican newspapers as well as a few American magazines.

The La Paz branch of **Libros Libros/Books Books** (Constitución at Madero, tel./fax 612/122-1410, Mon.–Sun. 9 A.M.–8:45 P.M.) has a limited selection of American newspapers, magazines, and books.

Accommodations

La Paz offers the most varied and least expensive selection of places to stay of any city in Baja, and new options are opening all the time. There are hotels in all budget categories, many with kitchenettes, plus bed and breakfast inns, condo complexes, and private vacation rental homes. Rates do not include tax or service fees. And many places offer discounts for stays of a week or longer.

Beach camping is available in several places outside the city limits.

HOTELS
Despite the planned construction of several large luxury hotels, most rooms in La Paz still fall in the US$50–125 range. Some of the older establishments could use a makeover, but the time warp is also part of their charm. You'll pay a bit more to stay right on the water rather than along the *malecón.* And none of the bay-front hotels are within easy walking distance of the *malecón* or downtown La Paz, although taxis are always available.

Most times of year, you can wing it and find a room when you arrive. But if you plan to visit during mid-November, check the Baja 1000 event schedule and make reservations well in advance. The tourist information office on the *malecón* is a good place to stop for updated information on most local hotels.

Under US$50
Budget accommodations often come without air conditioning—a significant inconvenience July–October. And since most of them are in the central commercial zone, they can be a bit noisy.

As old as the city itself, **Pensión California** (Degollado 209, tel. 612/123-3508, fax 612/122-2896, US$20) is housed in a former 18th-century convent between Revolución de 1910 and Madero. The interior courtyard of this rambling Moorish-style building contains a tropical garden of sorts and a display of old and new paintings that lend a distinctly Bohemian feel to the atmosphere. Rooms are basic—little more than a few worn sticks of furniture, fan, and hot shower—but reasonably comfortable. Practically every backpacker on the Baja circuit turns up at the Pensión California at one time or another. Discounts are possible for long-term stays, and there is Internet at the front desk.

The same family operates **Hostería del Convento** (Madero Sur 85, tel. 612/122-3508, fax 612/123-3525, misioner@prodigy.net.mx, US$20) in another former convent right around the corner. It has a similarly funky and faded feel, with a bit more greenery in the courtyard.

Seemingly undiscovered by visiting budget travelers is the family-run **Hotel Señorial** (Domínguez 254, no tel., US$16), which offers a cozy front balcony sitting area and 10 clean rooms with attached bath. The public areas aren't too charming, but the beds are comfortable. TV costs US$2 extra. The **Hotel San Carlos** (16 de Septiembre btw Serdán/Revolución de 1910, tel. 612/122-0444, fax 612/122-3991, US$20, US$25 with a/c) has 30 basic rooms.

La Paz has a youth hostel at the **Instituto de la Juventud y el Deporte** (Villa Juventil La Paz, tel. 612/122-4615, US$20), a sports complex on Boulevard Forjadores (Km 3) near Calzada 5 de Febrero. Facilities include a pool, gym, cafeteria, and volleyball and basketball courts. Beds are single bunks in gender-segregated, four-person dorm rooms. The hostel is distant from the town center and about the same cost for two people as some of the more centrally located hotels, considering the cost per bed. But it's closer to the main bus terminal than the downtown lodgings. All ages are welcome.

Posada Hotel Yeneka (Madero 1520 btw 16 de Septiembre/Av. Independencia, tel./fax 612/125-4688, ynkmacias@prodigy.net.mx, US$39) looks and operates much like a guesthouse. Long known on the backpacker circuit, the Yeneka is built around a courtyard filled with tropical vegetation, a rusting Model T, and an amazing collection of other items giving the appearance of an ongoing garage sale. The proprietors can arrange snorkeling, diving, fishing, boating, and horseback-riding excursions. A *lavandería* and car rental agency are also on the premises. Rooms are basic, dark, and a bit scruffy. You can find nicer accommodations for just a few dollars more per night.

Around the corner from Hotel Los Arcos, the friendly **Hotel Lorimar** (Bravo 110 btw Madero/Mutualisimo, tel. 612/125-3822, fax 612/125-3822, US$27–39) is a longtime budget favorite with European, Canadian, and U.S. visitors. Its 20 air-conditioned rooms are clean and well maintained. The proprietors speak English but are happy to let you practice your Spanish; they can also arrange kayaking and diving trips through local outfitters. The Lorimar is just a block off the *malecón;* guests often meet in the cozy upstairs dining area to exchange travel tips. Groups of three or four people can also be accommodated in some rooms.

The **Hotel Plaza Real** (Callejón de La Paz and Esquerro, tel. 612/122-9333, fax 612/122-4424, US$40), a block off the *malecón* and right around the corner from the Hotel Perla, is a three-story, modern hotel popular with middle-class Mexican businesspeople. Rooms have air conditioning and TV, and the downstairs coffee shop is a popular local spot for breakfast and Mexican food.

Hotel Restaurant Nuevo Pekin (Paseo Obregón 875 at Victoria, tel. 612/125-5335, www.nuevopekin.com.mx, US$47) occupies a pagoda-like building facing the *malecón*. It offers 30 clean rooms with TV and air conditioning (some with bay views). Credit cards are accepted.

Swimming pools and secure parking are hard to find in this price range, but you'll find both at the friendly ◖ **Hotel Gardenias** (Serdán Norte 520, tel. 612/122-3088, www.hotelgardenias.com.mx, US$45). Located in a residential neighborhood in the northwest part of the city, the hotel is a large, modern, two-story building set around a pleasant courtyard and pool. Popular among Mexicans, the Gardenias offers 56 clean rooms with TV and air conditioning. The attached restaurant is open for breakfast and lunch. *Note:* Although the hotel's street address reads Calle Serdán, the entrance is on Guerrero between Serdán and Guillermo Prieto.

If you're blazing through town on your way south to Los Cabos, well-kept **Hotel Calafía** (Km 4, tel. 612/122-5811, hotelcalafia@gmail.com, US$35) is a budget hotel along the highway that makes a convenient stop. It has 35 rooms, secure parking, and a pool. Rates include tax.

US$50-100

A block off Paseo Obregón, the three-story, apartment-style **Hotel Miramar** (5 de Mayo at Domínguez, tel. 612/122-8885, fax 612/122-0672, hmiramar@prodigy.net.mx, US$57) features clean but darkish rooms with air conditioning, minibar, and small TV with VCR. Beds rest on concrete platforms and slope a bit. Some rooms come with balconies and bay views at no extra charge, so be sure to ask what's available. The parking lot is a plus. Credit cards are accepted.

Hotel Posada Luna Sol (Topete 564 btw 5 de Febrero/Navarro, tel. 612/123-0559, U.S. tel. 800/355-7140, www.posadalunasol.com, US$60–130), located a half block from the bay and on the premises of Mar y Aventura, has 14 spacious, clean rooms decorated in Mexican kitsch. Enjoy a sunset cocktail under the rooftop *palapa*. In recent years, the property has added a new top-floor suite and a room with a small kitchen. Posada Luna also is one of the few hotels in this price range where rooms have satellite TV. Rates include tax. Credit cards are accepted.

The venerable **Hotel Perla** (Paseo Obregón 1570, tel. 612/122-0777 or 800/716-8799, U.S. tel. 888/242-3757, www.hotelperlabaja.com, US$75–100) has long been one of the city's most popular hotels, but unfortunately improvements haven't kept pace with rate increases. The two-story, tile-roofed hotel enjoys a prime location right at the center of the *malecón* and just a few steps away from the main shopping district. La Terraza, the hotel's downstairs, open-air restaurant, remains a favorite gathering place for power business lunches, while the upstairs nightclub draws a mostly local crowd. The mezzanine floor features a small pool. Clean, but plain and small, rooms have high ceilings, air conditioning, TVs, and telephones. Stay here if a central, waterfront location and secure indoor parking are important and the price is right. *Note:* There was no Internet service at last check.

Another *malecón* standby around since the dawn of La Paz's tourist industry is **Cabañas de los Arcos** (Paseo Obregón 498, tel. 612/122-2744 or 800/716-8644, U.S. tel. 800/347-2252, www.losarcos.com, US$75–100). Built in 1954, during La Paz's heyday as an exotic playground for Hollywood celebrities, *paceño*-owned Los Arcos became the city's first center for sportfishing trips. Today you can choose from among 52 air-conditioned rooms in the original cabaña section (fireplaces), junior suites behind the cabaña section (no fireplaces), and rooms and suites in the much larger **Hotel Los Arcos** section less than 100 meters down the street. Some rooms have bay views, others overlook the interior courtyard and pool. Both the new and original sections have swimming pools; the new one also offers a coffee shop, restaurant, bar, gift shop, sauna rooms, massage service, and whale-watching, diving, and sportfishing tours. Rooms at the Arcos are a bit nicer than the Perla for the same price, but still retain a 1970s feel. Friendly service and wireless Internet are two additional features.

Seven Crown Hotel (corner of Obregón and Lerdo de Tejada, tel. 612/128-9090, sevencrown@prodigy.net.mx, US$95), facing the *malecón,* looks like an office building from the outside, with a lobby one might mistake for an airlines office. Nonetheless, the rooms are quiet, clean, and well equipped. Amenities include a gym, parking, and wireless Internet.

Under Swiss ownership, the three-story, blue-and-white stucco **C** **Hotel Mediterrané** (Allende 36, tel./fax 612/125-1195, www.hotelmed.com, US$72–83) enjoys a great location, just a half block from the *malecón*. The small, well-managed hotel features large, airy, sparkling-clean rooms with air conditioning, refrigerator, and TV/VCR; each room is named for a different Greek island. Rooms with views are also the closest to the street and pick up a little more noise than those at the back of the hotel. There's also a rooftop sundeck with lounge chairs and a view of the bay. Kayaks and canoes are on hand for guests who would like to paddle in the bay. Bicycles are available for land-lovers. La Pazta restaurant and café are downstairs; the café has wireless Internet.

North of downtown, the **Hotel Suites Club El Moro** (Km 2 Carr. a Pichilingue, tel./fax 612/122-4084, www.clubelmoro.com, US$74–146) is a whitewashed, Moorish-style place on landscaped grounds. All rooms and kitchen-ette-equipped suites come with air conditioning, satellite TV with HBO, reliable wireless Internet, and private terrace. Standard rooms are a little small for the price (US$74 including tax), but at US$110, large junior suites are a great value. Other amenities include a pool, hot tub, offstreet and gated parking, and newly remodeled bar. The adjoining **Café Gourmet** serves great espresso, as well as breakfast and lunch every day. Hotel guests receive free coffee and a coupon for US$2.50 per day. Friendly staff and an attractive frequent-guest program bring repeat visitors back year after year. Buses heading downtown pass the hotel frequently during daylight hours; otherwise it's a two-kilometer (1.2-mi) walk to the town center.

Open since 1975, **Hotel La Concha Beach Club Resort and Condominiums** (Km 5 Carr. a Pichilingue, tel. 612/121-6161 or 800/726-8603, U.S. tel. 800/999-2252, www.laconcha .com, US$85) sits on Playa Caimancito, the city's closest swimming beach. All of the 94 well-kept rooms and suites have bay views. On the premises are two pools, tennis courts, an aquatic sports center, restaurant, bar, spa, and gift shop. The swimming pool in La Concha's newer condo section (see *Apartments, Condos, and Long-Term Rentals*) is nicer than the original hotel pool; both pools are open to hotel guests. The resort has equipment and services onsite for fishing, snorkeling, diving, sailing, and water skiing.

Next to the Baja Ferries terminal in Bahía Pichilingue, **Club Cantamar Resort and Sports Centre** (B.C.S. 11/Carr. a Pichilingue, tel. 612/122-7010, www.clubcantamar.com, US$80–102) caters to serious scuba divers and other water enthusiasts. This family business has grown steadily since it opened in 1994 with one 22-foot *panga* and an old 40-horsepower outboard engine. A boat ramp and tank-filling station paved the way to a full-scale resort.

Today, guests sleep in a four-story lodge with 45 standard rooms (11 of which were new in 2006), eight double condos, and two junior suites; a separate building contains four apartments, each with two bedrooms, two bathrooms, kitchenette, dining room, living room, and private balcony. Rooms are decorated in desert colors and stucco walls with rustic furnishings. Air conditioning and satellite TV are included, and most rooms have phones too. Other resort amenities include a 35-slip marina, swimming pool overlooking the ocean (deep enough for scuba training), bar, dockside restaurant, and swim-up bar. There are also a boat ramp, kayak rentals, private beach, fishing fleet, dive shop, scuba shop, and recompression chamber. Proximity to the industrial ferry terminal, with semi-trucks coming and going, is one disadvantage of the location. Night owls will find the Cantamar much to remote, but for those who want to maximize their time on the water, this resort is a fine home base. Rates include breakfast and taxes.

US$100-150

At Km 2.5 on the La Paz–Pichilingue Road, almost opposite Club de Yates Palmira, the palm-encircled **Hotel Palmira La Paz** (Km 2.5 Carr. a Pichilingue, tel. 612/121-6200 or 800/026-5444, U.S. tel. 877/727-2492, www .araizahoteles.com, US$135) caters to conventioneers as well as vacationers with its large meeting rooms, banquet halls, and quiet garden rooms. Other facilities include a pool, tennis court in good shape, restaurant, bar, and disco.

South of the *malecón* and Marina de La Paz is **Hacienda del Cortez** (formerly the Hotel La Posada de Engelbert, Nuevo Reforma and Playa Sur, tel. 612/129-9999, www.haciend-adelcortez.com, US$106–244). Originally built by pop crooner Engelbert Humperdinck for the Hollywood set, the recently renovated property offers 25 large suites and fireplace-equipped *casitas*. All rooms have satellite TV, phone, Internet, and air conditioning. A pool, tennis court, activities center, restaurant, and *palapa* bar fill out the compound. The quiet waterfront atmosphere is a plus. A full service spa was in the works at last check.

Opposite the Hotel Palmira La Paz (adjacent to the plush Club de Yates Palmira) is the **Hotel Marina** (Km 2.5 Carr. a Pichilingue, tel. 612/121-6254 or 800/685-8800, U.S. tel. 800/250-3186 or 800/826-1138, www.hotel-marina.com.mx, US$100–180) with 150 clean suites and master suites, somewhat saggy beds, and older furnishings. Facilities include tennis courts, a large pool, and an outdoor bar; boat slips are available nearby for visiting yachties.

At the center of the new 500-acre CostaBaja Resort & Marina (www.costabajaresort.com), the **Fiesta Inn La Paz** (Km 5.5 Carr. a Pichilingue, tel. 612/123-6000, www.fiestainn.com, US$95–163) is popular with families as well as boaters, who can anchor at the onsite marina. The resort has 120 guestrooms, including accessible rooms for handicapped guests; amenities include wireless Internet and a separate lap-swimming lane in addition to the main pool. To find the hotel, look for a signed entrance on a rise on the seaside of the road to Pichilingue.

US$150-250

Some of the nicest accommodations in town are found at the coral-hued **Posada de las Flores** (Obregón 440 btw Militar/Guerrero, tel./fax 612/125-5871, www.posadadelasflores.com, US$150–250). Well-tended landscaping and a small pool grace the entry, which faces the *malecón*. Rustic Mexican furniture and tile are used throughout, and the all-marble bathrooms feature a large bathtub and extra-thick towels. Rooms are outfitted with air conditioning, wireless Internet, cable TV, and a small refrigerator. A larger *casa* is next door. Bikes and kayaks for guest use at no extra charge. Rates include breakfast. Posada de las Flores also has sister properties in Loreto and Punta Chivato.

Southwest of town, at Km 5.5 on northbound Mexico 1 (it turns north eventually), the three-story **Grand Plaza Resort** (Lte. A, Marina Fidepaz, tel. 612/124-0830, U.S. tel. 866/357-9711, www.grandplazalapaz.com, US$150–200) is a typical airport business hotel with 50 bayside suites. Rooms are on the dark side, and beds sag a bit, but the pool is large, and bay views are a plus (no swimming). Notable amenities include free wireless Internet in the lobby and restaurant area, plus a sauna, pool tables, gym, hot tub, tennis court, massage room, and restaurant/bar. Rooms come with air conditioning and refrigerators. The hotel stands opposite the state tourism office and next to the nearly complete Marina Fidepaz.

BED-AND-BREAKFASTS

If you like cozier accommodations and the opportunity to socialize with your host, bed-and-breakfast-style accommodations can be a wonderful way to meet Mexican or expat families.

Under US$50

A branch of the same family that runs the popular Club El Moro hotel has opened **Baja Bed and Breakfast** (Madero 354, tel. 612/123-1370, www.bajabedandbreakfast.com, US$45–60) in a centrally located home just off the plaza. Two street-level rooms share a bath and a patio with a small swimming pool and barbecue. Above, a spacious first-floor apartment for rent by the night or week has a kitchen, separate bedroom, and living room. Rates include tax and wireless Internet.

Cecilia Moller serves a multicourse breakfast each morning on the third-floor terrace. You'll start your day filled with fresh breads, fruit, juice, coffee or tea, and eggs, quesadillas, *chilaquiles,* or other Mexican specialties. Some of La Paz's hottest new restaurants are less than a block away, and the *malecón* is a two-block walk. The inn is especially popular with kayakers preparing for a multiday paddle to Isla Espíritu Santo. Next door, the Mollers were building an additional four rooms with private baths, and there were plans to upgrade the existing rooms as well.

US$50-100

A half block off the *malecón,* **La Casa Mexicana Inn** (Bravo 106 btw Madero/Mutualismo, tel./fax 612/125-2748, www.casamex.com, US$65–95) offers five tastefully decorated rooms in a Moorish/art deco–style inn. All rooms come with remote-control air conditioning, fans, VCRs, and private baths. Rates include a breakfast of home-baked pastries, as well as tax. The property was up for sale and undergoing renovations in 2007.

Next door, a charming couple from down under, Patricia Lowe and Ken Bonner, have channeled their love for all things Italian into **Casa Tuscany Inn** (Bravo 110A, tel. 612/128-8103, www.tuscanybaja.com, US$90–125). Four colorful guestrooms overlook a garden courtyard behind the main house. Each has a comfortable queen bed, private bath, ceiling fan, and remote-control air conditioning. Prices include tax and breakfast.

US$100-150

El Ángel Azul (Independencia 518, tel./fax 612/125-5130, www.elangelazul.com, US$80–145) is housed in a historic building that once served as the La Paz courthouse. Carefully restored with INAH guidance, the hotel offers nine guestrooms and one suite around a large, landscaped courtyard. All rooms are air-conditioned and nonsmoking. The work of local artists is showcased throughout. Secure parking.

APARTMENTS, CONDOS, AND LONG-TERM RENTALS
US$50-100

Operated by La Concha Beach Resort, **Las Gaviotas** (Domínguez at Salvatierra, tel. 612/123-5298, US$135) is a five-story apartment-style complex in a residential neighborhood downtown. Each huge, two-bedroom apartment features a bay view, air conditioning, TV, phone, kitchen, two bathrooms, and private patio. There is Wi-Fi in the lobby and secure parking. Rates vary depending on whether or not the kitchen is used. You can also rent by the week. Electricity is billed separately.

US$150-250

On Playa Caimancito near Km 5 on La Paz–Pichilingue Road. **La Concha Beach Resort and Condos** (Km 5 Carr. a Pichilingue, tel. 612/121-6161 or 800/726-8603, U.S. tel. 800/999-2252, www.laconcha.com, US$85) rents large one- to three-bedroom condos with air conditioning, TV, and kitchenette. Condo residents have full use of hotel facilities, including two pools, a beach, restaurant/bar, and water-sports center.

CAMPING AND RV PARKS

Free beach camping is available north of the Pichilingue ferry terminal at Playas Pichilingue, Balandra (Puerto Balandra), El Tecolote, and El Coyote. Except for El Tecolote, none of these beaches has freshwater; all supplies must be brought from La Paz. Two restaurants at El Tecolote supply food and beverages. Though not common, theft unfortunately does occur at these beaches. A couple reported a pair of mountain bikes stolen from the locked bike rack on their car, just steps away from where they slept in December 2006. Keep valuables out of sight if at all possible.

Several trailer parks spread west from the city's edge out onto Mexico 1. Starting from the farthest away, just before Km 15 in El Centenario comes **Los Aripez (Oasis de Aripez) RV Park** (tel. 612/124-6090 or 612/125-6202), popular among Transpeninsular voyagers making short La Paz stopovers; 26 full-hookup slots here cost US$12–16. Facilities include hot showers, flush toilets, laundry, restaurant, bar, and boat access to Ensenada de la Paz. Tents are permitted. It's open year-round.

Five kilometers (3 mi) west of the city on Mexico 1, across from Motel Villa del Sol, is the well-maintained **Casa Blanca RV Park** (tel. 612/124-0009, fax 612/125-1142, open Nov.–May), where more than 46 full-hookup sites are US$16/night. The facility includes showers, flush toilets, a pool, tennis courts, spa, laundry, restaurant, and a small market.

A kilometer closer to the city center and surrounded by a high wall, **El Cardón Trailer Park** (Km 4, tel./fax 612/124-0078, elcardon@starmedia.com) features 80 shaded, well-tended *palapa* sites with full hookups for US$12–15 for two, depending on the size of your vehicle, plus US$2 for each additional person. Tent camping is permitted, and fees vary from US$3 for people on foot to US$4 for those arriving on bicycles, and a little bit more for those coming in on motorcycles. El Cardón offers a pool, groceries, bathrooms with flush toilets and hot showers, a children's play area, a dump station, and laundry. An Internet café in the park offers good rates and is open daily 6 A.M.–8 P.M. The park is open year-round.

Off Avenida Abasolo (Mexico 1) not far from the bayshore is the upscale, 96-slot **La Paz RV Park** (tel. 612/122-4480 or 612/122-8787, fax 612/122-9938). Full hookups alongside concrete pads cost US$17. Tent sites on the ground go for US$14. Facilities include showers, flush toilets, potable tap water, a small but clean pool, hot tub, tennis court, laundry, restaurant, and bar. Cash only. To find this well-kept RV park, go east on Avenida Abasolo and turn left (toward the bay) just before the VW dealer, then turn left on Calle Brecha California just before Posada Engelbert and continue three or four blocks. Open year-round.

A bit farther east toward the city center, off Calle Nayarit on the bay, is the smallish, palm-planted **Aquamarina RV Park** (Nayarit 10, tel. 612/122-3761, open Nov.–May). Though a bit run-down compared to La Paz RV Park, its shady spots are a favorite among boaters and divers. Aquamarina features its own marina, complete with boat ramp, storage facilities, and air for scuba tanks, plus showers, flush toilets, potable tap water, a pool, and laundry facilities. Nineteen full-hookup sites cost US$19. The Aquamarina also offers three apartments for rent.

Food

La Paz offers dining venues for all tastes and budgets, and, as might be expected in a coastal city, the seafood selection is particularly good.

ALTA COCINA MEXICANA

A new generation of chefs up and down the peninsula are working hard to create a more distinct identity for Baja regional cuisine. La Paz enjoyed its first such restaurant debut with the opening of **Las Tres Virgenes** (Madero at Constitución) in December 2006. The restaurant name refers to three mountains, one of which is a dormant volcano, visible in the distance on the drive from San Ignacio to Santa Rosalía. On the menu are innovative entrées like mesquite grilled baby octopus and *cabrillo* over garlic mint mashed potatoes. The restaurant gets rave reviews for the high quality of its food and a reasonably priced wine list. Indeed, local expats are calling it the best meal they've had in La Paz, period.

MEXICAN

A popular coffee shop–style place, **Restaurant Plaza Real** (Hotel Plaza Real, Esquerro at Callejón de la Paz, tel. 612/122-9333, daily 7 A.M.–3 P.M.) offers moderate prices, efficient service, and good Mexican food. The fresh orange juice is quite refreshing on a hot day.

Carlos'n Charlie's (Obregón at 16 de Septiembre, tel. 612/123-4547, daily noon–1 A.M., mains US$6–17) is part of the same chain as Squid Roe and Señor Frog's, but the atmosphere is much more low-key than the typical Grupo Anderson enterprise. The interior decor features old Mexican movie posters, while the menu emphasizes good Mexican fare, seafood (try the *ceviche paceño*), and steak dishes. Much of the clientele is Mexican. The terrace tables usually catch a breeze. Credit cards are accepted.

In a courtyard behind La Fabula Pizza on Obregón, **Peña La Pitahaya de Janicua** (Obregón 15, tel. 612/126-2234) is an almost hidden spot with a bohemian ambience and a Mexican menu. Artwork and Mexican crafts

food vendor stall in La Paz

LA PAZ AND VICINITY

are on display throughout, and there's live Latin folk music nightly.

The simple but pretty restaurant/bar **❬ El Zarape** (Av. México 3450 btw Oaxaca/Nayarit, tel. 612/122-2520, daily 7:30 A.M.–midnight, mains US$10–15) features a tiled entryway and a menu of traditional Mexican dishes. On Saturday evenings, El Zarape hosts a *cazuelada,* i.e., a buffet of *cazuelas* (large, open clay pans) filled with moles and other specialties of central and southern Mexico. A popular breakfast buffet is offered Tuesday–Sunday; a more modern Mexican buffet on Sunday noon–6 P.M. brings together recipes from all over the republic.

SEAFOOD

Restaurant La Costa (Navarro and Topete near La Marina Don José, daily 2 P.M.–2 A.M., mains US$10–15) is a simple *palapa*-roofed restaurant with some of the freshest seafood in La Paz. Operated by local seafood wholesalers Mar y Peña, **Restaurant La Mar y Peña** (16 de Septiembre btw Isabel la Católica/Albañez, tel. 612/122-9949, daily 9 A.M.–10 P.M.) is a small, air-conditioned place with a terrific menu that features practically everything that swims, including several *machaca* (dried and shredded) versions. The *sangría preparada* (homemade sangria) is also good. Prices are moderate to expensive. Credit cards are accepted.

Once a best-kept secret, **Bismark II** (Degollado at Altamirano, tel. 612/122-4854, daily 8 A.M.–10 P.M., mains US$10–20), has become one of the most popular tourist restaurants in La Paz in recent years, and locals no longer recommend it with as much enthusiasm. It specializes in lobster, abalone, and carne asada. The ceviche is also good. On the *malecón,* **Bismarkcito** (Paseo Obregón near Constitución, tel. 612/128-9900, mains US$10–15) is a waterfront offshoot of its parent restaurant. This casual eatery draws a crowd for weekday business lunches; however, when the exceptionally loud marching band starts playing on the sidewalk, conversation of any sort becomes impossible. The menu includes all manner of seafood cocktails, and fish and shellfish entrées; Peñafiel brand Mexican sodas are a treat.

One of the better hotel restaurants, **Restaurant Bermejo** (Hotel Los Arcos, Paseo Obregón, tel. 612/122-2744, Mon.–Sat. 7 A.M.–11 P.M., Sun. 8 A.M.–11 P.M., US$13–20) overlooks the *malecón*—ask for a window table. The Italian chef prepares a varied menu of seafood, steaks, and pastas. If you've had a successful day fishing, the restaurant will prepare your catch.

The popular (C **Mariscos Moyeyo's** (corner of Obregón and Calle Héores de 47, mains US$4–11), just past El Moro hotel, packs a crowd on weekend afternoons, when locals stop in for towering seafood cocktails. The floor is sand, and the tables and chairs are plastic. It takes a dozen wait staff to keep the fresh catch flowing. The restaurant has occasional live music.

Near the Posada las Flores on Obregón, **Las Brisas del Mar** (Obregón at Militar, tel. 612/123-5055, lasbrisasdelmbcs@hotmail.com, daily for dinner, mains US$13–27) serves seafood cocktails, fish *a la parilla, empanizado,* shrimp, lobster, and red meat from Sonora.

ITALIAN

Owned by a friendly Chinese/Italian couple, (C **Caffé Milano** (Esquerro 15, btw Callejón de la Paz/16 de Septiembre, tel. 612/125-9981, www.caffemilano.com.mx, Mon.–Sat. 4–11 P.M., mains US$6–18) prepares traditional Italian fare. Start with an order of fried oysters with caviar and move on to a homemade pasta or a hearty main dish like osso buco and *frutti di mare*. The restaurant received a AAA diamond rating in 2006. Look for the tall, light blue wooden doors.

La Pazta (Allende, adjacent to Hotel Mediterrané, tel. 612/125-1195, Wed.–Mon. 7 A.M.–11 P.M., Tues. 7 A.M.–3 P.M., mains US$10–15) is simply decorated with works of art, pastel stucco, and exposed brick. The light and airy restaurant offers breakfast, lunch, and dinner. The evening menu features a long list of pastas, pizzas, fondues, and other Swiss and Italian specialties. An extensive wine list includes Italian, U.S., Chilean, and *bajacaliforniano* labels.

Marine biologist Christian Liñan took time away from his studies to open **Toscana Pizza Gourmet** (Dominguez and Constitución, Mon.–Sat. 3–11 P.M., mains US$5–10)in 2006. This Italian pizzeria makes European-style pies for eating in or takeout; salads pasta, and drinks complete the menu. Dine at six pine picnic tables outside, or window counter seating inside.

ECLECTIC MENUS

Kiwi Restaurant Bar (on the *malecón* btw 5 de Mayo/Constitución, tel. 612/123-3282, daily 8 A.M.–midnight, mains US$6–15) offers a scenic bay view and varied menu of seafood, Mexican, and international recipes. The people-watching is better than the food, but this is not a bad choice for lobster. On weekends, the restaurant occasionally features live music.

The venerable **El Taste** (Paseo Obregón at Juárez, tel. 612/122-8121, daily 8 A.M.–midnight, mains US$10–20), while known for its breakfast, features steaks, Mexican food, and seafood. It's patronized by a mostly tourist and expat clientele.

Outdoors beneath the Hotel Perla, **La Terraza** (Paseo Obregón 1570, tel. 612/122-0777, mains US$10–20) features an extensive menu of seafood, Mexican, steak, and Italian dishes. A steady crowd of both tourists and locals comes for the best people-watching in town, as well as for the reasonably tasty, reasonably priced food.

Friendly **El Oasis Restaurant and Bar** (Paseo Obregón 115 btw 16 de Septiembre/Callejón de la Paz, tel. 612/125-7666, daily noon–midnight, mains US$6–17) is a sidewalk patio restaurant with great service and a large menu of well-prepared seafood, steaks, and Mexican dishes. Live music plays in the evening. Credit cards are accepted.

AMERICAN AND PIZZA

Near the plaza and across from Baja Bed and Breakfast, (C **Buffalo BAR-B-Q** (Madero 1240, tel. 612/128-8755, Mon.–Fri. 6 P.M.–midnight, Sat.–Sun. 2–10 P.M., mains US$10–20) gets high marks from locals for its steaks and burgers.

An upscale newcomer to the waterfront near the Marina de La Paz, **El Patrón Bar & Grill** (Plaza Vista Coral, tel. 612/125-9977, www.el-patronbarandgrill.com, Sun.–Wed. 2–11 P.M., Thurs.–Sat. 2 P.M.–midnight, mains US$12–24) serves lamb, Sonora beef, grilled fish, tequila shrimp, and Cornish game hens in a casual indoor/outdoor setting. Some say the quality of the food doesn't match the prices.

Visiting and resident yachties crowd **The Dock Café** (Marina de La Paz, corner Topete/Legaspy, tel. 612/125-6626, daily 8 A.M.–10 P.M., mains US$10–15), a small, casual diner serving fried chicken, hamburgers, fish-and-chips, bagels, salads, steaks, American breakfasts, some Mexican dishes, and homemade apple pie. A blues trio occasionally performs in the evening. (It's usually closed for two weeks at the end of August/beginning of September.)

Restaurant Grill Campestre (tel. 612/124-0454, daily for lunch and dinner, mains US$10–15), opposite the Fidepaz building on Mexico 1 north near Km 5.5, is popular with gringos and Mexicans alike for barbecued ribs, Cobb salad, and other American specialties.

ASIAN

La Cochinita (Forjadores and Veracruz, tel. 612/122-1600, daily 10 A.M.–10 P.M., mains US$5–10) is an extremely clean fast-food spot serving generous portions of Mexicanized Japanese dishes. It's a very popular lunch spot with the locals. A newer, smaller branch has opened on Calle Mutualismo, next to Bar El Misión.

ANTOJITOS

It's easy to find ◖ **Rancho Viejo** (Legaspy, half a block from the Marina de La Paz, tel. 612/128-4647, daily 24 hrs, dinner mains US$12–17) from the smell of the grill wafting up the street. Sit at a picnic table on the sidewalk, or in either of two dining rooms inside, to get away from the smoke. *Tacos de arranchera,* carne asada, or *pastor* arrive with the usual tray of fresh condiments. You can also order by the kilo. Service is prompt and friendly, and you can't beat the prices.

A half block from the *malecón* on 16 de Sep-

tiembre, **Restaurant Pichos** (tel. 612/128-9109, Tues.–Sun. 8 A.M.–11 P.M., mains US$3–6) serves delicious *tortas, licuados,* tacos, burgers, and *chilaquiles.* The *Hamburguesa Mexicana* comes with carne asada instead of ground beef, bacon bits, cheese, sliced avocado, tomato, and shredded lettuce, all on a lightly toasted bun. Two people can easily have lunch here for less than US$10, including sodas.

In the afternoons, the downtown area centered around the *malecón* and Calle 16 de Septiembre features street vendors serving fish tacos and *cocteles.* One of the best stands for fish, shrimp, and clam tacos, and *aguas frescas* is the extremely popular **Super Tacos de Baja California Hermanos González.** On Calle Esquerro beneath a big tree, opposite the side entrance of La Perla department store, this famous stand is still packed around lunchtime. Fish tacos and condiments are outstanding, and the *horchata* is delicious. Look for a second location on Degollado at Madero, next to Pensión California, and a larger restaurant location on Degollado at Mijares.

Taquería Los Superburros (Abasolo btw 5 de Febrero/Navarro) serves hamburgers, tacos (US$0.95), quesadillas (US$0.89), *huaraches* (US$3.50), and *papas rellenas.*

During the daytime, the cluster of *loncherías* in the **Mercado Municipal Francisco E. Madero** (Revolución and Degollado) serves as a very inexpensive grazing spot for *antojitos* and *comidas corridas.*

CAFÉS

The espresso business is booming in La Paz. Several chains now have multiple locations, and new ones seem to open every month. Starbucks look-a-like **5th Avenida Coffee** has wireless Internet in various locations, including 5 de Mayo on the plaza and Abasolo near the Marina de La Paz. **Café Exquisito** has a *malecón* location with sidewalk tables (Obregón south of La Fuente, Mon.–Sat. 6 A.M.–10:30 P.M., Sun. 8 A.M.–10:30 P.M., drinks US$1–3), plus two drive-through espresso stands north and south of town on Mexico 1, and one more at the airport. **Café Combate** has at least two locations in town: Serdán between Ocampo and Degollado, and on Bravo at the southeast entrance to Mercado Bravo.

Aside from these chains, a good place to enjoy coffee drinks and pastries in air-conditioned comfort is **Caffé Gourmet** (Esquerro and 16 de Septiembre, tel. 612/122-6037, Mon.–Sat. 8 A.M.–10 P.M.). The menu offers a long list of hot and cold coffee drinks, chai, smoothies, Italian sodas, pies, cookies, and pastries along with cigars and liquors. A cozy nonsmoking section can be found in the back. A second location was opening on the *malecón* in 2007.

Mareiros Café (Obregón north of Oasis, tel. 612/123-5439, Mon.–Sat. 8 A.M.–11 P.M., Sunday 9 A.M.–5 P.M.) is also air-conditioned, and the menu contains a whole page of coffee drinks, hot and cold, plus deli sandwiches, salads, snacks, and pastries. Mareiros has a few tables outside as well, and it is attached an Internet cafe. Air-conditioned **La Pazta Café** (daily 7 A.M.–11 P.M.), next to La Pazta Restaurant and Hotel Mediterrané serves excellent espresso drinks made from imported Italian Illy brand coffee, as well as cocktails, beer, and wine. Wireless Internet is free, and a desktop computer is available.

A café attached to the El Moro hotel (Km 2 Carr. a Pichilingue, tel./fax 612/122-4084, www.clubelmoro.com, daily 7 A.M.–4 P.M., mains US$5–15) is a good place to stop for breakfast on the way to Pichilingue.

El Quinto Sol (Domínguez and Independencia, tel. 612/122-1692) is a natural food/vegetarian store with a café section serving *tortas, comida corrida,* pastries, salads, granola, fruit and vegetable juices, and yogurt. The healthful breakfasts are particularly nice after extended travel. Readers also recommend **La Virtud** (Ramirez btw Bravo/Rosales, tel. 612/128-6940) for sandwiches, pastries, and healthy snacks.

GROCERIES

The **Mercado Municipal Francisco E. Madero** (Revolución de 1910 at Degollado) houses a collection of vendor stalls purveying fresh fish, meats, fruit, vegetables, and baked goods at non-subsidized free-market prices. Since prices are usually posted, no bargaining is necessary. At the corner of Revolución and Bravo is a *tortillería.* Other traditional markets include **Mercado Bravo** (Bravo at Guillermo Prieto) and **Mercado Abastos** (on Boulevard Las Garzas).

The government-subsidized **ISSSTE Tienda** (Revolución de 1910 at Bravo) has the city's best grocery prices, although the selection varies according to what ISSSTE bought cheaply that week. The **Tienda Militar** (Military Store, 5 de Mayo at Padre Kino) offers a larger selection than ISSSTE Tienda and is almost as inexpensive.

La Paz supermarkets include two large **CCC** (Centro Comercial California) outlets—one on Avenida Abasolo at Colima, the other on Isabel La Católica at Bravo. These carry American-brand packaged foods as well as Mexican products, but prices are about a third higher than what you'd usually pay elsewhere in town. Another good supermarket chain is **Supermercado Arámburo,** with three branches: 16 de Septiembre at Altamirano, Madero at Hidalgo y Costilla, and Durango 130 Sur (btw Ocampo/Degollado).

Plaza Ley, on the eastern outskirts of town on Las Garzas at Teotihuacán, carries a huge selection of groceries—at lower prices than CCC—as well as clothing, gardening supplies, small appliances, books, videos, housewares, and more. For buying in bulk, visit Walmart- and Costco-like **Soriana** (tel. 612/121-4771) and **City Club** (tel. 612/165-4990), owned by the same company, in a new shopping plaza on Boulevard Forjadores at the corner of Luis Donaldo Colosio.

NATURAL FOODS

El Quinto Sol (Domínguez at Av. Independencia) offers natural juices, wheat gluten, soybean meat substitutes (including soybean *chorizo),* whole-wheat flour, herbs, yogurt, and ice cream, as well as a few ready-to-eat items such as *tortas* and salads. More herbal medicines can be found at **Tonantzin** (Madero and 16 de Septiembre, Mon.–Sat. 10 A.M.–8 P.M.).

SWEETS

Downtown La Paz is packed with *tiendas* selling *nieves* (Mexican-style ice cream) and *paletas* (popsicles). **Paletería y Nevería La**

Michoacana is a big one, with branches on Paseo Obregón and Calle Madero. A personal favorite is tiny **❰ La Fuente** (Paseo Obregón btw Degollado/Muelle); though small, this place offers an amazing variety of flavors (including *capirotada,* a Mexican bread pudding), as well as *licuados, aguas frescas,* and all-fruit *paletas.* (The ones made from *pitahaya* are delicious.) Look for a polka dot tree in front of the entrance.

Two *dulcerías* (sweet shops) lie on two corners of the intersection of Calles Ocampo and Serdán. On a third corner is a large school, the obvious target market for these sweet shops. **Dulcería Perla** has a complete selection of traditional and modern Mexican sweets, while **Dulcería La Coneja** on the opposite corner specializes in candy-filled piñatas.

Information and Services

TOURIST ASSISTANCE

Baja California Sur's **Coordinación Estatal de Turismo** office (tel. 612/124-0100, turismo@correro.gbcs.gob.mx) lies between Km 6 and 5 on Mexico 1 (Avenida Abasolo), opposite the Grand Plaza Resort. The friendly staff can assist with most tourist inquiries; the Attorney for the Protection of Tourists is also stationed here. The office maintains an information booth on the *malecón* near the Los Arcos hotel, where you can pick up maps and brochures. The office on the highway is open Monday–Friday 8 A.M.–8 P.M., while the information booth on Obregón is open the same hours Monday–Saturday.

MONEY-CHANGING

Pesos are a must for everyday purchases in La Paz; city merchants are not as receptive to U.S.-dollar transactions as their counterparts in Cabo San Lucas, simply because they're not as used to them. Three banks with ATMs are clustered near the intersection of Calle 16 de Septiembre and the *malecón.* As elsewhere in Baja, the banks provide currency-exchange service only before noon Monday–Friday. The two branches of **Tony Money Exchange** (Mutualismo near La Perla, and nearby on 16 de Septiembre near the *malecón,* Mon.–Sat. 9 A.M.–9 P.M.) have decent rates. On Sundays, your only alternative is to change money at a hotel at lower rates.

The local American Express representative

is **Viajes Perla** (Obregón, tel. 612/122-8666, Mon.–Fri. 9 A.M.–5 P.M.), on the ground floor of Seven Crown Hotel.

POST AND TELEPHONE

The main post and telegraph office is at Revolución and Constitución, a block northeast of the cathedral; open Monday–Friday 8 A.M.–3 P.M., Saturday 9 A.M.–1 P.M.

DHL (Abasolo at Nayarit, tel. 612/122-8282) is the most reliable courier service in the city. The company picks up packages at no extra charge. If you are sending goods out of the country via DHL, you must first stop at the nearby Mexican customs office to have the parcel opened and inspected. Your parcel will then be sealed, and you'll receive an official customs form, which you must subsequently show to DHL before it can accept the parcel for shipping.

INTERNET ACCESS

Internet cafés can be found all over town, especially in the real estate offices along the stretch of waterfront between Hotel Los Arcos and Posada de las Flores. For example, **Omni Services** (Obregón 460-C, tel. 612/123-4888 or 877/805-7372) has Internet, PCs, copies, and fax services. Rates in La Paz are generally a reasonable US$2/hour. And many hotels and cafés now offer high-speed wireless Internet access for free. The 5th Avenida and Café Exquisito chains offer wireless access,

LA PAZ PHONE NUMBERS

La Paz area code: 612
Baja Ferries Office (Pichilingue): 123-0208
COTP (Captain of the Port): 122-0243 or 122-4364
Green Angels: 124-0100, 124-0199
Highway Patrol/Federal Police: 122-0369
Immigration: 125-3493, 124-6349
IMSS Hospital: 122-7377
Police, Fire Department, Red Cross (emergency): 066
SEMATUR Ferry Office (Pichilingue): 122-5005
State Tourism Department: 124-0100, 122-0199

as do most of the marinas. Hotels with wireless connections include the Los Arcos, Mediterrané, Fiesta Inn, Seven Crown, El Moro, and Posada de las Flores. Air-conditioned **La Pazta Café** (daily 7 A.M.–11 P.M.), next to La Pazta Restaurant and Hotel Mediterrané, has a desktop computer set up for customer use; wireless access if free if you bring your own computer.

PEMEX

The most central Pemex to downtown is located on 5 de Mayo between Serdán and Prieto. A second is 10 blocks away at the intersection of Isabel la Católica, and a third is on Avenida Abasolo as you leave La Paz headed toward the airport.

LAUNDRY

If you need to do some laundry, **La Paz Lava** (Ocampo at Mutualismo, tel. 612/122-3112, daily 8 A.M.–9:30 P.M.) is a good choice. This clean, modern, self-service launderette is within walking distance of the *malecón,* so you can stroll along the waterfront while waiting for your clothes. La Paz Lava also provides delivery service to home or hotel.

On Boulevard Forjadores adjacent to Supermercado Arámburo (opposite the youth hostel) is the enormous **Lavamática Cinthya;** you're sure to get a machine here. The marinas in town have their own laundry services as well.

LANGUAGE COURSES

If you'd like to study Spanish while you're in La Paz, Swiss-run **Centro de Idiomas, Cultura y Comunicación (CICC)** (Madero 2460 at Legaspy tel. 612/125-7554, www.cicclapaz.com, Mon.–Fri. 8:30 A.M.–1 P.M., Sat. 9:30 A.M.–1 P.M.) offers classes at all levels, from beginner to advanced. The standard course costs US$780 and includes four weeks of intensive classes (25 hours per week); book a homestay with a Mexican family at additional cost. Longer or shorter courses are available; a one-week travel Spanish course, for example, costs US$99. Business-Spanish and medical-Spanish courses are also offered.

Se Habla La Paz (Madero 540, tel./fax 612/122-7763, www.sehablalapaz.com) also offers more expensive classes and homestays for travelers and medical or legal professionals. Fees include a US$75 registration fee that covers student/family matching for homestays and airport pickup. Lessons run US$22/hour for a private session, US$16.50 for couples, and US$11 for group lessons. A one-week course is US$220 (20 hours), and a four-week program costs US$880 (80 hours). Payment is accepted via PayPal online.

NEWSPAPERS AND MAGAZINES

Two Spanish-language dailies are published in La Paz: *Diario Peninsular* and *El Sudcaliforniano.* **Librería Contempo** (Arrival at Paseo Obregón) carries Mexican newspapers, as well as a few American magazines. The La Paz branch of **Libros Libros/Books Books** (Constitución at Madero, tel./fax 612/122-1410, Mon.–Sun. 9 A.M.–8:45 P.M.) has a limited selection of American newspapers, magazines, and books.

IMMIGRATION

If you're planning to cross the Sea of Cortez by ferry and haven't yet validated your tourist card (see *Getting There*), stop by the immigration office on Paseo Obregón between Allende and Juárez, tel. 612/124-6349. It's usually open daily 8 A.M.–8:30 P.M. The immigration office at the airport is open seven days a week, while the one at the Pichilingue ferry terminal is open only an hour or so before each ferry departure.

Getting There and Around

GETTING THERE

By Air

Márquez de León International Airport (LAP) is 12 kilometers south of the city; the airport access road leaves Mexico 1 at Km 9. Although it's a small airport, facilities include a couple of gift shops, two snack bars, rental car booths, Ladatel phones (purchase cards from the snack bar), and an ATM machine. Although direct flights from the United States came to a halt for a number of years, Aero California, Aero Mexico, and Delta recently reinstated or added connections, making it easier and more affordable for travelers to reach La Paz without having to drive from Los Cabos. See the sidebar *Airlines Serving the Cape Region* in the *Essentials* chapter for specific connections and contact information.

Airport Transportation: Transporte Terrestre (tel. 612/125-3274) operates yellow-and-white vans between the city and the airport. The standard fare is US$15 *colectivo* (shared), US$30 for private service *(especial)*, and US$56 for a larger van. To Todos Santos the prices run US$200 *especial*, US$278 for a large van; to Los Cabos US$245/333; to San Carlos and López Mateos US$311/556. A regular taxi to the airport should cost around US$15. Some hotels operate airport vans that charge about US$5–10 per person.

By Bus

From the **Central Camionera** (Jalisco at Av. Independencia), **Águila** (tel. 612/122-3063 or 612/122-4270) runs northbound buses at least once a day to Ciudad Constitución, Puerto San Carlos, Puerto López Mateos, Loreto (US$32, twice daily), Mulegé, Santa Rosalía, San Ignacio, Vizcaíno Junction, Guerrero Negro (US$70, several times daily), San Quintín, Ensenada (US$85, four times daily), Tijuana (US$134, four times daily), Tecate, and Mexicali. These buses also stop at the much more convenient, centrally located terminal on the *malecón*.

Southbound, Águila buses depart from the **Terminal Malecón** (tel. 612/122-7898). Only one bus (5 P.M.) runs through the central Cape Region towns of El Triunfo, San Antonio, San Bartolo, Los Barriles (US$9), Santiago, and Miraflores, terminating in La Ribera/Las Cuevas. Most run via Mexico 19 through Todos Santos (nine buses per day, beginning at 7 A.M., US$7), continuing to Cabo San Lucas (US$14) and San José del Cabo (US$17); the 3 P.M. bus continues all the way to La Ribera.

If you're traveling southbound, you may find it more convenient to head to the centrally located terminal of **Autotransportes La Paz** (Degollado at Guillermo Prieto, tel. 612/122-2157), which has eight departures to Los Cabos via the West Cape. Fares are the same as listed above.

By Boat

The ferry port at Pichilingue, 16 kilometers (9.5 mi) northeast of downtown La Paz via Mexico 11, serves vehicle and passenger ferries between La Paz and Mazatlán or Topolobampo. Currently, the main passenger service is run by **Baja Ferries** (Pichilinque Terminal, tel. 612/123-0208, La Paz city office: Calle Isabel la Católica and Navarro, tel. 612/125-7443 or 800/122-1414, www.bajaferries.com). You can book tickets in advance online, in downtown La Paz, or at the ferry terminal. (See *By Ferry from Mainland Mexico* in the *Essentials* chapter for details.)

A temporary **vehicle import permit** is necessary for vehicular travel on the Mexican mainland. These permits aren't needed for Baja California travel, but if you've driven down to La Paz and decide you'd like to take your wheels on a mainland-bound ferry, you need to get one before buying a ticket. The whole process operates more smoothly in Tijuana, so if you anticipate using the ferry service, doing the paperwork in advance will save time and hassle.

If for whatever reason you decide to take the ferry and haven't done the paperwork in advance, you can obtain the proper permit in La Paz from the **Aduana Marítima** office (Mon.–Sat. 9 A.M.–1 P.M. and 5–7 P.M.), at the north end of the Pichilingue ferry terminal. To receive the permit, you need the original and three copies of your vehicle title or registration, a major credit card (in the vehicle owner's name), your driver's license, and your passport with valid Mexican visa. The permit can usually be processed on the spot (after a long wait in several lines), but budget a couple of days anyway, just in case all the right bureaucrats aren't in.

La Paz is an official Mexican port of entry, so the COTP office near Marina Palmira has authority to clear yachts for movement throughout Mexican waters. Unless you plan to anchor outside, the easiest way to arrange this is to check in at Marina de La Paz or Marina Palmira, and let the marina staff process all port clearance papers. Only one clearance in and out is required for entering and exiting the country; between Mexican ports the same papers can be presented. (See *Sports and Recreation* for information on La Paz marinas.)

GETTING AROUND

You can reach most points of interest downtown on foot. For outlying areas, you can choose city buses or taxis, or rent a car. *Note:* If you are driving into La Paz from the south and want to head directly to Peninsula Pichilingue

and the ferry terminal, you can take a shortcut just after the university on Boulevard Forjadores. Look for a sign for Libramiento Norte heading off to the right. If you get to Soriana and Office Depot, you've missed the turn. Best to continue on into the city and make your way to the waterfront.

By Bus

Regular city buses and *colectivos* radiate in all directions from the *zona comercial* surrounding the Mercado Municipal on Calle Degollado. Each bears the name of either the principal street along its run or the district where the route begins and ends. Any bus marked "El Centro," for example, will end up near the Mercado Municipal at Revolución and Degollado. For a few pesos, you can catch a bus out to the new Soriana shopping complex. These buses have signs in the windshield that say Soriana. Look on 16 de Septiembre, a few blocks in from the *malecón*.

From Terminal Malecón (Paseo Obregón 125), **Águila** (tel. 612/122-7898) runs seven buses daily between La Paz and various points along Península de Pichilingue. Buses to Playa Balandra and Playa El Tecolote operate at noon and 2 P.M., on weekends only.

By Taxi

Taxis can be found throughout El Centro, the downtown area between Calles 5 de Mayo and Degollado (especially along the west end of Calle 16 de Septiembre in the shopping district), and in front of the tourist hotels. On the *malecón* (Paseo Obregón), the main taxi stands are in front of Hotel Los Arcos and Hotel Perla. The average taxi hire downtown costs around US$2–3, a bit more after dark, and US$5 to Soriana. Trips to the airport are US$15, and to the ferry terminal, US$20. La Paz taxis don't have meters, so it's sometimes necessary to haggle to arrive at the correct fare. Longer trips are more economical if you use a shared taxi van, or *colectivo.*

By Car

A handful of international car rental agencies have airport and downtown locations in La

Paz. Rates start around US$25/day for unlimited miles, not including tax and insurance. See the sidebar *Where to Rent a Car in Baja* in the *Essentials* chapter for specific locations.

La Paz has plenty of Pemex stations, all offering Magna Sin (unleaded), Premium, and diesel.

Construction has been underway to widen Mexico 19 to a four-lane highway connecting La Paz and Cabo San Lucas. To date, about 20 miles have been widened near La Paz. There was talk at press time of a private corporation completing the expansion and then charging a toll.

Southeast of La Paz

State highway BCS 286 begins south of La Paz off Mexico 1 (at Km 211) and leads southeast 43 kilometers (26 mi) to the agricultural center of San Juan de los Planes. Along the way, this paved road climbs over the northeastern escarpment of the Sierra de la Laguna (here sometimes given its own name, Sierra de las Cacachilas), then descends toward the coastal plains, offering a panoramic view of aquamarine Bahía de la Ventana and Isla Cerralvo in the distance. At the crest of the ridge, you'll pass stands of live oak, several ranches, and the village of **La Huerta** (Km 17 on BCS 286). When the weather in La Paz seems intolerably hot, a drive up into the Sierra de las Cacachilas is a good way to cool off.

◖ BAHÍA DE LA VENTANA

At Km 38, a paved road branches northeast off BCS 286 and leads eight kilometers (5 mi) and 11 kilometers (6.8 mi), respectively, to the neighboring fishing villages of La Ventana and El Sargento on Bahía de la Ventana. About 1,000 people live here year-round, but the towns fill with American and Canadian windsurfers—and more recently, kiteboarders—during winter months. Wind sports are exceptionally good at La Ventana because of the strong *El Norte* northeasterlies channeled through Canal de Cerralvo to the north.

When the winds aren't blowing, onshore and inshore fishing is good all the way along the L-shaped bay; farther offshore in the Canal de Cerralvo, catches of marlin, skipjack, and dorado are common in the summer. The gently sloped beach offers easy small-boat launching. If you don't fish, the bayshore still makes

a worthwhile destination for camping, swimming, diving, and snorkeling, especially in the spring and fall (summers are hot). Isla Cerralvo lies about 16 kilometers (10 mi) offshore. Boats can easily be launched from the beach here.

The word is out on La Ventana, and the area is experiencing the beginnings of a real estate boom, with dozens of properties for sale, and many new buildings taking shape each year.

Windsurfing and Kiteboarding

Windsurfers discovered the ideal conditions at La Ventana a decade or two ago, but in recent years, the rising popularity of kiteboarding has brought many more adventure-seeking travelers to the area. Kiteboarders say La Ventana is

BAHÍA DE LA VENTANA

© AVALON TRAVEL PUBLISHING, INC.

© STEPHANIE HARGRAVE

the view from Mokie's

one of the best places in the world to learn the sport, because the shoreline of the bay curves around to catch those who drift downwind on white sand beaches. Experienced windsurfers say the wind at La Ventana isn't as strong as at Los Barriles, but it tends to be more consistent. The wind typically picks up around 11 A.M. and holds steady until just before sunset.

Several shops along the bay rent gear and offer lessons for windsurfing and kiteboarding. (They'll also come get you up if you have trouble staying upwind.) One of the first to set up shop in the early nineties was **Captain Kirk's Windsurfing** (U.S. tel. 310/833-3397, www.captainkirks.com), with headquarters in Los Angeles. The shop also rents a two-bedroom home with kitchen (US$275/day) and a *casita* with two double beds and bath (US$149/day). Rentals come with free use of mountain bikes, sea kayaks, and snorkeling equipment. A windsurfing or kiteboarding gear package is US$50.

With headquarters in Hood River, Oregon, the **New Wind Kite School** (U.S. tel. 541/387-2440, www.newwindkiteboarding.com, Nov.

15–Mar. 15) offers lessons for new and experienced kiteboarders (US$195–280/day, depending on the number of students). Custom instruction runs US$101 for one person for two hours. Board rentals cost US$40, but the school doesn't typically rent kites. This school also has a beach house next door. An upstairs room has its own bath and balcony, with access to a kitchen downstairs (US$89). Store your gear and use the air compressor to inflate your kite for free.

British Columbia–based **Elevation Kiteboarding School** (Canada tel. 604/848-5197, www.elevationkiteboarding.com) offers private lessons for CDN$100/hour and multiday kiteboarding camp packages. **Sheldon Kiteboarding** (U.S. tel. 707/374-3053, www.sheldonkiteboarding.com) provides beds and mattresses, a shared kitchen, and bath with a hot water shower. Bring your own sleeping bag.

Baja Adventures at Ventana Bay Resort replaces its rental gear each season, selling the previous year's equipment at reduced prices. In 2007, the shop had stocked up on 2007 North sails (3.7–6.7), 2007 Mistral Explosion, Syncros, and Screamers for boards, and custom boards by Open Ocean. Kiteboarding equipment includes North Rhino, Vegas, and Rebel kites and North Jamie Pros kiteboards. You can also rent K2 full suspension mountain bikes from the shop.

Scuba Diving

Palapas Ventana (tel. 612/114-0198, www.palapasventana.com) has opened a certified PADI dive shop onsite, for leading guided trips to Isla Cerralvo. The 26-foot super-*panga* has a four-stroke engine and takes up to six divers per trip. Scuba certification packages are available. Captain Tavo is a shark fisherman and dive instructor. Several of the windsurfing and kiteboarding resorts dabble in scuba trips, as well (see *Isla Cerralvo*).

Accommodations

Located about a half mile past El Sargento, the **Ventana Bay Resort** (tel. 612/128-4333, U.S. tel. 800/533-8452, www.ventanabay.com, US$110–140) completed its second phase of construction in late 2006 and now counts a few new rooms, plus an office, shop, and bar. Its bungalow-style guestrooms are set around a clubhouse, along with about a dozen private homes, a restaurant, bar, and full-service windsurfing, kiteboarding, and dive shop operated by Baja Adventures. The eco resort also offers kayaking, Hobie Cat sailing, mountain biking, sportfishing, and snorkeling. Room rates include breakfast and lunch. A seven-day package includes accommodations, two meals per day, and unlimited use of recreation equipment. Rates run US$695 for a "sports package," US$725 for a windsurfing package, and US$850 for a kiteboarding package. Wireless Internet is available at additional cost. The resort also manages a few of the private homes as vacation rentals.

Between La Ventana and El Sargento, **Palapas Ventana** (tel. 612/114-0198, www.palapasventana.com) has two types of newly constructed *palapa*-roof *casitas*. Regular ones sleep two in a king or two twin beds with shared shower and bath and no air conditioning (US$55 pp double occupancy). Specialty *casitas* sleep four

(in one room) with private tiled bath and air conditioning (US$77.50 pp double occupancy). Extra touches include high ceilings (with fans), Mission-style furnishings, hammocks, purified water dispensers, and rain showers. Also onsite are a dive shop, gated parking area, Internet café, and restaurant. Stay-and-dive packages include five days/four nights of accommodations; three days of diving (two tanks per day); breakfast everyday and lunch on dive days; and free use of kayak, snorkeling gear, and sailboat.

Mokie's (www.mokies.com) rents studio and one-bedroom (US$550/wk or US$1,500/mo) *casitas* on 3.5 fenced acres fronting the beach. Both *casitas* come with full-size bed, kitchen (including margarita glasses), two full-size futons, bath with large shower, mountain and sea views, and an outdoor terrace. Guests store their gear in a beachfront loft just 30 feet from the water's edge, or walk to shops that rent gear and offer lessons. When not on the water, enjoy a partially shaded beachfront terrace has a glass wall for shelter from the wind. Pay by credit card via PayPal.

Kurt-n-Marina (tel. 612/114-0010, U.S. tel. 509/590-1409, www.ventanakiteboarding.com) offer several *casitas* with *palapa* roofs and tiled baths, as well as camping and a shared outdoor kitchen.

Comfortable beds are a plus in relatively new and very clean rooms at ◖ **Casa Verde** (tel. 612/114-0214, U.S. tel. 509/590-4595, www.bahmahal.com, US$90). Enjoy natural light, private baths, small refrigerators, and seaviews in each one. Three Native American Lodges are set up for camping (US$30/40 s/d); guests may use a main kitchen or garden kitchen and shared bath with hot showers. Bikes, kayaks, and wireless Internet are included as well.

Steps from the sea, **Baja Joe's** (tel. 612/114-0001, www.bajajoe.com) has several *palapa*-roof cabins for rent (US$70–100). Some share a bath; others have their own. All have air conditioning and a small refrigerator. RV cabanas have private kitchens, and economical bunkhouse rooms go for US$30/40 s/d, with use of a shared outdoor kitchen and one of six baths on the property. Rates include mountain bikes, sea kayaks, snorkel equipment, and a storage area for gear. Baja

© STEPHANIE HARGRAVE

casita for rent

Joe's also manages a few private beach houses (US$600–1,200/week). No children under four. Discounts for long-term stays. Baja Joe's rents windsurfing (US$25/hour or US$40/day) and kiteboarding equipment as well.

La Ventana Campground, along the beach just north of the village of La Ventana, offers simple tent/camper sites, trash barrels, toilets, and showers for US$5 a night. Playas Miramar also offers sites for US$5, with no hookups but flush toilets.

Food

Each winter season brings a new wave of eateries to these sleepy bayside towns. Expect to find several small grocery stores (no supermarkets), a few traditional Mexican restaurants, several newer gringo establishments, a number of taquerías, and a *tortillería* (on the paved part of the road in El Sargento). Prices are generally low, and the atmosphere is casual. Mango margaritas at the Ventana Bay Resort clubhouse get especially high marks. If you plan to cook most of your own meals, stock up on supplies in La Paz.

Two hundred yards south of the trailer park, **Rincon del Bahia** (mains US$7–13) serves tasty seafood and Mexican fare on the beach. Owner Joaquin will serenade you while you dine. Fifty yards south of Palapas Ventana, **Tacos Rafa** grills fish tacos for US$6–13. The restaurant at **Palapas Ventana** (Fri.–Sat., mains US$8–13) prepares lasagna, steaks, BBQ ribs, fresh grilled fish, and you can enjoy local wines or an icy margarita. Reservations are recommended. **Ventanas del Sol** (mains US$6–12) is the place for ceviche and chicken mole, with a pool table and bar. Look for **Tacos en la Torre** (mains US$4–7) at the base of the radio tower in El Sargento, with a menu of *chilaquiles, tortas cubanas,* and flautas. On the west side of the road in El Sargento, **Tacos Leon** has hot dogs, *papas rellenas,* and enchiladas for US$4–10. Popular with RV park residents, **Viento del Norte** (mains US$4–9) serves hearty breakfasts, enchiladas, and jumbo margaritas.

Information and Services

Many local resorts and campgrounds now

have wireless Internet; some offer it for free, while others charge for access. Across from the main beachfront campground, **El Norte Restaurant** has satellite Internet for US$3/30 minutes. Use the restaurant's computers or bring your own. Mobile phones work here but get spotty signals. There are public pay phones here as well; pick up a Ladatel card at one of the mini-supers. **Palapas Ventana** has long-distance service.

Near the end of the pavement in El Sargento are a hardware store, mechanic, pharmacy, and Internet café, as well as **Miscelania Lupita.** A couple of launderettes offer drop-off or self service. El Sargento also has a Centro de Salud (Public Health Clinic) and a place where you can buy barrel gas.

ISLA CERRALVO

Across Bahía de la Ventana and Canal de Cerralvo lies Isla Cerralvo, one of the largest islands in the Sea of Cortez. At the time of early Spanish exploration, the island held large pearl-oyster beds and was inhabited by a small group of Pericú. Later, the rugged island reportedly became a favored final resting place for the *vagabundos del mar,* Amerindians who roamed the Sea of Cortez in dugout canoes until well into the 20th century.

Today Cerralvo remains one of the least visited of Baja's large coastal islands, simply because of its location on the far side of the Península de Pichilingue. Coral-encrusted **Roca Montaña,** off the southeastern tip of the island, is an excellent diving and fishing location, as is **Piedras Gordas,** marked by a navigation light at the southwestern tip. Depths at these sites range 3–15 meters (10–50 ft). Other good dive sites include the rock reefs off the northern end (average depth 18–21 m/60–70 ft), which feature a good variety of reef fishes, sea turtles, and shipwrecks. One of the reefs, **Arrecife de la Foca,** features an unidentified shipwreck with "Mazatlán" marked on the hull. **La Reina,** another reef at the north end of the island, is the site of a large steel-hulled freighter that sank a half century ago. Barely a hundred meters off the

island's west shore are two adjacent rock reefs known as **La Reinita.**

Access to Isla Cerralvo is easiest from Bahía de la Ventana or Punta Arenas, where beach launches are possible. From La Paz, it's a long haul around the Península de Pichilingue via Canal de San Lorenzo.

SAN JUAN DE LOS PLANES

Los Planes, as it's usually called, has several markets, a café, *dulcería, tortillería,* taxi stand, and around 1,500 inhabitants supported by farming (cotton, tomatoes, beans, and corn) or by fishing at nearby bays. There is a Pemex station where the road from San Antonio joins Mexico 286. During the windy season, dust blowing from cultivated fields on either side of the highway can cause a complete whiteout. Once you leave the main drag in Los Planes, there is little in the way of commercial businesses until you reach the Giggling Marlin on Bahía de los Muertos.

BAHÍA DE LOS MUERTOS

A graded road running east 21 kilometers (13 mi) from San Juan de los Planes leads to a pretty, curved bay. Historians don't know why a 1777 Spanish map named this shore "Bay of the Dead," but the name gained substance when a Chinese ship beached here in 1885. The ship had been refused entry at La Paz harbor because the crew was suffering from yellow fever; after putting in at this bay, all 18 crewmen died. Mexican fishermen buried the bodies above the tideline and marked their graves with wooden crosses, a few of which still stand. In the early 20th century, a community of American farmers tried unsuccessfully to cultivate the desert surrounding the bay; some died of thirst or hunger, adding to the bay's list of *muertos.*

Ensenada de los Muertos, an abandoned port at the north end of the bay, was built in the 1920s for the shipping of ore from El Triunfo mines in the Sierra de la Laguna.

Panga boats still line the shore, but the bay is changing little by little each year, as a 4,000-acre luxury real estate development takes shape to the south.

Bahía de los Sueños (Bay of Dreams)

When complete, the American-owned Bay of Dreams project will encompass an 18-hole golf course designed by Tom Doak, 432 homes, and 192 villas and condos. Inside the Bay of Dreams development, **Villas of Casa de los Sueños** sits on 25 landscaped acres with tennis courts, nine-hole golf course, multiple swimming pools, fitness facility, and a long list of luxury amenities including an onsite chef service and concierge. Its seven villas have king-size beds, rain showers, barbecues, satellite TV, wireless internet, and complimentary Internet calling to the United States. One-bedroom villas range US$450–700; two-bedrooms are US$650–1,200/night.

The crowd at the **Giggling Marlin Beach Club at Bay of Dreams** is much more sedate than at its parent bar and restaurant in Cabo San Lucas, though, should the mood strike, you can still get tangled upside down in its signature marlin hanging contraption.

PUNTA ARENAS DE LA VENTANA

A lesser road branches northeast about four kilometers before Los Muertos and leads eight kilometers (5 mi) to beautiful Punta Arenas de la Ventana and the abandoned **Las Arenas Resort.** The waters off Punta Arenas reputedly offer Baja's best roosterfish angling; wahoo, amberjack, grouper, dorado, and billfish are also in abundant supply. Guided *panga* trips may be available from the beach next to the resort, where local *pangeros* moor their boats, for US$60–85 per day. A bit south of the resort, off **Punta Perico** (Parakeet Point), is a lively reef with varied depths of 3–25 meters (10–82 ft).

The private **Aeromar las Arenas** airfield

offers tie down service and 24-hour security for guests of the Bay of Dreams resort.

GETTING THERE

Most travelers reach La Ventana by rental car or private vehicle (35–40 minutes from downtown La Paz, and about 45 minutes from the airport), but shuttles and bus service are available. A one-way shuttle from the La Paz airport to La Ventana runs US$120 (US$350 from Los Cabos). Pubic transportation is less expensive, but more complicated: First, you must get from the airport to the La Ventana bus stop (a US$15 cab ride). From there, you can catch a US$5 bus that leaves daily at 2 P.M.

Bahía de los Muertos can be reached from the south via a 47-kilometer (30-mi) dirt road between Los Barriles and San Juan de los Planes. The road is wide and flat from Los Barriles as far as Punta Pescadero and El Cardonal—13 kilometers (8 mi) and 22 kilometers (14 mi), respectively. North of El Cardonal, the road begins to rise along the Mesa Boca Alamo, eventually cutting inland and ascending steeply into the jagged, red Sierra El Carrizalito. Several kilometers of the road here wind around narrow, adrenaline-pumping curves with steep drop-offs. Contrary to popular belief, four-wheel drive is not a necessity for this section of road, but careful driving and good road clearance are. Twenty-four kilometers (15 mi) from El Cardonal, the road leaves the mountains and meets the paved end of BCS 286.

San Juan de los Planes, La Ventana, Punta Arenas de la Ventana, and Bahía de los Muertos can also be reached from Mexico 1 via a graded, unpaved road from San Antonio. (Construction was underway in 2007 to pave this stretch of road.) The road's east end begins on BCS 286 about 3.5 kilometers (2.2 mi) south of the turnoff for La Ventana and El Sargento.

LA PAZ AND VICINITY

WEST CAPE AND TODOS SANTOS

A few hundred meters past the modern Soriana shopping complex in Cabo San Lucas, the urban sprawl abruptly ends, cows reclaim the road, and the Pacific Ocean eventually pops into view. A lone trailer or two has set up camp along the shore, but you can't quite tell which dirt road they drove to get there. If it's late fall or early winter, wildflowers may still dot the landscape with a splash of color.

Don't get too lost in the scenery, however, or the Águila bus driver tailgating from behind might very well decide to pass on a blind turn just as an 18-wheeler approaches from the opposite direction. Welcome to the West Cape, the least developed coastal stretch on the lower part of the Baja Peninsula. Although a paved, two-lane highway (Mexico 19) extends the full 76 kilometers (47 mi) between Cabo San Lucas

and Todos Santos (and beyond all the way to La Paz), housing developments are still few and far between. Several large real estate projects are in the early stages near the farming community of El Pescadero and close to Cabo San Lucas, leaving the middle stretch to the pelicans, rancheros, fishermen, and the occasional ATV tour.

Once considered a stopover on the drive from La Paz to Cabo San Lucas, bohemian Todos Santos has become a destination in its own right. Surfers, artists, retirees, exotic bird rescuers, and yoga students all cross paths here, and at least several hundred of them are permanent expat residents. At press time, Todos Santos was basking in the attention of its recent designation as a Pueblo Mágico—one of only 23 small towns in Mexico given government funding to make their culture and history more accessible

© SUSAN HARPER

HIGHLIGHTS

◖ **La Candelaria:** Experience the rancho way of life in this rural village set in the foothills of the lower Sierra de la Laguna. Plan a day hike or a scenic drive from Cabo San Lucas on the way to Todos Santos (page 194).

◖ **Playa Los Cerritos:** Popular with novice surfers, swimmers, and sunbathers, this gently sloped beach lies comfortably protected from winter's northwest swell. Eagle rays, puffer fish, and other marinelife await discovery just below the surface (page 196).

◖ **Playa San Pedrito (Playa Las Palmas):** Rock cliffs at either end of the beach frame your view of the Pacific at this beach near Todos Santos. Bring a picnic and enjoy the secluded setting (page 198).

◖ **Todos Santos Historic District:** The most memorable postcards of Todos Santos depict rows of colorful, century-old facades with the signature large windows and doors of the Andalusian architecture style. Spend an afternoon exploring the town's galleries, shops, and restaurants on foot (page 205).

◖ **Playa Las Pocitas (La Poza de Lobos):** A small, freshwater lagoon within walking distance of Todos Santos is home to many types of waterfowl, as well as the area's finest boutique hotel, Posada La Poza (page 208).

LOOK FOR ◖ TO FIND RECOMMENDED SIGHTS, ACTIVITIES, DINING, AND LODGING.

to tourists and travelers. Gringo and Mexican locals alike were optimistic that the town would be able to preserve its artsy character even as the number of visitors increased.

PLANNING YOUR TIME

The drive from Cabo San Lucas to Todos Santos via Mexico 19 and the West Cape takes approximately one hour—making it an easy day trip for visitors who are staying in the Los Cabos area, or a slightly longer drive (90 minutes) directly from the airport.

You can take in most of what Todos Santos has to offer in a full day of sightseeing, cov-

ering the historic buildings and galleries in town and a beach or two along the coast. But as with most other towns in Baja, you'll enjoy the West Cape infinitely more if you stay long enough to wander miles of virgin, as-yet-undeveloped beaches stretching north and south from Todos Santos along the Pacific, explore the steep western escarpment of the Sierra de la Laguna, or simply hang out and soak up the small-town ambience.

Backpackers often plan multiday trips into the Sierra from the West Cape. If that sounds too challenging, guides also run half-day hikes as well as trail rides on ATVs. A day of

WEST CAPE

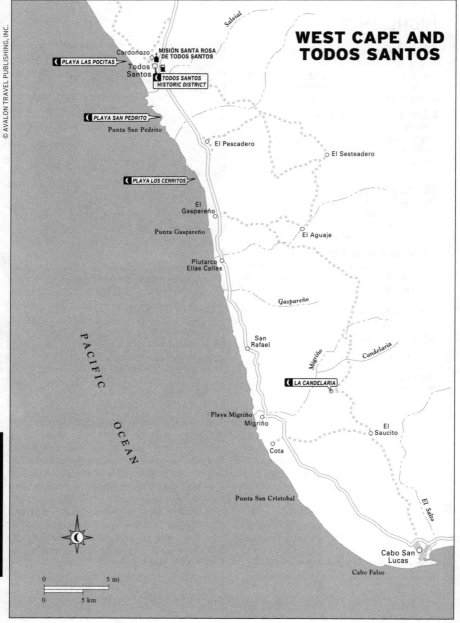

© AVALON TRAVEL PUBLISHING, INC.

WEST CAPE AND TODOS SANTOS

Salsial

Cardoñozo

☾ PLAYA LAS POCITAS

Todos
Santos

MISIÓN SANTA ROSA
DE TODOS SANTOS

☾ TODOS SANTOS
HISTORIC DISTRICT

☾ PLAYA SAN PEDRITO

Punta San Pedrito

El Pescadero

El Sesteadero

☾ PLAYA LOS CERRITOS

El
Gaspareño

Punta Gaspareño

El Aguaje

Plutarco
Elías Calles

Gaspareño

San
Rafael

Migriño

Candelaria

☾ LA CANDELARIA

P A C I F I C

Playa Migriño

Migriño

El
Saucito

O C E A N

Cota

Punta San Cristobal

El Salto

WEST CAPE

Cabo San
Lucas

Cabo Falso

0 ———— 5 mi

0 ———— 5 km

fishing or surfing could also lengthen your stay. Of course, if you're into these activities, a day probably isn't enough. Surfers can easily spend a week or a month trying to master the winter breaks here. And the fishing—whether by boat, surf rod, or hand line—is just as addictive.

GETTING THERE AND AROUND
By Air
Todos Santos is more or less equidistant from the Los Cabos and La Paz airports. A shuttle from Los Cabos costs approximately US$150, while a shuttle from La Paz runs US$200–300.

By Car
Though not essential, most travelers will want to have a car while staying in the West Cape and Todos Santos, as the beaches and sights are spread out from the two small towns. If you don't rent a car at the airport or drive your own from the States, you can rent one in Todos Santos. **Budget Car Rental** (Márquez de León 4, tel. 612/145-0062, egarcia@budgetbaja.com) has opened an office in Todos Santos next to the church and main plaza, and a second location inside the Milagro Real Estate office on Juárez.

Mexico 19 connects Todos Santos to Cabo San Lucas to the south and La Paz to the north. From the Los Cabos airport, follow the Transpeninsular Highway (Mexico 1) toward Cabo San Lucas, and take the turnoff for Todos Santos/Mexico 19. From La Paz, follow Mexico 1 south to the turnoff for Mexico 19. There are numerous Pemex stations in La Paz, Todos Santos, Pescadero, and Cabo San Lucas. If you need a car mechanic during your visit, there are a couple of options in Todos Santos, but you may have to head south to Cabo San Lucas for complicated transmission work.

By Taxi
As an alternative, a small fleet of blue vans parked next to the park in Todos Santos can provide taxi service around town for US$2 a trip. A van all the way to Los Cabos International Airport will cost around US$150; vans can hold 8–15 people with luggage. Call 612/145-0063 for more information.

By Bus
Nine Águila buses a day run between Todos Santos and La Paz to the north and Cabo San Lucas to the south. The La Paz and Cabo San Lucas bus trips take about two hours and cost about US$7 per person; a bus through to San José del Cabo costs US$10. In Pescadero, buses stop across the street from the Pemex. Tickets are sold on the buses, which arrive at and depart from Colegio Militar and Zaragoza (for San José del Cabo and Cabo San Lucas), or in front of Karla's Lonchería (for La Paz).

West Cape

Mexico 19 heads west out of Cabo San Lucas toward Cabo Falso before making a long, lazy arc to the north. An alternate route heads due north out of San Lucas, following unpaved ranch roads to the picturesque foothills village of La Candelaria. From there, those with four-wheel drive can follow a sandy arroyo road west, rejoining Mexico 19 near Playa Migriño. Those without four-wheel drive will find a visit to La Candelaria worthwhile but will have to return to Cabo San Lucas the way they came, then head north up Mexico 19. Both routes are covered in detail below.

CABO FALSO TO PLAYA MIGRIÑO

About three kilometers west of the Cabo San Lucas city limits is Cabo Falso, once incorrectly thought to be Baja California's southernmost point. Because the wide beach along Cabo Falso is protected as a nesting ground for sea turtles, visitors aren't permitted within 50 meters (165 ft) of the surf line. The dunes behind the beach, however, are a popular destination for rented ATVs from Cabo San Lucas. The abandoned lighthouse, **El Faro Viejo,** signaled ships 1895–1961; the original lens is now installed in a newer lighthouse higher on the beach. Surrounded by loose sand for at least a half mile, the old lighthouse can be approached only on foot, ATV, or horse.

Past Cabo Falso the highway begins climbing over the southwestern foothills and coastal plateaus of the Sierra de la Laguna to reach the small ranching settlement of Migriño after about 21 kilometers (13 mi). Playa Migriño, with access at Km 94 or 97, is a long section of beach next to Estero Migriño, a small estuary linked with Río Candelaria. In winter, surfers can catch a point break at the north end of the beach. Different sections of Playa Migriño are accessible via a network of sandy roads; several spots are suitable for camping.

◖ LA CANDELARIA

Palapa-roofed adobe and block homes, a small church, a school, split-rail and *carrizal* fences, and saddled burros tethered to paloverde and mesquite trees set the scene at this small village in the foothills of the lower Sierra de la Laguna. A palm oasis in a shallow canyon on the northwest edge of the quiet village holds an un-

© AVALON TRAVEL PUBLISHING, INC.

CLAYWARE OF CANDELARIA

Candelaria is widely known in the Cape Region for its rustic clay pottery, known as *trastes de barro* locally or, among foreign collectors, as "ranchware." No one's sure how or when the pottery tradition arrived here, but one theory speculates that when the southern Baja missions were secularized in the 19th century, many mestizos who had worked for the mission system chose to establish ranches farther into the sierra, where water was more abundant and the land more fertile. They may have brought with them the simple pottery techniques that were eventually lost to the cities that grew up along the coast.

Earth for Candelaria ranchware is dug from local hillsides, traditionally during the two weeks between the full and new moons (because of a belief that earth collected during this time makes better potting material). After grinding and sifting the earth by hand, potters add water and knead it into clay, which is then pinched, pulled, and punched into the desired pot shape. Some coiling techniques – rolling clay into ropelike lengths, then coiling them in layers along the rim – may be used near the tops of the vessels.

When the basic shape is finished, the potter smoothes the vessel's surfaces using a cow's rib, a thick piece of leather, or a dried corncob. The pot is left to dry for 12 hours, then polished by troweling the surface with stones and water. Cycles of drying and polishing continue until the artisan is satisfied with the overall aesthetic result, and then, after a final drying, the pots are taken out of the sun in late afternoon and warmed on a stove until they are too hot to touch. Pots are then placed on a grate and individually covered with "cow chips" (dried cow dung), which are carefully ignited.

The burning fuel functions as a natural kiln, firing the pots without benefit of an oven or other exterior structure. Potters tend the fire to make sure it burns evenly and steadily, all the while checking between layers of chips to see how the pot is progressing; when the entire pot glows red (usually this takes about one hour), it is fired. Pots created this way have a smooth, burnished terra-cotta appearance. Chips that touch the pot's surface during firing create blurred black "fire clouds," considered an error in the world of refined kiln techniques but valued by ranchware collectors.

Trastes de barro come in all shapes and sizes, from teacups to *frijoles* bowls to the rare *porrón*, a very large jar used for grain or water storage. The larger the piece, the more difficult it is to make and the more expensive it is to buy. *Tinajas*, medium-sized water jars, are easier to find and very functional. The slightly porous surfaces allow a little water to leak out and evaporate, thus keeping the vessel and its contents cooler than the ambient air temperature – call it ranch refrigeration.

---

derground stream, which has been dammed to irrigate mangoes, citrus, guavas, avocados, papayas, corn, and bamboo. Pigs wander in and out of the canyon, seeking cool mud around the pump house. Around 80 people live in the village full time; the population swells during school sessions when children from ranchos deeper in the sierra board here to attend the local school.

The area's hilly, tropical-arid thorn forest makes for good hiking. Bring plenty of water, even in winter, as the sun bakes everything unprotected by shade. At the edge of town near an old cane mill is a hill surmounted by a cemetery that can be reached on foot. Look for the headstone of Rafael Salvatierra, whose engraved dates of birth and death indicate he lived to the age of 130; opinions are divided as to whether the dates are accurate, although several generations ago residents in this area often passed the century mark.

Getting There

From Playa Migriño: The quickest way to La Candelaria is via a 9.1-kilometer (5.6-mi) sandy arroyo road that turns inland off Mexico 19 near Playa Migriño (just on the north side of Río Candelaria). The unsigned turnoff lies three kilometers (1.9 mi) south of the Km 94 marker, or about a half kilometer (0.3 mile) north of the main Playa Migriño turnoff. This road, suitable for four-wheel-drive vehicles only, parallels the deep, wide Río Candelaria arroyo. It's sandy and narrow in spots, so drivers must take care not to stray off the track into sand traps. And since the road runs across the bottom of the arroyo at one point, it would be risky during or after a hard rain. If you're two-wheeling it, stick to the San Lucas road both ways.

From Cabo San Lucas: This route is longer and more scenic than the road from Playa Migriño. From downtown Cabo San Lucas, begin driving toward San José along Boulevard Lázaro Cárdenas, then turn left at a sign marked La Paz Via Corta, directly opposite the entrance to Club Cascada. You are now heading northwest toward Todos Santos and La Paz. After passing a soccer field on the left, look for a power plant on your right and turn onto the wide dirt road near the plant (1.7 km/1.1 mi from the Via Corta intersection).

From this intersection, La Candelaria is 27.7 kilometers (17.2 mi) away (the highway sign says 23 km). Make another right 4.3 kilometers (2.7 mi) from the highway at a road signed La Candelaria and Los Pozos; you'll pass through a fence and cattle guard here. A military checkpoint has on occasion been set up near this gate.

As you ascend the sierra foothills into a relatively dense thorn forest (green in early fall) and stands of *cardón* and *pitahaya,* it's not unusual to see cattle or burros in the road, so drive slowly. The road forks about 12 kilometers (7.5 mi) from the highway; don't take the right fork signed for San Felipe and El Sauzal but rather the left one, which leads to the charming *ranchitos* and adobe ruins of Los Pozos. Pass a small chapel at 14 kilometers (8.9 mi) and follow signs for La Candelaria and La Trinidad. Stay with the main road and ignore any smaller forks from this point.

The road begins climbing, and 18.5 kilometers (11.5 mi) from the highway you'll see the Pacific Ocean to the west. Around 21 ki-lometers (13 mi) from the highway you pass a signed turnoff for Rancho San Ramón, and at 24 kilometers (15 mi) you come to a relatively major fork. The right branch is more direct to La Candelaria, though the left curves around to a *ranchito* and eventually cuts back onto the same road. About 800 meters (half a mile) farther (following the right branch), the road crosses an arroyo that could be problematic in heavy rain. Ignore a right turn to La Trinidad at 26.4 kilometers (16.4 mi). Less than 1.6 kilometers (1 mi) later you'll arrive at La Candelaria.

Note: Almost any type of vehicle can safely navigate the Cabo San Lucas–Candelaria road in dry weather. Low-lying Los Pozos—almost halfway to La Candelaria—may flood in heavy rains, so if it begins raining during the first half of the drive, turn back. Once you're past Los Pozos, keep going! Becoming stranded in La Candelaria would beat getting mired in Los Pozos.

Another way to visit La Candelaria is by guided ATV tour. Contact **Baja's Activities** (Km 104–105, tel. 624/143-2050, www .bajasactivities.com).

PESCADERO AND VICINITY
Playa Las Cabrillas
Of the many deserted beaches strung out along the Pacific coast between Playa Migriño and Todos Santos, one of the easiest to reach is **Playa Las Cabrillas,** south of El Pescadero (turnoff at Km 81). Flat and sandy, the beach was named for the plentiful sea bass that can be caught from shore. Grass-tufted dunes provide partial windscreens for beach camping, which is free.

◀ Playa Los Cerritos
A new official road sign points the way to Playa Los Cerritos at Km 64 (12.8 km/8 mi south of Todos Santos). From the turn, follow a good dirt road 2.7 kilometers (1.7 mi) southwest until you reach the sandy parking area. Sheltered by Punta Pescadero at its north end, the beach is usually safe for swimming. Throw on a pair of goggles and you may even catch a glimpse of a spotted eagle ray gliding

PESCADERO TO TODOS SANTOS

To San Pedro and La Paz

To La Pastora, El Carrizal, and Las Playitas

San Ignacio

19

Playa la Cachora

La Poza

Todos Santos

Cerro la Calera

Cerro la Poza

LIGHTHOUSE

Cerro Salado

Punta Lobos

Puerto Campechana

Puerto Algodones

GRADED ROAD

PLAYA SAN PEDRITO

Playa Las Palmas

Cerro San Pedro

CAMPO EXPERIMENTAL

Punta San Pedro

19

Cerro Los Viejos

Agua   Grande

Playa San Pedro

San Juan

GRADED ROAD

El Pescadero

GRADED ROAD

0   1 mi

0   1 km

Cerro Tecolote

Cerro el Gavilan

GRADED ROAD

Cuatro Vientos

Punta Pescadero

19

PLAYA LOS CERRITOS

To Cabo San Lucas

© AVALON TRAVEL PUBLISHING, INC.

by just offshore. Boogie boarding is another popular activity.

During the winter, the northwest swell tips a surfable point break, and during the summer, a mushy beach break sometimes occurs. Because wave size rarely intimidates, Cerritos is popular with novice surfers. The **Los Cerritos Surf Shop** (Degollado and Rangel, a half block up the hill from Miguel's) rents boards at the beach dawn till dusk.

Campers note: Change is afoot at this much-loved beach. Having received its title to the land, the local *ejido* has been selling property near the beach. Campers and RVers who set up camp were asked to leave in late 2006, and the **Los Cerritos Club** bar and beach restaurant opened in 2007 (see *Food*).

Three miles south near Km 75, a new real estate development, **Tortuga del Sol** (www.tortugadelsol.net) is taking shape with 123 home sites.

El Pescadero

As you approach El Pescadero from the south (Km 62), hilly terrain gives way on the west side of Mexico 19 to a series of flat, cultivated fields, most of which are bordered by a single row of tall corn stalks. Between fields of cherry tomatoes and basil, a number of palm-lined dirt roads meander to the water's edge. Though still much smaller and more spread out than its neighbor to the north, Pescadero has evolved in recent years from a cluster of simple *tiendas* and *loncherías* into a more developed business center with its own Pemex and Oxxo convenience store. The first major real estate development underway in the area is the 50-acre gated community of **Playa Agave Azul**. A tequila distillery and restaurant were in the plans, as well as a bar and restaurant at nearby Playa Los Cerritos (see *Food*).

Local expat residents here are getting involved with turtle conservation efforts, through egg collection and baby turtle release programs, as well as the building of an educational amphitheatre, designed in the shape of a turtle, to promote ecological awareness. Visit www.bajaturtle.com for more information.

WEST CAPE

Dirt roads heading to the beach can be a bit tricky to navigate. There are no street names or signs, and many roads dead-end at someone's driveway. The easiest way to find most of Pescadero's waterfront attractions is to follow a wide dirt road with a row of palms in the median that meets Mexico 19 just across from the Sandbar restaurant. If you've rented a place along this stretch of coast, be sure to get specific directions to find it.

Playa San Pedro

Just south of Punta San Pedro begins the long Playa San Pedro (7.4 km/4.6 mi south of the Todos Santos town limits), which is stony at the north end but sandy for a long stretch south. The beach's south end, toward Punta Pescadero, is sometimes called Playa Pescadero. Surfing toward the north end can be good, and it's a lot easier to find than Playa San Pedrito; the 3.1-kilometer (1.9-mi) access road west from Km 59 is clearly marked.

During the winter surfing season, the local *ejido* sometimes collects a nominal parking fee for vehicles parked in the small area at the end of the road near Punta San Pedro.

◖ Playa San Pedrito (Playa Las Palmas)

Just north of Pescadero between Km 56 and 57 is an unsigned, 2.5-kilometer (1.5-mi) dirt road west to Playa San Pedrito, called "Palm Beach" or Playa Las Palmas by local *norteamericanos*. Stretched between two rocky points and backed by Mexican fan palms and a salt marsh, this scenic beach offers good fishing and the occasional mushy beach break for surfing or body-boarding. For swimming, the middle 200 meters or so in the center of the cove is usually safest. Toward the north and south ends, the water looks deceptively shallow and inviting, but riptides have been known to carry swimmers out of the cove into open ocean or onto the rocks.

The best thing about San Pedrito/Las Palmas is that there is no easy vehicle access, so the sand isn't crisscrossed with vehicle tracks like many other beaches along the West Cape. However, the beach sand is often streaked with

black volcanic sediment from Puerto Algodones a little farther north.

Trails lead across the headlands at either end of the cove to beach vistas. In back of Punta San Pedro, the slopes of **Cerro Los Viejos** offer a rough but scenic hike.

This beach is sometimes incorrectly called "Playa San Pedro." Mexican topographic surveys confirm its original name as Playa San Pedrito, or "Little San Pedro Beach"—it's smaller than Playa San Pedro, immediately south of Punta San Pedro. Further proof can be found inside the Casa de la Cultura museum in Todos Santos, where a photo of this beach is clearly labeled Playa de San Pedrito. This same museum contains a historical photo of the Hacienda de San Pedrito—the hacienda now standing in ruins at the back of Playa San Pedrito. Nonetheless, most gringos and some locals confuse the names, chiefly because for years, a former campground on Playa San Pedro called itself San Pedrito.

Camping is no longer permitted in the palm grove or in the ruined hacienda behind it. Beach camping on the sand west of the palm grove is allowed, but don't leave any rubbish behind. Water is available from a spring at the south end of the beach; treat before drinking.

The more commonly used road to San Pedrito leaves Mexico 19 almost opposite the white buildings of the Campo Experimental on the east side of the highway between Km 56 and 57. A more direct road just a bit farther south is sometimes marked with a sign reading Road Closed; all the local residents use it anyway. Both roads intersect several other sandy tracks; when you see a ruined mansion just ahead, make sure you take the left fork that curves around to the south end of the palm orchard. If you head straight toward the middle or north end of the orchard you'll run into the salt marsh and have to hike a couple of hundred yards through tall salt grass and mud to reach the beach.

For information on beaches north of Playa San Pedrito, see *Sights* and *Beaches* in the *Todos Santos* section.

Exploring the Sierra

East of Pescadero, you can follow a network of dirt roads up into the sierra foothills to palm-filled arroyos, remote ranches, thick *cardonales* (*cardón* stands), and other delights. If you decide to explore the area, you should do so only in a high-clearance vehicle, preferably with four-wheel drive; better yet, park in the foothills and hike in. It's easy to become lost here, so you may be better off hiring a guide in Pescadero or in Todos Santos. Some of the best spots, such as **Cascada del Refugio,** a sparkling, palm-shaded waterfall, can be reached only by hiking across private land, for which you'll need permission—best arranged by someone local. At Rancho Pilar (Km 73, ranchopilar@yahoo.com), artisan and amateur naturalist Cuco Moyron can arrange mule trips into the Sierra de la Laguna and is a good source of information about sierra flora. He'll need about a week to make the arrangements. In Todos Santos, **Todos Santos Eco Adventures** (Juárez and Topete, tel. 612/145-0780, www.tosea.net) arranges one-day and multiday hikes.

One road leading southeast from south of town near Playa Los Cerritos continues approximately 56 kilometers (35 mi) across the Sierra de la Laguna to Mexico 1 between Santa Anita and Caduaño, about 16 kilometers (10 mi) south of Miraflores (see *Sierra de la Laguna* in the *East Cape and the Sierra de la Laguna* chapter). Parts of this road—properly called Ramal Los Naranjos but known by many Anglophone residents as the "Naranjas road"—are graded, but the middle section is passable only by sturdy four-wheel drive.

SURFING

Experienced surfers have several good options for waves along the West Cape. Playa Migriño offers an exposed right point and hollow beach break. Punta Gaspareño, around Km 73, catches a sandy right point break. Punta San Pedro (Km 59, site of the former San Pedrito RV park) offers consistent right reef and beach breaks; paddle out from the beach to avoid urchins on the reef. A little farther north, Playa San Pedrito has another beach break, best enjoyed during a west or north swell. Popular with novice surfers, Playa Los Cerritos has several left and right beach breaks. Experienced surfers will enjoy the right break off the point on larger northwest and south swells. Vacation rentals in the Pescadero area are popular with some surfers, while others prefer to camp north of Todos Santos. The **Pescadero Surf Camp** (Km 64, www.pescaderosurf.com) offers cabanas, camp sites, board rentals, and instruction.

SWIMMING

Most of the beaches along the West Cape are exposed to heavy surf; however, on calm days Playa Los Cerritos and Playa Las Palmas offer sheltered conditions for an ocean swim. At Las Palmas, the middle 200 meters or so in the center of the cove is usually safest. Toward the north and south ends, the water looks deceptively shallow and inviting, but riptides have been known to carry swimmers out of the cove into open ocean or onto the rocks.

SPA SERVICES

In a brick building three rows in from the beach, **Los Bules Day Spa** (Playa Congrejos, El Pescadero, tel. 612/108-4134, www.pescadise.com) offers deep tissue, hot stone, or Swedish massage (US$50), body wraps (US$45), and facials (US$40–70)—plus a native American *temazcal,* or sweat lodge (US$20). The proprietor, Maria, is also a gourd artist. Her gallery on the property contains pitchers, bowls, animals, candles, and teacups—all crafted from hard-shelled bottle gourds.

ENTERTAINMENT

These days, when Todos Santos residents want to go out for a night on the town, they head to Pescadero. Todos Santos may have more shops and restaurants, but Pescadero has the **Sandbar** (Km 63, tel. 612/130-3209, Mon.–Sat. 3 P.M. till late, Sun. 1–10 P.M.)—with a pool table, live music, and daily happy hour specials, as well as occasional cook-your-own kebab dinners.

SHOPPING

A string of *artesanías* selling such items as colorful Mexican blankets, hammocks, and pottery lines the highway in the Pescadero area.

Local artisans in Candelaria produce rustic ranchware pots, cane baskets, and *palo escopeta* chairs with palm-fiber bottoms. Look for a sign reading Pottery in the village if you're interested in buying these crafts. Candelaria resident Lorena Hankins sometimes leads pottery workshops; check with Lorena in La Candelaria, or inquire at Todos Santos Eco Adventures. At Km 80, **The Blanket Factory** is a popular stop for organized tours. Shop here for handmade rugs, blankets, clothing, and hammocks—or request a custom design.

Rancho Pilar

A sandy road near Km 73 leads to a trailer homestead where La Paz native Cuco Moyron (ranchopilar@yahoo.com) makes custom-fitted *bajacaliforniano*-style leather sandals with recycled tire-rubber soles for US$25–30 a pair. He can take your measurements one day and have the sandals ready the next. Cuco also makes clay pottery, and his wife, Pilar, makes beach rock and wire jewelry, as well as grass-woven hats. An amateur naturalist, Cuco can arrange mule trips into the Sierra de la Laguna and is a good source of information about sierra flora. He'll need about a week to make the arrangements. To find Rancho Pilar, follow the dirt road off Mexico 19 till it ends, then turn left and continue straight till you reach his gate; park outside the gate and walk in.

ACCOMMODATIONS

Several longtime Pescadero inns have changed hands in recent years, and new places are opening with each season. A number of private homes are also coming on the market as vacation rental properties.

US$50-100

On the beach in Pescadero, 3.5 kilometers from the wide dirt road that leaves Mexico 19

across from the Sandbar, the **San Pedrito Surf Hotel** (www.sanpedritosurf.com, US$65–150) is a remodel of the former Casa Cyrene. Now owned by two families from Hawaii, the property has five *casitas*. The surf bunkhouse has been converted into a two-bedroom family *casita*. All have full kitchens and king-size beds. Other amenities include bottled water, basic cooking utensils and spices, and linens. There is a washer/dryer on the property.

Right on the beach just south of the San Pedrito Surf Hotel, **Casa Simpatica** (http://todossantos.cc/casasimpatica.html, US$65) features three clean *casitas,* each with queen bed and private bath; amenities include a communal outdoor cooking area and Internet access. There's a three-night minimum.

At the San Pedrito surf break, **Las Palmas Tropicales** (www.tropicalcasitas.com, US$75–140) has four *palapa*-roof *casitas* (three with kitchens) with tiled baths and wireless Internet. Also close to the San Pedrito surf break, a couple from Santa Cruz, California own **Sierra de la Costa** (rcliv2surf@aol.com, US$70, three-night minimum), beach bungalow rentals with queen-size beds, tiled baths, private patios, and gas barbecues.

A little farther away from the beach and the surf breaks, **Rancho de Las Olas** (tel. 612/111-7121, ranchodelasolas@yahoo.com, www .bajacasitas.com, US$65–75) has three minimally furnished *casitas*. One is a stand-alone unit, while the others are second-story apartments. Weekly rates and longer-term discounts are available.

US$100-150

Near the San Pedrito Surf Hotel, **El Pozo Hondo** (pozohondobcs@yahoo.com, US$100–110) is a bed-and-breakfast with two *palapa*-roof bungalows surrounded by mango, avocado, and citrus trees.

US$150-250

Marble floors, robes, Egyptian cotton sheets, and fluffy towels are just a few of the luxury amenities at **La Alianza** (tel. 612/108-0436, www.bajaturtle.com, US$130–240), a five-room property near San Pedrito point. Guests share a third-floor *palapa*-roof deck and common kitchen. A separate, two-bedroom *casita* has two bedrooms, one bath, and a kitchen for US$150. Commissioned works from local artisan Cuco Moyron (see *Shopping*) add an authentic Baja twist to the grounds and home. This is the place to stay if you want privacy and that extra special touch. Owner Deborah McIntire is involved with local sea turtle conservation activities to protect the leatherbacks and olive ridleys that nest on the beach in Pescadero. Inquire about participating in a baby turtle release August–December.

Vacation Rentals

The Todos Santos community website, www.todossantos.cc, keeps a list of vacation rentals in the area. Here are a few of the most popular homes: For kids (and the young at heart), the highlight of a stay at **Villa del Faro** (U.S. tel. 707/468-0876, www.villadelfarobaja.com, US$3,000/week) is the curved waterslide that deposits swimmers into a 37-foot saltwater pool rimmed with fluorescent lights that glow after dark. Located at the south end of Pescadero Beach, the villa was built to handle a crowd, with three kitchens, five bedrooms, and a hot tub, plus massage, maid services, and catering available by request.

As the name implies, the **Beachfront Family Hacienda** (US$250/night or US$1,500/week), near the San Pedrito surf break, is a family-friendly 3,000-square-foot redbrick building with three bedrooms, two indoor baths, an outdoor shower, and a full kitchen. This home also comes with a washing machine and dishwasher, swing set, and beach gear.

Between the Los Cerritos and San Pedrito surf breaks, **Alhaja de Baja** is a recently remodeled two-bedroom house with king-size beds (www.alhajadebaja.com, US$990/week). **The Great Escape Ranch** at Los Cerritos (Km 66–67, US$125/night or US$700/week) has three rustically furnished bedrooms in a solar-powered home. Amenities include laundry, Internet, and satellite TV.

For luxury accommodations in a more remote location, **Noche de las Estrellas** (www.

nochedelasestrellas.com, US$350/night or US$5,000/week) sits on a bluff overlooking a sand beach at Elias Calles, 10 miles south of Pescadero. Four suites have private sitting areas, granite baths, and guest robes (for walking to the pool and hot tub). A shared living room has satellite TV and Wi-Fi, and the tiled kitchen has granite counters, an island and window bar with stools, and a table that seats eight. An outdoor kitchen is available for grilling.

Also in the Elias Calles area, **Casa Aqua Brillante** (Km 82, www.todossantos.cc/casaaquabrillante.html, US$3,500/week) is a luxury villa that sleeps six in three suites. Liberal use of marble, onyx, and granite set the stage. A 10-person dining table has ocean views. A fully equipped kitchen, satellite TV, and Wi-Fi complete the experience. The villa is off the grid, using solar power and propane for power and heat. Daily maid service is included in the rate. Inquire about food-stocking service and airport shuttles.

Surf and Fitness Camps

On the east side of the highway at Km 64, **Pescadero Surf Camp** (tel. 612/134-0480, www.pescaderosurf.com, US$60) is a good place for diehard surfers to meet kindred spirits. Besides tent and *palapa* camping, you can rent a cabaña that sleeps six and is equipped with kitchen and bath. Daily or weekly rates are available. Pescadero Surf Camp also offers campsites with shade *palapas* for US$7–10 per person per night. Amenities include water, electricity, bathrooms with hot showers, a pool with a swim-up bar, and a cooking area. The camp rents tents, as well as surfboards and boogie boards by the hour or day. Instruction is offered at all levels; guided "surfaris" are also available.

A raw-food diet and plenty of exercise define the detox experience at **Baja Life Camp** (Km 64, Barrio Las Palmitas, tel. 624/155-7057, U.S. tel. 858/764-4106, www.bajalifecamp.com). Run by a former NFL athlete, the camp has eight simple *palapa* structures set deep in the Pescadero *huerta*. Guests begin the day at sunrise with a warm-up and cardio workout and then relax for an afternoon siesta. Rates of US$1,000 per week for single occupancy in a private *casita* and US$800 per person double occupancy include meals, fitness instruction, lodging, airport transfer, and laundry.

Camping and RV Parks
RV Park Baja Serena (tel. 612/130-3006, US$20) in Pescadero offers eight spaces with water and sewer hookups (no electricity) that can be rented by the day, week, or month. The entrance is on Mexico 19 just south of Mini Super Los Arcos, which is where you check in.

Though the highway sign still stands, the popular **San Pedrito RV Park** was destroyed in 2003 by a hurricane. The property changed hands several times in 2006 and is likely to be developed soon.

Campers and trailers were asked to leave the former **Los Cerritos Trailer Park** in 2006–2007, as developers began work on a new oceanfront resort.

Free beach campsites along Mexico 19 can be found at the ends of dirt roads branching off Mexico 19 at Km 89–90, Km 86, Km 75, and Km 70–71.

FOOD
Simple **Restaurant Migriño,** on the ocean side of Mexico 19, just south of Km 102, serves *antojitos* and cold beer.

Lonchería Rosita (tel. 612/130-3094, daily 8 A.M.–8 P.M.), on the east side of Mexico 19 near the Pemex, is a small *palapa*-roofed place. Specialties include *pescado empanizado, tamales de puerco,* quesadillas, enchiladas, chicken and *machaca* burritos, and soft drinks.

Popular with locals and expats alike for its casual fare, ◖ **Felipe's Restaurant** (Km 61, mains around US$4) specializes in tasty Mexican dishes and seafood at nongringo prices for breakfast, lunch, and dinner.

Grill your own kebabs at the **Sandbar** (Km 63, tel. 612/130-3209, Mon.–Sat. 3 P.M. till late, Sun. 1–10 P.M.), or just pop in for daily happy hour specials, as well as weekly all-you-can-eat pizza.

The **Los Cerritos Club** (Km 66–67) at Playa Los Cerritos opened with multiple large-screen TVs just in time to host a Superbowl party in 2007. The preliminary menu included tacos, salads, and burgers.

Regulars praise **Art & Beer** (Km 69) for large signature cocktails—creative variations of the Bloody Mary, which comes generously garnished with all manner of shellfish. You must agree to buy a drink or a meal in order to view the art on display. When it's time to go, your eccentric hosts, Alfredo and Lourdes, may offer up a beer for the road.

Groceries
Mini Super Los Arcos is a *tienda* on Mexico 19 that carries a good selection of gringo items such as American cheese, nonfat milk, whole turkeys, yogurt, tofu, feta cheese, and balsamic vinegar. Special orders are welcomed.

Mini Super Los Cerritos (Km 63 Mexico 19) sells cold beer and ice, as well as some arts and crafts.

INFORMATION AND SERVICES
Pescadero has the only Pemex between Cabo San Lucas and Todos Santos, as well as an Oxxo convenience store. For emergencies, call 612/145-0445, or head to Todos Santos or the Los Cabos area for medical services. Buses en route to La Paz and Cabo San Lucas stop across from the Pemex. Many places in the Pescadero area now have wireless Internet, and a few of the networks were open at last check, but the closest Internet cafés were in Todos Santos.

WEST CAPE

Todos Santos

One of the more lushly vegetated arroyo settlements in the Cape Region, Todos Santos (pop. 5,000–7,000, depending on the season) sits on a *meseta* (low plateau) buttressing the sierra foothills. Looming over Todos Santos to the east, the sierra provides an underground stream that irrigates dozens of orchards laden with mangoes, avocados, guavas, papayas, citrus, coconuts, and other fruits. Most of these are cultivated along wide Arroyo de la Reforma to the town's immediate north, in an area commonly known as **La Huerta** or "The Orchard." At the west end toward the beach is **La Poza,** a small freshwater lagoon favored by resident and migrating waterfowl. North of town, amid a dense palm grove, is another natural pool where local children go swimming.

Beneath the town's sleepy surface, behind the century-old brick and adobe facades, lives a growing community of mostly American artists—with a few surfers and organic farmers mixed in—all of whom have found Todos Santos the ideal place to follow their independent pursuits. And discerning buyers say the art scene has come of age in Todos Santos in recent years, clearly setting itself apart from the typical retiree/artist community.

As a newly designated Pueblo Mágico, Todos Santos has received access to government funding for improving infrastructure and developing cultural tourism. To date, the money has been used to remodel the park and repair the auditorium. Next on the project list: burying wires and cables in the town center, repairing the theater, and protecting the oasis and lagoon.

In 2007, the town was also abuzz with talk of real estate development. One project near La Poza had run into problems with water and sewer rights; another at the San Pedrito surf break had changed hands three times in less than a year. There was talk of a fishing village at Punta Lobos. And new homes were popping up at the other end of town, along Playa Las Tunas, as power and water infrastructure crept northward. Locals remained optimistic that Todos Santos would retain its bohemian character, even in the wake of increased development—with Carmel and Santa Fe as the model, rather than Los Cabos or Cancun.

HISTORY

The earliest traces of human habitation in the Todos Santos area date back 3,000 years to "Matancita Man," the defleshed and painted remains (thus indicating a second burial) of a tall male who lived to at least 75 years on a vegetable and animal-protein diet. The first Spaniard to sight the oasis, Jesuit padre Jaime Bravo, found nomadic Guaicura availing themselves of the inland water source and collecting shellfish along the coast.

Padre Bravo established a farm community and a *misión de visita* (visiting mission) called Todos Santos here in 1724, to supply the water-poor mission community at La Paz with fruits, vegetables, wine, and sugarcane. By 1731 Todos Santos was producing 200 burro-loads of *panocha* (raw brown sugar) annually, along with figs, pomegranates, citrus, and grapes. Two years later, deeming the local Guaicura amenable to missionization, Padre Sigismundo Taraval founded Misión Santa Rosa de las Palmas at the upper end of the arroyo about two kilometers inland from the Pacific. Taraval fled to Isla Espíritu Santo near La Paz after a 1734 native rebellion, and the mission returned to visiting-chapel status the following year.

The local Guaicura population was soon wiped out by smallpox, and Pericú were brought in to work the fields. Reinstated as a *misión de visita* in 1735, Todos Santos outgrew La Paz by the mid-18th century; from 1737 until 1748, Padre Bernardo Zumziel actually spent more time in Todos Santos than at the mission in La Paz. Renamed Nuestra Señora del Pilar de Todos Santos in 1749, the town served as Spanish military headquarters for La Escuadra del Sur, the southern detachment of the Loreto presidio. This enabled the community to weather the Pericú rebellions

© PAUL ITOI

side street in Todos Santos

to the southwest in Santiago and San José del Cabo, although 49 Todos Santos inhabitants were killed defending the town in one related skirmish. Polish Jesuit padre Carlos Neumayer presided over the mission from 1752 until his death in Todos Santos in 1764. Todos Santos remained an important mission settlement until secularization in 1840.

When Governor Luis del Castillo Negrete ordered the distribution of church lands to the local community in 1841, he was contested by Padre Gabriel González, a local priest and former president of the mission who had used mission property for his own farming and ranching, becoming a powerful local trader in the process. González's armed rebellion was put down in 1842; the priest and his followers fled to Mazatlán.

Anglo whalers visiting Todos Santos in 1849 praised the town as "an oasis" with "friendly and intelligent people." In the post-mission era, Todos Santos thrived as Baja's sugarcane capital, supporting eight sugar mills by the late 19th century. While carrying out a survey of Cape Region flora

for the California Academy of Sciences in 1890, botanist T. S. Brandegee commented on the area's beauty and bounty. During this period handsome hotels, theaters, municipal offices, and homes for painters and sculptors were built.

Sugar prices dropped precipitously after World War II, and all but one mill closed when the most abundant freshwater spring dried up in 1950. The remaining mill closed in 1965, though smaller household operations continued into the early 1970s. The town faded into near obscurity.

Around 1981 the spring came back to life, and the arroyo once again began producing a large variety and quantity of fruits and vegetables. Three years later, Mexico 19 was paved between San Pedro and Cabo San Lucas, opening Todos Santos to tourists and expatriates for the first time.

SIGHTS
◖ Historic District

Although Todos Santos has been inhabited continually since 1731, the oldest standing structures date back only 100–150 years. The town's most historic buildings—a mixture

WEST CAPE

of one- and two-story affairs, all with court-yards—can be seen along the streets nearest the plaza, particularly along Pilar, Centenario, Legaspi, Topete, and Obregón. Most are constructed of fired Mexican brick laid in double or sometimes triple courses (some walls are plastered, some not) topped by flat parapet roofs. A few feature palm-thatched roofs. Large windows and doors bounded by *pilastres* in the classic Andalusian style (favored in provincial Mexico from the time of the Spanish until the middle of the 20th century) predominate in this area. The large building housing Café Santa Fé on Calle Centenario, facing the plaza, is one of the only substantial adobe structures downtown. Many of the buildings in this area are owned or occupied by foreigners. And the facades are likely to look more homogenous in coming years, as a uniform appearance is one of the contingencies of funding made available through the Pueblo Mágico program. Check *El Calendario* for the timing of the annual historic home tour, when owners open their doors to visitors.

On the hill overlooking town (off Mexico 19 on the way out of town toward La Paz) stand a few older adobe ruins. The newer eastern half of Todos Santos holds many small residences built of adobe brick or *chiname*—mud plastered over woven *palo de arco* (trumpetbush) branches. Brick ruins of several of the old sugar mills can be seen around town.

Iglesia Nuestra Señora del Pilar

Although the structure itself is rather plain, this church facing the southwest edge of the main plaza contains an important orange- and blue-garbed figure of the Virgin of Pilar, the focus of the town's biggest festival each year in October. In August, the famous Virgin of Loreto—considered the "mother" of all Baja churches founded by the Jesuits—is brought to the church from Loreto.

Centro Cultural Profesor Nestor Agúndez Martínez

Housed in a restored U-shaped brick building on Avenida Juárez at Obregón, the Centro Cultural (Mon.–Fri. 8 A.M.–5 P.M., Sat.–Sun. 9 A.M.–1 P.M., free admission) displays a modest collection of artifacts evoking the anthropology, ethnography, history, and natural history of the region, along with small displays of modern art and handicrafts. Named in honor of a venerated local high school teacher, the museum's pottery collection includes classic local ranchware, as well as older ceramics produced by the now-extinct Pericú. Some rare painted Amerindian skulls are also on display. One of the five exhibit rooms contains paintings by local artists, including a set of pastels of historic structures in Zacatecas.

BEACHES

None of the roads leading from Todos Santos to the beach are paved or even marked. To find them, you'll need good directions and a little patience for those inevitable moments when you realize you've taken a wrong turn and need to retrace your steps. The following list starts south of Todos Santos and proceeds north.

Punta Lobos

About two kilometers (1.2 mi) south of the town limits via Mexico 19, a signed, unpaved access road suitable for most vehicles leads 2.4 kilometers (1.5 mi) to Punta Lobos, a rocky point at the south end of a sandy cove. The point is named for a resident colony of sea lions. The surf here is usually okay for swimming, but take a good look at the currents before leaping in. This cove is used as a launching point for the local fishermen, so there's always a small fleet of *pangas* toward the point. The *pangas* usually bring the catch in after 3 P.M.; watching the pilots time the waves so that they can safely run the boats onto the beach is a treat. Sometimes fresh fish can be bought directly from the *pangeros*.

The ruins of an old stone-walled cannery lie at the side of the access road toward the beach; north along the beach stands a lighthouse. Swimming in the lighthouse area is not recommended because of strong currents. If you continue walking past the lighthouse you'll eventually reach Playa Las Pocitas and Playa La Cachora (described later in this section).

A small spring-fed lagoon lies behind the south end of the beach, marked by a large Virgin shrine. A narrow trail leads up and over the 215-meter (700-ft) headland to a panoramic view of the beach and sea below. On the other side of the headland you can see sandy **Puerto Campechano** and, farther south, Puerto Algodones.

Punta Lobos can be reached on foot from town by following Calle Pedrajo southwest one long block till you meet a wide dirt road. Turn left and follow the road until you can see the lighthouse on the right; take the next wide dirt road heading in that direction till you reach

WATER WARNINGS

While walking close to the surfline along any of the beaches north of Punta Lobos, watch out for "sneaker" waves that rise up seemingly out of nowhere to engulf the beach. Though rare, accidental drownings have occurred on these beaches.

Also beware – during the late *chubasco* season, especially September – of the small blue jellyfish, called *aguas malas*, that are commonly encountered in inshore waters.

Punta Lobos. This walk takes 20–30 minutes each way.

Hidden away two headlands south of Punta Lobos and almost surrounded by steep cliffs, this deep and secluded cove can be reached via a very rough, winding, and sometimes steep dirt and stone road that runs southwest off the Punta Lobos access road. According to local history, **Puerto Algodones** was used for the shipping of tomatoes, sugarcane, and canned fish from the 1930s through the 1950s, when a stone-block road was laid between the cannery and the bay. How it got the name "Algodones" (cotton) is a mystery; cotton was never cultivated in the Cape Region.

Along the north side of the U-shaped cove stands a tall pier made of rough-hewn stone blocks. The sure-footed can hike along a narrow trail at the bottom of a cliff and reach the rock pier—worth the effort for the view back into the bay. Smaller animal paths lead up a steep slope above the pier for more panoramic views. If you've got all day you could probably hike to Puerto Campechano and back from here.

A black-hued beach of rounded volcanic stones rims the middle reach of the bay, where the waves are sometimes suitable for bodysurfing. To reach the beach you can hike down a cliff or follow the old road. Snorkeling is good at the rocky headlands at each end of the bay, but currents and tidal surges can be too strong for some swimmers. Sea lions are sometimes seen along the rocks.

The old road to Algodones starts just east of the cannery ruins near Punta Lobos and climbs along the eastern rim of a large arroyo. You can hike to the bay from the cannery area in about 45 minutes at a steady pace, an hour if you take it slow. Start in the early morning and plan to spend the day there so that you can hike back in late afternoon, thus avoiding the hottest part of the day. If you have a sturdy off-highway vehicle that can take soft sand, you can drive about a fourth or a third of the way before the road becomes too rocky for anything but tractor tires.

For information on beaches south of Punta Lobos and Puerto Algodones, see *Pescadero and Vicinity*.

Playa La Cachora

Playa La Cachora is a broad swath of sand backed by verbena-trimmed dunes, a good spot for strolling and sunset-watching. From the Galería de Todos Santos, follow Calle Topete across the palm-filled arroyo known as La Huerta; the first sand road on the other side (turn left just before the low rock wall; if you start going uphill, you've gone too far) leads west to the beach after curving through a quiet residential section perched on a *meseta* above the northwest corner of the arroyo.

◖ Playa Las Pocitas (La Poza de Lobos)

If you walk south along Playa La Cachora, you'll come to scenic Las Pocitas, also known as La Poza de Lobos and a gold mine for bird-watchers. Along the back edge of the beach is a freshwater lagoon (La Poza), and toward the south end a rocky ridge heads inland. It's possible to walk back to town via a trail running along the base of the north side (the La Huerta side) of this ridge.

The undertow and shore break along La Cachora and Las Pocitas are usually too heavy for swimming, except during the summer when there are occasional long periods of relative calm.

COURTESY OF POSADA LA POZA, TODOS SANTOS

La Poza de Lobos

WEST CAPE

Playa La Pastora

A wider network of sand roads crosses the arroyo and runs north parallel to the beach for some 26 kilometers (16 mi). The roads pass small coconut and papaya orchards and larger farms at Las Playitas and El Carrizal, then head inland to join Mexico 19. Several sandy tracks branch west off this road to a lengthy succession of dune-lined beaches perfect for secluded sunbathing and beachcombing.

For much of the year the surfline here is too precipitous for swimming, though surfers can ride the waves at a break called La Pastora, named for a meadow some distance away. In winter, La Pastora offers a right point break in a northwest swell; in summer you'll find an occasional beach break in a southern swell, or a point break in a southwestern swell.

La Pastora is about 5.6 kilometers (3.5 mi) northwest of La Huerta via the only coastal road north; just past a wide arroyo that runs right up to the beach, look for a large, lone *palapa* next to a long, low stone wall.

Farther North

Beyond El Carrizal, a rough dirt road snakes north along and away from the coast 57 kilometers (36 mi) to a cluster of Ranchos—Los Inocentes, El Rosario, El Tepetate, and El Tomate—where another dirt road leads northeast 29 kilometers (18 mi) to meet Mexico 1. Sand beach lines the entire coastline here all the way north to **Punta Marqués** (about 24 km/15 mi north of Rancho El Tomate) and **Punta Conejo** (18 km/11 mi north of Punta Marqués). Both points offer excellent surfing and windsurfing in the winter and early spring. And surfable reef and point breaks can form in many other spots along the 58-kilometer (36-mi) stretch of sand extending south of Punta Marqués; check out **La Bocana,** an arroyo mouth near Los Inocentes. Self-contained beach camping is permitted anywhere along the shore.

FISHING

Many of the same game fish commonly found from Cabo San Lucas to La Paz can be caught offshore here. If you speak Spanish, you can go to Punta Lobos and ask the fishermen there about hiring *pangas* and fishing guides. The asking price is usually around US$30 per hour with a three-hour minimum. See *Organized Tours* for guided trips.

Surf casting, though possible at any of the Todos Santos area beaches, is safest and easiest at Playa San Pedrito (Palm Beach), Playa San Pedro, and Playa Los Cerritos (see *Pescadero and Vicinity*).

Ferreteria Oasis de Todos Santos (Rangel at Zaragoza, tel. 612/145-0754, Mon.–Fri. 8 A.M.–3 P.M. and 4–7 P.M., Sat. 8 A.M.–4 P.M.) carries some fishing supplies. You can buy live bait from the local fishermen at Punta Lobos.

WHALE-WATCHING

Although you won't see as many whales close to shore here as farther north in Bahía Magdalena (an important calving bay for the Pacific gray whale), newborn calves and their mothers do swim by on their "trial run" to the Sea of Cortez before beginning the long migration back to the Arctic Circle. The best months for spotting grays are December–April.

With a pair of binoculars and some luck, you can stand on any beach in the vicinity and spot grays (and other whales) spouting offshore. One of the best places to see them is near the rocky ridge at Playa Las Pocitas. For a much better view from shore, climb Punta Lobos (see *Beaches*). *Pangeros* at Punta Lobos will take up to five passengers out to see the whales for about US$25 an hour; inquire at the beach or at any of the hotels in town (see *Organized Tours*).

SURFING AND KAYAKING

Most of the Pacific breaks near Todos Santos hit their peak during the northwest swell, December–March. Experienced surfers who paddle around the larger points at Punta Lobos and Punta San Pedro during the late summer southern swell will sometimes turn up a nice break, although the usual summer custom is to head for the Corridor between Cabo San Lucas

© NIKKI GOTH ITOI

surf casting near Todos Santos

WEST CAPE

and San José del Cabo, or to lesser known spots around the east side of the Cape.

You may see auto window stickers bearing the label "Todos Santos Surfboards," but don't go looking for them—it's a small made-in-California brand. The **Todos Santos Surf Shop** (Degollado/Mexico 19 and Rangel, tel. 612/145-0882, mariosurfing@hotmail.com, daily 9 A.M.–5 P.M.) offers lessons, accessories, and ding repair; a satellite location at Playa Los Cerritos has rentals (open daily dawn till dusk). The newer **Costa Azul Surf Shop** on Juárez is an extension of same store at Playa Costa Azul in San Jose del Cabo.

La Sirena Kayak y Surf Aventuras (Olachea off Degollado, tel. 612/145-0353, www.lasirenakayaksurf.com) rents surfing equipment and supplies, offers surfing instruction (US$50/hour), and leads local kayak tours (US$50).

HIKING

Arrange guided day or overnight hikes into the Sierra de la Laguna at **Todos Santos Eco**

Adventures (Juárez and Topete, tel. 612/145-0780, www.tosea.net) or **La Sirena Kayak y Surf Aventuras** (Olachea off Degollado, tel. 612/145-0353, www.lasirenakayaksurf.com).

YOGA, MEDITATION, AND MARTIAL ARTS

Hatha and Ashtanga yoga classes meet several times a week at the La Arca building on Topete (US$4 per class). In the same location, **El Dharma de Todos Santos** (tel. 612/145-0676, www.eldharma.com) offers dharma talks and *vipassana* meditation classes 10–11:30 A.M. each Sunday. And Carlos Martinez Hererra offers Aikido classes to beginners and experienced students (cell 612/018-1052, ranchaiki@aikifarms.com, US$4 per class).

Tai chi chuan instruction is available at the Centro Cultural Monday and Friday October–June, for a fee of around US$6. Hours vary with the season.

The Elephant Tree (Obregón btw Centenario/Juárez, tel. 612/145-0299) is an inner-resource community center holding a variety of workshops including yoga, tarot, and writing.

SPA SERVICES

Kathleen Nelson offers massage treatments through **Todos Santos Oasis** (19 Legaspi at Hidalgo, tel. 612/145-0545, US$35/hr).

ORGANIZED TOURS

Todos Santos Eco Adventures (Juárez and Topete, tel. 612/145-0780, www.tosea.net) leads half-day outings to nearby waterfalls, cliff walks, and La Candelaria for US$55, as well as overnight trips to the Sierra Laguna, fishing trips (US$275 per boat for up to 6 hrs), and horseback riding (US$45/hr). A 90-minute walking tour of historic sites in Todos Santos is US$15 per person. The Eco Adventures office is also a friendly source of tourist information.

La Sirena Kayak y Surf Aventuras (Olachea off Degollado, tel. 612/145-0353, www.lasirenakayaksurf.com) leads similar trips, including whale-watching (US$35 pp for two hours), fishing (US$50/hour), and waterfall hikes (US$40 pp).

SHOPPING

Although Todos Santos hardly compares with Cabo San Lucas or San José del Cabo when it comes to variety and quantity, several interesting, high-quality shops have opened here, most of them clustered around the historic district near the plaza.

Home Furnishings and Gifts

Sun House (Pedrajo just off Mexico 19, tel. 612/145-0355) sells unique home furnishings and gifts produced by local artists.

In the same building as El Tecolote, **Fénix de Todos Santos** (Juárez at Hidalgo, tel./fax 612/145-0666) specializes in handcrafted Mexican art. Jewelry, rugs, leather bags, handwoven fabrics, *equipal* furniture, rugs, and decorative tinware are on display, as well as resortwear from Puerto Vallarta. In the same commercial center, **Tzintzuntzan** (Place of the Hummingbirds) is a small shop featuring un-

usual handcrafted *artesanías* and ornaments from Michoacán.

Emporio Hotel California (Juárez btw Morelos/Márquez de León, tel. 612/145-0525), attached to Hotel California, features an eclectic selection of decorative items, clothing, and jewelry.

In a refurbished historical building on Centenario opposite the Charles Stewart Gallery is **Mangos** (tel. 612/145-0451, Mon.–Sat. 10 A.M.–5 P.M.), a beautiful gift shop featuring Mexican folk art, ceramics, pewter ware, metal sculptures, silver jewelry, and beautiful Guatemalan textiles, rugs, and wood carvings.

On the opposite side of Centenario from El Perico Azul, **Manos Mexicanas** carries rustic Mexican furniture and an interesting selection of decorative accessories and unique jewelry, plus pottery made by Ruben Gutierrez.

Jewelry

El Filon de Taxco, opposite the Hotel California on Calle Juárez near Morelos, features a large selection of quality silver jewelry.

In the green building next to Mangos, **Arte Cactus** (Centenario, tel. 612/145-0773) offers a good selection of Mexican folk art and jewelry. Next door, check out **Joyería Brilanti** (Centenario near Topete, tel./fax 612/145-0726, www.brilanti.com) for good-quality silver jewelry. Brilanti has a second location nearby on the same street, next to El Perico Azul.

Clothing

El Perico Azul (Topete at Centenario, tel. 612/145-0222, Mon.–Sat. 11 A.M.–5 P.M., Sun. 11 A.M.–4 P.M.), opposite Caffé Todos Santos, features women's and men's clothing made from the best of Mexican textiles, handwoven and minimally processed. The shop also offers a few clothing items from Bali and India, local crafts, jewelry, and some leather pieces.

Beachwear and T-shirts, as well as imported perfumes, are sold at **Sisy's Boutique** (Hidalgo and Colegio Militar).

Books

In the Plaza de los Cardones commercial center,

El Tecolote Books/Libros (Juárez and Hidalgo, tel. 612/145-0295, fax 612/145-0288) carries a good selection of foreign and Mexican magazines (including surf magazines), new and used paperbacks (trades welcome), maps, and a large number of hardcover and softcover books on Mexican arts, architecture, and culture, as well as a good selection of books on tape and movies for sale or rent. The store also stocks art supplies such as paintbrushes and watercolor, acrylic, and oil paints. In a room in the back of El Tecolote is **Traditions,** a small shop featuring gifts, cards, and holiday decorations.

Arts and Crafts

Several shops in Todos Santos, all featuring typical Mexican art and crafts, seem to open in a new location with each successive season. Ones that have lasted longer than most are **La Iguana** and **Artesanías El Cardón,** *palapa*-roofed *artesanías* on the northwest corner of Márquez de León and Juárez opposite the church. They sell Mexican crafts, blankets, T-shirts, sterling silver, quartz, and onyx. Next door is **Bazar Agua y Sol** (tel. 612/145-0537) featuring exclusive jewelry designs, sculptures, pottery, and paintings. Credit cards are accepted here.

Artist Studios and Galleries

The art scene in Todos Santos has come of age in recent years, with more than a dozen galleries representing internationally-known artists from the United States and Mexico. One of the first artist arrivals was Charles Stewart, who has a home gallery, the **Charles Stewart Gallery & Studio** (Centenario and Obregón, tel./fax 612/145-0265, www.charlescstewart.com, Mon.–Sat. 11 A.M.–4 P.M.), usually referred to as "Stewart House." You can't miss this 1810-vintage, French-designed house smothered in foliage and enlivened by caged singing birds. Formerly of Taos, New Mexico, Stewart produces watercolor and oil paintings, wooden sculptures, and hand-carved doors; among his works are small *retablo*-style pieces that feature colorful *bajacaliforniano* pictograph motifs on salvaged wood. His home studio is open to the public daily 11 A.M.–4 P.M.

Newcomer **Galería On cé** (Hidalgo 11, tel. 612/145-0550) opened in November 2006 to showcase the photography of Howard Ekman and Jack Hamilton.

Galería de Todos Santos (Legaspi 33 at Topete, tel. 612/145-0500, www.galeriatodossantos.com, Mon.–Sat. 10 A.M.–4 P.M.), in the same building as the Todos Santos Inn, is owned by American artist Michael Cope and his wife, Pat. The high-ceilinged gallery focuses on the work of artists who live in Baja California. Look for pieces by Walker and Derek Buckner, Gloria Marie V., Carlos Uroz, Margaret Torres, Erick Ochoa, Anibal Angulo, Jack Smith, and Angelina Cimino. The works displayed are fine art and dimensional pieces, and the collection changes every six weeks or so. Michael and Pat have a second gallery at the site of a historic building at the corner of Centenario and Hidalgo that was formerly the town billiards hall; it once appeared in a Chris Isaak music video. This gallery features abstract pieces, while the original gallery displays more representational works of art.

A brightly hued house at Juárez and Morelos contains **Galería Logan** (tel. 612/145-0151, www.jilllogan.com, Mon.–Sat. 11 A.M.–4 P.M., Sun. by appointment), focusing on the work of artist Jill Logan, who creates dramatically colored landscapes, still lifes, and portraits in oil and acrylic.

La Paz native Ezra Katz, known for murals and etchings featured in a number of Cabo San Lucas restaurants and hotels, has opened **Ezra Katz Fine Art** (Juárez at Hidalgo, tel. 612/137-3473, Mon.–Sat. 10 A.M.–5 P.M., or by appt.), featuring John Comer, Lindy Duncan, Lesley Rich, and others, in addition to his own artwork.

Galería/Estudio de Kathleen Gambogi (Hidalgo btw Colegio Militar/Rangel, tel. 612/145-0460), near the Maria Bonita Hotel, features colorful paintings depicting Mexican scenes and still lifes by artist Kathleen Gambogi.

Galería/Studio de N. E. Hayles (Cuauhtémoc, tel./fax 612/145-0183, www.mexonline.com/hayles.htm, Mon.–Sat. 11 A.M.–4 P.M.) displays unique paper-tile mosaics, multimedia art, and tables fashioned by the artist/owner. **Galería Wall** (Juárez 4, tel. 612/145-0527, www.catherinewallart.com, Mon.–Sat. 11 A.M.–4 P.M.) shows Mexican-themed original oils by artist Catherine Wall.

Estudio Gabo (Verduzco 7 btw Olachea/Carrillo, tel. 612/145-0505, Mon.–Sat. 10 A.M.–4 P.M.) features paintings by La Paz native Gabo, whose work is inspired by Baja's colors and textures. His work can be found at Estudio Gabo and at the small **Gabo Galería** on Centenario near Topete.

Colores de México (Juárez at Hidalgo, tel. 612/145-0106, omommag@aol.com), opposite Los Adobes, is a photographic gallery featuring beautiful images by local residents Pat Gerhardt and Suzanne Hill. They specialize in photos of Mexico printed on watercolor paper in large format, suitable for framing.

ENTERTAINMENT AND EVENTS
Bars and Dancing
In 2007, **La Iguana Disco Bar** (Zaragoza and Rangel) opened after a period of closure, with live reggae and rock bands. The only real cantina in town is **Cañada del Diablo** (tel. 612/145-0022), a large, round, *palapa*-roofed place a little out of town at the northeastern end of Calle Centenario. Cañada del Diablo offers a fully stocked bar, including a few choice tequilas, and free popcorn. On occasion, local residents will hire a live *norteña* ensemble to play for a party here. Women and families, as well as men, patronize this bar, whose management is good about not letting the rare *borracho* get out of hand.

Near the Pemex station on Degollado, **Shut Up Frank's** (tel. 612/145-0707) is an expat bar featuring satellite broadcasts of sporting events. Happy hour is Monday–Friday 3–6 P.M.

In the gardens of the Todos Santos Inn, **La Copa** (Legaspi 33, tel. 612/145-0040, Tues.–Sat. 5–9 P.M.) is an upscale wine bar with a cozy romantic ambience. Owner Michael Cope has added a tapas menu Wednesday–Friday evenings (US$10/plate). The entrance is on Calle Topete.

The bar in Hotel California's uniquely decorated **La Coronela** (Juárez btw Morelos/Márquez de León, tel. 612/145-0525), frequented by local expats as well as the hotel's guests, is a fun place to have a few drinks. Live music on Saturday evenings.

Theater
The nicely restored **Teatro Márquez de León** (Calle Legaspi at Márquez de León) hosts musical and folkloric dance performances from time to time, especially during the annual October fiesta. Before the Teatro de la Ciudad in La Paz was built, this was the only proper theater in the state of Baja California Sur.

Simple outdoor cinemas—featuring grade-C Mexican films with the usual *ranchero/narcotraficante* themes—are sometimes set up next to the soccer field near La Huerta.

Events
Fiesta Todos Santos is held around the feast day of the town's patron saint, Virgen del Pilar, on October 12. For four days beginning the second Saturday of the month, residents enjoy dances, soccer and basketball games, fishing tournaments, cockfights, horse races, theater performances, amusement-park rides, and other merriment centered around the church and town plaza.

For 12 days beginning on the **Día de Guadalupe** (December 12), Todos Santos Catholics participate in nightly candlelight processions to the plaza church. The celebrations culminate in a midnight Mass on **Christmas Eve.**

In late January or early February, the government-funded **Todos Santos Art Festival** features sculptures, paintings, ceramics, and other visual works by local artists, as well as dancing, music, and other performing arts from out of town. Then, in early March, the **Todos Santos Latin Film Festival** comes to town.

Also once a year, usually in February or

WEST CAPE

March, historic homes in Todos Santos open to the public. Check *El Calendario* (www .todossantos-baja.com) for more information.

ACCOMMODATIONS

Overnight guests in Todos Santos can choose from a variety of modest hotels, bed-and-breakfast inns, and private vacation rentals. As more visitors arrive each year, new properties are opening, old ones are renovating, and others are just raising prices without making significant improvements. Many properties are now up for sale, and if water and sewer rights are worked out, several large resorts may be coming to the area in the not-too-distant future.

There are three accommodations in town with "Todos Santos" in their name: The Hacienda Todos Los Santos is located in the palm grove at the end of Avenida Juárez; the Todos Santos Inn is on Calle Topete, with its own wine bar; and the Hacienda Inn Todos Santos is north of town. Details for each are given below.

Hotels, Inns, and Bed-and-Breakfasts

Under US$50: In a dusty but quiet neighborhood in the town's southwestern quarter stands **Hotel Miramar** (Mutualismo at Pedrajo, tel. 612/145-0341, US$30). The two-story L-shaped motel contains 10 clean, small rooms, each with two twin beds. On the premises are a pool, small restaurant, and laundry. It's about a 20-minute walk from the beach via the dirt road to Punta Lobos. Off-street parking is available.

US$50-100: The former Hotel Misión del Pilar got a fresh coat of paint inside and out in 2006 and has opened under new ownership as the ◖ **Maria Bonita Hotel** (Colegio Militar at Hidalgo, tel. 612/145-0114, US$50–60). The office and 12 guestrooms are all on the second floor, above the popular Café Brown. Though rooms are plain, clean off-white walls, new curtains and bedspreads, and comfortable mattresses make for a pleasant stay. Small but clean bathrooms have shower stalls with glass

doors and hot water aplenty. Free and reliable wireless Internet will seal the deal for those who need to get online. A great value, this hotel is a wise choice for budget travelers who need a place to crash for the night. Through-traffic on Mexico 19 passes right by the hotel entrance, so expect to hear trucks and car radios unless you crank the fan on the air conditioner. Rates include tax.

On the road to La Pastora, the **Hacienda Inn Todos Santos** (tel./fax 612/145-0002, US$65–110) is about 2 kilometers from the center of town—a bit inconvenient for those without their own transportation. Amenities include a pool and restaurant/bar. The 14 rooms and suites come with cable TV, air conditioning, and bathrobes. Rates include continental breakfast. Turn right at the El Sol II grocery store to find the inn.

At **Hostería Las Casitas** (Rangel btw Obregón/Hidalgo, tel./fax 612/145-0255, www. lascasitasbandb.com, US$55–90), Canadian artist Wendy Faith has lovingly restored four *chiname* adobe cottages and one four-person suite over the last decade. Set among lush landscaping, rooms are small with low ceilings, one bed, and brightly colored walls and ceilings. Accommodations here are basic but artsy, with hand-painted murals in some rooms and the artist's own glasswork in others. Breakfast includes the B&B's own blend of coffee. An authentic *palo de arco casita* houses the owner's studio. This property was up for sale at last check.

The decade-old **Hotel Santa Rosa** (tel. 612/145-0394, www.hotelsantarosa.com.mx, US$60), on Calle Olachea near the south entrance to town, offers eight large, fairly well-maintained studio units with kitchenettes. Facilities include a good pool, laundry, and enclosed parking. Small discounts are available for long-term stays. The signed turnoff for the Santa Rosa is three blocks south of the Pemex station, after which it's another two blocks west to the hotel. Discounted monthly rates are available.

US$100-150: Set among towering palm, mango, and banana trees, **Jardin de Pilar**

(Pilar btw Topete/Hidalgo, tel. 612/145-0386, www.jardindepilar.com, US$105–120) has two beautifully appointed *casitas* for rent. Details include colorful high-end linens and bamboo accents, as well as wireless Internet.

Behind wrought-iron gates in a palm oasis at the south end of Juárez is **Hacienda Todos Los Santos** (Juárez, tel. 612/145-0547, www.mexonline.com/haciendatodoslossantos.htm). Operated as a hotel with daily housekeeping service, Hacienda Todos Los Santos has expanded to include eight rooms in four guesthouses. The original three guesthouses each have private terrace, fully equipped kitchen, and use of a swimming pool. Choose from Casa Santa Luz (US$185), with an air-conditioned bedroom with a queen-sized bed, TV, VCR, dining/day room with fireplace, living room with fireplace, and spacious bathroom; Casa del Palmar (US$165), a studio suite surrounded by terraces, with a king-sized bed, living area, spacious bathroom with shower and bathtub, and a TV/VCR; or Casita del Encanto (US$125), a studio suite with a queen-sized bed, wet bar, seating area, two patios, and a large bathroom. Access to a kitchen is available when Casita del Encanto is rented together with Casa del Palmar. A new four-bedroom/six-bath house, **Casa de Los Santos,** opened in 2007, has one room (US$125) and three suites (US$225–250), and the whole house rents for US$850/night. The upstairs suites have great views of the surrounding farmland. Owner Karen Rodriguez also rents a two-bedroom brick house with a *palapa* roof, called **Casa San Vicente,** on the corner of Pedrajo and Mutualismo.

US$150-250: The elegant **Ⓒ Todos Santos Inn** (Legaspi 33 at Topete, tel./fax 612/145-0040, www.todossantosinn.com, US$125–225) occupies a well-restored, 1880-vintage brick building. The original owner was said to have thrown his cashbox down the hole of an outhouse to keep it from marauding revolutionaries in 1910. Since then the building has served as a school, cantina, and movie house; the faded mural in the foyer dates to the 1930s. Large rooms with high adobe-brick ceilings and private baths are tastefully decorated with Mexican furniture, Saltillo tile, oriental rugs, mosquito nets, and ceiling fans. Larger suites offer sitting areas, private patios, and air conditioning. Common areas include an inviting pool and cozy wine bar called La Copa. Spanish-language instruction is available, either separately or as a package with accommodations (10 hours for US$200).

Before it closed in January 1999, the run-down, two-story **Hotel California** (Juárez btw Morelos/Márquez de León, tel. 612/145-0525, hotelcaliforniareservations@hotmail.com, US$125–200) was the most popular place to stay in Todos Santos for first-time visitors, some of whom mistakenly believed the hotel had some connection with the Eagles' song of the same name. Reopened in 2003, the hotel was beautifully renovated by new owners. It features 11 suites, a pool and garden, restaurant/bar **La Coronela** (see *Food*), and **Emporio Hotel California** (see *Shopping*).

A large outdoor patio set around a lagoon and saltwater swimming pool is the highlight of a stay at the smoke-free **Alegría Inn** (tel. 612/145-0700, www.alegriainn.net, US$125–185). Part bed and breakfast, part camp lodge, the inn is located north of town in a former private residence on the north side of the road leading to Playa La Cachora, off Calle Topete, past the Huerta. The layout works best for guests who like to spend more time outside than in their rooms. Quality sheets and towels, comfortable mattresses, and good lighting compensate for the small size of standard rooms, painted concrete shower stalls, and hard-to-clean fieldstone floors. Rooms are tastefully furnished with rustic Mexican pieces, and a hot breakfast is included in the price. Although the inn itself is quiet and secluded, this is not the place for privacy, as most rooms are steps away from the common kitchen and living room. Sound carries from inside out and outside in. There is a TV in the living room, and wireless Internet was installed but not working at last check. The Todos Santos Inn is a better value at this pricepoint.

Guests of Todos Santos' finest boutique hotel

Posada La Poza

WEST CAPE

receive a pair of binoculars and field guide to North American birds at check-in. Situated on the shore of a small lagoon, and set in a tropical desert garden, **(Posada La Poza** (tel. 612/145-0400, www.lapoza.com) blends the relaxed pace of life in Baja with a Swiss sensibility for quality and efficiency. Hosts Jörg and Libusche Wiesendanger opened the hotel in 2002. Guests stay in one of four garden suites (US$180), two junior suites with private hot tubs (US$240), or the honeymoon suite (US$440). All suites have ocean and lagoon views, air conditioning, and CD player, as well as Swiss linens and hypoallergenic blankets and pillows. Guestrooms and common areas also feature Libusche's oil and acrylic paintings. Splash around in a large saltwater swimming pool, watch for whales from the deck, or borrow a bicycle for a ride into town. And when you've had your fill of the great outdoors, you might give yourself an aromatherapy treatment in the onsite sweat lodge, which is filled with heated lava rocks topped with eucalyptus leaves, rosemary, or other herbs. Internet ac-

cess is available for travelers who can't entirely disconnect from the real world. Rates include continental breakfast; guests of the honeymoon suite also receive a fruit basket and bottle of champagne. The elegant **El Gusto!** restaurant serves hearty Mexican and international dishes like pork loin, rib eye, and lobster (see *Food*). The road to La Poza is well marked: Turn southwest off Degollado (Mexico 19) onto Calle Olachea or Calle Carrillo and follow the blue-and-white signs.

Guesthouses and Vacation Rentals

Several homes in town, most of them owned by American or Canadian expatriates, offer lodgings in cottages adjacent to, in back of, or attached to the principal house. Often the owners are happy to supply information about things to see and do in Todos Santos and environs. Price range US$65–225 for a one bedroom and US$200–400 for two bedrooms.

US$50-100: In a residential section of unpaved streets south of Mexico 19, **The Garden**

COURTESY OF POSADA LA POZA, TODOS SANTOS

Casita (Olachea and Mutualismo, tel./fax 612/145-0129, www.todossantos-baja.com/gardencasita.htm, US$85/395 day/week) is an owner-designed *palapa*-roofed guesthouse with a living area, dining area, kitchenette, bedroom, and patio surrounded by an enclosed courtyard. Wireless Internet as well as weekly and monthly rates are available. Long-term rates include weekly maid service.

In roughly the same neighborhood, **Las Flores Posada** (formerly Jane's Place, Pedrajo and Villarino, tel. 612/145-0216, www.todossantos.cc/lasfloresposada.html, US$55), offers four clean and comfortable apartments on a large, landscaped lot surrounded by a security wall. Three units come with kitchenettes and full-sized refrigerators. Pleasant indoor and outdoor sitting areas are found throughout.

Three blocks from the center of town, north of Mexico 19, **Las Palmas Casitas** (Hidalgo and Huerto, tel./fax 612/145-0213, janeLB3@yahoo.com, US$65–95) consists of two one-bedroom *casitas* and one two-bedroom, two-story *casita*, each with *palapa* roof. All *casitas* are smoke-free. All come with a kitchen, covered patio, tropical gardens, modern amenities, and secure parking.

Across the *huerta*, north of town near Café D'Licia, a fun-loving retired Italian couple, Sandra and Enrico Ugolini, have built several charming one-bedroom *casitas* with separate kitchens, beautiful landscaping, and fabulous ocean views. Gourmet potluck dinners are a tradition for guests and friends alike.

Behind the Pemex, near the sugarcane mill ruins, the **Posada del Molino** (off Rangel, tel. 612/145-0233, www.todossantos.cc/Posada DelMolino.html, US$75–90) was for sale at last check. The property has four comfortable, air-conditioned studios facing a swimming pool. Each studio sleeps two, and comes with satellite TV, CD player, and fully equipped kitchenettes. Maid service is included, and there are coin-operated laundry facilities on the grounds.

US$100-150: At **Los Colibrís** (tel. 612/145-0780, www.loscolibris.com, US$125), the proprietors of family-run Todos Santos

Eco Adventures have built three guest *casitas* on their hillside property, with stunning ocean views overlooking the freshwater estuary and Posada la Poza resort. Two twin beds in each *casita* can be arranged as a king. Meticulously tiled baths have rain showers and sculpted concrete countertops. Lampposts made of decorative tree trunks, colorful linens, and hummingbird feeders are few of the special touches. Rooms have ceiling fans (no air conditioner), bottled water, and CD players. Outdoor space is limited given the steep incline of the property, but the upper unit has its own balcony, and two others share a furnished patio. Two generations of the Jáuregui family attend to guest needs. (They also run Todos Santos Eco Adventures and manage Casa Colina, a separate stand-alone house with two bedrooms and a kitchen.) Breakfast room service and afternoon margaritas available upon request. The same family has also built **Casa Colina** (tel. 612/145-0780, www.casacolina-ts.com, US$150/890 night/week), a two-story, two-bedroom home located below Los Colibris *casitas* and above Posada la Poza. Large picture windows in the bedrooms and kitchen open to ocean views, while balconies on both bedrooms face the mountains. Each bedroom has a king-size bed with luxury linens, ceiling fan, and its own bath. The casa also has a fully equipped kitchen.

Another longtime Todos Santos property now up for sale, **Annie's Place** (tel. 612/145-0385, anniesplacebaja@yahoo.com, US$100–150/day, US$600–900/week, 3-night min) is north of town, on the north side of the road leading to Playa La Cachora. Casa de Arbol is a unique three-level "tree house" surrounded by coconut palms and mango trees. A perfect retreat for artists and writers, the tree house features a kitchen, sitting area, bathroom, and two patios on the first level. A light, airy bedroom fills the second level, while the third-level open deck boasts views of the ocean and mountains. Long-term stays are encouraged. Casa Amplia is a spacious two-bedroom *palapa*-roofed house with one and a half baths and a great room with fully equipped kitchen and a fireplace. Large covered patios extend the living space into true indoor/outdoor living.

Across the wide arroyo north of town, on the south side of the road leading to Playa La Cachora, the new owners of **Las Puertas** (tel./fax 612/145-0373, www.alaspuertas.com, US$135–175) are continuing to rent several *casitas:* a large two-bedroom, two-bath guesthouse with a fireplace; a smaller one-bedroom guesthouse; and an oceanview suite with a fireplace, all with thick adobe walls, *palapa* roofs, sunny patios, and custom, Baja-style furniture. Surrounded by mango and other fruit trees, all units have gourmet kitchens; one guesthouse comes with a separate, full kitchen while the other two have attached kitchens. Daily maid service is a plus. The beach is a five-minute walk away.

Property Managers

A number of part-time Todos Santos residents rent their houses by the day, week, or month. For current listings and availability, check with **El Centro de Mensajes** (The Message Center, in Hotel California (Avenida Juárez, tel. 612/145-0525, fax 612/145-0288, messagecenter1@yahoo.com); **Su Casa** (Degollado btw Pedrajo/Olachea, cell 612/157-5519, www.sucasa.cc); or **Como El Sol** (11 Hidalgo, tel./fax 612/145-0485, comoelsol@prodigy.net.mx, Mon.–Fri. 10 A.M.–2 P.M.) in the back of Colores de México.

Monthly rentals in town range from around US$400–700 a month for small, local-style cottages with few amenities to US$1,000–3,000 a month for larger, better-furnished houses.

Camping and RV Parks

El Litro RV Park (tel. 612/145-0389), a big dirt lot with 15 RV sites surrounded by palm trees, south of Mexico 19 at the end of Calle Olachea, invites campers and RVers to park alongside full hookups for US$12 a night or US$250 a month—the use of hot showers and clean bathrooms is included. The park also has 30 tent sites (US$8 per night) in an orchard camping area. From El Litro, it's a 15-minute walk to the beach. A washer and dryer were in

the plans at press time. The owners can store your rig for US$40/month.

North of town a maze of sandy roads leads to a string of undeveloped beaches suitable for camping (see *Sights* and *Beaches*). Camping, both free and fee, is also available at several of the beaches south of Todos Santos (see *Pescadero and Vicinity*).

FOOD

For a small town, Todos Santos has a surprising number of places to eat at every budget, though some seem to flourish and die with each successive tourist season.

Alta Cocina Mexicana

On the back patio of a beautifully restored adobe house, **Los Adobes** (Hidalgo btw Juárez/Colegio Militar, tel. 612/145-0203, www.losadobesdetodossantos.com, dail 11:30 A.M.–9 P.M., mains US$15–22), features upscale Mexican cuisine with prices to match. Under new ownership as of 2006, the menu includes grilled fish entrées, chicken mole, and steak fajitas. Visa and MasterCard are accepted.

Posada La Poza on Playa La Cachora features the elegant **El Gusto!** restaurant (tel. 612/145-0453, Fri.–Wed. 11:30 A.M.–4 P.M. and 6–9 P.M.), specializing in Mexican gourmet cuisine. The changing menu features a selection of delicious vegetarian dishes, as well as creative meat and seafood choices; all the produce used is organic and locally grown. Seating is available inside or out, with breathtaking views of the lagoon and ocean. The bar terrace and whale-watching deck are great spots for a sunset cocktail, and service is attentive. Tapas are available most days on the bar terrace.

Mexican

Made famous by a *New York Times* writeup several years ago, **Miguel's** (corner of Degollado and Rangel, daily 8 A.M.–9 P.M., mains US$6–10) has become known for lightly battered chiles rellenos smothered in sautéed tomatoes and onions. A dozen tables

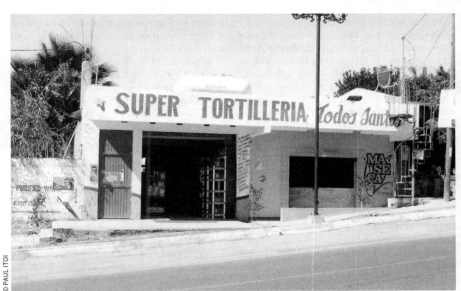

© PAUL ITOI

Todos Santos *tortillería*

are arranged on a sand floor under a *palapa* roof. The garrulous proprietor, Miguel, speaks excellent English and usually takes time to chat with repeat and first-time visitors. The menu also features enchiladas, burritos, and cheeseburgers.

You'll be hard pressed to find anything on the menu over US$6 at **Restaurant La Ramada** (Militar and Obregón, mains US$3–6). This relative newcomer serves tacos, tostadas, and the like in a clean kitchen with friendly service; it's open for breakfast, lunch, and dinner.

On Avenida Juárez opposite Hotel California, **Tequila Sunrise Bar & Grill** (daily 10 A.M.–9 P.M.) is a colorfully decorated, tourist-oriented restaurant featuring home-style Mexican food.

Pancho Banano (Hidalgo 11, tel. 612/145-0885, daily for breakfast, lunch, and dinner, mains US$6–10) across from Los Adobes on Hidalgo, offers standard Mexican food—and real estate pitches—to a mostly gringo clientele.

Seafood

The friendly **Mariscos Mi Costa** (Colegio Militar at Ocampo, daily 10 A.M.–8 P.M., mains US$8–15) is a casual seafood place with a raked sand-floor. The *sopa de mariscos* and *camarón al ajo* are particularly recommended.

Nestled in an alley on Juárez between Topete and Hidalgo is **Fonda El Zaguán,** a popular place specializing in fish tacos, vegetarian tacos, seafood soups, organic salads, and delicious Mexican seafood dishes. Daily specials are shown on a chalkboard out in front. The smoked marlin salad is popular. Closed Sunday.

Open since 1973, the old standby **Restaurant Santa Monica** (tel. 612/145-0204, daily 8 A.M.–9 P.M.), just north of the Pemex station on Mexico 19 (Calle Degollado), serves tasty shrimp, lobster, and carne asada dinners at reasonable prices. Service can be slow, but everything is made from scratch. One of the house specialties is *pollo estilo Santa Monica,* a quarter chicken braised in something akin to barbecue sauce.

WEST CAPE

Popular among locals as well as visitors for fresh seafood, tasty Mexican dishes, and cold beer served in frosted mugs is **Restaurant Las Fuentes** (at Calles Degollado and Colegio Militar, tel. 612/145-0257, Tues.–Sun. 7:30 A.M.–9:30 P.M.). The house specialty is *pescado empapelado,* fish baked in paper with tomatoes, mild chilies, and various other condiments, and the chiles rellenos are the best. This restaurant also offers a full bar. You can dine in the well-lighted indoor seating area or out on the *palapa*-roofed patio, surrounded by three fountains, bougainvillea, and palms. Service is friendly and efficient. Visa and MasterCard are accepted here.

International

Hotel California on Calle Juárez boasts the atmospheric **La Coronela** restaurant/bar (Juárez btw Morelos/Márquez de León, tel. 612/145-0525, daily 7 A.M.–1 A.M., dinner mains US$8–20). Prepared by a Belgian chef, the international menu has some creative dishes, such as almond crusted Pacific oyster tacos and yellowtail in an opal basil ginger coconut sauce. Visa and MasterCard are accepted.

One block south of the park, **Ana San Sushi Bar** (tel. 612/137-9856, Tues.–Sat. 1–9 P.M.) prepares sushi, sashimi, soups, and salads.

Café Luna (Hidalgo and Juárez, Thurs.–Tues. 11 A.M.–3 P.M. and 6–10 P.M.) offers a choice of secluded patio dining as well as indoor seating. The international menu lists tapas such as tomato and goat cheese tarts, Aztec soup, and gazpacho. Entrées include seafood dishes, pasta, chicken stuffed with goat cheese and mushrooms, filet mignon, and beef medallions with peanut sauce. Open in December only, **Suki's** (Hidalgo btw Rangel/Cuauhtemoc, generally Tues.–Sat. 5–9 P.M.) prepares a moderately priced menu of pan-Asian cuisine, with pad Thai, teriyaki, and Korean specialties.

American

Shut Up Frank's (tel. 612/145-0707, www.shutupfranks.com, Mon.–Sat. 10 A.M.–10 P.M., Sun. 10 A.M.–8 P.M.), on Degollado, is a sports bar and grill offering decent American-style dinners such as steak and lobster and a variety of burgers (even veggie), as well as burritos and other Mexican fare.

A little out of town at the northeastern end of Calle Centenario, **Cañada del Diablo** hosts cook-your-own T-bone steak night with all the trimmings (US$14) on Thursdays starting at 5 P.M., and fish-and-chips night (US$7) on Sundays also starting at 5 P.M.

Italian

Housed in a 150-year-old *casona* with 46-centimeter-thick (18-in-thick) adobe walls, the atmospheric **Café Santa Fé** (Centenario 4, tel./fax 612/145-0340, Wed.–Mon. noon–9 P.M.), on Calle Centenario off Márquez de León facing the plaza, is still *the* place to eat and be seen during the December–April high tourist season. The changing, mostly Italian menu emphasizes the use of fresh, local ingredients (including organic vegetables) to produce wood-fired pizza, ravioli (a shrimp and lobster version is the house specialty), pasta primavera, lasagna, fresh seafood, octopus salad, and the occasional rabbit. Complementing the menu are espresso drinks, a full wine list, tiramisu, and fresh fruits. Choose between interior tables or courtyard dining amid palm greenery. Prices match the café's aristocratic flair, starting at US$18 and going all the way up to US$40 for rabbit, which you must order four days in advance. The Santa Fé often closes in October during the town fiesta.

Around the corner from Todos Santos Eco Adventures, **Tres Gallines** (Topete and Juárez, tel. 612/145-0274, Mon.–Sat. noon–10 P.M.) serves northern Italian fare, including homemade pasta and imported espresso, at more reasonable prices. New in 2007, **Buena Vida,** in a historical brick building on Calle Centenario next to Mangos, opened to rave reviews for its dinner menu of pizzas (US$8), salads, and wines. Another popular newcomer is **Il Giardino** (Degollado btw Olochea/Carrillo, Tues.–Sun. 1–10 P.M.), serving wood-fired thin crust pizza (US$10) and other casual Italian fare.

Antojitos and Fast Food

Several vendors in town offer inexpensive but tasty fish tacos—usually either shark or dorado—and shrimp tacos. **Tres Hermanos** vendor stand at the corner of Márquez de León and Juárez is among the best. Tres Hermanos sells especially good fish, shrimp, and clam tacos 8 A.M.–2 P.M. most days, sometimes longer depending on the season.

Just outside of town, heading north toward La Paz is the friendly **Antojitos Veracruzanos,** featuring Veracruz-style *antojitos* such as chicken or beef *empanadas* (turnovers), *sopes, gorditas,* and tamales.

Near the southwest corner of Juárez and Hidalgo in the center of town, **Tacos Chilakos** (Mon.–Sat. 9 A.M.–9 P.M., mains US$4–6) serves dependable carne asada, tacos, quesadillas, *machaca* burritos, and coffee at a few outdoor tables on the sidewalk. *Papas rellenas* (stuffed potatoes) are available in the evening.

Local Mexican residents praise ◖ **Barajas Tacos** (Wed.–Mon. 8 A.M.–11 P.M.), on Degollado (Mexico 19) toward the south edge of town, for serving authentic *carnitas* and *tacos de pescado y camarones* during the day and *tacos de carne asada* and *papas rellenas* at night.

At least three or four hot dog vendor carts roll out in the evening—usually one each on Juárez, Colegio Militar, and Degollado. Most sell only turkey dogs—often wrapped in bacon (ask for *sin tocino* if you don't want the bacon wrap).

Cafés

Attention to detail and a love of improvisation set ◖ **Café Brown** (Hidalgo and Militar, tel. 612/145-0813, Tues.–Sun. 7:30 A.M.–9 P.M., mains US$4–9) apart from your average small-town café. Enjoy a limited menu of home-style cooking made from quality ingredients (Sonora beef, breads from a bakery in La Paz) while you check your email on the fastest wireless connection in town (US$2/hr). Friendly and attentive service sets the tone; good music completes the experience. Art that doesn't have permanent gallery space often finds a home here. And from informal cooking classes and independent films to percussion instruction and

salsa dancing, owners Ekerd and his wife love to throw a good party. Look for Café Brown in the back of the Maria Bonita Hotel (formerly Hotel Misión del Pilar) complex.

Above the Costa Azul Surf Shop, **Vonn Café** (Juárez near Hidalgo, mains US$4–6) is a second-story café with a small patio overlooking the busy street below. Tasty sandwiches come on soft, lightly toasted rolls with crispy lettuce and fresh tomato. Salads and smoothies are other options.

The smell of homemade bread wafts out of **Caffé Todos Santos** (Centenario 33, tel. 612/145-0300, Mon. 7 A.M.–2 P.M., Tues.–Sun. 7 A.M.–9 P.M., mains US$6–12) in the morning. Housed in a historic building on Centenario between Topete and Obregón, the café offers indoor seating, on chairs painted by local artists, or outdoor dining, either in the garden area out back or on the shaded veranda in front. The café offers excellent cappuccino and other coffee drinks, hot chocolate, fresh pastries, waffles, omelets, deli sandwiches (smoked turkey is a specialty), vegetarian sandwiches, ice cream, bagels, granola, fruit shakes (made with produce from the owner's farm), fresh-baked bread, salads, and other snacks. Delicious cheesy pizzas are available 5–9 P.M. on Friday only. Prices are a little high by local standards, but so is the quality of the food, and portions are large.

On the plaza next to Café Santa Fé, the **Santa Fé Deli** (tel./fax 612/145-0301, Wed.–Mon. 8 A.M.–3 P.M., mains US$4–9) serves waffles for breakfast, cobb salad, soup, and other light fare for lunch. The deli gourmet market stays open till 6 P.M. Walk through the Galería Santa Fe to get to the deli.

Worth a two-kilometer drive to *el otro lado,* the other side of town, ◖ **Café D'licia** (tel. 612/145-0862, Thurs.–Sun. 8:30 A.M.–2:30 P.M., mains US$5–12) in the Las Brisas area off Calle Topete, serves the best homemade cinnamon rolls and sticky buns on the peninsula, plus a full menu of breakfast and lunch specials, from eggs and pancakes to enchiladas and chiles rellenos. Drinks include smoothies, espresso, and fresh-squeezed juice.

Breads, salsas, and sauces are all homemade. This is a great place to bring young kids who like animals, as the owners rescue exotic birds, some of which have learned to speak a few words of Spanish. To find D'licia, follow Calle Topete past the Todos Santos Inn, across the lush *huerte,* past the primary school and into the dirt road that leads to Playa La Pastora. After the El Sol II market, look for a sign and driveway on the left.

If all you need is a cup of coffee, look for **Café Combate** on Juárez (Mexico 19) on the way to La Paz.

En Route to La Paz

If you're heading to La Paz along Mexico 19 and need a cup of java or a bite to eat, consider stopping off at **Lonchería La Garita** (daily 6 A.M.–6 P.M.), near Km 29, about 22.5 kilometers (14 mi) northeast of Todos Santos. With its large *palapa* roof and open-front *carrizo* eating area, it looks much like any other Baja highway truck stop. But the family operating La Garita seems to have a special flair for preparing humble but high-quality fare. The fresh ranch cheese and the bean or *machaca* burritos with *panela* are superb here, as are empanadas filled with slightly sweet, cinnamon-spiced *frijolitos.* Yet another major draw is the coffee, made from fresh-roasted and fresh-ground Chiapas beans; many people buy bags of coffee beans from La Garita.

Groceries

The usual assortment of staples can be bought at any of several markets in town, which include: **Mercadito Guluarte** (next to Hotel Guluarte), **Tienda Disconsa** (Calle Colegio Militar), **Super Mercado Hermanos González** (Calle Pedrajo), and **Supermercado El Sol** (Calle Degollado).

The friendly **Super Mercado Hermanos González,** off Mexico 19 at the south end of town on Calle Pedrajo, has the usual *tienda* items but also caters to the northern population by stocking such items as nonfat milk, bagels, yogurt, ricotta cheese, and balsamic vinegar, to name a few. Special orders are welcome. The larger **Supermercado El Sol** also stocks gringo items and is open until 10 P.M. A second El Sol is on the road to Playa La Pastora one block west of Hacienda Inn Todos Santos.

La Siempre Viva, at Calles Juárez and Márquez de León, opens around 7 A.M., which is an hour or two earlier than the others. La Siempre Viva stocks household wares and a few ranch supplies as well as groceries; the meats, cheeses, produce, and honey sold here come from local farms and ranches.

The government-subsidized **ISSSTE Tienda** (Juárez btw Zaragoza/Morelos) offers an ever-changing selection of inexpensive groceries and holds a fairly well-stocked pharmacy.

Panadería Todos Santos (Mon.–Sat. 2–8 P.M. or until sold out) sells *bolillos, pan dulce, coyotes, arepas,* and other Mexican-style baked goods cooked in the wood-fired oven, as well as *pan salado,* an Italian-style loaf. The bakery operates from an unsigned two-story brick building at the north end of Calle Rangel near Ocampo.

You can buy fresh and inexpensive corn tortillas for about US$0.50 per kilo at the **Tortillería de Todos Santos** (Colegio Militar btw Morelos/Márquez de León). Fresh seafood can often be purchased from the *pangeros* at Punta Lobos, south of town.

All the various *tiendas* mentioned here sell purified water in *garafónes,* 20-liter returnable containers, as well as the usual smaller-sized bottles. Beer is available from any market in town or from the *depositos* on Calle Colegio Militar adjacent to the post office; on Calle Degollado near the gas station; and also on Calle Degollado next to Super Pollo. Ice is available at most *tiendas,* as well as at the ice plant on Mexico 19 on the southern outskirts of town, and at beer *depositos.*

Fresh tropical fruits—mangoes, guavas, figs—are most abundantly available during the July–September rainy season, although certain fruits, such as papaya, are available year-round. Fresh vegetables peak in January and February. **Huerta Tropical,** on Colegio Militar across the street from Paletería la Paloma, sells locally grown produce in season.

Homemade ice cream can be found at **Paletería la Paloma** (daily 8 A.M.–9 P.M.), on Colegio Militar next to Hotel Maria Bonita, along with refreshing fresh-fruit *paletas* (popsicles). You may see pushcart vendors selling the *paletas* around town. A second location, **Paletería la Paloma 2,** is opposite the Pemex. **Nevería Rocco** (Hidalgo btw Centenario/Juárez), a small shop in a pink house, sells Carnation ice cream and *paletas*.

Just north of town on the way to La Paz, along the east side of Mexico 19, vendors sell candies and pastries made from local produce. Among the goodies available are tasty empanadas made from mango, guava, and *cajete* (goat milk caramel); *panocha* (brown-cane-sugar cakes); lemon peel and coconut candies; wild honey; and refreshing sugarcane juice.

INFORMATION AND SERVICES
Tourist Assistance
Although Todos Santos has no tourist office as such, you can usually find someone to answer your questions at El Tecolote Libros, El Centro de Mensajes, Eco Adventures, or Caffé Todos Santos. If you speak Spanish and seek information on the sierra backcountry, try La Siempre Viva at Calles Juárez and Márquez de León; this is where sierra ranchers traditionally come to supplement foods they produce at home.

The locally produced *El Calendario de Todos Santos* (www.todossantos-baja.com), issued monthly, is an excellent source of current events and short articles on regional culture; it's distributed free at El Centro de Mensajes, El Tecolote Libros, and many other establishments in town. *El Mirador* is a smaller, bilingual publication (tel. 612/145-0559, www.elmirador.tv) with much of the same, plus an online phone directory.

The Todos Santos Book, written by local residents Lee Moore and Janet Howe and available at El Tecolote Books, contains lots of information on things to see and do in the area.

Medical Services
The local emergency number for police, fire, and Red Cross is tel. 612/145-0445. The Centro de Salud (tel. 612/145-0095) is located on Mexico 19, at the corner of Juárez and Degollado.

Pharmacies
Farmacia Guadalupe (Av. Juárez, tel. 612/145-0300) can fill prescriptions any time of day or night. Other pharmacies in town include **Farmacia Hipocrates,** on Morelos opposite Mercado Guluarte, and **Farmacia Similares,** in the Hotel Maria Bonita complex, which offers discounted generic versions of most prescriptions.

Money-Changing
BANORTE, on Calles Juárez at Obregón, is open Monday–Friday 9 A.M.–2 P.M. To cash travelers checks or exchange dollars here you need to show your passport. A 24-hour *cajero* (ATM) is available outside the bank. Instructions are in English and Spanish, but the machine dispenses only pesos.

Post and Telephone
The post office in Todos Santos is literally a one-man operation. Located on Colegio Militar (Mexico 19) between Hidalgo and Márquez de León, it's supposed to open Monday–Friday 8 A.M.–1 P.M. and 3–5 P.M., but the hours can be erratic, since the manager is often out delivering mail.

Long-distance phone calls can be made from several Ladatel phones around town, including one on Hidalgo near Tecolote Books. **El Centro de Mensajes Todos Santos (The Message Center),** Juárez in the lobby of Hotel California (Apdo. Postal 48, Todos Santos, BCS 23305, tel. 612/145-0033, fax 612/145-0288, messagecenter1@yahoo.com, Mon.–Fri. 8 A.M.–3 P.M., Saturday 8 A.M.–2 P.M.), can give you a quick and honest rate comparison between Tel-Mex, AT&T, MCI, and other telephone companies. The office charges a reasonable surcharge over whichever long-distance service you choose. In addition to long-distance calling, this office offers fax, DHL courier, mail forwarding, reservations, travel agency, and answering services.

For mobile phone needs, two Telcel stores are located on Militar, between Hidalgo and Degollado.

Internet Access

Many Todos Santos guesthouses and hotels now have wireless Internet service. In addition, **Café Brown** (Hidalgo and Militar, tel. 612/145-0813, Tues.–Sun 7:30 A.M.–9 P.M.) in the Hotel Maria Bonita complex has high speed access on its own PC or via a wireless connection. The **Todos Santos Internet Café** (Juárez at Topete, tel. 612/145-0219, Mon.–Sat. 9 A.M.–5 P.M.), in the Milagro Real Estate office, has five desktop stations and two Ethernet connections for laptops.

Pemex

There is a Pemex in town located at the intersection of Militar and Degollado (Mexico 19), and a new one at Km 50–51 on the way north to La Paz.

Laundry

The *lavandería* (tel. 612/145-0006, daily 8 A.M.–6 P.M.) on Juárez in the Hotel Guluarte, offers wash-and-dry service for about US$4 per load; for US$0.50 less you can do it yourself. Hot water and soap are available. **Neptune Laundry** on Colegio Militar, is similar.

Language Courses

Guillermo Bueron (tel. 612/145-0119, g_bueron@yahoo.com) offers one-hour **Spanish, English,** and **French lessons** at the Centro Cultural. Guillermo uses the Berlitz total-immersion method of instruction. Group and individual classes are available at all levels.

Hardware Store

Ferre Todos Santos (Zaragoza at Rangel, tel. 612/145-0565, Mon.–Sat. 8 A.M.–2 P.M. and 3–6:30 P.M.) has employees who speak English, and stocks a decent selection of hardware goods. **Ferreteria Oasis de Todos Santos** (Rangel at Zaragoza, tel. 612/145-0754, Mon.–Fri. 8 A.M.–3 P.M. and 4–7 P.M., Sat. 8 A.M.–4 P.M.) has fishing supplies, as well as plumbing and electric parts.

BACKGROUND

The Land

BIRTH OF A PENINSULA

Baja California's Cape Region lies at the tip of the world's fourth-longest peninsula (after the Kamchatka, Malay, and Antarctic). Today the peninsula is separated from mainland Mexico by roughly 250 kilometers (155 mi) of ocean at the widest gap, but it wasn't always so. At one time Baja's entire length was attached to a broad tropical plain along Mexico's Pacific coast. The 23-ton duck-billed hadrosaur roamed the region (its fossilized bones have been found in northern Baja), as did the mammoth, bison, hyracotherium (a small, primitive horse), and camel. The peninsula's eventual divergence from the mainland came about as a result of the continual shifting of massive sections of the earth's surface, a process known as plate tectonics.

Like much of coastal California to the north, Baja California is part of the North Pacific Plate, while the rest of the North American continent belongs to the North American Plate. The boundary line between these two plates is the San Andreas Fault, which extends northward through the center of Mexico's Sea of Cortez and into California, where it parallels the coast on a southeast–northwest axis before veering off into the Pacific Ocean near San Francisco. The North Pacific and North American Plates have shifted along this gap for

© PAUL ITOI

millions of years, with the Pacific Plate moving in a northwesterly direction at a current rate of about 2–5 centimeters (1–2 in) a year.

This movement eventually tore basins in the earth's crust that allowed the Sea of Cortez to form, thus separating the land area west of the fault zone from land to the east. At one time the Sea of Cortez extended as far north as Palm Springs, California; the sea would have continued moving northward at a gradual pace had it not met with the Colorado River. Silting in the Colorado River delta reversed the northward movement of the basins, holding the northern limit of the Sea of Cortez at a point well below what is now the U.S.–Mexico border. Cut off by delta sedimentation, California's Salton Sea is a remnant of the northernmost extension of the Sea of Cortez.

As the peninsula moved slowly northwestward (257 km from the mainland by the time the Sea of Cortez became a stable feature—about five million years ago), the coastal plains tipped toward the west, creating a series of fault-block mountain ranges that includes one of the Cape Region's most outstanding features, the Sierra de la Laguna.

GEOGRAPHY

In many ways, Baja California's Cape Region boasts the peninsula's most distinctive geography. The area receives substantially more rainfall than any other part of Baja, save the Californian Region in the northeast. The Sierra de la Laguna catches most of this rainfall, so the highlands here are more lushly vegetated than the sierras to the north, while the coastal lowlands remain fairly dry for beachgoing tourists. And unlike the rest of the peninsula, about a fourth of the Cape Region falls below the Tropic of Cancer. The combination of tropical latitude with moist uplands and dry coastal areas has created two unique biomes in the region—the Cape Oak–Piñon Woodlands and the Cape Arid Tropical Forest (see *Flora*).

Mountains

Baja California's mountain ranges, or sierras, run down the center of the peninsula from northwest to southeast—a continuation of a mountain system that stretches southward from Alaska's Aleutian Islands to the spectacular rock formations at Cabo San Lucas. Because of the way the underground fault blocks tipped to create these sierras, the mountains tend to slope gradually toward the west and fall off more dramatically toward the east. The Cape Region's Sierra de la Laguna is an exception; it tips eastward so that its steepest slopes face west. It's also the only granitic fault-block range on the southern half of the peninsula—the others are volcanic.

The Sierra de la Laguna has been called an "island in the sky" because of its remarkable isolation from the Central Desert to the north and the Gulf Coast Desert to the east. Up to 100 centimeters (40 in) of rain falls annually on the peaks here, helping to support a unique ecosystem—the Cape Oak–Piñon Woodlands. These high-altitude woodlands harbor extensive stands of Mexican piñon pine, *madroño,* and *palmita.* Lower down, abundant runoff sustains communities on either side of the range. Substantial underground springs supply water for orchards near the pueblos of Todos Santos, El Triunfo, and San Antonio. The western escarpment, facing the Pacific Ocean, is dissected by stream-eroded canyons and arroyos (streambeds) that are dry most of the year. But the arroyos on the eastern slopes are filled with water much of the year, enabling the areas around Miraflores, Santiago, and San Bartolo to support fruit and vegetable farming.

Deserts

About 25 percent of the Cape Region's land area can be classified as desert, averaging less than 25 centimeters (10 in) of rain per year. The Cape's desert lands belong to the Sonoran Desert, which extends across northwestern Mexico into parts of southeastern California and southern Arizona. But any visitor who has previously traveled in other parts of the Sonoran Desert will note many subtle differences on the Cape. Because of the Cape's mountainous interior and the marine environment that surrounds it on three sides, the aridity of any given area can vary considerably. As a result, the Cape's desert lands belong to a subclassification of the Sonoran Desert known as the Gulf Coast Desert. This narrow subregion stretches along the Sea of Cortez from just below Bahía de los Ángeles to the tip of the peninsula near San José del Cabo.

On average, the elevation is substantially higher here (with peaks up to 1,500 meters) than in the deserts to the north, and the terrain is marked by several broken sierras of granitic and volcanic rock. These sierras contain numerous arroyos and a few perennial streams that allow for sustainable farming.

The southern reaches of the Gulf Coast Desert receive a bit of extra precipitation from the occasional tropical storm that blows in from the south. As a result of the added moisture and elevation, many more trees and flowering cacti are found here than in other Baja deserts. Sea of Cortez islands feature similar terrain, although the endemic vegetation varies from island to island.

Cape Arid Tropical Forest

The coastal areas of the Cape Region as well as the lower slopes of the Laguna and Giganta mountain ranges share characteristics typical of both tropical and arid biomes, hence the seemingly oxymoronic term "arid tropical forest." Like tropical forests worldwide, the lower Cape forests have trees, shrubs, and undergrowth of varying heights that create a canopied effect. Mixed with this tangled growth is a profusion of succulents more associated with arid climes, including the *cardón-barbón,* a shorter cousin of the towering *cardón* found throughout Baja's deserts.

Much of the vegetation in the Cape Arid Tropical Forest is normally associated with the tropical thorn forests of coastal Colima and Guerrero on the Mexican mainland. Prominent marker plants unique to the Cape subregion include the Tlaco palm, wild fig *(zalate),* wild plum *(ciruelo), mauto,* and the alleged aphrodisiac herb damiana.

Coastal Wetlands Region

Wetland pockets exist in shallow areas along bays and lagoons in numerous spots along the Cape coast. They usually consist of salt marshes (which contain high concentrations of salt-tolerant plants such as cordgrass, eelgrass, saltwort, and salt cedar) or mangrove *(mangle)* forests, containing one or more of the five species common in Baja. Within any given wetland, the water level, salinity, and temperature can vary considerably; hence, an extensive variety of plants and animals can adapt to wetland areas. Because of this environmental variation, salt marshes and mangrove wetlands support the highest biomass concentrations on the planet. For most visitors, the main attraction of the wetlands is the abundance of waterfowl.

Areas with substantial wetlands in the Cape Region include Bahía de la Paz (mangrove forests), Todos Santos (mixed saltwater/freshwater estuarine marshes), and Estero San José (mixed saltwater/freshwater estuarine marshes).

Islands

Most of the islands and islets surrounding the Baja California peninsula are found on the Sea of Cortez side; among the largest are Isla Espíritu Santo and Isla Cerralvo near La Paz. Many of these islands were created as the peninsula broke away from mainland Mexico and hence are "land-bridge" or "continental" islands rather than true oceanic islands. The islands are arid—their low elevation doesn't allow them to snag much of the rain that moves up from the south in summer. But because of their isolation, the Cortez islands feature a high number of endemic plant and animal species; at least half of the 120 cactus varieties found on the islands are endemic.

THE SEA OF CORTEZ

The Sea of Cortez was apparently named by Spanish sea captain Francisco de Ulloa, who sailed its entire perimeter 1539–1540 at the command of the most famous of all Spanish conquistadors, Hernán Cortés. Four years previously Cortés had himself sailed the sea in an aborted attempt to colonize the peninsula. The name Mar de Cortés henceforth appeared intermittently on maps of the region, alternating with Mar Vermejo (Vermillion Sea, in reference to the color reflected from huge numbers of pelagic crabs), until the Mexican government officially renamed it the Gulf of California (Golfo de California) early in the 20th century. Sailors, writers, and other assorted romantics, however, have continued to call it by its older name.

The sea is roughly 1,125 kilometers (700 mi) long, with an average width of 150 kilometers (93 mi). Its sea-bottom profile is one of the sheerest in the world; underwater valleys and canyons run its entire length, forming abysses that reach depths of up to 3.4 kilometers (2.1 mi). This abrupt relief causes some of the world's largest tidal margins, particularly in the north near the mouth of the Colorado River.

Oceanographers have divided the Sea of Cortez into four regions based on the prominent characteristics—depth, bottom contours, and marine productivity—of each zone. The northern quarter of the gulf, between the Colorado River delta and the Midriff Islands, is shallow in relation to the zones farther south because of silt deposited by the Colorado River. The silt has also rounded the bottom contours. The tidal range in this zone is up to 10 vertical meters (33 vertical ft), and the seawater is highly saline because of evaporation. Before the damming of the Colorado River, the bore created when the seaward river currents met the incoming tide was powerful enough to sink ships.

The next zone farther south encompasses the Midriff Islands, where basins reach depths of 820 meters (2,700 ft). Strong currents here bring nutrients up from the bottom while aerating the water. This leads to an unusually high level of biological productivity, otherwise known as "good fishin'."

From the Midriff Islands to La Paz, basin depth doubles, silting is minimal, and water temperatures begin decreasing dramatically.

The final sea zone below La Paz is oceanic, with trenches and submarine canyons more than 3,650 meters (12,000 ft) deep. Around the tip of the Cape, the Sea of Cortez meets the Pacific Ocean and their respective currents battle, producing some wicked riptides. This means that although the tip of the Cape is the warmest area on the peninsula during the winter, beach swimming can be treacherous.

The Sea of Cortez is biologically the richest body of water on the planet, supporting more than 900 species of marine vertebrates and more than 2,000 invertebrates at last count. The reported number rises with the publication of each new marine study. Scripps Institution of Oceanography in San Diego, California, has pronounced the Cortez "one of the most productive and diverse marine nurseries on Earth," while at the same time recognizing that greedy commercial interests may be devastating the natural balance in the Cortez through overfishing.

ENVIRONMENTAL ISSUES

The rapid growth of tourism and real estate development, especially in the Los Cabos area, has strained fragile ecosystems up and down the Baja Peninsula. Coastal development threatens mangrove habitat on the Mogote Peninsula near La Paz and the Estero San José. The delicate coral reef offshore from Cabo Pulmo could deteriorate rapidly if the water gets polluted from ongoing beachfront development. Even the pristine islands offshore from La Paz are showing early signs of stress from the increase in camping and organized trips.

ECOTOURISM

Environmentally friendly travel is an increasingly popular way to explore – and help protect – the natural wonders of Baja California. Trips range from whale-watching in Bahía Magdalena to helping with sea turtle conservation in the East or West Cape regions by participating in an egg harvest or baby turtle release. Birdwatchers will find abundant and rare species in the Todos Santos lagoon and the Estero San José.

On both sides of the peninsula, endangered sea turtles face poaching and loss of habitat for laying eggs. Commercial fishing has taken a toll on other species as well, with prize billfish reportedly now much smaller in size than in the early years of Baja's fishing camps.

Long-term, the scarcity of freshwater and ability of municipalities to keep up with water and sewage treatment needs pose another concern. The Escalera Náutica project, through which the Mexican government plans to build a network of 10 new ports and expand a dozen existing ports, may further disrupt ecosystems and local communities.

Residents and visitors, both Mexican and foreign, are getting involved to help conserve the environment for years to come. For example, Grupo Tortuguero (www.grupotortuguero.org) runs a turtle conservation program in Baja, and Pro Peninsula (www.propeninsula.org) publishes an informative website and quarterly newsletter about Baja's environmental concerns.

Climate

In satellite photographs of the North American continent snapped a hundred miles above the earth, Baja's Cape Region invariably jumps off the plate. The rest of the continent north and east may be obscured by whorls of clouds while the shores, plains, and mountains of the Cape are carved into the photographic image, remarkably clear. The chances of a day without rain in the winter are 95 percent in Baja, beating out Hawaii's 84 percent and Florida's 87 percent.

How does the Cape Region get so much sunshine? The simple answer is that it's positioned almost out of reach of the major weather systems that influence climate in western North America. Northwesterly storms from Eurasia and the Arctic bring rain and snow to the American Northwest and Midwest all winter long, while tropical storms roll across the South Pacific from Asia, dumping loads of rainfall along the lower Mexican coast and Central America in summer.

The Cape is only slightly affected by the outer edges of these systems. Anchored between the warm, fish-filled waters of the Sea of Cortez and the heaving Pacific Ocean, bisected by plains and mountains, the Cape's isolated ecosystems vary in climate from Mediterranean to desert to tropical. In some areas, overlapping microclimates defy classification, combining elements of semiarid, arid, subtropical, and tropical climes.

HOT AND COLD

Three variables influence temperatures at any given Cape location: elevation, latitude, and longitude. In plain talk, that means the higher you climb, the cooler it gets; the farther south you go, the warmer it gets; and it's usually cooler on the Pacific side of the peninsula and warmer on the Sea of Cortez side. The Tropic of Cancer (approximate latitude 23.5° N) slices across the Cape Region from Todos Santos on the west coast, through Santiago in the interior, to the East Cape south of Bahía de Palmas. Tropical temperatures are thus the norm throughout the Cape except in the high sierra.

Pacific Coast

Because of prevailing ocean currents, the Pacific coast shows the least overall variation in temperature, staying relatively balmy year-round. From March to July, the California Current flows southward along the coast, bringing cooler temperatures from the north that moderate seasonal atmospheric warming, while in December and January the coast is warmed by the northward movement of the Davidson Current. These seasonal currents stabilize the air temperatures so that Cabo San Lucas, for example, averages 18°C (64°F) in January and 29°C (84°F) in August, a range of only 11°C (20°F).

In winter, the West Cape and Cabo San Lucas usually enjoy the warmest temperatures of any coastal area in the Cape Region because of their relative protection from cool northern winds.

Sea of Cortez

The Sea of Cortez has its own set of currents—sometimes lumped together as the Gulf Current—that are fed by tropical waters of the South Pacific. The waters travel in a counterclockwise direction north along the mainland's upper Pacific coast and then south along the peninsular coast. As a result, the Sea of Cortez enjoys an average annual surface temperature of 24°C (75°F), significantly warmer than the Pacific's 18°C (64°F). The high rate of evaporation at the north end of the sea also contributes to warmer air temperatures; this combination of warm air and water temperatures means the Sea of Cortez can be classified as "tropical" over its entire length.

The weather along the East Cape is warm and sunny all winter long with average January temperatures around 23°C (74°F). In August, temperatures average 31°C (88°F) in San José del Cabo, although daily high figures in summer can easily reach 38°C (100°F) or more.

Winters on the Sea of Cortez coast can be cooler than you might suspect because of the coastline's relatively open exposure to northeastern winds. In La Paz and the East Cape, for example, it's not unusual for nighttime temperatures in January and February to drop as low as 14°C (57°F). At the same time, the Pacific coastline directly opposite may be as much as 5°C (10°F) warmer, especially along the West Cape. Cabo San Lucas has the warmest overall winter temperatures of any coastal location in the region.

The Corridor

What's the weather like in between? Geographers officially place the boundary between the Pacific Ocean and the Sea of Cortez at Land's End, the rock formation near the entrance of Bahía San Lucas, Cabo San Lucas. But the area stretching along the tip of the Cape from Cabo San Lucas to San José del Cabo—known in the tourist industry as the "Corridor" (*corredor náutico* or "nautical corridor" in local Spanish)—mingles both Pacific and Cortez influences to create a microclimate that's warmer than Pacific locations yet cooler than Cortez areas. Overall, however, temperatures along the Corridor tend to be more in line with southern Sea of Cortez zones.

Chubascos, Cordonazos, and Coromuels

Monthly average wind velocities for Baja California as a whole are moderate. Mid-May–mid-November, however, tropical storms from the south or east, known as *chubascos,* can bring high winds and rain to the coasts of the Cape Region. Although they usually blow over quickly, local mythology has it that if a *chubasco* lasts more than three hours, it will last a day; if it lasts more than a day, it will last three days; and if more than three days, it'll be a five-day blow.

Occasionally these storms escalate into hurricanes, which are much less frequent here than in the Gulf of Mexico and Caribbean. In 2006, Hurricane John made landfall at Los Frailes along the East Cape, causing severe wind and flood damage. Previous hurricanes hit the Cape in 1997 and 2001.

Another Sea of Cortez weather pattern is the *cordonazo,* a small but fierce summer storm that originates locally and is usually spent within a few hours. A more welcome weather phenomenon is the *coromuel* of Bahía de la Paz, a stiff afternoon breeze that blows from offshore during the hot summer and early fall. This wind was named for English Lord Protector Oliver Cromwell, identified with English pirates who took advantage of the wind's regular occurrence for the plunder of ships trapped in the bay.

WET AND DRY

The "Land of Little Rain," as Baja has been called, isn't unique in its aridity, since most of the earth's desert areas are found at latitudes between 15° and 30° either north or south of the equator; Baja is positioned roughly between 23° N and 31° N. Global convection currents in the atmosphere create a more or less permanent high-pressure shield over these zones, insulating them from the low-pressure fronts that bring rain clouds.

Rainfall in the Cape Region varies from less than 25 centimeters (10 in) per year in the driest areas east of the Sierra de la Laguna (from San José del Cabo north to La Paz) to upward of 100 centimeters (40 in) in the interior of the Sierra de la Laguna.

Variation in rainfall also occurs on a seasonal basis. In the Cape Region, rain usually arrives August–November, peaking at an average of 5.8 centimeters (2.3 in) in September for Cabo San Lucas and La Paz. Since mountain peaks trap rain clouds, the Cape's higher elevations invariably receive more rain than the low-lying coastal zones.

Flora

A thorough examination of all the plants and creatures of interest in the Cape Region might take volumes. The following sections cover some of either the most remarkable or most common forms of Cape plant life. The complex interconnecting ecosystems of the peninsula and its islands hold a high number of unique species and remain relatively unexplored by biologists. Several botanists, marine biologists, zoologists, and paleontologists have undertaken solo research in the area, but only since the 1990s has the first interdisciplinary team, sponsored by a Canadian university, begun studying the region.

CACTI
Cardón
One of the most common cacti throughout Baja, including the Cape Region, is the towering *cardón (Pachycereus pringlei),* the world's tallest species of cactus. Individuals can reach as high as 18 meters (60 ft) or more and weigh 12 tons, not counting the root system, which can spread up to 50 meters (165 ft) in diameter. More commonly they top out at 7–9 meters (23–30 ft). The giant, pale green trunks feature 11–17 vertical ribs and may measure one meter (3 ft) thick. Some live more than 400 years.

The *cardón* is often confused with the smaller saguaro cactus of Sonora and Arizona; one major difference is that the branches of the *cardón* tend to be more vertical than those of the saguaro. The hardwood cores of *cardón* columns have been used by *bajacalifornianos* for centuries as building beams and fence posts. Among Mexicans, a *cardón* forest is called a *cardonal.*

Biznaga
Another extremely common and highly visible cactus is the *biznaga,* or barrel cactus (genus *Ferocactus*). At least a dozen species—most of them endemic—grow in the Cape Region. The cactus's English name refers to its shape, which is short and squat like a barrel. Most common varieties reach about waist-high. One variety, however, *Ferocactus diguettii,* easily reaches four meters (13 ft) in height and a meter (3 ft) in diameter. It grows only on a few Sea of Cortez islands, sporting red-tinged spines and, in spring, gorgeous yellow to red flowers.

The Amerindians of Baja California Sur reportedly used hollowed-out *biznagas* as Dutch ovens, inserting food into the cavity along with heated stones, then sealing the cactus off till the food was cooked. The sturdy, curved spines also served as fishhooks on native fishing expeditions.

Pitahaya
Among Baja's original populations, another important cactus was the *pitahaya dulce,* known among Anglos as organ pipe cactus. It has slender, vertical ribs that grow in clusters, and its spiny, orange-size fruit contains a sweet, juicy,

pleasant-tasting pulp the color of red watermelon. According to accounts of Spanish missionaries, the Pericú Amerindians based their yearly calendar on the harvesting of the ripe fruit in late summer and early fall. During this season, the Amerindians engaged in a veritable fruit orgy, gorging themselves on the pulp until they fell asleep, then waking to begin eating again. The early Spanish explorers took the fruit along on long sea journeys—its vitamin C content helped to prevent scurvy.

The *pitahaya dulce* is commonly found in Baja California south of the Sierra de San Borja and on several Sea of Cortez islands. A similar species, *pitahaya agria* (*agria* means sour in Spanish; *dulce* is sweet), branches more densely and lower to the ground, hence its English name, galloping cactus. It grows throughout the peninsula and on most Sea of Cortez islands. The fruit of the *pitahaya agria* is similar in appearance to that of the *pitahaya dulce,* but, as implied by the Spanish name, it's less sweet, more acidic. Both types of *pitahaya* fruit remain popular among Cape residents and travelers; the sweet ones ripen in July.

Opuntia

Another cactus variety well represented throughout Baja is the genus *Opuntia,* which includes all types known as **cholla,** as well as the **nopal,** or prickly pear. Chollas are a bane to hikers because they're so prolific and densely covered with spines. A typical branch looks somewhat like braided or twisted rope. The cholla historically has had few domestic uses, although a tea made from the roots of the fuzzy-looking **teddy-bear cholla** (also called "jumping cholla" for its propensity to cling to the lower legs of hikers) is reportedly used by the Seri Amerindians as a diuretic.

In contrast, the much-loved prickly pear has broad, flat stems and branches and a sparser distribution of spines. In Northern Mexico and Baja its fleshy pads are a dietary staple. The most highly prized parts of the nopal are the young stem shoots, called *nopalitos,* and the ripe fruits, dubbed *tuna.* The flavor of the pads is a bit bland, like a cross between bell pepper and okra. The fruit, on the other hand, is juicy and sweet, and available in season in many Baja markets. If you want to taste it in the wild, remove the *tunas* carefully, cut them lengthwise with a sharp knife, and scoop out the insides with a spoon.

AGAVES

Several species of the sizable agave family are native to the Cape Region. All have long, spine-edged leaves, as well as flowers that bloom on tall stalks.

Yucca

One of the most common and striking desert plants is the yucca, which appears in several varieties throughout the Cape Region. The **tree yucca,** called *datilillo,* or "little date" for its resemblance to a date palm, is the largest of the agaves. *Datilillos* grow in clusters 3–7 meters (10–23 ft) tall, their daggerlike blades supported by long woody trunks. This endemic is found throughout the desert plains and chaparral subregions on the peninsula's Pacific side—just about anywhere except in the mountains.

Yuccas are extremely useful plants for rural *bajacalifornianos.* The fruit and flowers are edible (a candy called *colache* is made from the cooked flower buds), the roots can be boiled to make soap or leather softener, and the tough leaf fibers are used to make cordage, sandals, baskets, and mats.

Maguey

Also common are the many varieties of maguey, or century plant. The maguey has broad, closely clustered leaves that grow at ground level without a visible trunk. In most species, the plant flowers only once in its lifetime, sending up a tall, slender stalk after maturation—typically at 5–20 years, depending on variety and locale. Early Anglo settlers in the southwestern United States spread the myth that magueys bloomed only once in a hundred years, hence the fanciful name "century plant."

The maguey was an important food source for certain aboriginal populations, who harvested the plant just before it bloomed (when it's full of concentrated nutrients). Trimmed of its leaves, the heart of the plant was baked in an underground pit for 1–3 days, then eaten or stored. Some ranchers still prepare it in this manner. As with *datilillo,* the leaf fibers are used as cordage for weaving various household goods.

Sotol

Sotol is similar to yucca, but its leaves are narrower and softer. Some sotols produce long flower stalks like those of the century plant, though the flower buds occur along the stalk's entire length instead of only at the top.

One spectacular variety of sotol native to the Cape Region's higher elevations is the endemic *Nolina beldingii,* sometimes called *palmita* because of its resemblance to a small palm tree. *Palmitas,* whose flower stalks can reach seven meters (23 ft) in height, grow clusters of thick leaves branching from their short, woody trunks.

TREES
Palms

Five varieties of palm grow wild in the Cape Region; three are native, while two are introduced species. Palms are important to the local economy of the peninsula's southern half, where they're most common. The long, straight trunks are used as roof beams, the leaves are used in basketry and for roof and wall thatching, and the fruits provide nutrition.

Among the most handsome Baja palm trees is the endemic **Tlaco palm** (also called "taco palm," *palma palmía,* and *palma colorado*), common in the canyons and arroyos of the Cape Region mountains. The smooth, slender trunks, crowned by fan-shaped leaves, stand up to 20 meters (65 ft) tall. Its durable trunks have long been valued for house construction. A closely related species, the **Guadalupe Island palm,** is native to Isla Guadalupe; its self-shedding trunk leaves little or no shag, which has made the tree popular as a cultivated palm.

Baja's tallest palm variety is the endemic **Mexican fan palm** (also called Baja California fan palm, skyduster, or *palma blanca*), which reaches heights of 27–30 meters (90–100 ft).

As the name implies, its leaves are fan-shaped. Although it's not as durable as the Tlaco palm, the long trunk makes the tree useful for local construction. The fan palm's native habitats are north of the Cape Region in the Sierra de la Giganta and on Isla Ángel de la Guarda, but it is used as an ornamental throughout Baja.

Two palm varieties were imported to Baja for their fruit value. The **date palm** was introduced to Baja by Jesuit missionaries and is now common near former mission sites, including San José del Cabo. The tree typically reaches 15–20 meters (50–65 ft) tall at maturity; its oblong fruit grows beneath feather-shaped leaves in large clusters, turning from pale yellow to dark brown as it ripens. Baja dates are eaten locally and shipped to mainland Mexico but are generally not considered of high enough quality for export. The 30-meter (100-ft), featherleafed **coconut palm** commonly grows along coastal areas of the Cape Region and is an important local food source.

Oaks and Pines

Tens of thousands of visitors drape themselves along Cape Region beaches every year without any inkling that in the Sierra de la Laguna mountains rising behind the coastal plains stands one of Mexico's most remarkable relic piñon–live oak woodlands. Two endemic species of oak *(encino)* found in the sierra include the **cape oak,** usually seen growing in higher canyons and arroyos, and the **black oak,** confined to the Cape Region's lower slopes.

The **Mexican piñon pine** (known as *pino piñonero* in Mexico) grows profusely at higher elevations in the Sierra de la Laguna, where the wood is a commonly used building material and the nuts are sometimes gathered for food.

Mimosas

This subfamily of the Leguminosae, or pea family, includes dozens of genera common to arid and semiarid zones worldwide. Characterized by linear seedpods and double rows of tiny leaves, common varieties in the Cape Region include the **mesquite** and various endemic kinds of **acacia.**

Amerindians have long used the trunk, roots, leaves, beans, and bark of the mesquite tree for a variety of purposes, from lumber to medicine. Ground mesquite leaves mixed with water form a balm for sore eyes, a remedy still used by *curanderos* (healers) in rural Mexico today. Chewing the leaves relieves toothache. And mesquite gum has been used as a balm for wounds, a ceramic glue, a dye, and a digestive.

Mesquite beans are a good source of nutrition—a ripe bean pod, growing as long as 23 centimeters (9 in), contains roughly 30 percent glucose and is high in protein. Many animals and birds savor the beans; horses will eat them until they're sick. Rural Mexicans grind the dried pods into a flour, with which they make bread and a kind of beer. The Seri Amerindians, who live along the Sonoran coast of the Sea of Cortez, have separate names for eight different stages of the bean pod's development.

One of the prettiest endemic mimosas is the **palo blanco,** which has a tall, slender trunk with silver-white bark and a feathery crown that produces small, white, fragrant blossoms March–May. *Bajacalifornianos* use the bark of the *palo blanco* to tan leather; at the end of the 19th century the main industry at Cabo San Lucas was the shipping of *palo blanco* bark to San Francisco tanneries.

Wild Figs

Three types of wild fig trees *(zalates)*, one endemic, are common in the Cape Region's rocky areas. In the village of Pueblo La Playa, east of San José del Cabo, stands a vintage collection of *zalates* of impressive stature.

Cottonwoods and Willows

Various cottonwoods *(alamos)* and willows *(sauces)* grow at higher elevations throughout the Cape Region. The **huerivo** or **güeribo** *(Populus brandegeei)* is a beautiful endemic cottonwood found in sierran canyons and arroyos. Its tall, straight trunk reaches heights of 30 me-

ters and is a highly valued source of lumber for building construction and furniture-making.

Herbs

Baja's most famous herb is the reputed aphrodisiac **damiana.**

Another psychoactive plant found in Baja is **datura,** or **jimsonweed** *(toloache)*. A member of the potato family—a group that also includes nightshade and tobacco—jimsonweed produces large, fragrant, trumpet-shaped flowers that open in the evening and close by noon the following day. According to one folk remedy, the flowers will relieve insomnia if placed beside the pillow at night. All parts of the plant are considered toxic; in certain Yaqui Amerindian ceremonies, the seeds are eaten for their hallucinatory effect. Datura grows in abundance on rocky and sandy soils below 800 meters (2,600 ft) throughout the peninsula and on some Sea of Cortez islands.

LOVE HERB

Probably the most well-known herb native to Baja's Cape Region is **damiana** *(Turnera diffusa)*, a small shrub with bright, five-petaled yellow or golden flowers. The plant's aphrodisiac properties are its main claim to fame; these are often derided as nonsense by self-appointed Baja analysts. But according to botanist Norman C. Roberts, damiana "stimulates the genito-urinary tract and is used in the treatment of sexual problems such as impotence, frigidity, sterility, and sexual exhaustion." The herb is also used as a sedative and diuretic.

Damiana grows most commonly in rocky areas of the Cape Region but is also found as far away as Sonora, Texas, and the West Indies. The herb is usually ingested in sweetened tea made from the leaves or in a liqueur containing damiana extract. In resort areas, a "Baja margarita" substitutes damiana liqueur for triple sec.

Fauna

LAND MAMMALS

One of the most widespread carnivores on the peninsula as well as on some Sea of Cortez islands is the **coyote,** which seems to adapt itself equally well to mountain, desert, and coastal terrain. Anyone venturing into the interior of the peninsula is virtually guaranteed to spot at least one. In some areas they don't seem particularly afraid of humans, although they always maintain a distance of at least 15 meters (50 ft) between themselves and larger mammals. A coyote will sometimes fish for crab, placing a furry tail in the water, waiting for a crab to grab on, then, with a flick of the tail, tossing the crab onto the beach. Before the crustacean can recover from the shock, the coyote is enjoying a fine crab feast.

Rarely sighted is the **mountain lion**—also called cougar, panther, or puma—which, like all cats, is mostly nocturnal. These beautiful creatures occasionally attack humans, so those hiking in the sierras should avoid hiking at night. If you do meet up with a lion, wildlife experts suggest you convince the beast you are not prey and may be dangerous yourself. Don't run from the animal, as this is an invitation to chase. Instead, shout, wave your hands, and, if the lion acts aggressively, throw stones at it. If you're carrying a backpack, raise it above your shoulders so that you appear larger. One or more of these actions is virtually guaranteed to frighten the lion away. If not, grab the biggest, heaviest stick you can find and fight it out to avoid becoming cat food.

Smaller, less intimidating carnivores commonly encountered in the Cape Region include the gray fox, ringtail, bobcat, lynx, skunk, raccoon, and badger.

One of the largest ungulates still roaming wild in Baja is the **mule deer,** of which there is an endemic peninsular variety. Mule deer are most commonly seen on mountain slopes below 1,500 meters (5,000 ft). Lesser numbers of **white-tailed deer** inhabit higher elevations. Deer are a popular source of meat for ranchers living in the sierras; the ranchers also use deerskin to make soft, homemade boots called *teguas.*

At least four varieties of rabbit hop around the Cape Region: the brush rabbit, desert cottontail, black-tailed jackrabbit, and the rare, endemic black jackrabbit. Each is especially adapted to its particular habitat. The long, upright ears of the **black-tailed jackrabbit,** for example, enable it to hear sounds from a long distance, a necessity for an animal that is prey for practically every larger animal in the Cape Region. The more delicate ears of the **desert cottontail** act as radiators on hot desert days, allowing the rabbit to release excess body heat into the air. The **black jackrabbit** (*Lepus insularis*) is found only on Isla Espíritu Santo. Zoologists haven't yet been able to explain why the fur of this rabbit is mostly black, or why a cinnamon-red coloring appears along the ears and underparts.

The Cape supports a wide variety of common and not-so-common rodents—the white-tailed antelope squirrel, marsh rice rat, Botta's pocket gopher, and piñon mouse, to name a few. What may surprise some travelers is how many varieties manage to survive in the Gulf Desert. Among these are the desert pocket mouse, cactus mouse, desert wood rat, and five endemic species of kangaroo rat.

MARINE MAMMALS

The protected lagoons of Baja's Pacific coast and the warm waters of the Sea of Cortez are practically made for whales and dolphins. All told, 25 species of cetaceans frequent Baja waters, from the **blue whale,** the largest mammal on earth, to the **common dolphin** (*Delphinus delphis),* which is sometimes seen in the Sea of Cortez in pods as large as 10,000. Other whale species known to visit the Cape Region or make it their year-round habitat include minke, fin, Sei, Bryde's, humpback, gray, goose-beaked, sperm, dwarf sperm, false killer, killer, and pilot. Commonly seen dolphins include Pacific white-sided, bottle-nosed, spotted, Risso's, spinner, and striped.

California sea lions, or *lobos marinos,* are also plentiful; most live around the Sea of Cortez islands of San Estebán, San Jorge, Ángel de la Guarda, San Pedro Mártir, and Espíritu Santo.

Gray Whales

The marine mammal usually of most interest to Cape whale-watchers is the Pacific or California gray whale, which migrates some 19,300 kilometers (12,000 mi) a year between its feeding grounds above the Arctic Circle and its calving grounds in the Pacific lagoons of southern Baja. The gray is the easiest of the whales to view since it frequents shallow coastal waters. Although the lagoons used by the grays for calving are found north of the Cape Region in south-central Baja, the whales can sometimes be seen from shore as they make their way around the tip of the Cape to "exercise" the newly born calves.

Like many two-legged mammals, gray whales prefer to spend their winters south of the border. During the December–April calving season, **whale-watching tours** to the nearest calving lagoon (Bahía Magdalena, around 200 km/120 mi northwest of La Paz) can be arranged through hotels and travel agencies in La Paz, San José del Cabo, and Cabo San Lucas.

FISH

The seas surrounding Baja California contain an amazing variety of marinelife. In the Sea of Cortez alone, around 900 varieties of fish have been identified. Marine biologists estimate around 3,000 species, including invertebrates, between the Golfo de Santa Clara at the north end of the sea and the southern tip of Cabo San Lucas. This would make the area the richest sea, or gulf, in the world—a marine cornucopia that has inspired the nickname "God's Fishtank." The wide spectrum of aquatic environments along both coasts is largely responsible for this abundance and has led to Baja's reputation as a mecca for seafood aficionados as well as fishing and diving enthusiasts.

About 90 percent of all known Baja fish varieties are found close to the shores of the peninsula or its satellite islands. The Midriff

Islands area in the center of the Sea of Cortez is especially rich—tidal surges aerate the water and stir up nutrients, supporting a thick food chain from plankton to fish to birds and sea lions. The Cortez, in fact, has acted as a giant fish trap, collecting an assortment of marine species through thousands of years from the nearby Pacific, the more distant equatorial zones of South America, and even the Caribbean, through a water link that once existed between the two seas.

A brief guide to Baja's fish is provided here. Habitats are described as being onshore, inshore, or offshore. Onshore fish frequent the edge of the tidal zone and can be caught by casting from shore; inshore fish inhabit shallow waters accessible by small boat; and offshore fish lurk in the deep waters of the open Pacific or the southern Sea of Cortez.

Billfish

The Cape Region is the undisputed world billfishing capital; serious saltwater anglers from across the globe make the pilgrimage to La Paz or Cabo San Lucas in hopes of landing a swordfish, sailfish, or striped, blue, or black marlin. The sailfish and striped marlin are generally the most acrobatic, but all billfish are strong fighters. They inhabit a wide range of offshore waters in the Pacific and in the Sea of Cortez south of Bahía Magdalena and the Midriff Islands; the swordfish is found mostly on the Pacific side.

Corvinas and Croakers

About 30 species in Baja belong to this group of small- to medium-size fish that make croaking sounds. Varieties found inshore to onshore include white sea bass, Gulf corvina, orangemouth corvina, California corvina, yellowfin croaker, and spotfin croaker.

Jack

Popular jacks include yellowtail (one of the most popular fish used in *tacos de pescado*), Pacific amberjack, various pompanos, jack crevalle, and the strong-fighting roosterfish, named for its tall dorsal comb. These fish are most prevalent in inshore to onshore areas in the Sea of Cortez and in the Pacific south of Magdalena.

Dorado, Mackerel, and Tuna

Among the more sought-after food fish, found offshore to inshore throughout parts of both seas, are: dorado, sometimes called dolphin-fish (though it isn't related to mammalian dolphins or porpoises) or mahimahi (its Hawaiian name); sierra, especially good in ceviche; the knife-shaped wahoo, one of the fastest of all fish, reaching speeds of 50 knots; Pacific bonito; and three kinds of tuna—bluefin, albacore, and the highly prized yellowfin. Yellowfins can weigh up to 180 kilograms (400 pounds) and are among the best tasting of all tunas.

Bass

Sea bass are an inshore fish; different species dominate different Baja waters, and all commonly find their way into Mexican seafood restaurants. The larger bass are *garropa* (groupers), the smaller cabrilla.

Flatfish

These include flounder and halibut, usually called *lenguado* in Spanish. The most common variety on the Pacific side is California halibut; on the gulf side it's Cortez halibut. Both make good eating and are often used in tourist areas for *tacos de pescado.*

Snapper

Generally found south of Magdalena and round the Cape as far north as the upper Sea of Cortez, locally popular snappers include red snapper, yellow snapper, barred *pargo,* and dog snapper. All snappers are called *pargo* in Spanish, except for the red snapper, which is *huachinango.* All are common food fish.

Sharks, Rays, and Squid

Of the more than 60 species of sharks found in Baja waters, some are rare and most stay clear of humans. The more common species are found offshore to inshore from Magdalena to the Midriff, and include the smooth hammerhead, common thresher, bonito (mako),

sand, blue, blacktip, and the whale shark, the world's largest fish, which reaches 18 meters (59 ft) and 3,600 kilograms (almost four tons). Shark-fishing is an important activity in Baja, supplying much of the seafood eaten locally. Hammerhead, thresher, bonito, and leopard shark fillets are all very tasty.

Rays are quite common in warmer offshore-to-inshore waters throughout Baja. Many varieties have barbed tail spines that can inflict a painful wound. Contrary to myth, the barb is not actually venomous, although a ray "sting" can be extremely painful and easily becomes infected. Experienced beachgoers perform the "stingray shuffle" when walking on sandy bottoms: if you bump into a ray resting on the bottom, it will usually swim away; if you step on one, it's likely to give you a flick of the barb.

Common smaller rays found inshore include the butterfly ray and the aptly named shovelnose guitarfish, a ray with a thick tail and a flat head. Two species of rays—the mobula and the huge Pacific manta ray—are sometimes called "devilfish" because of their hornlike pectoral fins. The Pacific manta possesses a "wingspan" of up to seven meters (23 ft) and can weigh nearly two tons. Pacific mantas have become rare through overfishing. Another fairly large ray, the bat ray, is sometimes confused with the manta, though it doesn't have the manta's characteristic pectoral fins. A friendly manta will allow scuba divers to hitch rides by hanging on to the base of the pectorals, although most divemasters now discourage such activity.

Squids of various species and sizes, most under 30 centimeters (1 ft) in length, are found throughout the Pacific Ocean and Sea of Cortez. In deeper Pacific waters off the west coast glides the enormous Humboldt squid, which reaches lengths of 4.5 meters (15 ft) and may weigh as much as 150 kilograms (330 lbs). In the Cape Region, squid (*calamar* in Spanish) is popularly eaten in *cocteles* or used as sportfishing bait.

Elongated Fish

These varieties share the characteristics of long, slender bodies and beaklike jaws. The sharp-toothed California barracuda swims in the Pacific from the border down to Cabo San Lucas, while a smaller, more edible variety is found in the Sea of Cortez. In spite of their somewhat frightful appearance, barracudas rarely attack humans.

The silvery flying fish can be seen leaping above offshore waters throughout the Pacific and lower Sea of Cortez. It is not generally considered a food fish. The most edible of the elongated fish is probably the acrobatic Mexican needlefish, or *agujón,* which reaches two meters (6.5 ft) in length and has green bones.

Shellfish

Baja's shores abound with deep-water and shallow-water shellfish species, including multiple varieties of clams, oysters, mussels, scallops, and shrimp, many of which have disappeared from coastal California in the United States. Baja's most famous shellfish is undoubtedly the spiny lobster, which appears on virtually every *mariscos* menu on the peninsula.

BIRDS

Hosting around 300 known species of birds—one of the highest concentrations in North America—the peninsula and islands of Baja California provide undisturbed avian habitat par excellence. Ornithological research focusing on the Cape Region, however, is incomplete, and reference materials are difficult to come by; one of the most up-to-date works available is Ernest Preston Edwards's *The Birds of Mexico and Adjacent Areas,* published in 1998 (see *Suggested Reading*).

Coastal and Pelagic Species

The vast majority of the Cape's native and migrating species are either coastal or open-sea (pelagic) birds. The Sea of Cortez islands are particularly rich in bird life; the Mexican government has designated 49 of the islands as wildlife refuges to protect the many rare and endangered species there. Among the more notable island birds are the rare and clownish **blue-footed booby** and its more

common cousins, the **brown booby** and the **masked booby.**

Common throughout the coastal areas of southern Baja is the **magnificent frigate,** called *tijera* (scissors) in Mexico because of its scissors-shaped tail. In spite of their seafood diet, frigates can't swim or even submerge their heads to catch fish—instead, they glide high in the air on boomerang-shaped wings, swooping down to steal fish from other birds, especially slow-witted boobies.

Among the more commonly seen birds along the Sea of Cortez coast is the **brown pelican,** which in global terms is not so common. As a species, pelicans go back 30 million years; paleontologists use the modern pelican as a model for creating visual representations of the pteranodon, an extinct flying reptile with an eight-meter wingspan. Brown pelicans, the only truly marine species among the world's seven pelican species, dive 10–30 meters (30–100 ft) underwater to catch fish. Other pelicans only dip their beaks beneath the surface and tend to frequent inland waterways rather than marine habitats. Browns have almost entirely disappeared from the U.S. shores of the Gulf of Mexico, and they are declining in the coastal islands of California—apparently because of the pesticide content of the Pacific Ocean. Baja's Cortez and Pacific coasts are among the last habitats where the brown pelican thrives.

Another noteworthy bird along the coast is the **fisher eagle,** which, as its name implies, catches and eats fish. The fisher eagle is also occasionally seen along freshwater rivers and around the Pacific lagoons.

Other coastal birds of Baja include two species of cormorant, the long-billed curlew, four species of egret, four species of grebe, 10 species of gull, three species of heron, the belted kingbird, two species of ibis, three species of loon, the osprey, the American oystercatcher, six species of plover, six species of sandpiper, the tundra swan, and seven species of tern.

Certain fish-eating birds are usually seen only by boaters since they tend to fly over open ocean. These pelagics include two species of albatross, the black-legged kittiwake, the red phalarope, three species of shearwater, the surf scoter, the south polar skua, five species of storm petrel, the black tern, and the red-billed tropic bird.

Estuarine and Inland Species

Another group of waterfowl in southern Baja frequents only freshwater ponds, *tinajas* (springs), lakes, streams, and marshes. These birds include two species of bittern, the American coot, two species of duck, the snow goose, the northern harrier, six species of heron, the white-faced ibis, the common moorhen, two species of rail, five species of sandpiper, the lesser scaup, the shoveler, the common snipe, the sora, the roseate spoonbill, the wood stork, three species of teal, the northern waterthrush, and the American wigeon. Some of these birds are native; others only winter here. One of the best and most convenient places to view such bird life is the estuary in San José del Cabo.

In the sierras dwell the golden eagle, the western flycatcher, the lesser goldfinch, the black-headed grosbeak, the red-tailed hawk, two species of hummingbird, the pheasant, the yellow-eyed junco, the white-breasted nuthatch, the mountain plover, four species of vireo, eight species of warbler, the acorn woodpecker, and the canyon wren.

Common in the desert and other open country are three species of falcon (peregrine, prairie, and Cooper's), three species of flycatcher, six species of hawk, the black-fronted hummingbird, the American kestrel, the merlin, two species of owl, the greater roadrunner, eight species of sparrow, two species of thrasher, the vernon, the turkey vulture, the ladder-backed woodpecker, and the cactus wren.

REPTILES AND AMPHIBIANS

Among the slippery, slimy, scaly, crawly things that live in the Cape Region are around two dozen species of lizards, frogs, toads, turtles, and snakes.

Lizards

One four-legged reptilian of note is the **chuckwalla,** which is found on certain is-

lands in the Sea of Cortez; it sometimes grows to nearly a meter in length. The chuckwalla drinks freshwater when available, storing it in sacs that gurgle when it walks; when a freshwater source is not available, the lizard imbibes saltwater, which it processes through a sort of internal desalinator. Another good-sized lizard is the **desert iguana,** found throughout the Gulf Coast Desert and possibly farther north. Larger iguanas are sometimes eaten in ranchero stews and are said to taste better than chicken. The **coast horned lizard,** similar to the horny toad of the American Southwest, is another endemic.

Turtles

Of the six turtle varieties present, five are sea turtles: the leatherback, green, hawksbill, western ridley, and loggerhead. The **loggerhead** migrates back and forth between the Japanese island of Kyushu and the Sea of Cortez, a distance of 10,460 kilometers (6,500 mi). Because their eggs, meat, and shells are highly valued among coastal Mexican populations, all sea turtles are on the endangered species list. The Mexican government has declared turtle hunting and turtle egg collecting illegal; the devastation of the turtle population has slowed considerably but hasn't yet stopped. *Bajacalifornianos* say they're upholding the laws while anglers along the mainland coast of the Sea of Cortez still take sea turtles.

The main culprit has apparently been Japan, which is the world's largest importer of sea turtles—including the endangered ridley and hawksbill. The Japanese use the turtles for meat, turtle leather, and turtle-shell fashion accessories. In 1991, the Japanese government announced a ban on the importation of sea turtles, so perhaps the Sea of Cortez populations will eventually make a comeback.

Snakes

The rocky lowlands and chaparrals make perfect snake country. The bad news is that about half the known species are venomous; the good news is they rarely come into contact with

© PAUL ITOI

turtle nest

humans. Scorpion stings far outnumber snake-bites in Baja.

Harmless species include the western blind snake, rosy boa, Baja California rat snake, spotted leaf-nosed snake, western patch-nosed snake, bull snake, coachwhip, king snake, Baja sand snake, and California lyre snake.

The venomous kinds fall into two categories, one of which contains only a single snake species, the **yellow-bellied sea snake.** Sea snakes usually flee the vicinity when they sense human presence, but as a general precaution don't grab anything in the water that looks like a floating stick—that's how sea snakes deceive their prey.

The other venomous category comprises the rattlesnakes, of which there are supposedly 18 species stretched out along Baja California.

The most common species is the near-endemic **Baja California rattler,** whose range includes the lower three-fourths of the peninsula. Look for scaly mounds over the eyes if you care to make an identification. The most dangerous of Baja rattlers is the **Western diamondback;** it's the largest and therefore has the greatest potential to deliver fatal or near-fatal doses of venom. Fortunately, the diamondback is mostly confined to the canyons of the northern sierras.

The general all-inclusive Spanish term for snake is *serpiente;* a nonvenomous snake is referred to as *culebra,* the venomous sort *víbora.* A rattlesnake is *un serpiente de cascabel* or simply *un cascabel.* An encouraging factoid: According to Spanish records, no missionary ever died of a snakebite during the 300-year period of Spanish colonization of the New World.

History

PRE-CORTESIAN HISTORY

Because the Cape lacks spectacular archaeological remains, such as the Maya and Aztec ruins in the southern reaches of mainland Mexico, it has largely been ignored by archaeologists. It is highly likely, however, that the area was inhabited by human populations well before the rest of Mexico. Baja California Sur was the logical termination for the coastal migration route followed by Asian groups who crossed the Bering Strait land bridge between Asia and North America beginning around 50,000 B.C.

The Cochimís and Guaycuras

Amerindian groups living in the central and southern reaches of the peninsula when the Spanish arrived were apparently much less advanced technologically than the Yumanos of northern Baja, not to mention Amerindian groups found in central and southern mainland Mexico. Because of the lack of archaeological research in these areas, the only record we have of these cultures consists of Spanish accounts, which were undoubtedly biased in light of their mission to subordinate the peoples of the New World. Mission histories are full of lurid tales of Amerindian customs, many probably written to convince the Spanish crown of the desperate need to convert the natives. Nevertheless, the Amerindians of central and southern Baja appear to have been among the more "primitive" of the tribes encountered by the Spanish in Mexico or Mesoamerica. In modern archaeological terms, they hadn't progressed beyond the Paleolithic epoch (the early Stone Age).

According to these accounts, the Guaycuras, divided into the Pericú, Huchiti, and Guaicura tribes, occupied the Cape Region. One fringe anthropological view has suggested that part of the Guaycura tribes may have descended from Tahitian seafarers who were blown off course on their way to Hawaii. Whatever their place of origin, the Guaycuras spent most of their daylight hours searching for food; the men hunted small game or gathered shellfish while the women gathered fruit, seeds, and roots. If game was scarce, the people subsisted on a variety of insects and would even eat dried animal skins, including, according to reports, the leather boots of the conquistadors.

The southern Amerindians generally lived in the open and sought shelter only in the severest weather. Men wore little or no clothing, while women wore leather or yucca-fiber thongs around the waist with woven grasses or twigs suspended from the front and animal skins in the back. These garments were sometimes painted with bright colors. The tips of arrows and spears were generally of sharpened hardwood only, though chipped stone points were occasionally used. The Guaycuras also used reed blowguns. The most important time of year for these Amerindians was when the fruit of the *pitahaya* cactus ripened; the fruit was then so abundant the Amerindians allegedly abandoned all activities save sleeping and eating.

None of the Guaycuras apparently left behind any artwork. This has been attributed to their harsh living environment; they may have had little time or energy for artistic pursuits. However, in the inland areas of the south-central peninsula once inhabited by Cochimí and Guaycura tribes, numerous spectacular rock-art sites have been discovered. The Cochimís told the Spanish this rock art was created by a race of giants who'd preceded them. Almost nothing is known about this lost Amerindian culture, a people Baja rock-art expert Harry Crosby has dubbed "The Painters." Because rock-art sites in the Cape Region are less numerous than those found farther north in the Sierra de la Giganta and Sierra de San Francisco, modern researchers have almost totally neglected them.

THE SPANISH CONQUEST OF MEXICO

After 700 years of conflict with the Moors over control of the Iberian peninsula, Spain in the 15th century emerged as the most powerful nation in Europe. Convinced that a Roman Catholic God was destined to rule the world with Spain as His emissary, the Spanish monarchy sent Christopher Columbus in search of a new route to the Far East. His mission was to establish contact with a mythical "Great Khan" to develop an alternate trade route with the Orient, since Arabs controlled the overland route through the Middle East. Along the way as many pagans as possible would be converted to Christianity. Once the Arab trade monopoly was broken, the Holy Land would be returned to Christian control.

Columbus's landing in the West Indies in 1492 was followed by Pope Alexander VI's historic 1493 decree, which gave the Spanish rights to any new land discovered west of the Azores, as long as the Spanish made "God's name known there." Hence, the Spanish conquest of the New World started as a roundabout extension of the Holy Crusades.

A succession of Spanish expeditions into the Caribbean and Gulf of Mexico rapidly achieved the conquest of Mexico and Central America. Conquistador Hernán Cortés subdued the Valley of Mexico Aztecs in three years (1519–1521), and the allegiance—or decimation—of other Aztecs and the Maya followed quickly.

AMERINDIANS OF BAJA CALIFORNIA

© AVALON TRAVEL PUBLISHING, INC.

Early California Explorations

When the Spanish conquistadors came to the western edge of mainland Mexico and looked beyond toward the landforms they could see above the sea, they concluded that Baja California was a huge island and that the as-yet-unnamed Sea of Cortez led to the Atlantic. The idea of a "northwest passage" to the Atlantic persisted for years, even among seasoned explorers such as Cabrillo, Drake, and Vizcaíno. Cortés himself directed four voyages from the mainland to the island of La California, although he actually accompanied only the third. The history of these early expeditions exposes the enmity and extreme sense of competition among those conquistadors supposedly working toward a common cause.

The first voyage, launched in 1532, never made it to the peninsula. The ships were

captured in the Sea of Cortez by Nuño de Guzmán, an archrival of Cortés operating farther north in Mexico. The next year a second expedition, under Captain Diego Becerra of the *Concepción,* suffered a mutiny in which the captain was killed. Basque pilot Fortún Jiménez took charge, and the ship landed in Bahía de la Paz in early 1534. Thus the first European visitors to reach Baja California, a group of mutineers, arrived there just 42 years after Columbus touched down in the West Indies and nearly a century before the Pilgrims landed at Plymouth Rock.

Before they had much of a chance to explore, Jiménez and 22 of his crew were killed by Amerindians while filling their water casks at a spring. The survivors managed to sail the *Concepción* back to the mainland, where most were promptly captured by Guzmán. One of the escapees managed to reach Cortés with tales of rich caches of black pearls on a huge island with "cliffs and headlands and rocky coasts," as in the California of popular myth.

Cortés, inspired by these stories, organized and led a third expedition, partially financed by his own personal wealth. His party consisted of three ships and a group of 500 Spanish colonists that included women and children. They landed at the northeast end of Bahía de la Paz—which Cortés named Santa Cruz—in May of 1535, the same year New Spain was officially established. Although Cortés apparently found pearls in abundance, his attempt to colonize the peninsula lasted only two years, by which time disease, hostile Amerindians, and *chubascos* had driven the colonists back to the mainland.

The fourth attempt by Cortés to establish a Spanish foothold on California soil was led by the highly competent Captain Francisco de Ulloa, who'd accompanied Cortés on the failed Santa Cruz expedition. Cortés stayed behind on this one, hoping Ulloa's expedition would be able to find a more hospitable California beachhead. Ulloa set sail from Acapulco with two ships in July 1539, and in the next eight months he managed to explore the entire perimeter of the Sea of Cortez, reaching the mouth of the Río Colorado and rounding the Cape along the Pacific coast as far north as Isla Cedros.

Upon reaching Isla Cedros, Ulloa reportedly sent one ship back to Acapulco for supplies; it isn't known for certain what happened to the other vessel. According to some historical accounts, Ulloa found his way back to the mainland and was murdered by one of his own crew near Guadalajara; other accounts say he disappeared north of Isla Cedros. At any rate, his written report of the voyage—which indicated Baja was not an island but a peninsula—didn't surface until a hundred years later. His biggest contribution to the geography of the times was the naming of the Mar de Cortés, now the Sea of Cortez (or Gulf of California).

After squandering most of his wealth in futile attempts to explore Baja, Cortés was recalled to Spain in 1541, never to return to Mexican shores. In his place, Spain dispatched experienced Portuguese navigator Juan Rodríguez Cabrillo in 1542 with orders to explore the Pacific coast. Starting from the southern tip of the peninsula, his expedition made it as far north as the Oregon coast and mapped several major bays along the way, including those of San Diego and Monterey. Cabrillo himself never made it past California's Santa Barbara Islands, where he died after a mysterious fall.

Manila Galleons and Privateers

On the other side of the globe, events were unfolding that would influence Baja California's history for the next 250 years. Although Portuguese navigator Ferdinand Magellan reached the Philippines in 1521, it wasn't until 1565 that López de Legaspi defeated the archipelago's native defenders. Immediately thereafter, Esteban Rodríguez and Padre Andrés de Urdaneta pioneered a ship route from Manila to the New World that took advantage of the 14,500-kilometer (9,000-mi) Japanese Current across the northern Pacific, thus establishing a trade connection between the Orient and New Spain.

The ships making the annual round-trip voyages between Manila and Acapulco beginning in 1566 came to be called "Manila galleons." The lengthy sea journey was very difficult, however, because of the lack of freshwater during the final weeks of the five- to seven-month eastward crossing. This provided further impetus for establishing some sort of settlement in lower California where ships could put in for water and supplies.

A California landfall became even more desirable when in 1572 the Manila galleons started carrying shipments of gold, silks, and spices to New Spain. Laden with Asian exports, the ships were so heavy they became easy prey for faster pirate vessels. By 1580, England's Sir Francis Drake had entered the Pacific via the Straits of Magellan and circumnavigated the globe, thus ending Spanish dominion over the seas. Drake plundered Spanish ships with regularity, and as news of the treasure-laden ships spread, other English as well as Dutch privateers were lured into the Pacific.

Their raids on Spanish ships became an embarrassment to the crown and a drain on Spanish wealth, so the Spaniards were forced to seek out harbors in Baja's Cape Region where they could hide. Since the first land sighting on the east Pacific leg of the Manila–Acapulco voyage was below the peninsula's midpoint, the Cape Region was the logical choice for a landing. Following much experimentation, Bahía San Lucas and Bahía de la Paz became the two harbors most frequently used.

Eventually, however, the keen privateers figured out how to trap Spanish ships in the very bays their crews sought for protection. Thomas Cavendish plundered the Manila galleon *Santa Ana* at Cabo San Lucas in 1587, and so many ships were captured in Bahía de la Paz that the landfall there, originally called Santa Cruz by Cortés, eventually earned the name Pichilingue, a Spanish mispronunciation of Vlissingen, the provenance of most of the Dutch pirates.

Pirating continued off the Baja coast throughout the entire 250-year history of the Manila–Acapulco voyages. One of the more celebrated English privateers in later years was Woodes Rogers, who arrived in the Pacific in 1709 and captured the Manila galleon *Encarnación* off Cabo San Lucas. On his way to Baja California that same year Rogers rescued Alexander Selkirk, a sailor marooned on an island off the coast of Chile for four years. Selkirk served as shipmaster on Rogers's vessel and later became the inspiration for Daniel Defoe's 1719 novel *Robinson Crusoe*.

Further Exploration and Colonization Attempts

As the Spaniards' need for a permanent settlement in California grew more dire, coastal explorations were resumed after a hiatus of more than 50 years. Cabrillo was succeeded by merchant-turned-admiral Sebastián Vizcaíno, who in 1596 landed at the same bay on the southeast coast chosen by his predecessors, Jiménez and Cortés. This time, however, the natives were

SEBASTIÁN VIZCAÍNO EXPEDITIONS

——— Expedition of 1596
········· Expedition of 1602–03

© AVALON TRAVEL PUBLISHING, INC.

friendly (perhaps because it was *pitahaya* fruit season when they arrived), and Vizcaíno named the site La Paz (Peace). After loading up on *pitahaya* fruit—effective for preventing scurvy—and pearls, Vizcaíno continued north along the Sea of Cortez coast, stopping to gather more pearls before returning to the mainland.

In 1602 Vizcaíno commanded a second, more ambitious expedition that sailed along the Pacific coast to near present-day Mendocino, California. His names for various points and bays along the coasts of both Californias superseded most of those bestowed by Cabrillo and Cortés.

Upon his return Vizcaíno told his superiors that the Monterey Bay area of California was well suited to colonization. However, because he was no longer in favor with New Spain's fickle viceroys, no one paid much attention to his findings and he was reassigned to an obscure Sinaloa port. The cartographer for the voyage, Gerónimo Martínez, was beheaded for forgery, although his maps of the Californias remained the best available for more than 200 years.

This neglect of California's potential enabled an Englishman to put first claim to the territory. Sir Francis Drake, who landed at what is now Drake's Bay in northern California during his 1578–1580 voyage, christened the land New Albion on behalf of the English crown. Like the Spanish maps of the time, his maps depicted California as an island.

For a time Spain left both Californias unexplored. In 1615, Captain Juan de Iturbi obtained the first official concession for peninsular pearl diving, but no land settlement was established. After two of his ships were captured by Dutch privateers off Cabo San Lucas, de Iturbi sailed his remaining vessel northward in the Sea of Cortez as far as the 28th parallel, harvesting pearls along the way. Because of dwindling provisions, the expedition was forced to turn back to the mainland after only a few months.

The peninsula remained unconquered by the Spanish for another 80 years. In 1683, Spain's Royal Council for the Indies authorized an expedition under Admiral Isidor Atondo y Antillón and Padre Eusebio Francisco Kino, which managed to occupy an area of La Paz for three and a half months before being driven back to the mainland by dwindling provisions and hostile natives. After two months of rest and provisioning on the mainland, they crossed the Sea of Cortez again, this time establishing a mission and presidio just above the 26th parallel at a place they named San Bruno. Supported by a friendly Amerindian population, the mission lasted 19 months. Lack of water and food—they had to rely on supply ships from the mainland—forced Kino and Atondo back to the mainland.

Kino never returned to Baja California, but later became famous for his missionary efforts in northwestern Mexico and Arizona, where he is said to have converted thousands of Amerindians to Roman Catholicism. In 1701, he accompanied an expedition from the northwest of Sonora to the mouth of the Río Colorado that confirmed Ulloa's claim that Baja California was a peninsula. Kino died in Sonora in 1711.

THE MISSION PERIOD
The Founding of the Jesuit Missions

Padre Juan María Salvatierra finally succeeded in giving Spain and the Church what they wanted: a permanent Spanish settlement on the Baja California peninsula. Backed by the mainland missionary system, a 30,000-peso annual subsidy from the Royal Council of the Indies, and a contingent of Spanish soldiers, Salvatierra landed in San Bruno in October 1697, found a better water source 24 kilometers south of the original presidio, and proceeded to establish the mother of all California missions, Nuestra Señora de Loreto.

The founding of the Loreto mission initiated what Baja historians usually call "the Jesuit missionary period," lasting 1697–1767. During this interval, the Jesuits established 20 missions, stretching from the southern tip of the peninsula to near present-day Cataviña

© AVALON TRAVEL PUBLISHING, INC.

in central Baja. That wasn't a spectacular accomplishment compared with the progress of mainland colonization, but lower California was a much more difficult area to colonize. It had taken 167 years from the time the first Spaniard had set foot on the shore until the first successful settlement was established on Baja California soil.

The Spanish mission system basically worked like this: the padres, always in the company of armed escorts, approached groups of natives and offered them the protection of the Church and the Spanish crown in return for a willingness to undergo religious instruction. Those natives who agreed were congregated at a suitable spot and directed to build a mission. The mission in turn became a refuge for the Amerindians and a place for them to learn European farming techniques and other trades, as well as Catholic ways. Once pacification was complete, the mission became a secularized church community *(pueblo),* and the missionaries moved on to new areas.

The system worked well with the docile Amerindians of Central Mexico but was often unsuccessful among the nomadic, fiercely independent Amerindians of Northern Mexico and Baja. Elsewhere in Mexico and Latin America, the norm was to secularize after 10 years; in Baja, the Spanish Church never voluntarily secularized its missions.

Amerindian Revolts, Disease, and the Decline of the Jesuits

Several times during the Jesuit period, groups of Amerindians revolted against missionization. The most significant rebellion occurred in 1734–1736 among the Pericú of the southern peninsula. Apparently the revolt was triggered by Padre Nicolás Tamaral's injunction against polygamy—long a practice among the Pericú and Guaicura, tribes in which women outnumbered men. The punishment of a Pericú shaman under the injunction doubled the perceived assault on native culture, and a group of disaffected Amerindians organized themselves against the entire mission structure.

In October 1734, the Pericú attacked and burned the missions at Santiago and San José del Cabo, killing Padre Tamaral and his counterpart at Santiago; they also set fire to the mission in La Paz, although the padre there escaped unharmed and was able to send to the mainland for assistance. In Todos Santos, the rebels killed 49 Amerindian inhabitants who tried to defend their pueblo. The provincial governor of Sinaloa, after receiving letters from Loreto describing the uprising, dispatched a ship from the mainland with 60 Yaqui warriors and a number of Spanish soldiers. The troops marched from mission to mission, meeting little resistance from the poorly equipped Pericú.

Unrest among the Pericú continued for another two years, a situation that led to the founding of a large garrison at San José del Cabo. As a further precaution, the garrisons at every mission in the south were expanded by 10 soldiers each. Besides reinforcing the missions, this increased military presence encouraged Manila galleons to make Cabo San Lucas a regular stop on their return voyages from the Orient.

In the years to follow, epidemics of smallpox, syphilis, and measles—diseases borne by Europeans for which Amerindians had no natural immunity—devastated the Amerindian population. In 1738 Padre Jacobo Baegert of Misión San Luis Gonzaga estimated the Baja Amerindian population at about 50,000. In three outbreaks of smallpox in 1742, 1744, and 1748, an estimated 42,000 Amerindians—84 percent of the native population—perished. Gathering the Amerindians into mission settlements only hastened their demise, intensifying the spread of contagions. A significant number of Amerindians also lost their lives in continued rebellions against the padres. The La Paz mission was abandoned in 1748; by 1767 only one member of the entire Huchiti branch of the Guaycura nation survived.

As the southern Amerindians died out, the missionaries moved quickly northward, seeking new sheep for their flocks. The last four missions established by the Jesuits—Santa Gertrudis (1752), San Borja (1762), Calamajué (1766), and Santa María (1767)—were scattered widely in northern Baja in an obvious push toward California.

In 1767 King Charles III ordered the expulsion of the Jesuit Order from all Spanish dominions, including Baja California. Accounts of the expulsion disagree as to the reasons behind his action. According to crown representatives, the Jesuits were too power-hungry and would no longer be held accountable for their actions. The Jesuits themselves claimed persecution because they'd dared criticize corruption among the nobility and royalty of Europe. Whatever the reason, in 1768 the 16 Jesuit padres of Baja found themselves herded onto a ship bound for the mainland port of San Blas, where the same ship received a contingent of Franciscan padres sent to replace them.

Franciscan and Dominican padres succeeded the Jesuits, but by the end of the 18th century it was clear that Spain and the Church could no longer afford to support the Baja missions. The peninsula's Amerindian population had dwindled to less than 5,000 by 1800, and without an abundance of free native labor, maintaining a colony wasn't an easy task. The California missions to the north seemed much more promising—water was more readily available and the Amerindian labor force was more docile and plentiful. The growing unrest in Mexico placed the peninsula even lower on Spain's list of priorities.

INDEPENDENCE FROM SPAIN

The Catholic Church in Mexico had amassed huge amounts of wealth by the beginning of the 19th century and had become a lender to the colony's growing entrepreneurial class. At the other end of the economic spectrum, the increasing numbers of mestizos—Mexican-born residents of mixed Spanish and Amerindian ancestry—were denied land ownership and other rights and were generally treated as second-class citizens.

Fearing the Church was becoming too powerful, King Charles III of Spain decreed in 1804 that all Church funds be turned over to the royal coffers. To comply with the decree, padres all over Mexico were forced to call back

large sums of money lent out to entrepreneurs, and economic chaos ensued. Mexicans blamed their economic and social problems on Spain's remote rule; when Napoleon invaded Spain in 1808, limiting authority to Spanish loyalists in Mexico City, the disaffected clergy began planning a revolt.

Mexico's struggle for independence from Spain began on September 16, 1810, a date celebrated annually as Día de la Independencia, or Mexican Independence Day. On that day, Padre Miguel Hidalgo y Costilla issued a call for independence, today known as the Grito de Dolores (Dolores Cry) from the mainland city of Dolores, Guanajuato. Although the rebels who gathered around Hidalgo soon captured Zacatecas, Valladolid, and San Luis Potosí, Mexico wasn't completely free of Spanish rule for another 11 years. When Hidalgo was captured and executed by loyalists, another padre took his place, and the fighting continued until Mexico City acceded to the demands of the rebels in 1821.

The 1821 Plan de Iguala treaty between Spain and Mexico guaranteed three political underpinnings of the new regime: the religious dominance of the Catholic Church, a constitutional monarchy, and equal rights for mestizos as well as Mexican-born Spaniards. Former viceroy Agustín de Iturbide was appointed emperor of the new republic, but his reign lasted only two years before he was overthrown by another junta that established a short-lived federal republic called Los Estados Unidos de México—the United States of Mexico—in 1824.

During the next six years the Mexican republic endured two more coups; it wasn't until 1829 that all Spanish troops were expelled from Mexico. In 1832 all non-Dominican missions in Baja were secularized and converted to parish churches. The Dominican missions of the northern peninsula were allowed to remain because they were considered the only outposts of civilization north of La Paz and Loreto, and as such were important links with prospering Alta California. Another change in policy involved the encouragement of Anglo-American immigration to the northeastern Mexican state of Coahuila y Texas—a policy that would have profound implications later on.

The Mexican-American War

In 1833 Antonio López de Santa Anna, a megalomaniacal general in charge of enforcing the expulsion of Spanish troops, seized power and revoked the Constitution of 1824, thus initiating a series of events that eventually led to a war with the United States and the resultant loss of huge amounts of territory. During the first 30 years of Mexican independence, Mexico changed governments 50 times; Santa Anna—who called himself the "Napoleon of the West"—headed 11 of these regimes.

Mexican citizens everywhere were angry at the revocation of their republican constitution by a self-appointed dictator. But none were more frustrated than the Anglo-American immigrants who had voluntarily abandoned their U.S. citizenship to take Mexican citizenship under the Constitution of 1824 and live in the northern half of Coahuila y Texas. In 1836, the "Texicans" declared an independent Republic of Texas, fought and lost San Antonio's famous Battle of the Alamo, then routed Santa Anna's defending troops in San Jacinto, Texas.

Defeated and captured, Santa Anna signed the Velasco Agreement, which guaranteed Texas independence and recognized the Rio Grande as the border between Mexico and the new Texan republic. There matters lay until the United States granted statehood to the near-bankrupt republic in 1845. Santa Anna's government refused to recognize the Velasco Agreement, claiming Texas only extended as far south as the Nueces River, about 160 kilometers north of the Rio Grande at the widest gap. When the U.S. Army moved into the area south of the Nueces, Santa Anna retaliated by sending troops across the Rio Grande, thus initiating the Mexican-American War.

After a series of skirmishes along the Rio Grande, U.S. president James Polk ordered the army to invade Mexico. In Baja California, Mexican and American forces engaged at Santo Tomás, Mulegé, La Paz, and San José del Cabo. Mexico City finally fell to U.S. troops in March 1847, and Santa Anna signed the Treaty of Guadalupe Hidalgo in 1848. In the treaty, Mexico conceded not only the Rio Grande area of Texas but part of New Mexico and all of California for a payment of US$25 million and the cancellation of all Mexican debt.

In retrospect, it is likely the annexation of Texas was part of a U.S. plan to provoke Mexico into declaring war so the United States could gain more of the Southwest. The war so damaged Mexico's already weakened economy that in 1853 Santa Anna sold Arizona and southern New Mexico to the United States for another US$10 million. During that same year, American freebooter William Walker sailed to La Paz and declared himself "President of Lower California." He and his mercenary troops fled upon hearing that Mexican forces were on the way. He was later tried—and acquitted—in the United States for violation of neutrality laws. Walker was executed after a similar escapade in Nicaragua two years later.

For the Mexican population, already strongly dissatisfied with Santa Anna, these losses of territory became the final straw; in 1855 Santa Anna was overthrown by populist Benito Juárez.

Depopulation of the Peninsula, Civil War, and Reform

The second half of the 19th century was even more turbulent for Mexico than the first. At the end of the Mexican-American War, the California Gold Rush of 1849 lured many Mexicans and Amerindians away from the peninsula to seek their fortunes in California, reducing Baja's already scant population even further and transforming it into a haven for bandits, pirates, and an assortment of other outlaws and misfits. Only six Dominican padres remained on the peninsula by the 1880s.

Meanwhile, back on the mainland, a civil war (called the "War of Reform" in Mexico) erupted in 1858 after the removal of Santa Anna; self-appointed governments in Mexico City and Veracruz vied for national authority. Once again, Church wealth was the principal issue. The liberals, under Zapotec lawyer Benito Juárez, had promulgated a new constitution in 1857 and passed a law further restricting the financial powers of the Church; all Church property save for the church buildings themselves had to be sold or otherwise relinquished. A reactionary opposition group took control of Mexico City, and fighting continued until 1861, when the liberals won and Juárez was elected president.

Juárez immediately had to deal with the 1862 French invasion of Mexico, which came in response to Mexico's nonpayment of debts to France. Napoleon III's first invading force was defeated at Puebla on the Gulf of Mexico coast, but the following year the French captured the city and continued onward to take Mexico City, where they installed Austrian Ferdinand Maximilian as emperor of Mexico. Under U.S. pressure, the French gradually withdrew from Mexico, and Juárez was back in power by 1867.

Through the next four years Juárez initiated many economic and educational reforms. Upon his death in 1872, political opponent Porfirio Díaz took over and continued reforms begun by Juárez, albeit in a more authoritarian manner. Díaz and/or his cronies ruled for the next 28 years, suspending political freedoms but modernizing the country's education and transportation systems.

Foreign Investment in Baja California

In Baja, Díaz and the "Porfiriato" encouraged foreign investment on a large scale, and in the 1880s vast land tracts were sold to American or European mining, farming, manufacturing, and railway concessions. All but the mining concessions met failure within a few years, mainly because the investors weren't prepared to deal with the peninsula's demanding climate and lack of transportation.

Mineral excavation in late-19th-century Baja enjoyed a boom—gold, silver, copper, and gypsum were the main finds, along with graphite, mercury, nickel, and sulfur. One of the most successful mining endeavors was that of Compañía del Boleo, a French mining syndicate in Santa Rosalía that for many years was the largest copper-mining and smelting operation in Mexico.

THE 20TH CENTURY AND BEYOND
The Mexican Revolution

By the early 20th century, it was obvious that the gap between rich and poor was increasing, caused by the extreme procapitalist policies of the Díaz regime and the lack of a political voice for workers and peasants. In response to the situation, a liberal opposition group, using Texas as a base, formed in exile, organizing strikes throughout the country. This forced Díaz to announce an election in 1910; his opponent was Francisco Madero, a liberal from Coahuila. As it became clear that Madero was garnering mass support, Díaz imprisoned him on trumped-up charges.

Upon his release, Madero fled to Texas and began organizing the overthrow of the Díaz government. The rebels, with the assistance of the colorful bandit-turned-revolutionary Pancho Villa and peasant-hero Emiliano Zapata, managed to gain control of the Northern Mexico states of Sonora and Chihuahua. Unable to contain the revolution, Díaz resigned in May 1910 and Madero was elected president. His one-time allies, however, broke into several factions—the Zapatistas, Reyistas, Vasquistas, and Felicistas, named for the leaders of each movement—and Madero was executed in 1913. Baja California had its own faction, the Magonistas, who briefly held Tijuana in 1911.

For the next six years the various factions played musical chairs with national leadership; Mexico remained extremely unstable until revolutionary leader Venustiano Carranza emerged as president. Carranza held a historic convention that resulted in the Constitution of 1917, the current Mexican constitution. This document established the *ejido* program to return lands traditionally cultivated by the Amerindian peasantry, but taken away by rich ranch and plantation owners under Díaz, to local communities throughout Mexico. Three years later opponent Álvaro Obregón and his supporters overthrew Carranza.

Obregón managed to hang onto the office for four years, establishing important educational reforms; he was followed in 1924 by Plutarco Elías Calles. Calles instituted wide-reaching agrarian reforms, including the redistribution of three million hectares of land. He also participated in the establishment of the National Revolutionary Party (PNR), the forerunner of the Institutional Revolutionary Party (PRI), which remained Mexico's dominant party until the National Action Party (PAN) won the presidency in 2000.

U.S. Prohibition

About the same time Obregón took power in Mexico City, the U.S. government amended its own constitution to make the consumption, manufacture, and sale of alcoholic beverages a federal offense. This proved to be a disastrous experiment for the United States, ushering in an era of organized crime, but was a boon to Baja California development. Americans began rushing across the border to buy booze from the restaurants, cantinas, and liquor stores of Northern Mexico.

Border towns added casinos and brothels to the assortment of liquor venues and became so prosperous that the municipal leadership was able to lobby successfully for the division of Baja California into northern and southern territories. On the negative side, the border towns became renowned as world sleaze capitals. Their reputations persisted long after Prohibition ended in 1933 and the Mexican government outlawed gambling—prostitution remained legal—in 1938.

Nationalist Reforms and World War II

The year 1938 proved a turning point in modern Mexican history as PNR candidate Lázaro Cárdenas ascended to the presidency. Cárdenas, a mestizo with Tarascan Amerindian heritage, instituted the most sweeping social reforms of any national leader to date, effecting significant changes in education, labor, agriculture, and commerce.

His land reforms included the redistribution of 18.6 million hectares (46 million acres) among newly created *ejidos*—a legacy that is as hot a topic for debate today as it was then. Foreign-owned oil interests were expropriated, and a national oil company, Petróleos Mexicanos (Pemex), was established. Even though foreign investors were compensated for expropriations at fair market value (under a treaty signed by both the United States and Mexico), these reforms frightened off foreign investors for many years, and it has been only recently that Mexico has reattracted foreign capital. Cárdenas also reorganized the PNR as the Mexican Revolution Party (PRM—Partido de la Revolución Mexicana), which soon changed its name to the Institutional Revolutionary Party (PRI—Partido Revolucionario Institucional).

Between the Cárdenas period and the 2000 presidential election, Mexican political history was characterized by comparatively subtle shifts. Mexican leadership succession also had stabilized, a process often referred to as the oxymoronic "institutionalization of the revolution" (meaning the PRI had won every national election in that period).

Baja Statehood and the Transpeninsular Highway

After the war, Mexico continued to industrialize, and the economy remained relatively stable under one PRI president after another. In 1952 the Territory of (Northern) Baja California was declared Mexico's 29th state as its population moved past the 80,000 required for statehood. Northern Baja was, in fact, better off economically than most of the rest of the country. The boomtowns of Tijuana and Mexicali were servicing a fast-growing border economy, and Valle de Mexicali farming competed well with California's Imperial Valley. In 1958 it was determined that Baja was second only to Mexico City in the number of automobiles per capita.

Meanwhile, wealthy Americans had been flying to La Paz and Cabo San Lucas since the late 1940s to fish the teeming waters of the Sea of Cortez. In 1948 several Hollywood celebrities (including Bing Crosby, John Wayne, and Desi Arnaz) built a resort known as Las Cruces on the Cortez coast east of La Paz, and in 1958 a lone American investor constructed the Hotel Palmilla at Punta Palmilla on the Corridor. Others quickly followed, including the Hotel Cabo San Lucas, Hotel Hacienda, and Hotel Finisterra in Cabo San Lucas, and the Rancho Buena Vista on Bahía de Palmas.

Throughout the 1960s most of Baja south of Ensenada remained benevolently neglected, which led travel writers of the time to employ the famous catchphrase, "the forgotten peninsula." The Cape Region was a little-known beach and sportfishing destination limited to pilots, diehard anglers, and celebrities. The overall population of the Territory of Southern Baja California was stagnating, perhaps even decreasing; except for La Paz, it was limited to tiny collections of hardy souls here and there who scratched for cash as rancheros or *pescadores* (fishermen). Even La Paz was just a step above a sleepy backwater port, although its status as a duty-free port was beginning to attract a steady trickle of mainland Mexicans.

By the 1970s, it was obvious that southern Baja wasn't going to catch up with northern Baja unless transportation between the south, north, and mainland improved. Travel between Tijuana and La Paz took up to 10 days via rough dirt tracks. Construction of the Transpeninsular Highway (Mexico 1) was finally completed in 1973, connecting Tijuana with Cabo San Lucas for the first time. In less than a year, the population of Baja California Sur passed the 80,000 mark, and the territory became Mexico's 30th state.

The 1,700-kilometer-long (1,054-mi-long) Transpeninsular Highway has greatly contributed to the modernization of one of Mexico's last frontiers. Fishing and agricultural cooperatives can now transport their products to the border or to the ports of Santa Rosalía, Guerrero Negro, and La Paz. The highway has brought Americans, Canadians, and Europeans deep into the peninsula in greater numbers than ever before, and the revenue from their visits provides another means of livelihood for the people of Baja.

Like the border visitors of the Prohibition years, the foreigners who come to the Cape Region today are seeking something that's scarce in their own countries. For some it may be the unfenced desert solitude, for others the pristine beaches or historic mission towns. The challenge of the future for the Cape's burgeoning tourist industry is how to develop and maintain an adequate infrastructure without sacrificing those qualities that make Baja California Sur unique.

The People

Baja California Sur occupies a place in the Mexican psyche somewhat analogous to that of Hawaii for many Americans. It's seen as a place that's part of the nation yet almost out of reach—an exotic destination most of the population will never have an opportunity to see. Hence, mainlanders typically regard the *bajacalifornianos* of the southern peninsula as somehow "different" from themselves. And it's true that the people of Baja California Sur are in many ways a breed apart from their mainland compatriots. As Mexico's last frontier, El Sur continues to attract residents seeking a rugged, independent lifestyle they haven't been able to find in mainland Mexico.

The enticements of a highly favorable climate, bounteous sea, and wide-open spaces have drawn a mix of Baja natives, transplanted mainlanders, and gringos to the Cape Region.

Approximately a half million people live in Baja California Sur, most of them in La Paz, San José del Cabo, or Cabo San Lucas. Mexico's population growth rate is estimated at 1.16 percent per annum for 2006. But the growth rate for Los Cabos is a whoppping 15 percent, with 60 people a day moving to the area. Even so, Baja California Sur remains the country's least populated state.

ORIGINS

Bajacalifornianos (sometimes called *bajacalifornios*) are an unusually varied lot. Elsewhere in Mexico, the average citizen is a mix of Spanish and Amerindian bloodlines. In the Cape Region the mix is typically more complicated, mainly because southern Baja remained a frontier much longer than most of the mainland, attracting people who arrived in the New World long after the Spanish colonized the Mexican mainland. It was 167 years after the conquest of Mexico before the Spanish were able to maintain a permanent settlement on the peninsula; by this time, tales of the Californias were on the tongues of adventurers throughout

the world. The first paved highway between the Cape Region and the U.S. border was completed only a few decades ago.

By the end of the 19th century the Cape had become a favorite spot for sea-weary sailors to jump ship. The eastern shores of the peninsula were placid, and there was little chance deserters would be rounded up and incarcerated by local militia, who were scarce then and remain so today. Most of the ex-sailors who retired in this manner were English, but during World War I a few Germans and other Europeans

WHAT'S A GRINGO?

The Latin-American Spanish word "gringo," reportedly a corruption of the Spanish word *greigo,* or "Greek," has different meanings in different parts of Latin America. In Argentina and Uruguay, for example, it is used to refer to anyone of Italian descent. In Mexico and Central America, it's almost always reserved for people of northern European descent, especially Canadians and Americans. In spite of everyday linguistic evidence to the contrary, many non-Spanish speakers insist that only Americans are gringos. The Mexicans, however, have a more precise epithet for Americans: *yanquis,* or "Yankees."

Is "gringo" a derogatory term? It can certainly be used that way. Most of the time, however, it's simply an unconscious racial identification of neutral value. Educated Mexicans tend not to use it; instead they typically say *norteamericano* or *americano* for Americans. Some Mexicans insist on the former even though the term is a slight to Canadians and Mexicans, who, after all, are North Americans, too. *Canadiense* is used for Canadians, *alemán* for Germans, and so forth. A more precise term for U.S. citizens is *estadounidense.*

came ashore. Their ship captains might have considered them cowardly deserters, but survival in southern Baja in the 19th and early 20th centuries was possible only for the brave, hardy, and resourceful.

Since in a very real sense much of Baja is still a frontier area—with more immigrants wandering in year by year—Baja's demographics have yet to solidify into recognizable pie-graph proportions. About 2 percent of the residents aren't even Mexican citizens; many are American, Canadian, or European retirees, and a lesser number are gringos who've simply dropped out of the rat race. With the current relaxation of investment and trade laws, a growing number of foreigners are also setting up businesses on the Cape.

LANGUAGE

As in the rest of Mexico, Spanish is the primary language in Baja California Sur. English is widely spoken by merchants, hotel staff, and travel agents in La Paz, San José del Cabo, and Cabo San Lucas. Even in these cities, however, you can't count on finding English-speaking Mexicans outside the tourist districts.

If you restrict your daily schedule to hotel, beach, restaurant, and nightclub visits, you'll get by fine using English. But if you don't speak Spanish and you hope to do the Cape circuit or explore the interior, you'd be wise to learn at least enough of the language to cope with everyday transactions. Knowing a little Spanish will not only mitigate communication problems, it will also bring you more respect among the local Mexicans, who quite naturally resent foreign visitors who expect Mexicans to abandon their mother tongue whenever a gringo approaches. A popular sign seen in tourist restaurants reads "We promise not to laugh at your broken Spanish if you won't laugh at our broken English."

Dictionaries and Phrasebooks

The *Glossary* and *Spanish Phrasebook* at the back of this book will get you started on a basic vocabulary in *español*. For further study, you'll want a dictionary and a larger phrasebook. One of the best portable dictionaries for the Spanish student is the paperback *University of Chicago Spanish-English, English-Spanish Dictionary*, which emphasizes New World usages and contains useful sections on grammar and pronunciation. The 5th edition was published in 2003. If even this small volume is too large for your backpack, the *Collins Gem Dictionary: Spanish-English, English-Spanish* comes in a tiny 4-by-3.5-by-1-inch edition with a sturdy plastic cover and more than 40,000 entries. The 5th edition was published in 2001.

Berlitz's *Latin-American Spanish for Travellers* is a small phrasebook divided by topics and situations (e.g., grammar, hotel, eating out, post office). Not all the phrases and terms it contains are used in Baja, but it's better than nothing. The latest edition was published in 1998, and an audio edition came out in 2001.

One of the best references for off-the-road adventurers is Burleson and Riskind's *Backcountry Mexico: A Traveler's Guide and Phrase Book* (University of Texas Press, 1986). Although it's rather bulky for carrying in a backpack and is oriented toward travel in northern mainland Mexico, it contains many words and phrases of value to hikers and campers.

ESSENTIALS
Getting There

BY AIR
International Flights

The Cape Region boasts two international airports: **Los Cabos International Airport** (airport code: SJD) near San José del Cabo, and **Márquez de León International Airport** (LAP) near La Paz. Both field flights from the United States—the only country with direct international flights to the Cape—as well as from mainland Mexico. (For specific information on regularly scheduled flights, see the *Getting There* sections in *Los Cabos* and *La Paz*.) Both airports offer shuttles, taxis, and rental cars for transferring to your hotel, resort, or campground.

Air/Hotel Packages

Airlines serving Baja often offer package deals that include airfare, hotel, and airport transfers at money-saving prices. A typical package includes three nights' hotel accommodations, airfare, and airport transfers for about the same as airfare alone. Contact the airlines directly to inquire about such packages, or check with a good travel agent. Newspaper travel sections often carry advertisements for air/hotel deals in Los Cabos.

BY LAND

Most Cape visitors arrive by air, but a significant number—many of them repeat visitors—drive all the way down the peninsula from the

© NIKKI GOTH ITOI

U.S.–Mexico border. Public transportation by Mexican bus is also possible from the border. (Full details on the Transpeninsular road trip—by private vehicle and by bus—are available in *Moon Baja*.)

Buses

BUSES FROM SAN DIEGO TO TIJUANA

Greyhound Bus Lines (U.S. tel. 619/239-3266, www.greyhound.com) operates around 16 buses a day from the San Diego bus terminal to Tijuana's downtown bus terminal for US$12 one-way (approx. 1 hr) or US$24 round-trip. Greyhound also runs a number of buses daily to Tijuana's Central de Autobuses—where you'll find the greatest selection of buses heading to Baja California Sur—for about the same fare. San Diego's bus terminal is at 120 W. Broadway.

The cheapest bus to the border from San Diego is the Metropolitan Transit System's (www.sdcommute.com) city bus no. 932, which travels from the downtown area (Centre City) to San Ysidro every 30 minutes from around 5:40 A.M. to 10:52 P.M. (6:12 A.M.–10:52 P.M. weekends and holidays) for just US$2.25. Because it makes several stops along the way, the city bus takes 80 minutes to reach San Ysidro. For automated schedule information, call U.S. tel. 619/685-4900.

BUSES TO LA PAZ

See *Intercity Bus Service* under *Getting Around* for details on bus routes between the border and the Cape Region.

BUSES FROM MAINLAND MEXICO

Transportes Norte de Sonora (TNS, tel. 664/688-1979) and **Autotransportes Estrellas del Pacífico** (tel. 664/683-5022) operate long-distance express buses to Mexicali and Tijuana from various towns in Guanajuato, Nayarit, Sonora, Chihuahua, Michoacán, Jalisco, Sinaloa, Zacatecas, Querétaro, and Mexico City.

GREEN TORTOISE

To those who have never traveled by Green Tortoise (U.S. tel. 415/956-7500 or 800/867-8647, www.greentortoise.com), it's difficult to describe the experience. Imagine a sort of youth hostel on wheels, with a bit of a '60s spirit, and you'll begin to get the idea. The buses are refurbished Greyhounds with convertible beds and tables, comfortable but a bit of a tight squeeze at night when everyone's lying down. That's also when the bus travels. It's a great way to meet people.

Green Tortoise operates nine-day (from US$441) and 15-day (US$649) trips to Baja November–April that begin in San Francisco (pickups in L.A. and San Diego are possible) and range as far south as La Paz. Prices are reasonable and include transportation and lodging on the bus, plus guided hikes and side trips to remote Baja beaches. The food fund adds another US$9–10 per day to the trip; communal meals cover about 70 percent of the meals—some meals are left to the participants. The trips include an optional windsurfing and sailing program available for an additional fee. All things considered, it's a travel bargain and a novel introduction to Baja.

Driving

If you're contemplating the drive and have limited time, figure on making it from Tijuana to Cabo in three eight-hour days (Cataviña first night, Santa Rosalía or Mulegé second night) or two and a half dawn-to-dusk days (Guerrero Negro first night, La Paz second night). If you stretch your itinerary to include a week's driving time each way, you'll have a safer trip and more of an opportunity to enjoy the sights along the way.

The red tape for driving into Baja is minimal. No vehicle permits of any kind are required, no matter how long you stay in Baja, unless you plan to cross to the mainland by road (via San Luis Río Colorado) or ferry (Santa Rosalía or La Paz).

MEXICAN AUTO INSURANCE

There is a lot of confusion and misinformation in travel circles about why and how to insure your vehicle when driving in Mexico. Whether you are driving your own vehicle into Mexico,

AIRLINES SERVING THE CAPE REGION

© PAUL ITOI

Most direct flights from the United States arrive at Los Cabos International Airport; however, a few carriers have initiated routes between Los Angeles and La Paz International Airport.

AERO CALIFORNIA
(tel. 612/125-1023, U.S. tel. 800/237-6225, www.aerocalifornia.com)

La Paz: nonstop flights from Los Angeles and Tijuana

AEROLITORAL
(tel. 800/237-6639)

La Paz: nonstop flights from Los Angeles

AEROMÉXICO
(tel. 624/146-5097, 624/146-5098, or 800/021-4010, U.S. tel. 800/237-6639, www.aeromexico.com)

Los Cabos: direct flights from San Diego and Hermosilla

---

renting a car to drive over the border, or renting within Mexico, read this section carefully:

Before driving into Baja, all drivers should arrange for Mexican vehicle insurance. Why? Mexican law requires drivers to have proof of financial liability (a minimum of US$50,000 worth) for any property damage or bodily injury they cause to other parties in an accident. Unless you have a bond with a Mexican bank or cash in hand at the time of an accident, the only practical way to comply with the law is to purchase an insurance policy underwritten by a Mexican company. Without it, a minor traffic accident can turn into a nightmare, involving jail time and steep financial penalties. *No matter what your own insurance company*

nize foreign insurance policies for private vehicles in Mexico.

If you are planning to drive your own vehicle, you can purchase short-term insurance—as little as one day's worth—from one of 20 or so online vendors of Mexican Tourist Auto Insurance. Simply request a quote, complete an application, pay by credit card, and print a certificate from home before you leave for your trip. (You can purchase a policy in advance, and set it to begin on the day you plan to cross the border.) Policy terms and quality of service vary significantly, so be sure you are dealing with a reputable broker before you buy. A good way to tell is to call and speak to a live person, then complete the process online.

If you're not the plan-ahead type, or you prefer

ALASKA AIRLINES
(tel. 624/146-5210 or 624/146-5212, U.S. tel. 800/252-7522, www.alaskaairlines.com)

Los Cabos: nonstop flights from Los Angeles, San Francisco, San Jose, San Diego, Seattle/Tacoma, and Phoenix, with connecting flights from Portland and other cities

La Paz: new direct flight from Los Angeles

AMERICAN AIRLINES
(tel. 624/146-5300, U.S. tel. 800/433-7300, www.aa.com)

Los Cabos: nonstop daily from Dallas/Fort Worth, Los Angeles, Chicago

CONTINENTAL
(tel. 624/146-5050 or 624/146-5050, U.S. tel. 800/231-0856, www.flycontinental.com)

Los Cabos: daily flights from Houston; direct flights from Newark are daily or weekly, depending on the time of year

DELTA
(tel. 800/902-2100, U.S. tel. 800/221-1212, www.delta.com)

Los Cabos: daily direct flights from Atlanta and Salt Lake City

La Paz: new direct flight from Los Angeles

MEXICANA AIRLINES
(tel. 624/146-5001 or 800/509-8960, U.S. tel. 800/531-7921, www.mexicana.com.mx)

Los Cabos: direct flights from Los Angeles, Las Vegas, Chicago

UNITED AIRLINES
(tel. 800/003-0777, U.S. tel. 800/538-2929, www.ual.com)

Los Cabos: daily direct flight from Chicago and several direct flights per week from San Francisco

US AIRWAYS
(tel. 800/428-4322, U.S. tel. 800/622-1015, www.usairways.com)

Los Cabos: daily nonstop flights from Phoenix and connecting flights from Seattle and many other U.S. cities

---

found in nearly every border town between the Pacific Ocean and the Gulf of Mexico. Again, read the terms carefully before paying.

The first decision you'll need to make is between a liability-only policy (to comply with the law) or full coverage (to protect your vehicle). Liability-only policies typically cover third-party liability from a minimum of US$50,000, up to US$300,000; plus legal expenses (levels range widely from US$500 to US$30,000), medical payments for you and your passengers (US$2,000–5,000 per person; US$19,000–25,000 per accident), and some form of roadside assistance. Higher-end policies may include medical evacuation and a flight home if your car is stolen or not drivable. Standard deductibles begin at US$500

and scale to 2–10 percent of the value of the vehicle; a flat US$5,000 for motorcycles.

Full coverage adds physical damage and theft coverage to the list above. Since the cost of upgrading from liability-only to full coverage amounts to a few dollars more per day, it usually makes sense to add the theft coverage and enjoy the peace of mind. Theft coverage typically carries a higher deductible than just liability. See the sidebar *Mexican Auto Insurance Policy Checklist* for more on the fine print.

In business since 2001, Santa Cruz, California–based **Adventure Mexican Insurance** (U.S. tel. 831/477-9208 or 800/485-4075, www.mexadventure.com) provides daily, monthly, and annual Mexican auto insurance to individual travelers, as well as travel

MEXICAN AUTO INSURANCE POLICY CHECKLIST

Consider the following criteria before buying Mexican insurance for your private vehicle:

- Look for a U.S.-based claims office.

- Deductibles should be clearly stated, typically a minimum of $500 or 2 percent of the value of the vehicle.

- The better policies include legal coverage, roadside assistance, plane tickets home if your car cannot be driven, and medical evacuation.

- Some premium policies include extra coverage for uninsured drivers.

- Policies with a "combined single limit" (CSL) for bodily and property damage are preferred over "split limits," which are less flexible.

- The policy should allow you to handle repairs in the United States or Canada.

- The policy should clearly state an hourly labor rate high enough to cover the cost of repairs in the United States (the US$15/hour standard in Mexico will not be sufficient).

- Keep one copy of your policy in the glovebox and another in your wallet (in case the car is stolen).

- Call your claims number when you cross into Mexico to verify that it works.

- If you have a claim, report it before you leave Mexico within the time limit specified in your policy; some companies will not honor the policy once you have left the country.

- Claims adjusters can reach most parts of Baja within two hours.

- Driving on the beach is considered a non-conventional road: If you get stuck and the tide comes in and floods your car, it's probably not going to be covered.

- Any roads that require four-wheel drive are probably not covered.

When shopping online:

- Websites should display an insurance license logo.

- Check that the site is secure before you transmit personal data.

- When in doubt, call the vendor to verify services.

---

organizations. The company's website clearly explains Mexican insurance options and allows you to compare various policies from its three underwriters; well armed with information, you can then purchase online in a matter of minutes. For a long weekend trip to Baja, you'll pay around US$30 for liability only, and US$40 for full coverage (both at the minimum liability level of US$50,000). Full coverage monthly rates range US$150–250, depending on the value of the vehicle. Its policies cover repairs in the United States and include a bundled travel assistance package for medical evacuation of up to four passengers and plane tickets home if your vehicle is undrivable. Call toll-free for detailed information about insuring an RV, trailer, or other special circumstances. Short-term policies cover travel in all of Mexico, but for long-term policies, customers have the option of a regional North West policy covering Baja as well as the mainland states of Sonora, Chihuahua, and Sinaloa, at a reduced rate.

Several travel clubs offer discounted rates to members: For example, **Discover Baja Travel Club** (U.S. tel. 800/727-2252, www .discoverbaja.com) offers liability insurance for only US$75 per year and full coverage starting at US$122. AAA members can purchase Mexican auto insurance through the travel club website (www.aaa.com) or by phone.

If you forget to purchase insurance before you leave or prefer to purchase your policy in person, try **Instant Mexico Insurance Services** (223 Via de San Ysidro, U.S. tel. 619/428-4714, or 800/345-4701, www.instant-mex-auto-insur.com, open 24 hrs daily) at the last exit before the San Ysidro/Tijuana border crossing. You can also purchase tourist cards, fishing and boating permits, maps, guidebooks, and other Baja requisites here.

Whichever policy you choose, always make photocopies of it and keep originals and copies in separate, safe places. It's also a good idea to carry a photocopy of the first page—the "declaration" or "renewal of declaration" sheet—of your home country policy, as Mexican law requires that you cross the border with at least six months' worth of home country insurance.

TEMPORARY VEHICLE IMPORT PERMITS

If you're driving only in the states of Baja California and Baja California Sur, you won't need one of these. However, if you plan to take a vehicle aboard a ferry bound for the mainland from Santa Rosalía or La Paz, you will need a temporary vehicle import permit before you'll be allowed to book a ferry ticket. To receive this permit, simply drive your vehicle to a Mexican customs office (this can be done at any official border crossing or in La Paz) and present the following: a valid state registration for the vehicle (or similar document certifying legal ownership), a driver's license, and a credit card (Visa, MasterCard, American Express, or Diner's Club) issued outside Mexico.

If you are leasing or renting the vehicle, you also have to present a leasing or rental contract made out to the person bringing the vehicle into Mexico. If the vehicle belongs to someone else (e.g., a friend or relative), you must present a notarized letter from the owner giving you permission to take the vehicle to Mexico. Contrary to rumor, you aren't required to present the "pink slip" or ownership certificate unless the state registration certificate is for some reason unavailable.

Once Mexican customs officials have ap-proved your documents, you'll proceed to a Banjército (Banco del Ejército or Military Bank) office attached to the customs facilities, and your credit card account will be charged US$30 for the permit fee. This fee must be paid by credit card; cash is not accepted. If you don't have a credit card, you'll have to post a bond (1–2 percent of the vehicle's blue-book value) issued by an authorized Mexican bond company—a time-consuming and expensive procedure. Banjército is the bank used for all Mexican customs charges; the operating hours for each module are the same as for the border crossing at which it's located.

Once the fee has been charged to your credit card, the permit is issued, with a validity period equal to that shown on your tourist card or visa. You may drive back and forth across the border—at any crossing—as many times as you wish during the permit's validity. You are supposed to surrender the permit at the border when your trip is over, however.

BY FERRY FROM MAINLAND MEXICO

Private passenger and vehicle ferry services connecting southern Baja with the Pacific Coast of mainland Mexico allow anyone driving in the Mazatlán area to reach La Paz without a time-consuming trip all the way around the Sea of Cortez. Many drivers from the U.S. West Coast use Baja ferry services as an alternative way of reaching the mainland, since it allows them to avoid traffic-heavy Mexico 15 (or its expensive toll equivalent, Mexico 15-D) on the way to Mazatlán and points farther south. The ferries are comfortable and efficient in all classes. In heavy seas, you may want to consider taking motion sickness tablets before boarding.

The ferry services seem to change routes and schedules frequently, so check websites or visit offices at least a week before you plan to cross. At last check, **Baja Ferries** (Pichilinque Terminal, tel. 612/125-6324, U.S. tel. 915/833-3107, www.bajaferries.com, daily 8 A.M.–5 P.M.) was servicing two routes: A modern ship makes the crossing from La

Paz to Topolobampo/Los Mochis daily in six hours each way. This ferry has space for 1,000 passengers, including a choice of seats or cabins with two to four berths and attached bath. A seat on the ferry costs US$68. If you want a cabin berth, add US$76 to this fare. You can take a car or pickup truck along for US$100 (US$600 for an RV up to 10 meters). Baja Ferries has added a second route from La Paz to Mazatlán (Tues., Thurs., Sat., with return trips on Mon., Wed., Fri., US$77 one way) in a ship that holds 600 passengers in bus-style seats or cabins. Cars cost US$200 one way (US$1,200 for an RV up to 10 meters). All rates include tax. Pets are note allowed. Baja Ferries has a ticket office in downtown La Paz (Calle Isabel la Católica and Navarro, tel. 612/125-7443 or 800/122-1414). If you're starting from Topolobampo, the number is tel. 668/862-1003.

Transportación Marítima de California (TMC) (La Paz office tel. 800/744-5050, Mazatlán office tel. 800/700-0433, www.ferrytmc.com) also runs a car ferry between La Paz and Mazatlán (15.5 hrs). A car and driver cost US$237; RVs up to 10 meters cost US$600.

To book vehicle passage, you must hold a valid temporary vehicle import permit (see previous section). Show up three hours before the scheduled departure. You must drive the vehicle into the cargo hold yourself; this is usually the most unpleasant part of the journey, as most of the vehicles crossing are Mexican 18-wheeled trucks; the diesel fumes that accumulate in the hold while everyone gets in position (as directed by the ferry crew) can be intense. Soldiers or federal police are present on the piers at both ends of the journey, searching for arms and illegal drugs with the help of trained dogs.

Getting Around

If you've driven your own vehicle down to the Cape Region, you'll have a ready set of wheels for exploring all the Cape offers. If not, cars are easily rented in La Paz, San José del Cabo, and Cabo San Lucas, with limited options in Los Barriles and Todos Santos as well. You can also visit almost every town by public intercity bus.

BY BUS
Intercity Bus Service
Baja's reliable intercity bus transportation covers the peninsula from Tijuana to Cabo San Lucas. The longest direct ride available is the Tijuana–Cabo San Lucas route (about 30–32 hours), operated once daily by **Autotransportes Águila.** Many people break the bus trip up with an overnight stop in La Paz (25–28 hours from the Tijuana) and change to one of the many La Paz–Cabo San Lucas buses the following day.

Transportes Norte de Sonora (TNS) operates buses between Tijuana, Tecate, Mexicali, and points farther west, including destinations on the Mexican mainland as far away as Mexico City.

Special express buses with hostess service and air conditioning are used on long-distance trips. Shorter trips may or may not have air conditioning, but the buses are always tolerably comfortable. Schedules aren't always scrupulously kept, but even smaller bus terminals may feature public phones, restrooms, and cafés. The infamous "chicken buses" of Southern Mexico and Central America don't exist in Baja.

Fares are moderate. A Tijuana–La Paz ticket on a *primera,* or first-class, bus costs about US$134; second class is half that. The La Paz–Cabo San Lucas run is US$14–20, depending on whether you go via San José del Cabo or Todos Santos. Reservations aren't necessary—and in most cases aren't accepted—for bus travel. Buses usually depart several times daily, so you simply show up at the bus terminal around the time you want to leave. Buses ply the 35-kilometer (22-mi) stretch between

San José del Cabo and Cabo San Lucas frequently, all day long, for US$2 each way.

All the Spanish you need for riding a bus is *boleto* (ticket), the name of your destination (have a map handy just in case), and a reasonable command of spoken Spanish numbers for quoted fares (although the fare is always posted somewhere on the ticket office wall).

City Buses and *Colectivos*

La Paz has a comprehensive city bus system with fares of just a few pesos. City buses come in a variety of sizes and shapes, from 12-passenger vans *(colectivos)* to painted school buses and huge modern vessels with automatic doors. The destination or general route—typically a street name—is usually painted somewhere on the front of the bus or displayed on a marquee over the front windshield.

Printed bus schedules are either hard to come by or nonexistent. If you can't figure out which bus to take by comparing the destination sign with a map, just ask other waiting bus passengers or, if your Spanish isn't up to that, make inquiries at the tourist office.

BY TAXI

Regular-hire taxis congregate at hotels and designated taxi stands in La Paz, Todos Santos, San José del Cabo, and Cabo San Lucas. Sometimes fares are posted at the hotel or taxi stand, but often you must ask for a fare quote. If possible, try to find out the fare from hotel staff or a friendly resident before approaching a taxi driver—you'll feel more secure about not getting ripped off. If the quoted fare doesn't match what you've been told in advance, you can negotiate or try another driver. Fortunately, most Cape taxi drivers quote the correct fare immediately.

In smaller towns with no buses or route taxis, you may sometimes find a few regular hire taxis hanging out by the town plaza. They're generally used for reaching out-of-town destinations, since anyplace without a city bus system is small enough to wander around on foot. Although the locals pay a set fare based on distance, gringos are

sometimes quoted a much higher fare. Dig in and negotiate until it's reasonable. Even if you can afford the higher fare, you owe it to other foreign visitors not to encourage price gouging.

BY CAR

Before the 1973 completion of the Transpeninsular Highway (Mexico 1), only hardened off-road vehicles with equally sturdy drivers ever made it to the Cape. Nowadays, with paved Mexico 1 and paved Mexico 19 forming a loop around the Cape, the region is perfectly safe for ordinary folks driving ordinary passenger cars, as long as they employ a little ordinary common sense. For the adventurer, miles of unpaved roads remain that will take you as far from civilization as anyone would care to go. Such off-highway digressions are perfect for those who might agree with one of naturalist Joseph Krutch's famous Baja fiats:

> Baja California is a wonderful example of how much bad roads can do for a country. Bad roads act as filters. They separate those who are sufficiently appreciative of what lies beyond the blacktop to be willing to undergo mild inconvenience from that much larger number of travelers which is not willing. The rougher the road, the finer the filter.

Cape Roads

Two paved national highways grace the Cape Region: Mexico 1 (the Transpeninsular, from Tijuana to Cabo San Lucas) and Mexico 19 (between Cabo San Lucas and San Pedro, via Todos Santos). Both of these highways seem to be better maintained than their counterparts in central and northern Baja—this may be due to the fact that northern Baja roads are much more heavily trafficked, while central Baja may be too remote for regular upkeep by Mexican road crews.

The only paved state highway is BCS 286, the relatively short blacktop running between

CAPE DISTANCES

DISTANCE	DRIVING TIME
La Paz to San Pedro via Mex. 1 24 km (15 mi)	30 min
San Pedro to Todos Santos via Mex. 19 51 km (32 mi)	45 min
Todos Santos to Cabo San Lucas via Mex. 19 72 km (45 mi)	1 hr 30 min
La Paz to Cabo San Lucas via Mex. 1 and Mex. 19 147 km (92 mi)	2 hrs
La Paz to Los Barriles via Mex. 1 105 km (65 mi)	1 hr 45 min
Los Barriles to San José del Cabo via Mex. 1 81 km (50 mi)	1 hr 30 min
San José del Cabo to Cabo San Lucas via Mex. 1 34 km (21 mi)	30 min
La Paz to Cabo San Lucas via Mex. 1 221 km (137 mi)	2 hrs 30 min

La Paz and San Juan de los Planes. These three highways enable drivers to visit all of the Cape's major towns and resort areas, including La Paz, Los Barriles, Santiago, San José del Cabo, the Corridor (the 28-km/18-mi stretch between San José del Cabo and Cabo San Lucas), Cabo San Lucas, and Todos Santos.

An as-yet-unnamed paved road leads east of Mexico 1 at Las Cuevas to a point about six miles south of the East Cape community of La Ribera. Eventually, according to local authorities, this paved road will extend all the way down the East Cape to San José. Meanwhile, a decent unpaved, fair-weather road parallels this coastline.

The lower eastern escarpment of the Sierra de la Laguna is bisected by Mexico 1, which offers the only paved-road access to the mountains.

Off-Highway Travel

The Cape's unpaved roads vary considerably, from rutted jeep tracks to elevated, graded, gravel boulevards. The trouble with the graded unpaved roads is that they tend to degenerate quickly between gradings into washboard surfaces impossible to drive on at anything but very low speeds (8–16 kph/5–10 mph)—unless you want to risk crushed vertebrae and a dropped transmission.

The effect of these unpaved roads on you and your vehicle depends a lot on what you're driving. Some off-highway Baja navigators drive pickups with customized shocks and suspension that enable a driver to float over the worst washboard surfaces. Other drivers—like many of the local residents who can't afford heavy-duty, customized rigs—learn to drive slowly and appreciate the scenery.

The best unpaved roads are probably those that have evolved more or less naturally, with little or no grading. When the weather's dry, some of these roads ride better than the Transpeninsular. Of course, unpaved roads may sometimes start out nicely but get worse with each passing mile, to the point where even the most intrepid explorers are forced to turn around. At other times, a road will suddenly improve after a long stretch of cavernous potholes and caved-in sides. Weather is a big determining factor; even the best ungraded, unpaved roads are often impassable during or after a hard rain.

How do you know when to turn around? There's always an element of risk when driving down a dirt road for the first—or even the hundredth—time, but it helps to ask around before embarking on a road that doesn't see much traffic. A good road map can also assist with such decisions. The AAA map (see *Information and Services*) classifies unpaved roads into four categories: gravel, graded, dirt, and poor. The annotated ITM map uses a similar but more specific fourfold system: gravel, graded, unimproved dirt, and vehicular track.

Although neither of these maps is entirely up to date or 100 percent accurate, using one or both in conjunction with local input will greatly improve your decision-making. A topographical map could be of considerable value to a four-wheel-drive navigator as well, since sometimes it's the steep canyon grades that spell defeat.

Even with the best planning, there's always the possibility of getting stuck in muddy or sandy areas. Anyone engaging in serious off-highway driving should carry along a sturdy shovel for digging out mired wheels. Another handy trick for negotiating soft ground is to let the air out of your tires to a pressure of around 12–15 psi. This really works, but you should also carry along a 12-volt air compressor, one that will plug into the cigarette lighter, for pumping the tires back up after you're on firm ground again.

Driving Precautions

The first rule of Baja driving, no matter what kind of road you're on, is *never* take the road for granted. Any highway in Baja, including the Transpeninsular, can serve up 100 meters of smooth, seamless blacktop followed immediately by 100 meters of contiguous potholes or large patches of missing asphalt. A cow, horse, or burro could be right around the next curve, or a large dog can leap out in front of your vehicle just as you fasten your eyes on a turkey vulture drying its wings on top of a tall *cardón*.

The speed limits set by the Mexican government—80 kph (48 mph) on most highways—are reasonable for Baja's highway conditions. Obey them and you'll be much safer than if you try to keep the speedometer needle in the spot you're accustomed to. Wandering livestock, relatively narrow highway widths (6–8 m or 19–25 ft max), and inconsistent highway maintenance mean you simply can't drive at U.S./Canada speeds.

Many Cape roadways suffer from a conspicuous lack of shoulders. This doesn't mean you won't find any places to pull off—gravel turnouts appear fairly regularly, and in many areas

you can drive directly onto the roadside from the highway. It just means you can't count on a safe margin in an emergency. At the very least, an emergency turnout will raise a lot of rocks and dirt—small dangers in themselves—and in some spots, such as in the sierras around San Antonio, leaving the highway can launch you and your vehicle into a thousand-foot freefall. Guardrails are often flimsy or nonexistent.

Yet another reason not to take the road for granted is the high numbers of sometimes unmarked blind curves and blind hilltops frequently encountered. Never assume a clear path around a curve or over a hilltop—potential obstructions include an oblivious 18-wheeler or bus passing in the opposite direction, wandering livestock, rock slides, or road washouts. To be on the safe side, keep toward the outside edge of your own lane. Commercial truck drivers in Mexico roar down the road as if they're exempt from all speed limits, almost always flying at least 40 kph over the posted limit.

Rule number two is never drive the highways at night. Except along the Corridor section of Mexico 1 between San José and Cabo San Lucas, highways have no lighting. In addition, reflectors and even painted lines are absent from many highway sections; even if no other vehicles besides your own were on the road at night, you could easily overshoot an unexpected curve. Add to this the fact that many poorly maintained local vehicles have nonfunctioning headlights, taillights, or brake lights, and it should be obvious that trying to make highway miles after sundown is crazy. Some locals do it, but they're used to local conditions and know the roads relatively well. Still, a high proportion of car accidents in Baja—around 80 percent according to insurance companies—occur at night.

When you see road signs marked Vado or Zona de Vados, slow down. The word *vado* is most often translated as "dip," but in Baja it usually means more than a slight depression in the road—it's any place where the road intersects an arroyo, or dry stream wash. The danger lies not only in the sudden grade drop but in the potential for running into a recently accumulated body of water. Some *vados* feature measuring sticks marked in meters; when water is present, you'll know roughly how deep it is. If you come to a *vado* full of water with no measuring stick, get out of your vehicle and measure the depth yourself using a mesquite branch or other suitable object. *Vados* aren't always signposted, so stay alert—they appear even on relatively flat terrain.

In towns, pueblos, *ejidos,* or anywhere else people live in Mexico, you'll encounter *topes* (speed bumps). Often unpainted and unsigned, they can really sneak up on you. Some *topes* are real industrial-strength tire-poppers, so always take it slow when traversing them. You'll notice that Mexican drivers seem to have more respect for speed bumps than for stop signs or traffic lights.

Highway Signs

One of the pleasures of driving in the Cape Region is the relative absence of signs cluttering the roadside. Billboards, in fact, are virtually nonexistent. The Mexican government does have a system of highway signs, however, based on common international sign conventions followed throughout most of the world; these can be very helpful as long as you know what they mean. Most display self-explanatory symbols (e.g., a silhouette of a man holding a shovel means "men working").

Cautionary sign captions are especially helpful, including Curva Peligrosa (Dangerous Curve), Despacio (Slow), and Zona de Vados (Dip Zone). Other common highway signs include: Desviación (Detour), No Tire Basura (Don't Throw Trash), Conserve Su Derecha (Keep to the Right), Conceda Cambio de Luces (Dim Your Lights), No Rebase (No Passing), and No Hay Paso (Road Closed).

Along the highways as well as on many secondary roads, you can measure driving progress with the assistance of regularly spaced kilometer markers, usually black lettering on a reflective white background.

If you're having tire trouble, look for homemade signs reading *Llantera,* which indicate tire repair shops.

Traffic Offenses

Although Mexican traffic police don't go out of their way to persecute foreign drivers, it may seem that way when you're the foreigner who's stopped. The more cautiously you drive, the less likely you'll inadvertently transgress local traffic codes. This would seem like obvious advice, but for some reason many visiting motorists in Baja drive as if they think there are no traffic laws in Mexico.

If you're stopped by a *tránsito* (traffic cop), the first rule is to behave in a patient, civil manner. The officer might then let you off with just a warning. If the officer decides to make a case of it, you'll be asked to proceed to the nearest police post or station, where a fine will be assessed and collected. This is a perfectly legal request. But if the cop suggests or even hints at being paid on the spot, you're being hit up for *la mordida,* the minor bribe.

In Baja, requests for *la mordida* from foreigners—for traffic offenses, at least—have become increasingly rare, and the government is making admirable progress toward stamping out the practice altogether. If confronted with such a situation, you have two choices. Mexico's Attorney General for the Protection of Tourists recommends you insist on going to the nearest station to pay the fine, and that as you pay you request a receipt. Such a request may result in all charges being dropped. If you don't feel like taking the time for a trip to the station, you can choose to negotiate the "fine" on the spot. Doing so, however, won't contribute to the shrinking of the *mordida* phenomenon.

Speeding citations are rare, but when they are issued, the fine is usually equivalent to one day's Mexican minimum wage per each kilometer per hour above the speed limit you were estimated to be driving. Aside from speeding on Mexico 1-D, driving the wrong direction on one-way streets and running stop signs are the two most common traffic violations among foreign drivers in Baja. Some intersections may display no vertical stop (Alto) signs at all, only broad stripes painted on the pavement indicating where vehicles are supposed to stop. The best practice is to assume you're supposed to stop at every single intersection in the city, which is pretty close to the truth. A sign reading Cuatro Altos means the intersection is a four-way stop.

Mexican Auto Insurance

It's extremely important to carry a Mexican liability insurance policy on your vehicle while driving in Baja. In case of an accident, such a policy could keep you from going to jail. (For details, see *Mexican Auto Insurance* earlier in this chapter.)

Fuel

The only automotive fuel commercially available in Mexico is sold at government-owned Pemex stations. Unlike in many parts of Mexico, Pemex stations are fairly plentiful in the Cape Region, though it's always best to top off your tank whenever it reaches the half-empty mark and there's a Pemex station at hand.

Three kinds of fuel are available: an unleaded fuel with an octane rating of 87 (Magna Sin); a high-test unleaded rated at 89 (Premium); and diesel. All three are priced by Pemex according to standard rates and shouldn't vary from station to station. Since Pemex is government-owned, you don't see the week-to-week price fluctuations common in countries where oil companies are privately owned and rates are influenced by small changes in international oil prices. All are roughly equivalent in price to their U.S. or Canadian counterparts. The price should always be marked in pesos on the pump. Nearly all Pemex pumps in Baja now give readouts calibrated for the new peso, and they zero out automatically when the fuel nozzle is lifted from the pump.

Most Pemex stations are full-serve (though Los Cabos now has the first self-serve station on the peninsula), and a visit begins with two questions: How much, and what type of gas do you want? *"Lleno con premio/magna, por favor"* is the usual answer. Its customary to leave a small tip (up to US$1) for window washing or other extra services.

An early 2007 National Public Radio segment in the United States reported that Mexican authorities had determined that 9 out of 10 gas stations in the country were rigging their pumps, costing drivers some US$1 billion per year. Pay attention at the pump, but don't assume every attendant intends to rip you off.

Check to make sure the pump is zeroed before the attendant starts pumping your gasoline/diesel. If the nozzle hasn't been returned to the pump since the last sale, you could find your fuel total added to the previous customer's. This seems to be less of a problem now than in previous years; stations in the border towns are still the places most likely to overcharge. It helps to get out of your vehicle to keep an eye on the pumping procedures. If you're confused by the pump readout, currency conversion, or price per liter, carry a hand-held calculator to make sure it all adds up; a calculator held in clear view deters most potential grifters.

Another scam for gas overcharging at modern, auto-zeroing pumps is to use a gas hose that comes from an open pump on the opposite side, so you can't see whether the readout starts at zero.

Fuel must be paid for in cash, and you should count your change, especially when paying with large, 500-peso bills. On the mainland, a few stations now take Mexican bank cards such as Carnet. It's probably only a matter of time before Carnet acceptance at Pemex stations spreads to other cities across the nation, with perhaps Visa and MasterCard close behind. For the moment, however, be sure to carry plenty of pesos for fuel purchases. Mexican currency is the overwhelming preference of most Pemex stations; some stations near the U.S.–Mexico border take U.S. dollars, but the rate is always rounded down.

Rumors about the quality of Pemex fuels sometimes suggest an extra fuel filter or additive is necessary. This may have been the case 15 or more years ago, but nowadays Pemex fuel seems to perform well in all types of vehicles.

The main problem with Pemex fuel remains its availability, although in recent years the situation has improved considerably. Gas is

WHERE TO RENT A CAR IN BAJA

More than a dozen international brands and independent agencies rent vehicles for self-guided exploration of the Baja Peninsula. The major chains are listed below.

AGENCY	CONTACT	LOCATIONS
Advantage Rent a Car	tel. 624/143-0466	Cabo San Lucas (Ave. Lázaro Cardénas)
	www.arac.com	
Alamo	tel. 800/849-8001	San José del Sabo (Blvd. Castro)
	reservaciones@ alamorentacar.com.mx	Los Cabos Intl Airport
	www.alamorentacar.com	Cabo San Lucas (Ave. Lázaro Cardénas)
		La Paz (Obregón)
Avis	tel. 624/146-0201	Los Cabos Intl Airport (SJD)
	U.S. tel. 800/331-2112	Cabo San Lucas Airport
	www.avis.com	Cabo San Lucas (Ave. Lázaro Cardénas)
		Pueblo Bonito Sunset Beach (Los Cabos)
		Grand Baja Resort (Los Cabos)
		Hotel Pueblo Bonito Rose (Los Cabos)
		Pueblo Bonito Pacifica (Los Cabos)
		La Paz Intl Airport (LAP)
		La Paz (Obregón)
Budget	tel. 624/146-5333	La Paz Intl Airport (LAP)
	U.S. tel. 800/527-0700	Los Cabos Intl Airport
	www.budget.com	Marquis Hotel (Los Cabos)
	loscabos@budgetbaja.com	Todos Santos (Márquez de León 4)
Dollar Rent A Car	tel. 624/142-0100	La Paz Intl Airport (LAP)
	U.S. tel. 866/434-2226	La Paz (Obregón)
	www.dollar.com	Los Arcos Hotel (La Paz)
	www.dollarloscabos.com	Los Cabos Intl Airport (SJD)
		Hote Meliá Cabo Real (Los Cabos)
		Hotel Presidente (Los Cabos)
		San José del Cabo (Blvd. Castro)
		Cabo San Lucas (Blvd. Marina)
		Club Cascadas (Los Cabos)

Europcar	tel. 612/124-7011	La Paz Intl Airport
	U.S. tel. 877/940-6900	La Paz (Obregón)
	www.europcar.com	Los Cabos Intl Airport
Hertz	tel. 624/146-1803	Cabo San Lucas (Ave. Lázaro Cardénas 6)
	U.S. tel. 800/654-3001	La Paz Intl Airport (LAP)
	www.hertz.com	La Paz (Obregón 2130-D)
		Marina Costa Baja (Km 61 Carr. A Pichilingue)
		Los Cabos Intl Airport
		Westin Resort Los Cabos
National	tel. 624/146-5021	Cabo San Lucas (Ave. Lázaro Cardénas)
	U.S. tel. 800/227-7368	Hotel Casa del Mar (Los Cabos)
	www.nationalcar.com	Riu Palace (Los Cabos)
		Hilton Los Cabos
		Posada Real Los Cabos
		One&Only Palmilla (Los Cabos)
		Sheraton Hacienda del Mar (Los Cabos)
		Los Cabos Intl Airport
		La Paz Intl Airport
		La Paz (Obregón)
		Los Barriles (20 de Noviembre)
Payless Car Rental	tel. 624/146-5290	Cabo San Lucas (Camino Viejo a San José)
	www.paylesscarrental.com	Los Cabos Intl Airport (SJD)
	sanJosedelcabomexico@ paylesscarrental.net	San José del Cabo (Paseo San José)
Thrifty Car Rental	tel. 624/146-5030 or 800/021-2277	Cabo San Lucas (Blvd. Marina)
		La Paz Intl Airport
	www.thrifty.com	Westin Los Cabos
	gerencia.loscabos@ thrifty.com.mx	Crown Plaza Hotel (Los Cabos)
		Dreams Los Cabos
		San José del Cabo (Blvd. San José 20000A)

delivered to Baja from the mainland via the ferry service, so when the seas are rough, the gas doesn't always arrive on time. To notify customers, the hose is usually draped over the top of a pump when it's empty.

Liquefied petroleum gas (LPG) is available in Baja. The price per liter is about the same as for Magna Sin when bought for vehicular use. LPG sold for heating and cooking is subsidized and costs less than in the United States or Canada. The difficulty is finding it. Look for signs reading Butano.

Oil

Motor oil is widely available at *tiendas* and Pemex stations throughout the Cape. If your vehicle takes anything lower (thinner) than 30-weight, however, you'd better bring along your own; most places stock only 30- or 40-weight oil.

Parts and Repairs

Good auto shops and mechanics are available in La Paz, San José, and Cabo San Lucas. Elsewhere, if you have a breakdown, it's either do it yourself or rely on the mercy of passing drivers. In areas where you can find a mechanic, the following makes can usually be serviced: Chevrolet, Dodge, Ford, Nissan, Toyota, and Volkswagen. For anything else, you should carry spare filters, plugs, points, hoses, belts, and gaskets—even for the shortest of trips.

Green Angels (Roadside Assistance)

The Secretaría de Turismo operates a fleet of green trucks called **Ángeles Verdes** (Green Angels) that patrol Baja's highways and offer professional assistance to anyone with automotive problems. Each truck carries a first-aid kit, a shortwave radio, gasoline, and a variety of common auto parts. They're usually staffed by two uniformed employees, one of whom may speak some English. The drivers will perform minor repairs for the cost of the parts and can provide towing for distances up to 24 kilometers (15 mi). If they can't remedy the problem or tow your vehicle to a nearby me-

chanic, they'll give you a lift or arrange for other assistance.

The trucks supposedly patrol assigned highway sections at least twice a day; the author's experience is that the Green Angels are much more commonly seen in south-central Baja, where they're most needed because of the longer distances between towns.

Trailers and RVs

The Cape is a popular destination for RVers. Not only are there plenty of RV parks with services, but you can pull off the road and camp just about anywhere outside the cities, with few restrictions. The restrictions that do exist are largely physical; numerous places simply can't accommodate a wide trailer or motor home because of narrow roadways, steep grades, or sharp curves. Even the Transpeninsular is tight in some places. You shouldn't even attempt a Baja trip in any rig wider than three meters (9 ft).

The type of rig most suited to Baja travel is probably a well-equipped camper or van. With a bed, two 20-liter (five-gallon) water containers, a small propane stove and refrigerator, and a portable toilet, you can travel just as independently as someone driving a 12-meter (40-ft) motor home. Add a deep-cycle RV battery under the hood and you can run a variety of electrical appliances for at least a week without turning over your engine. For extra power, mount a solar panel on top of the cab or camper.

More complete information on managing the entire Transpeninsular journey by RV is available in *Moon Baja*.

Car Rental

Reserve a rental car for pickup at the Los Cabos and La Paz airports, as well as at downtown locations in La Paz, San José del Cabo, and Cabo San Lucas. Limited inventory is also available at a few places in Los Barriles, Loreto, and Todos Santos. Most of the international chains offer economy/compact cars for around US$30–45/day with unlimited miles or US$60–75 for an SUV or jeep. Rates in La Paz are slightly lower than in Los Cabos. Mexican liability insurance costs an additional US$25/day with these companies, and deductibles are often very high (US$1,000 and up). It pays to shop around. Book ahead online, or comparison shop when you arrive.

Online discount car rental services, such as Hotwire (www.hotwire.com), offer substantially lower rates than the major brands by selling excess inventory for their partner companies. Rentals through Hotwire come from names like Avis, Hertz, or Budget, but you won't know which company until you agree to purchase the rental. The other difference is that you prepay for the rental at the time of reservation, so you won't be able to change your mind once you get to Baja.

Independent agencies are another option, sometimes at lower cost but often with per-kilometer charges in addition to the daily rate.

Insuring Your Rental Car

The Mexican proof of financial responsibility law (see *Mexican Auto Insurance*) applies to drivers of rental cars in Mexico, except in this case, you don't get to choose a specific policy—rather, you agree to pay an additional US$25–40 per day for whatever coverage the rental car company provides. The exact amount depends on the size of the rental car. Terms and coverage limits vary among the various agencies, and they don't make it easy to see the fine print before you arrive at the counter. Deductibles at Thrifty were reportedly as high as US$2,500 at last check. To learn about the policy before you agree to rent the car, call the local office for the company you are considering. Read the contract carefully at the rental car counter, and be sure you understand the terms. If you drive farther than the contract permits, fail to report an accident within the time specified, or violate other clauses, your coverage may be nullified.

BY MOTORCYCLE

The entire Cape Region is excellent motorcycle country. The winding sierra roads are especially challenging, and since traffic is generally light you can really let it rip. Another advantage of motorcycle travel is that if your bike gets mired in soft ground, you can almost always extricate it without assistance.

As with automotive travel in Baja, predeparture planning is important. You should be able to carry enough gear in two panniers and a backpack (tied down on the rear) for a trip all the way down the peninsula.

Good motorcycle mechanics are hard to find in the Cape Region—you should be entirely self-reliant to make this trip safely and successfully. Besides the usual camping and first-aid gear, bikers should carry all tools needed for routine maintenance, spare brake shoes, a tire repair kit, spare levers, an extra battery, a clutch cable, spare light bulbs, a four-liter reserve gas can, and a spare helmet visor.

The same driving precautions that apply to four-wheel driving should be followed by bikers as well. Special care should be taken when negotiating blind curves because buses and trucks in Mexico aren't used to seeing motorcycles on the highway. As with bicycle touring, motorcyclists may find that an 11 A.M.–3 P.M. siesta is necessary to avoid the sun's worst rays.

BY BICYCLE

Among cyclists, Baja California Sur's Cape Region is the most popular area in all of Mexico. Traffic is relatively light, the scenery is striking, and cyclists can pull over and camp just about anywhere.

If you plan to stay on paved highways, a touring bike is the best choice, as it's lighter and faster than a mountain bike. On the other hand, the Cape offers so many great off-highway rides—such as the lower sierra and the Camino Rural Costero along the East Cape—that anyone who has the time and equipment should consider a mountain bike.

Many interesting trail rides lie within the 386-kilometer (240-mi) loop that circles the Cape from La Paz to Cabo San Lucas via the Sierra de la Laguna and back via Todos Santos and the west coastal plains. The lower eastern escarpment of the sierra in particular—west of Santiago and Miraflores—is fat-tire heaven, offering rides through tropical-arid thorn forests and, if you can handle steep grades and bike portage, subalpine meadows. The other side of the mountains, behind Pescadero on the West Cape, can also be rewarding. The unpaved road network along the coast between San José del Cabo and La Paz will astound even the most jaded dirt bikers as it takes them past deserted white-sand coves with coral reefs, over jagged desert peaks, and then down into lush San Juan de los Planes.

Because the sun can be particularly strong when you're on paved surfaces, which both reflect and radiate heat, you may find an 11 A.M.–3 P.M. siesta necessary no matter what time of year you ride. Don't forget to bring sunglasses and plenty of high-SPF sunscreen.

Equipment and Repairs

If you plan to camp along the way, you'll need the usual camping and first-aid gear, selected to fit your panniers. Camping is often your only choice on long coastal trips, because not all cyclists can make the mileage from hotel to hotel. On the other hand, if you're doing only the Cape loop you can easily bike from hotel to hotel.

Helmets are particularly important; a head injury is even more serious when you're in the middle of nowhere. A helmet also keeps direct sun off the top of your skull. A rearview mirror is a must for keeping an eye on motorists coming from behind on narrow roads. A locking cable is preferable to a clunky U-lock for long-distance trips because it weighs less. The only other security you might need is a removable handlebar bag for carrying your camera and valuables; you can take the bag with you when stopping at restaurants or *tiendas* and fill it with snacks for eating on the fly.

Water is the uppermost consideration on overnight trips. No matter what the time of year, cyclists should carry four one-liter bottles of water per day. The one-liter bottles used for cycling are more puncture-resistant than water containers designed for camping. Punctures are always a concern in Baja because of all the trees and plants bearing spines.

The puncture threat means you should out-

fit your bike with heavy-duty tires and tubes. Bring along two or three spare tubes, one spare tire, a tire gauge, and a complete tire repair kit. You should also carry duct tape and moleskin—or commercial plastic booting—to use as booting material against sidewall cuts caused by sharp rocks or cacti.

Check the nuts and bolts on your rack daily and retighten as necessary. Applying Locktite should lessen the need for retightening—carry a small supply along with extra nuts and bolts. Baling wire can be used for improvised repairs; carry two or three meters along with wire cutters.

Bike shops can be found in La Paz and Cabo San Lucas. Although the Mexicans who run these shops can sometimes perform miraculous repairs using nothing resembling a bike's original parts, it's safer to come prepared with spares, especially for parts that aren't easily jury-rigged. At a minimum, carry a spare freewheel, a rear derailleur, and all the wrenches and screwdrivers necessary to work on your bike. If in addition you bring along several extra spokes, cables, and a spare chain, you'll be ready for just about any repair scenario.

Bicycle Transportation

All airlines that fly to the Cape Region allow you to check bikes as luggage as long as they're boxed. Bus lines will transport bikes of paying passengers in bus luggage compartments for no additional cost, but again, bikes should be boxed. For return trips from Baja, you should be able to pick up a box from bicycle shops in La Paz or Cabo San Lucas or build your own from discarded cardboard boxes.

Guided Bicycle Trips and Equipment Rentals

If you're unsure of your off-road cycling skills, you might want to tackle the Cape with an experienced cycle guide. Several tour operators run cycling programs in Baja. In La Paz, Mexican-owned **Katún** (tel. 612/348-7758, www.katuntours.com) runs guided tours of the Sierra de la Laguna (US$1,980/two weeks, US$1,299/one week, US$50–75/day). Katún also rents 2006 Giant Yukon bikes with front suspension for US$10 an hour, US$15 for four hours, or US$20 per day.

In Los Cabos, **NaturAdventure** (tel. 624/105-2050, www.naturadventure.com) leads half-day and full-day trail rides of varying levels around the Los Cabos area on Gary

Fisher, Trek, and Specialized bikes. Destinations include Punta Gorda (US$65 pp), Cabo Pulmo (US$95 pp), and the Sierra de la Laguna (US$90 pp, US$75 half-day). Previous clients (only) can rent bikes for a self-guided tour (US$35–55 per day). MTB shoes and Shimano pedals area also available.

Visas and Officialdom

ENTRY REGULATIONS
Passports and Tourist Permits

Under the Western Hemisphere Travel Initiative, as of January 2007, all anyone traveling by air between the United States, Canada, Mexico, Central and South America, the Caribbean, and Bermuda is required to present a valid passport. The same applies to anyone traveling by land or sea as of January 2008.

Citizens of the United States or Canada (or of 42 other designated countries in Europe and Latin America, plus Singapore) visiting Mexico solely for tourism are not required to obtain a visa. Instead, they must carry validated "tourist cards" (*formas migratorias turistas,* or FMTs), which aren't actually cards but slips of paper. These are available free at any Mexican consulate or Mexican tourist office, from many travel agencies, on flights to Mexico, or at the border. The tourist card is valid for stays of up to 180 days and must be used within 90 days of issue. Your card becomes invalid once you exit the country—you're supposed to surrender it at the border—even if your 180 days hasn't expired. If you'll be entering and leaving Mexico more than once during your trip, you should request a multiple-entry tourist card, available from Mexican consulates only.

To obtain the FMT, you need proof of citizenship—a birth certificate (or certified copy), voter's registration card, certificate of naturalization, or passport. A driver's license doesn't qualify.

Once you cross the border (or land at an airport on an international flight), your tourist card must be **validated** by a Mexican im-

migration officer. You can arrange this at any *migración* office in Baja (many *municipio* seats have them), but it's accomplished most conveniently at the border crossing itself. *Note:* FMTs are occasionally inspected at the army checkpoint at the north end of Guerrero Negro, so you'd better have your papers in order before entering Baja California Sur.

At airports, you pass through immigration, where an officer stamps your paperwork with the date of entry and the number of days you're permitted to stay in Mexico.

Make sure you receive enough days to cover your visit. Some immigration officers, especially those at airports near tourist resorts, may fill in your FMT for 30 days, figuring that's sufficient for most holidays. If you want more than 30 days, it's best to mention it to the officer in advance.

In mid-1999, the Mexican government began collecting a fee (currently around US$22) from all tourists entering the country. If you fly in, this **tourist fee** is tacked on to your airfare. If you arrive by land or sea, the fee has been waived for visits of less than 72 hours. For longer stays, you can pay this fee at any bank in Mexico. The bank will issue a receipt, which you must show when you leave the country. In normal practice—at least so far—it's rare that anyone checks to see that you've paid the tourist fee. This laxity may change when Mexican authorities realize that very few road travelers bother to pay it. Or perhaps they'll be satisfied that everyone who flies into Mexico pays the fee.

Before 1991, Mexican regulations required children under the age of 18 crossing the border without one or both parents to carry a notarized letter granting permission from the absent parent, or both parents if both were absent. This regulation is no longer in effect, but we've heard that some Mexican border officers, as well as airline check-in crews, are still asking for the letter, apparently unaware the regulation has been rescinded. Hence, unaccompanied minors or minors traveling with only one parent should be prepared for all situations with notarized letters. In cases of divorce, separation, or death, the minor should carry notarized papers documenting the situation.

In reality, minors with tourist cards are rarely asked for these documents. Children under 15 may be included on their parents' tourist card, but this means that neither the child nor the parents can legally exit Mexico without the other.

Tourist Visas

Tourists from countries other than the 45 countries for which no visa is necessary must obtain tourist visas before arriving in Mexico. You must apply for your visa in person at a Mexican consulate; you usually can obtain a tourist visa within two weeks of filing an application. The Mexican Consulate General in San Diego can usually issue tourist visas on the day of application. Requirements include a valid passport, valid U.S. visa for multiple entries, form I-94, proof of economic solvency (such as an international credit card), a round-trip air ticket to Mexico, and a visa fee of around US$40.

Foreign visitors who are legal permanent residents of the United States do not need visas to visit Mexico for tourism. A free tourist card can be obtained by presenting your passport and U.S. residence card to any travel agency or at the airport or border crossing.

Business Travel

Citizens of Mexico's NAFTA (North American Free Trade Agreement) partners, the United States and Canada, are not required to obtain a visa to visit Mexico for business purposes. Instead, you receive a free NAFTA business permit (*forma migratoria nafta,* or FMN) similar to a tourist card at the point of entry (border crossing or airport); it's valid for 30 days. At the port of entry you must present proof of nationality (valid passport or original birth certificate plus a photo identification or voter's registration card) and proof that you are traveling for "international business activities," usually interpreted to mean a letter from the company you represent, even if it's your own enterprise.

Those who arrive with the FMN and wish to stay longer than the authorized period of 30 days must replace their FMN with an FM-3 form at an immigration office in Mexico. The FM-3 is valid for up to one year, for multiple entries, and may be extended. Note that the FMN is not valid for people who will be earning a salary during their stay in Mexico.

Citizens of other countries visiting for business purposes must obtain an FM-3 visa endorsed for business travel, which is valid for one year.

Overstays

If you overstay your visa and are caught, the usual penalty is a fine of around US$45 for overstays up to a month. After that the penalties become more severe. It's rare that a Mexican border official asks to see your FMT or visa when you're leaving the country. Your main risk comes if you get into trouble with the police somewhere in Mexico and they ask to see your immigration documents. Having expired papers only complicates your situation, so the best policy is to stay up to date in spite of the apparent laxity of enforcement.

Pets

Dogs and cats may be brought into Mexico if each is accompanied by a **vaccination certificate** that proves the animal has been vaccinated or treated for rabies, hepatitis, pip, and leptospirosis. You'll also need a **health certificate** issued no more than 72 hours before entry and signed by a registered veterinarian.

Since 1992, the requirement that the health certificate be stamped with a visa at a port of entry or at a Mexican consulate has been repealed. The certificate is still necessary; the visa isn't.

Upon recrossing the border into the United States, the U.S. Customs Service will ask to see the vaccination certificate.

Visitante Rentista and Inmigrante Rentista Visas

FM-3 visas may be issued to foreigners who choose to live in Mexico on a "permanent income" basis. This most often applies to foreigners who decide to retire in Mexico, though it is also used by artists, writers, and other self-employed foreign residents. With this visa, you're allowed to import one motor vehicle as well as your household belongings into Mexico tax-free.

The basic requirements for this visa are that applicants must forgo any kind of employment while living in Mexico and must show proof (bank statements) that they have a regular source of foreign-earned income amounting to at least US$1,000 per month (plus half that for each dependent over the age of 15, e.g., US$1,500 for a couple). A pile of paperwork, including a "letter of good conduct" from the applicant's local police department, must accompany the initial application, along with an immigration tax payment and various application fees totaling about US$211.

The visa must be renewed annually, but the renewal can be accomplished at any immigration office in Mexico. After five years in Mexico, you have to start over or move up to the FM-2 or *inmigrante rentista* visa, which has higher income requirements and signifies an intent to stay longer. After five years on an FM-2, an *inmigrante rentista* is eligible to apply for *inmigrado* status, which confers all the rights of citizenship (including employment in Mexico), save the rights to vote and hold public office.

Many foreigners who have retired in Mexico manage to do so on the regular 180-day tourist visa; every six months they dash across the border and return with a new tourist card (issued at the border) on the same day. This method bypasses all the red tape and income requirements of the retirement visa. If you own a home in Baja, however, some local immigration officials may interpret the law to mean that you must have an FM-2 or FM-3 visa—not an FMT or tourist visa—to be able to stay in that home for any period of time whatsoever. Although it's clear from a straight reading that Mexico's immigration laws do not require any special visas for home ownership (just as you don't need a particular visa to own property in the United States or Canada), each immigration district behaves like an individual fiefdom at the mercy of the local immigration chief.

Monthly income requirements for both *rentista* visas are keyed to the Mexican daily minimum wage (400 times minimum wage for the FM-2, 250 times for the FM-3), hence figures may vary according to the current dollar–peso exchange rate.

Reentering the United States

Overseas visitors need a passport and visa to enter the United States. Except for diplomats, students, or refugees, this means a nonimmigrant visitor's visa, which must be obtained in advance at a U.S. consulate or embassy abroad. Residents of Western European and Commonwealth countries are usually issued these readily; residents of other countries may have to provide the consulate with proof of "sufficient personal funds" before the visa is issued.

Upon a visitor's arrival in the United States, an immigration inspector decides how long the visa will be valid—the maximum for a temporary visitor's visa (B-1 or B-2) is six months. If you visit Mexico from California (or from anywhere else in the United States) for stays of 30 days or less, you can reenter the United States with the same visa, provided the visa is still valid, by presenting your stamped arrival/departure card (INS form I-94) and passport to a U.S. immigration inspector. If your U.S. visa has expired, you can still enter the country for a stay of 29 days or less on a transit visa—issued at the border—but you may be required to show proof of onward travel, such as an air ticket or ship travel voucher.

BORDER CROSSINGS

Baja California's U.S.–Mexico border has five official border crossings: Tijuana (24 hrs),

Otay Mesa (24 hrs), Tecate (5 A.M.–11 P.M.), Calexico/Mexicali (24 hrs), and Los Algodones (6 A.M.–10 P.M.). Tijuana is the largest and also the most heavily used, connecting Baja with U.S. Interstate 5, which extends all the way up the U.S. west coast to the Canadian border.

At any of the border crossings, you'll find the shortest waits (15–30 minutes at Tijuana) are 10 A.M.–3:30 P.M. or after 7 or 8 P.M. on weekdays. Weekends are the worst days in either direction, except late at night or before dawn, when traffic is light. If you're on your way out of Baja and find yourself near the border during rush hours, it might be best to find a restaurant and wait it out. A Saturday or Sunday morning wait at the Tijuana crossing can be as long as two hours in either direction; it's always longer going north.

If you're on foot, crossing is usually a breeze. Public and chartered buses also get through more quickly, using special traffic lanes.

Mexican Consulate in San Diego

San Diego's Mexican Consulate General (1549 India St., San Diego, CA 92101, tel. U.S. tel. 619/231-8414, www.consulmexsd.org, Mon.–Fri. 8 A.M.–1:30 P.M.) is relatively close to the Tijuana border crossing, about 30–45 minutes by car. The staff can assist with visas, immigration problems, special-import permits, and questions concerning Mexican customs regulations.

CUSTOMS
Entering Mexico

Officially, tourists are supposed to bring only those items into Mexico that will be of use during their trip. This means you can bring in practically anything as long as it doesn't appear in large enough quantities to qualify for resale. Firearms and ammunition, as well as boats, require special permits (see *Sports and Recreation*).

Technically speaking, you're allowed to import one camera and one video camera, up to 12 rolls of unused film or blank videocassettes for each, and used or developed film. Anything more is supposed to require

permission from a Mexican consulate. In everyday practice, however, Mexican customs officials rarely blink at more film or an extra camera or two. Professional photographers and others who would like to bring more cameras and film into Mexico can apply for dispensation through a Mexican consulate abroad. Regarding audio equipment, you're limited to one CD player and one audiocassette player (or combo), five laser discs, five DVDs, and up to 20 CDs or recording cassettes. Other per-person limitations include one typewriter, a cellular phone and a pager, a new or used laptop computer, a musical instrument, two used personal sports gear items, one tent and accompanying camping gear, one set of fishing gear, a pair of skis, a pair of binoculars, two tennis rackets, five "toys," and one sailboard.

Other limits include three liters of liquor, beer, or wine and two cartons (20 packs) of cigarettes or 25 cigars or 200 grams of tobacco.

Other than the above, you're permitted to bring in no more than US$300 worth of other articles. You will be subject to duty on personal possessions worth more than US$300, to a maximum of US$1,000 (except for new computer equipment, which is exempt up to US$4,000).

Foreign-registered motor vehicles—cars, trucks, RVs, motorcycles, etc.—do not require permits for travel anywhere on the Baja California peninsula. However, if you plan to take a vehicle registered outside Mexico onto one of the vehicle ferries that sail from Baja to the mainland, or if you plan to drive farther east than San Luis Río Colorado in Sonora, you must obtain an auto permit. These are available from any Mexican consulate abroad, or at the border, or from the ferry office in La Paz.

If you're bringing a vehicle across the border, you need Mexican auto insurance (see the *Getting There* and *Getting Around* sections).

Returning to the United States

Visitors returning to the United States from Mexico may have their luggage inspected by U.S. Customs officials. The hassle can be minimized by giving brief, straight answers to their questions (e.g., "How long have you been in Mexico?" "Do you have anything to declare?") and by cooperating with their requests to open your luggage, vehicle storage compartments, and anything else they want opened. Sometimes the officers use dogs to sniff luggage and/or vehicles for contraband and illegal aliens.

Nearly 3,000 items—including all handicrafts—made in Mexico are exempt from any U.S. Customs duties. Adults over 21 are allowed one liter (33.8 fluid ounces) of alcoholic beverages and 200 cigarettes (or 100 cigars) per person. Note that Cuban cigars may not be imported into the United States and will be confiscated at the border if discovered. Since an estimated 9 out of 10 cigars sold as Cubans in Mexico are reportedly fake, it's not worth the hassle, especially since a good hand-rolled cigar from Veracruz can challenge most Cubans. All other purchases or gifts up to a total value of US$400 within any 31-day period can be brought into the United States duty-free.

The following **fruits and vegetables** cannot be brought into the United States from Mexico: oranges, grapefruits, mangoes, avocados (unless the pit is removed), and potatoes (including yams and sweet potatoes). All other fruits are permitted (including bananas, dates, pineapples, cactus fruits, grapes, and berries of all types).

Other prohibited plant materials are straw (including packing materials and items stuffed with straw), hay, unprocessed cotton, sugarcane, and any plants in soil (this includes houseplants).

Animals and animal products that cannot be imported include wild and domesticated birds (including poultry, unless cooked), pork or pork products (including sausage, ham, and other cured pork), and eggs. Beef, mutton, venison, and other meats are permitted at up to 23 kilograms (50 lbs) per person.

Customs regulations can change at any time, so if you want to verify the regulations on a purchase before risking duties or confiscation at the border, check with a U.S. consulate in Baja before crossing or visit www.cbp.gov.

Returning to Canada

Duty-frees include 200 cigarettes (or 50 cigars or 200 grams of tobacco) and one bottle (1.1 liters) of booze or wine, 24 cans or bottles (355 ml) of beer or ale, and gifts to the value of C$60 per gift (other than alcohol or tobacco). Exemptions run from C$50 to C$750 depending on how long you've been outside Canada. To reach the maximum exemption of C$750 you must be gone at least one week. Because Canada is also signatory to NAFTA, customs legalities will change over the next decade.

LEGAL MATTERS

All foreign visitors in Mexico are subject to Mexican legal codes, which are based on Roman and Napoleonic law updated with U.S. constitutional theory and civil law. The most distinctive features of the Mexican judiciary system, compared to Anglo-American systems, are that the system doesn't provide for trials by jury (the judge decides) nor writs of habeas corpus (though you must be charged within 72 hours of incarceration or else released). Furthermore, bail is rarely granted to an arrested foreigner—for many offenses, not even Mexican nationals are allowed bail. Hence, once arrested and jailed for a serious offense, it can be difficult to arrange release. The lesson here is: Don't get involved in matters that might result in your arrest. This primarily means anything having to do with drugs or guns.

The oft-repeated saw that in Mexico an arrested person is considered guilty until proven innocent is no more true south of the border than north. As in Canada, the United States, or western Europe, an arrested person is considered a criminal *suspect* until the courts confirm or deny guilt. You have the right to notify your consulate if detained.

Mexican federal police *(federales* and *judiciales),* as well as the Mexican army, mostly under pressure from the United States, occasionally set up roadblocks to conduct searches for drugs and for arms. Such roadblocks used to be rare in Baja but have recently increased in number. On recent Transpeninsular drives we've been stopped at six or seven different military checkpoints *(puestos de control)* between Tijuana and Cabo San Lucas. In each case, the soldiers were courteous and the vehicle searches were brief and cursory. If your vehicle is stopped at a *puesto de control,* be as cooperative as possible. If there are any irregularities or if you object to the way in which the procedure is carried out, make note of the incident, including whatever badge numbers, names, or license numbers you can obtain discreetly, and later file a report with the Mexican Attorney General for Tourist Protection. So far I've not heard of any problems encountered by foreign visitors, although a couple of Americans were arrested for carrying unregistered firearms—a serious federal offense in Mexico—in 1996.

La Mordida

In the past, Mexican police had a reputation for hassling foreigners, especially those who drove their own vehicles in Mexico. Tales of the legendary *mordida* (literally, "bite"), or minor bribe, supposedly a necessary part of navigating one's way around Mexico, swelled way out of proportion to reality but were nonetheless based on real incidents.

For several years now, the Mexican police have for the most part ceased singling out foreigners for arrest, partly as a result of anticorruption efforts by the federal government but more important because of a conscious effort to attract more tourists. Most foreign visitors who drive in Mexico these days complete their trips without any police hassles. Tijuana is one notable exception. (See *Getting Around* for tips on traffic laws and dealing with traffic police.)

Military

In the last decade or so, the Mexican government has replaced many federal police officers around the country with active-duty army officers in an effort to clean up corruption among nonmilitary law enforcement agencies. In Baja, all 84 *judiciales* involved in antidrug operations were replaced with army officers in 1996. Opinions are sharply divided as to whether this is having a net positive or negative effect on law enforcement, but it's a fact that you can see more military around the country than at any time in Mexico's history since 1920. Roadblock inspection points, or *puestos de control,* along major and minor highways have become increasingly common. All manner of vehicles—buses, trucks, private autos—may be stopped and searched at such inspection points; if you get stopped at one the best thing to do is simply be patient until it's over, usually in five minutes or less. For the most part, soldiers stationed at these checkpoints perform their duties in a serious but respectful manner. Typically they speak very little English; this usually works in favor of the non-Spanish-speaking foreign visitor because it means they can't ask very many questions.

In Case of Arrest

If you get into trouble with Mexican law, for whatever reason, try to contact your nearest consulate in Baja. Embassies and consulates for each town are listed under the respective destination chapters. The state tourism office in La Paz (tel. 612/122-5939) is the best place to look for help. The office staff routinely handle emergency legal matters involving visiting foreigners; you stand a much better chance of resolving legal difficulties with their assistance.

Sports and Recreation

The Cape Region's major attractions largely fall under this heading—from trekking in the Sierra de la Laguna to scuba diving off Cabo Pulmo.

HIKING AND BACKPACKING Trails

Hiking trails, from wide, 150-year-old paths created by Amerindians or shepherds to smaller, more recent trails worn by hikers, crisscross the Sierra de la Laguna. Signposts are scarce—it's a good idea to scout an area first and ask questions locally about the best way to get from point A to point B. Although it's sometimes tempting to venture off established trails, that's a good way to get lost; you might also contribute to the destruction of delicate ecosystems. Light trails that don't seem to go anywhere may be cattle or coyote trails that connect surface water sources. (See the *East and Central Cape* chapter for information on specific trails.)

Maps

Topographic maps, which chart trails and elevation differentials, are essential for extended hiking and backpacking. **Map Link** (U.S. tel. 805/692-6777 or 800/962-1394, www.maplink.com) and **Map Centre** (U.S. tel. 619/291-3830 or 888/849-6277, www.mapcentre.com) carry a complete line of Baja topo maps in three scales (1:1,000,000, 1:250,000, and 1:50,000), sold separately according to region. The maps cost around US$13–15 each. **Mexico Maps** (U.S. tel. 805/687-1011, www.mexicomaps.com) offers GPS maps and digital maps, for some areas, as well as printed topo maps.

These same topographic maps are also available in Baja from the **Instituto Nacional de Estadística, Geografía e Informática (INEGI)** office in La Paz (Plaza Cuatro Molinos, Calle Altamirano 2790, Col. Centro, tel. 612/123-1545 or 612/122-4146, www.inegi.gob.mx) for about US$4 per sheet. Some topos may be out of print, in which case you can usually obtain a photocopy of archival prints from an INEGI office for US$6. These maps show not only trails and contour lines, but villages not normally marked on other maps.

Although you won't need a great deal of Spanish to read the INEGI maps, you might need to know the following translations for the map legend:

- *brecha*—gravel road
- *vereda*—path
- *terracería transitable en todo tiempo*—all-weather dirt road
- *terracería transitable en tiempo de secas*—dirt road passable only in dry weather
- *carretera pavimentada*—paved highway
- *carretera de más de dos carriles, caseta de pago*—toll highway of more than two lanes

What to Bring

For a hike of a day or less, all you need is sturdy footwear (light, high-topped hiking boots are preferable to sneakers in rocky terrain) and whatever food or water you plan to consume for the day. Count on at least two liters of water per person for chaparral or lower sierra day hiking, more if the weather is hot.

Longer hikes obviously require more preparation and equipment. Bring enough clothing to remain comfortable at both ends of the temperature spectrum; on the Pacific side of the sierra, days tend to be warm, nights chilly. A three-season backpacking tent and a light sleeping bag rated for temperatures down to 2°C (35°F) usually suffice for shelter.

Good hiking boots are essential. Thick lug soles with steel shanks are preferable, as they provide protection from sharp rocks and spiny plants. Bring along a first-aid kit that includes an elastic bandage for sprains and snakebite treatment as well as a pair of tweezers for removing thorns and cactus spines. Also pack a flashlight, compass, waterproof matches, a knife, extra batteries, foul-weather gear, and a signal device (mirror or whistle).

Always carry plenty of water: a minimum of five liters per person per full day of walking during hot weather, two liters in winter. Although springs and *tinajas* exist in the sierra, the water level varies considerably, and you shouldn't count on finding water sources along the way. If you need drinking water from one of these sources, always boil it first for at least 10 minutes or treat it with iodine or a water filter designed to remove impurities. Bring enough food for the duration of your hike (count on about 1.5 pounds of dry food per person per day), plus an extra one or two days' worth. One to three nestable pans will suffice for up to six hikers, along with a spoon, small plastic bowl, and cup for each person.

Camping Tips

In addition to all the usual rules for choosing campsites, don't camp beneath coconut palms (a falling coconut could knock down your tent or fracture your skull) or in arroyos (danger of flash floods).

Open fires are permitted just about anywhere in the Cape Region except within city limits. Dead or fallen hardwood is plentiful in the upper sierra; lower down, cactus skeletons—especially *pitahaya* and cholla—make excellent fuel. Scrap lumber suitable for firewood can sometimes be salvaged from town dumps. Imitate the locals and keep your fires small. Never leave hot coals or ashes behind; smother with sand—or water, if you can spare it—till cool to the touch.

Pack out all trash that won't burn, including cigarette butts; they take 10–12 years to decompose. Bury human waste six inches down, and don't use soap in streams or springs.

If you happen to have the blessed opportunity to camp on any of the Sea of Cortez islands such as Espíritu Santo, Cerralvo, or Partida, check your bags thoroughly before landing on the island to make sure you haven't inadvertently brought along any animal species (including insects or insect eggs) that aren't native to the island. Such introduced species can cause havoc on fragile island ecologies. Pack out all human waste as well as trash; carrying along a port-a-potty and deep-sixing its contents at sea after you leave the island is the most convenient way to deal with the former.

FISHING

The Cape Region's reputation as one of the world's best sportfishing regions is well deserved. Nowhere else will you find as many varieties of fish in an area as compact and accessible as the waters surrounding the Cape. Although it's most famous for acrobatic billfish—marlin, sailfish, and swordfish—and other deep-sea fishing, the Cape also offers opportunities for surf casters, small-boaters, and sport divers, as well as folks who don't yet know a rod from a reel. *The Baja Catch: A Fishing, Travel & Remote Camping Manual for Baja California,* by Neil Kell and Gene Kira, contains extensive discussions of lures and tackle, expert fishing techniques, and detailed directions to productive fisheries, plus numerous maps.

Onshore Fishing

Most accessible to travelers, since it doesn't require a boat, is onshore or surf fishing, which you can enjoy anywhere along the coast where you can get a line into the water.

Surf fishing is best along the Pacific coast between Playa El Migriño and El Carrizal (north of Todos Santos), at beaches along the Corridor, and almost anywhere on the Sea of Cortez between San José del Cabo and La Paz. Common onshore fish include surfperch, *cabezón,* sand bass, ladyfish, halibut, corvina, opaleye, leopard shark, and triggerfish. Surf fishing the submarine canyons along the shore of the East Cape can yield roosterfish, California yellowtail, and yellowfin tuna for anglers using the right tackle, and onshore catches of dorado and even marlin are not unknown. All of these except the marlin are considered excellent food fish, and even the marlin is edible when smoked.

One fish commonly caught onshore, the puffer, is *not* a good food fish; the meat is toxic to humans and can cause poisoning. The two puffer species common to Baja are easily identified, as their bodies expand like balloons when they're disturbed. Further identifiers: The bull's-eye puffer features a brownish body with black spots; depending on its stage of maturity, the golden puffer is either all golden or a dark purple-black with white spots and white fin trim. In Mexico, this fish is called *bolete.*

Inshore Fishing

Anyone with access to a small boat, either a skiff trailered in or a rented *panga* (an open fiberglass skiff that's usually 5–6 meters long and powered by a 40–60 hp outboard motor), can enjoy inshore fishing at depths up to 50–100 meters (165–330 ft). Common inshore catches include many of the surf fishes mentioned above, plus various kinds of groupers, sea bass, bonito shark, sculpin (scorpionfish), barracuda, sierra, pompano, amberjack, red and yellow snapper, *pargo,* and cabrilla. Cabrilla, however, must be released when caught.

Larger game fish occasionally taken inshore are the bluefin and yellowfin tuna, yellowtail, dorado, jack crevalle, and roosterfish. Again, all fish mentioned make good eating.

Offshore Fishing

The bigger game fish are found in deeper waters—more than 200 meters (650 ft)—and require bigger tackle and more technique, including specialized trolling methods prescribed for each type of fish. Larger boats—fishing cruisers—are usually necessary simply because of the distance from shore to the fishing area. In the Cape Region, however, you can reach depths of more than 200 meters less than 1.5 kilometer (1 mi) offshore. These areas are accessible by skiff or *panga,* though strong seasonal currents are sometimes a problem, requiring a larger outboard motor. Contrary to the popular image of Cabo San Lucas sportfishing, it isn't necessary to use a boat equipped with fighting chairs to catch the big ones, although it's undoubtedly more comfortable.

Because of the special tackle and techniques involved in offshore fishing, many Cape visitors hire local fishing guides, who usually provide boats and tackle, to transport them to offshore fishing grounds. A sometimes less expensive alternative involves signing up for fishing cruises, which take groups of tourist anglers out on big powerboats.

Most offshore anglers go after striped, blue, or black marlin, sailfish, swordfish, wahoo, dorado, roosterfish, yellowtail, and tuna. These fish are large, powerful fighters, requiring skill in handling rod and line. The billfish are the most acrobatic, performing high leaps and pirouettes when hooked; wahoo and roosterfish will also "greyhound," performing a series of long, low jumps while swimming rapidly in one direction.

Of the billfish, only the swordfish is considered good eating. The rest are traditionally regarded as trophy fish, meant to be stuffed and mounted in the den or living room. To their credit, an increasing number of anglers these days release billfish after catch; many outfitters discourage or even forbid the taking of these beautiful creatures unless the fish has been badly damaged in the fight.

The wahoo, dorado, roosterfish, yellowtail, and various tunas all make excellent eating.

Fishing Seasons

The Cape Region presents a complex set of fishing conditions that vary from month to month and year to year. Fish are biting somewhere in Cape waters year-round, but water temperature, ocean currents, weather patterns, fish migrations, and other variables mean you usually won't find the same type of fish in the same spot in, say, December as in July. An unusually dry year in the American Southwest, for example, lessens the outflow of nutrients from the Colorado River into the Sea of Cortez, diminishing the store of plankton and other small marine creatures at the bottom of the Cortez food chain. This in turn affects populations of larger fish, from sea bass to whale sharks.

Because of the numerous variables, all the "fishing calendars" can serve only as guidelines. A few generalizations are possible. The greatest variety and number of game fish swim the widest range of Cape waters April–October, when the water temperatures are relatively warm. In winter, many species migrate south, but fortunately for winter anglers, exceptions abound. The widely distributed California yellowtail, for example, is present year-round, migrating up and down the Sea of Cortez—La Paz and the East Cape in winter, central to northern Cortez in summer—as well as the lower Pacific coast. Sierra peak season is winter, when they're found in abundance along the Pacific coast. Wahoo generally spend December–April at the Cape, moving up toward Bahía Magdalena and the southern Cortez in the warmer months.

If your trip occurs December–April, head for Cabo San Lucas or San José del Cabo; May–November you can angle anywhere along a horseshoe-shaped loop extending from Bahía Magdalena on the Pacific side to above La Paz on the Cortez.

As a final caveat, remember that an unusually warm winter means better fishing all over Baja; likewise a particularly cold winter forces many fish far south, making even Cabo San Lucas, the "fisherman's paradise," less productive.

Tackle

Although bait and tackle are available at shops in La Paz and Cabo San Lucas, supplies are variable, and you can't count on finding exactly what you want. The more expensive fishing fleets supply or rent good fishing gear, while the budget-oriented outfits provide spotty equipment. If you're inclined toward using one of the no-frills outfitters to economize, it's wiser to have your gear assembled before arriving.

A full fishing kit containing tackle for every conceivable Cape Region sportfishing possibility would probably weigh in excess of 70 kilograms (150 lbs). Seasoned anglers claim you can get by in just about any situation with four basic rigs: two trolling rods with appropriate reels and 50- to 80-pound-test monofilament line for offshore fishing; one medium-duty eight- or nine-foot rod and spinner with 30-pound mono for surf casting and onshore fishing; and a six-foot light spinning rig loaded with four- to eight-pound line for bait fishing, freshwater fishing, or light surf casting. Two trolling rigs are recommended because these are the rods used against fish most likely to yank your outfit into the sea; it's always best to have a spare.

No matter how many rods you bring into Mexico, you're legally permitted to fish with only one at a time. Electric reels are permitted for use only by people with disabilities.

Bait

What a fish will take at any given moment is highly variable, hence the properly equipped angler comes prepared with an array of natural and artificial bait. Live or frozen bait—including everything from squid to mackerel to clams—is usually available near the more frequented fishing areas; you can also catch your own bait easily with a light rig. A cooler is necessary for keeping bait fresh; hired boats usually supply them. Among the vast selection of artificial lures available, the most reliable seem to be those perennials that imitate live bait, such as spoons, leadheads, candybars, swimmers, and, for offshore fishing, trolling heads. Bring along a few of each in different colors and sizes. You can buy a few highly specialized lures, such as marlin heads and wahoo specials, in Cabo San Lucas.

Tide Tables

Serious onshore-inshore anglers should bring along a set of current tide tables so they can decide what time to wake up in the morning.

Fishing Licenses

The red tape surrounding fishing in Mexico is minimal. The basic requirement is that anyone over 16 who intends to fish from a boat must possess a Mexican fishing license; technically, this includes all people aboard boats equipped with fishing tackle, whether they plan to fish or not. This is important to remember for anyone going along on fishing trips as a spectator. A license is not required for fishing from the shore.

A single license is valid for all types of fishing, anywhere in Mexico, and is issued for periods of one day, one week, one month, or one year. A license is usually included in the price of sportfishing cruises, but not necessarily on *panga* trips—if you don't have a license, be sure to ask if one is provided before embarking on a guided trip. The cost of a Mexican license has risen steadily through the last few years but remains less expensive than most fishing licenses in the United States or Canada. Last time we checked the cost was US$28.90 for a week, US$38.80 for a month, and US$48.70 for an annual license.

Fishing licenses are available from a number of sources, including tackle shops and Mexican insurance companies near the U.S.–Mexico border. They can be obtained by mail from the **Mexico Department of Fisheries (PESCA)** (2550 5th Ave., Suite 101, San Diego, CA 92103-6622, U.S. tel. 619/233-6956, fax 619/233-0344), or from California branches of the **American Automobile Association (AAA)** and **Discover Baja Travel Club** (3089 Clairemont Dr., San Diego, CA 92117, U.S. tel. 619/275-1836 or 800/727-2252, www.discoverbaja.com).

Mexican Regulations

The general daily bag limit is 10 fish per person, including no more than five of any one species. Certain fish varieties are further protected as follows (per-day limits): one full-grown marlin, sailfish, or swordfish; two dorado, roosterfish, shad, tarpon, or shark. Extended sportfishing by boat is limited to three consecutive days if the daily bag limit is reached each of the three days.

Bag limits are the same for free divers as for rod-and-reelers. Only hand-held spears and band-powered spearguns—no gas guns or powerheads—are permitted, and no tanks or compressors may be used. A further weight limitation permits no more than 25 kilograms (55 lbs) of fish in a day's catch of five specimens, or one specimen of unlimited weight. Gillnets, purse nets, and every other kind of net except for handling nets are prohibited for

use by nonresident aliens, as are traps, explosives, and poisons.

The taking of shellfish—clams, oysters, abalone, shrimp, and lobster—by nonresident aliens is officially prohibited. However, taking a reasonable amount—no more than can be eaten in a meal or two—is customarily permitted. This regulation is in place to protect Mexican fishing unions; even buying shellfish from local sources is prohibited unless you buy from a public market or *cooperativa*. Obtain a receipt in case of inspection.

Totuava, sea turtles, and cabrilla are protected species that cannot be taken by anyone. Nor can any fish be caught for "ornamental purposes" (i.e., for aquarium use). Mexican fishing regulations are subject to change; check with the Mexico Department of Fisheries for the latest version before embarking on a fishing expedition.

Two areas off limits to all fishing are Bahía Cabo San Lucas harbor and Pulmo Reef, the only official fish sanctuaries along the peninsular coast. Many other areas probably ought to be protected for educational and recreational purposes, since the government-regulated bag limits help to preserve fish species but not fish habitats. Fishing, boating, diving, and other aquatic activities can cause havoc in lagoons and to delicate reef systems; use special care when traversing these areas. Never drop an anchor or a fishing line on a coral reef; such contact can cause irreversible damage to reef systems.

U.S. Customs and California State Regulations

Once you've obeyed Mexican fishing regulations and bagged a load of fish, you still have to conform to U.S. Customs regulations if you wish to enter the United States with your catch. Fortunately, U.S. regulations conform with Mexican bag limits, so whatever you've legally caught south of the border can be transported north.

The U.S. state of California further requires anyone transporting fish into the state to present a completed California Declaration of Entry form, available at the border or at any international airport in California. To facilitate identification of the transported fish, some part of each fish—head, tail, or skin—must be left intact. In other words, you can't just show up at the customs station with a cooler full of anonymous fish fillets. You may also be asked to show a valid Mexican fishing license or a PESCA form confirming legal purchase of fish or shellfish. For more information, contact the California Department of Fish and Game (U.S. tel. 916/445-0411, www.dfg.ca.gov).

BOATING

Recreational boating along Baja's peninsular and island coastlines has been popular since the 1950s. In the days before the Transpeninsular Highway, it was one of the safest, if slowest, ways of traveling from California to the southern peninsula. Despite recent improvements in highway travel, interest in navigating Baja waters has only increased. The main difference now is that smaller vessels can be trailered or cartopped down the peninsula, saving days and weeks that might otherwise be spent just reaching your cruising destination.

An extremely wide range of pleasure boats plies Baja waters, from sea kayaks to huge motor yachts. The most heavily navigated areas lie along the northwest coast between San Diego and Ensenada and in the Cabo San Lucas to La Paz corridor, but even these waters are relatively uncrowded compared to the marinas and bays of California.

Cartopping

The most popular boats for short-range cruising, fishing, and diving are those that can be transported on top of a car, RV, or truck—aluminum skiffs in the four- to five-meter (12- to 15-ft) range. This type of boat can be launched just about anywhere; larger, trailered boats are restricted to boat launches with trailer access. The most appropriate outboard motor size for a boat this size is 15–20 hp; larger motors are generally too heavy to carry separately from the boat, a necessity for cartopping.

If you decide to transport a skiff or sea kayak on top of your vehicle, be sure to use a sturdy,

reliable rack or loader with a bow line to the front bumper and plenty of tie-downs. The rough road surfaces typical of even Baja's best highways can make it difficult to keep a boat in place; crosswinds are also a problem in many areas. Frequent load checks are necessary.

Inflatables

Rigid hull inflatable boats (RHIBs), such as those manufactured by Achilles or Zodiac, are also well suited to coastal navigation from Cabo San Lucas around to the East Cape. You can carry them on top or even in the cargo area of a large car or truck and inflate them with a foot pump or compressor as needed. A small 24-hp outboard motor is the best source of power. Inquire at **Pacific Marine Supply** (U.S. tel. 619/275-0508, www.pacmarinesupply.com) for the latest gear.

NavTec Expeditions (U.S. tel. 800/833-1278, www.navtec.com), organizes guided RHIB trips in the Sea of Cortez along the coast of Baja California Sur for US$2,000 per person for seven nights/eight days.

Trailering

Larger boats that require trailering because of their weight, and which then must be floated from the trailer at a launch site, are much less versatile than cartop boats. On the entire peninsula, fewer than 20 launches—five or six on the Pacific side, the remainder on the Sea of Cortez—offer trailer access. Another disadvantage to boat trailering is that Baja road conditions make towing a slow, unpleasant task. On the other hand, if one of these spots happens to be your destination and you plan to stay awhile, the added cruising range of a larger vessel might be worthwhile.

Ocean Cruising

The typical ocean cruiser on the Pacific side is a 12- to 24-meter (40- to 80-ft) powerboat; on the Cortez side, 10- to 18-meter (35- to 60-ft) sailboats are popular. Properly equipped and crewed, these boats can navigate long distances and serve as homes away from home. Smaller motor-powered vessels are usually prevented

© NIKKI GOTH ITOI

the *panga* lineup at Cabo Pulmo

from ocean cruising simply because of the lack of available fueling stations—their smaller fuel capacities greatly diminish cruising range. Sailboats smaller than nine meters (30 ft) have a similar problem because of the lack of storage space for food and water.

If you want to try your hand at ocean cruising, contact **Cortez Yacht Charters** (U.S. tel. 619/469-4255, www.cortezcharters.com), or **Baja SeaFaris** (tel. 612/125-9765, www.bajaseafaris.com) in La Paz.

Charts

The best nautical charts for Baja waters are those compiled by the U.S. government. They come in two series: the Coastal Series, which covers the entire Pacific and Cortez coastlines in three large charts (numbers 21008, 21014, and 21017) with a scale of around 1:650,000 each; and the Golfo de California Series, which offers much more detailed maps—in scales from 1:30,000 for La Paz to 1:290,610 for the entire Cape Region—of selected areas along the Cortez coast and around the Cape. Both

series are based on nautical surveys conducted 1873–1901, so many of the place-names are out of date.

You can buy these charts individually from the **Defense Mapping Agency (DMA)** (U.S. tel. 301/227-2000). Two of the Coastal Series are out of print, however, and others may eventually drop from sight as well. A much better and less expensive source of these charts is *Charlie's Charts: The Western Coast of Mexico (Including Baja),* which is a compilation of all U.S. nautical charts from San Diego to Guatemala, including those unavailable from the DMA. The charts have been extensively updated from the DMA originals, with more recent markings for anchorages, boat ramps, hazards, and fishing and diving spots. The spiral-bound volume is available from **Charles E. Wood** (Box 1244, Station A, Surrey, BC, Canada V3W 1G0). It's also available in many California marine supply stores, and from Amazon.com.

Waterproof, tear-resistant double-sided plastic charts published by **Fish-n-Map** (U.S. tel. 303/421-5994, www.fishnmap.com) are available in four sheets: Sea of Cortez North Chart (San Felipe to Mulegé, with inset maps of Bahía de los ángeles, Las Islas Encantadas, Bahía San Francisquito, Puerto Refugio, and Guaymas); Sea of Cortez South Chart (Loreto to Cabo San Lucas, with inset maps of Loreto south to Bahía Agua Verde, Bahía de la Paz, Isla Espíritu Santo, and Cabo San Lucas); the Baja California Chart North Pacific (Tijuana to Bahía Tortugas, with inset maps of the Coronado Islands, San Quintín area, Isla San Benito, and Isla Guadalupe); and Baja California Chart South Pacific (Punta Eugenia to Cabo San Lucas). Each of these measures 60 by 90 centimeters (24 by 36 in), or 10 by 22.5 centimeters (4 by 9 in) folded, costs US$7, and is available wherever Baja maps are sold.

Gerry Cruising Charts (U.S. tel. 520/394-2393, www.gerrycruise.com), produces 15 navigation charts for the entire Sea of Cortez (including the mainland Mexico side), plus a packet of charts for the Pacific side of Baja, costing US$21–45 depending on the number of charts per packet. Gerry Cunningham, who compiled these charts, also wrote *The Complete Guide to the Sea of Cortez,* which comes in three volumes and costs US$29–42 per volume or US$95 for the whole set. Also available on CD-ROM for US$95, the set contains 360 color photos.

Tide Tables

Tide tables are published annually; to cover the entire Baja coastline you'll need two sets: one that pertains to the Pacific tides and one for the Sea of Cortez tides. Both are available from **Map Link** (U.S. tel. 805/692-6777 or 800/962-1394, www.maplink.com), **Gerry Cruising Charts** (see *Charts*); or marine supply stores. You can also order Sea of Cortez tide tables from the **University of Arizona** (Printing and Graphics Services, 102 W. Stadium, Tucson, AZ 85721, tel. 520/621-2571, fax 520/621-6478).

Boat Permits

Any nonresident foreigner operating a boat in Mexican waters who intends to fish from that boat is required to carry a Mexican boat permit as well as a fishing permit. Even if you transport a boat to Baja with no fishing tackle and no plans to fish, it's a good idea to obtain a boat permit; first, because you might change your mind when you see all the fish everyone else is pulling in, and second, because you never know when you might end up carrying a passenger with fishing tackle. *All* boats used for fishing require a permit, whether cartopped, trailered, carried inside a motor vehicle, or sailed on the open seas.

Permits are available by mail from the Mexico Department of Fisheries (2550 5th Ave., Suite 101, San Diego, CA 92103-6622, tel. 619/233-6956, fax 619/233-0344), or from the Discover Baja Travel Club (3089 Clairemont Dr., San Diego, CA 92117, U.S. tel. 619/275-1836 or 800/727-2252, www.discoverbaja.com). A boat permit is valid for 12 months; fees vary according to the length of the craft.

Temporary Import Permits

These aren't necessary for Baja but are required if you plan to take a boat to mainland Mexico, whether by land or water. You can obtain the permit from offices in La Paz or Santa Rosalía or from a Registro Federal de Vehículos office in Tijuana, Mexicali, Ensenada, or La Paz.

Port Check-Ins

If you launch a boat at a Mexican port, specifically within the jurisdiction of a captain of the port (COTP), you must comply with official check-in procedures. This simply involves reporting to the COTP office and completing some forms. The only time it's a hassle is when the captain isn't present; you may have to wait around a few hours. Some ports charge filing fees of up to US$15.

Anytime you enter another COTP's jurisdiction, you're required to check in. Checking out is not required except when you leave the port of origin—i.e., the port at which you first launched. If you're on a cruise from a foreign country, you should check out at the last port with a COTP on your return itinerary. COTPs in Baja are found at Ensenada, Guerrero Negro, Bahía Magdalena (San Carlos), Cabo San Lucas, San José del Cabo, La Paz, Puerto Escondido, Loreto, Mulegé, Santa Rosalía, Bahía de los Ángeles, and San Felipe.

Fuel, Parts, and Repairs

At present only permanent marinas in Cabo San Lucas and La Paz (or farther north in Ensenada, Puerto Escondido, and Santa Rosalía) offer fuel year-round. Elsewhere you must count on your own reserves or try your luck at canneries, boatyards, and fish camps, where prices will probably exceed official Pemex rates. At places other than marinas you'll often have to go ashore and haul your own fuel back to the boat; come prepared with as many extra fuel containers as you can manage.

La Paz is the Cape Region's best source of marine supplies and repairs. As with all other motorized conveyances in Baja, it's best to bring along plenty of spare parts, especially props, filters, water pumps, shear pins, hoses, and belts. Don't forget to bring at least one life jacket per person—statistics show that in 80 percent of all boating fatalities, the victims weren't wearing them.

SEA KAYAKING

Kayaking is one of the best ways to experience the Cape Region coasts. Coves, inlets, water caves, and beaches inaccessible to skiffs or four-wheel-drive vehicles are easily approached in a kayak, especially on the Sea of Cortez. The Cortez is truly a world-class kayaking environment, as more and more kayakers discover each year. La Paz in particular is an excellent place to learn sea-kayaking skills because of the abundance of bays, coves, and islands nearby.

Kayaking on the Pacific side is for the experienced paddler only. High surf and strong currents require equal quantities of strength and expertise. Finding a beach campsite isn't too difficult, but reaching it through the surf might be.

Equipment

Sea kayaks can be rented from sports outfitters in La Paz and Cabo San Lucas. Outfitters in La Paz favor traditional closed-cockpit models designed for cold-water zones, even though nearby waters are quite warm most of the year. Cabo San Lucas outfitters often carry both closed- and open-cockpit styles. For extended winter touring, the closed-top boats are preferable—cool winds can make even warm spray feel cold on the skin. For shorter winter trips or summer excursions, the open-top has certain advantages. Since the paddler sits on top of the deck rather than underneath it, the open-top is much easier to exit and thus somewhat safer overall. Open-cockpit kayaks are also easier to paddle and more stable than traditional kayaks—just about anyone can paddle one with little or no practice. But they do maneuver a bit more slowly because of a wider beam and higher center of gravity.

If you're on your way to Baja by vehicle and need kayaking equipment or supplies, a convenient stop is **Southwind Kayak Center** (17855-A Sky Park Circle, Irvine, CA 92614, tel. 949/261-0200 or 800/768-8494, www.southwindkayaks.com). Southwind offers classes and rentals as well as sales.

Maps and Tide Tables

Nautical charts are of little use for kayak navigation. A better choice is 1:50,000-scale topo maps, available from Map Link, Map Centre, or Gerry Cruising Charts (see *Boating*). Tide tables are also invaluable.

Organized Kayak Trips

A great way to learn sea kayaking is to join an organized trip led by experienced kayakers. The Cape Region's best companies, **Baja Expeditions** and **Mar y Aventuras**, lead kayak trips out of La Paz year round (see the *La Paz and Vicinity* chapter).

Another good source of information on organized kayak trips and on Baja kayaking in general is **California Kayak Friends** (www.ckf.org).

KITEBOARDING AND WINDSURFING

From November through March, the Sea of Cortez is a windsurfing and kiteboarding paradise, particularly along the East Cape. La Paz is also a very good area, even in summer, when a strong breeze called *el coromuel* comes in just about every afternoon. The best spots here lie along the mostly deserted beaches of the peninsula northeast of town—Punta Balandra to Punta Coyote. When nothing's blowing in the Bahía de la Paz vicinity, dedicated windsurfers can shuttle west across the peninsula to check out the action at Punta Márquez on the Pacific side, only 72 kilometers (45 mi) away.

Los Barriles on Bahía de Palmas, along the East Cape, is one of the more accessible windsurfing areas in southern Baja. The wind blows a steady 18–30 knots all winter long, and wavesailing is possible in some spots. During the season, uphauling (pulling mast and sail up from the water) is usually out of the question because of chop and high winds, so the ability to waterstart (mount and launch from deep water) is a prerequisite for the area.

Los Barriles is also home to **Vela Windsurf Resorts** (U.S./Canada tel. 800/223-5443, www.velawindsurf.com), which offers highly rated instruction and package deals from mid-November through early March. Even if you're not a participant in one of its package vacations, you may be able to arrange for service and parts.

The Pacific side of Baja generally demands more experience. Those who can handle high surf and strong winds will love it. None of the Cape Region's Pacific shores, however, are protected from major swells, so the novice should attempt only fair-weather sailing.

SURFING

Cape Region surfers are blessed; they can enjoy both winter and summer wave action within a radius of roughly 100 kilometers.

In winter, a west-northwest groundswell combines with the year-round northwest windswell to stoke point breaks along the Pacific shore from Punta Márquez all the way to Migriño.

During summer's southern swell, the place to be is the Corridor between Cabo San Lucas and San José del Cabo, where beach breaks predominate at dependable spots such as Costa Azul ("Zippers"). When the southern swell is really happening, surfable waves wrap right around San José del Cabo as far north up the Sea of Cortez as Los Barriles.

There are more than 25 known point, reef, and beach breaks around the cape. Stop by the **Costa Azul Surf Shop** along the Corridor at Playa Costa Azul or in Todos Santos for a map with descriptions of the breaks, or buy a copy of the incredibly detailed *Surfer's Guide to Baja California,* by Mike Parise.

Equipment

For any extended trip down the coast, carry both a short and a long board—or a gun for the northwest shores of Isla Natividad or Islas de Todos Santos in winter. Long boards aren't used much in the Cape Region, however. Besides wax and a cooler, about the only other items you need to bring are a fiberglass-patching kit for bad dings and a first-aid kit for routine surf injuries. Most surf spots are far from medical assistance—don't forget butterfly bandages. Boards can be repaired at just about any boatyard on the coast, since most Mexican *pangas* are made of fiberglass and require a lot of patching.

Several surf shops in San José del Cabo and Cabo San Lucas sell boards, apparel, and accessories.

Airlines have made it more expensive these days to fly with your quiver; check the going rate before you head for the airport. Renting a board sounds pretty good when checking it costs US$100 each way. For longer trips, buying and reselling a board while you're there is another option.

Tide charts come in handy for predicting low and high tides; a pocket-sized tide calendar available from **Tidelines** (U.S. tel. 800/345-8524, www.tidelines.com) charts daily tide changes from Crescent City, California, to Manzanillo, Mexico, with +/- corrections from a Los Angeles baseline.

SCUBA DIVING AND SNORKELING

Because it lies at the intersection of the Pacific and the Cortez, the Cape Region makes a particularly varied dive location. The Sea of Cortez alone offers one of the world's richest marine ecosystems; sea lions, numerous whale and dolphin varieties, manta rays, amberjacks, and schooling hammerhead sharks are all part of a thick food chain stimulated by cold-water upwellings amid the more than 100 islands and islets that dot the Cortez.

Cabo San Lucas Diving

The diving here consists of wall dives and boulder fields along a vast underwater canyon, plus a one-of-a-kind dive around the point at Land's End, during which you descend in the Sea of Cortez and surface in the Pacific Ocean.

Cabo Pulmo Diving

The East Cape is known for Pulmo Reef, the only hard coral reef in the Sea of Cortez. This reef consists of eight volcanic ridges inhabited by profuse coral life. Because most underwater attractions are close to shore, this area is perfect for diving from small boats or open-cockpit kayaks. Some of the reef fingers can even be reached from shore.

La Paz Diving

Rock reefs are abundant throughout the lower Cortez islands near La Paz, where tidal conditions are generally calm and the water is relatively warm year-round. Marinelife is plentiful and varied at such sites.

Pacific Coast Diving

Heavy swells and surging along the Pacific coast mean that Pacific diving should be tackled only by experienced scuba divers or with an experienced underwater guide.

Cape Region Snorkeling

Several coves along the coast toward Cabo San Lucas make good snorkeling sites. Playa Santa María and Playa Chileno have soft corals at either end of a large cove. And Bahía Cabo San Lucas itself is a protected marine park; the rocks and points along the bayshore are suitable for snorkelers. To the north, snorkelers can explore the Sea of Cortez islands near La Paz and the coves along the Pichilingue Peninsula.

Equipment

Dive shops throughout the Cape Region are well stocked with standard diving and snorkeling equipment. Novice divers won't need to bring anything; experienced divers should bring along any specialized gear. Very little gear is available for sale. And since most equipment sold or rented in Cape dive shops is imported from the United States, stocks vary from season to season. Purchase prices are also generally a little higher in Mexico than north of the border.

Bottom line: If you're bringing your own gear, have it serviced before you leave home; check your computer batteries, and bring spare parts.

At Cabo San Lucas and around the Cape as far north as La Paz, most divers wear a 3 mm wetsuit late November–March; shorties or ordinary swimsuits will suffice the rest of the year. In summer, many Sea of Cortez divers wear Lycra skins to protect against *agua mala,* or small jellyfish stings.

Because divers and anglers occasionally use the same areas, a good diving knife is essential for dealing with wayward fishing line. Bring two knives so you'll have a spare. Also pack extra O-rings and bring a wetsuit patching kit if you plan to dive away from resort areas.

Dependable **air** for scuba tanks is available in La Paz, Cabo Pulmo, and Cabo San Lucas. Always check the compressor first to make sure it's well maintained and running clean. Divers with extensive Baja experience usually carry a portable compressor not only to avoid contaminated air but to use in areas where tank refills aren't available.

Buceo Medico Mexicano (tel. 624/143-3666) operates a **hyperbaric decompression chamber** in Cabo San Lucas at Plaza Marina (next to the Hotel Tesoro). The facility is equipped with two compressors, an oxygen analyzer, closed-circuit TV, and a hotline to Divers Alert Network (DAN). In La Paz, **Baja Diving and Service** (tel. 612/122-7010, www.clubcantamar.com) also operates a recompression chamber on the Pichilingue Peninsula. If these facilities aren't available, the next nearest full-time, dependable recompression facility is the **Hyperbaric Medicine Center** at the University of California Medical Center in San Diego (tel. 619/543-5222, Mon.–Fri. 7:30 A.M.–4:30 P.M. and for emergencies). Dive insurance for medical emergency assistance is available from the Divers Alert Network (DAN, www.diversalertnetwork.org).

Organized Dive Trips and Instruction

Cabo San Lucas boasts the Cape Region's greatest number of dive shops offering dive excursions. Many also offer instruction and PADI scuba certification (see *Sports and Recreation* in the *Los Cabos* chapter).

In Cabo Pulmo on the East Cape, three small operations offer guided dive trips. If you're planning on doing a Pulmo dive, it's considerably less expensive to arrange it here than in Cabo San Lucas on the other end of the Cape, assuming you can arrange your own transportation.

La Paz has several reliable outfitters that offer guided dives and instruction/certification (see *Sports and Recreation* in the *La Paz* chapter).

Accommodations

Places to stay in the Cape Region run the gamut from free beach camping to plush resort hotels. Visitors who plan on doing the Cape circuit will have a greater range of options at any given location if they bring along camping gear.

HOTELS, MOTELS, AND RESORTS

Unlike the closely spaced, vertical high-rises of Cancún, Acapulco, and other major Mexican resorts, Cape Region hotels tend more toward the organic than the geometric. Even in the Los Cabos area, they're more likely to hide behind a rocky cliff or occupy a secluded cove, spreading out along a sandy swath rather than towering over it. Often their shapes and colors mimic the surrounding environment.

For most Cape hotels, the high season runs November–March. Some places charge a higher peak-season rate January–March; in purely statistical terms, March usually scores the highest annual hotel occupancy. At many hotels and motels, midweek rates are lower than weekend rates.

Obviously, one way to save money on accommodations is to visit the Cape in the off-season, i.e., April–October. The Cape Region's climate is livable year-round; summer temperatures of 37°C (100°F) on the Cortez coast are usually mitigated by sea breezes and relatively low humidity. The exception is August–September, when high temperatures and high humidity are the norm all along the Cortez coast (see *Climate*).

Whatever the rack rate, you can usually get the price down by bargaining (except during peak periods, e.g., Christmas, spring break, and Easter). When making a reservation or checking in, be sure to clarify whether the room rate includes meals—occasionally it does. Asking for a room without meals is an easy way to bring the rate down, or you can simply ask if there's anything cheaper.

Most hotels add a 12 percent tax (10 percent valued-added tax, plus 2 percent lodging tax) to quoted rates. Some also add a 10 percent service charge. To avoid a 22 percent surprise over posted rates when you check out, be sure to ask whether the quoted rate includes tax and service.

Unless otherwise specified, the price ranges quoted are based on double-occupancy, high-season rates. Single occupancy prices may be lower, and suites may be avail-

© NIKKI GOTH ITOI

palapa-roofed *casita*

able at higher rates. All rates are per room, per night. Discounts may be offered for stays of a week or longer.

Under US$50

Many hotels and motels in the Cape Region are considerably less expensive than their counterparts in the United States, Canada, or Europe. You'll find a simple but clean room with private bath and double bed for around US$30–50 in La Paz, Cabo San Lucas, Todos Santos, and San José. Soap, towels, toilet paper, and purified drinking water are usually provided; in some places you may have to ask. Rooms in this price range don't always offer air conditioning (in San Lucas and San José they usually do), but fans may be available.

Lodging under US$25 per night is rare unless you stay at a *casa de huéspedes* or *pensión* (see *Alternatives to Hotels and Motels*), where bathrooms are usually shared *(baño colectivo)*. Only La Paz, the state capital, has such rock-bottom facilities.

US$50-100

The largest number of hotels and motels in the Cape Region fall into this price range. Some are older Mexican-style hotels just a bit larger than those in the budget range, while others are American-style motels. Everything in this price range comes with air conditioning.

US$100-150

Higher-end places are found all along the coast from La Paz around to Cabo San Lucas. Prices for "international-class accommodations" average US$100 and up. Some of these places are good values, while others are definitely overpriced. When in doubt, stick to the less expensive hotels. Or ask about "specials"; places that normally cost US$150 a night are sometimes available at 50 percent discounts.

US$150-250

A number of high-end boutique hotels and resorts are now scattered around the Cape Region, with the highest concentration in the Los Cabos area.

Over US$250

The most luxurious hotels in all of Baja—indeed among the best in all of Mexico—are found along the coast between San José del Cabo and Cabo San Lucas, in an area known as "the Corridor." Beach frontage, huge pools, spas, world-class restaurants, and golf course privileges are all part of the experience at these resorts.

Hotel Reservation Services

Most of the hotels and motels mentioned in this guidebook take reservations directly by phone or online. Many also accept reservations through booking agencies, such as **Mexico Travel Net** (U.S. tel. 800/511-4848, www.mexicotravelnet.com). Other options include **Delfin Hotels & Resorts,** also called **Cabo Hotels** (U.S. tel. 800/524-5104) and **Baja Properties** (Doblado and Morelos, San José tel. 624/142-0988, Cabo San Lucas tel. 624/143-2560, U.S. tel. 877/462-2226, www .bajaproperties.com).

Occasionally these agencies can arrange lower room rates or special packages not offered directly by the hotels themselves. Note that the lives of these kinds of booking agencies tend to be short. Your local travel agent may also be able to book lodging in Baja.

ALTERNATIVES TO HOTELS AND MOTELS
Casas de Huéspedes and Pensiones

Aside from free or very basic campgrounds, *casas de huéspedes* (guesthouses) and *pensiones* (boardinghouses) are the cheapest places to stay in the Cape Region. Unfortunately for budgeters, they're found only in La Paz. The typical *casa de huéspedes* offers rooms with shared bath *(baño colectivo)* for around US$15–20. A *pensión* costs about the same but may include meals. At either, most lodgers are staying for a week or more, but the proprietors are usually happy to accept guests by the night.

The main difference between these and budget hotels/motels—besides rates—is that they're usually in old houses or other buildings (e.g., convents) that have been converted

for guesthouse use. Soap, towels, toilet paper, and drinking water are usually provided, but you may have to ask.

Youth Hostel

A Hostelling International–affiliated youth hostel (*villa deportiva juvenil,* or youth sports villa) in La Paz offers shared dormitory-style rooms. Each guest is assigned a bed and a locker and has access to the hostel's sports facilities. Bathing facilities are communal, and guests must supply their own soap and towels. Rates are US$10–15 per night.

Staying at the hostel is a great way to meet young Mexicans and improve your Spanish; English is rarely spoken. About the only drawback is that the hostel is inconveniently located some distance from the center of town, so transportation can be a problem.

Condo/House Rentals and House-Sitting

For long-term stays of a month or more—and occasionally for stays as short as a week—house or condo rental may be significantly less expensive and more convenient than staying at a hotel or motel. Rents vary wildly according to facilities, neighborhood, and general location in Baja. The most expensive rentals are those found along the Corridor between San José del Cabo and Cabo San Lucas. Expect to pay a minimum of US$500 a month in these beach areas (in some instances you could easily pay that for a weekend), more typically US$1,000–1,500 a month for something quite simple.

Some of the best deals on beach houses can be found in Los Barriles, Buena Vista, and Todos Santos. At any of these places you can rent a furnished one- or two-bedroom with kitchen starting at around US$400–700 a month, more for places with air conditioning or lots of modern appliances. Property management services and real estate companies in these areas can help you find something in your price range (see the appropriate destination chapters for contact information).

Some of the same companies that manage

rentals may be able to offer house-sitting opportunities in homes whose seasonal residents want someone to take care of their property while they're away. Living rent-free in Baja may sound wonderful, but keep in mind that many homeowners have a list of chores they want carried out on a regular basis, such as tending plants, feeding and exercising pets, cleaning swimming pools, and so on.

CAMPING AND RV PARKS

For travelers who like the outdoors, camping is an excellent way to slash accommodations costs. The Cape Region has more campgrounds, RV parks, and other camping areas for its size than anywhere else in Mexico, although a few disappear with each passing year. Because the Cape's population density is so dramatically low, it's easy to find beach camp-

sites offering idyllic settings and precious solitude, often free of charge.

The Cape Region offers roughly 20 private campgrounds that charge fees ranging from around US$5 for a place with virtually zero facilities to as high as US$30 for a developed RV park with full hookups, wireless Internet, and recreation facilities. Most campgrounds charge around US$5–10 for tent camping, US$15–25 for full hookups.

If you can forgo permanent toilet and bathing facilities, you won't have to pay anything to camp, since there's a virtually limitless selection of free camping spots, from beaches to deserts to mountain slopes. You won't necessarily need four-wheel drive to reach these potential campsites, as plenty of turnouts and graded dirt *ramales* (branch roads) off the main highways can be negotiated by just about any type of vehicle.

Food and Drink

Much of what *bajacalifornianos* eat can be considered Northern Mexican cuisine. Because Northern Mexico is generally better suited to ranching than farming, ranch-style cooking tends to prevail in rural areas, which means that ranch products—beef, poultry, and dairy foods—are highly favored.

Unlike the northern mainland, however, just about any point in the Cape Region is less than a couple of hours' drive from the seashore, so seafood predominates here. In most places on the Cape, seafood is more common than meat or poultry. If there's anything unique about Cape cuisine, it's the blending of ranch cooking with coastal culture, which has resulted in such distinctive food creations as the *taco de pescado* (fish taco).

WHERE TO EAT

The Cape's larger towns—La Paz, San José del Cabo, and Cabo San Lucas—offer everything from humble sidewalk taco stands to *gran turismo* hotel restaurants. Elsewhere the choices are fewer and more basic. In small towns, there may

be only two or three restaurants serving standard Mexican dishes or, if near the coast, *mariscos* (seafood). Sometimes the best meals on the road come from what you improvise after a visit to a local *tienda de abarrotes* (grocery store).

Most hotels on the Cape have restaurants; in small towns and remote areas these may be among the best (and only) choices. A few hotel restaurants, such as the One&Only Palmilla's C, the Westin's Arrecife Restaurant or The Restaurant at Las Ventanas al Paraíso, all found in the Corridor between San José and San Lucas, are worthwhile culinary destinations in and of themselves. In Cabo San Lucas, the Cape's vacation capital, many restaurants cater to tourist tastes by serving a hybrid menu of common Mexican dishes, seafood, and burgers.

Local Color

Taquerías, small, inexpensive diners where tacos are assembled before your eyes (sort of the Mexican equivalent to the old-fashioned American hamburger stand), tend to be in areas with lots of foot traffic—near bus terminals, for

COOKING METHODS

Entrées, whether meat, poultry, or seafood, are most commonly prepared in one of the following styles:

adobo, adobada – marinated or stewed in a sauce of vinegar, chilies, and spices
albóndigas – meatballs
a la parrilla – broiled or grilled
a la veracruzana – seafood, often *al carbón* (charcoal-grilled)
al mojo de ajo – in a garlic sauce
al pastor – slowly roasted on a vertical spit
al vapor – steamed
asado/asada – grilled
barbacoa – pit-roasted
con arroz – steamed with rice
empanizada – breaded
encebollado – cooked with onions
entomado – cooked with tomatoes
frito – fried
guisado – in a spicy stew
machaca – dried and shredded

Ordering and Paying

You really don't need much Spanish to get by in a restaurant. Stating what you want, plus *por favor* (please), will usually do the trick (e.g., *"dos cervezas, por favor,"* "two beers, please"). Don't forget to say *"gracias"* ("thank you"). The menu is called *el menú* or, much less commonly in Baja, *la carta*.

La cuenta is the bill. A tip *(la propina)* of 10–15 percent is expected at any restaurant with table service; look to see if it's already been added to the bill before placing a tip on the table.

Costs

In this guidebook, we've tried to give some guidance as to the approximate meal cost at most sit-down restaurants. In most cases, a price range is given for the main dishes on the menu, leaving out the least expensive and most expensive items. Where prices cover a wide range, we've provided prices for a few representative entrées. At inexpensive places you can count on spending less than US$7 for an entrée (or for a *comida corrida*, where available), while a moderate meal will cost up to US$15, and an expensive one more cost than US$15.

WHAT TO EAT
Breakfasts

Menus at tourist restaurants are often confusing because some of the same "breakfast" dishes may end up on more than one section of the menu. Mexicans have two kinds of breakfasts, an early one called *desayuno,* eaten shortly after rising, and a second called *almuerzo* that's usually taken around 11 A.M. To further confuse the issue, Spanish-English dictionaries usually translate *almuerzo* as "lunch," while bilingual menus often read "breakfast."

The most common Mexican *desayuno* is simply *pan dulce* (sweet pastry) or *bolillos* (torpedo-shaped, European-style rolls) with coffee or milk. Cereal is also sometimes eaten for *desayuno;* e.g., *avena* (oatmeal), *crema de trigo* (cream of wheat), or *hojuelas de maíz* (corn flakes).

The heavier eggs-and-frijoles dishes known

example. The good ones are packed with taco-eaters in the early evening. In La Paz and San José del Cabo, another economical alternative is the *lonchería,* a small, café-style place that usually serves *almuerzo* (late breakfast/early lunch) and *comida* (the main, midday meal). *Lonchería* hours are typically 11 A.M.–5 P.M. Municipal markets in La Paz and San José feature rows of *loncherías* serving inexpensive basic meals and *antojitos* (snacks or one-plate dishes). Some *loncherías* offer *comida corrida,* a daily fixed-price meal that includes a beverage, an entrée or two, side dishes, and possibly dessert.

Cafés or *cafeterías* are similar to *loncherías* except that they may open earlier and serve *desayuno* (breakfast) in addition to other meals.

A *cenaduría* is yet another simple, café-style restaurant, this time concentrating on *la cena,* the evening meal. Often the menu will be similar to that of a *lonchería*—mostly *antojitos*—but the hours are later, typically 5–10 P.M.

widely as "Mexican breakfasts" in the United States and Canada are usually taken as *almuerzo,* the late breakfast, which is typically reserved for weekends and holidays. Eggs come in a variety of ways, including *huevos revueltos* (scrambled eggs), *huevos duros* (hard-boiled eggs), *huevos escafaldos* (soft-boiled eggs), *huevos estrellados* (eggs fried sunny side up), *huevos a la mexicana* (also *huevos mexicanos,* eggs scrambled with chopped tomato, onion, and chilies), huevos rancheros (fried eggs served on a tortilla), and *huevos divorciados,* two *huevos estrellados* separated by beans, each egg usually topped with a different salsa.

Eggs also come *con chorizo* (with ground sausage), *con machaca* (with dried, shredded meat), *con tocino* (with bacon), or *con jamón* (with ham). All egg dishes usually come with frijoles and tortillas. The biggest *almuerzo* package on the menu is typically called *almuerzo albañil* (brickmason's *almuerzo*) or *huevos albañil* (brickmason's eggs); this means eggs with one or more varieties of meat on the side.

One of the cheapest and tastiest *almuerzos* is *chilaquiles,* tortilla chips in a chili gravy with crumbled cheese on top. Eggs and/or chicken can be added to *chilaquiles* as options. Another economical choice is *molletes,* which consists of a split *bolillo* spread with mashed beans and melted cheese, served with salsa on the side.

Tortillas

A Mexican meal is not a meal without tortillas, the round, flat, pancakelike disks eaten with nearly any nondessert dish, including salads, meats, seafood, beans, and vegetables. Both wheat-flour and cornmeal tortillas are commonly consumed throughout Baja, although flour tortillas *(tortillas de harina)* are the clear favorite. Corn tortillas *(tortillas de maíz)* are more common in southern Mexico, where Amerindian populations (the first corn cultivators) are larger, while flour tortillas are more popular in the ranching areas of northern Mexico. Among northern Mexicans, it is said that meat and poultry dishes taste best with flour tortillas while vegetable dishes go best with corn. Most restaurants offer a choice. If you order tortillas without specifying, you may get *"¿de harina o de maíz?"* as a response.

Although prepackaged tortillas are available in *supermercados* (supermarkets), most *bajacalifornianos* buy them fresh from neighborhood *tortillerías* or make them at home. Many restaurants and cafés in Baja, and virtually all *loncherías* and taquerías, serve fresh tortillas.

Incidentally, a tortilla has two sides, an inside and an outside, that dictate which direction the tortilla is best folded when wrapping it around food. The side with the thinner layer—sometimes called the *pancita,* or belly—should face the inside when folding the tortilla. If you notice the outside of your tortilla cracking, with pieces peeling off onto the table, you've probably folded it with the *pancita* outside instead of inside.

Antojitos and Main Dishes

Antojitos literally means "little whims," thus implying snacks to many people. However, the word also refers to any food that can be ordered, served, and eaten quickly—in other words, Mexican fast food. Typical *antojitos* include tamales, enchiladas, burritos, flautas, chiles rellenos, *chalupas, picadillo,* quesadillas, *tortas,* and tacos.

The main dish, or *el plato fuerte,* of any meal can be a grander version of an *antojito,* a regional specialty from another part of Mexico (*mole poblano,* for example), or something the *cocineros* (cooks) dream up themselves. Typical entrées are centered around meats, seafood, or poultry.

Meats

Common meats include *carne de res* (beef), *puerco* (pork), and *borrego* (lamb). *Jamón* (ham), chorizo (sausage), and *tocino* (bacon) are usually reserved for *almuerzo.* Steak may appear on menus as *bistec, bistek, biftec,* or "steak." *Venado* (deer meat or venison) and *conejo* (rabbit) are commonly served on ranchos. Poultry dishes include *pollo* (chicken), *pavo* (turkey), and, less frequently, *pato* (duck) and *codorniz* (quail).

ANTOJITOS

No trip to Cabo would be complete without a sampling of traditional Mexican fast-food dishes.

birria – lamb or goat stew in a sauce spiced with cinnamon, cloves, cumin, and oregano

burrito – a flour tortilla rolled around meat, beans, or seafood fillings; Baja's lobster burritos are legendary

chalupa – a crisp, whole tortilla topped with beans, meat, etc. (also known as a tostada)

chile relleno – a mild poblano chili stuffed with cheese, deep-fried in egg batter, and served with a ranchero sauce (tomatoes, onions, and chilies)

enchilada – a corn tortilla dipped in chili sauce, then folded or rolled around a filling of meat, chicken, seafood, or cheese and baked in an oven

enfrijolada – same as enchilada except dipped in a sauce of thinned refried beans instead of chili sauce

entomatada – same as enchilada except dipped in a tomato sauce instead of chili sauce

flauta – a small corn tortilla roll, usually stuffed with beef or chicken and fried

gordita – a small, thick, corn tortilla stuffed with a spicy meat mixture

huarache – literally, "sandal"; a large, flat, thick, oval-shaped tortilla topped with fried meat and chilies

menudo – a thick soup made with cows' feet and stomachs (and less commonly, intestines) and seasoned with *chiles de árbol*, oregano, and fresh chopped onion; reputedly a sure hangover cure

pozole – hominy stew made with pork or chicken and garnished with radishes, oregano, onions, chili powder, salt, and lime

picadillo – a spicy salad of chopped or ground meat with chilies and onions (also known as *salpicón*)

quesadilla – a flour tortilla folded over sliced cheese and grilled; ask the cook to add *chiles rajas* (pepper strips) for extra flavor

sope – a small, thick, round corn cake with dimpled edges, topped with a spicy meat mixture and crumbled cheese

taco – a corn tortilla folded or rolled around anything and eaten with the hands; *tacos de pescado*, or "fish tacos," are a Baja specialty

tamal – plural *tamales;* cornmeal *(masa)* dough wrapped in a corn husk and steamed; sometimes stuffed with corn, olives, pork, or turkey

torta – a sandwich made with a Mexican-style roll *(bolillo/birote* or the larger *pan telera)*; one of the most popular is the *torta de milanesa,* made with breaded, deep-fried veal or pork

Seafood

Pescado (fish) entrées on the menu are often seasonal or dependent on the "catch of the day." Often just the word *pescado* and the method of cooking will appear (e.g., *pescado al mojo de ajo*). If you need to know exactly what kind of fish, just ask *"¿Hay qué tipo de pescado?"*—although in some cases the only response you get is something generic, like *"pescado blanco"* ("white fish"). For specific fish names, see the sidebar *Fish Translators* in the *Los Cabos* chapter.

Baja's number-one seafood specialty is the *taco de pescado* (fish taco). If you've never tried one, you're most likely wondering "What's the big deal—a fish taco?" Eat one, though, and you're hooked for life. Short, tender, fresh fish fillets are dipped in batter and fried quickly, then folded into a steaming corn tortilla with a variety of condiments, including *salsa fresca* (chopped tomatoes, onions, chilies, and lime juice), marinated cabbage (similar to coleslaw in the United States), guacamole (a savory avocado paste), and sometimes a squirt of mayonnaise or *crema* (fresh Mexican cream). *¡La última!* Any kind of white-fleshed fish can be used—the best fish tacos are those made from yellowtail *(jurel),* halibut *(lenguado),* or mahimahi *(dorado).*

Shellfish dishes *(mariscos)* popular on Baja menus include *ostiones* (oysters), *almejas* (clams), *callos* (scallops), *jaibas* (small crabs), *cangrejos* (large crabs), *camarones* (shrimp), *lan-*

gosta (lobster), *langostina* (crayfish, also called *cucarachas*), and *abulón* (abalone). They can be ordered as *cocteles* (cocktails—steamed or boiled and served with lime and salsa), *en sus conchas* (in the shell), or in many other ways.

Beans

The beans *(frijoles)* preferred in the Cape Region, as on the northern mainland, are pinto beans, usually dried beans boiled until soft, then mashed and fried with lard or vegetable oil (usually the former). Often this preparation is called *frijoles refritos* (refried beans), although they're not really refried except when reheated. Sometimes the beans are served whole, in their own broth, as *frijoles de olla* (boiled beans), or with bits of roast pork as *frijoles a la charra* (ranch-style beans). Frijoles can be served with any meal of the day, including breakfast.

Cheese

Even the most remote rancho usually has some cheese *(queso)* around, so if your appetite isn't stimulated by the *iguana guisada* simmering on the hearth, you can usually ask for chiles rellenos (mild poblano chilies stuffed with cheese and fried in an egg batter) or quesadillas (cheese melted in folded flour tortillas). A meal of beans, tortillas, and cheese provides a complete source of protein for travelers who choose to avoid meat, poultry, or seafood for health, economic, or moral reasons.

Vegetables and Vegetarian Food

Although vegetables are sometimes served as side dishes with *comidas corridas,* with restaurant entrées, or in salads *(ensaladas),* they're seldom listed separately on the menu. When they do appear on menus, it's usually at restaurants in towns near farming areas in northern Baja or else in the La Paz–Los Cabos area, where many vegetables come via boat from the mainland. The best place to add vegetables to your diet is at a market or grocery store.

It's difficult but not impossible to practice a vegetarian regime in Baja. Vegetarians can eat quesadillas (ask for corn tortillas, which unlike most flour tortillas do not contain lard) or *enchiladas de queso* (cheese enchiladas). With some luck, you'll stumble across restaurants that can prepare a variety of interesting cheese dishes, including *queso fundido con champiñones* (melted cheese with mushrooms, eaten with tortillas) and quesadillas made with *flor de calabeza* (squash flower). Some places make beans without lard *(sin manteca),* but you'll have to ask to find out. Many larger towns have at least one vegetarian/health food store (usually called *tienda naturista*) with a small dining section as well as bulk foods.

Vegans, for the most part, will do best to prepare their own food. Look for shops with signs reading *semillas* (seeds) to pin down a good selection of nuts and dried beans. You'll find plenty of fresh fruits and vegetables in markets and grocery stores.

Soup

The general menu term for soup is *sopa,* although a thick soup with lots of ingredients is usually a *caldo* or *caldillo. Menudo* is a soup of hominy *(nixtamal)* and cow's feet and stomach (or, less commonly, intestine) in a savory, reddish-brown broth, served with chopped onions, chilies, and crumbled oregano. It's seen throughout Mexico and is highly prized as a hangover remedy. *Pozole* is a similar soup with a much lighter-colored broth; some varieties of *pozole* are made with chicken instead of tripe.

Other tasty soups include *sopa de tortillas, sopa azteca,* and *sopa tlapeño,* all variations of artfully seasoned chicken broth garnished with *totopos* (tortilla wedges) and sliced avocado.

Salsas and Condiments

Any restaurant, café, taquería, or *lonchería* offers a variety of salsas. Sometimes only certain salsas are served with certain dishes, while at other times one, two, or even three salsas are stationed on every table. Often each place has its own unique salsa recipes—canned or bottled salsas are rarely used. The one ingredient common to all salsas is chili peppers, though these vary in heat from mild to incendiary.

There are as many types of salsas as there are Mexican dishes—red, green, yellow, brown, hot, mild, salty, sweet, thick, thin, blended, and chunky. The most typical is the *salsa casera* (house salsa), a simple, fresh concoction of chopped chilies, onions, and tomatoes mixed with salt, lime juice, and cilantro. This is what you usually get with the free basket of *totopos* (tortilla chips) served at the beginning of every Mexican meal. Another common offering is *salsa verde* (green sauce), made with a base of tomatillos (small, tart, green tomato-like vegetables). Some salsas are *picante,* or spicy hot (also *picosa*), so it's always a good idea to test a bit before pouring the stuff over everything on your plate.

Whole pickled chilies are sometimes served on the side as a condiment, especially with tacos. Salt *(sal)* is usually on the table, although it's rarely needed since Mexican dishes tend to be prepared with plenty of it. Black pepper is *pimiento negro,* and if it's not on the table it's normally available for the asking. Butter is *mantequilla,* sometimes served with flour tortillas.

In taquerías, guacamole (mashed avocado blended with onions, chilies, salt, and sometimes other ingredients) is always served as a condiment. In restaurants it may be served as a salad or with tortilla chips.

Desserts and Sweets

The most popular of Mexican desserts, or *postres,* is a delicious egg custard called flan. It's listed on virtually every tourist restaurant menu, along with *helado* (ice cream). Other sweet alternatives include pastries found in *panaderías* (bakeries) and the frosty offerings at the ubiquitous *paleterías*. Strictly speaking, a *paletería* serves only *paletas,* flavored ice on sticks (like American popsicles but with a much wider range of flavors), but many also serve *nieve,* literally "snow," which is flavored grated ice served like ice cream in bowls or cones.

Dulcerías, or candy shops, sell a huge variety of sticky Mexican sweets, usually wrapped individually. Often brightly decorated, *dulcerías* are oriented toward children and sometimes carry inexpensive toys as well as sweets. The larger ones sell piñatas, colorful papier-mâché figures filled with candy and small gifts and hung at parties (where children are allowed to break them with sticks, releasing all the goodies inside). Traditionally, piñatas are crafted to resemble common animals, but these days you'll see all kinds of shapes, including Pokémon, Santa Claus, and Batman.

In Todos Santos, once an important sugarcane-growing area, a local specialty is *panocha,* a candy made from raw sugar.

Fruits

A large variety of delicious fruits are available in local markets and grocery stores. Most common are mango *(mango),* banana *(plátano),* guava *(guayaba),* papaya *(papaya),* grapes *(uva),* pineapple *(piña),* and apple *(manzana),* but you may occasionally see more exotic fruits from the mainland. The *huertas* in Todos Santos and El Pescadero on the West Cape produce a variety of organic fruits, herbs, and vegetables for export to the United States, with some sold locally.

BUYING GROCERIES

The cheapest way to feed yourself while traveling in Baja is the same way you save money at home: Buy groceries at the store and prepare meals on your own. Even the smallest towns in Baja have a little grocery store or corner market. A ripe avocado, a chunk of *queso fresco,* and a couple of *bolillos* can make a fine, easy-to-fix meal.

The humblest type of store is the small family-owned *tienda de abarrotes,* usually recognizable by the single word *abarrotes* (groceries) printed somewhere on the outside (*tienda* means "store"). These stock the basics—tortillas, dried beans, flour, herbs and spices, bottled water, a few vegetables, possibly *bolillos* and *queso fresco*—as well as limited household goods such as soap and laundry detergent. As at convenience stores back home, the food at the average *tienda de abarrotes* is not particularly inexpensive. Cheaper, when you can find them, are government-sponsored Diconsa (Distribuidora Conasupo), *tienda rural,* and ISSSTE (Instituto de Seguridad y Servicios Sociales para Trabajadores del Estado) markets.

Privately run supermarkets are found in

larger towns. Like their American counterparts, they're usually well stocked with a wide variety of meats, baked goods, vegetables, household goods, and beer and liquor. Supermarket prices are often lower than those of smaller grocery stores.

Several towns and cities in Baja feature *mercados municipales* (municipal markets), large warehouse-type structures where meat, fruit, and vegetable producers sell their goods directly to the public. Prices are often very good at these markets, but it helps if you know how to bargain.

Another common *tienda* is the *ultramarinos,* which is primarily a place to buy beer and liquor along with a few food items.

Panaderías

Although you can often buy a few bakery items at the aforementioned stores, the best place to buy them is at their source—a *panadería* (literally, "breadery," i.e., bakery). The typical *panadería* produces tasty *bolillos* (Mexican rolls), *pasteles* (cakes), and *pan dulce* (cookies and sweet pastries). To select bakery items from the shelves of a *panadería,* simply imitate the other customers—pick up a pair of tongs and a tray from the counter near the cash register and help yourself, cafeteria-style.

Tortillerías

Unless you make them yourself, the best tortillas are found where they make them fresh every day. The automated process at a *tortillería* uses giant electric grinders and conveyor belts to transform whole corn into fresh tortillas, which you buy by weight, not number. A kilo yields about 40 average, 12-centimeter (5-in) tortillas; you may be able to order by the *cuarto* or *medio* (quarter or half kilo). The government-subsidized prices are low. Restaurants, *tiendas,* and home cooks buy tortillas from the local *tortillería* to avoid spending hours at a *metate* (grinder) and *comal* (griddle).

NONALCOHOLIC BEVERAGES
Water

Bottled drinking water is usually available at every *tienda de abarrotes* or supermarket throughout the region. If you're car camping, renting a house, or staying in one place for a long time, it may be more convenient to use the 20-liter (roughly five-gallon) reusable plastic containers of drinking water available in most Mexican towns. These typically cost US$6 for the first bottle of water and bottle deposit, then US$1.60 for each 20-liter refill. This is much cheaper than buying individual liter or half-liter bottles, which often cost as much as US$2 apiece, and you won't be throwing away so much plastic. The water will be easier to dispense if you also buy a *sifón* (siphon) designed for that purpose. These are available for around US$2.50 at many grocery stores.

The water and ice served in restaurants in the Cape Region is always purified—it's not necessary to order *agua mineral* (mineral water) unless you need the minerals. Likewise, the water used as an ingredient in "handmade" drinks, e.g., *licuados* or *aguas frescas,* also comes from purified sources. Actually, most Cape residents—Mexicans and foreigners alike—drink right out of the tap because the source, Sierra de la Laguna spring water, is perfectly safe.

Soft Drinks

Licuados are similar to American "smoothies"—fruit blended with water, ice, honey or sugar, and sometimes milk or raw eggs to produce something like a fruit shake. Any place that makes *licuados* will also make orange juice (*jugo de naranja*).

Aguas frescas are colorful beverages sold from huge glass jars on the streets of larger cities or at carnivals, especially during warm weather. They're made by boiling the pulp of various fruits, grains, or seeds with water, then straining it and adding sugar and large chunks of ice. *Arroz* (rice) and *horchata* (melon-seed) are two of the tastiest *aguas.*

American soft drinks *(refrescos)* such as 7-UP, Coke, and Pepsi are common; their Mexican equivalents are just as good. An apple-flavored soft drink called Manzanita is popular.

Hot Drinks

Coffee is served in a variety of ways. The best, when you can find it, is traditional Mexican-style coffee (ranchos sometimes serve it), which is made by filtering near-boiling water through fine-ground coffee in a slender cloth sack. Instant coffee *(nescafé)* is often served at small restaurants and cafés; a jar of instant coffee may be sitting on the table for you to add to hot water. When there's a choice, a request for *café de olla* (pot coffee) should bring you real brewed coffee. When you order coffee in a Mexican restaurant, some servers will ask *"¿de grano o de agua?"* (literally "grain or water?"), meaning "brewed or instant?" One of the better Mexican brands found in supermarkets is Café Combate. If you'd like a darker roast than normally available, buy a bag of green coffee beans (available at most supermarkets) and roast your own in a dry iron skillet.

Café con leche is the Mexican version of café au lait, i.e., coffee and hot milk mixed in near-equal proportions. *Café con crema* (coffee with cream) is not as available; when it is, it usually means a cup of coffee with a packet of nondairy creamer on the side. Espresso machines are popping up everywhere in the resort areas of Cabo San Lucas and San José del Cabo; most of the time the so-called "espressos" and "cappuccinos" produced bear only a passing resemblance to the real stuff. La Paz, too, is home to a growing number of Starbucks look-alikes.

Hot chocolate *(chocolate)* is fairly common on Mexican menus. It's usually served very sweet and may contain cinnamon, ground almonds, and other flavorings. A thicker version made with cornmeal—almost a chocolate pudding—is called *champurrado* or *atole.*

Black tea *(té negro)* is not popular among *baja-californianos,* although you may see it on tourist menus. Ask for *té helado* or *té frío* if you want iced tea. At home many Mexicans drink *té de manzanilla* (chamomile tea), *té de yerba buena* (mint tea), or *té de canela* (cinnamon tea) in the evenings.

ALCOHOLIC BEVERAGES

Drinking laws in Mexico are quite minimal. The legal drinking age in Mexico is 18 years. It's illegal to carry open containers of alcoholic beverages in a vehicle. Booze of every kind is widely available in bars, restaurants, grocery stores, and *licorerías* (liquor stores). *Borracho* means both "drunk" (as an adjective) and "drunkard."

Cerveza

The most popular and available beer brand in northern Baja is Tecate, brewed in Tecate, while in the south it's Pacífico, from Mazatlán, just across the Sea of Cortez from Cabo San Lucas. Both are good-tasting, light- to medium-weight brews, with Tecate holding a slight edge (more hops) over Pacífico. You can't compare either of these with their export equivalents in the United States, because Mexican breweries produce separate brews for American consumption that are lighter in taste and lower in alcohol content. It's always better in Mexico.

Other major Mexican brands such as Corona Extra (the number-one-selling beer in mainland Mexico and number-one-selling imported beer in the United States), Dos Equis (XX), Superior, Carta Blanca, Bohemia, and Negra Modelo are available in tourist restaurants, but you'll notice the locals stick pretty much to Tecate and Pacífico, perhaps out of regional loyalty.

The cheapest sources for beer are the brewery's agents or distributors (look for signs saying *agencia, subagencia, cervecería,* or *depósito*) where you can return deposit bottles for cash or credit. You can buy beer by the bottle *(envase),* can *(bote),* six-pack *(canastilla),* or 20-bottle case *(cartón).* Large, liter-size bottles are called *ballenas* (whales) or *caguamas* (sea turtles) and are quite popular. When buying beer at an *agencia* or *depósito,* specify *fría* if you want cold beer; otherwise you'll get beer *al tiempo* (at room temperature). Many *depósitos* offer free ice with the purchase of a case of beer.

Wine

Baja is one of Mexico's major wine-production areas, and Baja wines are commonly served in restaurants. A broad selection of varietals is available, including cabernet sauvignon, chardonnay, chenin blanc, pinot noir, barbera, tempranillo, and zinfandel. These and other grapes are also blended to produce cheaper *vino tinto* (red wine) and *vino blanco* (white wine). Better vintages may be labeled *reserva privada* (private reserve). When ordering wine in Spanish at a bar, you may want to specify *vino de uva* (grape wine), as *vino* alone can refer to distilled liquors as well as wine. *Vino blanco,* in fact, can be interpreted as cheap tequila.

Two of the more reliable and reasonably priced labels are L.A. Cetto and Santo Tomás, both produced in northern Baja. Better but more expensive—and hard to find—are Baja California's Monte Xanic and Château Camou. If you can find it, Monte Xanic's Cabernet y Merlot is considered one of the finest wines ever produced in Mexico. Camou makes an excellent *coupage* of cabernet franc, cabernet sauvignon, and merlot, labeled Gran Vino de Château Camou.

Cabo San Lucas has a very good restaurant/wine bar called Sancho Panza, part of Plaza Marina attached to Hotel Plaza Las Glorias, where you can taste almost any Baja vintage.

Liquor

Tequila is Mexico's national drink and also the most popular distilled liquor in Baja. If you're keen on sampling Mexico's best, head for Pancho's Restaurant in Cabo San Lucas, said to have the largest selection of tequilas in the entire country.

The second most popular liquor is brandy, followed closely by *ron* (rum), both produced in Mexico for export as well as domestic consumption. A favorite rum drink is the *cuba libre* (free Cuba), called *cuba* for short—a mix of rum, Coke, and lime juice over ice. Similar is the *cuba de uva,* which substitutes brandy for rum. Other hard liquors—gin, vodka, scotch—may be available only at hotel bars and tourist restaurants.

CANTINAS AND BARS

Traditionally, a cantina is a Mexican-style drinking venue for males only, but in modern urban Mexico the distinction between "bar" and "cantina" is becoming increasingly blurred. True cantinas are rare in the Cape Region. La Cañada del Diablo in Todos Santos is a rare example of a *cantina familiar* (family cantina) where everyone is welcome. In the smaller towns of the interior, you may occasionally stumble upon a more typical cantina, where blinking Christmas lights festoon a *palapa* roof and palm-thatch or ocotillo walls. Inside are a few tables and chairs and a handful of *borrachos;* if any women are present, they're either serving the booze or serving as hired "dates." The only drink choices will be beer, Mexican brandy, and cheap tequila or *aguardiente*—moonshine. Often when you order tequila in a place like this, you'll be served a large glass of *aguardiente,* considered an acceptable substitute.

Bars, on the other hand, are found in most hotels and in the downtown districts of La Paz, San José, and Cabo San Lucas. They've developed largely as social venues for tourists or for a younger generation of Mexicans for whom the cantina is passé. A bar, in contrast to a cantina, offers a variety of beer, wine, and distilled liquor. By Mexican standards, bars are considered very upmarket places to hang out, so they aren't extremely popular—many young Mexicans would rather drink at a disco where they can dance, too.

BAR LINGO

Do you want to order your margarita on the rocks? Wondering how to treat a hangover? Use this cheat-sheet to find your way around Baja's bar scene.

botanas – snacks
cantinero/cantinera – bartender
casco – empty bottle
cerveza – beer
envase, botella – bottle
con hielo – with ice
con sal – with salt
la cruda – hangover
lo mismo – the same
rocas – on the rocks
sin hielo – without ice
una copita, uno tragito – a drink
una mas – one more
una fría – a cold one
vaso, copa – glass

THE LIQUID HEART OF MEXICO

Tequila is a pallid flame that passes through walls and soars over tile roofs to allay despair.

Álvaro Mútis,
Tequila: Panegyric and Emblem

Mexico's national drink has been in production, in prototypical form, since at least the time of the Aztecs. The Aztecs, in fact, called themselves Mexicas in direct reference to the special spiritual role mescal – tequila's forerunner – played in their culture via Mextli, the god of agave (the desert plant from which *pulque*, mescal, and tequila are derived). These names, as interpreted by the Spanish, eventually yielded "Mexico."

The Spaniards levied a tax on tequila as early as 1608, and in 1795, King Carlos IV granted the first legal concession to produce tequila to Don José María Guadalupe Cuervo. The liquor's name was taken from the Ticuila Amerindians of Jalisco, who mastered baking the heart of the *Agave tequiliana weber,* or blue agave, and extracting its juice, a process employed by tequila distilleries today. Native to Jalisco, this succulent is the only agave that produces true tequila as certified by the Mexican government. Contrary to the myth that all true tequila must come from Tequila, Jalisco, Mexican law enumerates specific districts in five Mexican states where tequila may be legally produced, including as far away as Tamaulipas on the U.S.-Mexico border.

All liquors labeled "tequila" must contain at least 51 percent blue agave distillates. Sugarcane juice or extracts from other agaves usually make up the rest. Many tequila aficionados will caution you to look for the initials NOM – for Norma Oficial Mexicana – on the label to be sure it's "real" tequila, but we've never seen a bottle of tequila sold in Mexico that didn't bear those letters.

Despite the fact that tequila sales are booming today, much of the tequila-making process is still carried out *a mano* (by hand). In the traditional method, the mature heart of the tequila agave, which looks like a huge pineapple and weighs 18-56 kilograms (50-150 lbs), is roasted in pits for 24 hours, then shredded and ground by mule- or horse-powered mills. After the juice is extracted from the pulp and fermented in ceramic pots, it's distilled in copper stills to produce the basic tequila, which is always clear and colorless, with an alcohol content of 38-40 percent.

True "gold" tequilas are produced by aging the tequila in imported oak barrels to achieve a slightly mellowed flavor. The *reposado,* or "rested," type is oak-aged for at least two months, while *añejo,* or "aged," tequila must stay in barrels at least a year. Inferior "gold" tequilas may be nothing more than the silver stuff mixed with caramel coloring – always look for *reposado* or *añejo* on the label if you want the true gold.

José Cuervo, Sauza, and Herradura are well-established, inexpensive to medium-priced tequila labels with international notoriety. Of these three, Herradura is said to employ the most traditional methods; tequila connoisseurs generally prefer it over the other two. In 1983 Chinaco, based in the state of Tamaulipas, became the first label to produce a tequila made from 100 percent blue agave, a formula now considered standard for all high-end tequilas. Many tasters claim a label called Reserva del Patrón (sold simply as "Patrón" north of the Mexican border) is the finest and smoothest tequila tipple of them all. Other very fine *tequilas reposadas* include Don Eduardo, Ecuario Gonzales, La Perseverancia, Don Felipe, and our personal favorite for flavor and price, Las Trancas. To emphasize the limited production nature of these private reserve distillations, these brands are usually sold in numbered bottles with fancy labels. Less expensive but also very good are the Jimador, Centenario, and Orendain labels. As with wine, it's all a matter of personal preference; try a few *probaditos* ("little tastes," or shots) for yourself to determine which brand best tickles your palate. The fancier tequilas may be served in brandy snifters instead of the traditional tall, narrow shot glass *(caballito)*.

MESCAL AND THE WORM

The distillate of other agave plants – also known as magueys or century plants – is called mescal (sometimes spelled "mezcal"), not to be confused with the nondistilled mescal – *pulque* – prepared in pre-Hispanic Mexico. The same roasting and distilling process is used for today's mescal as for tequila. Actually, tequila is a mescal, but no drinker calls it that, just as no one in a United States bar orders "whiskey" when they mean to specify scotch or bourbon. Although many states in Mexico produce mescal, the best is often said to come from the state of Oaxaca.

The caterpillar-like grub, or *gusano de maguey* (maguey worm), floating at the bottom of a bottle of mescal lives on the maguey plant itself. They're safe to eat – just about anything pickled in mescal would be – but not particularly appetizing. By the time you hit the bottom of the bottle, though, who cares? Maguey worms are often fried and eaten with fresh corn tortillas and salsa – a delicious appetizer.

TEQUILA DRINKS

The usual way to drink tequila is straight up, followed by a water or beer chaser. Licking a few grains of salt before taking a shot and sucking a lime wedge afterward make it go down smoother. The salt raises a protective coating of saliva on the tongue while the lime juice scours the tongue of salt and tequila residues.

Tequila con sangrita, in which a shot of tequila is chased with a shot of *sangrita* (not to be confused with *sangría,* the wine-and-fruit punch), is a slightly more elegant method of consumption. *Sangrita* is a bright red mix of orange juice, lime juice, grenadine, red chile powder, and salt.

An old tequila standby is the much-abused margarita, a tart Tex-Mex cocktail made with tequila, lime juice, and Cointreau (usually "Controy" or triple sec in Mexico) served in a salt-rimmed glass. A true margarita is shaken and served on the rocks (crushed or blended ice tends to kill the flavor) or strained, but just about every other gringo in Baja seems to drink "frozen" margaritas, in which the ice is mixed in a blender with the other ingredients.

If you detect a noticeable difference between the taste of margaritas north or south of the border, it may be because bartenders in the United States and Canada tend to use bigger and less flavorful Persian limes *(Citrus latifolia),* while in Mexico they use the smaller, sweeter key or Mexican lime *(Citrus aurantifolia swingle).* A "Baja margarita" substitutes Baja's own damiana liqueur for the triple sec. The damiana herb is said to be an aphrodisiac.

Health and Safety

By and large, Baja California's Cape Region is a healthy place. Sanitation standards are high compared to many other parts of Mexico, and the tap water quality in many areas is superior to that in most of California. The visitor's main health concerns are not food or water sources but avoiding mishaps while driving, boating, diving, surfing, or otherwise enjoying the Cape's great outdoor life. Health issues directly concerned with these activities are covered under the relevant sections in this book.

FOOD AND WATER

Visitors who use common sense will probably never come down with food- or water-related illnesses while traveling in Cabo. The first rule is not to overdo it during the first few days of your trip—eat and drink in moderation. Shoveling down huge amounts of tasty, often heavy, Mexican foods along with pitchers of margaritas or strong Mexican beer is liable to make anyone sick from pure overindulgence. If you're not used to the spices and different ways of cooking, it's best to ingest small amounts at first.

Second, take it easy with foods offered by street vendors, since this is where you're most likely to suffer from unsanitary conditions. Eat only foods that have been thoroughly cooked and are served either stove-hot or refrigerator-cold. Many gringos eat street food without any problems whatsoever, but it pays to be cautious, especially if it's your first time in Mexico. Concerned with the risk of cholera, the Baja California Sur state government in July 1992 banned the sale of ice cream and ceviche (raw seafood salad) by street vendors.

Doctors usually recommend you avoid eating peeled, raw fruits and vegetables in Baja. Once the peel has been removed, it is virtually impossible to disinfect produce. Unpeeled fruits and vegetables washed in purified water and dried with a clean cloth are usually okay. After all, plenty of Mexican fruit is consumed daily in Canada and the United States.

Hotels and restaurants serve only purified drinking water and ice, so there's no need to ask for mineral water or refuse ice. Tap water, however, should not be consumed except in hotels where the water system is purified (look for a notice over the washbasin in your room). Most grocery stores sell bottled purified water. Water purification tablets, iodine crystals, water filters, and the like aren't necessary for Cape travel unless you plan on backpacking.

Turista

People who've never traveled to a foreign country may undergo a period of adjustment to the new gastrointestinal flora that comes with new territory. There's really no way to avoid the differences wrought by sheer distance. Unfortunately, the adjustment is sometimes unpleasant.

Mexican doctors call gastrointestinal upset of this sort *turista,* because it affects tourists but not the local population. The usual symptoms of turista—also known by the gringo tags "Montezuma's Revenge" and "the Aztec Two-Step"—are nausea and diarrhea, sometimes with stomach cramps and a low fever. Again, eating and drinking only in moderation will help prevent the worst of the symptoms, which rarely persist more than a day or two. And if it's any consolation, Mexicans often get sick the first time they go to the United States or Canada.

Many Mexico travelers swear by a **preventive regimen** of Pepto-Bismol begun the day before arrival in country. Opinions vary as to how much of the pink stuff is necessary to ward off or tame the foreign flora, but a person probably shouldn't exceed the recommended daily dose. Taper off after four days or so until you stop using it altogether.

Another regimen that seems to be effective is a daily tablet of 100-milligram doxycycline (sold as Vibramycin in the United States), a low-grade antibiotic that requires a prescription in most countries. It works by killing all the bacteria in your intestinal tract—including the ones that reside there naturally and help protect your bowels. It's available without a prescription in Mexican *farmacias,* but you should check with your doctor first to make sure you're not sensitive to it—some people have problems with sunlight while taking doxycycline. Consume with plenty of food and water. Some physicians believe when you stop taking the drug you're particularly susceptible to intestinal upset because there are no protective bacteria left to fight off infections.

Neither Pepto nor Vibramycin is recommended for travelers planning trips of three weeks or longer.

If you come down with a case of turista, the best thing to do is drink plenty of fluids. Adults should drink at least three liters a day, a child under 37 kilograms (80 lbs) at least a liter a day. Lay off tea, coffee, milk, fruit juices, and booze. Eat only bland foods—nothing spicy, fatty, or fried—and take it easy. Pepto-Bismol or similar pectin-based remedies usually help. Some people like to mask the symptoms with a strong over-the-counter medication such as Imodium AD (loperamide is the active ingredient), but though this can be very effective, it isn't a cure. Only time will cure traveler's diarrhea.

If the symptoms are unusually severe (especially if there's blood in the stools or a high fever) or persist more than one or two days, see a doctor. Most hotels can arrange a doctor's visit, or you can contact a Mexican tourist office, U.S. consulate, or Canadian consulate for recommendations.

SUNBURN AND DEHYDRATION

Sunburn probably afflicts more Cabo visitors than all other illnesses and injuries combined. The sunlight in Baja can be exceptionally strong, especially along the coast. For outdoor forays, sun protection is a must, whatever the activity. The longer you're in the sun, the more protection you'll need.

A hat, sunglasses, and plenty of sunscreen or sunblock make a good start. Bring along a sunscreen with a sun protection factor (SPF) of at least 25, even if you don't plan on using it all the time. Apply it to *all* exposed parts of your body—don't forget the hands, top of the feet, and neck. Men should remember to cover thinned-out or bald areas on the scalp. Sunscreen must be reapplied after swimming or after periods of heavy perspiration.

If you're going boating, don't leave shore with just a bathing suit. Bring along an opaque shirt—preferably with long sleeves—and a pair of long pants. Since you can never know for certain whether your boat might get stranded or lost at sea for a period of time (if, for example, the motor conks out and you get caught in an offshore current), you shouldn't be without extra clothing for emergencies.

It's also important to drink plenty of water or nonalcoholic, noncaffeinated fluids to avoid dehydration. Alcohol and caffeine—including the caffeine in iced tea and cola—increase your potential for dehydration. Symptoms of dehydration include darker-than-usual urine or inability to urinate, flushed face, profuse sweating or an unusual lack thereof, and sometimes headache, dizziness, and general feeling of malaise. Extreme cases of dehydration can lead to heat exhaustion or even heatstroke, in which the victim may become delirious or convulse. If either condition is suspected, get the victim out of the sun immediately, cover with a wet sheet or towel, and administer a rehydration fluid that replaces lost water and salts. If you can get the victim to a doctor, all the better—heatstroke can be serious.

If Gatorade or a similar **rehydration fluid** isn't available, you can mix your own by combining the following ingredients: one liter purified water or diluted fruit juice; two tablespoons sugar or honey; one-quarter teaspoon salt; and one-quarter teaspoon baking soda. If soda isn't available, use another quarter teaspoon salt. The victim should drink this mixture at regular intervals until symptoms subside substantially. Four or more liters may be necessary in moderate cases, more in severe cases.

MOTION SICKNESS

Visitors with little or no boating experience who join fishing cruises sometimes experience motion sickness caused by the movement of a boat over ocean swells. The repeated pitching and rolling affects a person's sense of equilibrium to the point of nausea. *Mareo* (seasickness) can be a very unpleasant experience not only for those green at the gills but for fellow passengers anxious lest the victim spew on them.

The best way to prevent motion sickness is to take one of the preventives commonly available from a pharmacist: promethazine (sold as Phenergan in the United States), dimenhydrinate (Dramamine), or scopolamine (Transderm Scop). The latter is available as an adhesive patch worn behind the ear—the time-release action is allegedly more effective than tablets. These medications should be consumed *before* boarding the vessel, not after the onset of symptoms. It's also not a good idea to eat a large meal before getting on a boat. (Experienced divers swear by a tablet called Bonine, taken the night before and morning of the boat ride, which doesn't have the same side effects—drowsiness—as Dramamine.)

If you start to feel seasick while out on the bounding main, certain actions can lessen the likelihood that it will get worse. First, do not lie down. Often the first symptom of motion sickness is drowsiness, and if you give in to the impulse you'll almost certainly guarantee a worsening of the condition. Second, stay in the open air rather than below deck—fresh air usually helps. Finally, fix your gaze on the horizon; this helps steady your disturbed inner ear, the proximate cause of motion sickness.

BITES AND STINGS
Mosquitoes and *Jejenes*

Mosquitoes breed in standing water. Since standing water isn't that common in arid Baja, neither are mosquitoes. Exceptions include palm oases, estuaries, and marshes when there isn't a strong breeze around to keep mosquitoes at bay. The easiest way to avoid mosquito bites is to apply insect repellent to exposed areas of the skin and clothing whenever the mossies are

out and biting. For most species, this means between dusk and dawn.

The most effective repellents are those containing a high concentration of DEET (N,N-diethyl-metatoluamide). People with an aversion to applying synthetics to the skin can try citronella (lemongrass oil), which is also effective but requires more frequent application.

More common than mosquitoes in estuarial areas are *jejenes*, tiny flying insects known as "no-see-ums" among Americans—you almost never see them while they're biting. The same repellents effective for mosquitoes usually do the trick with *jejenes*.

For relief from the itchiness of mosquito bites, try rubbing a bit of hand soap on the affected areas. For some people this works, for others it doesn't do a thing. Andantol, available in many Mexican pharmacies, is a German-made cream that relieves itchy insect bites. *Jejene* bites usually stop itching in less than 10 minutes if you refrain from scratching them. Excessive scratching of either type of bite can lead to infection, so be mindful of what your fingers are up to.

In spite of the presence of the occasional mosquito, the U.S. Centers for Disease Control has declared all of Baja California Sur malaria-free.

Wasps, Bees, and Hornets

Although stings from these flying insects can be very painful, they aren't of mortal danger to most people. If you're allergic to such stings and plan to travel in remote areas of Baja, consider obtaining anti-allergy medication from your doctor before leaving home. At the very least, carry a supply of Benadryl or similar over-the-counter antihistamine. Dramamine (dimenhydrinate) also usually helps mitigate allergic reactions.

For relief from a wasp/bee/hornet sting, apply a paste of baking soda and water to the affected area. Liquids containing ammonia, including urine, also help relieve pain. If a stinger is visible, remove it—by scraping, if possible, or with tweezers—before applying any remedies. If a stung limb becomes unusually swollen or if the victim exhibits symptoms of a severe allergic reaction—difficulty breathing, agitation, hives—seek medical assistance.

Ticks

If you find a tick embedded in your skin, don't try to pull it out—this may leave the head and pincers under your skin and lead to infection. Covering the tick with petroleum jelly, mineral oil, gasoline, kerosene, or alcohol usually causes the tick to release its hold to avoid suffocation.

Burning the tick with a cigarette butt or hot match usually succeeds only in killing it—when you pull the tick out, the head and pincers may not come with it. Stick with the suffocation method, and if the beast still doesn't come out, use tweezers.

Scorpions

The venom of the scorpion *(alacrán)* varies in strength from individual to individual and species to species, but the sting is rarely dangerous to adults. It can be very painful, however, resulting in partial numbness and swelling that lasts several days. In Baja, the small yellow scorpions inflict more painful stings than the larger, dark-colored ones.

The best treatment begins with persuading the victim to lie down and relax to slow the spread of the venom. Keep the affected area below the level of the heart. Ice packs on the sting may relieve pain and mitigate swelling; aspirin also helps.

Children who weigh less than about 13 kilograms (30 lbs) should receive medical attention if stung by a scorpion. Doctors in La Paz, San José, and Cabo San Lucas usually have ready access to scorpion antivenin *(anti-alacrán),* but it should be administered only under qualified medical supervision.

Scorpions prefer damp, dark, warm places—dead brush, rock piles, fallen logs—so exercise particular caution when placing your hands in or near such areas. Hands are the scorpion's most common target on the human body; campers should wear gloves when handling firewood in Baja.

Other favorite spots for scorpions are crumpled clothing and bedding. In Gulf Desert areas of the Cape, always check your bed sheets or sleeping bag for scorpions before climbing in. In the same environments, shake out your shoes and clothing before putting them on.

Poisonous Sea Creatures

Various marine animals can inflict painful stings on humans. In Baja, such creatures include jellyfish, Portuguese man-of-wars, cone shells, stingrays, sea urchins, and various fish with poisonous spines.

The best way to avoid jellyfish and Portuguese man-of-wars is to scope out the water and the beach before going in—if you see any nasties floating around or washed up on the sand, try another beach. You can avoid stingrays by shuffling your feet in the sand as you walk in shallow surf, which usually causes rays resting in the sand to swim away.

To avoid cone shell and sea urchin stings, wear shoes in the water; several sport shoe manufacturers now produce specialized water shoes, e.g., Nike's Aqua Socks. You can also often spot cones and urchins in clear water, especially when wearing a diving mask. Anglers should take care when handling landed fish to avoid poisonous spines.

The treatment for stings from all of the above is the same: Remove all tentacles, barbs, or spines from the affected area; wash the area with rubbing alcohol or diluted ammonia (urine will do in a pinch) to remove as much venom as possible; and wrap the area in cloth to reduce the flow of oxygen to the wound until pain subsides. If an acute allergic reaction occurs, get the victim to a doctor or clinic as quickly as possible.

Painful sting-ray wounds may require the famous hot-water treatment. If pain persists after thoroughly cleaning the wound, soak the affected limb in the hottest water the victim can stand. Continue soaking until the pain subsides—this can sometimes take up to an hour. The local folk remedy in Baja is to treat the wound with the sap of the *garambullo* cactus, often available from *botánicas* if not from a nearby patch of desert. Some stingray wounds may require medical treatment, even stitches.

MEDICAL ASSISTANCE

The quality of basic medical treatment, including dentistry, is relatively high in Cape cities and larger towns; ask at a tourist office or at your consulate for recommendations. Public IMSS hospitals can be found in La Paz, San José, and Cabo San Lucas; Cabo's hospital is quite modern. There are public IMSS clinics or Red Cross (Cruz Roja) stations in nearly every other town. In many areas, the Red Cross can be reached by dialing 066 (toll-free) from any pay phone.

Emergency Evacuation

Through the years, several U.S. companies have offered emergency 24-hour airlift service (accompanied by licensed physicians and nurses) from anywhere in Mexico to U.S. hospitals. Few have lasted more than a year or two. One of the longer-running operations is **Aeromedevac** (tel. 800/832-5087, U.S. tel. 619/284-7910 or 800/462-0911, www .aeromedevac.com). Aeromedevac accepts collect calls. Payment for the service can be made with a credit card or through your health insurance company.

Other companies with similar services include **Air Evac Services** (U.S. tel. 602/273-9348 or 800/421-6111, www.airevac.com), and **Advanced Aeromedical Air Ambulance Service** (P.O. Box 5726, Virginia Beach, VA 23471, tel. 757/481-1590 or 800/346-3556, www.aeromedic.com).

For information on other air evacuation services, contact the **Association of Air Medical Services** (U.S. tel. 703/836-8732, www.aams.org).

CRIME

Statistics clearly show that violent crime is overall less common in Mexico than anywhere in the United States. In Baja California Sur, crime statistics are estimated to be more than 90 percent lower than the U.S. national average. Yet Americans seem to be the most paranoid of all visitors to Mexico.

Historical reasons, to a large degree, account for this paranoia. Chief among them is the general border lawlessness that was the norm in the early 20th century—an era of border disputes and common banditry on both sides of the border. Americans living along the border came to fear *bandidos* who stole livestock and occasionally robbed the Anglo ranchers themselves, while the Mexicans feared American cattle rustlers, horse thieves, gunslingers, and the infamous Texas Rangers, a private militia whose conduct at the time fell somewhere between Hell's Angels motorcycle gang and the Los Angeles Police Department.

Soon after this era had begun to wane, as politics on both sides of the border stabilized, the U.S. Prohibition experiment sent millions of Americans scrambling into Mexican border towns for booze. In the illicit atmosphere, boozers were soon rubbing elbows with gamblers and pimps, and it wasn't long before Mexican border towns gained an even more unsavory reputation.

Once Prohibition was lifted, Americans no longer had reason to come to Mexico solely for drinking, and the border towns began cleaning up their acts. Among the uninformed and inexperienced, however, the border-town image remains, sadly mixing with the equally outdated *bandido* tales to prevent many Americans from enjoying the pleasures of life south of the border.

The **Secretaría de Turismo (SECTUR)** maintains a 24-hour travelers' aid hotline for emergencies of all kinds (tel. 55/5250-0123 or 800/903-9200.)

Precautions

Visitors to Cabo should take the same precautions they would when traveling anywhere in their own countries or abroad. Keep money and valuables secured, either in a hotel safe or safety deposit box, or in a money belt or other hard-to-reach place on your person. Keep an eye on cameras, purses, and wallets to make sure you don't leave them behind in restaurants, hotels, or campgrounds. At night, lock the doors to your hotel room and vehicle.

Private campgrounds usually have some kind of security, if only a night watchman, to keep out intruders. Secluded beach campsites seem to be safe because of their isolation—around the Cape Region it's rare for crime to occur in such areas. Nonetheless, don't leave items of value lying around outside your tent, camper, or RV at night.

Money

CURRENCY

The unit of exchange in Mexico is the **peso,** which comes in paper denominations of Mex$20, Mex$50, Mex$100, Mex$200, and Mex$500. Coins come in denominations of 5, 10, 20, and 50 centavos, and Mex$1, Mex$2, Mex$5, Mex$10, Mex$20, and Mex$100.

Prices

While it's highly unlikely you'll ever confuse dollar and peso prices because of the differing values, you should ask when in doubt, as they both use the same $ symbol. Sometimes the abbreviation *m.n.* will appear next to a price— this means *moneda nacional* (national money) and also refers to pesos. Coins smaller than one peso are often scarce, so payments often must be rounded off to the nearest peso or at least to the nearest 50 centavos.

Dollars vs. Pesos

Most places on the Cape will take U.S. dollars as well as pesos. Paying with pesos, however, usually means a better deal when the price is fixed in pesos; if you pay in dollars, the vendor can determine the exchange rate. If a can of motor oil, for example, is marked at Mex$18, and the bank rate is Mex$9 per dollar, you'll pay US$2 for the oil with pesos changed at the bank. However, if you ask to pay in dollars, the vendor may charge US$2.50 since vendors have the right—by custom rather than law— to charge whatever exchange rate they wish. If you're bargaining for price, it really doesn't matter what currency you use.

Some stores in smaller towns prefer not to take dollars since this means keeping track of two currencies and makes banking more com-plicated. Pemex stations sometimes refuse dollars—attendants are usually too busy to stop and calculate rates.

For anything larger than a Mex$100 note, getting change can sometimes be a problem in small towns, so try to carry plenty of notes and coins in denominations of Mex$50 or smaller. Small change is commonly called *morraya.*

CHANGING MONEY

The best way to obtain local currency is to withdraw cash from an ATM machine using your debit card from home, or pay with a credit card whenever possible (mainly at larger stores and moderate to upscale establishments in Los Cabos and La Paz). In some cases, however, you may need to exchange U.S. dollars or other currency for pesos. Several alternatives are dis-cussed below.

Debit Cards and ATM Cards

Most Mexican ATMs (automatic teller ma-chines) accept MasterCard or Visa debit cards as well as ATM cards on the Plus or Cirrus systems. Using an ATM card to obtain pesos from ATMs in Mexico is much more con-venient than cashing travelers checks. Most Mexican banks now charge nominal fees for withdrawing cash from their ATMs with cards from other banks. ATMs are called *cajeros au-tomáticos* (automatic cashiers) in Mexico.

At this time the most reliable machines seem to be those operated by **Banamex, Bancomer, HSBC, Banorte,** and **Banca Serfín,** whose ATMs accept cards coded for the Visa, Mas-terCard, Cirrus, and Plus systems.

Credit Cards

Visa and MasterCard are widely accepted in

the Cape region at large hotels, at restaurants catering to tourists or businesspeople, at car rental agencies (you can't rent a car without a credit card), and at shops in tourist centers or large cities. If in doubt, flash your card and ask *"¿Se aceptan tarjetas de crédito?"* A reply containing *"solo efectivo"* means "only cash."

It's important to keep in mind that many shops and some hotels add a 3–6 percent surcharge to bills paid with a credit card. Credit cards are not accepted at Pemex stations in Baja.

Cash advances on credit card accounts—a useful service for emergencies—are available at many Mexican banks.

Banks

Banks offer the best exchange rate for buying pesos, and they all offer the same rate, set by the Bank of Mexico. This rate is usually posted behind the counter where foreign exchange is handled. Banks also accept a wide range of foreign currencies, including euros, British pounds, Japanese yen, and Canadian dollars. Cash and travelers checks are accepted. The main drawbacks with banks are the long lines and short hours (Mon.–Fri. or Sat. 9 or 10 A.M.–1:30 or 3 P.M.); the foreign-exchange service usually closes at noon or 12:30 P.M.

Money Changers

The second best rate, generally speaking, is found at the *casa de cambio,* or private money-changing office. The *casa de cambio* (also called *servicio de cambio*) either knocks a few centavos off the going bank rate or charges a percentage commission. It pays to shop around for the best *casa de cambio* rates since some places charge considerably more than others. Rates are usually posted; *compra,* always the lower figure, refers to the buying rate for US$ (how many pesos you'll receive per dollar), while *vende* is the selling rate (how many pesos you must pay to receive a dollar).

Money changers are usually open much later than banks; some even work evening hours, which makes them immeasurably more convenient than banks. U.S. dollars are generally preferred, though many *casas* also accept Canadian dollars. However, Canadians should keep a reserve supply of U.S. dollars for instances when Canadian currency isn't accepted. Money changers usually accept travelers checks; some border-town *casas,* however, take only cash. The latter often offer the best exchange rates.

Only the larger towns and tourist centers offer money-changing offices. In smaller towns, you'll have to resort to a bank or local merchant. Many storekeepers are happy to buy dollars at a highly variable and sometimes negotiable rate. Few take traveler's checks, however, unless you make a purchase.

Money changers at Mexican airports offer notoriously low rates. Try to buy pesos in advance if arriving by air, or pay with dollars until you can get to a bank or *casa de cambio.*

Hotels

Hotels, motels, *pensiones,* and other lodgings generally offer the lowest exchange rates. If you're trying to save money, avoid changing currency where you stay. Pay for your room in pesos if possible, since the same low rate often applies to room charges paid in dollars.

MONEY MANAGEMENT
Estimating Costs

Inflation in Mexico runs high. This means that when estimating travel costs based on prices quoted in this book, some allowance must be made for inflation.

Because of fluctuations in the peso–dollar ratio, and in an effort to keep prices up to date, all prices in this book are quoted in dollars. This doesn't mean, however, that there won't be any increase in prices by the time you arrive. A couple of phone calls to hotels for price quotes should give you an idea of how much rates have increased, if at all; this difference can be applied as a percentage to all other prices for a rough estimate of costs.

Tipping

A tip of 10–15 percent is customary at restaurants with table service unless a service charge is added to the bill. Luggage handling at hotels or airports warrants a tip of US$0.50 per bag. A few hotels maintain a no-tipping policy; details will be posted in your room. The tipping of chambermaids is optional—some guests tip and some don't. Remember that these folks typically earn minimum wage; even a small tip may mean a lot to them.

You don't need to tip Pemex station attendants unless they wash your windows, check the oil, or perform other extra services beyond pumping gas. The equivalent of US$0.50–1 in pesos is sufficient. When the change due on a gasoline purchase is less than Mex$1, it's customary to let the attendant keep the change.

Taxes

The Mexican government collects an *impuesta al valor agregado* (IVA) or "value-added tax" (VAT) of 10 percent on all goods and services in Baja, including hotel and restaurant bills and international phone calls. On the mainland, the same tax is 15 percent, so Baja is a bargain in this respect. Although by American standards this may seem high, the tax is lower than the rate in other countries that employ value-added taxes, such as France, where the VAT runs more than 20 percent.

Hotels add a further 2 percent lodging tax. Many, but not all, hotel rate quotes include taxes, but to make sure, you might ask "*¿Se incluyen los impuestos?*"

Information and Services

BUSINESS HOURS

The typical small business is open Monday–Friday 9 A.M.–2 P.M., closed until 4 or 5 P.M., then open again until 7 or 8 P.M. Retail businesses are usually open on Saturday as well. Official government offices typically maintain an 8:30 A.M.–3:30 P.M. schedule, although Secretary of Tourism offices usually open again 5–7 P.M.

Bank hours vary. Most are open Monday–Friday 8:30 A.M.–3 P.M., though some banks in larger towns are open on Saturday. The foreign exchange service usually closes around noon—probably to lock in the exchange rate before afternoon adjustments.

TRAVEL SERVICES
Tourist Information

Mexico's federal tourist bureau, the Secretaría de Turismo (SECTUR), has an office in La Paz that stocks free brochures, maps, hotel and restaurant lists, and information on local activities (Km 5–6 Mexico 1 or Av. Abasolo, tel. 612/124-0100, turismo@correro.gbcs.gob.mx).

To contact the national office directly, call or write the **Secretaría de Turismo de México** (Presidente Mazaryk 172, 11587 México, D.F., tel. 55/3002-6300). Or call these toll-free information lines: SECTUR, Mex. tel. 800/903-9200, U.S. tel. 800/482-9832, www.sectur.gob.mx/wb2.

Outside Mexico, SECTUR operates Mexican Tourism Board (www.visitmexico.com) offices to handle requests for tourist information; several are in the United States.

Travel Clubs

Baja's popularity as a boating and RV destination has spawned California-based travel clubs that specialize in recreational travel on the peninsula. Membership benefits include discounts (usually 10–20 percent) at various hotels, restaurants, and other tourist-oriented establishments in Mexico; discounted group auto and boat insurance; the opportunity to participate in such club events as tours and fiestas; and subscriptions to newsletters containing tips from other club members, short travel features, and the latest information on road conditions and Mexican tourism policy. The clubs can also arrange tourist cards, boat permits, and fishing licenses by mail.

Such clubs come and go, some lasting only a year or two. **Discover Baja Travel Club** (3089 Clairemont Dr., San Diego, CA 92117, U.S. tel. 619/275-1836 or 800/727-2252, www.discoverbaja.com, US$39/yr), the largest and most successful club of this nature, invites members or potential members to visit its San Diego area office on the way to Baja for up-to-date road and weather information. DB publishes an online newsletter and printed color magazine, both packed with information on road travel, sightseeing, and new developments in Baja travel.

Vagabundos del Mar (190 Main St., Rio Vista, CA 94571, U.S. tel. 707/374-5511 or 800/474-2252, www.vagabundos.com, US$35/yr), the older of the two clubs, is oriented toward boaters and RVers and publishes its newsletter, *Chubasco,* every two months. Its 13,000 members enjoy reduced rates for Mexican insurance, organized trips and events, online discussion boards, and good prices on charts, maps, and books.

MAPS

For general road travel in the Cape Region, the maps in this guidebook should suffice. If you're planning to drive farther north than La Paz, pick up one of the many Baja California maps available to visitors. Two maps are particularly well-suited to general-purpose Baja road travel. One is published by the Automobile Club of Southern California and is available from most AAA offices; maps are free to AAA members, or available online for about US$5 through Baja Books and Maps (www.bajabooksandmaps.com) and other sellers. This map is easy to read, accurate, and detailed enough for any border-to-Cape auto trip. Its excellent graphics include topographic shading. At last check, the most recent edition had been published in 2004.

International Travel Maps and Books (ITM or ITMB) publishes a well-researched map (last updated 2003) that's a bit harder to find. Ashland, Oregon–based Travel Essentials stocks it for purchase online (US$8,

www.travelessentials.com), or it can be ordered from ITM (345 W. Broadway, Vancouver, BC V5Y 1P8, Canada). In spite of its smaller scale (1:650,000), the ITM map is far more detailed than the AAA map, and all distances are entered in kilometers as well as miles. Many dirt roads, trails, and destinations unmarked on the AAA map appear on the ITM map. In addition, the map features contour lines in 200-meter intervals and is annotated with useful historical and sightseeing information. The main drawback is that it's so detailed it's difficult to read. In addition, the map's graphics scheme uses far too much red, a color particularly difficult to read in low light (e.g., under a car dome light). A waterproof version with inset maps of Tijuana, Mexicali, and La Paz was revised in 2006; it's available from Amazon.com.

For getting around La Paz, **Guia Roji** (www.guiaroji.com.mx), the largest map publisher in Mexico, publishes a detailed city map (scale 1:20,000) with street index. Guia Roji also publishes state maps to Baja California Sur (scale 1:350,000; including a La Paz city map) and Baja California Norte (scale 1:1,000,000; include Tijuana and Mexicali city maps)—last updated in 2004 and both available from Amazon.com for US$7 each. The complete Mexico atlas is invaluable for extended trips that will include the mainland.

Topographical Maps

Because differences in elevation often determine backcountry route selection, hikers, kayakers, mountain bikers, and off-road drivers should consider obtaining topographical maps before arriving in the Cape Region (see *Sports and Recreation*). Topo maps are difficult to come by in the Cape Region; in La Paz, try the Instituto Nacional de Estadística Geografía e Informática (INEGI, in Plaza Cuatro Molinos at Calle Altamirano 2790, Col. Centro, tel. 612/123-1545 or 612/122-4146, www.inegi.gob.mx). INEGI sells topo maps for Baja California Sur at around US$4 a sheet.

Communications

TELEPHONE SERVICES

The national telephone company, TelMex, privatized in 1990 and has improved its services considerably in the last decade or so. Local phone calls are relatively cheap—a two-peso coin pays for a phone-booth call—as are long-distance calls *within* Mexico. If you can find a working phone (many public phones seem permanently "out of order") connections are usually good, though you may have to wait a while to get through to the operator during busy periods such as Sundays and holidays.

If you don't want to use a phone booth or a hotel phone (hotels usually add their own surcharges to both local and long-distance calls), you can make a call during business hours from a TelMex office. Only large towns offer TelMex offices with public telecommunications facilities; a small town may offer a private telephone office (usually called *caseta de teléfono* or *caseta*

de larga distancia), a local shop, whe hotels, private tele to calls, but rates

A public pay phone s (acronym for "Larga Distancia Telef fers phone booths where you can pay for local or long-distance calls with a *tarjeta de teléfono* (phone card) issued by TelMex. You can buy debit cards in denominations of Mex\$20, Mex\$30, Mex\$50, and Mex\$100 at many pharmacies, convenience stores, supermarkets, bus terminals, and airports.

Area Codes and Local Numbers

All area codes in Mexico now have three digits, except for Mexico City (area code 55). You may occasionally see phone numbers written using older numbering systems. The number 612/142-4274 in La Paz, for example, appeared

---

TELEPHONE CODES

Mastering telephone dialing codes in a foreign country can confuse even the most technically proficient traveler. Here's a list of the most frequently used access codes, emergency numbers, and area codes.

USEFUL NUMBERS

Long-distance operator (national): 020
Time: 030
Directory assistance (local): 040
Mexico City area code: 55
Police, Red Cross, fire: 060
Emergency response: 066
Spanish-English emergency info: 07
International operator: 090

BAJA CALIFORNIA AREA CODES

Ciudad Constitución/Puerto San Carlos: 613
Ensenada: 646
Guerrero Negro/San Ignacio/Mulegé: 615
La Paz/Todos Santos: 612

Loreto: 613
Mexicali: 686
Rosarito: 661
San Felipe: 686
San José del Cabo/Cabo San Lucas: 624
San Quintín/El Rosario: 616
Tecate: 665
Tijuana: 664

CALLING MEXICO FROM ABROAD

Mexico's country code is 52. To call Mexico direct from outside the country, dial your international access code + 52 + area code + number. For example, to call the number 684-0461 in Tijuana from the United States, dial 011 (international access code) + 52 (Mexico country code) + 664 (Tijuana area code) + 684-0461. To dial a Mexican cell phone number from abroad, add a 1 before the area code, and omit the prefix 044 (used only when calling within Mexico).

in 2000, and as 114/2-4274 be-
...ar.

...November 2001, all telephone num-
...ooth states of Baja California, and most
...e numbers elsewhere in Mexico, consist of
...ven digits. This means if you are in La Paz
and intend to call what would formerly have
been written as 114/2-4274 or 1/142-4274
under one of the earlier systems, you must now
dial 612/142-4274.

There's no standard way of hyphenating the
numbers in Mexico. You may see the number
in our La Paz example written as 1424274, 14-
24274, 14-24-274, and so on.

Long-Distance Domestic Calls

To make a long-distance call within Mexico,
dial 01 plus the area code and number.

If you have a calling-card number for Sprint,
AT&T, MCI, Bell Canada, or British Telecom,
you can use it to make long-distance calls. Each
has its own access code for direct dialing.

Mobile Phones

Most of the Cape Region now enjoys reliable mobile phone access through two competing companies: Telcel and Moviestar. Telcel has better
coverage and lower rates. For extended stays in
Baja, during which you plan to make a number
of local calls, buying a low cost GSM phone and
prepaid cards can make sense. Using it to call the
United States will cost a fortune, unless you are a
Cingular/AT&T customer in the United States.

Two U.S. carriers offer North America plans
that include calling to/from Mexico to the
U.S.: Cingular (www.cingular.com/mexico)
charges US$4.99/month and US$0.59/min-
ute for roaming in Mexico. Verizon (www.
verizonwireless.com/international) partners
with Moviestar to offer North America calling for US$60/month for 450 minutes, and
US$0.45/minute after the monthly allowance.
International roaming on a standard U.S. plan
through Verizon costs US$0.69/minute. Text
messaging is not supported.

In 2007, rates for calling a Mexican cell
phone from the United States jumped about
US$0.17 cents a minute, due to changes in the

Mexican government's regulation of the telephone industry. Also, a caller-pays policy began
in 2006. When calling a Mexican cell phone
number from the United States, it's now necessary to add a 1 after the country code: 52 1
612/xxx-xxxx. Within Mexico, you need to add
044 before the area code: 044 612/xxx-xxxx.

International Calls

To direct dial an international call to the
United States or Canada via TelMex, dial
001 plus the area code and number for a sta-
tion-to-station call. For international calls
to other countries, dial 00 plus the country
code, area code, and number. For operator-
assisted calls, dial 09 plus the country code,
area code, and number. Long-distance international calls are heavily taxed and cost more
than equivalent international calls from the
United States or Canada.

To reach toll-free 800 numbers in Mexico,
dial 01 first. Dial 001 first for numbers in the
United States, or 091 for Canada.

Internet Phones

In areas with Internet access, voice-over-IP
(VoIP) calling is fast replacing the need for satellite phones and Ladatel cards. Skype (www.
skype.com), Gizmo VoIP (www.gizmovoip.
com), and Crystal Voice (www.crystalvoice.
com) are three of many service providers out
there. Rates are about US$0.01–0.03 per
minute, plus an account setup fee of around
US$10. Some companies include a free U.S.
number for family and friends back home to
dial while you are on the road.

Long Distance the Old-Fashioned Way

If you don't have access to the Internet, you
can dial access numbers to reach operators
from AT&T, MCI, or Sprint for calling-card
or credit card calls. For Canada Direct, dial
01 800/010-1990, and for BT Direct dial *791
(see the sidebar *Telephone Codes*).

The appropriate long-distance operator can
then place a collect call on your behalf or charge
the call to your account if you have a calling

card for that service. If you try these numbers from a hotel phone, be sure the hotel operator realizes the call is toll-free; some hotel operators use their own timers to assess phone charges.

Warning: Since the deregulation of Mexican telephone service, several unscrupulous U.S.-based long-distance phone companies have set up shop in Mexico to take advantage of undiscerning tourists. The English-language signs next to the phone usually read "Call the U.S. or Canada Collect or With a Credit Card" or "Just Dial Zero to Reach the U.S. or Canada." Another clue is that the name of the company is not posted on the sign. If you try asking the operators on the line who they represent, you'll find the same company often operates under several different names in the same area, charging at least 50 percent more per international call than TelMex, AT&T, MCI, or Sprint—or even many times more, as much as US$10–20 for the first minute, plus US$4 each additional minute, even on weekends. A percentage of these charges usually goes to the hotel or private phone office offering the service. At most private phone offices, it's cheaper to use TelMex, even if you have to pay a service charge on top of TelMex rates, than to use these price-gouging U.S. companies. Or use MCI, Sprint, AT&T, or one of the other more well-known international companies, which charge around US$0.15–0.35/minute. Unless you're independently wealthy, always ask which company is being used before you arrange an international call through a hotel or private phone office. Some Mexican hotels are now cooperating with these cutthroat American companies—the tip-off is a card next to the phone that says you can use credit cards to make a call to the United States or Canada.

Collect Calls

For international service, calling collect often saves hassles. In Spanish, the magic words are *por cobrar* (collect), prefaced by the name of the place you're calling (e.g., *"a los Estados Unidos, por favor—por cobrar"*). This connects you to an English-speaking international operator. For best results, speak slowly and clearly. You may reach an international operator directly by dialing 090.

Satellite Phone

For the many areas of Baja where there are no regular telephone lines, no radio phones, no Internet, and no cellular phone service, the only solution is satellite phone—assuming you *have* to stay in phone contact at all times. California Baja Rent-a-Car rents GPS-satellite phones, as does Discover Baja Travel Club (3089 Clairemont Dr., San Diego, CA 92117, U.S. tel. 619/275-1836 or 800/727-2252, www.discoverbaja.com).

EMAIL AND INTERNET ACCESS

To the surprise of many first-time visitors, high-speed Internet access is almost ubiquitous in the Cape Region these days. Hundreds of miles of fibre-optic cable were buried alongside the Transpeninsular Highway in 2002–2003, replacing the need for slow dial-up connections in most towns, and connecting Baja residents and visitors to computers and websites around the world.

Reliability is another matter, however. Even at the most well-equipped business centers have trouble keeping their connections up 24/7. If all you need to do is check your email now and then, this won't be a problem. But if you intend to run business processes remotely while on the road, it may be difficult to find a good setup.

Five-star resorts, espresso bars, marinas, and RV parks all have set wireless antennas for guests who travel with their own laptop or other Internet-enabled device. Some charge extra by the hour or day; others throw it in for the price of a latte. In the larger condo complexes, you may be able to find an open (unsecured) Wi-Fi network to use. And for those traveling sans computer, there are dozens of Internet cafés in hotels, real estate offices, and business centers with desktop machines, as well as printers, copiers, and scanners for imaging needs.

Rates vary widely, from free with a food or beverage purchase to US$8/hour at one of the hotels in San José.

In more remote areas of the peninsula, some residents and RV owners have costly satellite Internet service through providers like HughesNet (formerly Direcway) and Starband.

POSTAL SERVICES

The Mexican postal service, though reliable, is relatively slow. Average delivery time between Mexico and the United States or Canada is about 10 days, while to Europe you must figure two weeks. Mail sent to Mexico from outside the country generally reaches its destination more quickly.

Most towns in the Cape Region have a post office *(correo)* where you can receive general-delivery mail. Have correspondents address mail in your name (last name capitalized), followed by a/c Lista de Correos, Correo Central, the town name, the state, and the country; e.g., Joe CUMMINGS, a/c Lista de Correos, Correo Central, La Paz, Baja California Sur, Mexico. Mail sent this way is usually held 10 days. If you want your mail held up to 30 days, substitute the words "Poste Restante" for Lista de Correos in the address. If you have the postal code for the town or city, insert it just after the state name. Since delivery time is highly variable, it's best to use *poste restante* just to be safe.

Many foreigners who are seasonal Cape residents have their mail sent in care of a hotel or RV park. You can rent boxes at larger Mexican post offices, but the initial application process often takes several weeks. Todos Santos, Cabo San Lucas, and La Paz have private mail companies that also rent boxes with minimal red tape.

The Mexican post office offers an express mail service (EMS) called Mexpost. International rates are relatively high; a Mexpost express letter to the United States or Canada, for example, costs US$15, to Europe US$18. Mexpost claims to deliver almost anywhere in Mexico within 48 hours, to major cities around the world within 72 hours.

UPS, Airborne Express, DHL, FedEx, and other courier services operate in La Paz and Cabo San Lucas. So far DHL and UPS seem to offer the lowest prices and best services. Local companies such as Estafeta and Aeroflash are also available, but reliability does not appear to match that of the international services.

Measurements and Standards

WEIGHTS AND MEASURES

Mexico uses the metric system as the official system of weights and measures. This means the distance between La Paz and San José del Cabo is measured in kilometers, cheese is weighed in grams or kilograms, a hot day in Cabo San Lucas is 32°C, gasoline is sold by the liter, and a big fish is two meters long. A chart at the end of this book converts pounds, gallons, and miles to kilograms, liters, and kilometers.

Bajacalifornianos used to dealing with American tourists often use the Anglo-American and metric systems interchangeably. Even rancheros in remote areas occasionally use *millas* (miles) as a measure.

In this book, distances are rendered in kilometers, often followed by miles in parentheses. All road markers in Mexico employ the metric system. Dimensions and weights are usually quoted using the metric system, but boat lengths and fishing line tests are quoted in feet and pounds (because of the influence of American boaters and anglers).

TIME

Baja California Sur lies in the mountain time zone and observes daylight saving time from the first Sunday in April to the last Sunday in October.

Time in Mexico is often expressed according to the 24-hour clock, from 0001 to 2359 (one minute past midnight to 11:59 P.M.). A restaurant posting hours of 1100–2200, for example, is open 11 A.M.–10 P.M.

ELECTRICITY

Mexico's electrical system is the same as that in the United States and Canada: 110 volts, 60 cycles, alternating current (AC). Electrical outlets are of the North American type, designed to work with appliances with standard double-bladed plugs.

RESOURCES
Glossary

abarrotes groceries

aduana customs service

alta cocina mexicana Mexican food prepared in a "high cuisine," or gourmet, style

antojitos literally "little whims," quick Mexican dishes like tacos and enchiladas

aparejo burro saddle

bahía bay

basura trash or rubbish; a sign saying No Tire Basura means Don't Throw Trash.

BCD buoyancy compensation device

BCN the state of Baja California Norte, more properly called just Baja California

BCS the state of Baja California Sur

boca literally "mouth," a geographic term describing a break in a barrier island or peninsula where sea meets lagoon

calle street

callejón alley or lane

cañon canyon

cardón Pachycereus pringlei, the world's tallest cactus

casa de huéspedes guesthouse

cerro mountain peak

cerveza beer

charreada Mexican-style rodeo

charro/charra horseman/horsewoman

colectivo van or taxi that picks up several passengers at a time for a standard per-person fare, much like a bus

correo post office

corrida de toros "running of the bulls" or bullfight

COTP captain of the port, capitanía del puerto in Spanish

curandero traditional healer

Diconsa Distribuidora Conasupo, S.A., a government-subsidized food distributor

efectivo cash payment

ejido collectively owned agricultural lands

ensenada cove or small bay

Fonatur Fondo Nacional de Fomento del Turismo (National Foundation for Tourism Development)

Gral. abbreviation for General (rank)

hostería hostelry, inn

IMSS Instituto Mexicano del Seguro Social (Mexican Social Security Institute)

INAH Instituto Nacional de Antropología e Historia (National Institute of Anthropology and History)

indios Mexicans of predominantly Amerindian descent; indígenas (indigenes) is the less common, but more politically correct, term

INEGI Instituto Nacional de Estadística, Geografía e Informática (National Institute of Statistics, Geography, and Information)

ISSSTE Instituto de Seguridad y Servicios Sociales para Trabajadores del Estado (Security and Social Services Institute for Government Workers)

laguna lagoon, lake, or bay

llano plains

lleno full

malecón waterfront promenade

maquiladora (maquila) a "twin-bond" or "in-plant" manufacturing enterprise where foreign components may be imported and assembled, then exported to a foreign country, free of customs duties in each direction; now that NAFTA has been enacted, the maquiladora may become extinct

mariscos literally "shellfish," but often used as a generic term for seafood

mercado market

mochila knapsack or backpack

mochilero backpacker

nopalitos strips of cooked or pickled prickly-pear cactus

PADI Professional Association of Dive Instructors

palacio municipal literally "municipal palace," equivalent to city or county hall in the United States

palapa thatched, umbrella-like shade shelter or roof

PAN Partido Acción Nacional

panadería bakery

parrada bus stop

Pemex Petroleos Mexicanos (Mexican Petroleum)

pensión boardinghouse

playa beach

plazuela smaller plaza

PRD Partido Revolucionario Democrático

pre-Cortesian a reference to Mexican history before the arrival of Spanish conquistador Hernán Cortés, i.e., before 1518; other terms with the same meaning include pre-Columbian (before Columbus's arrival) and pre-Hispanic (before the arrival of the Spanish)

PRI Partido Revolucionario Institucional

punta point

ramal branch road

rancheria a collection of small ranching households, most often inhabited by *indios*

ranchito small ranch

SECTUR Secretaría de Turismo (Secretariat of Tourism)

SEDESOL Secretaría de Desarrollo Social (Secretariat of Social Development)

SEMARNAT Secretaría de Medio Ambiente y Recursos Naturales (Secretariat of the Environment and Natural Resources)

tienda store

tinaja pool or spring

topes speed bumps

ultramarinos minimarket/delicatessen

ABBREVIATIONS

Av. Avenida

Calz. Calzada

Col. Colonia (neighborhood)

nte. *norte* (north)

ote. *oriente* (east)

pte. *poniente* (west)

s/n *sin número* ("without number," used for street addresses without building numbers)

Spanish Phrasebook

Your Mexico adventure will be more fun if you use a little Spanish. Mexican folks, although they may smile at your funny accent, will appreciate your halting efforts to break the ice and transform yourself from a foreigner to a potential friend.

Spanish commonly uses 30 letters – the familiar English 26, plus four straightforward additions: ch, ll, ñ, and rr, which are explained in "Consonants," below.

PRONUNCIATION

Once you learn them, Spanish pronunciation rules – in contrast to English – don't change. Spanish vowels generally sound softer than in English. (*Note:* The capitalized syllables below receive stronger accents.)

Vowels

a like ah, as in "hah": *agua* AH-gooah (water), *pan* PAHN (bread), and *casa* CAH-sah (house)

e like ay, as in "may:" *mesa* MAY-sah (table), *tela* TAY-lah (cloth), and *de* DAY (of, from)

i like ee, as in "need": *diez* dee-AYZ (ten), *comida* ko-MEE-dah (meal), and *fin* FEEN (end)

o like oh, as in "go": *peso* PAY-soh (weight), *ocho* OH-choh (eight), and *poco* POH-koh (a bit)

u like oo, as in "cool": *uno* OO-noh (one), *cuarto* KOOAHR-toh (room), and *usted* oos-TAYD (you); when it follows a "q" the **u** is silent; when it follows an "h" or has an umlaut, it's pronounced like "w"

Consonants

b, d, f, k, l, m, n, p, q, s,
t, v, w, x, y, z, and ch
pronounced almost as in English; **h** occurs, but is silent – not pronounced at all.

c like k as in "keep": *cuarto* KOOAR-toh (room), Tepic tay-PEEK (capital of Nayarit state); when it precedes "e" or "i," pronounce **c** like s, as in "sit": *cerveza* sayr-VAY-sah (beer), *encima* ayn-SEE-mah (atop).

g like g as in "gift" when it precedes "a," "o," "u," or a consonant: *gato* GAH-toh (cat), *hago* AH-goh (I do, make); otherwise, pronounce **g** like h as in "hat": *giro* HEE-roh (money order), *gente* HAYN-tay (people)

j like h, as in "has": *Jueves* HOOAY-vays (Thursday), *mejor* may-HOR (better)

ll like y, as in "yes": *toalla* toh-AH-yah (towel), *ellos* AY-yohs (they, them)

ñ like ny, as in "canyon": *año* AH-nyo (year), *señor* SAY-nyor (Mr., sir)

r is lightly trilled, with tongue at the roof of your mouth like a very light English d, as in "ready": *pero* PAY-doh (but), *tres* TDAYS (three), *cuatro* KOOAH-tdoh (four).

rr like a Spanish r, but with much more emphasis and trill. Let your tongue flap. Practice with *burro* (donkey), *carretera* (highway), and Carrillo (proper name), then really let go with *ferrocarril* (railroad).

Note: The single small but common exception to all of the above is the pronunciation of Spanish **y** when it's being used as the Spanish word for "and," as in "Ron y Kathy." In such case, pronounce it like the English ee, as in "keep": Ron "ee" Kathy (Ron and Kathy).

Accent

The rule for accent, the relative stress given to syllables within a given word, is straightforward. If a word ends in a vowel, an n, or an s, accent the next-to-last syllable; if not, accent the last syllable.

Pronounce *gracias* GRAH-seeahs (thank you), *orden* OHR-dayn (order), and *carretera* kah-ray-TAY-rah (highway) with stress on the next-to-last syllable.

Otherwise, accent the last syllable: *venir* vay-NEER (to come), *ferrocarril* fay-roh-cah-REEL (railroad), and *edad* ay-DAHD (age).

Exceptions to the accent rule are always marked with an accent sign: (á, é, í, ó, or ú), such as *teléfono* tay-LAY-foh-noh (telephone), *jabón* hah-BON (soap), and *rápido* RAH-pee-doh (rapid).

BASIC AND COURTEOUS EXPRESSIONS

Most Spanish-speaking people consider formalities important. Whenever approaching anyone for information or some other reason, do not forget the appropriate salutation – good morning, good evening, etc. Standing alone, the greeting *hola* (hello) can sound brusque.

Hello. *Hola.*
Good morning. *Buenos días.*
Good afternoon. *Buenas tardes.*
Good evening. *Buenas noches.*
How are you? *¿Cómo está usted?*
Very well, thank you. *Muy bien, gracias.*
Okay; good. *Bien.*
Not okay; bad. *Mal or feo.*
So-so. *Más o menos.*
And you? *¿Y usted?*
Thank you. *Gracias.*
Thank you very much. *Muchas gracias.*
You're very kind. *Muy amable.*
You're welcome. *De nada.*
Goodbye. *Adios.*
See you later. *Hasta luego.*
please *por favor*
yes *sí*
no *no*
I don't know. *No sé.*
Just a moment, please. *Momentito, por favor.*
Excuse me, please (when you're trying to get attention). *Disculpe or Con permiso.*
Excuse me (when you've made an error). *Lo siento.*
Pleased to meet you. *Mucho gusto.*
How do you say ... in Spanish? *¿Cómo se dice ... en español?*
What is your name? *¿Cómo se llama usted?*
Do you speak English? *¿Habla usted inglés?*
Is English spoken here? (Does anyone here speak English?) *¿Se habla inglés?*
I don't speak Spanish well. *No hablo bien el español.*
I don't understand. *No entiendo.*
How do you say ... in Spanish? *¿Cómo se dice ... en español?*
My name is ... *Me llamo ...*
Would you like ... *¿Quisiera usted ...*
Let's go to ... *Vamos a ...*

TERMS OF ADDRESS

When in doubt, use the formal *usted* (you) as a form of address.

I *yo*
you (formal) *usted*
you (familiar) *tu*
he/him *él*
she/her *ella*
we/us *nosotros*
you (plural) *ustedes*
they/them *ellos* (all males or mixed gender); *ellas* (all females)
Mr., sir *señor*
Mrs., madam *señora*
miss, young lady *señorita*
wife *esposa*
husband *esposo*
friend *amigo* (male); *amiga* (female)
sweetheart *novio* (male); *novia* (female)
son; daughter *hijo; hija*
brother; sister *hermano; hermana*
father; mother *padre; madre*
grandfather; grandmother *abuelo; abuela*

TRANSPORTATION

Where is ... ? *¿Dónde está ... ?*
How far is it to ... ? *¿A cuánto está ... ?*
from ... to ... *de ... a ...*
How many blocks? *¿Cuántas cuadras?*
Where (Which) is the way to ... ? *¿Dónde está el camino a ... ?*
the bus station *la terminal de autobuses*
the bus stop *la parada de autobuses*
Where is this bus going? *¿Adónde va este autobús?*
the taxi stand *la parada de taxis*
the train station *la estación de ferrocarril*
the boat *el barco*
the launch *lancha; tiburonera*
the dock *el muelle*
the airport *el aeropuerto*
I'd like a ticket to ... *Quisiera un boleto a ...*
first (second) class *primera (segunda) clase*
roundtrip *ida y vuelta*
reservation *reservación*
baggage *equipaje*

Stop here, please. *Pare aquí, por favor.*
the entrance *la entrada*
the exit *la salida*
the ticket office *la oficina de boletos*
(very) near; far *(muy) cerca; lejos*
to; toward *a*
by; through *por*
from *de*
the right *la derecha*
the left *la izquierda*
straight ahead *derecho; directo*
in front *en frente*
beside *al lado*
behind *atrás*
the corner *la esquina*
the stoplight *la semáforo*
a turn *una vuelta*
right here *aquí*
somewhere around here *por acá*
right there *allí*
somewhere around there *por allá*
road *el camino*
street; boulevard *calle; bulevar*
block *la cuadra*
highway *carretera*
kilometer *kilómetro*
bridge; toll *puente; cuota*
address *dirección*
north; south *norte; sur*
east; west *oriente (este); poniente (oeste)*

ACCOMMODATIONS
hotel *hotel*
Is there a room? *¿Hay cuarto?*
May I (may we) see it? *¿Puedo (podemos) verlo?*
What is the rate? *¿Cuál es el precio?*
Is that your best rate? *¿Es su mejor precio?*
Is there something cheaper? *¿Hay algo más económico?*
a single room *un cuarto sencillo*
a double room *un cuarto doble*
double bed *cama matrimonial*
twin beds *camas gemelas*
with private bath *con baño*
hot water *agua caliente*
shower *ducha*
towels *toallas*

soap *jabón*
toilet paper *papel higiénico*
blanket *frazada; manta*
sheets *sábanas*
air-conditioned *aire acondicionado*
fan *abanico; ventilador*
key *llave*
manager *gerente*

FOOD
I'm hungry *Tengo hambre.*
I'm thirsty. *Tengo sed.*
menu *carta; menú*
order *orden*
glass *vaso*
fork *tenedor*
knife *cuchillo*
spoon *cuchara*
napkin *servilleta*
soft drink *refresco*
coffee *café*
tea *té*
drinking water *agua pura; agua potable*
bottled carbonated water *agua mineral*
bottled uncarbonated water *agua sin gas*
beer *cerveza*
wine *vino*
milk *leche*
juice *jugo*
cream *crema*
sugar *azúcar*
cheese *queso*
snack *antojo; botana*
breakfast *desayuno*
lunch *almuerzo*
daily lunch special *comida corrida (or el menú del día depending on region)*
dinner *comida (often eaten in late afternoon); cena (a late-night snack)*
the check *la cuenta*
eggs *huevos*
bread *pan*
salad *ensalada*
fruit *fruta*
mango *mango*
watermelon *sandía*
papaya *papaya*
banana *plátano*

apple *manzana*
orange *naranja*
lime *limón*
fish *pescado*
shellfish *mariscos*
shrimp *camarones*
meat (without) *(sin) carne*
chicken *pollo*
pork *puerco*
beef; steak *res; bistec*
bacon; ham *tocino; jamón*
fried *frito*
roasted *asada*
barbecue; barbecued *barbacoa; al carbón*

SHOPPING

money *dinero*
money-exchange bureau *casa de cambio*
I would like to exchange traveler's checks. *Quisiera cambiar cheques de viajero.*
What is the exchange rate? *¿Cuál es el tipo de cambio?*
How much is the commission? *¿Cuánto cuesta la comisión?*
Do you accept credit cards? *¿Aceptan tarjetas de crédito?*
money order *giro*
How much does it cost? *¿Cuánto cuesta?*
What is your final price? *¿Cuál es su último precio?*
expensive *caro*
cheap *barato; económico*
more *más*
less *menos*
a little *un poco*
too much *demasiado*

HEALTH

Help me please. *Ayúdeme por favor.*
I am ill. *Estoy enfermo.*
Call a doctor. *Llame un doctor.*
Take me to . . . *Lléveme a . . .*
hospital *hospital; sanatorio*
drugstore *farmacia*
pain *dolor*
fever *fiebre*
headache *dolor de cabeza*

stomach ache *dolor de estómago*
burn *quemadura*
cramp *calambre*
nausea *náusea*
vomiting *vomitar*
medicine *medicina*
antibiotic *antibiótico*
pill; tablet *pastilla*
aspirin *aspirina*
ointment; cream *pomada; crema*
bandage *venda*
cotton *algodón*
sanitary napkins *use brand name, e.g., Kotex*
birth control pills *pastillas anticonceptivas*
contraceptive foam *espuma anticonceptiva*
condoms *preservativos; condones*
toothbrush *cepilla dental*
dental floss *hilo dental*
toothpaste *crema dental*
dentist *dentista*
toothache *dolor de muelas*

POST OFFICE AND COMMUNICATIONS

long-distance telephone *teléfono larga distancia*
I would like to call . . . *Quisiera llamar a . . .*
collect *por cobrar*
station to station *a quien contesta*
person to person *persona a persona*
credit card *tarjeta de crédito*
post office *correo*
general delivery *lista de correo*
letter *carta*
stamp *estampilla, timbre*
postcard *tarjeta*
aerogram *aerograma*
air mail *correo aereo*
registered *registrado*
money order *giro*
package; box *paquete; caja*
string; tape *cuerda; cinta*

AT THE BORDER

border *frontera*
customs *aduana*
immigration *migración*
tourist card *tarjeta de turista*

inspection *inspección; revisión*
passport *pasaporte*
profession *profesión*
marital status *estado civil*
single *soltero*
married; divorced *casado; divorciado*
widowed *viudado*
insurance *seguros*
title *título*
driver's license *licencia de manejar*

AT THE GAS STATION
gas station *gasolinera*
gasoline *gasolina*
unleaded *sin plomo*
full, please *lleno, por favor*
tire *llanta*
tire repair shop *vulcanizadora*
air *aire*
water *agua*
oil (change) *aceite (cambio)*
grease *grasa*
My . . . doesn't work. *Mi . . . no sirve.*
battery *batería*
radiator *radiador*
alternator *alternador*
generator *generador*
tow truck *grúa*
repair shop *taller mecánico*
tune-up *afinación*
auto parts store *refaccionería*

VERBS
Verbs are the key to getting along in Spanish. They employ mostly predictable forms and come in three classes, which end in *ar*, *er*, and *ir*, respectively:
to buy *comprar*
I buy, you (he, she, it) buys *compro, compra*
we buy, you (they) buy *compramos, compran*

to eat *comer*
I eat, you (he, she, it) eats *como, come*
we eat, you (they) eat *comemos, comen*

to climb *subir*
I climb, you (he, she, it) climbs *subo, sube*
we climb, you (they) climb *subimos, suben*

Here are more (with irregularities indicated):
to do or make *hacer* (regular except for *hago*, I do or make)
to go *ir* (very irregular: *voy, va, vamos, van*)
to go (walk) *andar*
to love *amar*
to work *trabajar*
to want *desear, querer*
to need *necesitar*
to read *leer*
to write *escribir*
to repair *reparar*
to stop *parar*
to get off (the bus) *bajar*
to arrive *llegar*
to stay (remain) *quedar*
to stay (lodge) *hospedar*
to leave *salir* (regular except for *salgo*, I leave)
to look at *mirar*
to look for *buscar*
to give *dar* (regular except for *doy*, I give)
to carry *llevar*
to have *tener* (irregular but important: *tengo*, *tiene, tenemos, tienen*)
to come *venir* (similarly irregular: *vengo*, *viene, venimos, vienen*)

Spanish has two forms of "to be":
to be *estar* (regular except for *estoy*, I am)
to be *ser* (very irregular: *soy, es, somos, son*)
Use *estar* when speaking of location or a temporary state of being: "I am at home." "*Estoy en casa.*" "I'm sick." "*Estoy enfermo.*" Use *ser* for a permanent state of being: "I am a doctor." "*Soy doctora.*"

NUMBERS
zero *cero*
one *uno*
two *dos*
three *tres*
four *cuatro*
five *cinco*
six *seis*
seven *siete*
eight *ocho*
nine *nueve*

10 *diez*
11 *once*
12 *doce*
13 *trece*
14 *catorce*
15 *quince*
16 *dieciseis*
17 *diecisiete*
18 *dieciocho*
19 *diecinueve*
20 *veinte*
21 *veinte y uno* or *veintiuno*
30 *treinta*
40 *cuarenta*
50 *cincuenta*
60 *sesenta*
70 *setenta*
80 *ochenta*
90 *noventa*
100 *ciento*
101 *ciento y uno* or *cientiuno*
200 *doscientos*
500 *quinientos*
1,000 *mil*
10,000 *diez mil*
100,000 *cien mil*
1,000,000 *millón*
one half *medio*
one third *un tercio*
one fourth *un cuarto*

TIME

What time is it? *¿Qué hora es?*
It's one o'clock. *Es la una.*
It's three in the afternoon. *Son las tres de la tarde.*

It's 4 A.M. *Son las cuatro de la mañana.*
six-thirty *seis y media*
a quarter till eleven *un cuarto para las once*
a quarter past five *las cinco y cuarto*
an hour *una hora*

DAYS AND MONTHS

Monday *lunes*
Tuesday *martes*
Wednesday *miércoles*
Thursday *jueves*
Friday *viernes*
Saturday *sábado*
Sunday *domingo*
today *hoy*
tomorrow *mañana*
yesterday *ayer*
January *enero*
February *febrero*
March *marzo*
April *abril*
May *mayo*
June *junio*
July *julio*
August *agosto*
September *septiembre*
October *octubre*
November *noviembre*
December *diciembre*
a week *una semana*
a month *un mes*
after *después*
before *antes*

(Courtesy of Bruce Whipperman, author of *Moon Pacific Mexico*.)

Suggested Reading

TRAVELOGUES

Amey, Ralph. *Wines of Baja California: Touring and Tasting Mexico's Undiscovered Treasures.* South San Francisco: The Wine Appreciation Guild, 2003. For those who plan to explore the Valle de Guadalupe, this small book gives a good overview of the wineries, with some history, as well as background on grapes and vintages.

Berger, Bruce. *Almost an Island: Travels in Baja California.* Tucson: University of Arizona Press, 1998. Berger, a pianist, poet, desert aficionado, and keen observer of human behavior, surveys Baja's social landscape, with a special focus on La Paz.

Burleson, Bob, and David H. Riskind. *Backcountry Mexico: A Traveler's Guide and Phrase Book.* Austin, TX: University of Texas Press, 1986. Part guidebook, part anthropological study covering Northern Mexico, with some relevance to Baja California backcountry travel.

Cudahy, John. *Mañanaland: Adventuring with Camera and Rifle Through California in Mexico.* New York: Duffie and Co., 1928. This hard-to-find text provides an interesting glimpse of pre–World War II Baja, but no outstanding revelations. Out of print.

Mackintosh, Graham. *Into a Desert Place.* New York: W. W. Norton & Co., 1994. A thoroughly engaging report of Mackintosh's walk around the entire coastline of Baja California during the course of two years. A classic of gringo-in-Baja travel literature for its refreshingly honest style and insights into Baja fishcamp and village life.

Mayo, C. M. *Miraculous Air: Journey of a Thousand Miles through Baja California, the Other Mexico.* University of Utah Press, 2002. Poignant, contemporary memoir by a fiction writer, Spanish/English translator, and editor, who lives in Mexico City.

Miller, Max. *Land Where Time Stands Still.* New York: Dodd, Mead, and Co., 1943. A classic travelogue that chronicles Baja life during World War II, when Mexicans alternately fell prey to German and American propaganda. Out of print.

Salvadori, Clement. *Motorcycle Journeys Through California and Baja,* 2nd Ed. North Conway, NH: Whitehorse Press, 2007. Having written more than 1,000 articles for dozens of motorcycle magazines in his 30-year career, this author does an admirable job of digesting the peninsula for other motorcyclists who might want to tackle the Holy Grail of North American road trips. Contains lots of invaluable tips.

Steinbeck, John. *The Log from the Sea of Cortez.* New York: Penguin USA, Viking, 1951. This chronicle of the author's Baja research voyage with marine biologist Ed Ricketts (the inspiration for *Cannery Row* protagonist "Doc") reveals Steinbeck as a bit of a scientist himself. Annotated with Latin, the book is full of insights into Pacific and Sea of Cortez marinelife as well as coastal *bajacaliforniano* society. Sprinkled throughout are expositions of Steinbeck's personal philosophy, implicit in his novels but fully articulated here. Also reveals the source for his novella *The Pearl.*

HISTORY AND CULTURE

Crosby, Harry. *Antigua California: Mission and Colony on the Peninsular Frontier, 1697–1768.* Albuquerque: University of New Mexico Press, 1994. This well-researched and detailed history covers the Jesuit period in Baja, from the mission planning stages in Sonora and Sinaloa through the expulsion from New Spain.

Francez, James Donald. *The Lost Treasures of Baja California*. Chula Vista, CA: Black Forest Press, 1997. A slim, hardbound volume containing chronicles of 19 Jesuit missions, in Spanish and English. Notable for its identification of some of the more obscure saints and iconographic elements in the mission sanctuaries and the inclusion of photos of models constructed by the author depicting missions—such as Comondú—that no longer exist.

Niemann, Greg. *Baja Legends*. San Diego, CA: Sunbelt Publications, 2002. A colorful gringo account of the people, events, and locations that shaped Baja California into the travel destination it is today.

Paz, Octavio. *The Labyrinth of Solitude: Life and Thought in Mexico*. New York: Grove/Atlantic Inc., Grove Press, 1961. Paz has no peer when it comes to expositions of the Mexican psyche, and this is his best work. Out of print.

Robertson, Tomás. *Baja California and Its Missions*. Glendale, CA: La Siesta Press, 1978. Robertson was the patriarch of an old Baja California–Sinaloa family of northern European extraction as well as a patron of Baja mission restoration. His useful amateur work synthesizes Baja mission history from several sources; like its sources, the book contains a few minor contradictions and muddy areas. Out of print.

NATURAL HISTORY AND FIELD GUIDES

Case, T. J., and M. L. Cody, eds. *A New Island Biogeography in the Sea of Cortez,* 2nd Ed. Oxford University Press, 2002. An updated and revised (from the 1983 original) collection of essays on the geography and wildlife of various Cortez islands.

Edwards, Ernest Preston. *The Birds of Mexico and Adjacent Areas*. Austin: University of Texas Press, 1998. A field guide to birds of Mexico, Belize, Guatemala, and El Salvador, with excellent illustrations and detailed descriptions for easy identification of all of Mexico's regular species.

Gotshall, Daniell W. *Sea of Cortez Marine Animals: A Guide to the Common Fishes and Invertebrates Baja California to Panama*. Sea Challengers, 1998. A good reference guide to divers, sailors, and snorkelers.

Krutch, Joseph Wood. *The Forgotten Peninsula: A Naturalist in Baja California*. Tucson: University of Arizona Press, 1986 (reprint from 1961). Combines natural history and a curmudgeonly travelogue style to paint a romantic portrait of pre–Transpeninsular Highway Baja.

Leatherwood, S., and R. R. Reeves. *The Sierra Club Handbook of Whales and Dolphins*. San Francisco: Sierra Club Books, 1983. A useful field guide for identifying cetaceans in Baja seas.

Nickerson, Roy. *The Friendly Whales: A Whalewatcher's Guide to the Gray Whales of Baja California*. San Francisco: Chronicle Books, 1987. A light study, with photographs, of the friendly whale phenomenon in Laguna San Ignacio, where gray whales often initiate contact with humans. Out of print.

Peterson, R. T., and E. L. Chaliff. *A Field Guide to Mexican Birds*. Boston: Houghton Mifflin Co., 1999. Although it may be a little weak on birds found in Baja, this updated edition is still one of the best handbooks for identifying Mexican bird life.

Roberts, Norman C. *Baja California Plant Field Guide*. Natural History Publishing Co., 1989. Contains concise descriptions of more than 550 species of Baja flora, more than half illustrated by color photos.

Scammon, Charles Melville. *The Marine Mammals of the Northwestern Coast of America*. Mineola, NY: Dover Publications reprint, 1968. Originally published in the 19th century by the whaler who almost brought about the gray whale's complete demise, this is *the* classic, pioneering work on Pacific cetaceans, including the gray whale. Out of print.

Thomson, Donald A. and Lloyd T. Findley, Alex N. Kerstitch. *Reef Fishes of the Sea of Cortez: The Rocky-Shore Fishes of the Gulf of California. Revised Edition.* University of Texas Press, 2000. Produced by an ecologist, a taxonomist, and an artist-photographer, the new version of this 1979 reference guide gives Spanish (and English) names for fish.

Wiggins, Ira L. *Flora of Baja California.* Stanford, CA: Stanford University Press, 1980. This weighty work, with listings of more than 2,900 species, is a must for the serious botanist. But for the average layperson with an interest in Baja vegetation, Norman Roberts's *Baja California Plant Field Guide* (see above) will more than suffice.

Zwinger, Ann Raymond. *A Desert Country near the Sea.* New York: Penguin USA, Truman M. Talley Books, 1983. A collection of poetic essays centered around Baja natural history (including a rare passage on the Sierra de La Laguna), with sketches by the author and an appendix with Latin names for flora and fauna. Out of print.

SPORTS AND RECREATION

Cummings, Joe and Nikki Goth Itoi. *Moon Baja,* 7th ed. Emeryville, CA: Avalon Travel Publishing, Inc., 2007. If you like the Cape Region, you'll probably love the rest of Baja California Sur and Baja California to the north. Now in its seventh edition, this guide covers the entire peninsula from Tijuana to Cabo San Lucas.

Fons, Valerie. *Keep It Moving: Baja by Canoe.* Seattle: The Mountaineers, 1986. Well-written account of a canoe trip along the Baja California coastline; recommended reading for sea kayakers as well as canoeists. Out of print.

Kelly, Neil, and Gene Kira. *The Baja Catch: A Fishing, Travel & Remote Camping Manual for Baja California,* 3rd Ed. Valley Center, CA: Apples and Oranges, 1997. Contains extensive discussions of lures and tackle, expert fishing techniques, and detailed directions to productive fisheries, plus numerous maps.

Lehman, Charles. *Desert Survival Handbook,* Revised Ed. Phoenix: Primer Publishers, 1998. A no-nonsense guide to desert survival techniques; should be included in every pilot's or coastal navigator's kit.

Parise, Mike. *The Surfer's Guide to Baja.* Surfpress Publishing, 2001. A must-have resource for Baja-bound surfers, the guide includes detailed directions to more than 75 breaks along the peninsula, plus maps and wave height charts.

Romano-Lax, Andromeda. *Sea Kayaking in Baja.* Berkeley, CA: Wilderness Press, 1993. This inspiring 153-page guide to Baja kayaking contains 15 one- to five-day paddling routes along the Baja coastline, plus many helpful hints on kayak camping. Each route is accompanied by a map; although these maps are too sketchy to be used for navigation, a list of Mexican topographic map numbers is provided so that readers can go out and obtain more accurate material. Out of print.

Tsegeletos, George. *Under the Sea of Cortez (Early Underwater Exploration and Spearfishing).* Chapel Hill, NC: Professional Press, 1998. Early in this case means starting in 1962, and the accounts make for fascinating, if a bit sorrowful (knowing how much marinelife has been lost in just 40 years), reading. Out of print.

Williams, Jack. *Baja Boater's Guide, Vols. I and II.* Sausalito, CA: H. J. Williams Publications, 2001 (Vol. I, 3rd Ed.) and 2003 (Vol. II, 4th Ed.). These ambitious guides, one each on the Pacific Ocean and the Sea of Cortez, contain useful aerial photos and sketch maps of Baja's continental islands and coastline.

Wong, Bonnie. *Bicycling Baja*. El Cajon, CA: Sunbelt Publications, 1988. Written by an experienced leader of Baja cycling tours, this book includes helpful suggestions on trip preparation, equipment, and riding techniques, as well as road logs for 17 different cycling routes throughout the peninsula. Out of print.

Wyatt, Michael. *The Basic Essentials of Sea Kayaking*, 3rd Ed. Falcon, 2005. A good introduction to sea kayaking, with tips on buying gear, paddling techniques, and safety.

REAL ESTATE AND LIVING ABROAD

Luboff, Ken. *Living Abroad in Mexico*. Emeryville, CA: Avalon Travel Publishing, 2005. This resource gives advice and tips for Americans thinking of moving to Mexico.

Peyton, Dennis John. *How to Buy Real Estate in Mexico*. San Diego: Law Mexico Publishing, 2006. The most thorough and in-depth reference available in English on buying Mexican property. Anyone considering real estate investments in Mexico should read this book before making any decisions.

Internet Resources

Most of the travel information you find on the Web today is clearly tailored to selling a tourism product—hotel, condo, restaurant, sports activity—without offering related information of much use. And many of these sites were designed in the mid-1990s and haven't been redesigned since. Forums, in which impassioned participants voice their many opinions, are a notable exception.

Baja.com
www.baja.com
One of the earliest Baja-focused online communities still ranks among the highest in traffic.

Baja Books and Maps
www.bajabooksandmaps.com
Online bookstore with an impressive collection of Baja-related titles.

Baja Bush Pilots
www.bajabushpilots.com
A must-read for pilots interested in flying a private aircraft to Baja.

Baja Nomad
www.bajanomad.com
Still the best all-around Baja site for hard infor-

mation that doesn't appear to have been paid for, with more nitty-gritty information than any rival. Great links page, copious information on hotels and restaurants, plus continually updated Baja news and essays.

BajaQuest
www.bajaquest.com
Mainly classified listings, with several active discussion boards.

Baja Travel Guide
www.bajatravel.com
An advertiser-driven site covering all of Baja, with telephone listings, maps, and calendar of events.

Cruise the Sea of Cortez
www.cruisecortez.com
A site for people who sail or who would like to sail the Cortez. Although the home page says the site was last updated in 2003, the messageboard has a number of current posts.

In Search of the Blue Agave
www.ianchadwick.com/tequila
An excellent website devoted to tequila connoisseurship, though it hasn't been updated in several years.

Instituto Nacional de Estadística, Geografía e Informática
www.inegi.gob.mx

This Mexican government agency publishes statistics on population and economics for all of Mexico, as well as complete topographical maps. Spanish only.

iWindsurf.com and iKitesurf.com
www.iwindsurf.com
www.ikitesurf.com

Daily Baja wind forecast and reports for windsurfers, plus a whole range of consumer weather delivery services, from the parent company WeatherFlow.

Los Cabos Guide
www.loscabosguide.com

Relatively up-to-date, advertiser-driven listings of hospitality and tourism businesses in the Los Cabos area, with some coverage of the East Cape and Todos Santos.

Mexico Online
www.mexonline.com/baja.htm

Advertiser-driven site that hosts home pages for many Baja businesses.

Mr.News.Mx
www.mrnewsmx.com

A news digest for Mexico news in English from many sources.

NaftaNet
www.nafta-sec-alena.org

Information pertinent to the North American Free Trade Agreement.

Olsen Currency Converter
www.oanda.com/converter/travel

For fast quotes on exchange rates for all international currencies, including the Mexican peso. Print out a "cheat sheet" to make easy conversions without having to do any math.

Sunbelt Publications
www.sunbeltpub.com

This book publisher specializing in upper and lower California has an online catalog of its Baja titles.

U.S. Embassy
http://mexico.usembassy.gov

Contains the home page for the U.S. Embassy in Mexico City, with information on consular services to U.S. citizens as well as State Department warnings.

Accommodations Index

Alegría Inn: 215
Alhaja de Baja: 201
Annie's Place: 217-218
Bahía Condo Hotel: 95-96
Baja Bed and Breakfast: 173
Baja Bungalows: 126
Baja Joe's: 186-187
Baja Life Camp: 201-202
Beachfront Family Hacienda: 201
Boca de Los Palmas: 129
Bungalows Breakfast Inn, The: 95
Cabañas de los Arcos: 171
Cabo Azul Resort & Spa: 40
Cabo Inn Hotel: 92
Cabo Pulmo Beach Resort: 27, 124, 125-126
Cabo Surf Hotel: 65
Cabo Villas: 96
Casa Agua Brillante: 201
Casa Colina: 217
Casa Contenta: 95
Casa del Jardín: 50
Casa del Mar Golf Resort and Spa: 67
Casa de Los Santos: 215
Casa Natalia: 23, 48
Casa Pablito Bed and Breakfast Hotel: 95
Casa Rafael's: 93
Casa San Vicente: 215
Casa Simpatica: 200
Casa Tuscany Inn: 174
Casa Verde: 186
Club Cabo Hotel and Campground Resort:
    92-93
Club Cantamar Resort and Sports Centre: 172
Club Cascadas: 96
CostaBaja Resort & Marina: 142, 173
Crowne Plaza Los Cabos Beach Resort: 49, 51
Desire Resort & Spa Los Cabos: 50, 51
Dreams Los Cabos: 23, 51, 66
El Ángel Azul: 174
El Cardonal's Hide-A-Way: 111
El Delfín Blanco: 52
El Dorado: 92
El Encanto Inn: 47
El Encanto Suites: 47
El Pozo Hondo: 200
Esperanza Resort: 23, 64, 68-69
Fiesta Americana Grand Los Cabos: 67
Fiesta Inn La Paz: 173
Garden Casita, The: 216-217
Grand Baja Resort & Spa: 49-50

Grand Plaza Resort: 173
Great Escape Ranch, The: 201
Hacienda del Cortez: 172-173
Hacienda Inn Todos Santos: 214
Hacienda Soleada del Mar: 129
Hacienda Todos Los Santos: 215
Hilton Los Cabos Beach & Golf Resort:
    66-67
Hostería del Convento: 170
Hostería Las Casitas: 214
Hotel Buena Vista Beach Resort: 119-120
Hotel Calafía: 171
Hotel California: 215
Hotel Casa Blanca: 91
Hotel Ceci: 47
Hotel Colli: 47
Hotel Diana: 47
Hotel Dos Mares: 91
Hotel Finisterra: 94
Hotel Gardenias: 170
Hotel La Concha Beach Club Resort and
    Condominiums: 172
Hotel Lorimar: 170
Hotel Los Arcos: 92, 171
Hotel Mar de Cortez: 92
Hotel Marina: 173
Hotel Mediterrané: 171-172
Hotel Miramar: 171, 214
Hotel Oasis: 91
Hotel Palmas de Cortez: 114
Hotel Palmira La Paz: 172
Hotel Perla: 171
Hotel Playa del Sol: 114
Hotel Plaza Real: 170
Hotel Posada Luna Sol: 171
Hotel Posada Real Los Cabos: 50, 51
Hotel Posada Terranova: 47
Hotel Punta Colorada: 120-121
Hotel Punta Pescadero: 110
Hotel Restaurant Nuevo Pekin: 170
Hotel San Carlos: 170
Hotel Santa Fe: 92
Hotel Santa Rosa: 214
Hotel Señorial: 170
Hotel Solmar Suites: 94, 96
Hotel Suites Club El Moro: 172
Instituto de la Juventud y el Deporte: 170
Jardin de Pilar: 214-215
Kurt-n-Marina: 186
La Alianza: 200-201

La Casa Mexicana Inn: 174
La Concha Beach Resort and Condos: 174
La Fonda del Mar Bed and Breakfast: 52
La Playita Inn: 52
Las Flores Posada: 217
Las Gaviotas: 174
Las Mañanitas: 51
Las Palmas Casitas: 217
Las Palmas Tropicales: 200
Las Puertas: 218
Las Ventanas al Paraíso: 23, 68
Los Barriles Hotel: 114
Los Colibrís: 217
Los Milagros Hotel: 92
Maria Bonita Hotel: 214
Marina Cabo Plaza: 94-95
Marina Fiesta Resort & Hotel: 95
Marina Sol Condominiums: 96
Marquis Los Cabos: 23, 64, 67-68
Martin Verdugo's Beach Resort: 114
ME Cabo: 93
Melía Cabo Real: 51, 67
Mira Vista Beachfront Condos: 51
Mokie's: 186
Mykonos Bay Resort: 51
Noche de las Estrellas: 201
Olas Hotel: 91
One&Only Palmilla: 69
Palapas Ventana: 186
Paraíso del Mar: 142
Pensión California: 169-170
Pescadero Surf Camp: 201
Posada de las Flores: 23, 173
Posada del Molino: 217
Posada Hotel Yeneka: 170
Posada La Poza: 23, 216
Posada Señor Mañana: 47
Presidente InterContinental Los Cabos Resort:
    50, 51
Pueblo Bonito Los Cabos: 93
Pueblo Bonito Pacifica: 23, 94
Pueblo Bonito Rosé: 93
Pueblo Bonito Sunset Beach: 94
Rancho Buena Vista: 119
Rancho de Las Olas: 200
Rancho Leonero Resort: 121
Riu Palace: 51, 93-94
Royal Solaris Los Cabos Hotel: 50, 51

Sampaguita Luxury Townhouse/
    Condominiums: 51
San Pedrito Surf Hotel: 200
Seven Crown Hotel: 171
Sheraton Hacienda del Mar: 65-66
Sierra de la Costa: 200
Siesta Suites Hotel: 92
Terrasol Condominiums: 96
Tesoro Los Cabos Hotel: 51, 95
Todos Santos Inn: 215
Tropicana Inn: 47-48
Vela Windsurf Resort: 114, 116
Ventana Bay Resort: 186
Villa and Casa del Mar: 126
Villa del Faro: 129, 201
Villa del Palmar Cabo Beach Resort & Spa: 93
Villa La Estancia: 93
Villa Los Frailes: 128
Villas del Arco: 93
Villas of Casa de los Sueños: 189
Viva Cabo Hotel: 92
Westin Los Cabos: 23
Westin Resort & Spa Los Cabos: 23, 64, 67

CAMPGROUNDS AND RV PARKS

Aquamarina RV Park: 175
Baja Joe's: 186-187
Casa Blanca RV Park: 174
Casa Verde: 186
Club Cabo Hotel and Campground Resort:
    92-93, 97
East Cape RV Resort: 116
El Cardón Trailer Park: 174-175
El Litro RV Park: 218
Kurt-n-Marina: 186
La Paz RV Park: 175
La Ventana Campground: 187
Los Aripez (Oasis de Aripez) RV Park: 174
Los Cerritos Trailer Park: 202
Martin Verdugo's Beach Resort: 116
Playa Norte RV Haven: 116
RV Park Baja Serena: 202
San Pedrito RV Park: 202
Vagabundos del Mar RV Park: 96-97
Villa Serena RV Park: 97

Restaurant Index

Agua Restaurant: 69, 70
Alfredo di Roma: 54
Ali's International Place: 56–57
Amarone: 100
Ana San Sushi Bar: 220
Antojitos Veracruzanos: 221
Arrecifes: 67, 70
Art & Beer: 202
Baan Thai: 54
Baja Cantina: 102
Baja Pizza Kitchen: 117
Barajas Tacos: 221
Billygan's Island, The: 102
Bismarkcito: 176
Bismark II: 176
Brasil Steakhouse: 100
Buena Vida: 220
Buffalo BAR-B-Q: 177
Buzzard Bay Sports Cantina: 117
Cabo Coffee Company: 102
Cabo Wabo: 88–89, 99
Café Brown: 221
Café Canela: 100
Café Combate: 178–179, 222
Café D'licia: 221–222
Café Exquisito: 178
Café Gourmet: 172
Café Luna: 220
Café Santa Fé: 220
Cafetería El Portón: 54
Cafetería El Recreo: 55–56
Caffé Gourmet: 179
Caffé Milano: 177
Caffé Todos Santos: 221
Campestre Triny: 117
Cañada del Diablo: 220
Canto del Mar: 23, 68, 70
Capo San Giovanni: 99
Carlos'n Charlie's: 98, 175
Carnitas El Michoacano: 101
Casa Rafael's: 98
Cascadas Beach & Grill: 99
Cheto Tacos: 101
Cilantro's Bar & Grill: 99
Coral Reef Bar and Grill: 126
Damiana: 53
Dock Café, The: 178
Don Emiliano: 52
Dulcería Arco Iris: 56
Dulcería Daniela's: 132

Dulcería La Coneja: 180
Dulcería Perla: 180
Edith's: 101
El Barrilito: 118
El Chilar: 53
El Gusto!: 216, 218
El Oasis: 132
El Oasis Restaurant and Bar: 177
El Palapa: 126–127
El Paraíso: 130
El Patrón Bar & Grill: 178
El Pin: 130
El Quinto Sol: 179
El Shrimp Bucket: 99
El Squid Roe: 98
El Taste: 177
El Tecolote: 151
El Tulipán: 54
El Zarape: 176
Felipe's Restaurant: 202
5th Avenida Coffee: 178
Fish House: 99
Flag's Sports Bar: 120
Fonda El Zaguán: 219
French Riviera: 56, 70, 100–101
Giggling Marlin: 100
Giggling Marlin Beach Club at Bay of Dreams: 189
Guacamaya: 55
Habañeros Mexican Bistro: 53
Hangman, The: 55
Il Giardino: 220
Karina's Hamburguesas: 118
Kenichi Sushi & Bar: 118
Kiwi Restaurant Bar: 177
La Bodega Steak and Wine House: 54
La Bonita del Señor San José: 56
La Cascada: 67, 70
La Cochinita: 178
La Coronela: 215, 220
La Dolce Ristorante Italiano & Pizzeria: 54, 100
La Europea: 101
La Fuente: 180
La Luna: 101
La Palma Taquería: 118
La Panga Antigua: 23, 52–53
La Pazta: 177
La Pazta Café: 179
La Perla: 97–98
La Picazón: 55

La Playita: 56
Las Brisas del Mar: 177
Las Gardenias: 98
Las Palmas: 99, 102
Las Queadillasss: 101
Las Tres Virgenes: 23, 175
La Terraza: 177
La Terraza Sidewalk Café: 53–54
Latitude 22+ Roadhouse: 100
Lenny's Deli: 101
Lolita's Restaurant: 98
Lonchería La Garita: 222
Lonchería Rosita: 202
Los Adobes: 218
Los Cerritos Club: 197, 202
Los Dos Ricardos: 56
Los Garcia: 99
Mareiros Café: 179
Mariscos El Puerto: 57
Mariscos Mazatlán: 99
Mariscos Mazatlán II: 54
Mariscos Mi Costa: 219
Mariscos Moyeyo's: 177
Martin Verdugo's Restaurant: 117
Mi Casa: 97
Mi Casa de Mariscos: 99
Mi Cocina: 52
Miguel's: 218–219
Mocambo de Los Cabos: 99
Morgan's Encore: 54
Morgan's Restaurant and Cellar: 54
Nancy's Restaurant and Bar: 126
Nevería Rocco: 223
Nick-San Restaurant: 101
Oasis Coffee Bar: 118
Olé Olé: 100
O Mole Mío: 97
Otra Vez: 118
Palapa Azul: 151
Paletería la Paloma: 223
Paletería la Paloma 2: 223
Paletería y Nevería La Michoacana: 56,
    179–180
Palomar Restaurant-Bar: 134
Pancho Banano: 219
Pancho's: 98
Peacocks Restaurant and Bar: 100
Peña La Pitahaya de Janicua: 175–176
Pitahayas: 65–66, 69–70
Posada Terranova: 54
Puerta Vieja: 70
Rancho Viejo: 178
Restaurant, The: 68

Restaurant Bar Jazmín: 53
Restaurant-Bar Pepe's: 60, 69
Restaurant Bermejo: 177
Restaurant C: 69, 70
Restaurant Calafia: 120
Restaurant El Caballero: 126
Restaurant El Descanso: 54
Restaurant El Paso: 132
Restaurant Grill Campestre: 178
Restaurant La Costa: 176
Restaurant La Mar y Peña: 176
Restaurant La Ramada: 219
Restaurant Las Bugambilias: 135
Restaurant Las Fuentes: 220
Restaurant Las Hornillas: 54–55
Restaurant Migriño: 202
Restaurant Miraflores: 135
Restaurant Pichos: 178
Restaurant Plaza Real: 175
Restaurant Santa Monica: 219
Rincon del Bahia: 187
Romeo & Julieta: 99–100
Ruth's Chris Steak House: 100
Sancho Panza Wine Bistro and Jazz Club
    Restaurant: 100
Sandbar: 202
San Francisco Coffee Company: 102
Santa Fé Deli: 221
Señor Greenberg's Mexicatessen: 101
7 Seas: 65, 70
Shrimp Factory, The: 99
Shut Up Frank's: 220
Siempre: 94
Signature Restaurant at Esperanza: 69
Solomon's Landing: 99
Stop Light Bar and Grill: 101
Suki's: 220
Sunset da Mona Lisa: 70
Sunset Grill: 101
Super Tacos de Baja California Hermanos
    Gonzales: 55
Super Tacos de Baja California Hermanos
    González: 178
Taco Loco: 101
Tacos Chilakos: 221
Tacos Condi: 101
Tacos en la Torre: 187
Tacos Leon: 187
Tacos Rafa: 187
Taquería El Ahorcado: 55
Taquería El Viejo: 118
Taquería Erika: 55
Taquería Los Barriles: 118

Taquería los Paisas: 101
Taquería Los Superburros: 178
Tequila Restaurant: 52
Tequila Sunrise Bar & Grill: 219
Theory Café: 102
Tío Pablo's: 117
Tomates: 66
Toscana Pizza Gourmet: 177

Tres Gallines: 220
Tres Hermanos: 221
Ventanas del Sol: 187
Viento del Norte: 187
Villa Serena Restaurant: 70
Voila! Bistro: 54
Vonn Café: 221
Yako's Sushi-Bar: 118

General Index

A

acacia: 234
accommodations: 288-291; Cabo San Lucas 51, 91-97; Corridor 51, 65-69; La Paz 169-175; Los Barriles 114; Los Cabos 31-32; San José del Cabo 40, 47-52; Todos Santos 214-218; West Cape 200-202; *see also* Accommodations Index; *specific place*
Aeromar las Arenas: 189
agaves: 232-233, 301
Agua Caliente: 134
aguas maias: 207
air travel: 254; airlines 256-257; La Paz 182; Los Cabos 32-33; Todos Santos 193
alcoholic beverages: 88, 298-299; *see also* bars
all-inclusive resorts: 50-51, 114
alta cocina mexicana: 16, 21, 52-53, 175, 218
alternative accommodations: 290
Amerindian groups: 144, 241
amphibians: 239-240
Ángeles Verdes: 268
animals: 235-240
antiques: 45
antojitos: 294
Arrecife de la Foca: 188
arrests: 275, 276
art galleries: Cabo San Lucas 90; itinerary tips 21; San José del Cabo 21, 44, 46; Todos Santos 17, 25, 212-213
Art Walk: 21, 44
ATMs: 57, 307
ATVs (all-terrain vehicles): 86, 113, 165
auto shops: 268

B

backpacking: 136-140, 277-278
Bahía de la Paz: 149, 151
Bahía de la Ventana: 142, 184-188
Bahía de los Fraires: 128
Bahía de los Muertos: 188
Bahía de los Sueños: 189
Bahía Las Palmas: 107, 108
Bahía Magdalena: 25
Bahía Pulmo: 122-123
Bahía San Gabriel: 154
Baja 1000: 167-168
Baja California rattlesnake: 240
Banco Golden Gate: 78

Banco San Jaime: 78
banks: 308; Cabo San Lucas 103; La Paz 180; San José del Cabo 57; Todos Santos 223
barracuda: 237-238
barrel cactus: 232
bars: 299; Cabo San Lucas 87-88; La Paz 166-167; San José del Cabo 44; Todos Santos 213; useful phrases 299
bass: 237
beaches: 16-17; accommodations 48-50; Cabo Pulmo 122-124; Cabo San Lucas 76-78; Corridor 60-61; itinerary tips 21-28; La Paz 149, 151-152; maps 152; safety tips 207; San José del Cabo 40-41; Todos Santos 207-209; West Cape 196-199
beach hotels: 48-50
bed-and-breakfasts: 50, 95, 173-174; *see also* Accommodations Index; *specific place*
beer: 298
bees: 304-305
Biblioteca de História de las Californias: 147, 149
bicycling: 269-271
billfish: 78-80, 236
birds/birdwatching: 238-239
biznaga: 231
black jackrabbit: 235
black oak: 233
black-tailed jackrabbit: 235
blue-footed booby: 238
blue whale: 235
boating/boat travel: 282-285; Cabo San Lucas 84-86; charters 165; East Cape 110; La Paz 163-165, 182-183; liveaboards 83; Los Cabos 34; marinas 34, 285; nautical charts 283-284; permits 284; port check-ins 284-285; supplies and repairs 285; tide tables 284; *see also* fish/fishing
Boca de la Sierra: 135
booking services/property management: 31-32, 51, 96, 218
bookstores: Cabo San Lucas 91, 104; La Paz 169, 181; San José del Cabo 46; Todos Santos 211-212
border crossings: 273-274
Boulevard Mijares: 21, 39-40
boutique hotels: 23
brandy: 299
bribes: 264, 276
brown booby: 238
brown pelican: 238

budget tips: 308
Buena Vista: 119-120
bullfights: 167
business hours: 309
business travel: 272
bus service: 255, 260-261; La Paz 182, 183; Los Cabos 34; San José del Cabo 58; Todos Santos 193

C

Cabo del Sol Golf Course: 63
Cabo Falso: 194
Cabo Pulmo: 24, 26-27, 107, 122-127, 287
Cabo Real Golf Course: 63
Cabo San Lucas: 16, 71, 74-75; accommodations 51, 91-97; beaches 76-78; entertainment and events 87-89; food/restaurants 97-103; itinerary tips 22, 25, 26; maps 72-73; outdoor recreation 26, 76-87, 287; shopping 89-91; tourist information and services 103-104; transportation services 105
Cabo San Lucas Country Club: 63-64
cacti: 231-232
cameras: 19
camping: 268, 291; environmental etiquette 156; travel tips 278; see also Accommodations Index; specific place
Cañon de la Zorra: 24, 107, 137
Cañon San Bernardo: 138
Cañon San Dionísio: 137-138
Cañon San Pablo: 138-139
cantinas: 299; see also bars
cape oak: 233
Cárdenas, Lázaro: 250
cardón: 231
Carnaval: 167
Carretera Transpeninsular: 74-75, 250-251
cartopping boats: 282
car travel: 255-259, 261-269; driving distances 262; driving tips 122, 255; gas stations 181, 202, 224, 265, 268; insurance 255-259, 265, 269; La Paz 183-184; Los Cabos 33-34; mechanics 268; off-road travel 262-263; roadblocks/checkpoints 275-276; road conditions 261-264; Rural Coastal Road 121-122; safety tips 262-264; San José del Cabo 58; Sierra de la Laguna 140; signage 264; Todos Santos 193; traffic offenses 264-265; vehicle import permits 183, 259; West Cape 193
Casa de Cultura (Miraflores): 134
casas de huéspedes: 290
Cascada del Refugio: 198

Catedral de Nuestra Señora de La Paz: 147
caves: 154
cell phones: 312
Centro Cultural Profesor Nestor Agúndez Martínez: 206
ceramics: 23, 168, 195
Cerro las Casitas: 135
Cerro La Vigía: 76
Cerro Los Viejos: 198
cerveza: 298
charreadas: 89, 167
charters: 157, 165
cholla: 232
chubascos: 230
chuckwalla: 239
cigars: 91
cinemas: 89, 167
city bus service: 261
civil wars: 248-249
clayware: 195
climate: 18, 139, 229-231
clothing stores: 211
clothing tips: 19-20
coast horned lizards: 239
Cochimís: 241
coconut palms: 233
collect telephone calls: 313
common dolphin: 235
condominiums/condotels: 50-51, 95-96, 174, 290-291; see also Accommodations Index; specific place
consulates/consular agents: 58, 104, 274
coral reefs: 16, 24, 26-27, 123-124
cordonazos: 230
coromuels: 230
Corral de los Frailes: 123
Corridor: 59-60; accommodations 51, 65-69; beaches 60-61; climate 230; food/restaurants 69-70; outdoor recreation 60-64, 287; shopping 65; tourist information and services 70-71
Cortés, Hernán: 144, 242-243
corvinas: 236
cost estimations: 308; food/restaurants 292; scuba diving 82, 158; snorkeling 82, 158
cottonwoods: 234
coyotes: 235
credit cards: 307-308
crime: 306-307
croakers: 236
Crossroads Country Club Beachfront Playa: 129
cruises: 85-86, 282-283
currency exchange: 307-308; Cabo San Lucas

103; La Paz 180; Los Barriles 119; San José del Cabo 57; Todos Santos 223
customs regulations: 274-275, 281-282
cycling: 269-271

D

damiana: 234
dance clubs: 22, 88-89, 166, 213
date palms: 233
datura: 234
debit cards: 307
dehydration: 303
demographics: 252-253
department stores: 168
desert cottontail: 235
desert iguana: 239
deserts: 226-227
diarrhea: 302-303
Díaz, Porfirio: 249
dinner cruises: 86
discos: see dance clubs
diving: see scuba diving
dolphins: 86, 235-236
dorado: 237
drinking water: 139, 278, 297, 302

E

East Cape: 16; itinerary tips 28; maps 4-5, 109; outdoor recreation 28, 110-111; planning tips 106-107; sightseeing tips 108
ecotourism: 119, 211, 228
El Aguaje: 140
El Arco: 75
El Bajito Reef: 27, 160
El Bajo de los Meros: 124
El Bajo Seamount: 27, 160-161
El Camino Rural Costero: 121-122
El Cantil: 123
El Cardonal: 111
El Chorro: 134
El Dorado Golf Club: 63
electricity: 314
El Embudo: 154
El Faro Viejo: 194
El Islote: 124
elongated fish: 237-238
El Pescadero: 17, 197-198
El Triunfo: 130, 132
email services: 313
emergency services: 58, 181, 306; see also medical services
Ensenada de los Muertos: 188
entertainment: Cabo San Lucas 87-89; La Paz 166-168; San José del Cabo 44; Todos Santos 199, 213
entry regulations: 271-273
environmental issues: 228-229
Estero San José: 21, 23, 30, 40
extended stay opportunities: 19

F

falcons: 239
fauna: 235-240
ferry service: 259-260; La Paz 182-183; Los Cabos 34
festivals and events: Cabo San Lucas 89; La Paz 167-168; San José del Cabo 44-45; Todos Santos 213-214
Fiesta de La Paz: 167
fine art: Cabo San Lucas 90; itinerary tips 23; San José del Cabo 46; Todos Santos 212-213
Finisterra: 75
fire opal: 23, 45-46
first-aid kits: 19
fisher eagle: 238
fish/fishing: 16, 236-238, 278-282; bait and tackle 81, 280; Buena Vista 120; Cabo Pulmo 125; Cabo San Lucas 78-81; charters 157; East Cape 110-111; festivals and events 89; Gorda Banks 129; government regulations 281-282; inshore fishing 279; itinerary tips 21-22, 24-27; La Paz 157; licenses 280-281; local terminology 79; Los Barriles 113; offshore fishing 279; onshore fishing 278-279; processing services 81, 118; San José del Cabo 41-42; seasons 279-280; surf casting 80-81; tide tables 280; Todos Santos 209; world records 80; see also sportfishing
fitness camps: 201-202
flatfish: 237
flora: 135-136, 227, 231-234
food/restaurants: 291-297; Cabo San Lucas 97-103; cooking methods 292; Corridor 69-70; costs 292; La Paz 175-180; Los Barriles 116-118; sanitation 302-303; San José del Cabo 52-57; Todos Santos 218-223; useful phrases 292, 294; see also Restaurant Index; specific place
footwear: 19
foreign investments: 249
foreign visitors: 272-273
fuel: 265, 268

G

gemstones: 23, 45-46
geography: 226-227

geologic history: 225-226
gift shops: 211
glass-bottomed tour boats: 85
golf courses: 16; Cabo San Lucas 87; Corridor 62-64; San José del Cabo 43
Gorda Banks: 107, 129
gray whales: 236
Green Angels (Ángeles Verdes): 268
gringos: 252
grocery stores: 296-297; Cabo Pulmo 127; Cabo San Lucas 102-103; Corridor 70; La Paz 179; Los Barriles 118; San José del Cabo 56; Todos Santos 222-223; West Cape 202
Guadalupe Island palm: 233
Guaycuras: 241
güeribo: 234
guesthouses: 216-218; see also Accommodations Index; specific place
guides: see outfitters
Guzmán, Nuño de: 144

H
hammerhead sharks: see sharks
handicrafts: 22; Cabo San Lucas 89-90; La Paz 168-169; San José del Cabo 45; Todos Santos 200, 212
harbor skiffs: 105
hardware stores: 224
health certificates (pets): 272-273
health issues: 302-307
herbs: 234
hiking: 16, 277-278; environmental etiquette 156; guides and outfitters 139-140; Isla Espíritu Santo 154; La Paz 165; maps 136; map sources 277; packing tips 277-278; planning tips 139; Sierra de la Laguna 136-140; Todos Santos 210; trails 277; West Cape 198-199
historical background: 241-251; see also specific place
home decor/interior design: Cabo San Lucas 90-91; San José del Cabo 46; Todos Santos 211
hornets: 304-305
horseback riding: 16; Buena Vista 120; Cabo San Lucas 86-87; charreadas 89, 167; itinerary tips 21; La Paz 165
hostels: see Accommodations Index; specific place
hot drinks: 298
hotels: see Accommodations Index; specific place
hot springs: 134

huerivo: 234

I
Ibarra's Pottery: 23, 168
Iglesia Nuestra Señora del Pilar: 206
Iglesia San José: 30, 40
iguanas: 239
immigration offices: 104, 182, 273
independence movements: 247-249
indigenous peoples: 144, 241
inflatable boats: 282
inmigrante rentistas: 273
insect bites and stings: 304-305
inshore fishing: 279
Instituto Tecnológico de La Paz: 149
insurance: 255-259, 265, 269
intercity bus service: 260-261
international telephone calls: 312
Internet access: 313; Cabo San Lucas 103-104; La Paz 180-181; Los Barriles 119; San José del Cabo 57; Todos Santos 224
Internet phones: 312
Internet resources: 326-327
Isla Ballena: 160
Isla Cerralvo: 161, 188
Isla Espíritu Santo: 25, 27, 142, 154-157, 160
islands: 17, 154-157, 227
Isla Partida: 27, 154, 155, 160
Isla Santa Cruz: 161
Islas Las Animas: 161
itinerary tips: 21-28

JK
jack fish: 236-237
jackrabbits: 235
jazz: 22
jejenes: 304
jellyfish: 207, 305
Jesuit missions: 245-247
jewelry: 22; Cabo San Lucas 89-90; San José del Cabo 45-46; Todos Santos 211
Jiménez, Fortún: 144, 242
jimsonweed: 234
Juárez, Benito: 249
kayaking: 16; Buena Vista 120; Cabo San Lucas 84; East Cape 111; equipment 285; guides and outfitters 285; itinerary tips 21-22, 24-25; La Paz 162-163; map sources 285; San José del Cabo 43; sea kayaking 285; tide tables 285; Todos Santos 209-210
Kino, Eusebio Francisco: 245
kiteboarding: 286; Bahía de la Ventana 184-186; itinerary tips 25; planning tips 18

L

La Bocana: 209
La Candelaria: 191, 194-196
La Concha Beach Club: 60-61
La Esperanza: 124
La Fortuna: 129
La Huerta: 184
La Laguna: 135
land mammals: 235
Land's End: 22, 26, 30, 75-76, 85
language: 253; dictionaries and phrasebooks
    253; fish/fishing terminology 79; glossary
    315-316; Spanish-language schools 181, 224;
    useful phrases 292, 294, 299, 317-322
La Paz: 17, 141-142, 144; accommodations 169-
    175; beaches 149, 151-152; entertainment
    and events 166-168; food/restaurants 175-
    180; historical background 144-146; islands
    154-157; itinerary tips 25, 27; maps 6, 143,
    148, 150-151, 152; outdoor recreation 17, 27,
    157-166, 287; planning tips 144; shopping
    168-169; tourist information and services
    180-182; transportation services 182-184
La Playita/Pueblo La Playa: accommodations
    52; food/restaurants 56-57; itinerary tips
    21; sightseeing tips 40-41
La Poza: 203
La Poza de Lobos: see Playa Las Pocitas (La
    Poza de Lobos)
La Reina: 188
La Reinita: 161, 188
La Ribera: 120
Las Casitas: 124
Las Cruces: 152
Las Cuevas: 134
Las Cuevitas: 154
Las Navajas: 123
laundry services: Cabo San Lucas 104; La Paz
    181; Los Barriles 118; San José del Cabo 58;
    Todos Santos 224
La Unidad Cultural Profesor Jesús Castro
    Argúndez: 149
La Vinorama: 129
leatherwork: 134, 200
legal matters: 275-276
Legend of The Flame: 38
licenses/permits: boating/boat travel 284; car
    travel 183, 259; fish/fishing 280-281; tourist
    permits 271-273
lighthouses: 194
liquefied petroleum gas (LPG): 268
liquor: 299
liveaboards: 83, 161-162

live music: 22, 166-167
lizards: 239
loggerhead turtles: 239
long-distance telephone calls: 312-313
Los Barriles: 25, 111-114, 116-119
Los Cabos: 16, 29-30; accommodations 31-32;
    Cabo San Lucas 71-105; Corridor 59-71;
    itinerary tips 28; maps 3, 32-33; outdoor
    recreation 28, 41-44, 60-64, 76-87, 287;
    planning tips 30-31; San José del Cabo
    35-59; transportation services 32-34
Los Cabos International Airport: 32-33, 254
Los Frailes: 75
Los Islotes: 27, 154, 155, 160
Los Manantiales: 134
love herbs: 234

M

mackerel: 237
Madero, Francisco: 249
magazines: 104, 181, 223
magnificent frigate: 238
maguey: 232-233, 301
malecón (La Paz): 17, 25, 142, 147
mammals: 235-236
Manila galleons: 243-244
manta rays: 27, 237
maps: 310; nautical charts 283-284; retail
    sources 277, 283-284
marinas: 34, 285
marine mammals: 235-236
markets: La Paz 179; San José del Cabo 56;
    Todos Santos 222-223; see also grocery
    stores
marlin: 78-80, 129, 236
Marlin Alley: 74-75
Márquez de León International Airport (LAP):
    182, 254
marriage ceremonies: 66
martial arts: 210-211
masked booby: 238
measurement systems: 314
mechanics: 268
medical services: 306; Cabo San Lucas 104;
    Los Barriles 118; San José del Cabo 57-58;
    Todos Santos 223; see also specific place
meditation classes: 210-211
mequite: 234
mescal: 301
Mexican-American War: 146, 248
Mexican fan palm: 233
Mexican piñon pine: 233
Mexican Revolution: 249-250

military presence: 276
mimosas: 233-234
Miraflores: 134-135
missionaries: 245-247
mobile phones: 312
money: 307-309; *see also* banks; currency exchange
mordidas: 264, 276
mosquitoes: 304
motels: *see* Accommodations Index; *specific place*
motion sickness: 304
motorcycle travel: 269
motor oil: 268
mountain biking: 269-271; Cabo San Lucas 86; La Paz 165; San José del Cabo 43
mountain lions: 235
mountains: 226
movie theaters: 89, 167
mule deer: 235
Museo Regional de Antropología e Historia: 25, 142, 147

NO

nautical charts: 283-284
needlefish: 238
newspapers: 104, 181
nightclubs/nightlife: 22, 44
Nine Palms: 28, 42
nonalcoholic beverages: 297-298
nopal: 232
oak trees: 233
Obregón, Álvaro: 250
O'Brien, John: 38
offshore fishing: 279
onshore fishing: 278-279
opal: 23, 45-46
opuntia: 232
organized tours: bicycling 270-271; kayaking 285; La Paz 165-166; Los Barriles 113; San José del Cabo 43-44; snorkeling 84, 162, 288; Todos Santos 211; *see also* outfitters
organ pipe cactus: 231-232
outdoor recreation: 277-288; Bahía de la Ventana 184-186; Cabo San Lucas 76-87, 287; Corridor 60-64; East Cape 28, 110-111; itinerary tips 21-22, 24-27; La Paz 17, 27, 157-166, 287; Los Cabos 28; planning tips 18, 139; San José del Cabo 41-44; Sierra de la Laguna 136-140; sports equipment 20, 46, 84, 91, 169; Todos Santos 28; West Cape 28
Outer Pulmo: 124
outfitters: Cabo San Lucas 79-80; kayaking 285; San José del Cabo 43-44; scuba diving 83, 288; Sierra de la Laguna 139-140; snorkeling 84, 162, 288; sportfishing 79-80; *see also* organized tours
overstays: 272

P

packing tips: 19-20
paddle-craft: 84
palapa restaurants: 102
Palmilla Golf Course: 63
palm trees: 233
palo blanco: 234
Palo Escopeta: 129
panga trips: 41-42, 80, 207
parasailing: 87
Paseo del Estero: 40
passports: 19, 271-273
pearls: 153
Pelican Rock: 75-76, 85
pelicans: 238
Pemex: 181, 202, 224
Península El Mogote: 152-153
pensiones: 290
performing arts: 213
pesos: 307
petroglyphs: 154
pets, traveling with: 272-273
pharmacies: 223
Picacho de la Laguna: 135
Piedras Gordas: 188
pine trees: 233
pirates: 145
pitahaya: 231-232
planning tips: 18-20
plants: 135-136, 227
Playa Acapulquito: 61; itinerary tips 28; outdoor recreation 42, 62
Playa Agave Azul: 197
Playa Balandra: 27, 149, 151
Playa Balconcito: 78
Playa Barco Varado: 61, 62; *see also* Shipwreck
Playa Buenos Aires: 61, 62
Playa Cabo Bello: 61, 62, 84
Playa Cabo Real: 62
Playa Caimancito: 149
Playa California: 21, 40
Playa Cantamar: 61, 62
Playa Cemeterio: 60, 61
Playa Chileno: 60; itinerary tips 21, 26; outdoor recreation 62, 81, 287; sightseeing tips 30
Playa Corral de los Frailes: 123
Playa Costa Azul: 61; food/restaurants 57;

itinerary tips 21, 23, 28; outdoor recreation 42, 62; sightseeing tips 41
Playa Costa Brava: 61
Playa Coyote: 151
Playa del Amor: itinerary tips 22, 25, 26; outdoor recreation 81; sightseeing tips 30, 76-77
Playa del Tesoro: 149
Playa el Coromuel: 149
Playa El Médano: 22, 76, 92-94
Playa El Mirador/Playa Bledito: 60, 61
Playa El Tecolote: 25, 142, 151
Playa El Tule: 61, 62
Playa El Zalate: 61
Playa Escondida: 78
Playa La Cachora: 208
Playa La Pastora: 25, 28, 209
Playa Las Cabrillas: 196
Playa La Sirenita: 123
Playa Las Palmas: see Playa San Pedrito (Playa Las Palmas)
Playa Las Pocitas: 23
Playa Las Pocitas (La Poza de Lobos): 191, 208
Playa Las Viudas: 60, 61
Playa Los Cerritos: 25, 28, 191, 196-197
Playa Migriño: 194
Playa Palmilla: 60, 61
Playa Palmira: 149
Playa Pichilingue: 149
Playa Punta Colorada: 149
Playa San Carlos: 61
Playa San Pedrito (Playa Las Palmas): 191, 198
Playa San Pedro: 198
Playa Santa María: 60, 61; itinerary tips 21, 26; outdoor recreation 62, 81, 287; sightseeing tips 30
Playa Solmar: 23, 78
Plaza Constitución (Jardín Velazco): 147, 149
Plaza Mijares: 21, 30, 39-40
poisonous animals: 240, 305-306
population: 252-253
post offices: 314; Cabo San Lucas 103; La Paz 180; San José del Cabo 57; Todos Santos 223
pottery: 23, 168, 195
prickly pear cactus: 232
prohibition (U.S.): 250
property managers: 218
Pueblo La Playa: 129; see also La Playita/Pueblo La Playa
Puerto Algodones: 207
Puerto Campechano: 207
Puerto Paraíso: 90

Punta Arena: 28, 121
Punta Arenas de la Ventana: 189
Punta Bella: 61
Punta Chileno: 61, 62
Punta Colorada: 120-121
Punta Conejo: 209
Punta El Mechudo: 157
Punta Gorda: 129
Punta Lobos: 207-208
Punta Marqués: 209
Punta Palmilla: 62
Punta Perico: 189
Punta Pescadero: 110
Punta San Pedro: 28, 209

QR

race and sports betting: 89
rainfall: 18, 139, 229, 231
Rancho Boca de la Vinorama: 129
Rancho Pilar: 200
Rancho San Dionísio: 134
Rancho San Luis: 129
Rancho Santa Elena: 129
Rancho Tule: 129
Rancho Verde: 132
ranchware: 195
rattlesnakes: 240
rays: 27, 237, 305-306
reading suggestions: 323-326
real estate purchases: 115
recompression services: 84
recreational activities: see outdoor recreation; specific place
reform movements: 250
rental cars: 268-269; agencies 266-267; insurance 269; La Paz 183-184; Los Barriles 118; Los Cabos 33-34; San José del Cabo 58; Todos Santos 193
reptiles: 239-240
reservation services: 290
resorts: 288-290; all-inclusive resorts 50-51, 114; Buena Vista 119-120; Cabo Pulmo Beach Resort 27; Cabo San Lucas 93, 95; Los Barriles 114; Los Cabos 16; romantic resorts 23; San José del Cabo 40, 49-50, 51; see also Accommodations Index; specific place
restaurants: see Restaurant Index; specific place
road races: 167-168
Roca Montaña: 188
Roca Pelícanos: 75-76, 85
Rock, The: 42
rodeos: see charreadas

romantic escapes: 23, 66
rum: 299
RV services: 58, 268; *see also* Accommodations Index

S

safety tips: beaches 207; bicycling 270; car travel 262-264; crime 306-307
sailing: 84
Salvatierra shipwreck: 27, 161
San Antonio: 130, 132
San Antonio de la Sierra: 132
San Bartolo: 107, 132
San Evaristo: 157
sanitation: 302-303
San José del Cabo: 16, 35, 38-39; accommodations 40, 47-52; entertainment and events 44-45; food/restaurants 52-57; itinerary tips 21, 24; maps 36-37; outdoor recreation 41-44; shopping 45-46; sightseeing tips 39-41; transportation services 58-59
San Juan de Los Planes: 188
San Pedro: 130
Santa Rita: 134
Santiago: 132, 134
Santo Domingo: 132
satellite phones: 313
schools: 181, 224
scorpions: 305
scuba diving: 16, 287-288; Bahía de la Ventana 186; Buena Vista 119, 120; Cabo Pulmo 124-125, 287; Cabo San Lucas 81-84, 287; Corridor 62, 287; costs 82, 158; dive operators 27, 159-161; East Cape 110-111; equipment 84, 287-288; Gorda Banks 129; guides and outfitters 83, 288; itinerary tips 21-22, 24-27; La Paz 157-162, 287; liveaboards 83, 161-162; Pacific Coast 27, 287; planning tips 18, 27, 161; recompression services 84; San José del Cabo 42
sea bass: 237
sea lions: 26-27, 85, 123, 154, 236
Sea of Cortez: 227-228, 230
seasons: 18, 139, 229-231
sea urchins: 305
sharks: 27, 237
shellfish: 238
Shipwreck: 61; itinerary tips 28; outdoor recreation 42, 62
shipwrecks: 27, 62, 161, 188
shopping: Cabo San Lucas 89-91; Corridor 65; itinerary tips 23; La Paz 168-169; Los

Barriles 114; San José del Cabo 45-46; Todos Santos 200, 211-213; *see also specific place*
shopping malls: 90
shrimp by the bucket: 22, 99
shuttle services: 59
Sierra de la Laguna: 16, 135-140, 226; maps 4-5, 131; planning tips 106-107; sightseeing tips 130, 132, 134-135
silver jewelry: 22; Cabo San Lucas 89-90; Todos Santos 211
skydiving: 87
snakes: 239-240
snapper: 237
sneaker waves: 207
snorkeling: 287-288; Buena Vista 120; Cabo Pulmo 287; Cabo San Lucas 81-84, 287; costs 82, 158; dive operators 159-161; East Cape 111; equipment 84, 287-288; guides and outfitters 84, 162, 288; Isla Espíritu Santo 154; itinerary tips 21-22, 24-27; La Paz 157-162, 287; liveaboards 83, 161-162; Pacific Coast 27, 287; planning tips 161; recompression services 84; San José del Cabo 42
soft drinks: 297
sotol: 233
souvenirs: 45
Spanish Conquest: 145-146, 241-245
Spanish-language schools: 181, 224
spa services: Cabo San Lucas 87, 94; Corridor 64-65; itinerary tips 21, 23; La Paz 165; Los Barriles 113-114; San José del Cabo 43; Todos Santos 211; West Cape 199
sportfishing: Buena Vista 120; Cabo San Lucas 78-80; guides and outfitters 79-80; Los Barriles 113; planning tips 18; *see also* fish/fishing
sports equipment: 20, 46, 84, 91, 169
squid: 237
statehood: 250
stingrays: *see* rays
submarine canyons: 26, 81
sunburn/sunscreen: 303
sunset cruises: 86
sunset views: 22
surf casting: 80-81
surfing: 17, 286; Cabo San Lucas 84; Corridor 61-62; equipment 42-43, 286; itinerary tips 21, 28; planning tips 18; Punta Arena 121; San José del Cabo 42-43; surf camps 201; Todos Santos 209-210; West Cape 198
swimming: with dolphins 86; itinerary tips 26; West Cape 196-197, 199; *see also* beaches

T

tannery: 134
taxes: 309
taxis: 261; Cabo San Lucas 105; La Paz 183; San José del Cabo 59; Todos Santos 193
Teatro de la Ciudad: 149
Teatro Márquez de León: 213
teddy-bear cholla: 232
telegraph offices: 57, 180
telephone service: 311-313; area codes 311-312; Cabo San Lucas 103; La Paz 180; San José del Cabo 57; Todos Santos 223-224; useful numbers 311
temperatures: 18, 139, 229-231
tequila: 299, 300-301
ticks: 305
tide tables: 280, 284, 285
time: 314
timeshares: 48-49, 96
tipping: 308-309
Tlaco palm: 233
Todos Santos: 17, 190-191, 203; accommodations 214-218; beaches 207-209; entertainment and events 199, 213-214; food/restaurants 218-223; historical background 203, 205; historic district 25, 191, 205-206; itinerary tips 22, 25, 28; maps 7, 204, 206; outdoor recreation 28; planning tips 191, 193; shopping 200, 211-213; sightseeing tips 205-206; tourist information and services 223-224
toiletries: 19
topographical maps: 310
Tortuga del Sol: 197
tourist information and services: 309-310; Bahía de la Ventana 187-188; Cabo Pulmo 127; Cabo San Lucas 103-104; Corridor 70-71; La Paz 180-182; Los Barriles 118-119; San José del Cabo 57-58; Todos Santos 223-224
tourist permits: 271-273
tours: see organized tours; outfitters
traffic offenses: 264-265
trailered boats: 282
Transpeninsular Highway: 74-75, 250-251
transportation services: 254-271; Bahía de la Ventana 189; Cabo Pulmo 127; Cabo San Lucas 105; Los Cabos 32-34; San José del Cabo 58-59; Todos Santos 193; West Cape 193
trastes de barro: 195
travel clubs: 309-310
trees: 233-234
tree yucca: 232
tropical forests: 227
Tropic of Cancer: 134
tuna: 237
turista: 302-303
turtles: 239

UV

uninhabited islands: 17, 154-157, 227
Universidad Autonomía de Baja California Sur: 149
vacation rentals: Los Barriles 116; Todos Santos 216-218; West Cape 201; see also Accommodations Index; *specific place*
vaccinations (pets): 272-273
value-added tax (VAT): 309
vegetation: 135-136, 227
vehicle import permits: 183, 259
villas: 96
visas: 271-273
visitante rentistas: 273
Vizcaíno, Sebastián: 145, 244-245
voltage: 314

WXYZ

Waborita: 88
wasps: 304-305
waterfalls: 16, 24, 198
waterfowl: 238-239
water taxis: 25
WaveRunners: 86
weather: 18, 139, 229-231
wedding ceremonies: 66
weights and measures: 314
West Cape: 17, 190-191; food/restaurants 202; itinerary tips 28; maps 7, 192; outdoor recreation 28; planning tips 191, 193; sightseeing tips 194-199
Western diamondback rattlesnake: 240
wetlands: 227
whales: 235-236
whale-watching: 236; Cabo San Lucas 86; itinerary tips 25; La Paz 162; planning tips 18; Todos Santos 209
white-tailed deer: 235
wild figs: 234
wildlife: 235-240
willows: 234
windsurfing: 16, 286; Bahía de la Ventana 184-186; Cabo San Lucas 84; East Cape 111; itinerary tips 25; Los Barriles 113; planning tips 18
wine: 91, 100, 298-299
World War II: 250

yellow-bellied sea snakes: 240
yoga classes: Cabo San Lucas: 87; San José del
    Cabo: 43; Todos Santos: 210-211
youth hostels: 290; *see also* Accommodations
    Index; *specific place*

yucca: 232
Zippers: 42, 57
Zona Hotelera: 40

Acknowledgments

Besides our own adventures, family, friends, and kindred spirits contributed their many travel experiences to shape this edition of *Moon Cabo*. Adrienne Mohadjerin and Kristina Curtis accompanied us to Cabo San Lucas for their first spring break and lived to tell the tale. Susan Harper came along for a fun-filled week in San José del Cabo. Sandra and Vinny Creta abandoned family in Phoenix to spend Thanksgiving in Los Cabos—and got the lowdown on Mexican fire opals.

Hally and Greg Bayer recalled details of their first Cape Region tour and reported on a New Year's trip to Rosarito. Judy and Kellen Glinder contributed photos from Todos Santos. Kristi Kull sent notes from a first trip to Los Cabos, while newlywed Jennifer Librach shared advice on planning a Los Cabos destination wedding.

Photographer Tomas Spangler lent the use of his beautiful Baja images and also reported from the road. And Jeff Nordahl helped us understand the ins and outs of Mexican car insurance.

Many Baja residents helped us separate fact from fiction this time around. Cecilia Moller told us about the hot new places in La Paz, while Nancy Delerey enlightened us on the current real estate climate there. Tim Hatler sent detailed notes from nearby La Ventana. And we commiserated with Los Barriles retiree Lon Fitter while stuck in traffic outside Los Barriles during the weekend of the Baja 1000.

Over the past couple of years, we've enjoyed several chances to socialize with new friends in Cabo Pulmo, Marly Rickers and Clint Fultz, as well as dive instructors Carmel Lamar and Pablo Nobili.

Alessandra and Enrico Ugolini introduced us to Todos Santos years ago, inviting us to sample produce from their garden and teaching us how to fish from the beach. On our most recent visit, Don Mitchell and Alicia Dufaux filled us in on recent developments in town and gave us sweets for the road. Lynne Cummings and Howard Ekman generously helped complete our coverage of the area.

Special thanks to Joe Cummings for the many years of research and on-the-ground reporting that have made *Moon Cabo* the comprehensive and authoritative guide it is today. It is going to be a tough act to follow. The friendly and capable team at Avalon, led by editor Kathryn Ettinger, helped transform raw text files into a printable manuscript.

On a personal note, Paul Itoi shouldered much of the weight of the project, logging thousands of miles behind the wheel as we ventured up and down the peninsula—and later, hours in front of the computer as we worked our way through maps and manuscript. His passion for outdoor adventure prompted our first trip to Baja California nearly a decade ago and has shaped our coverage of sports and recreation in this edition.

Baby Emmett Itoi completed his first international road trip at the age of five months. He let us dip his feet in the Pacific at Playa Los Cerritos, rode patiently in the backpack while we walked through towns, and made friends at just about every stop. We could not have imagined a more perfect travel companion.

Acknowledgments